MICROSOFT® *Word* 2000

Comprehensive Course

Mastering and Using

H. Albert Napier
Philip J. Judd

VISIT US ON THE INTERNET
www.swep.com

South-Western Educational Publishing
an International Thomson Publishing company I(T)P®
www.thomson.com

Cincinnati • Albany, NY • Belmont, CA • Bonn • Boston • Detroit • Johannesburg • London • Madrid
Melbourne • Mexico City • New York • Paris • Singapore • Tokyo • Toronto • Washington

ISBN: 0-538-42772-8 (spiral bound, hard cover)
ISBN: 0-538-42608-X (perfect bound, soft cover)

4 5 6 7 BM 03

Managing Editor: Carol Volz
Project Manager/Editor: Cheryl L. Beck
Marketing Manager: Larry Qualls
Consulting Editor: Robin Romer, Pale Moon Productions
Production Services: GEX Publishing Services
Graphic Designer: Brenda Grannan, Grannan Graphics

I(T)P®

International Thomson Publishing

South-Western Educational Publishing is a division of International Thomson Publishing, Inc. The ITP logo is a registered trademark herein used under license by South-Western Educational Publishing.

Microsoft® Word 2000 Comprehensive for Windows®

Journey into the Future . . .

Our NEW Napier & Judd series™, *Master Using Microsoft Word 2000 Comprehe Course* is the most comprehensive, in tional tool designed for the user who wants t and use the application software. This exper ten product provides all the instruction nece be certified as a Microsoft Office User Specia (MOUS) Core and Expert user.

Mastering and Using Microsoft Word 2000 Comprehensive
◆ Student Text (spiral bound, hard cover)   0-538-42772-8
◆ Student Text/data CD-ROM Package (soft cover, perfect)   0-538-42608-X
◆ Activities Workbook (perfect bound, soft cover)   0-538-42622-5
◆ Electronic Instructor Package(Manual and CD-ROM)   0-538-42609-8
◆ Testing Package   0-538-42673-X

A new feature is the Electronic Instructor, a CD-ROM which includes less SCANS correlations, scheduling charts, presentations slides, and much m Books complementary to this book include the following:

Mastering and Using Microsoft Word 2000 Beginning Course
◆ Student Text (perfect bound, soft cover)   0-538-42815-5
◆ Student Text/Data CD-ROM Package (soft cover, perfect)   0-538-42812-0
◆ Activities Workbook (perfect bound, soft cover)   0-538-42622-5
◆ Electronic Instructor Package (Manual and CD-ROM)   0-538-42609-8
◆ Testing Package   0-538-42673-X

Mastering and Using Word 2000 Intermediate Course
◆ Student Text (perfect bound, soft cover)   0-538-42816-3
◆ Student Text/Data CD-ROM Package (soft cover, perfect)   0-538-42813-9
◆ Activities Workbook (perfect bound, soft cover)   0-538-42622-5
◆ Electronic Instructor Package (Manual and CD-ROM)   0-538-42609-8
◆ Testing Package   0-538-42673-X

Mastering and Using Word 2000 Advanced Course
◆ Student Text (perfect bound, soft cover)   0-538-42817-
◆ Student Text/Data CD-ROM Package (soft cover, perfect)   0-538-42814-
◆ Activities Workbook (perfect bound, soft cover)   0-538-42622-5
◆ Electronic Instructor Package (Manual and CD-ROM)   0-538-42609-8
◆ Testing Package   0-538-42673-X

Mastering and Using Microsoft Office 2000
◆ Student Text (spiral bound, hard cover)   0-538-42771-X
◆ Student Text/data CD-ROM Package (soft cover, perfect)   0-538-42605-X
◆ Activities Workbook (perfect bound, soft cover)   0-538-42621-7
◆ Electronic Instructor Package (Manual and CD-ROM)   0-538-42606-3
◆ Testing Package   0-538-42673-X

South-Western Educational Publishing

N&J NAPIER & JUDD Series

For more information about these South-Western products a
Join us On the Internet at www.swep.co

What's New in Word 2000

Office

- ▶ Different Office 2000 suites
- ▶ Personalized menus and toolbars
- ▶ Multi-language support
- ▶ Web-based analysis tools
- ▶ Improved Office Assistant
- ▶ Online collaboration with NetMeeting and Web discussions from inside Office applications
- ▶ E-mail from inside Office applications
- ▶ Collect and Paste and Office Clipboard toolbar
- ▶ New Open and Save As dialog box features
- ▶ Saving directly to Web server
- ▶ Improved Clip Gallery format and new clips

Word

- ▶ Web themes
- ▶ Web Page Preview
- ▶ Web Layout View (formerly Online Layout View)
- ▶ Print Layout View (formerly Page Layout View)
- ▶ 12-point default font size
- ▶ Nested tables
- ▶ Vertical and horizontal text alignment on Tables and Borders toolbar
- ▶ AutoFit table options on menu
- ▶ New Tables Properties dialog box
- ▶ Click and Type feature
- ▶ Web Page Wizard to create professional-looking Web pages and multipage Web sites

Napier & Judd

In their over 48 years of combined experience, Al Napier and Phil Judd have developed a tested, realistic approach to mastering and using application software. As both academics and corporate trainers, Al and Phil have the unique ability to help students by teaching them the skills necessary to compete in today's complex business world.

H. Albert Napier, Ph.D. is the Director of the Center on the Management of Information Technology and Professor in the Jones Graduate School of Administration at Rice University. In addition, Al is a principal of Napier & Judd, Inc., a consulting company and corporate trainer in Houston, Texas, that has trained more than 90,000 people in computer applications.

Philip J. Judd is a former instructor in the Management Department and the Director of the Research and Instructional Computing Service at the University of Houston. Phil now dedicates himself to corporate training and consulting as a principal of Napier & Judd, Inc.

Philip J. Judd

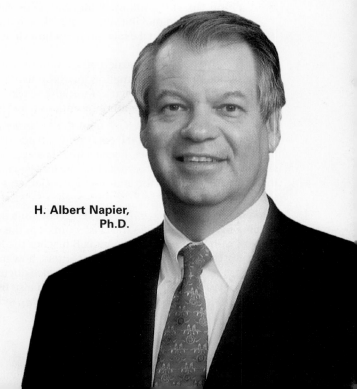

H. Albert Napier,
Ph.D.

Preface

At South-Western Educational Publishing, we believe that technology will change the way people teach and learn. Today there are millions of people using personal computers in their everyday lives—both as tools at work and for recreational activities. As a result, the personal computer has revolutionized the ways in which people interact with each other. The Napier and Judd series combines the following distinguishing features to allow people to do amazing things with their personal computers.

Distinguishing Features

All the textbooks in the *Mastering and Using* series share several key pedagogical features:

Case Project Approach. In their more than twenty years of business and corporate training and teaching experience, Napier and Judd have found that learners are more enthusiastic about learning a software application if they can see its real-world relevance. The textbook provides bountiful business-based profiles, exercises, and projects. It also emphasizes the skills most in demand by employers.

Comprehensive and Easy to Use. There is thorough coverage of new features. The narrative is clear and concise. Each unit or chapter thoroughly explains the concepts that underlie the skills and procedures. We explain not just the *how*, but the *why*.

Step-by-Step Instructions and Screen Illustrations. All examples in this text include step-by-step instructions that explain how to complete the specific task. Full-color screen illustrations are used extensively to provide the learner with a realistic picture of the software application feature.

Extensive Tips and Tricks. The author has placed informational boxes in the margin of the text. These boxes of information provide the learner with the following helpful tips:

▶ Quick Tip. Extra information provides shortcuts on how to perform common business-related functions.

▶ Caution Tip. This additional information explains how a mistake occurs and provides tips on how to avoid making similar mistakes in the future.

▶ Menu Tip. Additional explanation on how to use menu commands to perform application tasks.

▶ Mouse Tip. Further instructions on how to use the mouse to perform application tasks.

▶ Internet Tip. This information incorporates the power of the Internet to help learners use the Internet as they progress through the text.

▶ Design Tip. Hints for better presentation designs (found in only the PowerPoint book).

End-of-Chapter Materials. Each book in the *Mastering and Using* series places a heavy emphasis on providing learners with the opportunity to practice and reinforce the skills they are learning through extensive exercises. Each chapter has a summary, commands review, concepts review, skills review, and case projects so that the learner can master the material by doing. For more information on each of the end-of-chapter elements see page viii of the How to Use this Book section in this preface.

Appendixes. Mastering and Using series contains three appendixes to further help the learner prepare to be successful in the classroom or in the workplace. Appendix A teaches the learner to work with Windows 98. Appendix B teaches the learner how to use Windows Explorer; Appendix C illustrates how to format letters; how to insert a mailing notation; how to format envelopes (referencing the U.S. Postal Service documents); how to format interoffice memorandums; and how to key a formal outline. It also lists popular style guides and describes proofreader's marks.

Microsoft Office User Specialist (MOUS) Certification. The logo on the cover of this book indicates that these materials are officially certified by Microsoft Corporation. This certification is part of the MOUS program, which validates your skills as a knowledgeable user of Microsoft applications. Upon completing the lessons in the book, you will be prepared to take a test that could qualify you as either a core or expert user. To be certified, you will need to take an exam from a third-party testing company called an Authorization Certification Testing Center. Call **1-800-933-4493** to find the location of the testing center nearest you. Tests are conducted at different dates throughout the calendar year. To learn more about the entire line of training materials suitable for Microsoft Office certification, contact your South-Western Representative or call **1-800-824-5179**. Also visit our Web site at *www.swep.com*. To learn more about the MOUS program, you can visit Microsoft's Web site at *www.microsoft.com/train_cert/cert/*.

SCANS. In 1992, the U.S. Department of Labor and Education formed the Secretary's Commission on Achieving Necessary Skills, or SCANS, to study the kinds of competencies and skills that workers must have to succeed in today's marketplace. The results of the study were published in a document entitled *What Work Requires of Schools: A SCANS Report for America 2000*. The in-chapter and end-of-chapter exercises in this book are designed to meet the criteria outlined in the SCANS report and thus help prepare learners to be successful in today's workplace.

Instructional Support

All books in the *Mastering and Using* series are supplemented with the following items:

Instructor's Resource Package. This printed instructor's manual contains lesson plans with teaching materials and preparation suggestions, along with tips for implementing instruction and assessment ideas; a suggested syllabus for scheduling semester, block, and quarter classes; and SCANS workplace know how. The printed manual is packaged with an Electronic Instructor CD-ROM. The Electronic Instructor CD-ROM contains all the materials found in the printed manual as well as:

- ► Student lesson plans
- ► Data files
- ► Solutions files
- ► Test questions
- ► Transparencies
- ► PowerPoint presentations
- ► Portfolio assessment/worksheets
- ► Learning styles strategies
- ► Career worksheets
- ► Tech prep strategies

Testing Tools Package. Testing Tools is a powerful testing and assessment package that enables instructors to create and print tests from test banks designed specifically for South-Western Educational Publishing titles. In addition, instructors with access to a networked computer lab (LAN) or the Internet can administer, grade, and track tests online. Learners can also take online practice tests.

Course. Course is a template-based platform to deliver a Web-based syllabus. It allows instructors to create their own completely customized online syllabus, including lesson descriptions, dates, assignments, grades, and lesson links to other resources on the Web. To access this Web tool, an instructor must be a South-Western customer and contact sales support at 1-800-824-5179 for an access code. After the instructor has set up the online syllabus, students can access the Course.

Learner Support

Activity Workbooks. The workbook includes additional end-of-chapter exercises over and above those provided in the main text.

Data CD-ROM. To use this book, the learner must have the data CD-ROM (also referred to as the Data Disk). Data Files needed to complete exercises in the text are contained on this CD-ROM. These files can be copied to a hard drive or posted to a network drive.

How to Use This Book

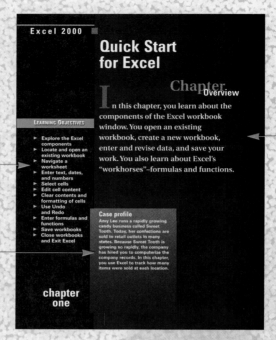

Excel 2000

Quick Start for Excel

Chapter Overview

In this chapter, you learn about the components of the Excel workbook window. You open an existing workbook, create a new workbook, enter and revise data, and save your work. You also learn about Excel's "workhorses"–formulas and functions.

LEARNING OBJECTIVES

► Explore the Excel components
► Locate and open an existing workbook
► Navigate a worksheet
► Enter text, dates, and numbers
► Select cells
► Edit cell content
► Clear contents and formatting of cells
► Use Undo and Redo
► Enter formulas and functions
► Save workbooks
► Close workbooks and Exit Excel

Case profile

Amy Lee runs a rapidly growing candy business called Sweet Tooth. Today, her confections are sold to retail outlets in many states. Because Sweet Tooth is growing so rapidly, the company has hired you to computerize the company records. In this chapter, you use Excel to track how many items were sold at each location.

chapter one

Learning Objectives — A quick reference of the major topics learned in the chapter

Case profile — Realistic scenarios that show the real world application of the material being covered

Chapter Overview — A concise summary of what will be learned in the chapter

Full color screen illustrations provide a realistic picture to the user

Caution Tip — This additional information explains how a mistake occurs and provides tips on how to avoid making similar mistakes in the future

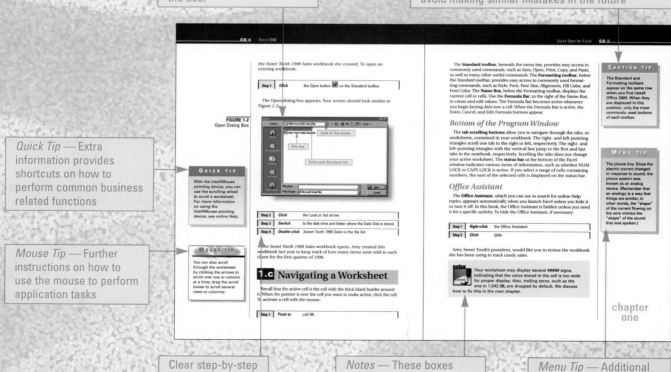

Quick Tip — Extra information provides shortcuts on how to perform common business related functions

Mouse Tip — Further instructions on how to use the mouse to perform application tasks

Clear step-by-step directions explain how to complete the specific task

Notes — These boxes provide necessary information to assist you in completing the exercises

Menu Tip — Additional explanation on how to use menu commands to perform application tasks

End-of-Chapter Material

Concepts Review — Multiple choice and true or false questions help assess how well the reader has learned the chapter material

Summary — Reviews key topics discussed in the chapter

Commands Review — Provides a quick reference and reinforcement tool on multiple methods for performing actions discussed in the chapter

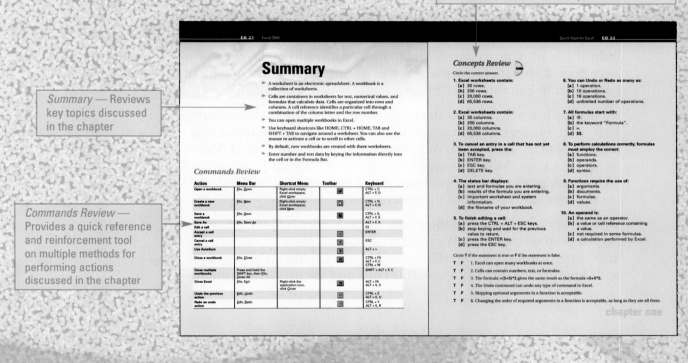

Skills Review — Hands-on exercises provide the ability to practice the skills just learned in the chapter

SCANS icon — Indicates that the exercise or project meets a SCANS competencies and prepares the learner to be successful in today's workplace

Case Projects — Asks the reader to synthesize the material they learned in the chapter and complete an office assignment

Internet Case Projects — Allow the reader to practice using the World Wide Web

MOUS Certification icon — indicates that the exercise or project meets Microsoft's certification objectives that prepare the learner for the MOUS exam

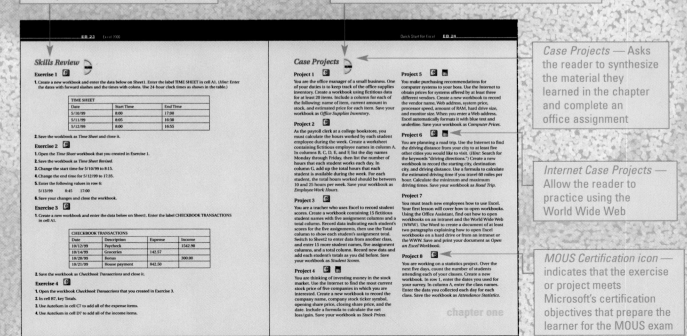

Acknowledgments

We would like to thank and express our appreciation to the many fine individuals who have contributed to the completion of this book. We have been fortunate to have a reviewer whose constructive comments have been so helpful: Paul Fletcher.

No book is possible without the motivation and support of an editorial staff. Therefore, we wish to acknowledge with great appreciation the project team at South-Western Educational Publishing: Cheryl Beck, project manager; Mike Broussard, art and designer coordinator; Angela McDonald, production coordinator; Kathy Hampton, manufacturing coordinator, and Carol Volz, managing editor.

We are very appreciative of the personnel at Napier & Judd, Inc., who helped prepare this book. We acknowledge, with great appreciation, the assistance provided by Ollie Rivers and Nancy Onarheim in preparing and checking the many drafts of this book and the instructor's manual.

Contents

APPENDIX ———————————————————— AP 1

Microsoft
Office 2000

Getting Started with Microsoft Office 2000

Chapter Overview

- ► **Describe Microsoft Office 2000**
- ► **Determine hardware and software requirements**
- ► **Identify common Office elements**
- ► **Start Office applications**
- ► **Get help in Office applications**
- ► **Close Office applications**

Microsoft Office 2000 provides the ability to enter, record, analyze, display, and present any type of business information. In this chapter you learn about the capabilities of Microsoft Office 2000, including its computer hardware and software requirements and elements common to all its applications. You also learn how to open and close those applications and get help.

For more information on how to prepare for the MOUS certification exam, check out the MOUS certification grids located on the data CD-ROM under the MOUS correlation folder for each book.

chapter one

1.a What Is Microsoft Office 2000?

Microsoft Office 2000 is a software suite (or package) that contains a combination of software applications you use to create text documents, analyze numbers, create presentations, manage large files of data, create Web pages, and create professional-looking marketing materials. Table 1-1 lists four editions of the Office 2000 suite and the software applications included in each.

Applications	Premium	Professional	Standard	Small Business
Word	X	X	X	X
Excel	X	X	X	X
PowerPoint	X	X	X	
Access	X	X		
Outlook	X	X	X	X
Publisher	X	X		X
FrontPage	X			

TABLE 1-1
Office 2000 Editions

The **Word 2000** software application provides you with word processing capabilities. **Word processing** is the preparation and production of text documents such as letters, memorandums, and reports. **Excel 2000** is software you use to analyze numbers with worksheets (sometimes called spreadsheets) and charts, as well as perform other tasks such as sorting data. A **worksheet** is a grid of columns and rows in which you enter labels and data. A **chart** is a visual or graphic representation of worksheet data. With Excel, you can create financial budgets, reports, and a variety of other forms.

PowerPoint 2000 software is used to create **presentations,** a collection of slides. A **slide** is the presentation output (actual 35mm slides, transparencies, computer screens, or printed pages) that contains text, charts, graphics, audio, and video. You can use PowerPoint slides to create a slide show on a computer attached to a projector, to broadcast a presentation over the Internet or company intranet, and to create handout materials for a presentation.

Access 2000 provides database management capabilities, enabling you to store and retrieve a large amount of data. A **database** is a collection of related information. A phone book or an address book are common examples of databases you use every day. Other databases include a price list, school registration information, or an inventory. You can query (or search) an Access database to answer specific questions about the stored data. For example, you can determine which customers in a particular state had sales in excess of a particular value during the month of June.

CAUTION TIP

This book assumes that you have little or no knowledge of Microsoft Office 2000, but that you have worked with personal computers and are familiar with Microsoft Windows 98 or Windows 95 operating systems.

QUICK TIP

Microsoft Office 2000 is often called Office and the individual applications are called Word, Excel, PowerPoint, Access, Outlook, Publisher, and so on.

chapter
one

Outlook 2000 is a **personal information manager** that enables you to send and receive e-mail, as well as maintain a calendar, contacts list, journal, electronic notes, and an electronic "to do" list. **Publisher 2000** is desktop publishing software used to create publications, such as professional-looking marketing materials, newsletters, or brochures. Publisher wizards provide step-by-step instructions for creating a publication from an existing design; you also can design your own publication. The **FrontPage 2000** application is used to create and manage Web sites. **PhotoDraw 2000** is business graphics software that allows users to add custom graphics to marketing materials and Web pages.

A major advantage of using an Office suite is the ability to share data between applications. For example, you can include a portion of an Excel worksheet or chart in a Word document, use an outline created in a Word document as the starting point for a PowerPoint presentation, import an Excel worksheet into Access, merge names and addresses from an Outlook Address Book with a Word letter, or import a picture from PhotoDraw into a newsletter created in Publisher.

1.b Hardware and Software Requirements

You must install Office 2000 applications in Windows 95, Windows 98, or Windows NT Workstation 4.0 with Service Pack 3.0 installed. The applications will not run in the Windows 3.x or the Windows NT Workstation 3.5 environments.

Microsoft recommends that you install Office on a computer that has a Pentium processor, at least 32 MB of RAM, a CD-ROM drive, Super VGA, 256-color video, Microsoft Mouse, Microsoft IntelliMouse, or another pointing device, and at least a 28,800-baud modem. To access certain features you should have a multimedia computer, e-mail software, and a Web browser. For detailed information on installing Office, see the documentation that comes with the software.

1.c Identifying Common Office Elements

Office applications share many common elements, making it easier for you to work efficiently in any application. A **window** is a rectangular area on your screen in which you view a software application, such as Excel. All the Office application windows have a similar look and arrangement of shortcuts, menus, and toolbars. In addition, they share many features, such as a common dictionary to use for spell checking your work and identical menu commands, toolbar buttons, shortcut menus, and keyboard shortcuts that enable you to perform tasks such as copying data from one location to another. Figure 1-1 shows the common elements in the Office application windows.

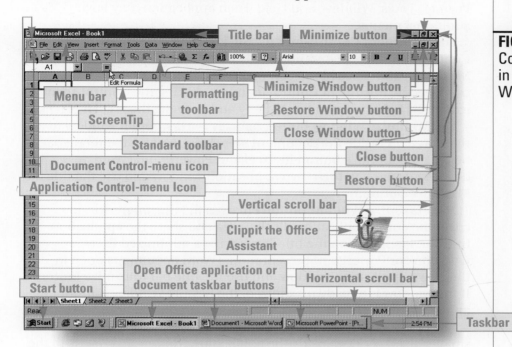

FIGURE 1-1
Common Elements in Office Application Windows

Title Bar

The application **title bar** at the top of the window includes the application Control-menu icon, the application name, the filename of the active document, and the Minimize, Restore (or Maximize), and Close buttons.

The **application Control-menu** icon, located in the left corner of the title bar, displays the Control menu. The Control menu commands manage the application window, and typically include commands such as: Restore, Move, Size, Minimize, Maximize, and Close. Commands that are currently available appear in a darker color. You can view the Control menu by clicking the Control-menu icon or by holding down the ALT key and then pressing the SPACEBAR key.

The **Minimize** button, near the right corner of the title bar reduces the application window to a taskbar button. The **Maximize** button, to the right of the Minimize button, enlarges the application window to fill the entire screen viewing area above the taskbar. If the window is already maximized, the Restore button appears in its place. The **Restore** button reduces the application window size. The **Close** button, located in the right corner of the title bar, closes the application and removes it from the computer's memory.

CAUTION TIP

In order to save hard disk space, Office installs many features and components as you need them. Shortcuts, toolbar buttons, and menu commands for these features appear in the application window or dialog boxes, indicating that the feature is available.

chapter
one

QUICK TIP

Office 2000 file formats (except Access) are compatible with the previous version of Office (Office 97), which means Office 97 users can open Office 2000 files without a converter, although some Office 2000 formatting features will be lost. For a list of Office 2000 formatting features not supported by Office 97, see online Help in each application.

MOUSE TIP

If you are left-handed, you can switch the operation of the left and right mouse buttons in the Mouse Properties dialog box. Double-click the My Computer icon on the desktop, double-click the Control Panel folder, and then double-click the Mouse icon to display the dialog box.

Menu Bar

The **menu bar** is a special toolbar located below the title bar and contains the menus for the application. A **menu** is list of commands. The menus common to Office applications are File, Edit, View, Insert, Format, Tools, Window, and Help. Each application may have additional menus.

The **document Control-menu** icon, located below the application Control-menu icon, contains the Restore, Move, Size, Minimize, Maximize, and Close menu commands for the document window. You can view the document Control menu by clicking the Control-menu icon or by holding down the ALT key and pressing the HYPHEN (-) key.

The **Minimize Window** button reduces the document window to a title-bar icon inside the document area. It appears on the menu bar below the Minimize button in Excel and PowerPoint. (Word documents open in their own application window and use the title bar Minimize button.)

The **Maximize Window** button enlarges the document window to cover the entire application display area and share the application title bar. It appears on the title-bar icon of a minimized Excel workbook or PowerPoint presentation. (Word documents open in their own application window and use the title bar Maximize button.) If the window is already maximized, the Restore Window button appears in its place.

The **Restore Window** button changes the document window to a smaller sized window inside the application window. It appears to the right of the Minimize Window button in Excel and PowerPoint. (Word documents open in their own application window and use the title bar Restore button.)

The **Close Window** button closes the document and removes it from the computer's memory. It appears to the right of the Restore Window or Maximize Window button. (In Word, the Close Window button appears only when one document is open. Otherwise, Word uses the title bar Close button.)

Default Toolbars

The **Standard** and **Formatting toolbars,** located on one row below the menu bar, contain a set of icons called buttons. The toolbar buttons represent commonly used commands and are mouse shortcuts used to perform tasks quickly. In addition to the Standard and Formatting toolbars, each application has several other toolbars available. You can customize toolbars by adding or removing buttons and commands.

When the mouse pointer rests on a toolbar button, a **ScreenTip** appears identifying the name of the button. ScreenTips, part of online Help, describe a toolbar button, dialog box option, or menu command.

Scroll Bars

The **vertical scroll bar,** on the right side of the document area, is used to view various parts of the document by moving, or scrolling, the document up or down. It includes scroll arrows and a scroll box. The **horizontal scroll bar**, near the bottom of the document area, is used to view various parts of the document by scrolling the document left or right. It includes scroll arrows and a scroll box.

Office Assistant

The **Office Assistant** is an animated graphic you can click to view online Help. The Office Assistant may also anticipate your needs and provide advice in a balloon-style dialog box when you begin certain tasks, such as writing a letter in Word.

Taskbar

The **taskbar,** located across the bottom of the Windows desktop, includes the Start button and buttons for each open Office document. The **Start button,** located in the left corner of the taskbar, displays the Start menu or list of tasks you can perform and applications you can use.

You can switch between documents, close documents and applications, and view other items, such as the system time and printer status, with buttons or icons on the taskbar. If you are using Windows 98, other toolbars—such as the Quick Launch toolbar—may also appear on the taskbar.

QUICK TIP

You can use the keyboard to access Office application features. This book lists all keys in uppercase letters, such as the TAB key. This book lists keystrokes as: Press the ENTER key. When you are to press one key and, while holding down that key, to press another key, this book lists the keystrokes as: Press the SHIFT + F7 keys.

1.d Starting Office Applications

You access the Office applications through the Windows desktop. When you turn on your computer, the Windows operating system software is automatically loaded into memory. Once the process is complete, your screen should look similar to Figure 1-2.

notes The desktop illustrations in this book assume you are using Windows 98 with default settings. Your desktop may not look identical to the illustrations in this book. For more information on using Windows 98 see Appendix A or information provided by your instructor.

chapter
one

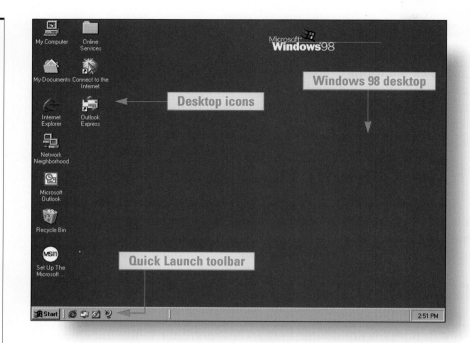

FIGURE 1-2
Default Windows 98
Desktop

You begin by opening the Excel application. To use Start button to open Excel:

Step 1	*Click*	the Start button [Start] on the taskbar
Step 2	*Point to*	Programs
Step 3	*Click*	Microsoft Excel on the Programs menu

The Excel software is placed into the memory of your computer and the Excel window opens. Your screen should look similar to Figure 1-1.

You can open and work in more than one Office application at a time. When Office is installed, the Open Office Document command and the New Office Document command appear on the Start menu. You can use these commands to select the type of document on which you want to work rather than first selecting an Office application. To create a new Word document without first opening the application:

Step 1	*Click*	the Start button [Start] on the taskbar
Step 2	*Click*	New Office Document
Step 3	*Click*	the General tab, if necessary

The dialog box that opens should look similar to Figure 1-3.

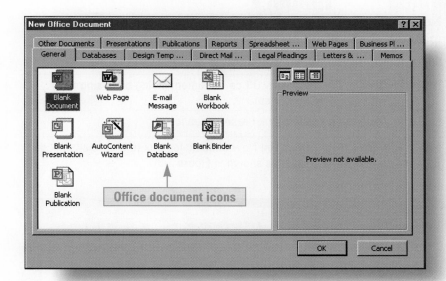

FIGURE 1-3
General Tab in
the New Office
Document Dialog Box

QUICK TIP

A **dialog box** is a window
that contains options
for performing specific
tasks. The New Office
Document dialog box
contains **icons** (or
pictures) for creating a
blank Word document,
Web page (in Word),
e-mail message (using
Outlook or Outlook
Express), Excel
workbook, PowerPoint
presentation, Access
database, or Publisher
publication. The available
icons depends on the
Office applications you
have installed.

To create a blank Word document:

| Step 1 | *Click* | the Blank Document icon to select it, if necessary |
| Step 2 | *Click* | OK |

The Word software loads into your computer's memory, the Word
application opens with a blank document, and a taskbar button
appears for the document. Your screen should look similar to Figure 1-4.

FIGURE 1-4
Word Application Window

chapter
one

Next you open a blank presentation. To open the PowerPoint application and a blank presentation:

Step 1	*Open*	the New Office Document dialog box using the Start menu
Step 2	*Double-click*	the Blank Presentation icon
Step 3	*Click*	OK in the New Slide dialog box to create a blank title slide, as shown in Figure 1-5

FIGURE 1-5
Blank PowerPoint
Presentation

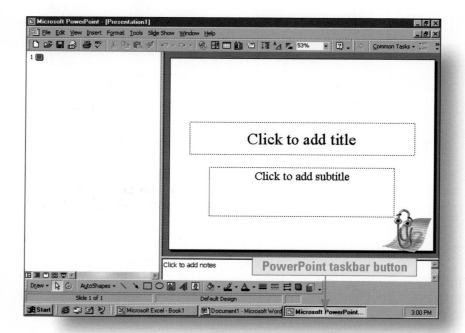

You can also open an Office application by opening an existing Office document from the Start menu. To open an existing Access database:

Step 1	*View*	the Start button **Start** on the taskbar
Step 2	*Click*	Open Office Document
Step 3	*Click*	the Look in: list arrow in the Open Office Document dialog box
Step 4	*Switch*	to the disk drive and folder where the Data Files are stored
Step 5	*Double-click*	*International Sales* to open the Access application and database, as shown in Figure 1-6

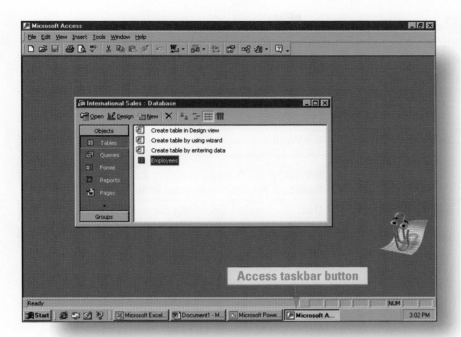

FIGURE 1-6
International Sales
Database in
Access Window

You can switch between open Office documents by clicking the appropriate taskbar button. To switch to the Excel workbook and then the Word document:

Step 1	*Click*	the Excel button on the taskbar
Step 2	*Observe*	that the Excel window and workbook are visible
Step 3	*Click*	the Word Document1 button on the taskbar
Step 4	*Observe*	that the Word window and document are visible

1.e Getting Help in Office Applications

There are several ways to get help in any Office application. You can display the Office Assistant, get context-sensitive help, or launch your Web browser and get Web-based help from Microsoft.

Using the Office Assistant

The **Office Assistant** is an interactive, animated graphic that appears in the Word, Excel, PowerPoint, and Publisher application windows. When you activate the Office Assistant, a balloon-style dialog box

> **QUICK TIP**
>
> If multiple windows are open, the **active window** has a dark blue title bar. Inactive windows have a light gray title bar.

chapter
one

opens containing options for searching online Help by topic. The Office Assistant may also automatically offer suggestions when you begin certain tasks. As you begin to key a personal letter to Aunt Isabel, the Office Assistant automatically asks if you want help writing the letter. To begin the letter:

MENU TIP

You can display the Office Assistant from the Help menu. You can also press the F1 key.

Step 1	*Verify*	the Word document is the active window
Step 2	*Click*	the Microsoft Word Help button [?] on the Standard toolbar, if the Office Assistant is not visible
Step 3	*Key*	Dear Aunt Isabel: (including the colon)
Step 4	*Press*	the ENTER key

The Office Assistant and balloon appear. Your screen should look similar to Figure 1-7.

FIGURE 1-7
Office Assistant Balloon

The Office Assistant balloon contains three options you can click with the mouse. If you click the "Get help with writing the letter" option, the Letter Wizard dialog box opens. A **wizard** is a series of dialog boxes you can use to complete a task step-by-step. If you click the "Just type the letter without help" option or the Cancel option, the balloon closes.

CAUTION TIP

After you cancel the balloon, the letter-writing help options will not appear again until you create a new, blank document.

| Step 5 | *Click* | Cancel to close the balloon |

If you prefer to use the Microsoft Help window to access online Help, you can choose to show or hide the Office Assistant or you can turn off the Office Assistant completely. To hide the Office Assistant:

| Step 1 | *Right-click* | the Office Assistant |
| Step 2 | *Click* | Hide |

You can activate the Office Assistant at any time to search online help for specific topics or to customize the Office Assistant. Custom options affect all Office applications. To review the Office Assistant customization options:

Step 1	*Click*	the Microsoft Word Help button 🔲 on the Standard toolbar
Step 2	*Click*	the Office Assistant to view the balloon, if necessary
Step 3	*Click*	Options in the Office Assistant balloon
Step 4	*Click*	the Options tab, if necessary

The dialog box that opens should look similar to Figure 1-8.

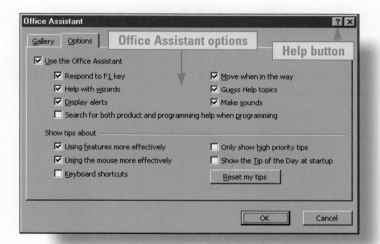

FIGURE 1-8
Options Tab in the Office Assistant Dialog Box

To learn about dialog box options, you can use the dialog box Help button or you can right-click an option. To view the ScreenTip help:

Step 1	*Drag*	the Office Assistant out of the way, if necessary
Step 2	*Right-click*	the Keyboard shortcuts option
Step 3	*Click*	What's This? to view a ScreenTip help message for this option
Step 4	*Press*	the ESC key to close the ScreenTip help message

The default Office Assistant image is Clippit. But you can select from a gallery of animated images. To view the Office Assistant image options:

| Step 1 | *Click* | the Gallery tab |

MENU TIP

You can hide the Office Assistant by clicking the Hide the Office Assistant command on the Help menu. You can redisplay the Office Assistant by clicking the Show the Office Assistant on the Help menu.

MOUSE TIP

You can drag the Office Assistant to a new location with the mouse pointer.

chapter
one

Step 2	*Click*	the Next> and <Back buttons to view different image options
Step 3	*Click*	Cancel to close the dialog box without changing any options

You can use the Office Assistant to search an application's online Help. Suppose you want to learn how to turn off the Office Assistant. To search online Help:

Step 1	*Click*	the Office Assistant to activate the balloon
Step 2	*Key*	turn off the Office Assistant in the text box
Step 3	*Press*	the ENTER key to view a list of help options in the balloon dialog box
Step 4	*Click*	the Hide, show, or turn off the Office Assistant option

The Microsoft Word Help window opens and contains information about how to manage the Office Assistant. Your screen should look similar to Figure 1-9.

FIGURE 1-9
Microsoft Word
Help Window

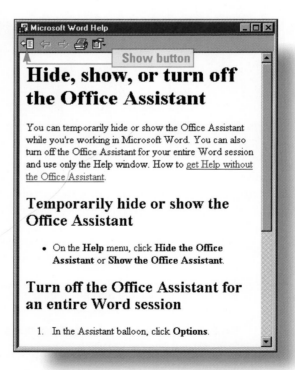

You can scroll the Help window to view all the information. You can click the Show button to view the Contents, Answer Wizard, and Index tabs that access other help topics. If you have Internet access, you can view a Microsoft Help Web page from inside the Help window. To view the additional tabs:

| Step 1 | *Click* | the Show button in the Help window, if necessary, to display the Contents, Answer Wizard, and Index tabs |
| Step 2 | *Click* | the Close button ☒ in the upper-right corner of the window |

Using the Help Menu

The Help menu provides commands you can use to view the Office Assistant or Help window, show or hide the Office Assistant, connect to the Microsoft Web site, get context-sensitive help for a menu command or toolbar button, detect and repair font and template files, and view licensing information for the Office application. To review the Help menu commands:

Step 1	*Click*	Help
Step 2	*Observe*	the menu commands
Step 3	*Click*	in the document area outside the menu to close the Help menu

Using What's This?

You can get context-sensitive help for a menu command or toolbar button using the What's This? command on the Help menu. This command changes the mouse pointer to a help pointer, a white mouse pointer with a large black question mark. When you click a toolbar button or menu command with the help pointer, a brief ScreenTip help message appears describing the command or toolbar button. To a ScreenTip help message for a toolbar button:

Step 1	*Press*	the SHIFT + F1 keys
Step 2	*Observe*	that the help mouse pointer with the attached question mark
Step 3	*Click*	the Save button 🖫 on the Standard toolbar
Step 4	*Observe*	the ScreenTip help message describing the Save button
Step 5	*Press*	the ESC key to close the ScreenTip help message

chapter
one

1.f Closing Office Applications

There are many ways to close the Access, Excel and PowerPoint applications (or the Word application with a single document open) and return to the Windows desktop. You can: (1) double-click the application Control-menu icon; (2) click the application Close button; (3) right-click the application taskbar button and then click the Close command on the shortcut menu; (4) press the ALT + F4 keys; or (5) click the Exit command on the File menu to close Office applications (no matter how many Word documents are open). To close the Excel application from the taskbar:

| Step 1 | *Right-click* | the Excel button on the taskbar |
| Step 2 | *Click* | Close |

You can close multiple applications at one time from the taskbar by selecting the application buttons using the CTRL key and then using the shortcut menu. To close the PowerPoint and Access applications:

Step 1	*Press & Hold*	the CTRL key
Step 2	*Click*	the PowerPoint button and then the Access button on the taskbar
Step 3	*Release*	the CTRL key and observe that both buttons are selected (pressed in)
Step 4	*Right-click*	the PowerPoint or Access button
Step 5	*Click*	Close

Both applications close, leaving only the Word document open. To close the Word document using the menu:

Step 1	*Verify*	that the Word application window is maximized
Step 2	*Click*	File
Step 3	*Click*	Exit
Step 4	*Click*	No in the Office Assistant balloon or confirmation dialog box to close Word without saving the document

Summary

► The Word application provides word processing capabilities for the preparation of text documents such as letters, memorandums, and reports.

► The Excel application provides the ability to analyze numbers in worksheets and for creating financial budgets, reports, charts, and forms.

► The PowerPoint application is used to create presentation slides and audience handouts.

► You can use Access databases to organize and retrieve collections of data.

► Publisher provides tools for creating marketing materials, such as newsletters, brochures, flyers, and Web pages.

► The Outlook application helps you send and receive e-mail, maintain a calendar, "to do" lists, organize the names and addresses of contacts, and perform other information management tasks.

► One major advantage of Office suite applications is the ability to integrate the applications by sharing information between them.

► Another advantage of using Office suite applications is that they share a number of common elements, such as window elements, shortcuts, toolbars, menu commands, and other features.

► You can start Office suite applications from the Programs submenu on the Start menu and from the Open Office Document or New Office Document commands on the Start menu.

► You can close Office applications by double-clicking the application Control Menu icon, clicking the application Close button on the title bar, right-clicking the application button on the taskbar, pressing the ALT + F4 keys, or clicking the Exit command on the File menu.

► You can get help in an Office application by clicking commands on the Help menu, pressing the F1 or SHIFT + F1 keys, or clicking the Microsoft Help button on the Standard toolbar.

chapter one

Concepts Review

Circle the correct answer.

1. ScreenTips do not provide:
[a] the name of a button on a toolbar.
[b] help for options in a dialog box.
[c] context-sensitive help for menu commands or toolbar buttons.
[d] access to the Office Assistant.

2. To manage a Web site, you can use:
[a] Outlook.
[b] FrontPage.
[c] PhotoDraw.
[d] Publisher.

3. The title bar contains the:
[a] document Control-menu icon.
[b] Close Window button.
[c] Standard toolbar.
[d] application and document name.

4. The Excel application is best used to:
[a] prepare financial reports.
[b] maintain a list of tasks to accomplish.
[c] create newsletters, brochures, and flyers.
[d] create custom graphics.

Circle **T** if the statement is true or **F** if the statement is false.

T F 1. You use Publisher to create newsletters and brochures.
T F 2. Excel is used to create presentation slides.
T F 3. The default Office Assistant graphic is Clippit.
T F 4. Access is used to create and format text.

Skills Review

Exercise 1

1. Identify each common element of Office application windows numbered in Figure 1-10.

FIGURE 1-10
Excel Application Window

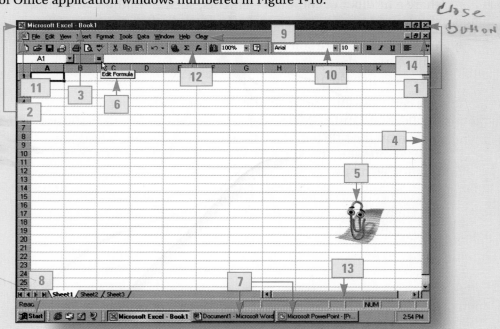

Exercise 2

1. Open the Word application using the Programs command on the Start menu.
2. Close the Word application using the taskbar.

Exercise 3

1. Open the Excel application and then the PowerPoint application using the <u>P</u>rograms command on the Start menu.
2. Open the Access application and the *International Sales* database using the Open Office Document command on the Start menu.
3. Switch to the PowerPoint application using the taskbar button and close it using the Close button on the title bar.
4. Close the PowerPoint and Access applications at the same time using the taskbar.

Exercise 4

1. Create a new, blank Word document using the New Office Document command on the Start menu.
2. Create a new, blank Excel workbook using the New Office Document command on the Start menu.
3. Switch to the Word document using the taskbar and close it using the title bar Close button.
4. Close the Excel workbook using the taskbar button.

Exercise 5

1. Open the Word application using the Start menu.
2. Show the Office Assistant, if necessary, with a command on the <u>H</u>elp menu.
3. Hide the Office Assistant with a shortcut menu.
4. Show the Office Assistant with the Microsoft Word Help button on the Standard toolbar.
5. Search online Help using the search phrase "type text." Open the Type text help page.
6. Click the underlined text <u>typing text</u> to view a help page of subtopics. Scroll and review the help page.
7. Close the Help window. Hide the Office Assistant with a shortcut menu.

Case Projects

Project 1

You are the secretary to the marketing manager of High Risk Insurance, an insurance brokerage firm. The marketing manager wants to know how to open and close the Excel application. Write at least two paragraphs describing different ways to open and close Excel. With your instructor's permission, use your written description to show a classmate several ways to open and close Excel.

Project 2

You work in the administrative offices of Alma Public Relations, and the information management department just installed Office 2000 Professional on your computer. Your supervisor asks you to write down and describe some of the Office Assistant options. Open the <u>O</u>ptions tab in the Office Assistant dialog box. Review each option using the dialog box Help button or the What's This? command. Write at least three paragraphs describing five Office Assistant options.

Project 3

As the new office manager at Hot Wheels Messenger Service, you are learning to use the Word 2000 application and want to learn more about some of the buttons on the Word toolbars. Open Word and use the What's This? command on the <u>H</u>elp menu to review the ScreenTip help for five toolbar buttons. Write a brief paragraph for each button describing how it is used.

Project 4

As the acquisitions director for Osiris Books, an international antique book and map dealer, you use Publisher to create the company's catalogs and brochures. A co-worker, who is helping you with a new brochure, opened Publisher and did not know why the Catalog window appeared. She has asked you for an explanation. Open the Publisher application and review the Catalog window. Close the Catalog window leaving the Publisher window open. Use the Office Assistant to find out more about the Catalog by searching online Help using the keyword "catalog." Write your co-worker a short note explaining how the Catalog is used.

chapter one

Working with Menus and Toolbars

Chapter Overview

Office 2000 tries to make your work life easier by learning how you work. The personalized menus and toolbars in each application remember which commands and buttons you use, and add and remove them as needed. In this chapter, you learn how to work with the personalized menus and toolbars, how to customize the menu bar and toolbars, and how to view and customize the Office Shortcut Bar.

LEARNING OBJECTIVES

► Work with personalized menus and toolbars
► View, hide, dock, and float toolbars
► Customize the menu bar and toolbars
► View and customize the Office Shortcut Bar

chapter two

2.a Working with Personalized Menus and Toolbars

A **menu** is a list of commands you use to perform tasks in the Office applications. Some commands also have an associated image, or icon, shown to the left of a command. A **toolbar** contains a set of icons (the same icons you see on the menus) called **buttons** that you click with the mouse pointer to quickly execute a menu command.

When you first open Excel, Word, or PowerPoint, the menus on the menu bar initially show only a basic set of commands and the Standard and Formatting toolbars contain only a basic set of buttons. These short versions of the menus and toolbars are called **personalized menus and toolbars**. As you work, the commands and buttons you use most frequently are stored in the personalized settings. The first time you select a menu command or toolbar button that is not part of the basic set, it is added to your personalized settings and appears on the menu or toolbar. If you do not use a command for a while, it is removed from your personalized settings and no longer appears on the menu or toolbar. To view the personalized menus and toolbars in PowerPoint:

Step 1	*Click*	the Start button ![Start] on the taskbar
Step 2	*Click*	the New Office Document command on the Start menu
Step 3	*Click*	the General tab in the New Office Document dialog box
Step 4	*Double-click*	the Blank Presentation icon
Step 5	*Click*	OK in the New Slide dialog box to create a blank title slide for the presentation
Step 6	*Click*	Tools on the menu bar
Step 7	*Observe*	the short personalized menu containing only the basic commands, as shown in Figure 2-1

CAUTION TIP

The activities in this chapter assume the personalized menus and toolbars are reset to their default settings. In this chapter, you select menu commands and toolbar buttons by clicking them with the mouse pointer. You learn how to use menu commands and toolbar buttons to perform tasks in the application chapters.

QUICK TIP

FrontPage and Access also provide the personalized menus and toolbars options. When you first open FrontPage, you see the Standard and Formatting toolbars. When you first open Access, you see only the Standard toolbar. Publisher does not provide the personalized menus and toolbars options.

FIGURE 2-1
Personalized Tools Menu

chapter
two

If the command you want to use does not appear on the short personalized menu, you can expand the menu by pausing for a few seconds until the menu expands, clicking the expand arrows at the bottom of the menu, or double-clicking the menu name.

| Step 8 | *Pause* | until the menu automatically expands, as shown in Figure 2-2 |

FIGURE 2-2
Expanded Tools Menu

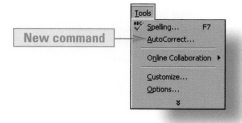

You move a menu command from the expanded menu to the personalized menu, simply by selecting it. To add the AutoCorrect command to the short personalized Tools menu:

Step 1	*Click*	AutoCorrect
Step 2	*Click*	Cancel in the AutoCorrect dialog box to cancel the dialog box
Step 3	*Click*	Tools on the menu bar
Step 4	*Observe*	the updated personalized Tools menu contains the AutoCorrect command, as shown in Figure 2-3

FIGURE 2-3
Updated Personalized Tools Menu

When you first open Word, Excel, or PowerPoint, the Standard and Formatting toolbars appear on one row below the title bar and some default buttons are hidden. You can resize a toolbar to view a hidden button by dragging its **move handle**, the gray vertical bar at the left edge of the toolbar, with the **move pointer,** a four-headed black arrow. To resize the Formatting toolbar:

Step 1	*Move*	the mouse pointer to the move handle on the Formatting toolbar
Step 2	*Observe*	that the mouse pointer becomes a move pointer
Step 3	*Drag*	the Formatting toolbar to the left until nine Formatting toolbar buttons are visible
Step 4	*Observe*	that you see fewer buttons on the Standard toolbar

The buttons that don't fit on the displayed area of a toolbar are collected in a More Buttons list. To view the remaining the Standard toolbar default buttons:

| Step 1 | *Click* | the More Buttons list arrow 🔽 on the Standard toolbar |
| Step 2 | *Observe* | the default buttons that are not visible on the toolbar, as shown in Figure 2-4 |

| Step 3 | *Press* | the ESC key to close the More Buttons list |

If you want to display one of the default buttons on a personalized toolbar, you can select it from the More Buttons list. To add the Format Painter button to the personalized Standard toolbar:

Step 1	*Click*	the More Buttons list arrow 🔽 on the Standard toolbar
Step 2	*Click*	the Format Painter button
Step 3	*Observe*	that the Format Painter button is turned on and added to the personalized Standard toolbar, as shown in Figure 2-5

C A U T I O N   T I P

When updating the personalized Standard or Formatting toolbar with a new button, a button that you have not used recently might move to the More Buttons list to make room for the new button.

FIGURE 2-4
More Buttons List

chapter
two

FIGURE 2-5
Updated Personalized
Standard Toolbar

| Step 4 | *Click* | the Format Painter button on the Standard toolbar to turn it off |

If you want to view all the menu commands instead of a short personalized menu and all the default toolbar buttons on the Standard and Formatting toolbars, you can change options in the Customize dialog box. To show all the toolbar buttons and menu commands:

Step 1	*Click*	<u>T</u>ools
Step 2	*Click*	<u>C</u>ustomize
Step 3	*Click*	the <u>O</u>ptions tab, if necessary

The dialog box that opens should be similar to Figure 2-6.

FIGURE 2-6
<u>O</u>ptions Tab in the
Customize Dialog Box

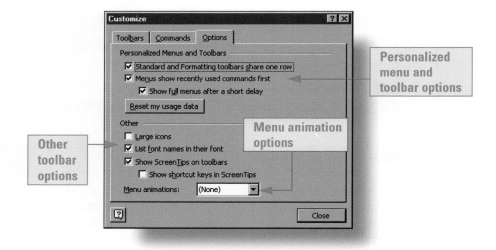

Step 4	*Click*	the Standard and Formatting toolbars <u>s</u>hare one row check box to remove the check mark and reposition the Formatting toolbar below the Standard toolbar
Step 5	*Click*	the Me<u>n</u>us show recently used commands first check box to remove the check mark and show the entire set of commands for each menu
Step 6	*Click*	Close to close the dialog box

Step 7	*Observe*	the repositioned Standard and Formatting toolbars
Step 8	*Click*	Tools to view the entire set of Tools menu commands
Step 9	*Press*	the ESC key

You can return the menus and toolbars to their initial (or **default**) settings in the Customize dialog box. To reset the default menus and toolbars:

Step 1	*Open*	the Options tab in the Customize dialog box
Step 2	*Click*	the Standard and Formatting toolbars share one row check box to insert a check mark
Step 3	*Click*	the Menus show recently used commands first check box to insert a check mark
Step 4	*Click*	Reset my usage data
Step 5	*Click*	Yes to confirm you want to reset the menus and toolbars to their default settings
Step 6	*Close*	the Customize dialog box
Step 7	*Observe*	that the Tools menu and Standard toolbar are reset to their default settings

2.b Viewing, Hiding, Docking, and Floating Toolbars

Office applications have additional toolbars that you can view when you need them. You can also hide toolbars when you are not using them. You can view or hide toolbars by pointing to the Toolbars command on the View menu and clicking a toolbar name or by using a shortcut menu. A **shortcut menu** is a short list of frequently used menu commands. You view a shortcut menu by pointing to an item on the screen and clicking the right mouse button. This is called right-clicking the item. The commands on shortcut menus vary—depending on where you right-click—so that you view only the most frequently used commands for a particular task. An easy way to view or hide toolbars is with a shortcut menu. To view the shortcut menu for PowerPoint toolbars:

| Step 1 | *Right-click* | the menu bar, the Standard toolbar, or the Formatting toolbar |
| Step 2 | *Observe* | the shortcut menu and the check marks next to the names of currently visible toolbars, as shown in Figure 2-7 |

> **CAUTION TIP**
>
> When you choose the Menus show recently used commands first option, it affects all the Office applications, not just the open application.
> Resetting the usage data to the initial settings does not change the location of toolbars and does not remove or add buttons to toolbars you have customized in the Customize dialog box.

chapter
two

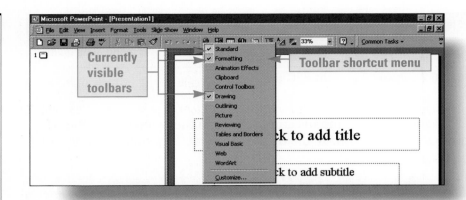

FIGURE 2-7
Toolbars Shortcut Menu

QUICK TIP

Some of the toolbars
that appear on the
toolbars list vary from
Office application to
application.

Step 3	*Click*	Tables and Borders in the shortcut menu
Step 4	*Observe*	that the Tables and Borders toolbar appears on your screen

The Tables and Borders toolbar, unless a previous user repositioned it, is visible in its own window near the middle of your screen. When a toolbar is visible in its own window it is called a **floating toolbar** and you can move and size it with the mouse pointer just like any window. When a toolbar appears fixed at the screen boundaries, it is called a **docked toolbar**. The menu bar and Standard and Formatting toolbars are examples of docked toolbars. In PowerPoint, the Drawing toolbar is docked above the status bar. You can dock a floating toolbar by dragging its title bar with the mouse pointer to a docking position below the title bar, above the status bar, or at the left and right boundaries of your screen. To dock the Tables and Borders toolbar below the Standard and Formatting toolbars:

Step 1	*Position*	the mouse pointer on the blue title bar in the Tables and Borders toolbar window
Step 2	*Drag*	the toolbar window slowly up until it docks below the Standard and Formatting toolbars

Similarly, you float a docked toolbar by dragging it away from its docked position toward the middle of the screen. To float the Tables and Borders toolbar:

Step 1	*Position*	the mouse pointer on the Tables and Borders toolbar move handle until it becomes a move pointer
Step 2	*Drag*	the Tables and Borders toolbar down toward the middle of the screen until it appears in its own window

When you finish using a toolbar, you can hide it with a shortcut menu. To hide the Tables and Borders toolbar:

| Step 1 | *Right-click* | the Tables and Borders toolbar |
| Step 2 | *Click* | Tables and Borders to remove the check mark and hide the toolbar |

2.c Customizing the Menu Bar and Toolbars

Recall that you can add a button to a personalized toolbar by clicking the More Buttons list arrow on the toolbar and then selecting a button from the list of default buttons not currently visible. You can also add and delete buttons and commands on the menu bar or other toolbars with options in the Customize dialog box. To customize the menu bar:

Step 1	*Right-click*	any toolbar (the menu bar, Standard toolbar, or Formatting toolbar)
Step 2	*Click*	Customize
Step 3	*Click*	the Commands tab, if necessary

The dialog box on your screen should look similar to Figure 2-8.

FIGURE 2-8
Commands Tab in the Customize Dialog Box

You add a button on the menu bar to route the active presentation to other users on the network via e-mail.

chapter
two

Step 4	*Verify*	that File is selected in the Categories: list
Step 5	*Click*	Routing Recipient in the Commands: list (scroll the list to view this command)
Step 6	*Click*	Description to view the ScreenTip
Step 7	*Press*	the ESC key to close the ScreenTip
Step 8	*Drag*	the Routing Recipient command to the right of Help on the menu bar
Step 9	*Click*	Close to close the dialog box and add the Routing Recipient button to the menu bar
Step 10	*Position*	the mouse pointer on the Routing Recipient icon to view the ScreenTip, as shown in Figure 2-9

FIGURE 2-9
Button Added to Menu Bar

You can remove a button from a toolbar just as quickly. To remove the Routing Recipient button from the menu bar:

Step 1	*Open*	the Customize dialog box
Step 2	*Drag*	the Routing Recipient button from the menu bar into the dialog box
Step 3	*Close*	the dialog box
Step 4	*Close*	the PowerPoint application and return to the Windows desktop

2.d Viewing and Customizing the Office Shortcut Bar

The **Office Shortcut Bar** is a toolbar that you can open and position on your Windows desktop to provide shortcuts to Office applications and tasks. It can contain buttons for the New Office Document and Open Office Document commands on the Start menu, shortcut buttons to create various Outlook items like the New Task button, and buttons to open Office applications installed on your computer.

You can view and use the Office Shortcut Bar as needed or you can choose to have it open each time you start your computer. To view the Office Shortcut Bar:

Step 1	*Click*	the Start button 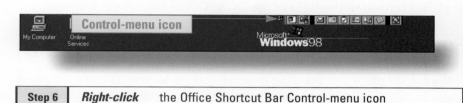 on the taskbar
Step 2	*Point to*	Programs
Step 3	*Point to*	Microsoft Office Tools
Step 4	*Click*	Microsoft Office Shortcut Bar
Step 5	*Click*	No in the Microsoft Office Shortcut Bar dialog box to not open the Office Shortcut Bar each time you start your computer

The Office Shortcut Bar may appear docked in the upper-right corner or along the right edge of your Windows desktop. Your screen may look similar to Figure 2-10.

Step 6	*Right-click*	the Office Shortcut Bar Control-menu icon

The Office Shortcut Bar Control-menu contains commands you can use to customize or close the Office Shortcut Bar. If your Shortcut Bar does not already contain buttons to open the individual Office applications, you may want to customize it for the Office applications you use frequently. To open the Customize dialog box:

Step 1	*Click*	Customize
Step 2	*Click*	the Buttons tab

The dialog box on your screen should look similar to Figure 2-11.

FIGURE 2-10
Office Shortcut Bar

FIGURE 2-11
Buttons Tab in the Customize Dialog Box

chapter
two

QUICK TIP

You can enlarge the
Shortcut Bar buttons
by clicking the Large
Buttons check box; this
inserts a check mark
on the View tab in the
Customize dialog box.
You can place the
Shortcut Bar in its own
window, and then move
and size the window by
clicking the Auto Fit into
Title Bar area check
box; this removes the
check mark on the View
tab in the Customize
dialog box.

The shortcut button for a particular application or file is visible on the Office Shortcut Bar if a check mark appears in the check box to the left of the application icon in the Show these Files as Buttons: list. To add a shortcut button that opens the Word application:

Step 1	*Scroll*	the Show these Files as Buttons: list to view the check boxes for the Office applications
Step 2	*Click*	the Microsoft Word check box to insert a check mark
Step 3	*Observe*	that a button for the Word application immediately appears on the Office Shortcut Bar

You can easily reposition a button on the Office Shortcut Bar by moving the item into the Show these Files as Buttons: list. To reposition the Word button to the right of the Open Office Document button:

Step 1	*Click*	the Microsoft Word application name to select it in the list
Step 2	*Click*	the Move up arrow until the Microsoft Word application and check box appear immediately below the Open Office Document icon and check box
Step 3	*Observe*	that the Word button on the Office Shortcut Bar is repositioned

You can also delete an application button from the Office Shortcut Bar. To remove the Word application button:

Step 1	*Click*	the Microsoft Word check box to remove the check mark
Step 2	*Move*	the Microsoft Word check box back to its original position above the Excel check box by selecting it and clicking the Move down arrow
Step 3	*Click*	OK

The Office Shortcut Bar may be in the upper-right corner of your screen and sized to fit within an application title bar. This means that Office Shortcut Bar always shows on top of the active application's title bar with small buttons. You can enlarge the buttons and place the Shortcut Bar in its own window so you can move it elsewhere on the screen. You can also hide and redisplay the Shortcut Bar as needed. To close the Office Shortcut Bar:

| Step 1 | *Right-click* | the Office Shortcut Bar Control-menu icon |
| Step 2 | *Click* | Exit |

Summary

► When you first start Word, Excel, or PowerPoint, you see personalized menus containing basic commands. As you use different commands, they are automatically added to the personalized menu. Commands that are not used for some time are removed from the personalized menus.

► When you first start Word, Excel, or PowerPoint, the Standard and Formatting toolbars share one row below the menu bar. You can reposition the Formatting toolbar to view more or fewer toolbar buttons. The remaining default toolbar buttons that are not visible on the toolbars can be added from the More Buttons list.

► FrontPage and Access also provide the personalized menus and toolbars options.

► You can turn off or reset the personalized menus and toolbars in the Options tab of the Customize dialog box.

► You can hide or view toolbars as you need them by using a shortcut menu.

► Toolbars can be docked at the top, bottom, or side of the screen or they can remain floating on the screen in their own window.

► You can customize toolbars by adding or deleting buttons and commands, displaying larger-sized buttons, and turning on or off the display of ScreenTips, or adding keyboard shortcut keys to ScreenTips.

► The menu bar is a special toolbar that can be customized just like other toolbars.

► The Office Shortcut Bar is a customizable toolbar you can position on the desktop and contains shortcuts for opening Office documents and applications.

chapter two

Commands Review

Action	Menu Bar	Shortcut Menu	Toolbar	Keyboard
To display or hide toolbars	View, Toolbars	Right-click a toolbar, click the desired toolbar to add or remove the check mark		ALT + V, T
To customize a toolbar	View, Toolbars, Customize	Right-click a toolbar, click Customize		ALT + V, T, C

Concepts Review

SCANS

Circle the correct answer.

1. A menu is:
- [a] a set of icons.
- [b] a list of commands.
- [c] impossible to customize.
- [d] never personalized.

2. The Options tab in the PowerPoint Customize dialog box does not include an option for:
- [a] turning on or off ScreenTips for toolbar buttons.
- [b] turning on or off Large icons for toolbar buttons.
- [c] adding animation to menus.
- [d] docking all toolbars.

3. A toolbar is:
- [a] a list of commands.
- [b] always floating on your screen.
- [c] a set of icons.
- [d] never docked on your screen.

4. When you right-click an item on your screen, you see:
- [a] the Right Click toolbar.
- [b] animated menus.
- [c] expanded menus.
- [d] a shortcut menu.

Circle **T** if the statement is true or **F** if the statement is false.

T   F   1. The Standard and Formatting toolbars must remain on the same row.

T   F   2. When updating docked personalized toolbars, some buttons may be automatically removed from view to make room for the new buttons.

T   F   3. Resetting your usage data affects your toolbars regardless of their size or position.

T   F   4. You cannot add animation to menus.

Skills Review

SCANS

Exercise 1

1. Open the Word application.

2. Open the Options tab in the Customize dialog box and reset the usage data, have the Standard and Formatting toolbars share one row, and the menus show recently used commands first.

3. Add the Show/Hide button to the personalized Standard toolbar using the More Buttons list.

4. Add the Font color button to the personalized Formatting toolbar using the More Buttons list.

5. Open the Customize dialog box and reset your usage data in the Options tab.

6. Close the Word application.

Exercise 2   C

1. Open the Excel application.

2. Open the Options tab in the Customize dialog box and reset the usage data, have the Standard and Formatting toolbars share one row, and the menus show recently used commands first.

3. View the personalized Tools menu.

4. Add the AutoCorrect command to the personalized Tools menu.

5. Reset your usage data.

6. Close the Excel application.

Exercise 3

1. Open the Office Shortcut Bar. (Do not set it to automatically open when you start your computer.)

2. Customize the Office Shortcut Bar to add the Word, Excel, and PowerPoint shortcut buttons or remove them if they already appear.

3. Customize the Office Shortcut Bar to have large buttons and position it in its own window vertically at the right side of the desktop.

4. AutoFit the Office Shortcut Bar to the title bar with small buttons.

5. Remove the Word, Excel, and PowerPoint application shortcut buttons or add them back, if necessary.

6. Close the Office Shortcut Bar.

Exercise 4

1. Open the Word application.

2. Add the Clear command icon from the Edit category to the menu bar.

3. Reset the menu bar back to its default from the Toolbars tab in the Customize dialog box.

4. Close the Word application.

Exercise 5

1. Open the Excel application.

2. View the Drawing, Picture, and WordArt toolbars using a shortcut menu.

3. Dock the Picture toolbar below the Standard and Formatting toolbars.

4. Dock the WordArt toolbar at the left boundary of the screen.

5. Close the Excel application from the taskbar.

6. Open the Excel with the New Office Document on the Start menu. (*Hint:* Use the Blank Workbook icon.)

7. Float the WordArt toolbar.

8. Float the Picture toolbar.

chapter two

9. Hide the WordArt, Picture, and Drawing toolbars using a shortcut menu.

10. Close the Excel application.

Case Projects

Project 1

As secretary to the placement director for the XYZ Employment Agency, you have been using Word 97. After you install Office 2000, you decide you want the menus and toolbars to behave just like they did in Word 97. Use the Office Assistant to search for help on "personalized menus" and select the appropriate topic from the Office Assistant list. (*Hint:* You may need to view all the topics presented in the Office Assistant balloon.) Review the Help topic you select and write down the steps to make the personalized menus and toolbars behave like Word 97 menus and toolbars.

Project 2

You are the administrative assistant to the controller of the Plush Pets, Inc., a stuffed toy manufacturing company. The controller recently installed Excel 2000. She prefers to view the entire list of menu commands rather than the personalized menus and asks for your help. Use the Office assistant to search for help on "full menus" and select the appropriate topic in the Office Assistant balloon. Review the topic and write down the instructions for switching between personalized menus and full menus.

Project 3

As administrative assistant to the art director of MediaWiz Advertising, Inc. you just installed PowerPoint 2000. Now you decide you would rather view the complete Standard and Formatting toolbars rather than the personalized toolbars and want to learn a quick way to do this. Use the Office Assistant to search for help on "show all buttons" and select the appropriate topic from the Office Assistant balloon. Review the topic and write down the instructions for showing all buttons using the mouse pointer. Open an Office application and use the mouse method to show the complete Standard and Formatting toolbars. Turn the personalized toolbars back on in the Customize dialog box.

Project 4

You are the training coordinator for the information technology (IT) department at a large international health care organization, World Health International. The information technology department is planning to install Office 2000 on computers throughout the organization within the next two weeks. Your supervisor, the IT manager, asks you to prepare a short introduction to the Office 2000 personalized menus and toolbars to be presented at next Monday's staff meeting. He wants you to emphasize the advantages and disadvantages of using the personalized menus and toolbars. Write down in at least two paragraphs the advantages and disadvantages of using the personalized menus and toolbars.

Working With Others Using Online Collaboration Tools

I Chapter Overview

In today's workplace many tasks are completed by several co-workers working together as part of a team called a workgroup. Office applications provide tools to assist workgroups in sharing information. In this chapter you learn about scheduling and participating in online meetings and conducting Web discussions with others in your workgroup.

LEARNING OBJECTIVES

▶ Schedule an online meeting
▶ Participate in Web discussions

chapter three

CAUTION TIP

The activities in this chapter assume you have access to directory servers and Web servers with Office Server Extensions installed, Microsoft NetMeeting, and Outlook with Exchange Server service installed. If you do not have access to the appropriate servers and software, you will be able to read but not do the hands-on activities. Your instructor will provide additional server, e-mail address, NetMeeting, and Outlook instructions as needed to complete the hands-on activities.

3.a Scheduling an Online Meeting

Many organizations assign tasks or projects to several workers who collaborate as members of a **workgroup**. Often these workgroup members do not work in the same office or some members travel frequently, making it difficult for the group to meet at one physical location. Office applications, together with Microsoft NetMeeting conferencing software, provide a way for workgroup members to participate in online real-time meetings from different physical locations—just as though everyone were in the same meeting room. In an online meeting, participants can share programs and documents, send text messages, transfer files, and illustrate ideas.

You can schedule an online meeting in advance using Outlook or you can invite others to participate in an online meeting right now by opening NetMeeting directly from Word, Excel, PowerPoint, and Access and calling others in your workgroup. To participate in an online meeting, invitees must have NetMeeting running on their computers.

Calling Others from Office Applications Using NetMeeting

Suppose you are working on an Excel workbook and want to discuss the workbook with another person in your workgroup. You know that they are running NetMeeting on their computer. You can call them while working in the workbook. To open NetMeeting and place a call from within Excel:

Step 1	*Click*	the Start button ▓Start on the taskbar
Step 2	*Click*	the Open Office Document command on the Start menu
Step 3	*Double-click*	the *International Food Distributors* workbook located on the Data Disk
Step 4	*Click*	Tools
Step 5	*Point to*	Online Collaboration
Step 6	*Click*	Meet Now to open NetMeeting and the Place A Call dialog box

The directory server and list of names and calling addresses in the Place A Call dialog box on your screen will be different, but the dialog box should look similar to Figure 3-1.

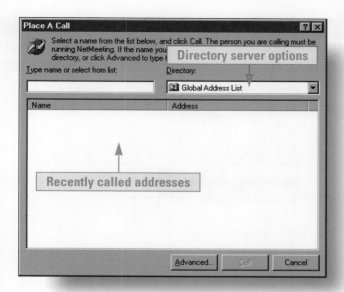

FIGURE 3-1
Place A Call Dialog Box

The person who initiates the meeting call is called the **host**. The person or persons receiving the call are called **participants**. Because you are initiating a call about the open Excel workbook, you are the host for this meeting. You can select a specific directory server and then select the participant to call from a list of persons logged onto the server or select someone from the list of frequently called NetMeeting participants. The *host* now calls a participant in the list:

| Step 1 | *Right-click* | the name of the person in the list specified by your instructor and click Call |

NetMeeting dials the participant. Depending on the participant's NetMeeting configuration, he or she can automatically accept the call or manually accept or ignore the call. If the NetMeeting configuration is set up to manually answer calls, an announcement appears on the participant's screen, allowing him or her to click a button to accept or decline the call.

For the activities in this chapter, the participant's NetMeeting software is configured to automatically accept incoming calls. When the call is accepted, the *International Food Distributors* workbook and the Online Meeting toolbar automatically display on the participant's screen, even if the participant does not have Excel installed. Only the host needs to have the application installed and the file available. Both the *host's* and the *participant's* screens should look similar to Figure 3-2.

The host has **control** of the *International Foods Distributors* workbook when the meeting starts, which means the host can turn on or off collaboration at any time, controlling who can edit the document. When collaboration is turned on, any one participant can control the workbook for editing. When collaboration is turned off,

**chapter
three**

FIGURE 3-2
Host's and Participant's
Screens

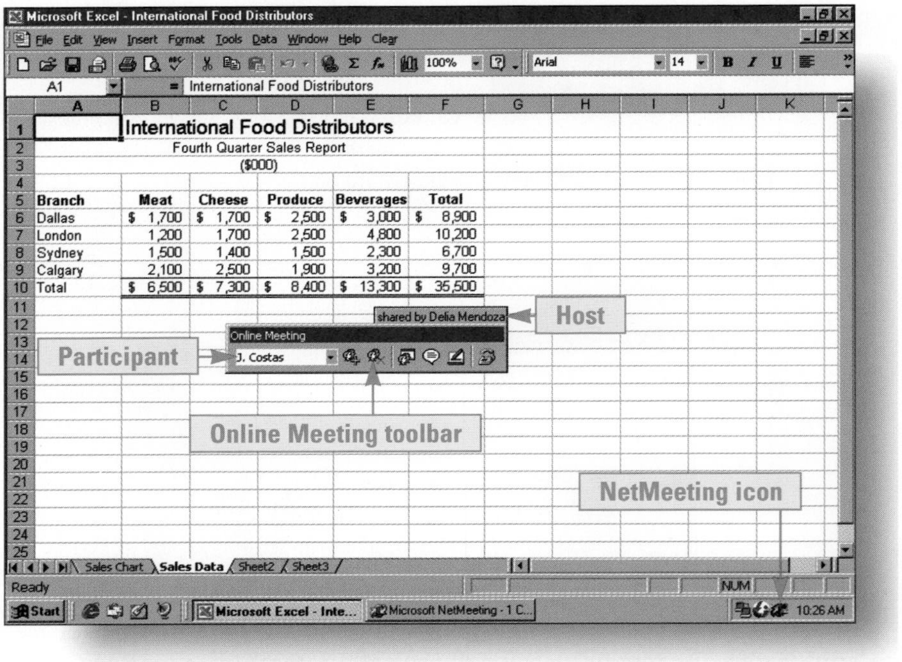

Q U I C K   T I P

Only the host of the
meeting can use all the
features on the Online
Meeting toolbar.

only the host can edit the workbook but all participants can see it. The
host now turns on collaboration:

Step 1	**Click**	the Allow others to edit button ⊞ on the Online Meeting toolbar

The first time a participant wants to take control of the workbook,
they double-click it. The host can regain control of the workbook at
any time simply by clicking it. To regain control of the workbook after
the first time they control it, a participant also clicks it. The initials of
the person who currently controls the workbook appear beside the
mouse pointer. The *participant* takes control of the workbook for the
first time to edit it:

C A U T I O N   T I P

When someone else
controls a document
during an online
meeting, you cannot
use your mouse pointer
to access commands or
edit the document until
you regain control of it.

Step 1	**Double-click**	the workbook to take control and place your user initials beside the mouse pointer
Step 2	**Click**	Tools
Step 3	**Click**	Options
Step 4	**Click**	the View tab
Step 5	**Click**	the Gridlines check box to remove the check mark
Step 6	**Click**	OK to turn off the gridlines in the workbook

The *host* regains control of the workbook:

| Step 1 | *Click* | the workbook to regain control and place your initials beside the mouse pointer |
| Step 2 | *Turn on* | the gridlines on the View tab in the Options dialog box |

The **Whiteboard** is a tool that participants can use to illustrate their thoughts and ideas. Only the host can display the Whiteboard during an online meeting that originates from within an Office application. All participants can draw on the Whiteboard at the same time only when the host turns off collaboration. The *host* turns off collaboration:

Step 1	*Click*	the workbook to regain control, if necessary
Step 2	*Click*	the Allow others to edit button to turn off collaboration
Step 3	*Click*	the Display Whiteboard button on the Online Meeting toolbar

Your screen should look similar to Figure 3-3.

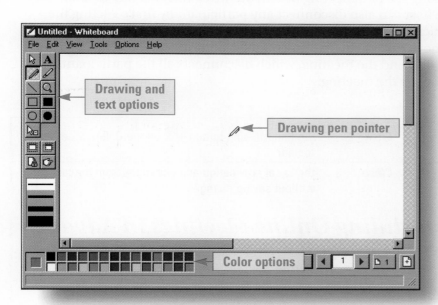

FIGURE 3-3
Whiteboard Window

> ### QUICK TIP
> When collaboration is turned off, meeting participants can use **Chat** to send and respond to keyed messages in real time. With a sound card and a camera attached to their computer, the host and participants in an online meeting can both hear and see one another. For more information on using Chat, audio, and video in online meetings see NetMeeting online Help.

> ### QUICK TIP
> The meeting host can turn off collaboration when someone else has control of the document by pressing the ESC key.

All participants, including the host, add text, draw shapes, add color, and insert additional pages in the Whiteboard window. The host can save and print Whiteboard pages. The host and participant explore using the drawing, text, and color options for the Whiteboard. First, the *host* selects a color and draws a shape:

chapter
three

MENU TIP

The host can send a copy of the active document to all participants by clicking the File menu, pointing to Send To, and clicking the Online Meeting Recipient command. All participants then receive the file as an e-mail attachment. The host can send the document to one participant by clicking the E-mail button on the Standard toolbar and attaching the document file to an e-mail message.

CAUTION TIP

Only the host can save and print the document during an online meeting. If a participant in control attempts to print or save the workbook, it is printed at the host's printer and saved to the host's hard disk or originating server.

| Step 1 | *Click* | Red in the color options |
| Step 2 | *Draw* | a shape by dragging the drawing pen pointer in the Whiteboard drawing area |

The *participant* now takes control of the drawing pen, selects a color, and draws a shape:

| Step 1 | *Click* | the Whiteboard to take control of the drawing pen |
| Step 2 | *Click* | Blue in the color options and draw a shape |

The *host* and the *participant*:

| Step 1 | *Continue* | to share the Whiteboard and explore the different Whiteboard options |
| Step 2 | *Click* | the Close button ⊠ on the Whiteboard window title bar to close the Whiteboard |

Each participant can disconnect from the meeting at any time by clicking the End Meeting button on the Online Meeting toolbar. The host can also disconnect any participant by first selecting the participant from the Participants List button and then clicking the Remove Participants button on the Online Meeting toolbar. The host can also end the meeting, which disconnects all the participants. The *host* ends the meeting:

| Step 1 | *Click* | the End Meeting button 🗗 on the Online Meeting toolbar |
| Step 2 | *Close* | the Excel application and workbook from the taskbar without saving changes |

Scheduling Online Meetings in Advance Using Outlook

As a host, you can schedule online meetings in advance using Outlook directly or from inside other Office applications. Suppose you are putting the finishing touches on a PowerPoint presentation and want to schedule an online meeting in advance with other workgroup members. You can do this from inside the PowerPoint application. To open a PowerPoint presentation and invite others to an online meeting:

Step 1	**Open**	the PowerPoint application and the *International Food Distributors* presentation located on the Data Disk using the Open Office Document command on the Start menu
Step 2	**Click**	Tools
Step 3	**Point to**	Online Collaboration
Step 4	**Click**	Schedule Meeting

The Outlook Meeting window opens, similar to Figure 3-4.

This window provides all the options for setting up the meeting. You address the message to one or more e-mail addresses, key the subject of the meeting, and select the directory server where the meeting will be held. You also select the date and time of the meeting. The current document is selected as the Office document to be reviewed and a meeting reminder is set to be delivered to the host and attendees 15 minutes prior to the scheduled meeting.

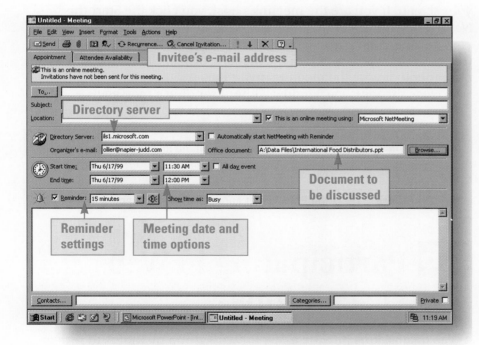

FIGURE 3-4
Outlook Meeting Window

As long as all invitees are using Outlook for their scheduling, you can determine the best time to schedule the meeting by clicking the Attendee Availability tab and inviting others from the Outlook global address book. To review the Attendee Availability tab:

Step 1	**Click**	the Attendee Availability tab

**chapter
three**

| Step 2 | *Observe* | the meeting scheduling options you can use to compare each invitee's free and busy times from their Outlook calendars and select the best meeting time |
| Step 3 | *Click* | the Appointment tab |

You send the completed meeting invitation by clicking the <u>S</u>end button on the Standard toolbar. Each invitee receives an e-mail message with the meeting information. They can choose to accept, decline, or tentatively accept the invitation by clicking a button inside the message window. If they accept, an Outlook appointment item is added to their calendar. Because you are the host, an appointment item is automatically added to your Outlook calendar. If invitees accept, decline, or accept tentatively, you receive an e-mail notification of their attendance choice and your meeting appointment item is updated to show who is attending and who declined.

Fifteen minutes prior to the scheduled online meeting (if Outlook is running on your computer) a meeting reminder message opens on your screen. If you are the meeting's host, you click the Start this NetMeeting button in the reminder window to begin the meeting. If you are an invited participant, you click the Join the Meeting button in the reminder window to join the meeting or you click the Dismiss this reminder to ignore the meeting invitation.

To close the message window without sending a message:

Step 1	*Click*	the Close button [X] on the message window title bar
Step 2	*Click*	<u>N</u>o
Step 3	*Close*	the PowerPoint application and presentation

QUICK TIP

For more information on scheduling meetings using Outlook, see Outlook online Help.

CAUTION TIP

Special software called Office Server Extensions must be installed on a Web server before discussion items can be created and stored there. For more information on Office Server Extensions software, see the documentation that accompanies Office or online Help.

3.b Participating in Web Discussions

Web discussions provide a way for workgroup members to review and provide input to the same document by associating messages, called **discussion items**, with the document. Discussion items are saved in a database separate from the associated document. This enables the group to consider multiple discussion items related to the same document; it also allows the document to be edited without affecting any discussion items. Discussion items are **threaded**, which means that replies to an item appear directly under the original item. Discussion items are saved as they are entered and are available immediately when the associated document is opened.

Suppose you are working on a Word document and want to solicit input from others in your workgroup. Instead of sending a copy to everyone in the workgroup or routing a single copy to everyone, you decide to use the Web discussion feature. To start a Web discussion:

Step 1	*Open*	the Word application and the *Dallas Warehouse Audit* document located on the Data Disk using the Open Office Document command on the Start menu
Step 2	*Click*	<u>T</u>ools
Step 3	*Point to*	<u>O</u>nline Collaboration
Step 4	*Click*	<u>W</u>eb Discussions

After you connect to your discussion server, the Web Discussions toolbar opens docked above the status bar. See Figure 3-5.

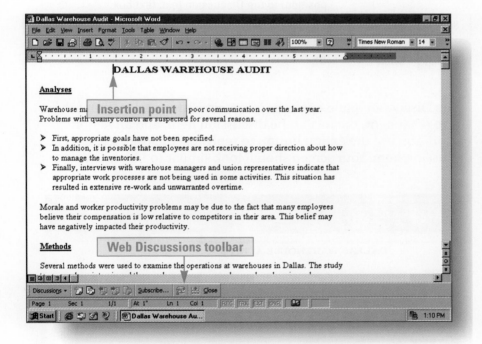

FIGURE 3-5
Document with Web Discussions Toolbar

QUICK TIP

There are two types of discussion items: an **inline discussion item** relates to a specific paragraph, picture, or table, and a **general discussion item** relates to the entire document. Word supports both inline and general discussion items. Excel and PowerPoint support only general discussion items.

First, you add a general discussion item identifying the issues to be discussed in the document. To add a general discussion item:

Step 1	*Press*	the CTRL + HOME keys to move the keying position (called the insertion point) to the top of the document
Step 2	*Click*	the Insert Discussion about the Document button 🔲 on the Web Discussions toolbar

The dialog box that opens should look similar to Figure 3-6.

chapter three

FIGURE 3-6
Enter Discussion Text
Dialog Box

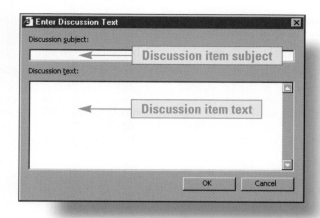

Step 3	*Key*	Problems in Dallas in the Discussion subject: text box
Step 4	*Press*	the TAB key to move the insertion point (the keying position) to the Discussion text: text box
Step 5	*Key*	We have only three weeks to resolve the problems in Dallas.
Step 6	*Click*	OK

The Discussion pane opens and contains information about the active document, the text of the discussion item, and an Action button. You use the Action button to reply to, edit, or delete a discussion item. Your screen should look similar to Figure 3-7.

FIGURE 3-7
Document with
Discussion Pane

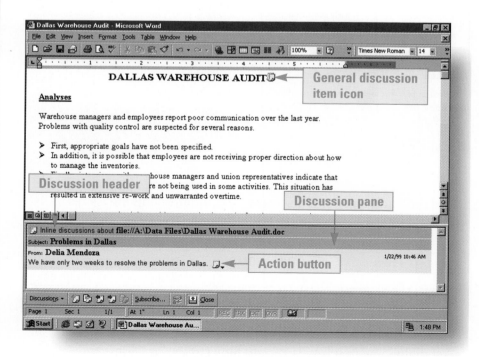

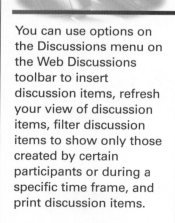

MOUSE TIP

You can use options on the Discussions menu on the Web Discussions toolbar to insert discussion items, refresh your view of discussion items, filter discussion items to show only those created by certain participants or during a specific time frame, and print discussion items.

Next you add an inline discussion item to a specific paragraph. To close the Discussion pane and add an inline discussion item:

Step 1	*Click*	the Show/Hide Discussion Pane button 🔼 on the Web Discussions toolbar
Step 2	*Click*	at the end of the first bulleted item ending in "specified." to reposition the insertion point
Step 3	*Click*	the Insert Discussion in the Document button 🗐 on the Web Discussions toolbar
Step 4	*Key*	Goals in the Discussion <u>s</u>ubject: text box
Step 5	*Key*	Doesn't Yong's group have responsibility for setting warehouse goals? in the Discussion <u>t</u>ext: text box
Step 6	*Click*	OK

The inline discussion item icon appears at the end of the bulleted text and the Discussion pane opens. Your screen should look similar to Figure 3-8.

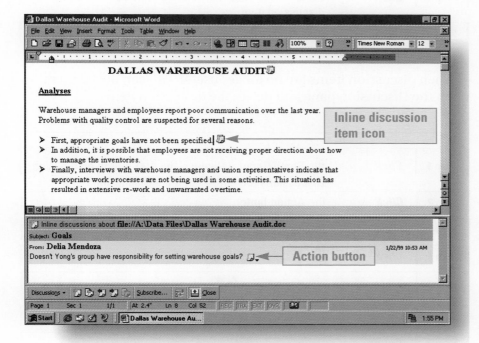

FIGURE 3-8
Inline Discussion Item

| Step 7 | *Click* | the Show/Hide Discussion Pane button 🔼 on the Web Discussions toolbar to close the Discussion pane |

CAUTION TIP

You can modify a document that contains threaded discussions. If you make changes in an area that is not associated with a discussion item, the inline and general discussions are not affected. If you change or delete part of the document associated with a discussion item, any inline discussions are deleted but general discussions are not affected. If you move, rename, or delete a document, all inline and general discussions are lost.

**chapter
three**

Others in the workgroup can now open the *Dallas Warehouse Audit* document, log on to the discussion server, and review the inline and general discussion items. They can reply to existing items and create new items. They can edit or delete any discussion items they create. Now assume you are a different member of the workgroup and you just opened the *Dallas Warehouse Audit* document, logged on to the discussion server, and want to participate in the discussion. To thread a reply to the inline discussion item at the end of the bulleted list:

Step 1	*Press*	the CTRL + HOME keys to move the insertion point to the top of the document
Step 2	*Click*	the Next button ⬇ twice on the Web Discussions toolbar to select the second discussion item and open the Discussion pane
Step 3	*Click*	the Action button in the Discussion pane
Step 4	*Click*	Reply
Step 5	*Key*	Yong's group is currently understaffed and behind schedule. in the Discussion text: text box
Step 6	*Click*	OK to thread your reply immediately below the original discussion item
Step 7	*Close*	the Discussion pane

When discussion items are no longer useful, you can delete them. To open the Discussion pane and delete the discussion items:

Step 1	*Click*	the Show General Discussions ⬜ button on the Web Discussions toolbar to open the Discussion Pane
Step 2	*Click*	the Action button
Step 3	*Click*	Delete
Step 4	*Click*	Yes to confirm the deletion
Step 5	*Click*	the Next button ⬇ on the Web Discussions toolbar
Step 6	*Delete*	the first inline discussion item
Step 7	*Delete*	the second inline action item
Step 8	*Click*	Close on the Web Discussions toolbar to close the discussions session
Step 9	*Close*	the Word application and the document without saving any changes

Summary

▶ You can work with others to complete tasks using Office applications' online collaboration tools: NetMeeting and Web Discussions.

▶ You can use the NetMeeting conferencing software directly from inside Office applications to host or participate in an online meeting.

▶ During an online meeting using NetMeeting, participants can take turns editing the current document when the meeting's host turns on collaboration.

▶ When collaboration is turned off, participants in a NetMeeting online meeting can use the Whiteboard.

▶ You can chat in real-time during an online meeting and, with a sound card and camera, both see and hear other attendees.

▶ You can schedule a meeting in advance, either using Outlook or from inside Office applications.

▶ Another way to work with others on a document is to participate in a Web discussion by associating text comments, called discussion items, with a specific document.

▶ Inline discussion items relate to specific paragraphs, pictures, or tables in a document. General discussion items relate to the entire document. Only the Word application supports inline discussion items.

Commands Review

Action	Menu Bar	Shortcut Menu	Toolbar	Keyboard
Schedule a meeting using NetMeeting inside Office applications	Tools, Online Collaboration, Meet Now			ALT + T, N, M
Schedule a meeting in advance using Outlook inside Office applications	Tools, Online Collaboration, Schedule Meeting			ALT + T, N, S
Participate in Web Discussions from inside Office applications	Tools, Online Collaboration, Web Discussions			ALT + T, N, W

chapter three

Concepts Review

Circle the correct answer.

1. Workgroup members:
[a] always work in the same physical location.
[b] never travel on business.
[c] always work independently of each other.
[d] often work in different physical locations or travel frequently.

2. A participant in an online meeting:
[a] can turn collaboration on and off.
[b] controls access to the Whiteboard.
[c] can save and print to their own hard drive or printer.
[d] is the person receiving the call.

3. The first time a participant takes control of a document during an online meeting, the participant must:
[a] open the Chat window.
[b] click the document.
[c] double-click the document.
[d] press the CTRL + HOME keys.

4. NetMeeting participants use the Whiteboard to:
[a] key real-time text messages.
[b] share and edit documents.
[c] add inline discussion items.
[d] illustrate their ideas and thoughts.

Circle **T** if the statement is true or **F** if the statement is false.

T   T   1. To participate in an online meeting, invitees must be running NetMeeting on their computer.

T   F   2. When collaboration is turned on, the host of an online meeting always maintains control of the active document.

T   F   3. To gain control of a document during collaboration, participants must double-click it.

T   F   4. The active document can be printed and saved to any participant's printer, hard disk, or server during an online meeting.

notes You must be connected to the appropriate directory and discussion servers and have NetMeeting and Outlook running with Exchange server to complete these exercises. Your instructor will provide the server and e-mail address information and any NetMeeting and Outlook instructions needed to complete these exercises.

Skills Review

Exercise 1

1. Open the Word application and the *Dallas Warehouse Audit* document located on the Data Disk.

2. Invite three other people to an online meeting now.

3. Take turns making changes to the document.

4. End the meeting. Close the Word application and document without saving any changes.

Exercise 2

1. Open the Excel application and the *International Food Distributors* workbook located on the Data Disk.

2. Invite four other people to an online meeting next Thursday at 2:00 PM.

3. Open Outlook and read their automatic meeting reply messages.

4. Open the Outlook appointment item created for the message and view the updated attendee information.

5. Delete the appointment item and send a message to all attendees canceling the meeting.

6. Close Outlook. Close the Excel application and workbook without saving any changes.

Exercise 3

1. Open the PowerPoint application and the *International Food Distributors* presentation located on the Data Disk.

2. Create a general Web discussion item using the text "This is an important presentation."

3. Close the Web discussion and the PowerPoint application and presentation without saving any changes.

Exercise 4

1. Open the PowerPoint application and the *International Food Distributors* presentation located on the Data Disk.

2. Reply to the general discussion item using the text "What is the project due date?"

3. Print the discussion items using a command on the Discussions menu.

4. Delete the general discussion items created for the *International Food Distributors* presentation.

5. Close the Web discussion and the PowerPoint application and presentation without saving any changes.

Case Projects

Project 1

As assistant to the accounting manager at Wilson Art Supply, you are asked to find out how to select a discussion server. Open the Word application and use the Office Assistant to search for discussion server topics using the keywords "Web discussions" and select the appropriate topic from the Office Assistant balloon. Review the topic and write down the instructions for selecting a discussion server.

Project 2

You work in the marketing department at International Hair Concepts, a company that imports professional hairdresser supplies. Your department is going to start scheduling online meetings to collaborate on Word documents and you want to be prepared for potential problems. Open the Word application and use the Office Assistant to find the "troubleshoot online meetings" topic. Write down a list of potential problems and their possible solutions.

Project 3

A co-worker at Merton Partners, a public relations firm, mentions that you can subscribe to documents and folders stored on a Web server and then be notified when changes are made to them. Using Word online Help to search for Web discussion topics; review the topic, "About subscribing to a document or folder on a Web server." Write a paragraph about how subscribing to documents and folders could help you in your work.

Project 4

The Women's Professional Softball Teams annual tournament is in two months and 30 teams from around the world will participate. The director wants to review the schedule (created in Word) at one time with the team representatives in the United States, England, France, Holland, Germany, China, Argentina, Mexico, and Australia. Write at least two paragraphs recommending an online collaboration tool and explaining why this is the best choice.

chapter three

Introduction to the Internet and the World Wide Web

Chapter Overview

Millions of people use the Internet to shop for goods and services, listen to music, view artwork, conduct research, get stock quotes, keep up-to-date with current events, and send e-mail. More and more people are using the Internet at work and at home to view and download multimedia computer files containing graphics, sound, video, and text. In this chapter you learn about the origins of the Internet, how to connect to the Internet, how to use the Internet Explorer Web browser, and how to access pages on the World Wide Web.

chapter four
4

4.a What Is the Internet?

To understand the Internet, you must understand networks. A **network** is simply a group of two or more computers linked by cable or telephone lines. The linked computers also include a special computer called a **network server** that is used to store files and programs that everyone on the network can access. In addition to the shared files and programs, networks enable users to share equipment, such as a common network printer. See Figure 4-1.

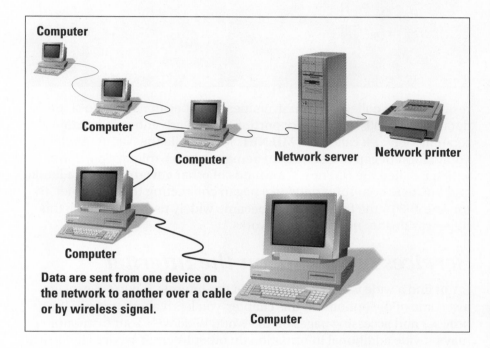

Computer

Computer

Computer

Network server   Network printer

Computer

Data are sent from one device on the network to another over a cable or by wireless signal.

Computer

FIGURE 4-1
Computer Network

The **Internet** is a worldwide collection of computer networks that enables users to view and transfer information between computers. For example, an Internet user in California can retrieve (or **download**) files from a computer in Canada quickly and easily. In the same way, an Internet user in Australia can send (or **upload**) files to another Internet user in England. See Figure 4-2.

The Internet is not a single organization, but rather a cooperative effort by multiple organizations managing a variety of computers.

A Brief History of the Internet

The Internet originated in the late 1960s, when the United States Department of Defense developed a network of military computers called the **ARPAnet**. Quickly realizing the usefulness of such a network,

chapter
four

FIGURE 4-2
The Internet

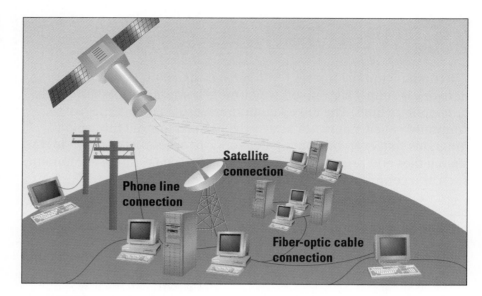

researchers at colleges and universities soon began using it to share data. In the 1980s the military portion of the early Internet became a separate network called the **MILNET**. Meanwhile the National Science Foundation began overseeing the remaining non-military portions, which it called the **NSFnet**. Thousands of other government, academic, and business computer networks began connecting to the NSFnet. By the late 1980s, the term Internet became widely used to describe this huge worldwide "network of networks."

Services Available on the Internet

You find a wide variety of services on the Internet. Table 4-1 explains just some of the options. In this chapter, you learn about using a Web browser and accessing pages on the World Wide Web. Your instructor may provide additional information on other Internet services in the list.

CAUTION TIP

During peak day and evening hours, millions of people are connecting to the Internet. During these hours, you may have difficulty connecting to your host computer or to other sites on the Internet.

4.b Connecting to the Internet

To connect to the Internet you need some physical communication medium connected to your computer, such as network cable or a modem. You also need a special communication program that allows your computer to communicate with computers on the Internet and a Web browser program, such as Microsoft Internet Explorer 5, that allows you to move among all the Internet resources. See Figure 4-3.

Category	Name	Description
Communication	E-mail	Electronic messages sent or received from one computer to another
	Newsgroups	Electronic "bulletin boards" or discussion groups where people with common interests (such as hobbyists or members of professional associations) post messages (called **articles**) that participants around the world can read and respond to
	Mailing Lists	Similar to Newsgroups, except that participants exchange information via e-mail
	Chat	Online conversations in which participants key messages and receive responses on their screen within a few seconds
File Access	FTP	Sending (uploading) or receiving (downloading) computer files via the File Transfer Protocol (FTP) communication rules
Searching Tools	Directories	Tools that help you search for Web sites by category
	Search Engines	Tools to help you find individual files on the Internet by searching for specific words or phrases
World Wide Web (Web)	Web Site	A subset of the Internet that stores files with Web pages containing text, graphics, video, audio, and links to other pages

TABLE 4-1
Internet Services

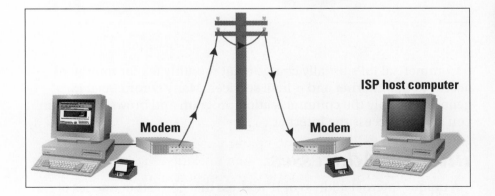

FIGURE 4-3
Internet Connection

chapter
four

Internet Service Providers

After setting up your computer hardware (the network cable or modem) and installing the Internet Explorer Web browser, you must make arrangements to connect to a computer on the Internet. The computer you connect to is called a **host**. Usually, you connect to a host computer via a commercial Internet Service Provider, such as America Online or another company who sells access to the Internet. An **Internet Service Provider (ISP)** maintains the host computer, provides a gateway or entrance to the Internet, and provides an electronic "mail box" with facilities for sending and receiving e-mail. See Figure 4-4.

FIGURE 4-4
Internet Service Providers

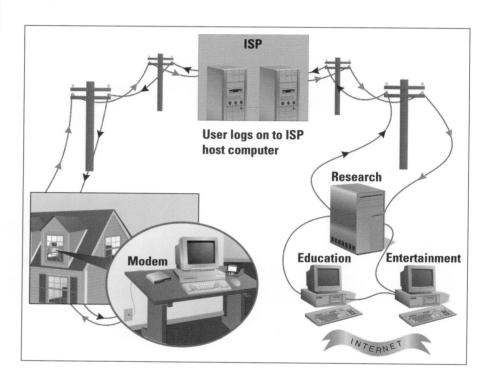

Commercial ISPs usually charge a flat monthly fee for unlimited access to the Internet and e-mail services. Many commercial ISPs generally supply the communication program and browser program you need to access the Internet.

Internet Addresses

A unique Internet address or IP address that consists of a series of numbers identifies each host computer on the Internet. Computers on the Internet use these IP address numbers to communicate with each other, but you will probably need to use one only when you install dial-up networking instructions on your computer. The more important address is the host computer's descriptive address. This address specifies the individual computer within a level of organization, or **domain**, on the Internet. For example, a host computer in the math department at a university might be identified as: *raven.math.uidaho.edu* where "raven" identifies the specific computer, "math" identifies the department, "uidaho" identifies the university, and the suffix "edu" identifies that the address is for an educational institution. You'll find that the descriptive host name is much easier to use and remember than the IP address. Table 4-2 identifies the top-level domain (or highest organizational unit on the Internet) names you see as you work with Internet resources. Other top-level domain names are under consideration but not yet in use.

Top-Level Domain	Organization
.com	Commercial enterprise
.gov	Government institution
.edu	Educational institution
.mil	Military institution
.net	Computer network
.org	Other organizations

TABLE 4-2
Top-Level Domains

User Names

When you make arrangements to access the Internet via an ISP, you also set up a user name that identifies your account with the ISP. Your user name consists of a name you select and the host's descriptive name. User names can be full names, first initial and last names, nicknames, or a group of letters and numbers. For example, the user name for Beth Jackson who accesses the Internet via a commercial ISP named Decon Data Systems might be: *Beth_Jackson@decon.net* where "Beth_Jackson" is the user's name, and "decon.net" is the descriptive name for the ISP's host computer.

4.c Challenges to Using the Internet

Using the Internet to send e-mail, read and post articles to newsgroups, chat online, send and receive files, and search for information is fun and exciting. However, because people use the Internet all over the world, there is a seemingly endless source of data and information available. The sheer size of the Internet can sometimes be intimidating.

Another potential difficulty is the time it takes for messages and files to travel between computers on the Internet. Communication speeds

QUICK TIP

There are several commercial networks that are separate from the Internet. These commercial networks provide users with features such as online newspapers and magazines, chat groups, access to investment activities, computer games, and special-interest bulletin boards as well as Internet access. Popular commercial networks include America Online and the Microsoft Network.

chapter
four

QUICK TIP

Many college and university libraries have Web sites with excellent tips on how to use and evaluate information on the Internet.

INTERNET TIP

To change the start page for the Internet Explorer Web browser, click the Internet Options command on the View menu and then click the General tab. Define the start page by keying the URL in the Address: text box or clicking the Use Current, Use Default, or Use Blank buttons. For more information on designating a start page, see Internet Explorer online Help.

can be improved by using high-speed modems and special telephone lines. Faster Internet communication via cable is also becoming more widely available.

You should also be aware that the Internet is a cooperative effort, with few widely accepted presentation standards. As a result, the presentation of information on the Internet is varied and inconsistent. Some Web sites are well-designed and easy to use, while some are not. The Internet is a dynamic environment that changes daily with new host computers and Web sites being added and existing ones being removed. This means new or different information is available constantly. Also, old or outdated information may still be available on Web sites that are not properly maintained.

Also, there may be questions about the accuracy of information you find on the Internet. Remember that the Internet is a largely unregulated environment with few, if any, controls over what information is published on the Web or contained in files at FTP sites. It is a good idea to get supporting information from another source before using any information you find on the Internet to make critical business decisions.

Another challenge to using the Internet is the lack of privacy and security for your e-mail and file transmissions. Information sent from one computer to another can travel through many computer systems and networks, where it could be intercepted, copied, or altered. When you access a page on the World Wide Web, it is possible that information such as your e-mail address, which Web pages you view, the type of computer, operating system, and browser you are using, and how you linked to that page can be captured without your knowledge. If you are concerned, you can take advantage of security software that prevents this type of information from being captured.

Certain browser and server programs on Internet computers can encrypt (or scramble) information during transmission and then decrypt (or unscramble) it at its destination. Commercial activities, such as buying an item via credit card or transferring money between bank accounts, can occur in this type of secure environment. However, be advised that much Internet activity takes place in an insecure environment. Government regulations, as well as technological methods to assure privacy and security on the Internet, continue to be developed.

4.d Using Internet Explorer

A **Web browser** is a software application that helps you access Internet resources, including Web pages stored on computers called Web servers. A **Web page** is a document that contains hyperlinks (often called links) to other pages; it can also contain audio and video clips. A **hyperlink** is text or a picture that is associated with the location (path and filename) of another page. To open the Internet Explorer Web browser:

| Step 1 | **Connect** | to your ISP, if necessary |

| Step 2 | **Double-click** the Internet Explorer icon 🅔 on the desktop |

When the Web browser opens, a Web page, called the **start page**, loads automatically. The start page used by the Internet Explorer Web browser can be the Microsoft default start page, a blank page, or any designated Web page. Figure 4-5 shows the home page for the publisher of this book as the start page.

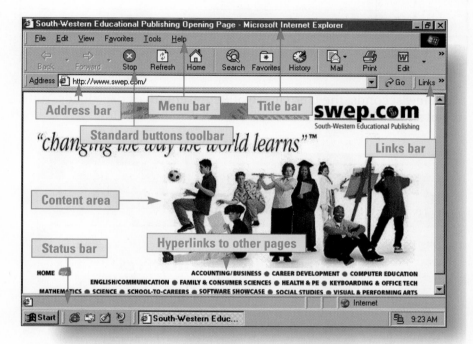

FIGURE 4-5
Internet Explorer
Web Browser

MOUSE TIP

The **Address bar** contains a text box in which you key the path and filename of the Web page you want to load and a drop-down list of recently loaded Web pages and files.

The **Links bar** is a customizable bar to which you can add shortcuts to frequently loaded Web pages.

QUICK TIP

As a Web page loads, the progress bar illustrates the progress of the downloading process. When you place the mouse pointer on a link in the current Web page, its URL appears in the left side of the status bar.

Loading a Web Page

Loading a Web page means that the Web browser sends a message to the computer (called a Web server) where the Web page is stored, requesting a copy of the Web page. The Web server responds by sending a copy of the Web page to your computer. In order to load a Web page, you must either know or find the page's **URL** (Uniform Resource Locator)—the path and filename of the page that is the Web page's address. One way to find the URL for a Web page is to use a search engine or directory or you might find a particular company's URL in one of the company's advertisements or on their letterheads and business cards. Examples of URLs based on an organization's name are:

South-Western Educational Publishing   *www.swep.com*
National Public Radio   *www.npr.org*
The White House   *www.whitehouse.gov*

**chapter
four**

You can try to "guess" the URL based on the organization's name and top-level domain. For example, a good guess for the U.S. House of Representatives Web page is *www.house.gov.*

You can key a URL directly in the Address bar by first selecting all or part of the current URL and replacing it with the new URL. Internet Explorer adds the "http://" portion of the URL for you. To select the contents of the Address bar and key the URL for the U.S. House of Representatives:

Step 1	*Click*	the contents of the Address bar
Step 2	*Key*	www.house.gov
Step 3	*Click*	the Go button or press the ENTER key

In a few seconds, the U.S. House of Representatives page loads. Your screen should look similar to Figure 4-6.

FIGURE 4-6
U.S. House of
Representatives Web Page

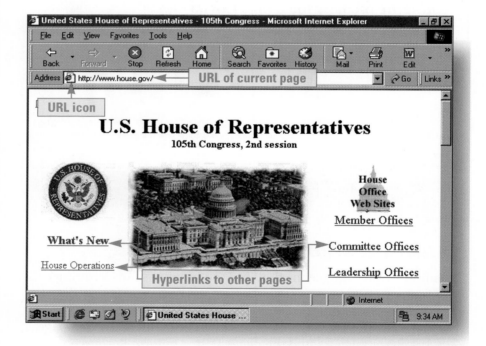

Creating Favorites

Web pages are constantly being updated with new information. If you like a certain Web page or find a Web page contains useful information and plan to revisit it, you may want to save its URL as a **favorite**. Suppose you want to load the U.S. House of Representatives home page frequently. You can create a favorite that saves the URL in a file on your hard disk. Then at any time, you can quickly load this Web page by clicking it in a list of favorites maintained on the Favorites menu.

The URLs you choose to save as favorites are stored in the Favorites folder on your hard disk. You can specify a new or different folder and you can change the name of the Web page as it appears in your list of favorites in this dialog box. To add the U.S. House of Representatives Web page as a favorite:

Step 1	*Click*	Favorites
Step 2	*Click*	Add to Favorites
Step 3	*Click*	OK
Step 4	*Click*	the Home button 🏠 to return to the default start page

One way to load a Web page from a favorite is to click the name of the favorite in the list of favorites on the Favorites menu. To load the U.S. House of Representatives home page from the Favorites menu:

Step 1	*Click*	Favorites
Step 2	*Click*	the U.S. House of Representatives favorite to load the page
Step 3	*Click*	the Home button 🏠 to return to the default start page

The Back and Forward buttons allow you to review recently loaded Web pages without keying the URL or using the Favorites list. To reload the U.S. House of Representatives Home page from the Back button list:

Step 1	*Click*	the Back button list arrow ⬅▾ on the toolbar
Step 2	*Click*	United States House of Representatives

4.e Using Directories and Search Engines

Because the Web is so large, you often need to take advantage of special search tools, called search engines and directories, to find the information you need. To use some of the Web's numerous search engines and directories, you can click the Search button on the

QUICK TIP

Another way to load a favorite is to use the Favorites button to open the Favorites list in the **Explorer bar**, a pane that opens at the left side of your screen.

CAUTION TIP

Any Web page you load is stored in the Temporary Internet Files folder on your hard disk. Whenever you reload the Web page, Internet Explorer compares the stored page to the current Web page either each time you start the browser or each time you load the page. If the Web page on the server has been changed, a fresh Web page is downloaded. If not, the Web page is retrieved from the Temporary Internet File folder rather than downloaded. To view and change the Temporary Internet File folder options (and other Internet Explorer options), click the Internet Options command on the Tools menu.

chapter
four

Standard toolbar to open the Search list in the Explorer bar. To view the Search list:

| Step 1 | *Click* | the Search button 🔍 on the toolbar |
| Step 2 | *Observe* | the search list options |

Search engines maintain an index of keywords used in Web pages that you can search. Search engine indexes are updated automatically by software called **spiders** (or **robots**). Spiders follow links between pages throughout the entire Web, adding any new Web pages to the search engine's index. You should use a search engine when you want to find specific Web pages. Some of the most popular search engines include AltaVista, HotBot, and Northern Light.

Directories use a subject-type format similar to a library card catalog. A directory provides a list of links to broad general categories of Web sites such as "Entertainment" or "Business." When you click these links, a subcategory list of links appears. For example, if you click the "Entertainment" link you might then see "Movies," "Television," and "Video Games" links. To find links to Web sites containing information about movies, you would click the "Movies" link. Unlike search engines, whose indexes are updated automatically, directories add new Web sites only when an individual or a company asks that a particular Web site be included. Some directories also provide review comments and ratings for the Web sites in their index. Most directories also provide an internal search engine that can only be used to search the directory's index, not the entire Web. You use a directory when you are looking for information on broad general topics. Popular directories include Yahoo and Magellan Internet Guide.

To search for Web pages containing "movie guides:"

Step 1	*Key*	movie guides in the search list text box
Step 2	*Click*	the Search button or press the ENTER key
Step 3	*Observe*	the search results (a list of Web pages in the search list)

The search results list consists of Web page titles as hyperlinks. To load a page from the list, simply click the hyperlink. To close the Explorer bar and search list:

| Step 1 | *Click* | the Search button 🔍 on the toolbar |

Guidelines for Searching the Web

Before you begin looking for information on the Web, it is a good idea to think about what you want to accomplish, establish a time frame in which to find the information, and then develop a search strategy. As you search, keep in mind the following guidelines:

1. To find broad, general information, start with a Web directory such as Galaxy or Yahoo.

2. To find a specific Web page, start with a search engine such as Alta Vista or HotBot.

3. Become familiar with a variety of search engines and their features. Review each search engine's online Help when you use it for the first time. Many search engine features are revised frequently so remember to review them regularly.

4. Search engines use spider programs to index all the pages on the Web. However, these programs work independently of each other, so not all search engines have the same index at any point in time. Use multiple search engines for each search.

5. **Boolean operators** allow you to combine or exclude keywords when using a search engine. **Proximal operators** allow you specify that search keywords be close together in a Web page. Boolean and proximal operators are words that allow you to specify relationships among search keywords or phrases using (brackets), OR, NOT, AND, NEAR, and FOLLOWED BY. Not all search engines support Boolean and proximal operators, but use them to reduce the scope of your search when they are available. For example, if you are looking for gold or silver and don't want Web pages devoted to music, try searching by the keywords *metals* not *heavy*. To make sure the keywords are in close proximity use the NEAR or FOLLOWED BY proximal operators.

6. Use very specific keywords. The more specific the phrase, the more efficient your search is. For example, use the phrase "online classes" plus the word genealogy (*"online classes" + genealogy*) rather than simply *genealogy* to find Web pages with information about classes in how to trace your family tree.

7. Watch your spelling. Be aware how the search engine you use handles capitalization. In one search engine "pear" may match "Pear", "pEaR", or "PEAR." In another search engine, "Pear" may match only "Pear."

8. Think of related words that might return the information you need. For example, if you search for information about oil, you might also use "petroleum" and "petrochemicals."

9. Search for common variations of word usage or spelling. For example, the keywords deep sea drilling, deepsea drilling, and deep-sea drilling may all provide useful information.

10. The search returns (or **hits**) are usually listed in order of relevance. You may find that only the first 10 or 12 hits are useful. To find more relevant Web pages, try searching with different keywords.

CAUTION TIP

You get varying results when using several search engines or directories to search for information on the same topic. Also, search tools operate according to varying rules. For example, some search engines allow only a simple search on one keyword. Others allow you to refine your search by finding words within quotation marks together, by indicating proper names, or by using special operators such as "and," "or," and "not" to include or exclude search words. To save time, always begin by reviewing the search tool's online Help directions, then proceed with your search.

After you find the desired information, "let the user beware!" Because the Web is largely unregulated, anyone can put anything on a Web page. Evaluate carefully the credibility of all the information you find. Try to find out something about the author and his or her credentials, or the about validity of the origin of the information.

chapter four

Summary

▶ A network is a group of two or more computers linked by cable or telephone lines and the Internet is a worldwide "network of networks."

▶ The Internet began in the late 1960s as the military Internet ARPAnet. By the 1980s the National Science Foundation assumed responsibility for the non-military portions and the term Internet became widely used.

▶ The World Wide Web is a subset of the Internet that uses computers called Web servers to store documents called Web pages.

▶ To access the Internet, your computer must have some physical communication medium, such as a cable or dial-up modem and a special communication program.

▶ An Internet Service Provider (or ISP) maintains a host computer on the Internet. In order to connect to the Internet, you need to connect to the host computer.

▶ Each host computer has an Internet address or IP address consisting of a series of numbers and a descriptive name based on the computer name and domain of the host. In addition to the host computer IP address and descriptive name, each user has a name that identifies their account at the Internet Service Provider.

▶ Large commercial enterprises, colleges, and universities may have a computer network on the Internet and can provide Internet access to their employees or students.

▶ There are many challenges to using the Internet—including the amount of available information, communication speed, the dynamic environment, lack of presentation standards, and privacy/security issues.

▶ You should carefully evaluate the source and author of information you get from the Internet and confirm any business-critical information from another source.

▶ Other external networks related to the Internet are large commercial networks, such as America Online, the Microsoft Network, and USENET.

▶ You use Web browsers, such as Internet Explorer, to load Web pages.

▶ Web pages are connected by hyperlinks, which are text or pictures associated with the path to another page.

▶ Directories and search engines are tools to help you find files and Web sites on the Internet.

Commands Review

Action	Menu Bar	Shortcut Menu	Toolbar	Keyboard
Load a Web page	File, Open			ALT + F, O Key URL in the Address bar and press the ENTER key
Save a favorite	Favorites, Add to Favorites	Right-click hyperlink, click Add to Favorites	Drag URL icon to Links bar or Favorites command	ALT + A, A CTRL + D
Manage the Standard toolbar, Address bar, and Links bar	View, Toolbars	Right-click the Standard toolbar, click desired command	Drag the Standard toolbar, Address bar, or Links bar to the new location	ALT + V, T
Load the search, history, or favorites list in the Explorer bar	View, Explorer Bar			ALT + V, E

Concepts Review

SCANS

Circle the correct answer.

1. To post messages of common interest to electronic bulletin boards, use:
[a] search tools.
[b] e-mail.
[c] file access.
[d] newsgroups.

2. A network is:
[a] the Internet.
[b] a group of two or more computers linked by cable or telephone wire.
[c] a group of two or more computer networks linked by cable or telephone lines.
[d] a computer that stores Web pages.

3. The Internet began as the:
[a] MILNET.
[b] NSFnet.
[c] SLIPnet.
[d] ARPAnet.

4. Which of the following is not a challenge to using the Internet?
[a] chat groups.
[b] dynamic environment and heavy usage.
[c] volume of information.
[d] security and privacy.

Circle **T** if the statement is true or **F** if the statement is false.

T F   1. An IP address is a unique identifying number for each host computer on the Internet.

T F   2. A host computer's descriptive name identifies it by name and organizational level on the Internet.

T F   3. Commercial networks that provide specially formatted features are the same as the Internet.

T F   4. USENET is the name of the military Internet.

Skills Review

SCANS

Exercise 1

1. Open the Internet Explorer Web browser.

2. Open the Internet Options dialog box by clicking the Internet Options command on the View menu.

3. Review the options on the General tab in the dialog box.

4. Write down the steps to change the default start page to a blank page.

5. Close the dialog box and close the Web browser.

chapter four

Exercise 2

1. Connect to your ISP and open the Internet Explorer Web browser.

2. Open the search list in the Explorer bar. Search for Web pages about "dog shows."

3. Load one of the Web pages in the search results list. Close the Explorer bar.

4. Print the Web page by clicking the Print command on the File menu and close the Web browser.

Exercise 3

1. Connect to your ISP and open the Internet Explorer Web browser.

2. Load the National Public radio Web page by keying the URL, *www.npr.org*, in the Address bar.

3. Print the Web page by clicking the Print command on the File menu and close the Web browser.

Exercise 4

1. Connect to your ISP and open the Internet Explorer Web browser.

2. Load the AltaVista search engine by keying the URL, *www.altavista.digital.com*, in the Address bar.

3. Save the Web page as a favorite. Search for Web pages about your city.

4. Print at least two Web pages by clicking the Print command on the File menu and close your Web browser.

Case Projects

Project 1

Your supervisor asks you to prepare a fifteen-minute presentation describing the Internet Explorer toolbar buttons. Review the toolbar buttons and practice using them. Write an outline for your presentation that lists each button and describes how it is used.

Project 2

Your manager is concerned about Internet security and wants to know more about Internet Explorer security features. Click the Contents and Index command on the Internet Explorer Help menu to locate and review the topics about security. Write a note to your manager discussing two security topics.

Project 3

You are working for a book publisher who is creating a series of books about popular movie actors and actresses from the 1920s to the 1950s, including Humphrey Bogart and Lionel Barrymore. The research director asks you to locate a list of movies on the Web that the actors starred in. Use the Explorer bar search list and the Yahoo directory search tool to find links to "Entertainment." Close the Explorer bar and then, working from the Yahoo Web page, click "Movies" within the Entertainment category, scroll down and click the Actors and Actresses link. Search for Humphrey Bogart in the Actors and Actresses portion of the database. Link to the Web page that shows the filmography for Humphrey Bogart. Print the Web page that shows all the movies he acted in. Use the History list to return to the Actors and Actresses search page. Search for Lionel Barrymore, link to and print the filmography for him. Close the Internet Explorer Web browser.

Project 4

You are the new secretary for the Business Women's Forum. The association's president asked you to compile a list of Internet resources. Connect to your ISP, open Internet Explorer, and search for pages containing the keywords "women in business" (including the quotation marks). From the search results, click the Web page title link of your choice. Review the new Web page and its links. Create a favorite for that page. Use the Back button list to reload the search results and click a different Web page title from the list. Review the Web page and its links. Create a favorite for the Web page. Load and review at least five pages. Return to the default home page. Use the Go menu and the History bar to reload at least three of the pages. Print two of the pages. Delete the favorites you added, and then close Internet Explorer.

Microsoft
Word 2000

Quick Start for Word

Chapter Overview

This chapter gives you a quick overview of creating, editing, printing, saving, and closing a document. To learn these skills, you create a new document, save and close it, then you open an existing document, revise the text, and save the document with both the same and a different name. This chapter also shows you how to view formatting marks, zoom the document window, and move the insertion point. In addition, you learn to identify the components of the Word window and create a folder on your hard drive to store your documents. You use these basic skills every time you create or edit a document in Word.

Learning Objectives

- Identify the components of the Word window
- Compose a simple document
- Edit a document
- Save a document
- Preview and print a document
- Close a document
- Locate and open an existing document
- Create a new document
- Close Word
- Send a Word document via e-mail

Case profile

Today is your first day as a new employee at Worldwide Exotic Foods, Inc., one of the world's fastest growing distributors of specialty food items. The company's mission is to provide customers with an unusual selection of meats, cheeses, pastries, fruits, and vegetables from around the world. You report to Chris Lofton, the word processing department manager, to complete an introduction to the Word 2000 word processing application.

chapter one

notes This text assumes that you have little or no knowledge of the Word application. It also assumes that you have read Office Chapters 1–4 of this book and that you are familiar with Windows 95 or Windows 98 concepts.

1.a Identifying the Components of the Word Window

Before you can begin to work with Word, you need to open the application. When you open the application, a new, blank document opens as well. To open the Word application and a new, blank document:

Step 1	*Click*	the Start button ⊞ Start on the taskbar
Step 2	*Point*	to Programs
Step 3	*Click*	Microsoft Word

When the Word application opens, it contains a blank document with the temporary name *Document1*. Your screen should look similar to Figure 1-1, which identifies the specific components of the Word application window.

notes For the activities in this text, you view your documents in Normal view unless otherwise instructed.

Word has many different ways to view a document. Figure 1-1 shows a new, blank document in Normal view. Changing document views is discussed in more detail in Chapter 2. However, for now, if you need to change the view to Normal view:

| Step 1 | *Click* | View |
| Step 2 | *Click* | Normal |

**chapter
one**

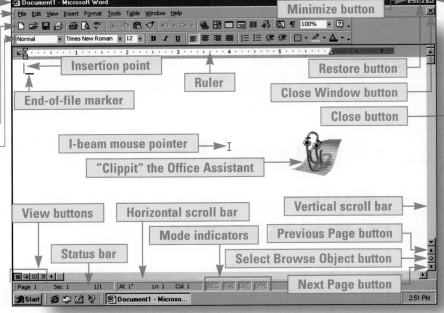

FIGURE 1-1
Word Application Window
with a Blank Document

Menu Bar

The **menu bar**, located below the title bar, contains nine drop-down menu commands that contain groups of additional, related commands. For example, the File menu contains commands for opening, closing, previewing, and printing files. You can use the mouse or the keyboard to select a command from the menu bar. The activities in this book instruct you to select menu bar commands with the mouse. The Commands Review section at the end of each chapter provides a summary of both mouse and keyboard techniques to select a menu command.

Standard Toolbar

The **Standard toolbar** is located under the menu bar and is made up of buttons that represent commonly used commands. For example, the Standard toolbar contains buttons for opening, saving, previewing, and printing a file. The Standard toolbar allows you to perform commands quickly by clicking the button that represents that command. You can customize the Standard toolbar (or any other toolbar) by adding or deleting buttons.

Formatting Toolbar

The **Formatting toolbar** is located under the Standard toolbar in Figure 1-1 and is made up of buttons that represent commonly used formats. For example, the Formatting toolbar contains buttons for changing text appearance, such as the font or text alignment.

Ruler

The horizontal **ruler,** located under the Formatting toolbar, provides features you can use to change the tab settings, margins, and indentations in your document.

Insertion Point

The blinking vertical bar in the upper-left corner below the horizontal ruler is the insertion point. The **insertion point** marks the location where text is entered in a document.

End-of-file Marker

The short horizontal line below the insertion point is the **end-of-file marker** that marks the point below which you cannot enter text. This marker moves down as you insert additional lines of text into the document. The end-of-file marker is visible only in Normal view.

Select Browse Object Button

You can use the **Select Browse Object button,** located below the vertical scroll bar, to choose the specific item—such as text, graphics, and tables—you want to use to move or browse through a document.

Previous Page and Next Page Buttons

You use the **Previous Page button** and **Next Page button,** also located below the vertical scroll bar, to move the insertion point to the top of the previous or next page in a multi-page document. When you specify a different browse object, the button name changes to include that object, such as Previous Comment or Next Comment. Clicking the buttons moves you to the previous or next browse object you specified.

View Buttons

Word has several editing views or ways to look at a document as you edit it. The Normal View, Web Layout View, Print Layout View, and Outline View buttons, located to the left of the horizontal scroll bar, can be used to view and work with your document in a different way. Normal view is the best view for most word-processing tasks, such as keying, editing, and basic formatting. Web Layout view shows how your document will look if displayed in a Web browser. Print Layout view shows how your document will look when printed on paper. Outline view displays your document in outline format so you can work on its structure and organization.

QUICK TIP

The Standard and Formatting toolbars appear on the same row when you first install Office 2000. In this position, only the most commonly used buttons of each toolbar are visible. All the other default buttons appear on the More Buttons drop-down lists. As you use buttons from the More Buttons drop-down list, they move to the visible buttons on the toolbar, while the buttons you don't use move into the More Buttons drop-down list. If you arrange the Formatting toolbar below the Standard toolbar, all buttons are visible. Unless otherwise noted, the illustrations in this book show the full menus and the Formatting toolbar below the Standard toolbar.

chapter
one

Status Bar

The **status bar** appears at the bottom of the screen above the taskbar and provides information about your document and a task in progress. It indicates the current page number (Page 1), the current section of the document (Sec 1), and the current page followed by the number of pages in the document (1/1). In the center of the status bar you see indicators for the current vertical position of the insertion point measured in inches (At 1"), the current line number of the insertion point on that page (Ln 1), and the horizontal position of the insertion point (Col 1).

There are five mode indicators at the right of the status bar. These indicators provide mouse shortcuts to: record a macro (REC), track changes (TRK), extend a text selection (EXT), key over existing text (OVR), and check the spelling and grammar in the document (Spelling and Grammar Status). (Note that the Spelling and Grammar Status mode indicator is blank unless the document contains text).

Office Assistant

The **Office Assistant**, which you can use to search for online Help topics, may appear automatically when you work in Word unless you hide it or turn it off. In the illustrations in this book, the Office Assistant is hidden. To hide the Office Assistant, if necessary:

Step 1	*Right-click*	the Office Assistant
Step 2	*Click*	Hide

After you hide the Office Assistant multiple times, you may get a dialog box that asks if you want to turn the Office Assistant off completely. If you turn the Office Assistant off completely, you can then turn it back on by clicking the Show the Office Assistant command on the Help menu.

With the blank document open, you are ready to work. Chris asks you to key in a short company profile that Worldwide Exotic Foods can use in a press release.

1.b Composing a Simple Document

Chris gives you a short paragraph to key. As you key the text, it is visible on the screen and resides in your computer's memory. Word uses a feature called **word wrap** to automatically move words that do not fit on the current line to the next line. As a result, you can key the text without worrying about how much text fits on a line. You do not press the ENTER key at the end of each line. You press the ENTER key only to create a blank line or to end a paragraph.

The paragraph in Step 1 below contains two intentional errors. Key the text exactly as it appears. If you make additional errors, just continue keying the text. You learn two methods of correcting keying errors in the next section. Remember, do not press the ENTER key at the end of each line. To key the text:

| Step 1 | *Key* | Worldwide Exotic Foods, Inc. is one of the fastest-growing distributors of specialty food items. Worldwide Exotic Foods branch offices in Chicago, Illinois, Melbourne, Australia, Vancouver, Canada, and London, England, and specializes in supplying high-quality and unusual food products too customers around the world. |

Next, you correct any keying errors in the paragraph.

1.c Editing a Document

One of the important benefits of using Word is the ability to easily modify a document by inserting, removing, or editing text without having to key the document again. When you position the mouse pointer in a text area, it changes shape to look like a large "I" and is called the **I-beam**. You use the I-beam to position the insertion point in the text area where you want to correct keying errors or add new text. Recall that the insertion point is the blinking vertical bar on your screen that indicates where the next keyed character will appear. The text you just entered contains at least two errors. The first error you need to correct is a missing word in the second sentence. To insert the word "has:"

| Step 1 | *Move* | the I-beam before the "b" in the word "branch" in the second sentence |
| Step 2 | *Click* | the mouse button to position the insertion point |

Your screen should look similar to Figure 1-2.

> **CAUTION TIP**
>
> When you key text in a document, certain words or phrases may appear with a red or green wavy line underneath. The red line indicates the word is misspelled or it is not in the Word English-language dictionary or in any custom dictionaries being used. The green line indicates a possible error in grammar. Chapter 3 discusses the Spelling and Grammar features.

> **QUICK TIP**
>
> Another way to remove a character is to move the insertion point to the right of the character and press the BACKSPACE key.

chapter
one

FIGURE 1-2
Repositioned
Insertion Point

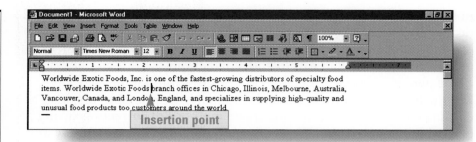

Step 3	*Key*	has
Step 4	*Press*	the SPACEBAR

The second error is an extra letter "o" in the word "too" in the last sentence, which you need to delete. To delete the letter "o":

Step 1	*Move*	the I-beam before the second "o" in the word "too" in the last sentence
Step 2	*Click*	the mouse button to position the insertion point
Step 3	*Press*	the DELETE key
Step 4	*Correct*	any additional errors, if necessary, by repositioning the insertion point and inserting or deleting text

While you are creating or editing a document, every change you make is stored temporarily in your computer's memory. If the power to your computer fails or you turn off the computer, your work will be lost. You can prevent such a loss by frequently saving the document to a disk.

 1.d Saving a Document

Word enables you to save files to a floppy disk, an internal hard disk, or a network server. When you save a file for the first time, it does not matter whether you choose the Save command or the Save As command on the File menu or you click the Save button on the Standard toolbar. Regardless of which method you use, the Save As dialog box opens—providing a way for you to give your document a new name and specify the disk drive and folder location where you want to save the document.

After you have specified the location for saving your document, you key the name of the document in the File name: text box. A filename can have up to 255 characters—including the disk drive reference and path—and can contain letters, numbers, spaces, and some special characters in any combination. Filenames cannot include the following special characters: the forward slash (/), the backward slash (\), the colon (:), the semicolon (;), the pipe symbol (|), the question mark (?), the less than symbol (<), the greater than symbol (>), the asterisk (*), and the quotation mark (").

Using longer descriptive filenames helps you locate specific documents when you need to open and print or edit them. For example, the filename *Letter* won't mean much if you have written many letters, but the filename *Mendez Hire Letter* has meaning even months later.

 notes
Be sure to check with your instructor if you do not know the disk drive and folder in which to save your documents.

To save your document:

| Step 1 | *Click* | the Save button 🖫 on the Standard toolbar |

The Save As dialog box on your screen should look similar to Figure 1-3.

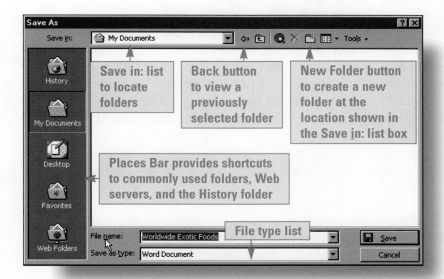

You can quickly locate a folder with the Save in: list, move to the previously viewed folder contents with the Back button, move up one level in the Save in: list, launch the Internet Explorer Web browser and search the Web, delete selected folders, add a new folder to the current location, change the viewing options for the folder icons, and change

---

INTERNET TIP

You can save your documents as HTML documents (or Web pages) by clicking the Save As Web Page command on the File menu. You can also change the file type to Web Page in the Save As dialog box.

FIGURE 1-3
Save As Dialog Box

MOUSE TIP

You can click the General Options command on the Tools button drop-down list in the Save As dialog box to view only the Save tab in the Options dialog box.

chapter one

the file type with options in this dialog box. For easier access to commonly used folders, the Save As dialog box also contains a **Places Bar**, which provides shortcuts for opening the My Documents and Favorites folders. You can view the My Computer, My Documents, and Online Services desktop icons with the Desktop shortcut in the Places Bar. The Web Folders shortcut in the Places Bar allows you to save Web pages you create in Word directly to a Web server.

Step 2	*Click*	the Save <u>i</u>n: list arrow
Step 3	*Switch*	to the appropriate disk drive and folder, as designated by your instructor
Step 4	*Key*	*Company Profile* in the File <u>n</u>ame: text box
Step 5	*Click*	<u>S</u>ave

After the document is saved, the document name *Company Profile* appears in place of *Document1* on the title bar.

1.e Previewing and Printing a Document

After you create a document, you usually print it. Before printing a document, you can preview it to see what it will look like when printed. You do not have to preview the document before printing it. However, you can save paper by previewing your document and making any necessary changes before you print it.

To preview the *Company Profile* document and then print it:

| Step 1 | *Click* | the Print Preview button 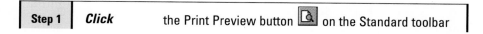 on the Standard toolbar |

The Print Preview window opens. Your screen should look similar to Figure 1-4.

FIGURE 1-4
Print Preview Window

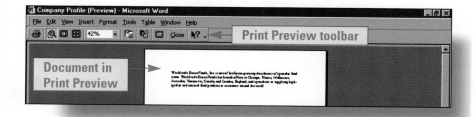

When you preview a document, you are verifying that the document text is attractively and appropriately positioned on the page. If necessary, you can change the document layout on the page, key additional text, and change the appearance of the text as you preview it. For now, you should close Print Preview and return to the original view of the document.

| Step 2 | *Click* | the Close button Close on the Print Preview toolbar |
| Step 3 | *Click* | the Print button 🖨 on the Standard toolbar |

You are finished with the *Company Profile* for now, so you can close the document.

1.f Closing a Document

When you use the Word application, you can have as many documents open in the memory of your computer as your computer resources will allow. However, after you finish a document you should close it or remove it from the computer's memory to conserve those resources. To close the *Company Profile* document:

| Step 1 | *Click* | the Close Window button ☒ in the upper-right corner of the menu bar |

When documents are closed from the File menu or the Close Window button on the menu bar, the Word application window remains open. This window is sometimes called the **null screen**. To continue working in Word from the null screen, you open an existing document or create a new, blank document.

CAUTION TIP

If you edit a document and then try to close it without saving, Word opens a message window prompting you to save your changes.

1.g Locating and Opening an Existing Document

When you want to edit an existing document, you need to open a copy of it from the disk where it is stored. From inside the Word application, you can open a document in two ways: (1) with the Open command on the File menu, or (2) with the Open button on the Standard toolbar. Either method opens the Open dialog box. In this dialog box you first select the disk drive and folder where the document is located. Then you can select the specific document you

chapter one

want from a list of documents available at that location. Each document you open in Word has its own taskbar button.

Chris asks you to open an existing document that contains several paragraphs so that you can see how to scroll and move the insertion point in a larger document. To open an existing document:

QUICK TIP

You can also open a document by double-clicking the document's filename or icon in the Open dialog box. This is the same as clicking the filename to select it and then clicking the Open button to open it.

Step 1	*Click*	the Open button 📂 on the Standard toolbar
Step 2	*Click*	the Look in: list arrow
Step 3	*Switch*	to the disk drive and folder where the Data Files are stored
Step 4	*Double-click*	New Expense Guidelines

The document contains characters you can see as well as characters you cannot see.

Viewing Formatting Marks

When you create a document Word automatically inserts some characters that you do not see called **formatting marks**. For example, each time you press the ENTER key to create a new line, a paragraph mark character (¶) is inserted in the document. Other formatting marks include tab characters (→) and spaces (·) between words. Sometimes these formatting marks are called **nonprinting characters** because they do not print, but they can be viewed on the screen. You may want to view the formatting marks to help you edit a document. The Show/Hide button on the Standard toolbar turns on or off the view of formatting marks. To show the formatting marks:

| Step 1 | *Click* | the Show/Hide button ¶ on the Standard toolbar |

Your screen should look similar to Figure 1-5.

FIGURE 1-5
Formatting Marks

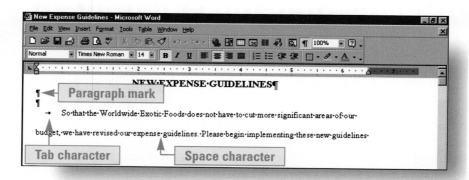

Notice the paragraph marks at the end of each paragraph, the tab character at the beginning of each paragraph, and the space indicators between each word. You won't be formatting this document now, so you can turn off the view of formatting marks. To turn off the view of formatting marks:

Step 1	*Click*	the Show/Hide button ¶ on the Standard toolbar

Whether the formatting marks are visible or not, you can take a closer look at your document.

Zooming the Document Window

When creating a document, you may want to view your document more closely or look at a miniature view of an entire page to see how the text is arranged on the page. This is called **zooming** the document.

You can zoom a document from 10% to 500% of the actual size. You can also resize the view to show the document's entire width by using the Page Width option. To make the text appear larger on the screen, increase the zoom percentage. To make the text appear smaller on the screen, decrease the zoom percentage. Zooming your document changes only the view on the screen; it does not change the size of characters on the printed document. To zoom the *New Expense Guidelines* document:

Step 1	*Click*	the Zoom button list arrow 100% ▾ on the Standard toolbar
Step 2	*Click*	200%

Notice that the Zoom text box indicates 200% and the text is very large.

Step 3	*Click*	the Zoom button list arrow 100% ▾ on the Standard toolbar
Step 4	*Click*	Page Width to view the entire width of the document

Being able to change the document view is helpful when you are formatting a document. However, with large zoom percentages or large documents you might need to scroll to view other parts of your document.

chapter one

Using the Scroll Bars

When you want to view different parts of a document without moving the insertion point, use the vertical and horizontal scroll bars. Scrolling changes only that part of the document you see in the document window; it does not change your keying position in the document. The scroll bars appear on the right side and bottom of the window above the status bar. The **vertical scroll bar** enables you to scroll up and down in your document. The **horizontal scroll bar** allows you to scroll left and right in your document. A scroll bar has two scroll arrows. A gray shaded area containing a scroll box separates these scroll arrows. The **scroll box** represents your viewing position in the document. For example, if the vertical scroll box appears in the middle of the vertical scroll bar, you are viewing the middle of your document. (Figure 1-1 identifies the parts of the vertical and horizontal scroll bars.) Table 1-1 summarizes how to view a document using the scroll bars.

TABLE 1-1
Navigating a Document
with the Scroll Bars

To Scroll	Do This
Down one line	Click the down scroll arrow
Up one line	Click the up scroll arrow
Down one screen	Click the gray shaded area below the vertical scroll box
Up one screen	Click the gray shaded area above the vertical scroll box
Up or down one page	Click and hold the scroll box on the vertical scroll bar to see the current page number. Drag the scroll box to a new page and the new page number will show in a ScreenTip.
End of a document	Drag the vertical scroll box to the bottom of the vertical scroll bar
Beginning of a document	Drag the vertical scroll box to the top of the vertical scroll bar
Right side of document	Click the right scroll arrow
Left side of document	Click the left scroll arrow
Far right side of document	Click the gray shaded area right of the horizontal scroll box
Far left side of document	Click the gray shaded area left of the horizontal scroll box
Beyond the left margin (in Normal view)	SHIFT + Click the left scroll arrow on the horizontal scroll bar
Beyond the right margin (in Normal view)	SHIFT + Click the right scroll arrow on the horizontal scroll bar
To hide the area beyond the left margin (in Normal view)	Click the horizontal scroll box

QUICK TIP

If you are using the IntelliMouse pointing device, you can use the scrolling wheel to scroll a document. For more information on using the IntelliMouse pointing device, see online Help.

In addition to scrolling, you can move the insertion point within a document.

Moving the Insertion Point

You have already learned how to move the insertion point using the I-beam. You can also use the Next Page, Previous Page, and Select Browse Object buttons to move the insertion point, as explained in Table 1-2. (Note that you must be working in a multi-page document to move the insertion point to another page.)

To Move the Insertion Point To	Do This
A new page	Click the Select Browse Object button below the vertical scroll bar and then click the Browse by Page button
The top of the next page	Click the Next Page button below the vertical scroll bar
The top of the previous page	Click the Previous Page button below the vertical scroll bar

TABLE 1-2
Moving the Insertion Point

You can also use the keyboard to move the insertion point in your document. Table 1-3 summarizes the ways you can do this.

To Move	Press	To Move	Press
Right one character	RIGHT ARROW	To the top of the next page	CTRL + PAGEDOWN
Left one character	LEFT ARROW	To the top of the previous page	CTRL + PAGEUP
Right one word	CTRL + RIGHT ARROW	Up one line	UP ARROW
Left one word	CTRL + LEFT ARROW	Down one line	DOWN ARROW
Down one paragraph	CTRL + DOWN ARROW	Up one screen	PAGEUP
Up one paragraph	CTRL + UP ARROW	Down one screen	PAGEDOWN
Beginning of the line	HOME	To the beginning of a document	CTRL + HOME
End of the line	END	To the end of a document	CTRL + END
Back to the previous position of the insertion point or to a previous revision	SHIFT + F5	To go to a specific line or page or section or table or graphic	F5
To the top of the window	ALT + CTRL + PAGEUP	To the bottom of the window	ALT + CTRL + PAGEDOWN

TABLE 1-3
Moving the Insertion Point with the Keyboard

chapter
one

When instructed to scroll to change the view or move the insertion point to a different location, use one of the methods described in Tables 1-1, 1-2, and 1-3. To move the insertion point:

| Step 1 | *Practice* | using the mouse and keyboard to move the insertion point in the *New Expense Guidelines* document |
| Step 2 | *Close* | the *New Expense Guidelines* document without saving any changes |

Chris asks you to add some text to the *Company Profile* document.

Using the Save Command

You can open a copy of an existing document, edit it, and then save it with the same name to update the document on the disk. You want to edit the *Company Profile* document you created earlier. To open the *Company Profile* document:

Step 1	*Click*	the Open button 📂 on the Standard toolbar
Step 2	*Switch*	to the appropriate disk drive and folder
Step 3	*Double-click*	*Company Profile*

The file you selected opens in the document window. You edit the document by inserting text. To add an additional paragraph:

Step 1	*Move*	the insertion point to the end of the last sentence
Step 2	*Press*	the ENTER key twice
Step 3	*Key*	Contact us 24 hours a day, seven days a week at our Web site, www.exoticfoods.com.
Step 4	*Press*	the SPACEBAR

Notice that when you press the SPACEBAR after keying the Web site address and period, Word underlines the Web site address *www.exoticfoods.com* and changes the color to blue. This indicates the text is a hyperlink. A **hyperlink** is text or a picture that is associated with the path to another page. For now, you don't want the Web site address text in your document blue and underlined, so you remove the hyperlink formatting by clicking the Undo button on the Standard toolbar or pressing the CTRL + Z shortcut key combination. Then you save the document to update the copy on the disk.

| Step 5 | *Click* | the Undo button ⟲ on the Standard toolbar |
| Step 6 | *Click* | the Save button 💾 on the Standard toolbar |

The copy of the document on disk is updated to include the additional paragraph.

Creating a Folder and Using the Save As Command

Sometimes you may want to keep both the original document and the edited document in different files on the disk. This allows you to keep a backup copy of the original document for later use or reference. To do this, you can save the edited document with a different name. If you want to create a new folder in which to store the modified document, you can create it from Windows Explorer or from inside the Word Save As dialog box.

notes Check with your instructor, if necessary, for additional instructions on where to create your new folder.

You need to make an additional edit to *Company Profile* by adding the telephone number. This time, after you edit the document you save it to a new location and with a new name so that the document is available both with and without the phone number. To edit the document, create a new folder, and save the document with a new name:

Step 1	*Key*	You may also contact us at (312) 555-1234.
Step 2	*Click*	File
Step 3	*Click*	Save As
Step 4	*Click*	the Create New Folder button on the dialog box toolbar
Step 5	*Key*	Completed Files Folder in the Name: text box
Step 6	*Click*	OK to create and open the new folder
Step 7	*Key*	*Company Profile Revised* in the File name: text box
Step 8	*Click*	Save

chapter one

You leave this new copy of the document open while you create a new, blank document.

1.h Creating a New Document

From inside the Word application, you can create a new, blank document in two ways: (1) click the <u>N</u>ew command on the <u>F</u>ile menu or (2) click the New Blank Document button on the Standard toolbar. Each document you create in Word is based on a model document called a **template**. When you create a new document using the New Blank Document button on the Standard toolbar, the document is based on the **Normal template**, which is the basic, default Word document model. When you create a document with the <u>N</u>ew command on the <u>F</u>ile menu, Word provides a selection of templates for special documents such as letters, memos, and reports. To create a new, blank document:

Step 1	*Click*	the New Blank Document button 🗋 on the Standard toolbar

You should have two documents open, *Company Profile Revised* and a blank document. You can switch easily between open Word documents with the <u>W</u>indow command on the menu bar or from the taskbar. To switch to the *Company Profile Revised* document:

Step 1	*Click*	the *Company Profile Revised* taskbar button

You are now viewing the *Company Profile Revised* document. You could work in this document, or return to the new, blank document and work in that document. For now, however, you are finished. When you finish using Word, you should exit or close the application and any open documents.

1.i Closing Word

You can close the Word application without first closing the open documents. If you modify open documents and then attempt to close the Word application without first saving the modified documents, a dialog box prompts you to save the changes you have made.

To close the application:

Step 1	*Click*	File
Step 2	*Click*	Exit

The Word application and both open documents close. Because you did not use the blank document, Word did not prompt you to save changes. Also, because you saved the *Company Profile Revised* document after you last modified it, Word closed the document without prompting you to save.

1.j Sending a Word Document via E-mail

If you have Outlook 2000 or Outlook Express 5.0 designated as your e-mail client, you can send e-mail messages directly from Word by clicking the E-mail button on the Standard toolbar. This displays an e-mail message header in which you key the recipient's e-mail address. The open Word document appears in the message content area. To send a Word document as an attachment when working in Word, click the New command on the File menu, and click the General tab in the New dialog box. Then double-click the E-mail icon to open the message header. Use the Attach File button in the message header to attach the file.

QUICK TIP

For more information on sending e-mail messages from Word, see the Word Integration chapter or online Help.

chapter
one

Summary

► The components of the Word window in Normal view include the title bar, the Standard and Formatting toolbars, the horizontal ruler, the insertion point, the end-of-file marker, the Previous Page and Next Page buttons, the Select Object Browser button, the View buttons, the vertical and horizontal scroll bars, and the status bar.

► Pressing the ENTER key creates a blank line or a new paragraph.

► You can remove text from your document with the DELETE or BACKSPACE keys.

► When you create or edit text, Word temporarily stores changes in your computer's memory.

► Word wrap is a word processing feature that automatically moves words that do not fit on the current line to the next line.

► To preserve changes to your document, you should save the document frequently.

► To save documents, you must use unique filenames that can be up to 255 characters long, including the disk drive reference and path.

► When you save a document for the first time, you must specify the disk drive and folder where the document will be stored.

► Before printing a document, it is a good practice to preview it to see what it will look like when it is printed.

► You can have as many documents open as your computer's resources will allow; however, it is a good practice to close a document when you finish working with it to conserve those resources.

► You can move the insertion point with both the mouse and the keyboard.

► You can view the special formatting marks inserted by Word with the Show/Hide button.

► Zooming the document window allows you to increase or decrease the viewing size of the text.

► The vertical and horizontal scroll bars enable you to view different parts of a document without moving the insertion point.

► When all documents are closed, the Word application remains open and you see the null screen.

► To edit an existing document, you open a copy of the document stored on a disk.

▶ After opening and editing an existing document, you usually save it again with the same name and in the same location; however, you can save it with a new name or new location.

▶ You can easily create a new folder for storing documents from the Save As dialog box.

▶ When you finish using Word, you should close the application.

Commands Review

Action	Menu Bar	Shortcut Menu	Toolbar	Keyboard
Create a new line or end a paragraph				ENTER
Remove a character to the left of the insertion point				BACKSPACE
Remove a character to the right of the insertion point				DELETE
Save a document for the first time or save a document with a new name or to a new location	File, Save As			ALT + F, A F12
Save a document for the first time or save a previously named and saved document	File, Save		🖫	ALT + F, S CTRL + S SHIFT + F12 ALT + SHIFT + F2
Preview a document	File, Print Preview		🔍	ALT + F, V CTRL + F2
Print a document	File, Print		🖨	ALT + F, P CTRL + P CTRL + SHIFT + F12
Close a document	File, Close	Right-click the document taskbar button, click Close	Close button ☒ on the title bar Close Window button ☒ on the menu bar	ALT + F, C CTRL + W CTRL + F4
Open an existing document	File, Open		📂	ALT + F, O CTRL + O CTRL + F12 ALT + CTRL + F2
Create a new, blank document	File, New		▯	ALT + F, N CTRL + N
Zoom a document	View, Zoom		100% ▾	ALT + V, Z
Show formatting marks	Tools, Options, View tab, All		¶	ALT + T, O, A
Close the Word application	File, Exit		Application Close button ☒	ALT + F, X ALT + F4
Send e-mail	File, New		📧	ALT + F, N

chapter one

Concepts Review

Circle the correct answer.

1. **The Standard toolbar appears in the Word application window below the:**
   [a] menu bar.
   [b] status bar.
   [c] Formatting toolbar.
   [d] scroll bar.

2. **When you are completely finished working with a document you should:**
   [a] edit it.
   [b] hide formatting marks.
   [c] key it.
   [d] save it.

3. **Zooming the document window:**
   [a] shows the formatting marks.
   [b] allows you to delete text.
   [c] moves text to the bottom of the document.
   [d] increases or decreases the viewing size of text.

4. **The insertion point:**
   [a] is located under the Standard toolbar and contains shortcut buttons.
   [b] indicates the location where text is keyed in a document.
   [c] provides features for changing margins, tabs, and indentations.
   [d] always appears at the bottom of the screen above the taskbar.

5. **To preserve any changes to the document currently visible on your screen, it is a good idea to:**
   [a] save the document frequently.
   [b] preview the document.
   [c] move the document to the null screen.
   [d] scroll the document.

6. **The Select Object Browse button is located:**
   [a] below the Formatting toolbar.
   [b] on the menu bar.
   [c] in the lower-left corner of the Word screen.
   [d] below the vertical scroll bar.

7. **To save a document for the first time, you can click the:**
   [a] Select Browse Object button.
   [b] New Blank Document button.
   [c] Print button.
   [d] Save button.

8. **When you key a document that contains errors, you should:**
   [a] close the document.
   [b] preview and print the document.
   [c] save the document.
   [d] edit the document.

9. **Which of the following characters can be used in a filename?**
   [a] period (.)
   [b] asterisk (*)
   [c] pipe symbol (|)
   [d] question mark (?)

10. **If you edit a document and then try to close the Word application, Word:**
    [a] automatically saves the changes without a message prompt.
    [b] closes without saving any changes to the document.
    [c] opens a message prompt dialog box asking you to save changes.
    [d] requires you to save the changes to the document.

Circle **T** if the statement is true or **F** if the statement is false.

T F   1. If you are creating or editing a document, any changes you make are stored temporarily in your computer's memory.

T F   2. When using Word, you need to press the ENTER key at the end of each line of text to move the insertion point back to the left margin.

T F   3. When you have finished working on a document, Word automatically saves the document to disk.

T F   4. The Formatting toolbar is located below the ruler and consists of buttons that represent commonly used commands.

T F   5. The Save As command is used to save a document for the first time.

T F   6. You cannot use the keyboard to select commands from the menu bar.

T F   7. When you finish using Word, you should close the application.

T F   8. You can use letters, numbers, and some special characters in a filename.

T F   9. When all documents are closed, the null screen appears.

T F   10. You can move the insertion point to the top of individual pages of a multiple page document with the scroll arrows.

notes The Skills Review exercises sometimes instruct you to create a document. The text you key is shown in italics. Do not format the text with italics unless specified to do so. Your text may word wrap differently from the text shown. Do not press the ENTER key at the end of a line of text to force it to wrap the same way.

Skills Review

Exercise 1 Ⓒ

1. Create a new, blank document and key the following text exactly as shown, including the intentional errors. You correct the text in Exercise 2.
Spreadsheet software is a commmon type of computer application software. Other types of applications include word processing, database management, presentation, communication, and Internet browser.

2. Save the document as *Application Software*.

3. Preview, print, and close the document.

Exercise 2 Ⓒ

1. Open the *Application Software* document you created in Exercise 1.

2. Delete the extra "m" in the word "common" in the first sentence and delete the word "applications" and replace it with the word "software" in the second sentence.

chapter one

3. Delete the word "Internet" and replace it with the word "Web" in the second sentence.

4. Save the document as *Application Software Revised*.

5. Preview, print, and close the document.

Exercise 3

1. Create a new, blank document and key the following text exactly as shown, including the intentional errors. You correct the text in Exercise 4.
Word processing provides an individual with an effective and efficient means of preparing documents. You can create documents and quickly make needed changes prior to printing the document. The software allows your to save the document in a file for later use.

2. Save the document as *Word Processing*.

3. Preview, print, and close the document.

Exercise 4

1. Open the *Word Processing* document you created in Exercise 3.

2. Delete the words "and efficient" in the first sentence.

3. Delete the words "the document" and replace them with the word "them" in the second sentence.

4. Delete the character "r" in the word "your" in the last sentence.

5. Save the document as *Word Processing Revised*.

6. Preview, print, and close the document.

Exercise 5

1. Create a new, blank document and key the following text exactly as shown, including the intentional errors. You correct the text in Exercise 6.
The purchasing department will be ordering employee handboooks for the new employees hired during the month of May. Please determine how many handbooks you need and contact Kelly Armstead at ext. 154 by Monday.

2. Save the document as *Employee Handbooks*.

3. Preview, print, and close the document.

Exercise 6

1. Open the *Employee Handbooks* document you created in Exercise 5.

2. Delete the extra "o" in "handboooks" in the first sentence.

3. Insert the word "next" before the word "Monday" in the last sentence.

4. Save the document as *Employee Handbooks Revised*.

5. Preview, print, and close the document.

Exercise 7

1. Create the following document making the noted changes.

> You monthly sales projection is due on ~~Wednesday~~. Please note that the minimum number of units sold per month must be 1,000. Contact Betty McManners or Jim Davidson if you have any questions about preparing your report.

(handwritten changes: insert "report" after "projection", change "Wednesday" to "Thursday", caret after "Davidson")

2. Save the document as *Sales Report*.

3. Preview, print, and close the document.

Exercise 8

1. Open the *New Expense Guidelines* document located on the Data Disk.

2. Practice using the following keyboard movement techniques to move the insertion point in the document:

a. Move the insertion point to the end of the document using the CTRL + END keys.

b. Move the insertion point to the beginning of the document using the CTRL + HOME keys.

c. Move the insertion point to the word "Foods" in the first line of the first paragraph using the CTRL + RIGHT ARROW keys.

d. Move the insertion point to the end of the first line of the first paragraph using the END key.

e. Move the insertion point to the beginning of the first line of the first paragraph using the HOME key.

f. Move the insertion point to the second paragraph (down one paragraph) using the CTRL + DOWN ARROW keys.

g. Move the insertion point to the first paragraph (up one paragraph) using the CTRL + UP ARROW keys.

h. Move the insertion point to the top of the next page using the CTRL + PAGEDOWN keys.

3. Close the document without saving any changes.

Exercise 9

1. Create a new, blank document.

2. Key a paragraph of text describing your favorite hobby.

3. Save the document as *My Favorite Hobby*.

4. Preview, print, and close the document.

chapter one

5. Open *My Favorite Hobby* document you saved in Step 3.

6. Add a second paragraph further describing why you enjoy the hobby.

7. Open the Save As dialog box.

8. Create a new folder named Hobby (check with your instructor, if necessary, to select the appropriate location for the new folder).

9. Save the document in the new Hobby folder with the new name *Why I Enjoy My Hobby*.

10. Preview, print, and close the document.

Case Projects

Project 1

Chris Lofton, the word processing manager at Worldwide Exotic Foods, has asked you to create a new document containing a short paragraph describing two methods of correcting keying errors to include in the Word Processing Training Handbook for new employees. Create, save, preview, and print the document.

Project 2

Create a new document for the Word Processing Training Handbook that contains a short paragraph describing the two methods of opening an existing document from inside the Word application. Save, preview, and print the document.

Project 3

You are working with another new employee at Worldwide Exotic Foods (choose a classmate) to learn how to customize the Office Assistant. Together, review the Office Assistant dialog box options and online Help. Then you and your co-worker each create a document and write at least three paragraphs that describe ways to customize the Office Assistant. Save, preview, and print your documents.

Project 4

Chris asks you to review online Help for several of the buttons on the Standard toolbar and suggests you use the What's This? command on the Help menu to do it. Use the What's This? command on the Help menu to get online Help for three buttons on the Standard toolbar. Create a new document and for each button write one paragraph that describes what the button does and how to use it. Save, preview, and print the document.

Project 5

If you have not yet done so, read Chapter 4 in the Office Unit in this book to learn about the Internet and the World Wide Web (the Web). Many of your assignments at Worldwide Exotic Foods require using the Web to locate information. Chris asks you to learn how to locate information on the Web by using different search engines and directories. Connect to your ISP and use your Web browser's search feature to load the home page for several search engines. Review each search engine's home page and online Help. Print at least three search engine Help Web pages. Close the browser and disconnect from your ISP. Key a brief description of the World Wide Web into a new document. Save, preview, and print the document.

Project 6

Chris asks you to show several new employees how to print multiple documents at one time from the Open dialog box. Using the various tools available on the Help menu, research how to do this. Create a new document with a short paragraph describing how to print multiple documents from the Open dialog box. Save, preview, and print the document. Using your document as a guide, demonstrate to several co-workers how to print multiple documents at one time from the Open dialog box.

Project 7

Because many of your work assignments at Worldwide Exotic Foods require you to use the Web and your Web browser, Chris wants you to become more familiar with your Web browser's features. Connect to your ISP and load the default home page for your Web browser. Review your Web browser's options to learn how to change the default start page to a page of your choice. With your instructor's permission, change the default start page and close the browser. Open the browser and load the new start page. Reset the option to load the original default start page. Close the browser and disconnect from your ISP. Create a new document and key the steps for changing the default start page in your browser. Save, preview, and print the document.

Project 8

Connect to your ISP and load the home page for a search engine. Use what you learned in Case Project 5 to search for companies on the Web who are similar to Worldwide Exotic Foods. Print at least three Web pages for similar companies. Close the browser and disconnect from your ISP. Create a new document and key the names and URLs of the Web pages you found. Save, preview, and print the document.

chapter one

Creating and Editing a Word Document

Chapter Overview

The basic foundation for every document is creating and editing. This chapter discusses these skills in more detail. You learn to insert dates and text and to select, cut, copy, and delete text. In addition, you learn to use the Overtype mode, the Undo and Repeat commands, and different editing views. With these skills, you can produce finished letters and other documents with minimal rekeying and maximum accuracy.

LEARNING OBJECTIVES

- ► Create a letter
- ► Select text
- ► Cut, copy, insert, move, and paste text
- ► Delete text
- ► Use the Undo, Redo, and Repeat commands
- ► Use Overtype mode
- ► Switch between different editing views

Case profile

B. D. Vickers, the Administrative Vice President of Worldwide Exotic Foods, requests an assistant in the purchasing department and you get the assignment. You work with Kelly Armstead, Vickers' executive assistant, in preparing correspondence for the department. The first letter is a reply to someone inquiring about distribution possibilities for the company.

chapter two

notes You should review Appendix C, Formatting Tips for Business Documents, before beginning this chapter.

2.a Creating a Letter

Most organizations follow specific formatting for their letters. A common letter format widely used for both business and personal correspondence is the **block format**. When you create a letter in block format, all the text aligns against the left side of the page. This includes the date, the letter address, the salutation, the body, the complimentary closing, the writer's name, reference initials, and any special letter parts such as an enclosure or subject line. The body of the letter is single spaced with a blank line between paragraphs.

Three blank lines separate the date from the letter address information, one blank line separates the letter address information and the salutation, one blank line separates the salutation from the body of the letter, and one blank line separates the body of the letter from the complimentary closing. There are three blank lines between the complimentary closing and the writer's name line. If reference initials appear below the writer's name, a blank line separates them. If an enclosure or attachment is noted, the word "Enclosure" or "Attachment" appears below the initials with two blank lines separating them. Finally, when keying the letter address information, one space separates the state and the postal code (ZIP+4).

Most companies use special paper for their business correspondence called **letterhead** paper because the organization's name and address are preprinted at the top of each sheet. When you create a business letter, you determine the initial keying position based on the depth of the letterhead information on the paper (most letterheads are between one inch and two inches deep) and the amount of the letter text. Figure 2-1 illustrates the parts of a block format business letter.

Kelly asks you to create a new letter in the block format. Before you begin keying the text in your letter, you set the appropriate margins for the document.

Setting Margins

Margins are the distance from the top, bottom, left, and right edges of the page to the text. All text in a document appears within the margins you specify. When printing on letterhead paper, you must consider the depth of the preprinted letterhead when setting top margins and the amount of letter text when setting left and right margins.

> **QUICK TIP**
>
> Block format is also called block style.

chapter two

FIGURE 2-1
Block Format
Business Letter

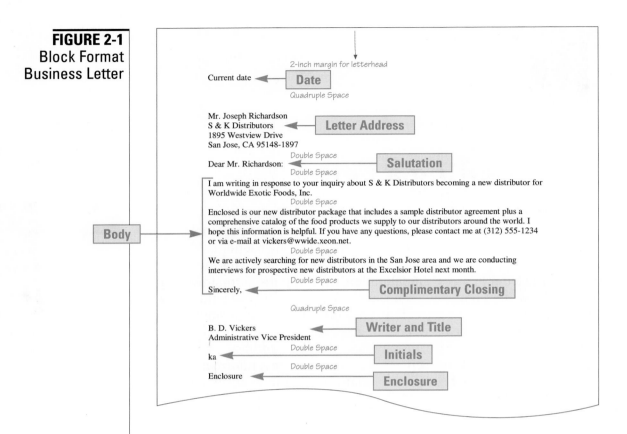

You can change the document margins by clicking the Page Setup command on the File menu to open the Page Setup dialog box. Each margin, Top, Bottom, Left, and Right has a text box indicating the current margin setting. You can key a new margin size number in the text box. You can also click the up and down arrow buttons at the right side of each text box to increase or decrease the margin setting. The new margins you set affect the entire document by default. However, you can change the document margins from the position of the insertion point or for a section of a document.

First, you create the letter shown in Figure 2-1 by creating a new, blank document and then setting the appropriate margins. Then you key the letter text. Worldwide Exotic Foods uses letterhead paper that requires a 2-inch top margin. To create a new, blank document and set the margins:

Step 1	*Click*	the New Blank Document button ▫ on the Standard toolbar, if necessary
Step 2	*Click*	File
Step 3	*Click*	Page Setup

| Step 4 | *Click* | the Margins tab, if necessary |

The dialog box on your screen should look similar to Figure 2-2.

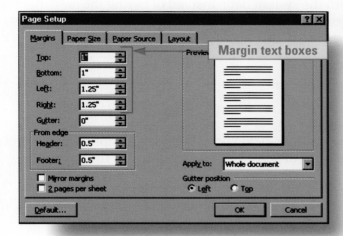

FIGURE 2-2
Margins Tab in the Page
Setup Dialog Box

You can use the dialog box Help button to review the options on the Margins and other tabs in this dialog box. Notice that the blank document is created with preset 1-inch top and bottom margins, and 1.25-inch left and right margins. These **default** margins are preset in the Normal template. You can change the margins as necessary by keying the correct margin in each text box. For this letter, you need to change the top margin to two inches, and the left and right margins to one inch. You can use the TAB key to quickly select the next option in a dialog box.

Step 5	*Key*	2 in the Top: text box
Step 6	*Press*	the TAB key twice
Step 7	*Key*	1 in the Left: text box
Step 8	*Press*	the TAB key
Step 9	*Key*	1 in the Right: text box
Step 10	*Verify*	the Apply to: list box displays Whole document
Step 11	*Click*	OK

After setting the appropriate margins, you begin the letter by inserting the current date.

chapter
two

Inserting the Date and Time

Word provides a variety of special options that allow you to insert a date or date and time without keying it. You can insert the date or date and time as text or as a field of information that is automatically updated with the system date. Instead of keying the date manually in the letter, you can have Word insert the date for you.

Step 1	*Click*	Insert
Step 2	*Click*	Date and Time

The Date and Time dialog box opens. Except for the dates, the dialog box you see on your screen should look similar to Figure 2-3.

FIGURE 2-3
Date and Time Dialog Box

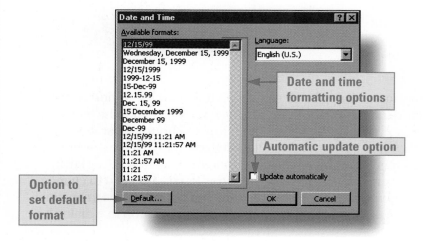

You can change the format of the date by selecting a format option in the Date and Time dialog box. The Update automatically check box provides an option to insert the date as text or as a date field, which automatically updates with the current system date whenever the document is printed. The Default button allows you to set a selected date/time format as the default format for all your Word documents. You use the third date/time format option.

QUICK TIP

To update a date inserted as a Word date field, select the date and press the F9 key.

Step 3	*Verify*	the Update automatically check box is blank
Step 4	*Double-click*	the third date format

When the current date is inserted, you are ready to complete the letter by keying the letter text. By default, Word is in **Insert mode**. This means that when you insert text the characters are entered at the position of the insertion point. When you insert text within an existing line of text, the text to the right of the insertion point shifts to make room for the new text. You continue with the letter by inserting the letter address, salutation, body, complimentary closing, initials, and enclosure notation you see in Figure 2-1.

notes

By default, Word capitalizes the first character in the first word of a sentence. When you key your initials, Word automatically capitalizes the first initial. You can manually correct it to lowercase by pressing the SPACEBAR and pressing the CTRL + Z keys after you key your initials.

Also by default, Word changes the color and underlines the path to a Web page or an e-mail address. This allows someone reading the document online to click the e-mail address to open his or her e-mail program. When you press the ENTER key or SPACEBAR after keying an e-mail address, Word changes the e-mail address to a hyperlink. You can remove the hyperlink formatting by clicking the Undo button on the Standard toolbar or pressing the CTRL + Z keys.

To complete and save the letter:

Step 1	*Press*	the ENTER key four times
Step 2	*Key*	the remaining letter text, as shown in Figure 2-1
Step 3	*Save*	the document as *Richardson Letter*

When you create a Word document, it is possible to make changes to characters, complete words, or groups of words at the same time by first selecting the text.

2.b Selecting Text

Selecting text is one of the most important word processing techniques. **Selecting** means to highlight one or more characters of text so that you can edit, format, or delete them. Once a character, word, or group of words is selected, Word recognizes the selected text as one unit that you can modify using Word editing features. For example, if you wanted to underline a group of words for emphasis, you would first select the words and then apply an underline format. You can select text with both the mouse and the keyboard.

chapter
two

Selecting Text with the Mouse

One way to select text with the mouse is to drag the I-beam across the text. To select text by dragging, click at the beginning of the text, hold down the left mouse button, and move the mouse on the mouse pad in the direction you want to highlight. When the desired text is highlighted, release the mouse button.

The **selection bar** is the vertical area to the far left of the document between the horizontal ruler and the View buttons. When the mouse pointer is in the selection bar, it appears as a right-pointing arrow and you can use it to select text. Figure 2-4 identifies the selection bar and the shape of the mouse pointer when it is in the selection bar.

FIGURE 2-4
Selection Bar

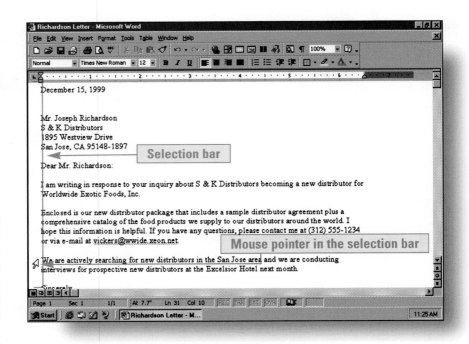

Word includes many mouse and keyboard shortcuts for selecting text. Table 2-1 lists some of these frequently used shortcuts.

Deselecting text means to remove the highlighting. You can deselect text by clicking anywhere in the document area outside the selection, by selecting new text, or by pressing a **pointer-movement key** (UP ARROW, DOWN ARROW, LEFT ARROW, RIGHT ARROW) on the keyboard.

notes

Chapter 1 and the previous sections of this chapter provided step-by-step instructions for repositioning the insertion point. From this point forward, you are instructed to move the I-beam or insertion point to the appropriate position. Review Chapter 1 to see the step-by-step process for repositioning the insertion point, if necessary.

To Select	Do This
A word and the trailing space	Double-click a word
A sentence and the trailing space	Hold down the CTRL key and click inside the sentence
A line of text	Move the mouse pointer into the selection bar next to the line and click
Multiple lines of text	Drag in the selection bar next to the lines
A paragraph	Move the mouse pointer into the selection bar next to the line and double-click, or triple-click the paragraph
Multiple paragraphs	Drag in the selection bar
The document	Hold down the CTRL key and click in the selection bar, or triple-click in the selection bar
A vertical selection of text	Hold down the ALT key and drag the mouse down and left or right
A variable amount of text	Place the insertion point at the beginning of the text to be selected then move the I-beam to the end of the text to be selected and hold down the SHIFT key and click the mouse button
The text from the insertion point to the end of the document	Press the CTRL + SHIFT + END keys
The text from the insertion point to the beginning of the document	Press the CTRL + SHIFT + HOME keys

TABLE 2-1
Keyboard and Mouse Shortcuts for Selecting Text

QUICK TIP

You can find comprehensive lists of keyboard shortcuts in online Help by using the Office Assistant to search using the keyword phrase "keyboard shortcuts."

To select a paragraph of your document by dragging:

Step 1	**Move**	the I-beam before the "E" in "Enclosed" in the second body paragraph
Step 2	**Drag**	down until you have highlighted the entire paragraph and the following blank line
Step 3	**Press**	the RIGHT ARROW key to deselect the text

Compare the dragging selection technique to using the selection bar. To select the second body paragraph using the selection bar:

Step 1	**Move**	the mouse pointer into the selection bar before the "E" in "Enclosed" until the mouse pointer becomes a right-pointing arrow
Step 2	**Double-click**	the selection bar
Step 3	**Click**	outside the selected text to deselect it

chapter
two

Selecting Text with the Keyboard

You can select text using the keyboard by pressing F8 (EXT mode) and then pressing a pointer-movement key, or by holding down the SHIFT key and pressing a pointer-movement key. Either method turns on the **Extend mode** at the location of the insertion point. For example, move the insertion point to the beginning of a word, press the F8 key to turn on the Extend mode, then press the CTRL + RIGHT ARROW key to highlight the word. To remove a selection you highlighted with the F8 key, press the ESC key and then press a pointer-movement key.

After text is selected, you can perform other tasks such as deleting it, formatting it, replacing it by keying new text, and copying or moving it to another location.

2.c Cutting, Copying, Inserting, Moving, and Pasting Text

You can move, or **cut and paste,** text from one location to another in a Word document. You can duplicate, or **copy and paste,** text from one location to another in a Word document. You can also cut and paste or copy and paste text into a different Word document or into another Office application document.

Using Collect and Paste

You use the Cut command to remove text, the Copy command to duplicate text, and the Paste command to insert the cut or copied text. The Cut and Copy commands collect selected text from your Word document and insert it in the Office Clipboard. The **Office Clipboard** is a reserved place in the memory of your computer that can be used to store text temporarily. The Office Clipboard can hold up to twelve cut or copy actions.

To cut or copy text, you first select the desired text and then click Cut or Copy on the Edit menu or shortcut menu, or click the Cut or Copy button on the Standard toolbar. To insert the cut or copied text at a new location in your document, first move the insertion point to the location. Then click the Paste command on the Edit menu or shortcut menu, or click the Paste button on the Standard toolbar. You can also use the Clipboard toolbar to paste. The Clipboard toolbar usually appears automatically after you cut or copy a second selection without pasting the first selection you cut or copied.

Kelly reviewed the *Richardson Letter* document and wants you want to move the third body paragraph to the second body paragraph position. To move text with the shortcut menu:

Step 1	*Select*	the third paragraph beginning with "We are" and the following blank line
Step 2	*Move*	the mouse pointer to the selected text
Step 3	*Right-click*	the selected text

A shortcut menu for the selected text appears. Your screen should look similar to Figure 2-5.

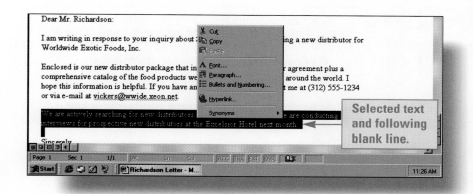

FIGURE 2-5
Text Shortcut Menu

Step 4	*Click*	Cut
Step 5	*Observe*	that the third body paragraph no longer appears in the document because it is temporarily stored on the Office Clipboard
Step 6	*Move*	the I-beam before the "E" in "Enclosed" in the second body paragraph
Step 7	*Right-click*	at the I-beam position to view the shortcut menu
Step 8	*Click*	Paste

The paragraph is inserted in the new location. Kelly also wants you to copy two of the letter address lines to the end of the document. You can copy and paste both lines at one time or you can copy and paste each line separately using the Clipboard toolbar. Before you begin the copy process, you add some additional blank lines at the end of the document. To insert additional blank lines at the bottom of the letter:

Step 1	*Move*	the insertion point to the end of the document

QUICK TIP

When you want to embed or link data copied from another Office application, you use the Paste Special command on the Edit menu. For more information on embedding and linking, see the Word Integration chapter or online Help.

chapter
two

| Step 2 | *Press* | the ENTER key three times |

The **Collect and Paste** feature is a simple way to copy individual lines of the letter address and then paste them all at once. To collect and paste text:

Step 1	*Scroll*	to view the letter address
Step 2	*Select*	the first line of the letter address using the selection bar; include the paragraph mark at the end of the line (turn on the formatting marks, if desired)
Step 3	*Click*	the Copy button 📋 on the Standard toolbar
Step 4	*Select*	the last line of the letter address using the selection bar; include the paragraph mark at the end of the line
Step 5	*Click*	the Copy button 📋 on the Standard toolbar

The Clipboard toolbar appears. The Clipboard toolbar you see on your screen should look similar to Figure 2-6.

FIGURE 2-6
Clipboard Toolbar

Clipboard (2 of 12)

Paste All

Items copied to the Office Clipboard

CAUTION TIP

If the Clipboard toolbar was previously turned off, it might not appear automatically. You can right-click the Standard or Formatting toolbar and click Clipboard to show it, if necessary.

With the two selections of text copied, you can paste one or both in a new location. To paste text:

Step 1	*Move*	the insertion point to the end of the document
Step 2	*Move*	the mouse pointer to the copied item icons on the Clipboard toolbar and observe the ScreenTip for each item
Step 3	*Click*	the Clipboard toolbar icon for the first line of the letter address (Mr. Joseph Richardson)
Step 4	*Observe*	that the text is pasted into the document and the insertion point moves to the next line
Step 5	*Click*	the Clipboard toolbar icon for the last line of the letter address (San Jose, CA 95148-1897)
Step 6	*Observe*	that the text is pasted into the document and the insertion point moves to the next line

You can clear the Clipboard after you no longer need to paste the items stored there. To clear the Clipboard:

Step 1	*Click*	the Clear Clipboard button 🖾 on the Clipboard toolbar
Step 2	*Click*	the Close button ☒ on the Clipboard toolbar
Step 3	*Save*	the document as *Revised Richardson Letter* and close it

After reviewing the *Revised Richardson Letter* Kelly wants to make some additional changes. She asks you to work from the original *Richardson Letter*.

Moving and Copying Text with the Mouse

A shortcut for moving and copying text is called the **drag-and-drop** method. This method uses the mouse and does not store the any items on the Office Clipboard. To move text using drag-and-drop, first select the text and then drag the selection to its new location. To copy text using drag-and-drop, select the text, hold down the CTRL key, and then drag the text to its new location, releasing the mouse button before you release the CTRL key.

When you are using the drag-and-drop method, the insertion point changes to a small, dashed, gray vertical line. A small box with a dashed, gray border appears at the base of the mouse pointer. If you are copying text, a small plus sign (+) appears below of the mouse pointer.

You open the *Richardson Letter* from the File menu and move the third body paragraph to the second body paragraph position using the mouse pointer. You can quickly open a recently closed document by clicking the document name on the File menu list of recently closed documents. To use the drag-and-drop method to move text:

Step 1	*Click*	File
Step 2	*Click*	the *Richardson Letter* at the bottom of the File menu
Step 3	*Select*	the paragraph beginning with "We are" and the following blank line
Step 4	*Move*	the mouse pointer to the selected text (the pointer is a left-pointing arrow)
Step 5	*Click*	and hold the mouse button
Step 6	*Observe*	the dashed-line insertion point at the tip of the mouse pointer

chapter
two

Step 7	*Drag*	up until the dashed-line insertion point is positioned before the "E" in "Enclosed" in the second body paragraph
Step 8	*Release*	the mouse button
Step 9	*Deselect*	the text

As you edit documents, you often need to delete text previously keyed in a document.

2.d Deleting Text

There are several ways to delete text from a document. The BACKSPACE and DELETE keys delete individual text characters in your document to the left and right of the insertion point, respectively. You can also use the BACKSPACE or DELETE keys to delete selected text. To delete the word "new" in the first body paragraph in the *Richardson Letter* document:

| Step 1 | *Double-click* | the word "new" in the first body paragraph |
| Step 2 | *Press* | the DELETE key |

The text is deleted. You can use this method to delete both small and large selections of text. If you delete a large selection inadvertently, you won't need to re-key the selection. Fortunately, it is possible to reverse your last action.

C 2.e Using the Undo, Redo, and Repeat Commands

The Undo and Repeat commands come in handy as you edit documents. The **Undo** command enables you to reverse a previous action. The **Repeat** command enables you to duplicate your last action.

You think the word "new" should stay in the letter. Because you just deleted the text, you can use the Undo command on the Edit menu or Undo button on the Standard toolbar to reverse the action. To restore the word "new" to the letter:

| Step 1 | *Click* | the Undo button 🔙 on the Standard toolbar |

The word reappears in the letter in the original location. You can undo multiple actions sequentially beginning with the last action you performed; just click the Undo button for each command you want to reverse. Similarly, you can also repeat actions and redo actions that were previously undone. Click the <u>R</u>epeat command on the <u>E</u>dit menu to repeat your last action. Click the **Redo** button on the Standard toolbar to redo an action previously undone. After rereading the letter, you decide the word "new" doesn't need to be in the letter. To redo your last undo action:

| Step 1 | *Click* | the Redo button 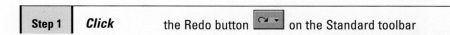 on the Standard toolbar |

The word "new" is again deleted from the letter. Another way to replace text is to use the Overtype mode and key new text over old text.

2.f Using the Overtype Mode

Word has an **Overtype mode** that allows you to key new text over existing text. When you are in Overtype mode, any character you key replaces the character to the right of the insertion point. The OVR mode indicator on the status bar allows you to turn on or off Overtype mode. To turn on Overtype mode, double-click the OVR mode indicator on the status bar. The OVR mode indicator appears boldfaced to indicate Overtype mode is turned on. When you want to return to Insert mode, double-click the OVR mode indicator to turn off Overtype mode.

You look at Mr. Richardson's original letter and discover his street address is 1895 Westview Place. To edit the street address line using Overtype mode:

Step 1	*Move*	the insertion point before the "D" in "Drive" in the street address line
Step 2	*Double-click*	the OVR mode indicator on the status bar to turn on Overtype mode
Step 3	*Observe*	that the OVR mode indicator is bold, indicating the feature is turned on
Step 4	*Key*	Place

**chapter
two**

The characters in the word "Place" replace the characters in the word "Drive." Because you are replacing existing characters with new characters, it is important that you turn off Overtype mode and return to Insert mode as soon as you are finished with your changes. This way you won't replace text unintentionally.

| Step 5 | *Double-click* | the OVR mode indicator on the status bar to turn off Overtype mode |
| Step 6 | *Save* | the document as *Final Richardson Revision* and close it |

Word has many ways to view a document for editing. The appropriate editing view depends on the kind of editing you are doing.

2.g Switching Between Different Editing Views

You can view documents in several ways for editing: Normal view, Web Layout view, Print Layout view, Full Screen view, Outline view, and Print Preview. The two most commonly used views for entering and editing text are Normal view and Print Layout view.

Normal View

Normal view is commonly used for keying, editing, and formatting text. It does not display margins, headers and footers, drawing objects, graphics, and text in column format.

Print Layout View

In **Print Layout view**, your document looks more like it looks on the printed page, including headers and footers, columns, graphics, drawing objects, and margins. You also see a vertical ruler in Print Layout view. To view a document in Print Layout view:

Step 1	*Open*	the *Vancouver Warehouse Report* located on the Data Disk
Step 2	*Click*	the Print Layout View button 🔲 to the left of the horizontal scroll bar
Step 3	*Zoom*	the document to Whole Page

Your screen should look similar to Figure 2-7.

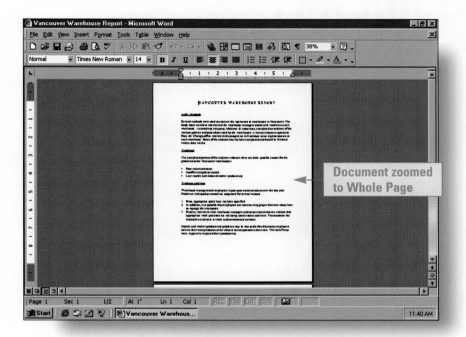

FIGURE 2-7
Print Layout View

Step 4	*Click*	the Normal View button to the left of the horizontal scroll bar
Step 5	*Close*	the document without saving any changes

Full Screen View

When you need to maximize the number of text lines you see on your screen use **Full Screen view**, which hides the title bar, menu bar, toolbars, scroll bars, status bar, and taskbar. You can view a document in Full Screen view by clicking the F̲ull Screen command on the V̲iew menu.

CAUTION TIP

You may notice that the I-beam sometimes appears with a text alignment indicator in Print Layout view. This is the Click and Type feature. You use the **Click and Type** feature to double-click anywhere in your document in Print Layout view and key your text.

QUICK TIP

For more information on changing Word options click the O̲ptions command on the T̲ools menu, then click the General and View tabs. You can use the dialog box Help button to view a description of each option on each tab.

chapter
two

Summary

▶ The block format is a commonly used format for business correspondence.

▶ Word has preset top, bottom, left, and right margins that you can change in the Page Setup dialog box.

▶ The date and time can be inserted in a document as text or as a field that automatically updates to the current system date when the document is printed.

▶ You can select characters, words, or groups of words with the mouse or keyboard.

▶ Selected text can be cut, copied, pasted (inserted), and deleted.

▶ You can collect several cut or copied selections and then paste them individually or all at one time using the Office Clipboard.

▶ You can repeat or undo your last action.

▶ Word has several ways you can view your document, including: Normal view, Web Layout view, Print Layout view, Print Preview, Outline view, and Full Screen view. Use Normal view to key, edit, and format text. Use Print Layout to view and work with margins, headers and footers, columns, graphics, and drawing objects. Use Web Layout view to see how a Web page looks in a Web browser.

Commands Review

Action	Menu Bar	Shortcut Menu	Toolbar	Keyboard
Set margins	File, Page Setup			ALT + F, U
Insert date	Insert, Date and Time			ALT + I, T ALT + SHIFT + D
Update a selected date field		Right-click, then click Update Field		F9
Cut, Copy, Paste	Edit, Cut or Copy or Paste	Right-click then click Cut or Copy or Paste		ALT + E, T or C or P CTRL + C (copy) CTRL + X (cut) CTRL + V (paste)
Turn on or off Overtype			Double-click the OVR mode indicator	INSERT
Undo or Redo actions	Edit, Undo			ALT + E, U CTRL + Z
Repeat actions	Edit, Repeat			ALT + E, R CTRL + Y
Cancel an action				ESC
Change editing views	View, Normal or Web Layout or Print Layout or Outline or Full Screen			ALT + V, N or W or P or U, or O ALT + CTRL + P ALT + CTRL + O ALT + CTRL + N

Concepts Review

Circle the correct answer.

1. You can remove text by selecting the text and pressing the:
[a] EXT key.
[b] ALT + PAGEUP keys.
[c] CTRL key.
[d] DELETE key.

2. You cannot add a date to a document by:
[a] keying the date manually.
[b] inserting a date field that updates automatically.
[c] inserting the date as text.
[d] pressing the Insert key.

3. The selection bar is:
[a] located below the status bar.
[b] used to open other Office applications.
[c] used to select text in different ways.
[d] used to set left and right margins.

4. When you use the block format for a business letter, the:
[a] date and complimentary closing are centered on their respective lines.
[b] letter address is positioned below the salutation.
[c] letter components all begin at the left margin.
[d] letter components all begin at the right margin.

5. Margins refer to the:
[a] distance from the center of the page to the edge of the page.
[b] distance from the top, bottom, left, and right edges of the page to the text.
[c] number of lines you can have on a page.
[d] size of the text on a page.

6. By default, Word is in the:
[a] Overtype mode.
[b] Edit mode.
[c] Online Review mode.
[d] Insert mode.

7. Which of the following is not a selection technique in Word?
[a] Pressing the CTRL + SHIFT + END keys to select from the insertion point to the end of the document.
[b] Double-clicking the selection bar opposite the paragraph you wish to select.
[c] Double-clicking a word.
[d] Pressing the ALT key and clicking a word.

8. Using the mouse to move or copy text is called:
[a] cut-and-drag.
[b] select-and-cut.
[c] copy-and-cut.
[d] drag-and-drop.

9. Overtype mode allows you to:
[a] select text.
[b] key over existing text.
[c] move text.
[d] copy text.

10. Which of the following is not an editing view?
[a] Full Page view
[b] Web Layout view
[c] Print Layout view
[d] Normal view

Circle **T** if the statement is true or **F** if the statement is false.

T   F   1. When you are in the Overtype mode and enter new text, any character you key replaces the character to the right of the insertion point.
T   F   2. Word automatically defaults to the Edit mode.
T   F   3. Word can undo multiple actions.

chapter two

T	**F**	4.	The mouse and the keyboard can both be used to select text in a document.
T	**F**	5.	The EXT mode indicator appears boldfaced when you are using the Extend mode feature.
T	**F**	6.	You can restore text that has been deleted.
T	**F**	7.	You can maximize the number of lines of text displayed on the screen by switching to Full Screen view.
T	**F**	8.	Normal view displays your document closely to the way it looks when printed.
T	**F**	9.	You can insert the date and the time together in a Word document.
T	**F**	10.	The Office Clipboard is a reserved place in the memory of your computer you can use to temporarily store up to 12 items you have cut or copied.

Skills Review

Exercise 1

1. Create the following document. Use the block format with 2-inch top margin and 1-inch left and right margins. Insert the current date in the format of your choice at the top of the document. As you key the text, use the movement techniques and insert/delete actions you learned in this chapter to correct any errors.

Current date

Ms. Gail Jackson
Corporate Travel Manager
International Travel Services
1590 W. Convention Street
Chicago, IL 60605-1590

Dear Ms. Jackson:

Thank you for helping plan business trip to London this winter. I am really looking forward to seeing the sites, as well as taking care of some business. This is my first trip to London, and you were quite courteous in answering my questions.

Yours truly,

Kelly Armstead
Executive Assistant to B. D. Vickers

ka

---

2. Save the document as *Travel Letter*.

3. Preview, print, and close the document.

Exercise 2   C

1. Open the *Travel Letter* document created in Exercise 1 in this chapter.

2. At the end of the street address line, add ", Suite 16A"; in the first sentence, add the word "me" after the word "helping"; in the first sentence, add the word "my" after the word "plan" and delete the word "business"; in the first sentence, delete the word "winter" and replace it with the word "summer."

3. Save the document as *Travel Letter Revised*.

4. Preview, print, and close the document.

Exercise 3   C

1. Create the following document. Use the block format with 2-inch top margin and 1-inch left and right margins. Insert the date as a field at the top of the document. As you key the letter, use the movement techniques and insert/delete actions to correct any errors.

Current date

Mr. Taylor Schreier
J & H Electronic Wholesalers
4578 Main Street
Cleveland, OH 78433-6325

Dear Mr. Schreier:

Thank you for inquiry about our holiday basket special offers. I am enclosing our most recent holiday catalog that explains and illustrates our special offers.

Please call our Sales Department at (312) 555-5555 when you are ready to place your order.

Yours truly,

P.L. Brown
Marketing Vice President

pb

Enclosure

2. Save the document as *Schreier Letter*.

3. Preview, print, and close the document.

chapter two

Exercise 4

1. Open the *Schreier Letter* document created in Exercise 3 in this chapter.

2. In the first sentence, add the word "your" after the word "for" and delete the word "about" and replace it with the word "regarding."

3. Using Overtype mode, replace the text "Yours truly," with the text "Sincerely," in the complimentary close. Delete any extra characters and then turn off Overtype mode.

4. Save the document as *Schreier Letter Revised*.

5. Preview, print, and close the document.

Exercise 5

1. Open the *Employment Application Letter* document located on the Data Disk.

2. Move the second body paragraph to the first body paragraph position using a shortcut menu.

3. Undo the move action.

4. Move the second body paragraph to the first body paragraph position using drag-and-drop.

5. Combine the third body paragraph with the second body paragraph by viewing the formatting marks and deleting the paragraph marks at the end of the second body paragraph and the blank line between the second body paragraph and the third body paragraph. Don't forget to add a space between the two sentences of the revised second body paragraph.

6. Replace the words "Current date" with the current date in the 12 November 1999 format.

7. Save the document as *Employment Application Letter Revised*.

8. Preview, print, and close the document.

Exercise 6

1. Open the *Business Solicitation Letter* located on the Data Disk.

2. Change the margins to a 2-inch top margin and 1-inch left and right margins.

3. Delete the word "own" in the first sentence of the first body paragraph. Use the Repeat command on the Edit menu to delete the text "explaining and" in the first sentence of the second body paragraph.

4. Replace the words "Current date" with the current date in the format of your choice.

5. Save the document as *Business Solicitation Letter Revised*.

6. Preview, print, and close the document.

Exercise 7

1. Create the following document. Use the block format with 1½-inch top margin and 1¼-inch left and right margins. Insert the current date in the format of your choice at the top of the document. As you key the letter, use the movement techniques and insert/delete actions to correct any errors.

Current date

BCH Software Company
4000 Skywalk Way
Ventura, CA 91015-4657

Dear Sir:

Please send by return mail all of products brochures, technical specifications, and price
list for your software related to word processing for IBM PS2/ and IBM-compatible
personal computers.

Additionally, please add your mailing list to update us on any future changes in your
product line.

Sincerely,

B. D. Vickers
Administrative Vice President

ka

2. Save the document as *BCH Software Letter*.

3. Preview, print, and close the document.

Exercise 8

1. Open the *BCH Software Letter* document created in Exercise 7 in this chapter.

2. Edit the document following the proofing notations.

3. Save the document as *BCH Software Letter Revised*.

4. Preview, print, and close the document.

Current date

Mr. James Wilson
BCH Software Company
4000 Skywalk Way
Ventura, CA 91015-4657

                    Mr. Wilson
Dear ~~Sir:~~

Please send by return mail all of products brochures, technical specifications, and price list for ~~your~~ software related to ~~word processing~~ for IBM PS2/ and IBM-compatible personal computers.

Additionally, please add your mailing list to update us on any ~~future~~ changes in your product line.

Sincerely,

B. D. Vickers
Administrative Vice President

ka

Case Projects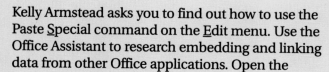

Project 1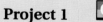

B. D. Vickers is traveling on business to Melbourne, Australia in three weeks. Prepare a letter to Mr. David Melville, Reservations Manager at the Excelsior Hotel, 3500 Wayburne Drive, Melbourne, VIC, 30001, Australia, requesting accommodations for a week beginning three weeks from today. Insert the date as text using the Day, Month (in text), Year format. Save, preview, and print the document.

Project 2

Kelly Armstead asks you to find out how to use the Paste Special command on the Edit menu. Use the Office Assistant to research embedding and linking data from other Office applications. Open the

Vancouver Branch Sales workbook (located on the Data Disk) in Excel, copy the data to the Office Clipboard, switch to a blank document, and embed the data using the Paste Special command. Save, preview, and print the document.

Project 3

Kelly Armstead has asked you to find a list of keyboard shortcuts you both can use to prepare correspondence. Using the Office Assistant, search Word online Help for a list of keyboard shortcut keys for moving the insertion point in a document and selecting text in a document. Print the lists. Use the lists to demonstrate the keyboard shortcuts to a classmate.

Project 4

B. D. Vickers is considering ordering several IntelliMouse pointing devices for the Purchasing Department and has asked you to find out how the devices are used to increase productivity in the department. Using the <u>H</u>elp menu resources, including Web resources, search for information on the IntelliMouse pointing device. Create a new document containing at least three paragraphs describing how the Purchasing Department employees can improve their productivity by using the IntelliMouse pointing device. Insert the current date as text using the mm/dd/yy format. Save, preview, and print the document.

Project 5

There have been several power failures because of storms in the area and Kelly is concerned that she may lose documents she is working on if the power fails. She has asked you to find out what options Word has to automatically back up documents as she is working and to automatically recover documents lost during a power failure. Using the <u>H</u>elp menu, research what backup and document recovery features Word provides. Create a new document, containing at least four paragraphs, that describes how to set backup procedures and recover lost or damaged documents. Insert the date as a field using the format of your choice. Save, preview, and print the document.

Project 6

B. D. Vickers has extended the business trip discussed in Project 1 and now plans to spend two days in Hong Kong and three days in London before returning. Kelly needs a list of possible accommodations in Hong Kong and London and has asked you to search the Web for information on hotels in these cities. She also needs you to review flight schedules and suggest flights from Melbourne to Hong Kong, from Hong Kong to London, and from London to Chicago. Connect to your ISP and search the Web for the information you need. Save at least two URLs as "favorites." Print at least five

Web pages. Disconnect from your ISP and close your browser. Create a new, blank document and key the title and URL of the pages you printed. Insert the date as text in the format of your choice. Save, preview, and print the document.

Project 7

Open the document of your choice. Practice using various selection techniques to select text. Delete and restore text using the Delete key and the Undo, Redo, and Repeat commands. Close the document without saving any changes.

Project 8

Worldwide Exotic Foods, Inc. participates in a summer internship program for graduating seniors and has a new group of interns starting the program next week. Margie Montez, the program director, has asked you to make a ten-minute presentation on creating business letters using Word 2000. The presentation is scheduled for next Thursday, at 3:00 PM. Create a new document listing the topics you plan to discuss and the order in which you plan to discuss them. Insert the date and time using the format of your choice. Save, preview, and print the document. Ask a classmate to review the document and provide comments and suggestions on the topics to be covered and the organization of the presentation. With your instructor's approval, schedule a time to give your presentation to your class.

Project 9

Kelly has subscribed to an e-mail mailing list and gets Word 2000 user tips every day via e-mail. You would like to also subscribe to this kind of mailing list and want to know more about how to do this. Connect to your ISP and search the Web for information on locating and subscribing to mailing lists. Create a new, blank document that lists titles and URLs for pages that provide mailing list information. Insert the date using the Day (in text), Month (in text) and Date, Year format. Save, preview, and print the document.

chapter two

Using the Proofing Tools

Chapter Overview

Documents with misspellings and grammar errors indicate sloppiness and inattention to detail—two traits no company wants to convey. Proofing a document before you print it helps ensure it is error-free, allowing readers to focus on its content. Word has several tools to help you proof your documents. In this chapter you learn to use the Spelling and Grammar, Thesaurus, and AutoCorrect proofing tools. You also learn to insert dates automatically with AutoComplete and create, insert, edit, print, and delete AutoText entries.

Case profile

Worldwide Exotic Foods requires that all correspondence and documents sent out from the company have accurate spelling and grammar. Kelly Armstead asks you to correct any errors in a letter she keyed quickly before it is printed and mailed.

chapter three

3.a Using the Spelling and Grammar Features

Kelly tells you that it is company policy to check the spelling and grammar of any document before you print it. You can check the spelling and grammar in a document with a menu command, a toolbar button, a status bar mode indicator, or a shortcut menu. By default, Word checks the spelling and grammar in your document as you key the text. Using this automatic spelling and grammar feature saves time in editing your document. When you misspell a word or key text that may be grammatically incorrect and then press the SPACEBAR, a wavy red or green line appears below the text. The red line indicates a spelling error and the green line indicates a possible grammar error.

Kelly's letter contains several keying errors. You open the letter and then use the Spelling and Grammar command to correct those errors. To open the letter containing errors:

| Step 1 | *Open* | the *IAEA Letter* document located on the Data Disk |

Notice the wavy red and green lines below text that may be misspelled or grammatically incorrect. In this letter the proper names are correct; therefore, you can ignore the wavy red or green lines underneath them if they appear. When necessary, you can add words like proper names to a custom dictionary. *For the activities in this chapter, do not add any words to a custom dictionary.*

There is one grammar error in the letter, indicated by a wavy green line. To correct the grammar error "an" in the second body paragraph:

| Step 1 | *Right-click* | the word "an" |

The Grammar shortcut menu that appears on your screen should look similar to Figure 3-1.

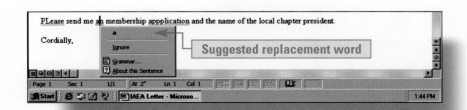

FIGURE 3-1
Grammar Shortcut Menu

chapter
three

MENU TIP

You can right-click a misspelled word or grammar error to correct it. You can also click the Spelling and Grammar command on the Tools menu to correct spelling or grammar errors.

Notice the shortcut menu suggestion to replace the word "an" with "a." You can quickly replace a word by clicking the suggested word in the shortcut menu, or you can display the Grammar dialog box to get more information about the error message. Because this is an obvious error, you can quickly correct it by replacing "an" with "a."

Step 2	*Click*	a on the shortcut menu

Next, you correct the misspellings in the letter. To correct the spelling of the word "intereting" in the first body paragraph:

Step 1	*Right-click*	the word "intereting"

The Spelling shortcut menu that appears on your screen should look similar to Figure 3-2.

FIGURE 3-2
Spelling Shortcut Menu

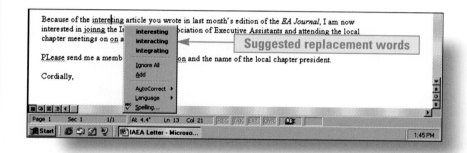

You can click a suggested spelling, ignore the spelling, add the word to a custom dictionary, add the error and suggested replacement word to the AutoCorrect tool, or open the Spelling dialog box. Because the correct spelling is on the shortcut menu, you click it to fix the error.

MOUSE TIP

You can click the Spelling and Grammar button on the Standard toolbar or the Spelling and Grammar Status mode indicator on the status bar to correct spelling or grammar errors.

Step 2	*Click*	interesting on the shortcut menu

You can display the spelling or grammar shortcut menu with the Spelling and Grammar Status mode indicator on the status bar.

To correct the next error, the word "joinng," using the Spelling and Grammar Status mode indicator:

Step 1	*Click*	the word "joinng" to position the insertion point in the word
Step 2	*Double-click*	the Spelling and Grammar Status mode indicator on the status bar

| Step 3 | *Click* | joining on the shortcut menu |

Another way to correct spelling and grammar is to use the Spelling and Grammar dialog box, which shows each error and provides options for you to correct it. To correct the remaining errors using the Spelling and Grammar dialog box:

| Step 1 | *Click* | the Spelling and Grammar button ![ABC] on the Standard toolbar |

The dialog box on your screen should look similar to Figure 3-3.

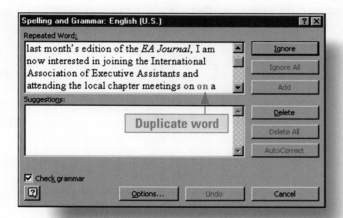

FIGURE 3-3
Spelling and Grammar Dialog Box

The Spelling and Grammar tool detected the duplicate word "on" in the first body paragraph. You want to delete the duplicate word.

| Step 2 | *Click* | D̲elete |

Word deletes the extra word and moves to the next spelling error. The word "PLease" appears in the dialog box and Word provides a list of possible corrections in the Suggestio̲ns: list. Word highlights the most likely suggested correction "Please" for the irregular capitalization.

| Step 3 | *Click* | C̲hange |

The next misspelled word "appplication" appears in the dialog box and Word suggests the correct spelling "application."

| Step 4 | *Click* | C̲hange |

chapter
three

Word highlights the proper name "Armstead." Because this spelling is correct, you can ignore it and proceed to the next error. You can choose to ignore words that are correct but do not appear in the dictionaries. To ignore the remaining possible errors:

Step 5	*Click*	Ignore until the spelling and grammar checking is complete and a dialog box opens indicating the process is complete
Step 6	*Click*	OK
Step 7	*Save*	the document as *IAEA Letter Revised*

In addition to checking the spelling and grammar, you read Kelly's letter and want to find new words to replace certain words in the letter.

3.b Using the Thesaurus

The **Thesaurus** enables you to replace a selected word with another word that has the same or a very similar meaning. Kelly suggests that you substitute a different word for the word "article" in first body paragraph of her letter. To find a synonym:

Step 1	*Right-click*	the word "article" in the first body paragraph
Step 2	*Point*	to Synonyms

A shortcut menu of replacement words appears along with the Thesaurus command. You can select a replacement word from the shortcut menu or open the Thesaurus dialog box for additional replacement options. You decide to replace "article" with "commentary."

Step 3	*Click*	commentary on the shortcut menu
Step 4	*Observe*	that the word "commentary" replaces the word "article"
Step 5	*Save*	the document

Another Word proofing tool, AutoCorrect, can automatically correct your keying errors.

3.c Using AutoCorrect

The **AutoCorrect** tool fixes common errors as you key in the text. For example, if you commonly key "adn" for "and," AutoCorrect corrects the error as soon as you press the SPACEBAR. AutoCorrect also corrects two initial capitalized letters (DEar), capitalizes the first letter of a sentence, capitalizes the names of days, and corrects errors caused by forgetting to turn off the CAPS LOCK key (aRTICLE). The AutoCorrect tool contains an extensive list of symbols and words that are inserted whenever you type an abbreviation for the symbol or word and then press the SPACEBAR. You can specify certain words as exceptions to this automatic correction. To verify AutoCorrect is turned on:

Step 1	*Click*	Tools
Step 2	*Click*	AutoCorrect
Step 3	*Click*	the AutoCorrect tab, if necessary

The AutoCorrect dialog box on your screen should look similar to Figure 3-4.

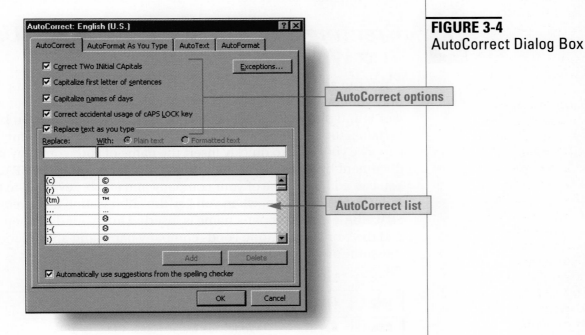

FIGURE 3-4
AutoCorrect Dialog Box

Remember that you can use the dialog box Help button to review the all the options on the AutoCorrect tab.

**chapter
three**

| Step 4 | *Verify* | a check mark appears in the Replace text as you type check box |
| Step 5 | *Click* | OK |

To test AutoCorrect, you first delete the word "the" before the word "International" in the first body paragraph and then deliberately key the word "teh:"

Step 1	*Delete*	the word "the" before the word "International" in the first body paragraph
Step 2	*Key*	teh
Step 3	*Verify*	that the word is misspelled
Step 4	*Press*	the SPACEBAR
Step 5	*Observe*	the word "teh" is automatically corrected to "the" when you press the SPACEBAR
Step 6	*Save*	the *IAEA Letter Revised* document and close it

QUICK TIP

If AutoCorrect makes a change you do not want, press the CTRL + Z keys or click the Undo button on the Standard toolbar to undo the AutoCorrect action.

Sometimes it is necessary to alter the AutoCorrect tool by adding or removing AutoCorrect items or by setting AutoCorrect exceptions.

Creating and Applying Frequently Used Text With AutoCorrect

You can add and delete items in the AutoCorrect list. You can add not only your own common keying errors or misspelled words, but also words and phrases that you would like to insert whenever you key a certain letter combination and press the SPACEBAR. For example, suppose you want to quickly insert the name of your company into a document by keying an abbreviation and then pressing the SPACEBAR. You can add the name of your company and an abbreviation to the AutoCorrect list. Then, when you key the abbreviation and press the SPACEBAR, your company name is inserted into your document. To add the Worldwide Exotic Foods company name and abbreviation to the AutoCorrect list:

Step 1	*Create*	a new, blank document
Step 2	*Key*	Worldwide Exotic Foods, Inc.
Step 3	*Select*	the text (do not include the paragraph mark at the end of the text)
Step 4	*Click*	Tools

Step 5	*Click*	AutoCorrect
Step 6	*Click*	the AutoCorrect tab, if necessary
Step 7	*Observe*	that the company name is already entered in the With: text box
Step 8	*Key*	wef in the Replace: text box
Step 9	*Click*	Add
Step 10	*Observe*	that the company name and abbreviation are added to the AutoCorrect list
Step 11	*Click*	OK
Step 12	*Delete*	the selected company name text

You decide to test the abbreviation you added to the AutoCorrect list. To insert the company name using AutoCorrect:

Step 1	*Key*	wef
Step 2	*Press*	the SPACEBAR
Step 3	*Observe*	the company name is automatically inserted

Adding words you key frequently to the AutoCorrect list is a great timesaver. When you no longer need an AutoCorrect entry, you should delete it. To delete the company name from the AutoCorrect list:

Step 1	*Click*	Tools
Step 2	*Click*	AutoCorrect
Step 3	*Click*	the AutoCorrect tab, if necessary
Step 4	*Key*	wef in the Replace: text box to scroll the AutoCorrect list
Step 5	*Click*	Worldwide Exotic Foods, Inc. in the AutoCorrect list
Step 6	*Click*	Delete
Step 7	*Click*	OK

You can also create a list of words or exceptions that AutoCorrect leaves untouched.

**chapter
three**

Setting AutoCorrect Exceptions

AutoCorrect comes with a list of **exceptions**, words or abbreviations that AutoCorrect does not correct automatically. Whenever you key a period (.) in a commonly used abbreviation, AutoCorrect may interpret the period as the end of a sentence and then capitalize the following word. To avoid this, you can set an AutoCorrect exception to ignore capitalization following the period (.) in a specific abbreviation. Worldwide Exotic Foods frequently uses the abbreviation "Qtr." for "quarter" in its documents. You can set an exception for this abbreviation so that the AutoCorrect feature does not automatically capitalize next word. To use AutoCorrect before setting an exception:

Step 1	*Press*	the ENTER key to move the insertion point to the next line
Step 2	*Verify*	the Capitalize the first letter of sentences option is turned on in the AutoCorrect tab of the AutoCorrect dialog box
Step 3	*Key*	Qtr.
Step 4	*Press*	the SPACEBAR
Step 5	*Key*	is
Step 6	*Press*	the SPACEBAR
Step 7	*Observe*	the letter "I" in the word "Is" is capitalized
Step 8	*Delete*	the Qtr. Is text

Many Worldwide Exotic Foods documents use the Qtr. abbreviation for quarters, such as the financial reports. To create an exception for the abbreviation "Qtr.":

Step 1	*Click*	Tools
Step 2	*Click*	AutoCorrect
Step 3	*Click*	the AutoCorrect tab, if necessary
Step 4	*Click*	Exceptions
Step 5	*Click*	the First Letter tab, if necessary

The AutoCorrect Exceptions dialog box on your screen should look similar to Figure 3-5.

QUICK TIP

If the Automatically add words to list option is turned on in the AutoCorrect Exceptions dialog box, you can backspace over the incorrectly capitalized word and key it again. Word then adds the exception to the list. To keep the AutoCorrect feature from automatically correcting text with mixed upper and lowercase letters, you can click the INitial CAps tab in the AutoCorrect Exceptions dialog box and add your exception to the list.

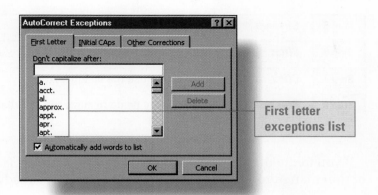

FIGURE 3-5
First Letter Tab in the
AutoCorrect Exceptions
Dialog Box

First letter
exceptions list

> **QUICK TIP**
>
> You can also add
> formatted text and
> graphics to an
> AutoCorrect entry.

You add the words AutoCorrect cannot automatically correct in this dialog box. AutoCorrect exceptions are not case sensitive, so you can enter the text in lowercase letters, uppercase letters, or a combination.

Step 6	*Key*	qtr. in the D<u>o</u>n't capitalize after: text box
Step 7	*Click*	<u>A</u>dd
Step 8	*Click*	OK twice to close the dialog boxes

With the AutoCorrect exception added to the list, you decide to try it out. To test the exception:

Step 1	*Key*	Qtr.
Step 2	*Press*	the SPACEBAR
Step 3	*Key*	is
Step 4	*Press*	the SPACEBAR
Step 5	*Observe*	the word "is" is not capitalized

You can delete exceptions when you no longer need them. To delete the Qtr. exception:

Step 1	*Open*	the AutoCorrect dialog box and view the AutoCorrect tab
Step 2	*Click*	<u>E</u>xceptions
Step 3	*Click*	the <u>F</u>irst Letter tab, if necessary
Step 4	*Key*	qtr. in the D<u>o</u>n't capitalize after: text box to scroll the AutoCorrect list

chapter
three

Step 5	*Observe*	that qtr. is selected in the list
Step 6	*Click*	Delete
Step 7	*Click*	OK twice to close the dialog boxes
Step 8	*Press*	the ENTER key twice to move the insertion point in the document

If you frequently key larger amounts of text, AutoText is a better option than AutoCorrect for inserting text that has already been keyed.

3.d Using AutoText

An **AutoText** entry is a segment of stored text that you can insert into your documents. In this way, it is similar to AutoCorrect; however, AutoText is often used for large amounts of preformatted standard text. Word provides standard AutoText entries or you can create custom AutoText entries.

Inserting Standard AutoText

Word provides standard AutoText entries, such as complimentary closings or mailing instructions for letters. To view the standard AutoText options:

| Step 1 | *Click* | Insert |
| Step 2 | *Point to* | AutoText |

Your screen should look similar to Figure 3-6.

FIGURE 3-6
Standard AutoText Menu

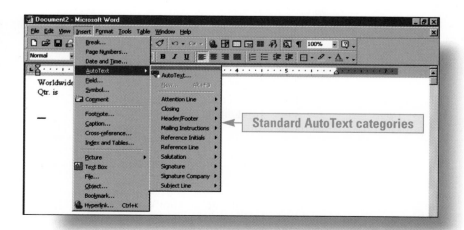

Step 3	*Point to*	Mailing Instructions
Step 4	*Click*	CERTIFIED MAIL
Step 5	*Observe*	the text CERTIFIED MAIL is inserted into the document
Step 6	*Continue*	to explore the standard AutoText entries by viewing the AutoText categories and inserting an AutoText entry into the current document
Step 7	*Press*	the ENTER key twice to move the insertion point

You can create your own custom AutoText entries such as the closing for a letter or standard paragraph text for letters and contracts.

Inserting Custom AutoText

Because you use the same letter closing text for all B. D. Vickers' letters, Kelly suggests you create a custom AutoText closing for the letters instead of keying the closing at the end of each letter. To create a custom AutoText entry, first you create and select the text that you want to insert in documents. If you want the text to have a certain format, you must format the text before you select it.

Each custom AutoText entry must have a unique name that can contain spaces. AutoText names are not case sensitive. If you name an AutoText entry with uppercase letters, you can insert the entry into the document using lowercase letters.

You create a custom AutoText complimentary closing for B. D. Vickers. To key the text for a custom AutoText entry:

> **CAUTION TIP**
>
> Unless you specify another template, an AutoText entry is saved with the Normal template and is available for all documents created with the Normal template.

Step 1	*Key*	Sincerely,
Step 2	*Press*	the ENTER key four times
Step 3	*Key*	B. D. Vickers
Step 4	*Press*	the ENTER key twice
Step 5	*Key*	your initials and press the SPACEBAR
Step 6	*Press*	the CTRL + Z keys to undo the AutoCorrect capitalization
Step 7	*Press*	the ENTER key twice
Step 8	*Key*	Enclosure

**chapter
three**

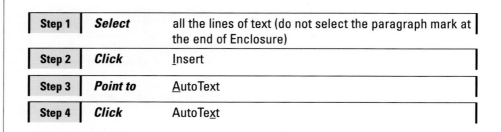

After you key the text, and format it if necessary, you can turn it into
an AutoText entry. To create the AutoText entry:

Step 1	*Select*	all the lines of text (do not select the paragraph mark at the end of Enclosure)
Step 2	*Click*	Insert
Step 3	*Point to*	AutoText
Step 4	*Click*	AutoText

The dialog box on your screen should look similar to Figure 3-7.

FIGURE 3-7
AutoText Tab in the
AutoCorrect Dialog Box

By default, Word inserts text from the first line of the selection as the
AutoText name. You can change this to a more descriptive, but brief
and unique name that will remind you of its contents.

Step 5	*Key*	closing in the Enter AutoText entries here: text box
Step 6	*Click*	Add
Step 7	*Delete*	the selected text

Now you can insert the closing AutoText entry into your document. You can insert a custom AutoText entry by displaying the AutoText dialog box or by keying the name of the entry and pressing the F3 key. You can also key just enough characters for AutoComplete to identify an AutoText entry's unique name and display an AutoComplete tip, then press the F3 key or the ENTER key. To insert AutoText using the keyboard:

Step 1	*Key*	clos (for closing)
Step 2	*Observe*	the AutoComplete tip that appears above the text with two lines of the AutoText entry
Step 3	*Press*	the F3 key
Step 4	*Observe*	that the AutoText closing entry is inserted into the document

AutoText can be modified to add text or formatting.

Editing AutoText Entries

You can easily edit AutoText entries. You need to include B. D. Vickers' job title in the closing AutoText entry. You can edit an AutoText entry by first changing the text, then selecting the changed text, and adding new AutoText with the same name. To edit the closing AutoText entry:

Step 1	*Move*	the insertion point after the text "B. D. Vickers" in the closing text
Step 2	*Press*	the ENTER key
Step 3	*Key*	Administrative Vice President
Step 4	*Select*	all the lines of the closing, beginning with Sincerely and ending with Enclosure (do not select the paragraph mark following Enclosure)
Step 5	*Click*	Insert
Step 6	*Point to*	AutoText
Step 7	*Click*	AutoText
Step 8	*Click*	closing in the list
Step 9	*Click*	Add
Step 10	*Click*	Yes to redefine the entry with Vickers' title

**chapter
three**

To test the closing entry AutoText:

Step 1	*Delete*	the closing text you just inserted into the document
Step 2	*Key*	Clos
Step 3	*Press*	the F3 key or the ENTER key

The redefined AutoText closing entry is inserted into the document.

Deleting AutoText Entries

When you no longer need an AutoText entry, you should delete it. To delete an AutoText entry, open the AutoText dialog box. Then click the AutoText name in the AutoText list box and click the Delete button. To delete the "closing" AutoText entry:

Step 1	*Click*	Insert
Step 2	*Point to*	AutoText
Step 3	*Click*	AutoText
Step 4	*Click*	closing in the AutoText list
Step 5	*Click*	Delete
Step 6	*Click*	OK

Word has another feature, called AutoComplete, you can use to automatically insert dates and standard AutoText.

3.e Inserting Dates with AutoComplete

The **AutoComplete** feature automatically completes the text of the current date, a day of the week, a month, as well as AutoText entries. As you start to key a date, weekday, month name, or AutoText entry, an AutoComplete tip appears above the insertion point. You press the F3 key or the ENTER key to enter the text or continue keying the text to ignore the AutoComplete suggestion.

To enter the current date using AutoComplete:

Step 1	*Press*	the ENTER key twice to move the insertion point down two lines
Step 2	*Key*	the name of the current month and press the ENTER key when the AutoComplete tip appears
Step 3	*Press*	the SPACEBAR
Step 4	*Observe*	that the AutoComplete tip suggests the current date in the month/day/year format
Step 5	*Press*	the ENTER key to insert the current date as text and then press the ENTER key to move the insertion point to the next line

You can continue keying text as if you had keyed the date yourself. To insert the day of the week using AutoComplete:

Step 1	*Key*	the first four characters of a day of the week
Step 2	*Observe*	the AutoComplete tip suggests the complete name of the day of the week
Step 3	*Press*	the ENTER key to accept the complete name of day of the week
Step 4	*Close*	the document without saving changes

AutoComplete, along with all the proofing tools, will help you ensure all your documents are free from errors.

QUICK TIP

You can turn on or off the display of AutoComplete tips for AutoText and dates in the AutoText tab of the AutoCorrect dialog box.

chapter
three

Summary

► By default, Word automatically checks the spelling and grammar in your document as you type.

► When you display the Spelling and Grammar dialog box, you can choose to ignore the selected word, change it to another word, add the word to a custom dictionary, delete the word from the document, or add the word and its correction to the AutoCorrect list.

► The Thesaurus tool allows you to substitute a word having the same or similar meaning in place of the word that contains the insertion point.

► The AutoCorrect tool allows you to automatically correct commonly misspelled or mistyped words as you type, or to insert text by keying an abbreviation for the text and then pressing the SPACEBAR.

► The AutoCorrect tool is turned on by default.

► You can add items to the AutoCorrect list and create exceptions to the AutoCorrect list.

► The AutoText features allow you to insert standard text—such as mailing instructions—or to create and save custom text, then insert it as needed.

► The Spike is a special AutoText feature that allows you to cut text selections from different documents and insert them at one time.

► The AutoComplete feature allows you to automatically insert the current month, day of the week, and date by pressing the F3 or ENTER key.

Commands Review

Action	Menu Bar	Shortcut Menu	Toolbar	Keyboard
Turn on or off the AutoCorrect tool	Tools, AutoCorrect			ALT + T, A
Check spelling and grammar	Tools, Spelling and Grammar	Right-click a word with a wavy red or green line underneath		ALT + T, S F7 ALT + F7
Substitute words with same or similar meaning	Tools, Language, Thesaurus	Right-click a word, point to Synonyms		ALT + T, L, T SHIFT + F7
Create, edit, insert, delete custom AutoText entry	Insert, AutoText, AutoText			ALT + I, A, X ALT + F3
Insert standard AutoText	Insert, AutoText			ALT + I, A
Print AutoText entries	File, Print			ALT + F, P

Concepts Review

Circle the correct answer.

1. The AutoCorrect tool:
  [a] provides statistics about your document.
  [b] checks for misspelled words as you key and underlines them with a wavy red line.
  [c] checks the grammar in the document.
  [d] corrects Caps Lock errors when you press the SPACEBAR.

2. The Thesaurus tool:
  [a] adds new words to the custom dictionary.
  [b] corrects two initial capitalization.
  [c] checks for misspelled words as you type.
  [d] allows you to substitute words.

3. The Spelling and Grammar tool does not:
  [a] indicate grammatical errors.
  [b] identify words with capitalization problems.
  [c] show you spelling and grammar errors as you type.
  [d] automatically complete dates.

4. The AutoComplete feature:
  [a] presents a tip with contents you can insert by pressing the ENTER key.
  [b] checks the readability of the document.
  [c] checks the spelling in the document.
  [d] checks the grammar in the document.

5. An AutoText entry:
  [a] must have a unique name.
  [b] cannot be saved for future use.
  [c] cannot be changed once it is created.
  [d] replaces text as soon as you press the SPACEBAR.

6. You can create a new AutoText entry with the:
  [a] F3 key.
  [b] AutoText subcommand on the Insert menu.
  [c] AutoComplete tool and the ENTER key.
  [d] INSERT key.

7. The Spike:
  [a] allows you to edit text.
  [b] allows you to format text.
  [c] allows you to cut text from several documents and then insert all the text at one time.
  [d] is an AutoComplete feature.

chapter three

8. **You can check the grammar in your document with the:**
   - [a] AutoComplete command.
   - [b] Thesaurus command.
   - [c] Synonyms command.
   - [d] Spelling and Grammar Status mode indicator.

9. **You can turn on or off the automatic checking of spelling and grammar in the:**
   - [a] AutoCorrect dialog box.
   - [b] Options dialog box.
   - [c] Format dialog box.
   - [d] AutoText dialog box.

10. **Which of the following options are not available in the Spelling and Grammar dialog box:**
    - [a] selecting suggested spellings for a word from a list.
    - [b] ignoring the selected word.
    - [c] adding the word to the AutoCorrect list.
    - [d] adding the word to the AutoText list.

Circle **T** if the statement is true or **F** if the statement is false.

T   F   1. You can use the Spelling and Grammar tool to find synonyms for selected words in your document.

T   F   2. The AutoText feature allows Word to check for spelling errors as you type.

T   F   3. The Synonyms command displays words with the same or similar meaning as that of a selected word.

T   F   4. You can check the spelling and grammar of your document only with a toolbar button.

T   F   5. The Spelling and Grammar tool presents a ScreenTip containing the complete text of the word you are keying.

T   F   6. When the Spelling and Grammar tool does not find a word in the dictionaries, a wavy green line appears underneath the word.

T   F   7. AutoText names are case sensitive.

T   F   8. The AutoComplete tool finds spelling errors.

T   F   9. The AutoCorrect tool automatically corrects commonly misspelled words as you key them.

T   F   10. It is not possible to add words to the AutoCorrect list.

Skills Review

Exercise 1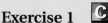

1. Open the *Vancouver Report With Errors* document located on the Data Disk.

2. Correct the spelling errors using the Spelling and Grammar command on the Tools menu.

3. Save the document as *Vancouver Report Revised*.

4. Preview, print, and close the document.

Exercise 2

1. Open the *Solicitation Letter With Errors* document located on the Data Disk.

2. Select the text "Current date" and use AutoComplete to replace it with the actual date.

3. Correct the spelling and grammar errors using the Spelling and Grammar Status mode indicator.

4. Use the Synonyms command to choose another word for "growth" in the first body paragraph.

5. Save the document as *Solicitation Letter Revised*.

6. Preview, print, and close the document.

Exercise 3   C

1. Open the *Personal Letter With Errors* document located on the Data Disk.

2. Select the text Current date and use AutoComplete to replace it with the actual date.

3. Correct the spelling and grammar errors using the shortcut menus.

4. Use the Thesaurus tool to select another word for "arrangements" in the last paragraph (*Hint*: Right-click the word, point to Synonyms, and then click Thesaurus).

5. Save the document as *Personal Letter Revised*.

6. Preview, print, and close the document.

Exercise 4   C

1. Create a new, blank document.

2. Create an AutoText entry to insert a standard complimentary closing for the letters signed by R. F. Williams. Use the "Sincerely yours" closing text. Add an Attachment line and your initials. Name the AutoText entry "Williams Closing."

3. Insert the "Williams Closing" AutoText entry into a new, blank document using the F3 key or the ENTER key.

4. Save the document as *Williams Closing*.

5. Preview and print the document.

6. Edit the "Williams Closing" AutoText entry to include the job title "Vice President Marketing."

7. Save the document as *Williams Closing Revised*.

8. Preview, print, and close the document.

Exercise 5   C

1. Open the *Client Letter* document located on the Data Disk.

2. Select the text "Current date" and use AutoComplete to replace it with the current date.

3. Insert the "Williams Closing" AutoText entry created in Exercise 4 at the bottom of the document. Add any additional blank lines as necessary.

4. Save the document as *Williams Letter*.

5. Preview, print, and close the document.

Exercise 6   C

1. Print all the current AutoText entries.

2. Delete the "Williams Closing" AutoText entry you created in Exercise 4 in this chapter.

3. Close the Word application to update the Normal template.

Exercise 7   C

1. Open the *Application Letter With Errors* document located on the Data Disk.

2. Select the text "Current date" and use AutoComplete to replace it with the actual date.

chapter three

3. Move the second body paragraph beginning "Per our conversation" to the first body paragraph position.

4. Move the last body paragraph beginning "If you have" and make it the second sentence of the second body paragraph. Delete any extra blank lines, if necessary.

5. Correct the spelling and grammar using the Spelling and Grammar button on the Standard toolbar.

6. Use the Synonyms command to select another word for "department" in the first paragraph.

7. Save the document as *Application Letter Revised*.

8. Preview, print, and close the document.

Exercise 8   C

1. Create the following document. Use appropriate margins for a letter to be printed on 2-inch letterhead paper. Correct any spelling or grammar errors as you key the text using the Spelling and Grammar shortcut menus. Use the AutoComplete and standard AutoText features where appropriate to complete the letter—for example, to enter the current date.

Current date

Ms. Lavonia Jackson
Gift Baskets Galore!
1001 Kirby Drive
Houston, TX 77043-1001

Dear Ms. Jackson:

congratulations on starting your own gift shop. I know you will be successful because of the tremendos the growth of the gift basket market.

We would like to order our holiday gifts from your shop and are lookin forward to receiving your holiday catalog as soon as it is available.

Sincerely,

Tom McGregor
Personnel Manager

mj

2. Save the document as *McGregor Letter*.

3. Preview, print, and close the document.

Case Projects

Project 1

You have been assigned to work in the legal department at Worldwide Foods for two weeks. The department manager has asked you to find some way for the three secretaries in the department to save time using Word to create and proof their documents. Prepare a document describing how the secretaries can use the AutoComplete, AutoText, and AutoCorrect tools to save time. Include spelling and grammar shortcuts. Use the Spelling and Grammar tool to correct any spelling and grammar errors in your document. Use the AutoCorrect tool to quickly enter symbols and text. Use the Thesaurus tool to replace words with more appropriate or descriptive ones. Use the AutoComplete tool to enter the current date. Save and print the document.

Project 2

As Kelly's assistant, you are often called on to solve user problems with the Word application. You received the following list of problems from the secretaries in the Tax Department about the AutoText and AutoCorrect features:

1. How can I store an AutoCorrect entry without its original formatting?

2. My AutoComplete tips are not displaying when I insert AutoText.

3. How can I share AutoText entries with other secretaries in my department?

Using the Office Assistant, research the answers to these questions. Use the keywords "AutoComplete," "AutoText," and "templates" for your search. Create, save, and print a document that describes how to solve these problems. Use the Spelling and Grammar tool to correct any spelling and grammar errors in your document. Use the AutoCorrect tool to quickly enter symbols and text. Use the Thesaurus tool to replace words with more appropriate or descriptive ones. Use the AutoComplete tool to enter the current date. Discuss your proposed solutions with a classmate.

Project 3

One of the legal secretaries asks for your help creating AutoCorrect exceptions. Using the Office Assistant, research the AutoCorrect exceptions list feature. Create a new document containing a short paragraph describing how to use this feature. Use the Spelling and Grammar tool to correct any spelling and grammar errors in your document. Use the AutoCorrect tool to quickly enter symbols and text. Use the Thesaurus tool to replace words with more appropriate or descriptive ones. Use the AutoComplete tool to enter the current date. Save and print the document. Open the AutoCorrect dialog box and add two items of your choice to the AutoCorrect Exceptions list.

Project 4

Mark Lee, a human resources consultant, is giving a 30-minute presentation on creating professional resumes at the next meeting of the International Association of Executive Assistants. He asks you to help prepare a list of topics by looking for Web pages that discuss how to create a resume. Connect to your ISP and open your Web browser. Search the WWW for information about writing a resume. Save at least two URLs as "favorites." Print at least two Web pages. Disconnect your ISP connection and close your Web browser.

Project 5

Using the research on creating resumes you prepared in Project 4, create, print, and save a document Mark can use to prepare his presentation. Use the Spelling and Grammar tool to correct any spelling and grammar errors in your document. Use the AutoCorrect tool to quickly enter symbols and text. Use the Thesaurus tool to replace words with more appropriate or descriptive ones. Use the AutoComplete tool to enter the current date.

chapter three

Project 6

B. D. Vickers has noticed that some letters and reports that contain spelling and grammatical errors are being mailed to clients. He asks you to prepare instructions on using the Spelling and Grammar tool, which he will give to all administrative assistants and secretaries during a special luncheon next week. Create a new document that contains at least four paragraphs outlining how to use the Spelling and Grammar tool *including* custom/special dictionaries, how to add a word to the AutoCorrect list during the spell-checking process, and how to use the various options in the Spelling and Grammar dialog box. Use the Spelling and Grammar tool to correct any spelling and grammar errors in your document. Use the AutoCorrect tool to quickly enter symbols and text. Use the Thesaurus tool to replace words with more appropriate or descriptive ones. Use the AutoComplete tool to enter the current date. Save, preview, and print the document.

Project 7

Kelly wants to purchase several reference books for the company library on how to use Microsoft Word. She doesn't have time to check out the local bookstores so she has asked you to look for the books at several online bookstores. Connect to your ISP and load your Web browser. Search for online bookstores. Load several online bookstore Web pages and search each Web site for books on how to use Microsoft Word. Use the information you gather from the bookstores to prepare a document containing a list of books by title. Include the author's name, the price of the book, and the proposed shipping time. Use the Spelling and Grammar tool to correct any spelling and grammar errors in your document. Use the AutoCorrect tool to quickly enter symbols and text. Use the Thesaurus tool to replace words with more appropriate or descriptive ones. Use the AutoComplete tool to enter the current date. Save and print the document.

Project 8

B. D. Vickers wants to know something about the readability of the documents the administrative staff is preparing and has asked you to find out what feature in Word can provide that information. Using the Office Assistant, research the readability statistics displayed by the Spelling and Grammar tool. Create a new document containing at least three paragraphs describing the readability statistics and formulas. Use the Spelling and Grammar tool to correct any spelling and grammar errors in your document. Use the AutoCorrect tool to quickly enter symbols and text. Use the Thesaurus tool to replace words with more appropriate or descriptive ones. Use the AutoComplete tool to enter the current date. Save, preview, and print the document.

Formatting Text

Chapter Overview

The ability to format text provides a word processing program much of its power. Word's formatting features give you the ability to create professional-, unique-looking documents. In this chapter you learn how to change the appearance of text using AutoFormat and the character formatting features: fonts, font size, bold, underline, italic, text effects, and text animation. You also learn to repeat and copy character formats and change the case of text. Finally, you learn to add bullets and numbering to text.

Case profile

Because of your successful performance in the purchasing department, the marketing department has requested you to fill in for Elizabeth Chang, the assistant secretary, who is going on a short holiday. Before she left, Elizabeth left several documents for you to format.

LEARNING OBJECTIVES

► Format characters as you type
► Select and change fonts and font sizes
► Apply font formats
► Apply character effects
► Apply character spacing and animation effects
► Duplicate character formats
► Change the case of text
► Add bullets and numbering
► Highlight text in a document
► Insert Symbols and special characters

chapter four

4.a Formatting Characters as You Type

Word has an **AutoFormat As You Type** feature (in addition to the symbol characters in the AutoCorrect list) that automatically formats certain characters as you type such as replacing ordinals (1st) with superscript (1st), fractions (1/2) with fraction characters (½), and "straight quotes" with "curly quotes." The automatic formatting is applied when you press the SPACEBAR and is turned on by default. You can turn off the automatic formatting of characters on the AutoFormat As You Type tab in the AutoCorrect dialog box.

Before you start formatting the *Library Bulletin* document for Elizabeth, you review the AutoFormat As You Type options. To review the AutoFormat As You Type options:

Step 1	*Open*	the *Library Bulletin* document located on the Data Disk
Step 2	*Click*	Tools
Step 3	*Click*	AutoCorrect
Step 4	*Click*	the AutoFormat As You Type tab

The dialog box you see on your screen should look similar to Figure 4-1.

FIGURE 4-1
AutoFormat As You Type
Tab in the AutoCorrect
Dialog Box

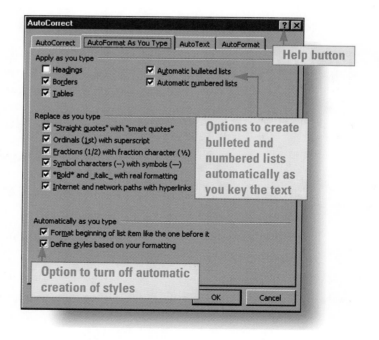

| Step 5 | *Click* | the dialog box Help button to review the options on the AutoFormat As You Type tab |

A **style** is a group of formats you apply to selected text. For now, you turn off the option that automatically creates styles as you format text.

| Step 6 | *Click* | the Define styles based on your formatting check box to remove the check mark |
| Step 7 | *Click* | OK |

Elizabeth wants you to add "on the 1st day of the month" to the document. As you enter the text with an ordinal number, Word automatically formats the number. To add an ordinal number:

| Step 1 | *Select* | the text "on a monthly basis" at the end of the *Library Bulletin* document |
| Step 2 | *Key* | on the 1st day of the month |

The ordinal number "1st" was replaced with "1st." The text on your screen should look similar to Figure 4-2.

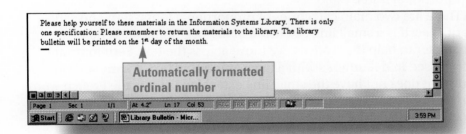

| Step 3 | *Save* | the document as *Library Bulletin Revised* |

You can determine the type of font and the font size you want to use in your documents.

QUICK TIP

The AutoFormat tab in the AutoCorrect dialog box contains options that control how Word automatically formats an entire document. For more information on automatically formatting an entire Word document, see online Help.

FIGURE 4-2
Automatic Number Formatting

chapter
four

4.b Selecting and Changing Fonts and Font Sizes

A **font** is a set of printed characters with the same size and appearance. A font has three characteristics: typeface, style, and point (font) size.

1. **Typeface** refers to the design and appearance of printed characters. Some typefaces include:

   Times New Roman   Courier New
   Arial   *Brush Script MT*

2. **Style** refers to bold or italic print. *Italic print is slanted to the right* and **bold print is darker**.

3. **Point (font) size** refers to the height of the printed characters. There are 72 points to an inch and the larger the point size, the larger the characters. Some common point sizes include:

   8 point   10 point   12 point

A font may be **monospaced** with the same amount of space between characters or **proportional** with a varying amount of space between characters. Courier is an example of a monospaced font and Times New Roman is an example of a proportional font. Most people who use a word processing application to create text documents use proportional fonts.

There are two main categories of proportional fonts: serif and sans serif. A **serif** is a small line extension at the beginning and end of a character to help the reader's eye move across the text. Serif fonts are often used in documents with a large amount of text. A **sans serif** font is one that does not have the small line extension (*sans* is the French word for without). Sans serif fonts are often used for paragraph headings and document titles. The Times New Roman font is an example of a serif font and the Arial font is an example of a sans serif font.

The default font and font size in Word are the Times New Roman font and 12-point font size. The *Library Bulletin Revised* document, according to Elizabeth's notes, should be in 10-point font size, with the title in Arial font.

notes

This book assumes that your computer is connected to a Hewlett-Packard LaserJet printer and you use TrueType fonts. If you have a different printer, make the appropriate selections for your printer.

Changing Fonts

To change the font, first select the text to be changed. For example, if you want to change the font for the entire document, select the entire document. Then select the font you want to use. If the document has not been keyed yet, you can select the font before you key the text. That font selection is then used throughout the document.

Currently, the entire *Library Bulletin Revised* document is formatted with the Times New Roman, 12-point font. To change the font of the title text, "INFORMATION SYSTEMS LIBRARY BULLETIN," to the Arial TrueType font:

| Step 1 | **Select** | the title "INFORMATION SYSTEMS LIBRARY BULLETIN" |

| Step 2 | **Click** | the Font button list arrow  on the Formatting toolbar |

The font list on your screen should look similar to Figure 4-3.

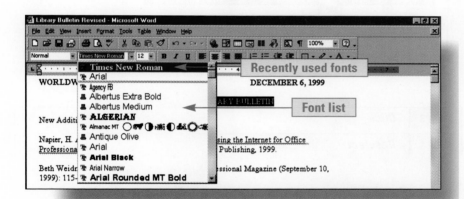

FIGURE 4-3
Font List

Notice that some fonts on the Font drop-down list have a symbol to the left of the font name. A "TT" symbol indicates that the font is a **TrueType font** that prints text exactly the way it is displayed on your screen. A printer symbol next to a font indicates that the assigned printer supports the font. A list of the most recently used fonts may appear at the top of the font list followed by a narrow double line.

| Step 3 | **Click** | Arial (scroll to view this option, if necessary) |

| Step 4 | **Deselect** | the text |

The document title font is different from the text font, making it distinct. You can also change the font size for your documents.

**chapter
four**

Changing Font Sizes

The point (font) size for the text of the entire document is currently 12 point. The *Library Bulletin Revised* document should be in 10 point. To change the point size for the entire document to 10 point:

Step 1	*Select*	the entire document

Step 2	*Click*	the Font Size button list arrow 12 ▼ on the Formatting toolbar

The Font Size drop-down list that appears on your screen should look similar to Figure 4-4.

FIGURE 4-4
Font Size List

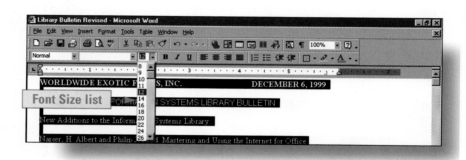

Step 3	*Click*	10

Step 4	*Deselect*	the text

The entire document changes to 10 point. Next you need to add emphasis to certain text by applying font styles, such as bold and italic.

> **Q U I C K   T I P**
>
> You can use keyboard shortcuts to apply font styles. For example, press the CTRL + B keys to apply the bold style to selected text. Use the Office Assistant to view and print a complete list of keyboard shortcuts.

4.c **Applying Font Formats**

Elizabeth wants certain words emphasized in *Library Bulletin Revised* document. You can do this by applying the bold or italic font formats, or styles, to the text. Font styles are part of **character formatting**, which means only the selected character or characters are affected when you apply the font style.

Applying Bold

The **bold** style makes the selected text darker than other text to attract a reader's attention. When you apply bold style, Word makes the text appear darker on the screen as well as on the printed page.

To apply bold style to the text "New Additions to the Information Systems Library:"

Step 1	*Select*	New Additions to the Information Systems Library (do not select the colon)
Step 2	*Click*	the Bold button **B** on the Formatting toolbar
Step 3	*Deselect*	the text leaving the insertion point in the paragraph

The text appears darker. Notice that the Bold button on the Formatting toolbar appears pressed, indicating the bold style is applied. You remove the bold format the same way you applied it. The first line of the document contains the company name and date formatted with the bold style. Elizabeth's notes tell you to remove the bold. To remove the bold style:

Step 1	*Select*	the first line of the document using the selection bar
Step 2	*Click*	the Bold button **B** on the Formatting toolbar
Step 3	*Deselect*	the text leaving the insertion point in the in the first line

The text is no longer bold and the Bold button on the Formatting toolbar is no longer pressed.

Applying Italic

Italicizing text allows you to emphasize text by slanting the text to the right. You apply and remove italic formatting the same way you do bold formatting: by selecting the text and applying the italic style.

Elizabeth's notes indicate the magazine title in which Beth Weidman's article appears should be italicized. To italicize the magazine title:

Step 1	*Select*	the magazine title "Web Site Professional Magazine" in the second item in the list
Step 2	*Click*	the Italic button *I* on the Formatting toolbar
Step 3	*Deselect*	the text leaving the insertion point in the title

The magazine title is italicized. Notice the Italic button on the Formatting toolbar is pressed, indicating that the italic style is applied to the text. You can remove the italic style the same way you applied it.

M E N U   T I P

You can apply the bold style to text by clicking the <u>F</u>ont command on the Format menu or shortcut menu.

M O U S E   T I P

You can apply character formatting to a single, complete word by clicking the word to place the insertion point in it, and then applying the format.

Q U I C K   T I P

You can apply or remove italic formatting from selected text in the Font tab in the Font dialog box.

chapter four

MENU **TIP**

You can underline selected text by clicking the <u>F</u>ont command on the F<u>o</u>rmat menu to open the Font dialog box, clicking the Fo<u>n</u>t tab, clicking the <u>U</u>nderline Style list arrow, and then clicking the underline style of your choice.

Applying Underlines

Emphasizing text by placing a line underneath the text is called **underlining**. You can choose to underline selected letters, selected words, or selected words and the spaces between them. Word also provides a variety of underlines you can use to enhance text.

You want to add a thick single line below the title "New Additions to the Information Systems Library." The Underline button on the Formatting toolbar formats text and spaces between the text with a thin single line. Instead, you must open the Font dialog box to see a complete list of underline styles.

To apply a thick single underline to text:

Step 1	*Select*	New Additions to the Information Systems Library (do not select the colon)
Step 2	*Right-click*	the selected text
Step 3	*Click*	<u>F</u>ont
Step 4	*Click*	the Fo<u>n</u>t tab, if necessary

The Fo<u>n</u>t tab in the Font dialog box that opens on your screen should look similar to Figure 4-5.

FIGURE 4-5
Fo<u>n</u>t Tab in the Font Dialog Box

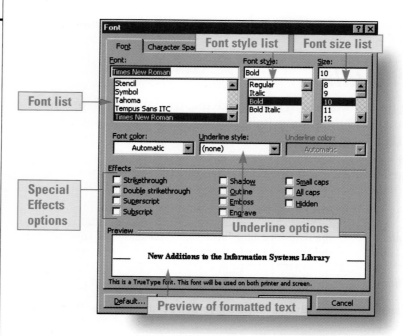

MOUSE **TIP**

You can underline selected words and spaces with a single underline by clicking the Underline button on the Formatting toolbar.

You can change fonts, font style, font size, underlining, underline color, and color of selected text in the Fo<u>n</u>t tab. The Effects group provides options for applying special effects to selected text. The Preview area provides a sample of the formatting options before they are applied to the selected text.

Step 5	*Click*	the <u>U</u>nderline style: list arrow
Step 6	*Click*	the thick single line option (the fifth option in the list)
Step 7	*Preview*	the underline formatting in the dialog box
Step 8	*Click*	OK
Step 9	*Deselect*	the text

The text is underlined with a thick single line. The book title in the first item in the list should be italicized instead of underlined. You can add or remove a thin single underline to words and spaces with the Underline button on the Formatting toolbar. To remove the underline from the book title and italicize it:

Step 1	*Select*	the book title "Mastering and Using the Internet for Office Professionals"
Step 2	*Click*	the Underline button on the Formatting toolbar
Step 3	*Click*	the Italic button *I* on the Formatting toolbar
Step 4	*Deselect*	the text leaving the insertion point in the text
Step 5	*Save*	the document

In addition to using bold, italic, and underline to emphasis text, you can use other special text effects such as Superscript, Subscript, Outline, and Small Caps.

4.d Applying Character Effects   C

Another way to emphasize text is to add special text effects like superscript, subscript, small caps, outline, and strikethrough effects. Elizabeth asks you to add these formats to specified text in the *Library Bulletin Revised* document.

chapter
four

Applying Superscript and Subscript

The **Superscript** format places text slightly above a line of normal printed text. The **Subscript** format places text slightly below a line of normal printed text. This is superscript, and this is subscript. You can apply Superscript or Subscript formats to selected text in the Font tab in the Font dialog box. To experiment with the Superscript and Subscript formats:

Step 1	*Move*	the insertion point to the left margin before the "B" in "Beth"
Step 2	*Key*	1
Step 3	*Select*	the number 1
Step 4	*Click*	Format
Step 5	*Click*	Font
Step 6	*Click*	the Font tab, if necessary
Step 7	*Click*	the Superscript check box to insert a check mark
Step 8	*Click*	OK
Step 9	*Deselect*	the text

The number 1 appears in Superscript format and the text on your screen should look similar to Figure 4-6.

FIGURE 4-6
Superscript Format

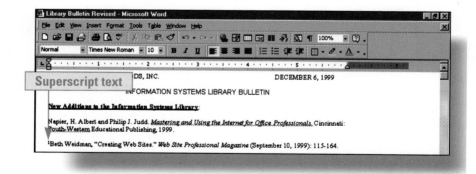

You apply the Subscript format the same way. To apply the Subscript format:

Step 1	*Move*	the insertion point to the left margin before the "R" in "Robert"
Step 2	*Key*	2

Step 3	*Select*	the number 2
Step 4	*Open*	the Font tab in the Font dialog box
Step 5	*Click*	the Subscript check box to insert a check mark
Step 6	*Click*	OK
Step 7	*Deselect*	the text
Step 8	*Observe*	the placement of the superscript and subscript text in relation to the text
Step 9	*Delete*	the superscript and subscript text
Step 10	*Save*	the document

QUICK TIP

You can remove Superscript and Subscript formatting from selected text by removing the check mark from the appropriate check box on the Font tab in the Font dialog box.

Applying Strikethrough

When you edit a document online, you might want to indicate text that should be deleted. One way to do this is to format the text with the **Strikethrough** effect, which draws a line through selected text. To add the Strikethrough effect to the first sentence of the last paragraph:

Step 1	*Select*	in the Information Systems Library
Step 2	*Open*	the Font tab in the Font dialog box
Step 3	*Click*	the Strikethrough check box to insert a check mark
Step 4	*Click*	OK

The selected text now has a line through it, indicating it could be deleted from the document. Because you don't want to delete the text, you remove the Strikethrough.

Step 5	*Click*	the Undo button [icon] on the Standard toolbar
Step 6	*Deselect*	the text

Elizabeth indicated that the library name needs to be distinguished from the rest of the text. You decide to apply the Small Caps effect.

Applying Small Caps

The **Small Caps** effect is a special text effect that displays selected text in uppercase characters and any characters keyed with the SHIFT key pressed are slightly taller than the remaining characters. The

chapter four

Small Caps format is appropriate for headings and titles, such as Information Systems Library. To apply the Small Caps effect:

Step 1	*Select*	the text "Information Systems Library" in the first sentence of the last paragraph
Step 2	*Open*	the Font tab in the Font dialog box
Step 3	*Click*	the Small Caps check box to insert a check mark
Step 4	*Click*	OK

The text is in uppercase characters, with the first character of each word slightly taller than the remaining characters in the word.

Step 5	*Continue*	by applying the Small Caps effect to each instance of "Information Systems Library"

Another special text effect you can use to emphasize text is the Outline effect.

Applying Outline

The **Outline** effect shows both the inner and the outer border of each character and leaves the interior white. The effect is good for large fonts usually used in titles. To change the font size of the first line and apply the Outline effect:

Step 1	*Select*	the first line beginning "Worldwide" at the top of the document
Step 2	*Open*	the Font tab in the Font dialog box
Step 3	*Change*	the font size to 14 point
Step 4	*Click*	the Outline check box to insert a check mark
Step 5	*Click*	OK
Step 6	*Observe*	the new formatting
Step 7	*Deselect*	the text
Step 8	*Save*	the document

Adding extra spacing between text characters in titles adds variety and interest to a document. Special animation effects are a great way to draw attention to documents that will be read online, such as the *Library Bulletin Revised* document.

4.e Applying Character Spacing and Animation Effects

Character spacing is the amount of white space that appears between characters. You can change the character spacing by scaling the characters to a specific percentage, expanding or condensing the characters a specific number of points, or by kerning. **Kerning** adjusts the space between particular pairs of characters depending on the font.

You want the title of the *Library Bulletin Revised* document to stand out more, so you scale the text. To scale the title text so that it is stretched horizontally to be 120% of its original width:

Step 1	*Select*	the title "INFORMATION SYSTEMS LIBRARY BULLETIN"
Step 2	*Open*	the Font dialog box
Step 3	*Click*	the Character Spacing tab
Step 4	*Key*	120 in the Scale: text box
Step 5	*Press*	the ENTER key

The text is "stretched" horizontally to 120% of its original width. Upon her return, Elizabeth is going to attach the *Library Bulletin Revised* document to e-mail messages so the recipients can read the document online. She wants you to add animation effects to the *Library Bulletin Revised* document that draw attention to the document's title. To add animation effects:

Step 1	*Verify*	the title text is still selected
Step 2	*Open*	the Font dialog box
Step 3	*Click*	the Text Effects tab
Step 4	*Click*	Marching Red Ants in the Animations: list box
Step 5	*Click*	OK
Step 6	*Observe*	that a red dashed moving box now appears around the title
Step 7	*Deselect*	the text
Step 8	*Save*	the document

QUICK TIP

Pressing the ENTER key when working in a dialog box is the same as clicking the dialog box selected button. For example, the OK button is the selected button in most dialog boxes. You can press the ENTER key instead of clicking the OK button to accept your option choices and close the dialog box.

chapter
four

The red marching ants will attract immediate attention to the document. Once you have applied character formatting to text it's often easier to duplicate that formatting to other text rather than reapplying it each time.

4.f Duplicating Character Formats

Word can duplicate character formats by repeating or copying the formats. If you have already formatted text with a certain character formats (such as font styles) and want to immediately format additional text the same way, you can repeat the character formats with the Repeat command on the Edit menu. If you want to duplicate formats, but you have performed several commands since the formatting command, you can use the Format Painter button on the Standard toolbar to *copy* the formats from one text and paste it to other text.

Repeating Character Formats

You can repeat multiple character formats that have been applied to selected text with the options on the Font tab in the Font dialog box. For example, if you apply the Small Caps and underlining formats with the Font dialog box options, you can then apply both formats to new text at the same time simply by clicking the Repeat command on the Edit menu.

You apply the bold, single underline, and font size formats to selected text and then immediately repeat that formatting to unformatted text. To apply and repeat multiple character formats:

Step 1	*Select*	the phrase "There is only one specification" in the last paragraph (do not select the colon)
Step 2	*Open*	the Font tab in the Font dialog box
Step 3	*Click*	Bold in the Font style: list box
Step 4	*Click*	14 in the Size: list box (scroll to view this option)
Step 5	*Click*	the Underline style: list arrow
Step 6	*Click*	Words only
Step 7	*Click*	OK
Step 8	*Deselect*	the text

CAUTION TIP

Multiple formatting options applied with buttons on the Formatting toolbar cannot be repeated. If you use the Formatting toolbar to apply multiple formats, only the last format applied is repeated. For example, if you apply font size and underline formatting with the Formatting toolbar buttons, select new text, and click the Repeat command on the Edit menu, only the last format applied is repeated.

The text is formatted with multiple formats. Now you repeat the formats on the next phrase in the document.

Step 9	*Select*	the phrase "Please remember to return the materials to the library" in the last paragraph (do not select the period)
Step 10	*Click*	Edit
Step 11	*Click*	Repeat Font Formatting
Step 12	*Deselect*	the text

The bold, underline, and font size formatting are applied to the selected phrase. You can also apply multiple formats from the Formatting toolbar; just remember that, when you do this, *only the last format applied is repeated.* To apply bold and underline formatting to the last sentence using the Formatting toolbar and then repeat the formatting in the title:

Step 1	*Select*	the last sentence in the document (do not select the period)
Step 2	*Click*	the Bold button **B** on the Formatting toolbar
Step 3	*Click*	the Underline button **U** on the Formatting toolbar
Step 4	*Select*	the title "INFORMATION SYSTEMS LIBRARY BULLETIN"
Step 5	*Click*	Edit
Step 6	*Observe*	that the Repeat command says "Repeat Underline" although you applied both bold and underline formats to the original text

Because you applied multiple formats with the Formatting toolbar buttons, the Repeat Font Formatting command on the Edit menu becomes the Repeat Underline command. Only the last format applied, the underline format, can be repeated. You close the menu and undo the formatting.

Step 7	*Press*	the ESC key to close the menu
Step 8	*Click*	the Undo button on the Standard toolbar twice to undo the bold and underline formats

When you want to apply the multiple character formatting to different text long after you originally applied the formatting, you can save time by copying the formatting from one text selection to another.

chapter
four

Copying Formats using the Format Painter

Copying formats, rather than recreating them, ensures consistency and saves time. You can copy and paste character formats quickly with the Format Painter button on the Standard toolbar. To use the Format Painter to copy formats, first place the insertion point in the text that contains the formats to be copied. Then click the Format Painter button. When you move the mouse pointer into the keying area, the mouse pointer changes to an I-beam with a paintbrush icon. To paste the formats, drag the Format Painter I-beam across the text to be formatted. The Format Painter pastes *all* the formats from the original text, including *all* formats applied with the Formatting toolbar. You want to copy the formats from "There is only one specification" to different text. To copy formats using the Format Painter:

Step 1	*Move*	the insertion point to the text "There is only one specification"
Step 2	*Click*	the Format Painter button on the Standard toolbar
Step 3	*Select*	New Additions to the Information Systems Library (do not select the colon)
Step 4	*Observe*	the copied formats
Step 5	*Deselect*	the text
Step 6	*Save*	the document

4.g Changing the Case of Text

Elizabeth wants you to change the case of the title in the *Library Bulletin Revised* document. You can change the case of text by first selecting the text you want to change, and then clicking the Change Case command on the Format menu. To change the case of the title text:

Step 1	*Select*	the title "INFORMATION SYSTEMS LIBRARY BULLETIN"
Step 2	*Click*	F<u>o</u>rmat
Step 3	*Click*	Change Cas<u>e</u>

The dialog box on your screen should look similar to Figure 4-7.

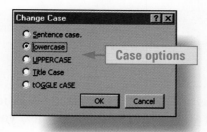

FIGURE 4-7
Change Case Dialog Box

QUICK TIP

You can remove character formatting from selected text by pressing the CTRL + SHIFT + Z keys.

Step 4	*Click*	the <u>T</u>itle Case option button
Step 5	*Click*	OK
Step 6	*Deselect*	the text

Notice that you can now see the small cap formatting you applied earlier to the title.

Step 7	*Save*	the document and close it

Sometimes you need to organize text in a list and add symbols or numbers to each paragraph.

4.h Adding Bullets and Numbering

Special symbols called **bullets** or numbers can precede lists of text, to make the lists more attractive and easier to read. The second document Elizabeth left for you to format is named *Enhanced Text*. Your instructions are to create bulleted and numbered lists from certain paragraphs.

Creating Bulleted Lists

The *Enhanced Text* document contains several short paragraphs to which you must add bullets. The bullets help indicate that the paragraphs are related items. To create a bulleted list:

MENU TIP

You can add numbers or bullets to selected text with options in the Bullets and Numbering dialog box, which you open by clicking the <u>B</u>ullets and Numbering command on the F<u>o</u>rmat menu or a shortcut menu.

Step 1	*Open*	the *Enhanced Text* document located on the Data Disk
Step 2	*Select*	the text beginning with "Apply" and ending with "listed items." (do not select the title text)

chapter
four

| Step 3 | *Click* | the Bullets button 🔳 on the Formatting toolbar |
| Step 4 | *Deselect* | the text |

A bullet symbol is automatically inserted to the left of the paragraphs, which are indented ½ inch. The text you see on your screen should look similar to Figure 4-8.

FIGURE 4-8
Bulleted List

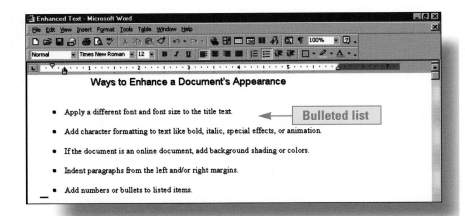

Creating Numbered Lists

Numbered lists are used to organize items sequentially. It is very easy to replace a bulleted list with a numbered list. Simply select the bulleted list paragraphs and then click the Numbering button on the Formatting toolbar. To replace the bullets with numbers:

| Step 1 | *Select* | the bulleted paragraphs beginning with "Apply" and ending with "listed items." |
| Step 2 | *Click* | the Numbering button 🔳 on the on the Formatting toolbar |

Numbers now precede the paragraphs instead of bullets. To change the bullet or numbering style, you can click the Bullets and <u>N</u>umbering command on the F<u>o</u>rmat menu, click the appropriate tab, and select a different bullet or numbering style. You can remove the bullets or numbers from a list by selecting the list and clicking the Bullets or Numbering button on the Formatting toolbar to turn off the formatting.

| Step 3 | *Select* | the numbered paragraphs beginning with "Apply" and ending with "listed items.", if necessary |
| Step 4 | *Click* | the Numbering button 🔳 on the Formatting toolbar |

QUICK TIP

You can create a multilevel bulleted or numbered list by pressing the TAB key to indent a paragraph to the next lower level or pressing the SHIFT + TAB keys to return a paragraph to the next higher level.

The AutoFormat As You Type feature allows you to create numbered or bulleted lists automatically as you type. Word turns on these AutoFormat features by default; the settings are located on the AutoFormat As You Type tab in the AutoCorrect dialog box. For more information on automatic numbering or bullet options, see online Help.

Step 5	*Reapply*	the Bullets formatting
Step 6	*Deselect*	the text
Step 7	*Save*	the document as *Enhanced Text Revised* and close it

Another way to draw a reviewer's attention to important text in a document being read on a computer screen is to highlight the text.

4.i Highlighting Text in a Document

Elizabeth wants to draw attention to the text "Warning! Warning! Warning!" in the *Policy #152* document. To do this, she asks you to highlight the text in color. To highlight the text:

Step 1	*Open*	the *Policy #152* document located on the Data Disk
Step 2	*Select*	the text Warning! Warning! Warning!
Step 3	*Click*	the Highlight button list arrow on the Formatting toolbar
Step 4	*Click*	Bright Green
Step 5	*Observe*	that the text is highlighted in color

You can also select a highlighter color and then drag the mouse pointer over text to apply the color highlighting. To change the highlighted text color to yellow:

Step 1	*Click*	the Highlight button list arrow on the Formatting toolbar
Step 2	*Click*	Yellow
Step 3	*Position*	the mouse pointer over text and observe that it is now a color pen pointer
Step 4	*Drag*	the color pen pointer over the bright green highlighted text to change the color to yellow
Step 5	*Click*	the Highlight button to turn off the color pen pointer
Step 6	*Save*	the document as *Policy #152 With Highlighted Text* and close it

chapter
four

Another way to enhance text appearance is to insert symbols and special characters into your document.

4.j Inserting Symbols and Special Characters

Symbols and special characters can be inserted into a document using the AutoCorrect feature or the Symbol command on the Insert menu. Elizabeth left instructions for you to complete a new marketing department training class announcement by inserting the appropriate symbols and special characters.

Inserting Symbols

First, you need to insert the copyright symbol in the document. To insert the copyright symbol using the AutoCorrect feature:

Step 1	*Open*	the *Quality 2000 Training* document located on the Data Disk
Step 2	*Move*	the insertion point to the end of the "Quality 2000" text in the third title line
Step 3	*Key*	(c) to insert the copyright symbol using AutoCorrect

You can also insert the copyright symbol from a dialog box. To insert the copyright symbol using the Symbol dialog box:

Step 1	*Move*	the insertion point to the end of the "Quality 2000" text in the second body paragraph
Step 2	*Click*	Insert
Step 3	*Click*	Symbol
Step 4	*Click*	the Symbols tab, if necessary
Step 5	*Select*	Symbol from the Font: list, if necessary
Step 6	*Double-click*	the © symbol (12th symbol in the 7th row)
Step 7	*Close*	the dialog box

Now you need to insert a special character.

Inserting Special Characters

Other special characters like the en dash (used in dates), the nonbreaking space, and the em dash (used to insert a break in thought) as well as the copyright symbol can also be inserted from the Special Characters tab in the Symbol dialog box. You want to replace the hyphen in the first paragraph with an em dash character. To select the hyphen and open the dialog box:

Step 1	*Select*	the hyphen following the word "now" in the last sentence of the first body paragraph
Step 2	*Open*	the Symbol dialog box
Step 3	*Click*	the Special Characters tab
Step 4	*Double-click*	the Em Dash option in the list
Step 5	*Close*	the dialog box
Step 6	*Observe*	that the em dash replaces the hyphen in the document
Step 7	*Save*	the document as *Quality 2000 With Symbols* and close it

With Word's formatting features you can make any document look professionally formatted.

chapter four

Summary

▶ The AutoFormat As You Type feature automatically formats certain characters you key—such as quote marks, fractions, and ordinals—when you press the SPACEBAR.

▶ Fonts are sets of printed characters that have the same size and appearance.

▶ A font has three aspects: typeface, style, and point (font) size.

▶ The default font in Word is Times New Roman, 12-point font.

▶ You can apply bold, italic, and underline character formats to selected text for emphasis.

▶ Superscript or subscript character formats can be applied to selected characters to position the characters slightly above or below the line of normal text.

▶ You can add animation effects, such as red marching ants, to documents to emphasize text when the document is displayed online.

▶ Character formats can be duplicated to new text using the Repeat command on the Edit menu or the Format Painter button on the Standard toolbar.

▶ The case of text characters can be changed to Sentence case, lowercase, UPPERCASE, Title Case, or tOGGLE cASE.

▶ You can add bullets to group a list of items or add numbers to organize a list of items.

▶ You can draw attention to text in a document being read on a computer screen by highlighting it in color.

▶ Symbols and special characters, such as © or ® or em dash, can be inserted into your document.

Commands Review

Action	Menu Bar	Shortcut Menu	Toolbar	Keyboard
Change font	Fo̲rmat, F̲ont	Right-click the selected text, click F̲ont	Times New Roman	ALT + O, F CTRL + D CTRL + SHIFT + F, then DOWN ARROW to select the font
Change font size	Fo̲rmat, F̲ont	Right-click the selected text, click F̲ont	12	ALT + O, F CTRL + SHIFT + P, then DOWN ARROW to select the font size
Apply or remove bold formatting	Fo̲rmat, F̲ont	Right-click the selected text, click F̲ont	**B**	ALT + O, F CTRL + B
Apply or remove italic formatting	Fo̲rmat, F̲ont	Right-click the selected text, click F̲ont	*I*	ALT + O, F CTRL + I
Apply or remove underline formatting	Fo̲rmat, F̲ont	Right-click the selected text, click F̲ont	U̲	ALT + O, F CTRL + U
Apply or remove superscript or subscript formatting	Fo̲rmat, F̲ont	Right-click the selected text, click F̲ont		ALT + O, F CTRL + = (sub.) CTRL + SHIFT + + (sup.)
Repeat formats	E̲dit, R̲epeat			ALT + E, R CTRL + Y
Copy formats			🖌	CTRL + SHIFT + C, then CTRL + SHIFT + V
Change case	Fo̲rmat, Change Case̲			ALT + O, E SHIFT + F3
Remove character formatting				CTRL + SHIFT + Z CTRL + SPACEBAR
Apply or remove bullets and numbering to lists	Format, Bullets and N̲umbering	Right-click the selected text or at the insertion point and click Bullets and N̲umbering	≣ ≣	Key a number followed by a space or tab character and the text Key an asterisk followed by a space or tab character and the text
Highlight text			🖊▾	
Insert symbols and special characters	Insert, S̲ymbol			ALT + I, S Press the appropriate shortcut keys

Concepts Review

Circle the correct answer.

1. You can apply a double underline to text with the:
  [a] Underline style: list box in the Font dialog box.
  [b] Su̲perscript option in the Font dialog box.
  [c] Su̲bscript option in the Font dialog box.
  [d] Underline button on the Formatting toolbar.

2. Typeface refers to the:
  [a] amount of space between the characters.
  [b] height of the characters.
  [c] design and appearance of the characters.
  [d] slant of the characters.

chapter four

3. You can copy character formats by:
[a] clicking the Bullets button.
[b] using the Format Painter feature.
[c] clicking the Numbering button.
[d] pressing the DELETE key.

4. The Bold, Underline, and Italic buttons on the Formatting toolbar cannot be used to:
[a] apply formats.
[b] remove formats.
[c] emphasize text.
[d] repeat multiple formats.

5. When you use the Repeat command on the Edit menu to repeat formats applied from the Font dialog box:
[a] all the formats are repeated.
[b] none of the formats are repeated.
[c] the text is changed to uppercase.
[d] only the last format is repeated.

6. Which of the following is not a special font effect?
[a] Emboss
[b] Engrave
[c] Hidden
[d] Bold

7. Character spacing options are found in the:
[a] Font dialog box.
[b] AutoCorrect dialog box.
[c] Formatting dialog box.
[d] AutoText dialog box.

8. The Underline button on the Formatting toolbar applies the following underline style:
[a] Dotted.
[b] Single, words only.
[c] Single, words and spaces.
[d] Double wavy.

9. Italics emphasizes text by:
[a] making the text darker.
[b] slanting the text to the right.
[c] placing the text above the baseline.
[d] slanting the text to the left.

10. Which of the following is not an option for changing the case of text?
[a] Uppercase
[b] Lowercase
[c] Triple case
[d] Sentence case

Circle **T** if the statement is true or **F** is the statement is false.

T F   1. The Italic button on the Formatting toolbar allows you to create text that looks and prints darker than the rest of the text.

T F   2. You must underline both words and the spaces between them when you apply underlining.

T F   3. Subscript formatting places text slightly below a line of normal printed text.

T F   4. Superscript formatting places text slightly above a line of normal printed text.

T F   5. The Format Painter button on the Standard toolbar allows you to copy only one format at a time.

T F   6. The three characteristics of fonts are: typeface, weight, and point (font) size.

T F   7. You can add Superscript and Subscript buttons to the Formatting toolbar.

T F   8. You can add numbers but not bullet symbols to lists.

T F   9. You cannot turn off the automatic formatting of characters.

T F   10. Typeface refers to the design and appearance of printed characters.

Skills Review

Exercise 1

1. Open the *Interoffice Meeting Memo* document located on the Data Disk.

2. Replace the text Current date with the actual date.

3. Apply bold style to the text TO, FROM, DATE, and SUBJECT in the memo form headings. (Do not apply bold to the colons.)

4. Apply bold to the day and time for the meeting in the first paragraph.

5. Single underline the number 20 in the third paragraph.

6. Italicize the topic assignments. (Select only the topic assignments.)

7. Save the document as *Interoffice Meeting Memo Revised*.

8. Preview, print, and close the document.

Exercise 2

1. Open the *Marketing Department Memo* document located on the Data Disk.

2. Replace the text Current date with the actual date.

3. Remove the bold format from the memo form headings. (Do not select the colon.)

4. Remove the italic format from the topic assignments. (Select only the topic assignments.)

5. Select the entire document and change the font to Arial 12 point.

6. Save the document as *Marketing Department Memo Revised*.

7. Preview, print, and close the document.

Exercise 3

1. Open the *Vancouver Sales Report* document located on the Data Disk.

2. Format the title "VANCOUVER BRANCH OFFICE" with the Outline effect.

3. Bold and underline the column titles.

4. Select the entire document and change the font to Arial 12 point.

5. Save the document as *Vancouver Sales Report Revised*.

6. Preview, print, and close the document.

Exercise 4

1. Open the *Commonly Misused Words* document located on the Data Disk.

2. Apply bold style to the commonly misused words. (Do not include the example and definition.)

3. Remove the italic format from the definitions.

4. Highlight in yellow the text "commonly misused words" in the second sentence.

5. Save the document as *Commonly Misused Words Revised*.

6. Preview, print, and close the document.

chapter four

Exercise 5

1. Open the *Company Correspondence Memo* document located on the Data Disk.

2. Replace the text Current date with the actual date.

3. Change the case of "Memorandum" to all uppercase.

4. Change the character spacing scale of "MEMORANDUM" to 200%.

5. Apply bold style to the text MEMORANDUM, TO, FROM, DATE, and SUBJECT. (Do not apply bold to the colons.)

6. Select the text MEMORANDUM and change the font to Arial 14 point.

7. Select the memo form headings and change the font to Times New Roman 12 point.

8. Save the document as *Company Correspondence Memo Revised*.

9. Preview, print, and close the document.

Exercise 6

1. Open the *Market Research* document located on the Data Disk.

2. Check the spelling and grammar and make the appropriate changes.

3. Insert a superscript number 1 after the word Davidson in the first paragraph.

4. Insert two lines at the end of the document and key the following text (including the superscript; do not apply the italic style to the text):
   ¹ One of the leading market research firms in the country.

5. Create a new paragraph beginning with the text "Telephone support" in the last paragraph.

6. Add bullets to the paragraphs beginning "Surveys" and "Telephone support."

7. Change the case of Vancouver branch in the first paragraph to all uppercase.

8. Save the document as *Market Research Revised*.

9. Preview, print, and close the document.

Exercise 7

1. Open the *Policy #152* document located on the Data Disk.

2. Select the text Warning! Warning! Warning! and change the case to uppercase.

3. Apply bold style to the text WARNING! WARNING! WARNING!

4. Select the text WARNING! WARNING! WARNING! and change the font to Arial 24 point.

5. Add animation effects of your choice to the text WARNING! WARNING! WARNING!

6. Change the case of "Only Authorized Personnel" and "May Proceed Beyond This Point" to all uppercase.

7. Select the text "Only Authorized Personnel" and "May Proceed Beyond This Point" and change the font to Arial 14 point bold.

8. Select the remainder of the text and change the font to Arial 12 point.

9. Single underline only the words in the third sentence beginning "Surveillance."

10. Save the document as *Policy #152 Revised*.

11. Preview, print, and close the document.

Exercise 8

1. Open the *Business Information Management* document located on the Data Disk.

2. Select the entire document and change the font to Arial 12 point.

3. Apply bold style to the text BUSINESS INFORMATION MANAGEMENT.

4. Select the text BUSINESS INFORMATION MANAGEMENT and change the font to Arial 18 point.

5. Apply bold style and underline the course number and title for BIM 160.

6. Use the Format Painter feature to copy the formatting to the remaining course numbers and titles.

7. Underline the last two lines in the document.

8. Save the document as *Business Information Management Revised*.

9. Preview, print, and close the document.

Exercise 9

1. Create the following document.

Introduction

Types of Stores
The Mall
The Strip Center
The Boutique
The Gourmet Store

Shopper Personalities
The Sales Hunter
The Gourmet
The Browser
The Catalog Shopper

Conclusion

2. Using the Font dialog box, change the text Introduction, Types of Stores, Shopper Personalities, and Conclusion to all caps, bold, and Arial 14 point. (*Hint:* Use the copy or repeat formatting methods to save time.)

3. Select the text beginning with "The Mall" and ending with "The Gourmet Store" and add bullets.

4. Select the text beginning with "The Sale Hunter" and ending with "The Catalog Shopper" and add bullets.

chapter four

5. Save the documents as *Stores Outline*.

6. Preview and print the document.

7. Replace the bullets with numbers.

8. Change the text "INTRODUCTION" to "SHOPPING SUMMARY."

9. Save the document as *Shopping Summary*.

10. Preview, print, and close the document.

Exercise 10

1. Open the *Symbols And Special Characters* document located on the Data Disk.

2. Insert the appropriate symbol or special characters as indicated in the text using the Symbol dialog box.

3. Save the document as *Symbols And Special Characters Revised*.

4. Preview, print, and close the document.

5. Open the *Chicago Warehouses Audit* document located on the Data Disk.

6. Highlight the first bulleted list in bright green.

7. Highlight the second bulleted list in pink.

8. Save the document as *Important Chicago Information*.

9. Preview, print, and close the document.

Case Projects

Project 1

Kelly Armstead asks you to show her the different font effect options available in Word. Open an existing document of your choice. Experiment with the special font effects options in the Font dialog box by selecting text and applying special effects formats and animation effects. Create a new Word document listing, describing, and showing the different effects. Use bulleted and numbered lists and character formats as appropriate. Save, preview, and print the document. With your instructor's permission, give a printed copy of the document to a classmate and, using the document as your guide, show your classmate how to use the different fonts and animation options.

Project 2

Marcy Wainwright, who works in the purchasing department, suggests you could save time in applying character formatting to text by using keyboard shortcuts. You decide to research which keyboard shortcuts to use to apply character formatting. Using the Office Assistant, locate, review, and print a list of keyboard shortcut keys used to apply character formatting. Open the document of your choice and apply different character formatting using keyboard shortcuts. Use bulleted and numbered lists and character formats in the document as appropriate. Save, preview, and print the document.

Project 3

You have been assigned to key the text of a new client proposal. Because of the proposal format, you want to use special character spacing for some of the proposal titles but aren't certain what character spacing options are available. Using the Office Assistant and other Word Help features, research how to use the character spacing options. Create a new document, containing at least two paragraphs, to describe how you can use these character spacing options in the client proposal. Include some sample titles with special character spacing. Use bulleted and numbered lists and character formats in the document as appropriate. Save, preview, and print the document.

Project 4

Albert Navarro, in Human Resources, wants to have a "brown bag" lunch for his staff that includes a short presentation on troubleshooting character formatting and using bullets and numbering in documents. He asked Kelly for help and she assigned the presentation to you. Using the Office Assistant, search online Help for tips on how to troubleshoot problems with these topics. Create a new document containing at least three paragraphs that describe possible problems and solutions associated with character formatting or bullets and numbering. Use bulleted and numbered lists and character formats in the document as appropriate. Save, preview, and print the document. With your instructor's permission, present your troubleshooting tips to several classmates.

Project 5

The administrative offices are moving to a new floor in the same building and B. D. Vickers asks you to create a letter announcing the move. The letter should contain the department's new address, phone number, fax number, and e-mail address. Create the letter for B. D. Vickers' signature. Set the appropriate margins, use fictitious data, and apply appropriate character formatting features discussed in this chapter to make the text attractive and easy to read. Use different text effects from the Font dialog box. Use bulleted and numbered lists and character formats in the document as appropriate. Save, preview, and print the letter.

Project 6

Elizabeth left you instructions to create a list of Web sites that are marketing and selling their products on the Web. Connect to your ISP and open your Web browser. Search the Web for pages that contain information on Web-based marketing and direct sales. Print at least three Web pages. Create a new, blank document and list the title of the Web pages and their URLs. Use bulleted and numbered lists and character formats in the document as appropriate. Save, preview, and print the document.

Project 7

Kelly Armstead needs the mailing addresses or e-mail addresses of the senators and congressmen from Illinois. You know that this information is available on the Web. Connect to your ISP and load your Web browser. Locate the home page for the U. S. Senate and U. S. House of Representatives. Follow the links to the names and addresses of the senators and congressmen. Print the appropriate pages. Create a new, blank document and key the information you found. Use bulleted and numbered lists and character formats in the document as appropriate. Save, preview, and print the document.

Project 8

You want to know more about how to use the keyboard to create bulleted and numbered lists automatically. Using the Office Assistant and other Word Help features, research how to create bulleted and numbered lists automatically. Create a new document and practice creating bulleted and numbered lists automatically with the fictitious data of your choice. Save, preview, and print the document.

chapter four

Using the Tabs Command

Chapter Overview

Some information is more clearly presented in columns and rows than in paragraph text. For example, it's easier to compare monthly expenses when the figures are arranged in columns by month and in rows by item. In this chapter you learn to organize information attractively on the page in rows and columns using tab stops and tab formatting marks.

LEARNING OBJECTIVES

► Understand tabs
► Set left tabs
► Set center tabs
► Set decimal tabs
► Set right tabs
► Set tabs with leaders

Case profile

The accounting department is overwhelmed with special projects and deadlines. Elizabeth Chang was so pleased with your work in the marketing department that she recommended you to Bill Wilson, the accounting manager. Bill wants you to create a summary memo to include with the quarterly sales report.

chapter
five

notes Before beginning the activities in this chapter you should review Appendix C, Formatting Tips for Business Documents, if you have not already done so.

5.a Understanding Tabs

When you need to prepare written communication to someone inside your organization, you can create an interoffice memorandum (or memo) instead of a letter document. Interoffice memorandums generally follow the standard format shown in Figure 5-1. The memorandum should have a 2-inch top margin, 1-inch left and right margins, and the double-spaced heading text TO:, FROM:, DATE:, and SUBJECT: at the beginning of the memorandum followed by paragraphs separated by a blank line. The variable TO:, FROM:, DATE:, and SUBJECT: text that follow each heading should be aligned. You do this with tabs.

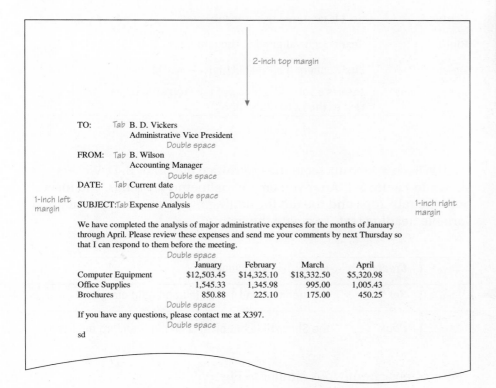

FIGURE 5-1
Standard Interoffice Memorandum

After each heading, you insert a **tab formatting mark,** a nonprinting character you key in your document by pressing the TAB key. Each tab

chapter five

QUICK TIP

To set custom tab stops that affect all the paragraphs in a new document, set the tab stops before you begin keying the first paragraph. When you press the ENTER key to begin a new paragraph, the tab settings are added to the new paragraph.

formatting mark you insert moves the text to the right of the tab formatting mark to the next tab stop. **Tab stops** are text-alignment icons positioned on the horizontal ruler that indicate where text should align. By default, Word documents have tab stops set at every ½ inch. You can also set custom tab stops at any position between the left and right margins for one or more selected paragraphs or the entire document.

Tab stops are part of **paragraph formatting**. This means that only the selected paragraph or paragraphs are affected when you set or modify tabs stops. To set custom tab stops for individual paragraphs, you must first select the paragraphs. To select a single paragraph, simply move the insertion point into the paragraph. To select multiple paragraphs, use the selection techniques you learned in Chapter 2.

Word has five types of tab alignments: Left, Center, Right, Decimal, and Bar. Text is left-aligned at default tab stops and can be left-, center-, right-, or decimal-aligned at custom tab stops. Table 5-1 describes the five tab text alignments. For more information on Bar alignment, see online Help.

TABLE 5-1
Tab Alignment Options

Tab	Alignment	Icon
Left	Text is left-aligned at the tab	
Center	Text is centered over the tab	
Right	Text is right-aligned at the tab	
Decimal	Text is aligned at the decimal character	
Bar	Inserts a vertical line at the tab stop and aligns text to the right of the line	

MOUSE TIP

You can set the left, center, right, decimal, and bar tab stops by selecting the appropriate tab alignment icon on the Tab Alignment button located to the left of the horizontal ruler, and then clicking at the appropriate position on the horizontal ruler.

Bill Wilson asks you create the interoffice memo to B. D. Vickers shown in Figure 5-1. After you create the memo headings, you insert both the tab stops and the tab formatting marks necessary to align the variable heading text. To create the memo:

Step 1	*Create*	a new, blank document
Step 2	*Set*	a 2-inch top, and 1-inch left and right margins
Step 3	*Click*	the Show/Hide button ¶ on the Standard toolbar

Your screen should look similar to Figure 5-2.

FIGURE 5-2
Formatting Marks, Default
Tab Stops, Tab Alignment
Button

M ENU TIP

You can set custom tab stops with the Tabs command on the Format menu by specifying where each tab formatting mark is inserted on the page, where each the tab alignment icon is inserted on the horizontal ruler, and the addition of leader characters.

By default, Word sets tab stops every ½ inch on the horizontal ruler. As you key the heading text, you press the TAB key to insert a tab formatting mark, which moves the insertion point to the next default tab stop on the horizontal ruler. Because you displayed the non-printing characters, you'll be able to see the tab formatting marks when you key them. To view the tab formatting marks and create the memo headings:

Step 1	*Observe*	the paragraph formatting mark at the first line
Step 2	*Observe*	the default tab stops set at every ½ inch on the horizontal ruler
Step 3	*Observe*	the Tab Alignment button to the left of the horizontal ruler
Step 4	*Key*	TO:
Step 5	*Press*	the TAB key
Step 6	*Observe*	the tab formatting mark
Step 7	*Observe*	that the insertion point moves to the next default tab stop at the ½-inch position on the horizontal ruler

Your screen should look similar to Figure 5-3.

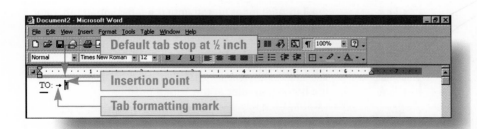

FIGURE 5-3
Insertion Point, Tab
Formatting Mark, and
Default Tab Stop

| Step 8 | *Key* | B. D. Vickers |
| Step 9 | *Press* | the ENTER key |

chapter
five

Step 10	*Press*	the TAB key
Step 11	*Key*	Administrative Vice President
Step 12	*Press*	the ENTER key twice
Step 13	*Continue*	to key the remaining headings and variable heading text you see in Figure 5-1, inserting one tab formatting mark between each heading and the variable text for that heading
Step 14	*Press*	the ENTER key twice following the SUBJECT: heading and variable text
Step 15	*Save*	the document as *Expense Memorandum*

C 5.b Setting Left Tabs

Notice that the variable heading text is not properly aligned because each line aligned at the first available default tab setting. To properly align the heading text, you need to add a custom left tab stop to the horizontal ruler for all the heading lines. A **left-aligned tab** aligns text along the left at the tab stop position. The quickest way to set custom tab stops is to use the mouse, the Tab Alignment button, and the horizontal ruler. Before you set custom tab stops, you must select the appropriate paragraph or paragraphs, then select the appropriate tab alignment icon with the Tab Alignment button, and finally, click the horizontal ruler to insert the tab stop at the appropriate position. When you click the ruler, the tab alignment icon you select from the Tab Alignment button appears on the ruler. To set a custom left tab for all the heading lines at one time:

Step 1	*Select*	the text beginning with the "TO:" paragraph and ending with the "SUBJECT:" paragraph
Step 2	*Click*	the Tab Alignment button until the left-aligned tab icon appears, if necessary
Step 3	*Move*	the mouse pointer to the 1-inch position on the horizontal ruler
Step 4	*Click*	the horizontal ruler at the 1-inch position
Step 5	*Deselect*	the text

A left-align tab icon appears on the horizontal ruler and the variable text in the heading lines aligns at the 1-inch position. Your screen should look similar to Figure 5-4.

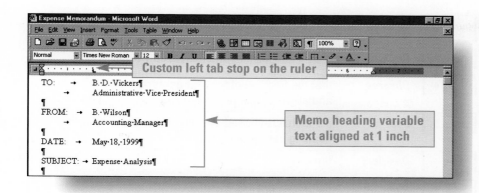

FIGURE 5-4
Custom Left Tab at 1 Inch

You remove tab stops or change the location of tab stops on the horizontal ruler by selecting the appropriate paragraphs and then dragging the tab stops with the mouse pointer. To move the custom left tab to 1½-inch for all the heading paragraphs:

Step 1	*Select*	the heading paragraphs
Step 2	*Position*	the mouse pointer on the left-align tab icon at the 1-inch position on the horizontal ruler (the ScreenTip "Left Tab" appears)
Step 3	*Drag*	the left-align tab icon to the 1½-inch position on the horizontal ruler

The variable text in each heading paragraph shifts to the 1½-inch position. You remove a tab stop by dragging it completely off the ruler. To remove the custom tab at 1½-inch position:

| Step 1 | *Verify* | the heading paragraphs are still selected |
| Step 2 | *Drag* | the tab icon at the 1½-inch position down off the horizontal ruler |

When you remove custom tab stops, the tab settings return to the default settings.

| Step 3 | *Observe* | that the tab stops on the horizontal ruler indicate the ½ inch default settings and the variable heading text is no longer properly aligned |

You set custom tab stops for individual paragraphs just as you do multiple paragraphs. To set a left tab for the first heading paragraph only:

| Step 1 | *Click* | in the heading paragraph beginning "TO:" to position the insertion point (this selects the paragraph) |

chapter
five

Step 2	*Verify*	the Tab Alignment button is set for a left tab
Step 3	*Click*	the 1-inch position on the horizontal ruler
Step 4	*Observe*	that the first line of the first paragraph *only* moves right and aligns at the new custom tab stop position
Step 5	*Set*	a 1-inch left-aligned custom tab for the remaining heading paragraphs
Step 6	*Deselect*	the text
Step 7	*Save*	the document

You now key the paragraph text in the body of the memo and then organize the expense analysis data in columns using tab formatting characters and tab stops on the horizontal ruler.

C **5.c** Setting Center Tabs

Center-aligned tabs center text over the tab stop, which is appropriate for creating column headings. Figure 5-1 includes text in columns separated by tab formatting marks. The text is arranged in five columns and includes column headers for the last four columns. You key the first body paragraph and the column headings: To key the first body paragraph:

Step 1	*Key*	the first body paragraph from Figure 5-1 on the second line following the SUBJECT: heading line
Step 2	*Press*	the ENTER key twice

Next you set custom center-aligned tab stops for the expense analysis column headings and key the headings.

Step 3	*Click*	the Tab Alignment button until the center-aligned tab icon appears
Step 4	*Click*	the 2.5-, 3.5-, 4.5-, and 5.5-positions on the horizontal ruler to insert the center-aligned tab icons
Step 5	*Press*	the TAB key
Step 6	*Key*	January
Step 7	*Press*	the TAB key

Step 8	*Key*	February
Step 9	*Press*	the TAB key
Step 10	*Key*	March
Step 11	*Press*	the TAB key
Step 12	*Key*	April
Step 13	*Press*	the ENTER key

When you press the ENTER key to create a new paragraph, Word remembers the previous paragraph tab settings. Because you use different tab setting for the text you key in the columns, you should remove the center-aligned tab icons from the ruler for this paragraph. To remove the center-aligned tab icons:

Step 1	*Drag*	each tab stop for the current paragraph off the ruler
Step 2	*Save*	the document

Now you are ready to set tab stops to align the expense analysis data.

5.d Setting Decimal Tabs

You want the expense data to align attractively on the decimal point in each column when you key the data in the columns. This makes reading columns of numbers much easier. A **decimal tab** aligns numbers at the decimal point.

To set decimal tab stops and enter the expense data text in the columns:

Step 1	*Click*	the Tab Alignment button until the decimal-aligned tab icon appears
Step 2	*Click*	the horizontal ruler at approximately the 2.6-, 3.6-, 4.6-, and 5.6-inch positions to insert the decimal-aligned tab stops using the ALT key to view the numbers on the horizontal ruler
Step 3	*Key*	Computer Equipment
Step 4	*Press*	the TAB key
Step 5	*Key*	$12,503.45

chapter
five

Step 6	*Press*	the TAB key
Step 7	*Key*	$14,325.10
Step 8	*Press*	the TAB key
Step 9	*Key*	$18,332.50
Step 10	*Press*	the TAB key
Step 11	*Key*	$5,320.98
Step 12	*Press*	the ENTER key

When you press the ENTER key, the next paragraph retains the tab stop settings from the previous paragraph. These tabs are appropriate for the remaining rows of data. To create the remaining lines:

Step 1	*Key*	Office Supplies
Step 2	*Press*	the TAB key
Step 3	*Observe*	the insertion point moves to the tab and aligns on the decimal point of the number above it
Step 4	*Continue*	to add the remaining two lines of tabbed text and the rest of the memo, as shown in Figure 5-1
Step 5	*Save*	the document and close it

Bill asks you to update the accounting department telephone extension list and add the revision date at the right margin below the phone numbers. You can use a right-aligned tab stop to add the revision date.

5.e Setting Right Tabs

A **right-aligned tab** is appropriate for text that should be aligned at the right of the tab, such as a date at the right margin of a document. To position the date at the right margin, set a right-aligned tab, press the TAB key, and then key or insert the date. To set a right tab and right-align the date at the right margin of the first line:

Step 1	*Open*	the *Telephone List* document located on the Data Disk
Step 2	*Move*	the insertion point to the bottom of the document and add two new blank lines

Step 3	*Click*	the Tab Alignment button to the left of the horizontal ruler until the right-aligned tab icon ▣ appears
Step 4	*Click*	the 5½-inch position on the horizontal ruler to insert the right-aligned tab icon
Step 5	*Drag*	the right-aligned tab icon to the 6-inch position (the right margin)

Your screen should look similar to Figure 5-5.

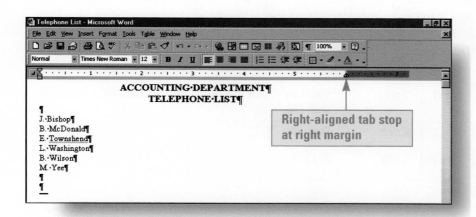

FIGURE 5-5
Right-Aligned Tab

Step 6	*Press*	the TAB key
Step 7	*Key*	today's date using AutoComplete
Step 8	*Observe*	that as you key the date the text flows left from the tab position
Step 9	*Save*	the document as *Telephone List Revised*

Bill asks you to continue the telephone extension list revision by positioning each employee's name at the left margin and their telephone number at the right margin in the telephone list document. He also wants you to insert a dotted or dashed line between the employee's name at the left margin and their extension at the right margin to help guide the reader's eye across the page. You can use right-aligned tab stops with tab leaders to do this.

5.f Setting Tabs with Leaders

Documents that have a large amount of white space between columns of text, such as a table of contents or a phone list, can be difficult for a reader's eye to follow across the page from column to column. **Tab leaders** are dashed or dotted lines you can add to a tab to provide a visual guide for the reader as they read the text from column to column. You add a leader character to a tab in the Tabs dialog box. Before you open the Tabs dialog box to set tab stops and add leaders, you must remember to select the appropriate paragraphs to be formatted. To set a right-aligned tab at the 6-inch position and add the second leader style:

Step 1	*Select*	the lines of text beginning with "J. Bishop" and ending with "M. Yee"
Step 2	*Click*	F<u>o</u>rmat
Step 3	*Click*	<u>T</u>abs

The Tabs dialog box that opens on your screen should look similar to Figure 5-6.

FIGURE 5-6
Tabs Dialog Box

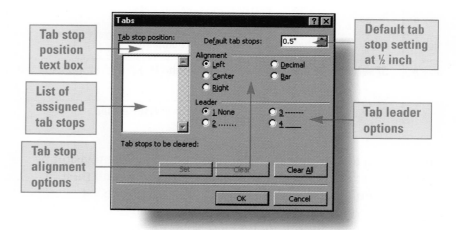

You can use the dialog box Help button to review the options in the dialog box. You set tab stops in the dialog box by keying the tab position and selecting an alignment option. Then you can select a leader style.

Step 4	*Key*	6 in the <u>T</u>ab stop position: text box
Step 5	*Click*	the <u>R</u>ight option button

| Step 6 | *Click* | the <u>2</u> .... leader option button |
| Step 7 | *Click* | OK |

With the tab stops and leader set, you can enter the tab formatting marks and telephone extensions for each item. To key the telephone extensions list:

Step 1	*Move*	the insertion point to the end of the J. Bishop text
Step 2	*Press*	the TAB key
Step 3	*Observe*	the leader characters that appear from the J. Bishop text to the tab
Step 4	*Key*	X388
Step 5	*Press*	the DOWN ARROW key to move the insertion point to the end of the B. McDonald text
Step 6	*Continue*	to key the telephone extensions to the document, pressing the TAB key between the name and extension B. McDonald, X391 E. Townshend, X402 L. Washington, X455 B. Wilson, X397 M. Yee, X405
Step 7	*Save*	the document and close it

No matter what type of document you create, you can use tabs to precisely align text in columns.

chapter
five

Summary

► You can reposition and organize text in columns by setting tab stops on the horizontal ruler and inserting tab formatting marks in the text.

► Tab stops are text-alignment icons positioned on the horizontal ruler that indicate where text should align.

► Tab formatting marks are nonprinting characters you key in your document by pressing the TAB key.

► Left-aligned tab stops position text at the tab and then flow the text to the right.

► Right-aligned tab stops position text at the tab and then flow the text to the left.

► Center-aligned tab stops are appropriate for column headings and position text at the tab and then flow the text left and right as necessary to center at the tab.

► Decimal-aligned tab stops are appropriate for columns of numbers containing decimal points and align the numbers on their decimal points.

► To assist the reader's eye in following text from column to column, you can add leader characters to a tab.

Commands Review

Action	Menu Bar	Shortcut Menu	Toolbar	Keyboard
Set custom tab stops	Format, Tabs		Click the Tab Alignment button to select an alignment icon, then click the horizontal ruler at the appropriate position ⌊ Left ⌋ Right ⊥ Center ⊥ Decimal	ALT + O, T

Concepts Review

Circle the correct answer.

1. **Which of the following is not a tab alignment?**
   [a] Left
   [b] Right
   [c] Justify
   [d] Decimal

2. **To align text at the right of a tab using the Tab Alignment button and the horizontal ruler, select the:**
   [a] Left alignment icon.
   [b] Justify alignment icon.
   [c] Right alignment icon.
   [d] Center alignment icon.

3. **You can insert a tab formatting mark by pressing the:**
   [a] ENTER key.
   [b] TAB key.
   [c] HOME key.
   [d] END key.

4. **To quickly set custom tab stops that affect one paragraph, first:**
   [a] select the entire document.
   [b] select multiple paragraphs.
   [c] move the insertion point to the paragraph.
   [d] click the horizontal ruler then select the paragraph.

5. **The default tab stops are positioned every:**
   [a] ½ inch.
   [b] 1 inch.
   [c] ¾ inch.
   [d] ¼ inch.

6. **To assist the reader's eye in following text from column to column, you can add:**
   [a] length to the line.
   [b] less space between the characters.
   [c] leader characters.
   [d] lending characters.

7. **To view the tab formatting marks in a document, click the:**
   [a] Show Tabs button.
   [b] Show/Hide button.
   [c] Format Marks button.
   [d] Tab Alignment button.

8. **You can manually enter the tab position, change the default tab settings, and add leaders to tab stops with the:**
   [a] Format, Paragraph commands.
   [b] Insert, Tabs commands.
   [c] Tools, Options commands.
   [d] Format, Tabs commands.

Circle **T** if the statement is true or **F** is the statement is false.

T   F   1. The default setting for tab stops is every ⅛ inch.

T   F   2. You can set tab stops with the mouse and the horizontal ruler.

T   F   3. The Tab Alignment button has four alignment settings.

T   F   4. Use a center-aligned tab to position the date at the right margin.

T   F   5. Use a left-aligned tab to start a new paragraph.

T   F   6. When you create text column headings, you can use the decimal-aligned tab to center the headings over the column.

T   F   7. You cannot remove tab stops with the mouse pointer.

T   F   8. Tab leader characters can be added by clicking the Tab Alignment button.

chapter five

Skills Review

Exercise 1

1. Create a new, blank document and key the text in columns below:

	1998	1999	2000
Division 1	$200,000	$90,000	$180,000
Division 2	212,000	205,000	79,000
Division 3	140,000	400,000	120,000
Division 4	304,000	107,000	105,000
Division 5	201,000	148,000	195,000

2. Use right-aligned tab stops to align the numbers.

3. Use center-aligned tab stops to align the column headings.

4. Save the document as *Division Data*.

5. Preview, print, and close the document.

Exercise 2

1. Open the *Media Memo* document located on the Data Disk.

2. Replace the text Current date with the actual date.

3. Set the appropriate margins for an interoffice memorandum.

4. Insert tab formatting marks in the heading paragraphs so you can align the variable heading text.

5. Set a left-aligned tab at 1 inch on the horizontal ruler for all the heading paragraphs to align the variable heading text.

6. Insert a new line below R. F. Jones and then insert a tab formatting mark and key the title "Media Buyer."

7. Insert a new line below B. Wilson and then insert a tab formatting mark and key the title "Accounting Manager."

8. Spell check the document.

9. Save the document as *Media Memo Revised*.

10. Preview, print, and close the document.

Exercise 3

1. Create a new, blank document and key the text in columns below:

Branch	Meat	Cheese	Produce
Chicago	$55,900	$125,000	$77,000
Vancouver	33,000	7,890	15,000
London	22,500	12,500	18,000
Melbourne	34,333	40,100	48,550

2. Use right-aligned tab stops to align the numbers.

3. Use center-aligned tab stops to align the column headings.

4. Save the document as *Branch Sales*.

5. Preview, print, and close the document.

Exercise 4

1. Open the *Vendor Phone List* document located on the Data Disk.

2. Select the four lines of text and set a right-aligned tab with the leader of your choice at the 6-inch position on the horizontal ruler.

3. Insert a new line at the top of the document and remove the right-aligned tab from the horizontal ruler.

4. Insert a tab formatting mark, key the column title "<u>Vendor</u>" with the underline, insert a tab formatting mark, and key the column title "<u>Phone List</u>" with the underline.

5. Set two center-aligned tab stops on the horizontal ruler to center the column titles attractively over their respective columns.

6. Save the document as *Vendor Phone List Revised*.

7. Preview, print, and close the document.

Exercise 5

1. Create a new, blank document and key the text in columns below:

Sales District	Telephone	Supplies	Misc.
1	$1,450.25	$744.33	$225.45
2	1,645.33	525.88	214.55
3	985.22	275.90	243.89
4	1,112.98	210.66	423.67
5	1,967.34	678.23	313.56

2. Use decimal-aligned tab stops to align the telephone, supplies, and miscellaneous expense numbers.

3. Use center-aligned tab stops to align the column headings and the sales district numbers.

4. Save the document as *Sales District Expenses*.

5. Preview, print, and close the document.

Exercise 6

1. Create a new, blank document and key the following text in columns.

Item	Budgeted	Actual	Difference
Executive Secretaries	$1,234,000	$1,145,000	$(89,000)
Administrative Assistants	289,500	364,800	75,300
Equipment	850,000	730,000	(120,000)
Telecommunications	365,000	340,500	(24,500)
Miscellaneous	65,000	50,000	(15,000)

2. Use the appropriate tab stops to center the column headings and align the budgeted, actual, and difference numbers.

3. Save the document as *Budget Variance*.

4. Preview, print, and close the document.

Exercise 7

1. Open the *Regional Expenses Memo* document located on the Data Disk.

2. Replace the text Current date with the actual date.

chapter five

3. Select the heading paragraphs and then set a left-aligned tab at 1½ inches on the horizontal ruler.

4. Move the left-aligned tab to 1 inch.

5. Insert the following columnar text separated by tab stops below the first body paragraph of the memo. Use center-aligned tab stops for the column titles. Use decimal-aligned tab stops for the selling, employee, and overhead numbers. Remember to add a single blank line before and after the columnar text.

Region	Selling	Employee	Overhead
Central	$42,000.50	$2,210.00	$12,825.98
Eastern	32,545.78	3,412.44	7,890.66
Midwest	53,897.75	3,508.34	8,454.88
Mountain	49,154.33	6,974.76	5,221.44
Southern	34,675.21	11,242.88	15,111.75
Western	40,876.21	8,417.77	10,445.29

6. Save the document as *Regional Expenses Memo Revised*.

7. Preview, print, and close the document.

Exercise 8

1. Create the following interoffice memorandum.

TO: D. Ingram
            Sales Director

FROM: B. Wilson
            Accounting Manager

DATE: Current date

SUBJECT: Sales Summary   Analysis

I have completed the sales analysis you requested and the data appear below.

Name	January	February	March
Davis, Stephen	$65,000	$45,000	$78,000
McCarthy, Rachel	45,000	58,000	76,000
Mills, Cheryl	95,000	99,000	92,000

Please contact me at X397 if you have any questions.

sd

2. Key the current date in the memorandum using AutoComplete.

3. Set appropriate margins for an interoffice memorandum.

4. Set the appropriate tab stops for the text in columns.

5. Apply bold style to the TO:, FROM:, DATE:, and SUBJECT: headings.

6. Save the document as *Ingram Memo*.

7. Preview, print, and close the document.

Case Projects

Project 1

Bill Wilson asks you to prepare an interoffice memorandum from him to all regional sales managers advising them of the semi-annual sales meeting to be held in two weeks in the main conference room at corporate headquarters in Chicago. Additionally, everyone attending the meeting must contact you to arrange hotel accommodations, rental cars, and airline tickets. Use character and tab formatting features to make the memo interesting to read and professional in appearance. Save, preview, and print the document.

Project 2

You are preparing a sales analysis for Bill Wilson to take to the semi-annual sales conference and you would like to change the default tab position from every ½ inch to every ¼ inch. Using the Office Assistant and the keyword "tabs" search for help topics on changing the default tab position in a document. Create an interoffice memorandum to Bill Wilson from yourself with the subject line "Default Tabs." Add at least two body paragraphs describing how to change the default tab settings. Save, preview, and print the document.

Project 3

Benji Hori, one of the accounting assistants, asks you if there is a way to vary the alignment of text in a single line. He needs to create a document with the document title, date, and page number all on the same line. He wants the document title left-aligned, the date center-aligned, and the page number right-aligned. If necessary, look up the "Troubleshoot

paragraph formatting" topic in online Help using the Office Assistant and review how to align text differently on the same line. Create a sample document with the title "Quarterly Sales Report" left-aligned, the current date center-aligned, and the text "Page Number" right-aligned. Save, preview, and print the document. With your instructor's permission, show a classmate how to align text differently on the same line.

Project 4

Before you begin keying a new accounting report for Bill Wilson, you want to practice setting and removing tab stops in a document. Open an existing document that contains tab stops and tab formatting marks. Remove all the tab stops for the entire document at one time. Explore using left, center, right, and decimal tabs to make the document easier to read. Save the document with a new name, then preview and print it.

Project 5

Bill Wilson is planning an auto trip to Houston, Texas, and he asks you to use the Web to look up the mileage and print driving instructions and a city-to-city trip map from Chicago to Houston. Connect to your ISP, load your Web browser and, using a directory or search engine, locate Web pages that help you plan auto trips by calculating the mileage and creating driving instructions and maps from city to city. Save and print the driving instructions and trip map. Create an interoffice memorandum to Bill outlining the mileage and driving instructions. Save, preview, and print the memorandum.

chapter five

Project 6

Katrina Levy, one of the accounting assistants, asks you for help. She has an old document with tab stops set differently for each of the paragraphs. She wants to remove all the tab stops for the entire document at one time but isn't certain how to do this. Open the Tabs dialog box and use the dialog box Help button to get more information about the Clear and Clear All buttons. Using the Office Assistant and the keywords "clear tabs" search online Help for information on clearing all the tab stops in a document. Create an interoffice memorandum to Katrina describing how to clear all the tabs in document at one time. Save, preview, and print the memo.

Project 7

Kelly Armstead called to ask you how to find someone's e-mail address using the Web. Connect to your ISP, load your Web browser and—using several directories and search engines—locate Web pages that include a feature that allows you to search for e-mail addresses. Print at least three pages. Create an interoffice memorandum to Kelly listing the Web pages and describing how to use them to search for e-mail addresses. Save, preview, and print the memo.

Project 8

Bill Wilson is attending a meeting with the branch vice presidents to discuss the quarterly sales figures. He wants you to create a document he can hand out at the meeting. Using fictitious data for the Chicago, London, Melbourne, and Vancouver branches, create a document with two columns for branch names and total sales data for each branch. Use tab stops with leaders to organize the data attractively on the page. Save, preview, and print the document.

Setting Spacing, Aligning Text, and Using Indentation Options

Chapter Overview

Poorly arranged text can distract readers from the information in a document. When text is attractively spaced and positioned on the page, readers can concentrate on the document content. You can use line spacing, text alignment, and indentation options to position text in your documents. In this chapter you learn different ways to change the line spacing and text alignment, and different ways to indent paragraph text.

Learning Objectives

▶ Set character, line, and paragraph spacing
▶ Align text vertically
▶ Align text in paragraphs
▶ Use indentation options

Case profile

After completing your assignment in the accounting department, you are asked to return to the purchasing department to help Kelly Armstead create and format the department's correspondence and reports. You begin by keying and formatting the new audit report from the Melbourne branch office.

chapter
six

notes   For this chapter, the automatic creation of styles based on formatting is turned off in the AutoFormat As You Type tab in the AutoCorrect dialog box.

Before beginning the activities in this chapter you should review Appendix C, Formatting Tips for Business Documents, if you have not already done so.

6.a Setting Character, Line, and Paragraph Spacing

Line spacing indicates the vertical space between lines of text. The default setting for line spacing in Word is single spacing. Table 6-1 describes single spacing as well as the other line-spacing options available in Word. The paragraph text in letters and memorandums is usually single spaced. Double spacing is most often used for long reports so that they are easier to read. Also, documents in progress are often double spaced so reviewers can use the extra white space to write their comments and proofing notations.

> **MENU TIP**
>
> You can change the line spacing for selected paragraphs by clicking the Paragraph command on the Format menu or shortcut menu.

TABLE 6-1
Line-spacing Options

Option	Description
Single	Accommodates the largest font size in the line plus a little extra space, depending on the font.
1.5 Lines	Sets the line spacing to 1.5 times the single-line spacing.
Double	Sets the line spacing to twice the single-line spacing.
At Least	Sets a minimum line spacing that will adjust to accommodate larger font sizes or graphics.
Exactly	Sets a fixed line spacing that will not adjust for larger font sizes or graphics.
Multiple	Sets the line spacing by a percentage of the single-line spacing. A multiple of 1.3 increases the single-line spacing by 30%. A multiple of 0.7 decreases the single line spacing by 30%.

> **MOUSE TIP**
>
> You can add the single-, 1.5-, and double-line spacing buttons to the Formatting toolbar by clicking the More Buttons list arrow on the Formatting toolbar, pointing to Add or Remove Buttons, and then clicking the desired line-spacing button.

Figure 6-1 illustrates a report document in the unbound report format with a 2-inch top margin and 1-inch left and right margins. Kelly wants you to key the Melbourne audit report document in Figure 6-1 and then format the text using line spacing and vertical text alignment options to make the text more attractive and easier to read.

FIGURE 6-1
Unbound Report

↓ 2-inch top margin

Several methods were used to examine the operations at warehouses in Melbourne. The study team members interviewed the warehouse managers and several workers in each warehouse. A consulting company, Wadell & Associates, completed an analysis of the various policies and procedures used by the warehouses. A human resources specialist from the Chicago office interviewed managers as well as labor union representatives at each warehouse. Some of the analysis has not been completed and should be finished within three weeks.

The completed portion of the analysis indicates there are three possible causes for the problems at the Melbourne warehouses:

1-inch left margin

- Insufficient quality control
- Low morale and reduced worker productivity
- Poor communication

1-inch right margin

Warehouse managers and employees report poor communication over the last year. Problems with quality control are suspected for several reasons.

1. Appropriate goals have not been specified.
2. Appropriate work processes are not being used in some activities.
3. Employees are not receiving proper direction about how to manage the inventories.

Morale and worker productivity problems may be due to the fact that many employees believe their compensation is low relative to competitors in their area. This belief may have negatively impacted their productivity.

In contrast, interviews in Vancouver, Chicago, and London indicate that warehouses in these areas do not seem to have the problems found in Melbourne. Managers and union representatives at these locations stated that all personnel work together in a cooperative manner.

Communications between all warehouse personnel regarding goals, policies, and procedures are effective and employees believe they are fairly compensated.

QUICK TIP

Line spacing is included in paragraph formatting. Whenever you change the line spacing, the new line spacing affects only the selected paragraphs. To change the spacing for a single paragraph, simply move the insertion point to that paragraph. To change the spacing for several paragraphs, you must first select the paragraphs. To set line spacing that affects all the paragraphs in a new document, set the line spacing before you begin typing the first paragraph.

To create the document:

Step 1	*Create*	a new, blank document, if necessary
Step 2	*Set*	2-inch top and 1-inch left and right margins
Step 3	*Key*	the text in Figure 6-1 (do not add any blank lines between the paragraphs)
Step 4	*Create*	the bulleted and numbered lists in the document, as shown in Figure 6-1
Step 5	*Save*	the document as *Melbourne Audit Report*

notes
If you are using a 14-inch monitor with 640x480 resolution, you can zoom documents with 1-inch left and right margins to Page Width. This allows you to see all the text at the right margin. For the remainder of this book it is assumed you have zoomed the document to Page Width, if necessary.

chapter
six

To set the line spacing in your document, first select the entire document or the paragraphs you wish to change. Then change the line spacing in the Paragraph dialog box. Kelly wants the entire report double-spaced. To change the line spacing of the entire document to double:

Step 1	*Select*	the entire document
Step 2	*Right-click*	the selected text
Step 3	*Click*	<u>P</u>aragraph
Step 4	*Click*	the <u>I</u>ndents and Spacing tab, if necessary

The dialog box on your screen should look similar to Figure 6-2.

FIGURE 6-2
Paragraph Dialog Box

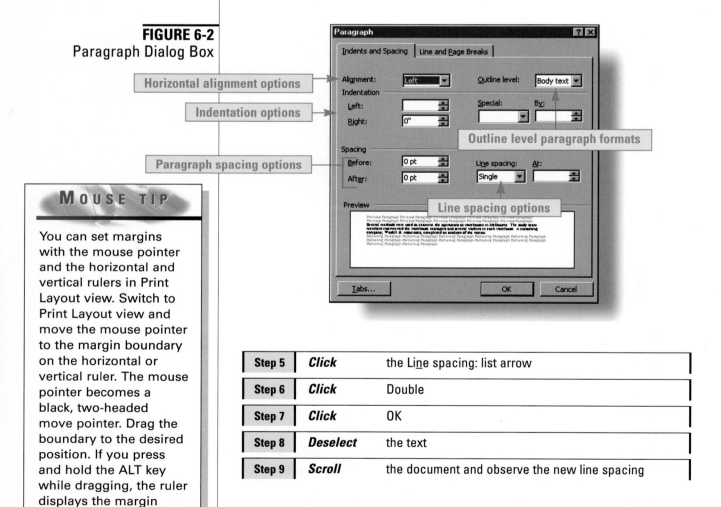

Horizontal alignment options

Indentation options

Paragraph spacing options

Outline level paragraph formats

Line spacing options

Step 5	*Click*	the Li<u>n</u>e spacing: list arrow
Step 6	*Click*	Double
Step 7	*Click*	OK
Step 8	*Deselect*	the text
Step 9	*Scroll*	the document and observe the new line spacing

Notice that the spacing between each line of text is now two lines, causing the document to extend into a second page. Word inserts a dotted line indicating a page break, which marks the end of page one and the start of page two.

The bulleted and numbered paragraphs in the *Melbourne Audit Report* would look better if they were spaced 1.5 times the single-line spacing. You change only the first two paragraphs in each list because Word inserts the additional space below the line. You want to leave the third paragraph with double spacing so the lists are separated equally from paragraphs above and below them. To change the line spacing for the bulleted and numbered lists:

Step 1	*Select*	the first two bulleted list paragraphs (scroll to view these paragraphs, if necessary)
Step 2	*Right-click*	the selected text
Step 3	*Click*	Paragraph
Step 4	*Click*	the Indents and Spacing tab, if necessary
Step 5	*Click*	the Line spacing: list arrow
Step 6	*Click*	1.5
Step 7	*Click*	OK
Step 8	*Select*	the first two numbered paragraphs (scroll to view the paragraphs, if necessary)
Step 9	*Open*	the Paragraph dialog box
Step 10	*Change*	the line spacing to 1.5
Step 11	*Scroll*	the document and observe the line spacing
Step 12	*Save*	the document

The new line spacing is making the report much easier to read. Kelly wants the *Melbourne Audit Report* to be attractively spaced on one page instead of two pages. She suggests you change the line spacing and use vertical alignment to do this.

6.b Aligning Text Vertically

Vertical alignment affects how the text is placed on the page in relation to the top and bottom margins. Kelly wants the *Melbourne Audit Report* to be attractively spaced on one page. Because the double-spaced report falls onto two pages, you need to change the line spacing to reduce the amount of space between the lines. Once the report is on one page, you can align the text vertically between the

MOUSE TIP

To view the character and paragraph formats applied to a paragraph, press the SHIFT + F1 keys to change the mouse pointer to a "What's This?" help pointer. Then click the paragraph. Press the ESC key to return the mouse pointer to its original shape and close the Reveal Formats box.

QUICK TIP

C You can increase or decrease spacing between characters with options on the Character Spacing tab in the Font dialog box.

You can increase or decrease the white space above or below paragraphs with options on the Indents and Spacing tab in the Paragraph dialog box.

chapter
six

top and bottom margins. To view the document in Print Layout view and change the line spacing:

Step 1	*Switch*	to Print Layout view
Step 2	*Zoom*	the document to Two Pages and observe the two-page layout
Step 3	*Set*	the line spacing for the entire document to 1.5 lines
Step 4	*Observe*	the document is now on one page, but the text is not yet distributed evenly between the top and bottom margins
Step 5	*Zoom*	the document to Whole Page
Step 6	*Click*	File
Step 7	*Click*	Page Setup
Step 8	*Click*	the Layout tab
Step 9	*Click*	the Vertical alignment: list arrow

The dialog box on your screen should look similar to Figure 6-3.

FIGURE 6-3
Layout Tab in the Page
Setup Dialog Box

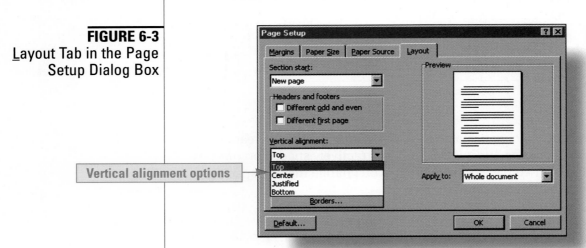

Vertical alignment options

The **Top** vertical alignment option aligns text with the top margin. The **Center** vertical alignment option allows you to center the text between the margins. This option is good for creating report title pages or signs. The **Bottom** vertical alignment option aligns the text at the bottom margin, leaving the extra white space at the top of the page. The **Justified** vertical alignment option distributes full-page text evenly between the top and bottom margins by adding additional line spacing. This option will give the report the look that Kelly wants.

Step 10	*Click*	Justified
Step 11	*Click*	OK
Step 12	*Observe*	the text is distributed evenly between the 2-inch top and 1-inch bottom margins
Step 13	*Switch*	to Normal view and deselect the text
Step 14	*Save*	the document

With the new vertical alignment, the *Melbourne Audit Report* fits nicely on the page. Next Kelly wants the body paragraph text to have evenly aligned left and right margins, the bulleted paragraphs to be centered between the left and right margins, and the numbered paragraphs to be positioned attractively on the page. To create these effects, you must align the text horizontally.

6.c Aligning Text in Paragraphs

Horizontal text alignment affects how the text is placed on the page in relation to the left and right margins. Like line spacing and vertical alignment, horizontal alignment is included in paragraph formatting, which means any horizontal alignment changes affect only selected paragraphs.

The four horizontal text alignment options are left, center, right, and justify. The default horizontal text alignment is left. **Left alignment** lines up text along the left margin and leaves the right margin "ragged," or uneven. **Right alignment** lines up the text along the right margin and leaves the left margin ragged. **Center alignment** centers the text between the left and right margins and leaves both margins ragged. **Justified alignment** aligns the text along both the left and right margins; Word adjusts the spaces between words so that the each line is even at both margins. The quickest way to change the alignment of selected paragraphs is to use the alignment buttons on the Formatting toolbar.

You use each of these alignments in the *Melbourne Audit Report*.

Setting Justified Alignment

Kelly asks you to justify the body text of the report. This way the *Melbourne Audit Report* document will have perfectly even left and right margins for each full line. Justification affects only full lines of

QUICK TIP

To change the horizontal alignment of a single paragraph, simply move the insertion point to that paragraph. To change the horizontal alignment of more than one paragraph, you must first select the desired paragraphs. To set horizontal alignment that affects all the paragraphs in a new document, set the alignment before you begin keying the first paragraph.

MENU TIP

You can change the horizontal text alignment by clicking the Alignment: list arrow in the Paragraph dialog box and selecting the appropriate alignment format.

text; partial lines are even along the left margin and ragged along the right. To justify all the paragraphs in the document:

Step 1	*Select*	the entire document
Step 2	*Click*	the Justify button on the Formatting toolbar
Step 3	*Deselect*	the text and scroll the document to verify that all the paragraphs are justified

Although the entire report is justified, notice that the partial lines at the end of each paragraph and the short bulleted and numbered list paragraphs are ragged along the right margin.

Setting Center Alignment

Paragraphs that are center-aligned have each line centered between the left and right margins. Center alignment is appropriate for single-line paragraphs, such as titles, paragraph headings, or bullets. You want to center the bullet paragraphs. To do this:

Step 1	*Select*	the bulleted paragraphs (scroll to view, if necessary)
Step 2	*Click*	the Center button on the Formatting toolbar and deselect the text

Each bulleted paragraph is centered between the left and right margins. Next you format the numbered list.

Setting Right Alignment

When paragraphs are right-aligned, each line of the paragraph is aligned at the right margin. Right alignment is appropriate for dates, page numbers, or to add a special effect to short one-line paragraphs. You decide to try right alignment for the numbered list. To right-align the numbered paragraphs:

Step 1	*Select*	the numbered paragraphs (scroll to view, if necessary)
Step 2	*Click*	the Align Right button on the Formatting toolbar and deselect the text

Each numbered paragraph is aligned along the right margin. Kelly comments that right alignment is not the most attractive position for the numbered paragraphs and suggests you realign them to their original position.

Setting Left Alignment

You can remove the horizontal alignment formatting or apply a different horizontal alignment to paragraphs by selecting the paragraphs you want to realign and then clicking the appropriate alignment button. To left-align the numbered paragraphs:

Step 1	*Select*	the numbered paragraphs
Step 2	*Click*	the Align Left button on the Formatting toolbar and deselect the text
Step 3	*Save*	the document

The numbered list looks better left-aligned, but you want to shift the paragraphs right so they stand out more.

6.d Using Indentation Options

Indenting, or moving text away from the margin, helps draw attention to that text. The Word indentation options position some or all lines of a paragraph to the right of the left margin (or to the left of the right margin). Indenting is part of paragraph formatting, which means only selected paragraphs are indented. The other paragraphs in the document remain unchanged.

There are four types of indents: left, right, first line, and hanging. A **Left Indent** moves all the lines of a paragraph to the right away from the left margin. A **Right Indent** moves all lines of a paragraph to the left away from the right margin. A **First Line Indent** moves the first line of a paragraph to the right or the left. A **Hanging Indent** leaves the first line of the paragraph at the left margin and moves the remaining lines to the right away from the left margin.

A tab stop and an indent are very different formatting features. Recall that when you press the TAB key, Word inserts a nonprinting tab formatting mark and moves only that line to the next tab stop on the horizontal ruler. When you apply an indent option, you can specify which lines to move and how many spaces to move them.

Setting a Left Indent

You can use left indents to draw attention to an entire paragraph or to set off quoted material. You indent paragraphs from the left margin by clicking the Increase Indent button on the Formatting toolbar. You

C

chapter
six

MENU TIP

You can indent paragraphs from the left or right margins by keying the indent position in the Indents and Spacing tab of the Paragraph dialog box.

want to indent the first paragraph of the *Melbourne Audit Report* 1½ inches from the left margin. To indent the first paragraph:

| Step 1 | *Move* | the insertion point to the first paragraph to select it |
| Step 2 | *Click* | the Increase Indent button ▦ on the Formatting toolbar |

All the lines of the first paragraph are indented to the first tab stop at the ½-inch position on the horizontal ruler. Your screen should look similar to Figure 6-4.

FIGURE 6-4
Indented Paragraph

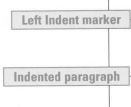

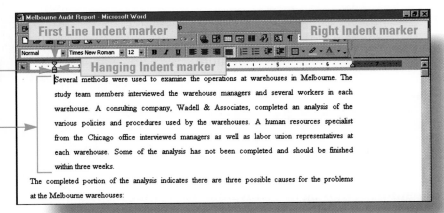

| Step 3 | *Click* | the Increase Indent button ▦ on the Formatting toolbar twice to indent the paragraph to the 1½-inch position. |

Each time you click the Increase Indent button, the selected paragraphs are indented to the next tab stop. The paragraph would look better if it were not indented as far. To return the paragraph to the left margin:

| Step 1 | *Verify* | the insertion point is in the first paragraph |
| Step 2 | *Click* | the Decrease Indent button ▦ on the Formatting toolbar three times |

You can indent paragraphs from the left or right margin to any position on the horizontal ruler by dragging the indent markers shown in Figure 6-4. These indent markers give you the flexibility of indenting text a specific distance instead of indenting to the next tab stop on the horizontal ruler. To indent all the lines of the first paragraph ¾ inch:

| Step 1 | **Click** | in the first paragraph to select it, if necessary |
| Step 2 | **Move** | the mouse pointer to the Left Indent marker ▭ on the horizontal ruler (see Figure 6-5) |

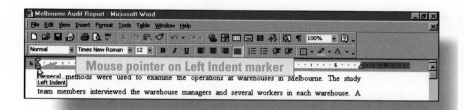

FIGURE 6-5
Left Indent Marker

| Step 3 | **Drag** | the Left Indent marker to the ¾-inch position on the horizontal ruler |

To add even more emphasis to the paragraph, you can indent it from both the left and right margins.

Setting a Right Indent

You can indent a paragraph from the right margin by dragging the Right Indent marker to the left to any position on the horizontal ruler. Most commonly, a right indent is used with a left indent to separate quoted materials in a report and to emphasize numbered or bulleted lists. To indent the first paragraph ¾ inch from the right margin using the Right Indent marker:

| Step 1 | **Move** | the mouse pointer to the Right Indent marker ⌂ on the horizontal ruler (see Figure 6-6) |

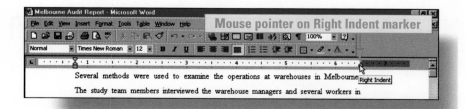

FIGURE 6-6
Right Indent Marker

| Step 2 | **Drag** | the Right Indent marker left to the 5¾-inch position on the horizontal ruler |

chapter
six

CAUTION TIP

It's easy to accidentally drag the First Line, Hanging, or Left Indent markers on the ruler beyond the document's left margin. In Normal view, if you can still see the indent marker, drag it back to the appropriate position. Then click the scroll box on the horizontal scroll bar to reposition the screen. If you can no longer see the indent markers, switch to Print Layout view, drag the indent markers to the right, and then return to Normal view.

The first paragraph is now indented ¾ inch from both the left and right margins. You can remove the indents by selecting the paragraph and dragging the indent markers back to the left or right margin. To remove the left and right indents from the first paragraph:

Step 1	Click	in the first paragraph to select it, if necessary
Step 2	Drag	the Right Indent marker back to the right margin
Step 3	Drag	the Left Indent marker back to the left margin

The first line of any paragraph can be repositioned to the left or right of the other lines by using the First Line Indent option.

Setting a First Line Indent

You can use the First Line Indent marker on the horizontal ruler to indent just the first line of a paragraph leaving the remaining lines in their original position. You often see first-line indents in long text documents, such as books and reports. You decide to indent the first line of each paragraph in the report. To indent the first line of each text paragraph with the First Line Indent marker:

| Step 1 | Verify | that the insertion point is in the first text paragraph |
| Step 2 | Move | the mouse pointer to the First Line Indent marker on the horizontal ruler (see Figure 6-7) |

FIGURE 6-7
First Line Indent Marker

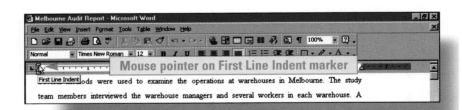

Step 3	Drag	the First Line Indent marker to the ½-inch position on the horizontal ruler
Step 4	Observe	that the first line of the paragraph is indented to the ½-inch position
Step 5	Continue	to indent the first line of each of the other five text paragraphs (turn on the formatting marks, if necessary, to see each paragraph mark)

QUICK TIP

By default Word uses a First Line Indent when you press the TAB key for a line of text that is already keyed in the document. You can turn this feature on or off in the Edit tab of the Options dialog box.

It's easier to find the beginning of each paragraph with the first line indented.

Setting a Hanging Indent

Certain paragraphs need a special kind of indent—a hanging indent, which leaves the first line at its original position and moves all the remaining lines to the right. Hanging indents are often used to create bulleted lists, numbered lists, and bibliographies. You can create a hanging indent with the Hanging Indent marker on the horizontal ruler. To create a hanging indent for the first paragraph:

Step 1	*Move*	the insertion point to the first paragraph
Step 2	*Move*	the mouse pointer to the Hanging Indent marker 🔺 on the horizontal ruler (see Figure 6-8)

FIGURE 6-8
Hanging Indent Marker

Step 3	*Drag*	the Hanging Indent marker to the 1-inch position
Step 4	*Observe*	that the first line remains at the ¾-inch position and the remaining lines of the paragraph move to the 1-inch position on the horizontal ruler

To undo the hanging indent:

Step 1	*Press*	the CTRL + Z keys to undo the hanging indent
Step 2	*Save*	the document and close it

Indents enable you to position text on the page exactly where you want it.

QUICK TIP

Don't forget that you can quickly reverse your previous action with the Undo button on the Standard toolbar or the CTRL + Z shortcut key combination.

chapter
six

Summary

▶ Paragraph formatting includes line spacing, vertical and horizontal text alignment, and indents.

▶ When applying paragraph formatting, you must select the paragraph or paragraphs to be formatted before you select the formatting option.

▶ You can select different line-spacing options such as Single, Double, and 1.5 from the Line spacing: list in the Paragraph dialog box.

▶ Text can be aligned vertically from the top margin, centered between the top and bottom margins, and justified between the top and bottom margins.

▶ Horizontal alignment is positioning text between the left and right margins. There are four horizontal alignment options: left, center, right, and justified.

▶ You can indent paragraphs from the left margin, the right margin, or both margins.

▶ Paragraphs can be indented with options in the Paragraph dialog box, buttons on the Formatting toolbar, and by dragging the indent markers on the horizontal ruler. Indentation options include First Line, Hanging, Left, and Right Indents.

Commands Review

Action	Menu Bar	Shortcut Menu	Toolbar	Keyboard
Change line spacing	F<u>o</u>rmat, <u>P</u>aragraph	Right-click selected paragraph(s), click <u>P</u>aragraph		ALT + O, P CTRL + 1 (single) CTRL + 2 (double) CTRL + 5 (1.5)
Change alignment	F<u>o</u>rmat, <u>P</u>aragraph	Right-click selected paragraph(s), click <u>P</u>aragraph	Align Left Center Align Right Justify	ALT + O, P CTRL + L (Left) CTRL + E (Center) CTRL + R (Right) CTRL + J (Justify)
Indent paragraphs	F<u>o</u>rmat, <u>P</u>aragraph	Right-click selected paragraph(s), click <u>P</u>aragraph	Drag the indent marker on the horizontal ruler	ALT + O, P CTRL + M (from Left) CTRL + T (Hanging)
Remove paragraph formatting				CTRL + Q
Review text formatting				SHIFT + F1

Concepts Review

Circle the correct answer.

1. The default line spacing is:
[a] Justified.
[b] Single.
[c] Double.
[d] Center.

2. To change the line spacing for multiple paragraphs, you must first:
[a] center the paragraphs.
[b] justify the paragraphs.
[c] select the paragraphs.
[d] apply bold formatting to the paragraphs.

3. The Justified vertical alignment option:
[a] aligns text with the top margin.
[b] centers text between the left and right margins.
[c] distributes text evenly between the top and bottom margins.
[d] centers text evenly between the top and bottom margins.

4. To format a document with even left and right margins, you should apply the:
[a] Center vertical alignment.
[b] Center horizontal alignment.
[c] Justify horizontal alignment.
[d] Justified vertical alignment.

5. You cannot indent selected paragraphs by:
[a] dragging an indent marker on the horizontal ruler.
[b] clicking the Increase Indent button.
[c] keying the indent position in the Paragraph dialog box.
[d] keying the indent position in the Font dialog box.

6. A hanging indent moves:
[a] all the lines of a paragraph to the right.
[b] all the lines of a paragraph to the left.
[c] only the top line.
[d] all lines except the top line.

7. Which of the following is not part of paragraph formatting?
[a] underlining
[b] indenting
[c] line spacing
[d] horizontal alignment

8. The Multiple line-spacing option sets the line spacing to:
[a] twice the single line spacing.
[b] double the single line spacing.
[c] 1.5 times the single line spacing.
[d] a percentage of the single line spacing.

9. Ragged margins are:
[a] even.
[b] centered.
[c] justified.
[d] uneven.

10. When document text aligns at the left margin and has a ragged right margin, the text is:
[a] center-aligned.
[b] left-aligned.
[c] right-aligned.
[d] justified.

Circle **T** if the statement is true or **F** is the statement is false.

T   F   1. The default horizontal alignment is left alignment.

T   F   2. You can set line spacing with the mouse and the horizontal and vertical ruler.

T   F   3. Word double-spaces your document unless you change the line spacing.

T   F   4. Justified alignment means that text is aligned only along the left margin.

T   F   5. You must press the TAB key to indent a paragraph.

T   F   6. A paragraph can be indented from the right margin.

T   F   7. You can add line-spacing buttons to the Formatting toolbar.

T   F   8. Line spacing means to specify the horizontal space between characters.

T   F   9. Vertical text alignment specifies where the text appears in relation to the top and bottom margins.

T   F   10. When applying paragraph formatting to an entire document, only the first paragraph must be selected.

notes   For the remainder of this text, when you open a letter or memo document from the Data Disk or key a new document from a figure, replace the text "Current date" with the actual date using the AutoComplete feature or the Date and <u>T</u>ime command on the <u>I</u>nsert menu.

Skills Review

Exercise 1

1. Open the *Expense Guidelines* document located on the Data Disk.

2. Set the appropriate margins for an unbound report.

3. Format the Expense Guidelines title to change the case to uppercase and apply bold, 14 point, centered alignment formats.

4. Justify the body paragraphs between the left and right margins.

5. Double-space the body paragraphs.

6. Save the document as *Expense Guidelines Revised*.

7. Preview, print, and close the document.

Exercise 2

1. Open the *Interoffice Training Memo* located on the Data Disk.

2. Change the margins to the appropriate margins for an interoffice memorandum.

3. Set a tab stop to line up the heading paragraphs.

4. Change the case of the To, From, Date, and Subject headings to uppercase.

5. Indent the two paragraphs beginning "Samantha" and "Steve" ½ inch from both the left and the right margins.

6. Save the document as *Interoffice Training Memo Revised*.

7. Preview, print, and close the document.

Exercise 3

1. Open the *District C Sales Decline* document located on the Data Disk.

2. Set a 2-inch top margin and 1.5-inch left and right margins.

3. Double-space and justify the entire document.

4. Single-space and center the stores paragraphs.

5. Save the document as *District C Sales Decline Revised*.

6. Preview, print, and close the document.

Exercise 4

1. Create the following document.

2. Use the default margins.

3. Right align the current date on the first line.

4. Center align the title four lines below the date and format it with bold, 14-point font.

5. Apply bold formatting to the NAME, ADDRESS, TELEPHONE NUMBER, AGE, and GENDER text.

6. Set left tab stops to position the AGE and GENDER text attractively.

7. Set center tab stops for the column titles to center them over the column text.

8. Set left tab stops for the column text to align the text evenly in columns.

9. Triple-space all the text except the text in columns using the Multiple line-spacing option.

10. Use the 1.5 line-spacing option for the columnar text.

11. Center the text vertically between the top and bottom margins.

12. Save the document as *Order Form*.

13. Preview, print, and close the document.

chapter six

Current date

ORDER FORM

Please fill out the information below using a ballpoint pen. Please print legibly.

NAME:

ADDRESS:

TELEPHONE NUMBER: **AGE:**   **GENDER:**

Please circle the items you wish to order:

Item	Size	Box	Color
12D345	3 pound	round	red
89C367	4 pound	square	green
44F890	6 pound	triangle	black
78B779	2 pound	circle	yellow

Exercise 5

1. Open the *Vancouver Draft* document located on the Data Disk.

2. Set margins for an unbound report.

3. Change the font for the entire document to Times New Roman, 12 point.

4. Center-align, bold, and format with Times New Roman 14-point font the title "Vancouver Warehouse Report."

5. Double-space the entire document.

6. Justify the body paragraphs between the left and right margins.

7. Apply the Small Caps effect and bold formatting to the paragraph heading "Audit Methods."

8. Copy the Small Caps effect and bold formatting to the "Problems," "Problem Analyses," and "Summation" paragraph headings.

9. Create a center-aligned bulleted list with the three paragraphs beginning "Poor Communication."

10. Single-space the bulleted list.

11. Right-align the current date on the second line below the body paragraphs.

12. Save the document as *Vancouver Draft Revised*.

13. Preview, print, and close the document.

Exercise 6

1. Open the *Vancouver Draft Revised* document you created in Exercise 5.

2. Select the entire document.

3. Press the CTRL + Q keys to remove the paragraph formatting.

4. Press the CTRL + SPACEBAR keys to remove the character formatting.

5. Save the document as *Vancouver Draft Without Formatting*.

6. Preview, print, and close the document.

Exercise 7

1. Open the *Policy #113* document located on the Data Disk.

2. Use the default margins.

3. Set the line spacing for the entire document to 4 times the single line spacing.

4. Center-align, apply 14-point Times New Roman font, and apply bold formatting to the text "DANGER! DANGER! DANGER!"

5. Center-align the "Authorized Personnel Only" paragraph.

6. Center-align and apply the All Caps and italic effect to the last line of text.

7. Vertically center the text on the page.

8. Save the document as *Policy #113 Revised*.

9. Preview, print, and close the document.

Exercise 8

1. Open the *Word Division* document located on the Data Disk.

2. Set margins for an unbound report.

3. Set the line spacing for the entire document to 1.5 lines.

4. Format the title "Word Division" with bold, 14-point font, and center align it.

5. Justify the body paragraphs horizontally.

6. Indent the first line of the body paragraphs ½ inch from the left margin using the First Line Indent marker on the horizontal ruler.

7. Create a numbered list with the three paragraphs beginning "A one-letter syllable" and ending with "the contraction doesn't." Right indent the numbered list paragraphs to the 5½-inch position on the horizontal ruler.

8. Save the document as *Word Division Revised*.

9. Preview, print, and close the document.

Exercise 9

1. Create the following document.

2. Set the appropriate margins.

3. Set the appropriate line spacing.

4. Use the appropriate horizontal and vertical alignment.

5. Indent the body paragraphs.

6. Format the title.

7. Save the document as *Investment Analysis*.

8. Preview, print, and close the document.

INVESTMENT ANALYSIS

This is an excellent time for you to take a close look at the income you are receiving from the tax-exempt bonds in your portfolio. When you bought the bonds, did you buy fixed income or lifetime maturation?

Essentially any person can earn funds today, but only an informed person will know how to correctly invest their extra money to gain utmost safety of principal and gain the greatest growth in investment appreciation.

To many investors, earnings are the most important part of their investment program. It is their maintenance income, their retirement plan, their self-insurance for children and grandchildren, as well as their trust for charities.

Current date

Case Projects

Project 1

Kelly Armstead asks you how to use different paragraph spacing options in the Paragraph dialog box and character spacing options in the Font dialog box. Using Word help features, review information on character and paragraph spacing. Create a new interoffice memorandum to Kelly, containing at least four paragraphs, that describes how to use the character and paragraph spacing options. Open an existing document and change the character and paragraph spacing. Save the document with a new name, and then preview and print it.

Project 2

B. D. Vickers believes you can purchase and print postage over the Internet. Connect to your ISP, launch your Web browser, and search the Web for pages containing information about purchasing and printing postage on the Web. Create a favorite or bookmark for the home page at each site you visit. Create an interoffice memorandum to B. D. Vickers describing how to purchase and print postage from pages on the Web. Save, preview, and print the document.

Project 3

One of the new employees in the purchasing department is having a problem creating evenly spaced lines in a document that contains large text characters on various lines. Using the Office Assistant, search for help topics on setting line spacing for this type of document. Create a new unbound report document containing a title and a numbered list of instructions on changing the line spacing to create evenly spaced lines with mixed-size characters. Save, preview, and print the document. With your instructor's permission, demonstrate these instructions to a classmate.

Project 4

Kelly asks you to prepare an interoffice memorandum to all purchasing department employees reminding them of the annual purchasing conference to be held in three weeks in Vancouver. Anyone who plans to attend the conference must contact her no later than next Thursday to arrange for someone to handle their responsibilities while they are at the conference. Use character, paragraph, and document formatting features to make the memo interesting to read and professional in appearance. Save, preview, and print the document.

Project 5

Kelly tells you that Word provides a special toolbar you can use to open your Web browser and load Web pages from inside Word. Connect to your ISP and view the Web toolbar using the toolbar shortcut menu. Use the Favorites button to display a Web page with information about purchasing and printing postage on the Web. Create an interoffice memorandum to Kelly describing how to view and use the Web toolbar. Save, preview, and print the document.

Project 6

Kelly wants you to create a one-page cover sheet for an audit report on the Melbourne branch that she is completing. She wants the title of the report to contain B. D. Vickers name and title and the current date triple spaced, in a 14-point font, and centered vertically and horizontally on the page. Create, save, preview, and print the cover sheet.

Project 7

Kelly asks you to present some troubleshooting tips on indenting text at the next meeting of the International Association of Executive Assistants. Using Word help features, review how to indent text. Create a new document containing a list of at least five indenting troubleshooting tips. Save, preview, and print the document. With your instructor's approval demonstrate these troubleshooting tips to several classmates.

Project 8

Rick Johns, a new employee in the purchasing department, asks for your help in setting line-spacing options in a document. Using Word help features, research how to set all the different line-spacing options. Create an interoffice memorandum to Rick containing a description of each of the line-spacing options and how to use them in a document. Include examples of each option in your document. Save, preview, and print the document.

chapter six

Previewing and Printing a Document

Chapter Overview

Previewing documents before printing them enables you to find errors you might otherwise not notice until you print. You can fix any problems you find right in Print Preview, whether they are text edits or formatting changes. In this chapter you learn how to edit a document in Print Preview and set print options.

LEARNING OBJECTIVES

► **Use Print Preview**
► **Print a document**

Case profile

Worldwide Exotic Foods requires all employees to preview their documents and make necessary changes before printing to prevent reprinting and keep costs down. Kelly Armstead needs your help in previewing, editing, and printing several documents previously created.

chapter seven

7.a Using Print Preview

Print Preview displays your document onscreen exactly as it will print on paper. When viewing a document in Print Preview, you can see one or more pages of your document. Headers, footers, margins, page numbers, text, and graphics can also be seen in Print Preview.

The first document Kelly asks you to finalize and print is an *Analysis Report*. To open and preview a document:

Step 1	*Open*	the *Analysis Report* document located on the Data Disk
Step 2	*Verify*	the insertion point is at the top of the document
Step 3	*Click*	the Print Preview button on the Standard toolbar
Step 4	*Click*	the One Page button on the Print Preview toolbar to view only the first page of the document, if necessary

The first page of the *Analysis Report* document appears in Print Preview. Your screen should look similar to Figure 7-1.

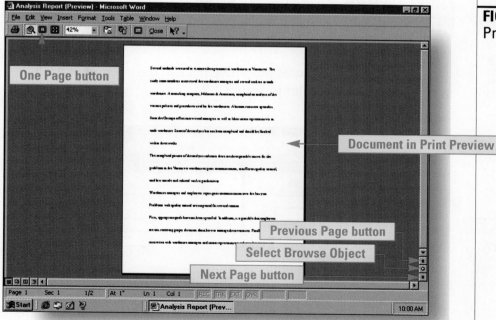

FIGURE 7-1
Print Preview

When viewing only one page of a multiple-page document, you can use the vertical scroll bar or the Previous Page or Next Page buttons located below the vertical scroll bar to scroll among the pages.

You view the second page of the *Analysis Report* document.

C

MENU TIP

You can click the Print Pre̲view command on the F̲ile menu to see how your document looks before it is printed.

chapter
seven

QUICK TIP

The Next and Previous buttons are controlled by the options in the Select Browse Object button. The default option is Page. When the Page option is selected in the Select Browse Object grid, the Next and Previous buttons have black arrows and are used to browse by page in all editing views including Print Preview. When a different option is selected in the Select Browse Object grid, the Next and Previous buttons have blue arrows and become the Next and Previous browse buttons for the option selected in the Select Browse Object grid. To reset the buttons to Next and Previous Page, click the Select Browse Object button and then click Page on the grid.

| Step 5 | *Click* | the Next Page button [icon] below the vertical scroll bar to view page two |
| Step 6 | *Click* | the Previous Page button [icon] below the vertical scroll bar to view the first page again |

The One Page button on the Print Preview toolbar displays a single page at a time. You can use the Multiple Pages button on the Print Preview toolbar to view two or more small, thumbnail-sized pages at one time. When you view several thumbnail-sized pages at one time you can compare how the text appears on subsequent pages and where the page breaks occur. To view both pages of the *Analysis Report* document side by side:

Step 1	*Click*	the Multiple Pages button [icon] on the Print Preview toolbar to view the Multiple Pages grid
Step 2	*Point to*	the second square in the top row of the grid
Step 3	*Observe*	the 1×2 Pages notation at the bottom of the grid
Step 4	*Click*	the second square in the top row
Step 5	*Observe*	both pages of the document display side by side
Step 6	*Observe*	the dark blue border around the first page

The dark border indicates the active page of the document. Your screen should look similar to Figure 7-2.

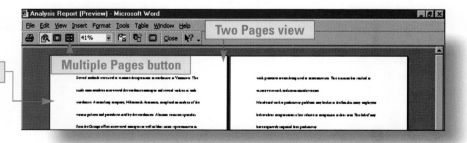

Active Page

FIGURE 7-2
Two Pages View

You can zoom or edit individual pages when viewing more than one page by first making a page the active page. To activate a page, simply click it with the mouse pointer.

| Step 7 | *Click* | page two |
| Step 8 | *Click* | page one |

Not only can you see how your document looks before you print it, you can also edit your document in Print Preview. You can key text, apply formatting, set tab stops and paragraph indents, and change margins in Print Preview. For easier viewing, you can magnify, or zoom, a portion of the document with the magnifying pointer or the Zoom button on the Print Preview toolbar.

The **Magnifier** button on the Print Preview toolbar is a toggle switch that turns on or off the zoom pointer. By default, the Magnifier button and the zoom pointer are turned on when you Print Preview a document. When the Magnifier button is turned on and the mouse pointer is positioned on a selected page, it changes into the zoom pointer. If multiple pages are displayed, you should first select a page by clicking it and then position the mouse pointer on it.

To view just single pages and zoom the first page:

Step 1	*Click*	the One Page button 🔲 on the Print Preview toolbar
Step 2	*Move*	the mouse pointer to the beginning of the first paragraph on the page
Step 3	*Observe*	that the mouse pointer changes into a zoom pointer (a magnifying glass with a plus sign in the middle)

Your screen should look similar to Figure 7-3.

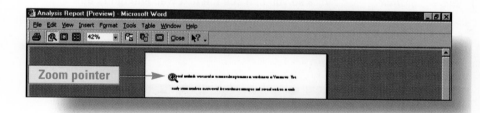

FIGURE 7-3
Zoom Pointer

Step 4	*Click*	the paragraph with the zoom pointer
Step 5	*Observe*	that the document is zoomed to 100% and you are viewing the portion of the first paragraph you clicked
Step 6	*Observe*	that the mouse pointer is still the zoom pointer (a magnifying glass with a minus sign in the middle)
Step 7	*Click*	the document with the zoom pointer

The document is zoomed to one page. You need to change the margins for the *Analysis Report* document. Because you are already viewing the document in Print Preview, you decide to do make the change here. The same formatting features that are available in Normal or Print Layout view are available in Print Preview. For example, you can open the Page

QUICK TIP

You can select and view individual pages of a multiple-page document by pressing the PAGE UP or PAGE DOWN keys. You can show additional toolbars in Print Preview with the toolbar shortcut menu or you can customize the Print Preview toolbar by clicking the More Buttons list arrow and then pointing to Add or Remove Buttons.

You can close the Print Preview of the current document with the taskbar shortcut menu. This does not close the document. It returns you to previous Normal or Print Layout view.

chapter
seven

Setup dialog box from the <u>F</u>ile menu in Print Preview just as you can in Normal or Print Layout view. To set the margins for an unbound report:

Step 1	*Open*	the Page Setup dialog box and click the <u>M</u>argins tab, if necessary
Step 2	*Set*	the appropriate margins for an unbound report
Step 3	*Observe*	the new margins

To key or format selected text in Print Preview, you must first have an insertion point and an I-beam. When you turn off the Magnifier button, the insertion point appears and the mouse pointer becomes an I-beam when you position it over the document. To see the insertion point and the I-beam:

Step 1	*Click*	the Magnifier button 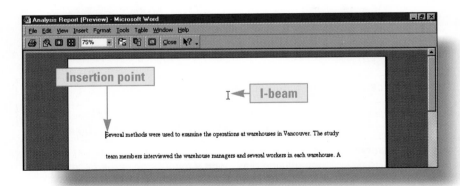 on the Print Preview toolbar to turn off the zoom pointer
Step 2	*Move*	the mouse pointer to the top of the page
Step 3	*Observe*	the mouse pointer is now an I-beam and you can see the small, flashing insertion point at the top of the document
Step 4	*Click*	the Zoom button list arrow on the Print Preview toolbar
Step 5	*Click*	75% so you can see the text well enough to edit it

Your screen should look similar to Figure 7-4.

FIGURE 7-4
Document Zoomed to 75%

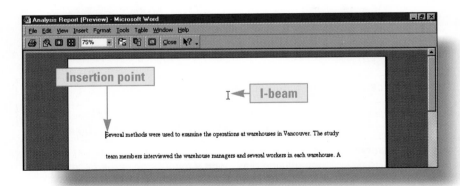

Now you can see the text and the insertion point more easily. You want to indent the first line of all the paragraphs. You can show the horizontal and vertical rulers in Print Preview and then indent individual paragraphs or you can select the entire document, open the Paragraph dialog box, and indent all the paragraphs at the same time.

To indent the first line of each paragraph ½ inch from the left margin:

Step 1	**Select**	the entire document
Step 2	**Open**	the Indents and Spacing tab in the Paragraph dialog box
Step 3	**Click**	the Special: list arrow
Step 4	**Click**	First line
Step 5	**Key**	.5 in the By: text box, if necessary
Step 6	**Click**	OK
Step 7	**Deselect**	the text
Step 8	**Click**	the Zoom button list arrow on the Print Preview toolbar
Step 9	**Click**	Two Pages
Step 10	**Observe**	the indented paragraphs
Step 11	**Zoom**	the first page to 75%

You believe the *Analysis Report* document should have a title. You can key and format that title when the Magnifier button is turned off and you see the insertion point and the I-beam. To key and format a title:

Step 1	**Insert**	a blank line at the top of the first page
Step 2	**Move**	the insertion point to the new blank line
Step 3	**Key**	the title Analysis Report
Step 4	**Select**	the title text using the I-beam
Step 5	**Format**	the title text with Bold using a shortcut menu and the Font dialog box
Step 6	**Center**	the title text using a shortcut menu and the Paragraph dialog box
Step 7	**Zoom**	the first page to One Page (See Figure 7-5)

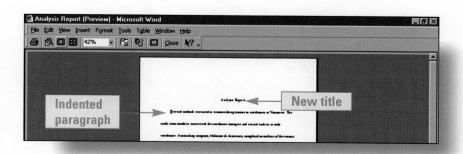

FIGURE 7-5
New Title and
Indented Paragraphs

chapter
seven

Step 8	*Click*	the Close button Close on the Print Preview toolbar
Step 9	*Save*	the document as *Revised Analysis Report*

The document looks good with the correct margins, paragraph indentation, and title. Now you're ready to print it.

 ## 7.b Printing A Document

After you correct the margins and paragraph indentations, you are ready to print the document. However, before you print it, you might need to change the paper size, paper orientation, or paper source. The Page Setup dialog box provides options for you to change the paper size, paper orientation, and the paper source before you print a document. Word provides a list of common paper sizes from which to choose, including Letter 8½ × 11 in; Legal 8½ × 14 in, and Envelope #10 4⅛ × 9½ in. You can also choose a paper **orientation** (the direction text is printed on the paper): Portrait or Landscape. **Portrait orientation** means that the short edge of the paper is the top of the page. **Landscape orientation** means that the long edge of the paper is the top of the page. To review the current settings in the Page Setup dialog box:

Step 1	*Open*	the Page Setup dialog box
Step 2	*Click*	the Paper Size tab

The dialog box on your screen should look similar to Figure 7-6.

FIGURE 7-6
Paper Size Tab in the Page
Setup Dialog Box

The Paper size: list box provides a list of pre-set paper sizes. You can also select a Custom size from the list and then specify the paper dimensions in the Width: and Height: text boxes. By default, the paper size is Letter (8½ × 11 in) and the orientation is Portrait. You can change the orientation by clicking the appropriate option button. By default, the paper size and orientation settings apply to the whole document. You can change this option with the Apply to: list. As you change the options, the Preview area shows a sample of the document. After you review the options, you can close the dialog box without making changes.

| Step 3 | *Click* | Cancel |

Printing is usually your final activity in document creation. You can print a document by clicking the Print button on the Print Preview toolbar or the Standard toolbar. However, when you click the Print button, you do not get an opportunity to change the print options in the Print dialog box.

The Print command on the File menu opens the Print dialog box, which contains options and print settings you can modify before printing a document. To set the print options for the *Revised Analysis Report*:

| Step 1 | *Click* | File |
| Step 2 | *Click* | Print |

The dialog box on your screen should look similar to Figure 7-7.

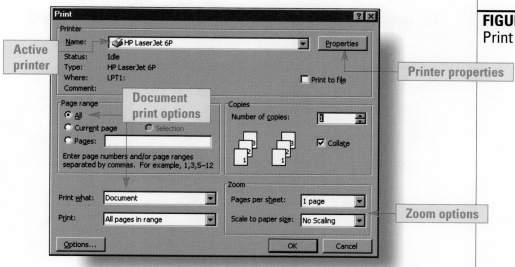

FIGURE 7-7
Print Dialog Box

> **CAUTION TIP**
>
> If the requested theme is not available, you can install themes using Office 2000 CDROM or substitute a different theme.

chapter
seven

The active printer is identified in the Name: list box. You can select from a list of available printers by clicking the list arrow and clicking the printer you want to use.

By default, Word prints one copy of your entire document. The Print what: list box provides a list of items you can print other than your document. For example, to print a list of AutoText entries stored in the Normal template, select AutoText entries from this list.

You can specify the number of copies to print in the Number of copies: text box. The Page range group contains options for printing All pages, the Current page that contains the insertion point, the Selection of highlighted text, or the Pages you specify by page number. The Print: list box allows you to print only odd or even pages in a selected page range. By default, Word **collates** or orders copies of a multiple-page document in binding order as it prints. You can turn off the collating option by removing the check mark from the Collate check box.

Printing your document to a file is helpful if you want to print on a higher-quality printer at a different location or on a computer that does not have the Word program. You can print your document to a file on a disk, rather than send it to a printer, by inserting a check mark in the Print to file check box.

Text can be scaled to fit multiple pages on one sheet of paper or scaled to fit to various paper sizes in the Zoom group. Use this feature to scale larger documents to fit smaller paper or print several miniature document pages on one sheet of paper.

| Step 3 | *Click* | Print to print the document |
| Step 4 | *Save* | the document and close it |

The printed *Revised Analysis Report* is ready to be duplicated and distributed to the Worldwide Exotic Foods branch managers.

Summary

► In order to avoid printing a document that contains errors—which can waste time and money—it is a good practice to preview your document before you print it.

► You can view one page or multiple pages of your document in Print Preview.

► Print Preview enables you to view headers, footers, margins, page numbers, text, and graphics.

► You can edit a document by keying text, applying formatting, setting tab stops, indenting paragraphs, and changing margins in Print Preview.

► You can turn off the Magnifier button in Print Preview and then key and edit text in the document.

► In Print Preview, you can zoom in for a closer view of a document either by turning on the Magnifier button and clicking the document with the mouse pointer or by using the Zoom button on the Print Preview toolbar.

► Before you print your document, you can set print and page setup options in the Print and Page Setup dialog boxes.

► The Print button on the Print Preview or Standard toolbars prints the document without allowing you to review the settings in the Print dialog box. The Print command on the File menu allows you to open the Print dialog box and confirm or change print options before you print a document.

Commands Review

Action	Menu Bar	Shortcut Menu	Toolbar	Keyboard
Preview a document	File, Print Preview			ALT + F, V CTRL + F2
View multiple pages in Print Preview				
View one page in Print Preview				
Magnify a document in Print Preview				
Print a document	File, Print			ALT + F, P CTRL + SHIFT + F12 CTRL + P

chapter seven

Concepts Review

Circle the correct answer.

1. By default, Print Preview displays your document:
[a] in two pages.
[b] in multiple pages.
[c] exactly as it will print on paper.
[d] in Landscape orientation.

2. The Magnifier button:
[a] scrolls to a new page.
[b] shows the horizontal and vertical rulers.
[c] shows two pages side by side.
[d] allows you to zoom your document with the mouse pointer.

3. You set the default print orientation in the:
[a] printer Properties dialog box.
[b] Page Setup dialog box.
[c] Page Layout dialog box.
[d] Options dialog box.

4. The default paper size and orientation is:
[a] 11 × 18 inch, Portrait.
[b] 8½ × 12 inch, Landscape.
[c] 8½ × 11 inch, Portrait.
[d] A4, Portrait.

5. To key or format selected text in Print Preview, you must use the:
[a] zoom pointer.
[b] horizontal ruler.
[c] I-beam.
[d] Magnifier button.

6. When Word automatically collates a printed document it:
[a] saves the document to a file.
[b] prints AutoText entries.
[c] prints copies of multiple-page documents in binding order.
[d] scales larger documents to fit on smaller paper.

7. The actions of the Next and Previous buttons in Print Preview are controlled by the:
[a] vertical scroll bar.
[b] Magnifier button.
[c] Zoom button.
[d] Select Browse Object button.

8. You can key text in your document in Print Preview by first:
[a] minimizing the window.
[b] viewing multiple pages.
[c] zooming the document.
[d] turning off the Magnifier button.

9. You can view and change print options by clicking the:
[a] Printer command on the File menu.
[b] Options command on the Tools menu.
[c] Print Options command on the Print Preview menu.
[d] Set Print Options button in the Print dialog box.

10. Which of the following options is not available in the Print dialog box?
[a] Print to file
[b] Collate copies
[c] Set the paper orientation
[d] Print selected text

Circle **T** if the statement is true or **F** if the statement is false.

T   F   1. To print only the page containing the insertion point, you should select the <u>A</u>ll option in the Print dialog box.

T   F   2. To print the entire document that you are currently editing, you should select the Curre<u>n</u>t Page option in the Print dialog box.

T   F   3. If you key 1-4 in the Pages text box in the Print dialog box, Word prints only pages 1 and 4 of the document.

T   F   4. The Letter (8½ × 11 in) paper size is the default paper size.

T   F   5. It is not possible to print only odd or even pages.

T   F   6. You can change margins, tab stops, or paragraph indents in Print Preview.

T   F   7. The Print button on the Print Preview toolbar opens the Print dialog box.

T   F   8. You can scale text to fit multiple pages on one sheet of paper.

T   F   9. You can view additional toolbars in Print Preview.

T   F   10. It is possible to print a document in reverse page number order.

Skills Review

Exercise 1

1. Open the *Vancouver Warehouse Report* document located on the Data Disk.

2. Print Preview the document.

3. Print only page 2 and close the document.

Exercise 2

1. Open the *Analysis Report* document located on the Data Disk.

2. Print the entire document using the Print button on the Standard toolbar in Normal view and close the document.

Exercise 3

1. Open the *Interoffice Meeting Memo* document located on the Data Disk.

2. Print Preview the document.

3. Apply bold formatting to the meeting day and time in the first paragraph in Print Preview.

4. Save the document as *Interoffice Meeting Memo Edited*.

5. Print the document from Print Preview and close the document.

Exercise 4

1. Open the *New Expense Guidelines* document located on the Data Disk.

2. Print Preview the document.

chapter seven

3. Format the title with the Arial, 16-point font in Print Preview and leave the insertion point in the title paragraph.

4. Save the document as *New Expense Guidelines Revised*.

5. Print only the current page from Print Preview and close the document.

Exercise 5 C

1. Open the *Research Results* document located on the Data Disk.

2. Print Preview the document.

3. Change the top margin to 2 inches and the left and right margins to 1 inch in Print Preview.

4. Create numbered paragraphs with the last two single spaced paragraphs in Print Preview.

5. Indent the numbered paragraphs ½ inch from the right margin in Print Preview.

6. Horizontally justify all the paragraphs in the document.

7. Save the document as *Research Results Revised*.

8. Print the document from Print Preview and close the document.

Exercise 6 C

1. Open the *Understanding The Internet* document located on the Data Disk.

2. Print pages 1 and 3 in Normal view and close the document.

Exercise 7 C

1. Open the *Understanding The Internet* document located on the Data Disk.

2. Print Preview the document.

3. View the document in multiple pages with 4 pages on 2 rows.

4. Remove the bold, italic formatting and apply bold, Small Caps effect to the side (paragraph) headings in Print Preview. (*Hint:* After selecting and formatting the first bold, italic paragraph heading, use the CTRL + Y shortcut keys to copy the formatting to the other bold, italic paragraph headings.)

5. Save the document as *The Internet And The Web*.

6. Print pages 2, 4, and 6 in Normal view.

7. Use the Zoom options in the Print dialog box to print the entire document two pages per sheet of paper and close the document.

Exercise 8 C

1. Create the following document.

2. Use the default margins and set the appropriate tab stops for the memo headings.

3. Print Preview the document.

4. Change the margins to the appropriate margins for an interoffice memorandum in Print Preview.

5. Change the font for the entire document to Arial, 12 point in Print Preview.

TO: Marketing Department

FROM: J. D. Collins

DATE: Current date

SUBJECT: Holiday Gift Baskets

There will a meeting on Tuesday, October 2 at 1:00 p.m. to discuss how to introduce our line of holiday gift baskets. Please bring any ideals you have to the meeting.

ke

6. bold formatting to the memo heading text TO, FROM, DATE, and SUBJECT (do not include the colon) in Print Preview.

7. Save the document as *Holiday Gift Baskets.*

8. Print the document from Print Preview and close the document.

Case Projects

SCANS

Project 1

Kelly wants you to review setting different print options and then create a memo to all summer interns describing the print options and how to set them. Using the Word Help tools, review setting print options. Create a new interoffice memorandum to all summer interns, containing at least three paragraphs, that describes how to use at least three print options. Save, preview, and print the document.

Project 2

Dale Metcalf, a purchasing agent, asks you how to view and change the properties for his printer, which is the same model as your printer. Open the Print dialog box and review the Properties for your printer. Create an unbound report document containing at least four paragraphs describing the properties that are set for your printer. Save, preview, and print the document. With your instructor's permission, use the unbound report document as a guide to demonstrate viewing and changing printer properties to one of your classmates.

chapter seven

Project 3

You recently read an article in the company newsletter describing Internet newsgroups (online discussion groups) and would like to know more about how to participate in them. Connect to your ISP, launch your Web browser, and search for Web pages containing information on newsgroups. Save at least two Web pages as favorites or bookmarks. Print at least two Web pages. Create an unbound report, containing at least five paragraphs, that describes newsgroups and how to subscribe to them. Use vertical and horizontal alignment, line spacing, and indentation options to give the report a professional appearance. Save, preview, and print the report.

Project 4

B. D. Vickers needs to purchase several new laser printers for Worldwide Exotic Foods and wants to review which models are currently available. He asks you to use the Web to prepare a list of printers, their features, and cost. Connect to your ISP, launch your Web browser, and search for Web pages for vendors who sell laser printers. Gather printer information on at least three different vendors. Create an interoffice memorandum to B. D. Vickers discussing the results of your research. Save, preview, and print the memo.

Project 5

You are having lunch with Bob Garcia, the new administrative assistant, and he describes several problems he has when printing documents. He frequently gets a blank page at the end of his documents, sometimes the text runs off the edge of the page, he gets a "too many fonts" error when he prints a document, and occasionally the printed text he prints looks different from the text on the screen. You offer to look into the problems and get back to him. Using the Office Assistant, search for troubleshooting tips for printing

documents and find suggested solutions to Bob's problems. Write Bob a memo describing each problem and suggesting a solution to the problem. Save, preview, and print the memo.

Project 6

Kelly wants a document she can use to train new employees how to set print options. She also wants to train the new employees to use the Zoom options in the Print dialog box. Open the Options dialog box and click the Print tab. Using the dialog box Help button, review each of the print options. Open the Print dialog box and review the Zoom options. Create an unbound report document titled "Print Options" and describe each of the options on the Print tab and the Print Zoom feature. Save, preview, and print the document. Attach a sample of a two-page document printed on one sheet of paper using the Zoom options.

Project 7

You just purchased a new printer, but do not know how to set up it up and define it as your default printer. Using online Help , research how to set up a new printer and define it as the default printer. Write Kelly Armstead a memo discussing the process. Save, preview, and print the memo.

Project 8

The Melbourne branch office manager is ill and B. D. Vickers wants to send flowers using a shop that accepts orders on the Web but isn't certain how to do this. Connect to your ISP, launch your Web browser, and search for Web pages with information about ordering and paying for flowers for international delivery to Melbourne, Australia. Print at least three Web pages. Create a memo to B. D. Vickers describing how to order and pay for flowers on the Web. Save, preview, and print the memo. Attach the Web pages you print to the memo.

Preparing and Printing Envelopes and Labels

Chapter Overview

E very business depends on its correspondence. Letters and packages need to be sent daily. Each needs an envelope or mailing label before it can be mailed. In this chapter you create, format, and print envelopes and labels.

LEARNING OBJECTIVES

► **Prepare and print envelopes**
► **Prepare and print labels**

Case profile

Kelly Armstead asks you to print envelopes and mailing labels. Worldwide Exotic Foods uses the U. S. Postal Service (USPS) guidelines for envelopes and mailing labels that do not have a corresponding letter. Envelopes and labels that do have a corresponding letter follow the punctuation and case of the letter address. You create an envelope that does not have a corresponding letter, an envelope for an existing letter, an envelope and label from a list of addresses, and a sheet of return address labels for B. D. Vickers.

chapter eight

notes Before you begin the activities in this chapter, you should review Appendix C, Formatting Tips for Business Documents, if you have not already done so.

C 8.a Preparing and Printing Envelopes

Printing addresses on envelopes is a word processing task that almost everyone must perform at one time or another. Envelopes do not use the standard 8½ × 11 inch paper on which you normally print letters and reports. A standard Size 10 business envelope is 4⅛ × 9½ inches, and a standard short Size 6¾ envelope is 3⅝ × 6½ inches. You can create envelopes by opening an existing letter and letting Word identify the letter address as the envelope delivery address, or you can key the envelope delivery address in a blank document.

notes Because different printers have varying setup requirements for envelopes and labels, your instructor may provide additional printing instructions for the activities in this chapter.

Kelly needs an envelope for which there is no corresponding letter. She gives you a copy of the U. S. Postal Service (USPS) guidelines for envelopes and mailing labels to review before you begin (see Appendix C). The USPS delivery address guidelines require a sans serif font, uppercase characters, and no punctuation except for the hyphen in the ZIP + 4 code. Worldwide Exotic Foods uses the USPS guidelines for envelopes and labels that do not have a corresponding letter.

You can create an individual envelope by first creating a blank document. To create an envelope from a blank document:

Step 1	*Create*	a new, blank document, if necessary
Step 2	*Click*	Tools
Step 3	*Click*	Envelopes and Labels
Step 4	*Click*	the Envelopes tab, if necessary

The dialog box you see on your screen should look similar to Figure 8-1.

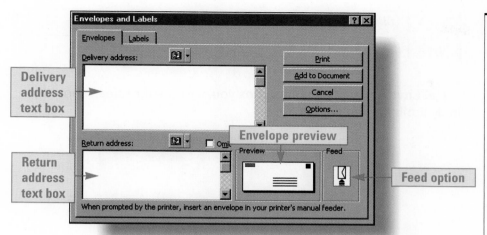

FIGURE 8-1
Envelopes and Labels
Dialog Box

You key the delivery address in the <u>D</u>elivery address: text box. You can edit or key the return address in the <u>R</u>eturn address: text box, which contains information from the User Information tab in the <u>O</u>ptions dialog box. If you are using envelopes with a preprinted return address, you can omit printing the return address by inserting a check mark in the O<u>m</u>it check box. The Feed image illustrates how to insert envelopes in the current printer. You click the <u>O</u>ptions button to change envelope size, select manual or tray feed for blank envelopes, change the feed position, print the Delivery point <u>b</u>arcode, or add character formatting to the address text. You send the envelope directly to the printer with the <u>P</u>rint button. The <u>A</u>dd to Document button attaches the envelope to the current document for saving and printing with the document.

A **style** is a group of formatting attributes saved with a unique name. Word automatically formats the text you key in the <u>D</u>elivery address: text box with the Envelope Address style and the return address with the Envelope Return style. The Envelope Address style contains the sans serif Arial font with a 12-point font size. Next, you key the delivery address using the USPS guidelines. To key the envelope text:

Q UICK   TIP

You can change the font of the delivery or return address in the Envelopes and Labels dialog box by selecting the text and then opening the Font dialog box with a shortcut menu.

| Step 1 | *Verify* | the insertion point is in the <u>D</u>elivery address: text box |

| Step 2 | *Key* | MS ELAINE CHANG
719 EAST 35TH STREET
ST PAUL MN 55117-1179 |

Because Worldwide Exotic Foods uses preprinted envelopes for all correspondence, you omit the return address. Then you select the envelope size.

| Step 3 | *Click* | the O<u>m</u>it check box to insert a check mark, if necessary |

chapter
eight

Step 4	*Click*	Options
Step 5	*Click*	the Envelope Options tab, if necessary

The Envelope Options dialog box you see on your screen should look similar to Figure 8-2.

FIGURE 8-2
Envelope Options
Dialog Box

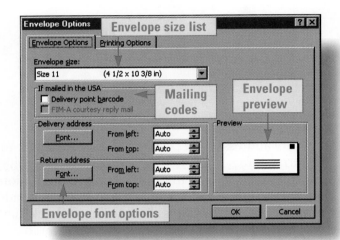

You can select the envelope size in the Envelope size: list box. Options for using the Facing Identification Mark (FIM-A) and Delivery point barcode to speed mail delivery are in the If mailed in the USA group. For a more detailed explanation of these two codes, see online Help. You can also change the font and position of the envelope addresses. To change the envelope size:

Step 6	*Click*	the Envelope size: list arrow
Step 7	*Click*	Size 6¾ (3⅝ × 6½ in), if necessary
Step 8	*Observe*	that the sample envelope now displays the 6¾ size

You also set printing options in this dialog box. The current options are set for your printer. However, if necessary, you can specify envelope rotation, face up or down, and manual or tray feed in this tab. You accept the current printing options and envelope size. To review print options:

Step 1	*Click*	the Printing Options tab
Step 2	*Observe*	the different Feed method options
Step 3	*Click*	OK

In order to print the envelope, you may have to manually feed a blank envelope or blank sheet of paper in your printer. If your instructor tells you to print the envelope, follow your printer's envelope setup instructions and print the envelope by clicking the Print button in the Envelopes and Labels dialog box. Otherwise you cancel the Chang envelope by closing the Envelopes and Labels dialog box. To close the dialog box:

Step 1	*Click*	Close

Another way to create an envelope is to open a document that contains a list of frequently used delivery addresses, move the insertion point to one of the addresses, and open the Envelopes and Labels dialog box. Word enters the delivery address for you. Kelly maintains a list of delivery addresses for members of the International Association of Executive Assistants and asks you to create an envelope from this list. To open the address list document and create an envelope:

Step 1	*Open*	the *Envelope And Label List* document located on the Data Disk
Step 2	*Move*	the insertion point to the address for Elaine Fitzsimmons (scroll to view this address)
Step 3	*Click*	Tools
Step 4	*Click*	Envelopes and Labels
Step 5	*Click*	the Envelopes tab, if necessary

The Envelopes tab in the Envelopes and Labels dialog box opens with Elaine Fitzsimmons address in the Delivery address: list box. Unless instructed to print the Fitzsimmons envelope by your instructor, you cancel it by canceling the dialog box.

Step 6	*Click*	Cancel
Step 7	*Close*	the document without saving any changes

When you open an existing letter and then open the Envelopes and Labels dialog box, Word automatically selects the letter address exactly as it appears in the document and places it in the Delivery address: text box. When creating an envelope for an existing letter, Worldwide Exotic Foods uses the letter address punctuation and case in the envelope delivery address. B. D. Vickers' letter to Ms. Neva Johnson needs an envelope.

chapter eight

To create and format an envelope for an existing letter:

Step 1	*Open*	the *Johnson Letter* located on the Data Disk
Step 2	*Open*	the Envelopes tab in the Envelopes and Labels dialog box
Step 3	*Observe*	the letter address is automatically placed in the Delivery address: text box

You modify the return address text for B. D. Vickers, and select the envelope size and options.

Step 4	*Click*	the Omit check box to remove the check mark, if necessary
Step 5	*Select*	the all text in the Return address: text box or move the insertion point to the text box if it is blank
Step 6	*Key*	B. D. Vickers Administrative Vice President Worldwide Exotic Foods, Inc. Gage Building, Suite 2100 Riverside Plaza Chicago, IL 60606-2000
Step 7	*Click*	Options and click the Envelope Options tab, if necessary
Step 8	*Click*	the Envelope size: list arrow
Step 9	*Click*	Size 6¾ (3⅝ × 6½ in), if necessary
Step 10	*Observe*	the envelope preview
Step 11	*Click*	OK

Often you want to add an envelope to the letter document so that you edit or print both the letter and the envelope at the same time. To add the envelope to the letter:

Step 1	*Click*	Add to Document

A confirmation dialog box opens asking if you want to save the new return address as the default return address for all future envelopes. If you click the Yes button, Word adds the return address information to the User Information tab in the Tools, Options dialog box. You do *not* want to change the default return address.

Step 2	*Click*	No

The envelope is added as Page 0 at the top of the document with a section break separating the envelope from the document. **Section breaks** divide your document into differently formatted parts. You can view and edit both the envelope and the letter in Print Layout view. To view the envelope in Print Layout view:

| Step 1 | *Verify* | the insertion point is in the envelope text |
| Step 2 | *Switch* | to Print Layout view |

Your screen should look similar to Figure 8-3.

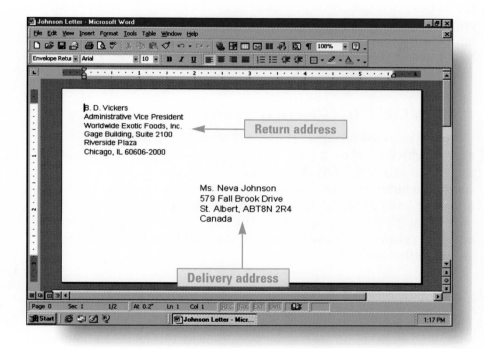

FIGURE 8-3
Envelope in Print Layout View

> **QUICK TIP**
>
> If necessary, you can reposition the delivery address from Print Layout view by moving the frame that Word inserts around the address. A **frame** is a box added to text, graphics, or charts that you drag to reposition these items on a page. To view the frame, move the insertion point into the delivery address. You reposition the delivery address on the envelope by dragging and then deselecting the frame.

| Step 3 | *Scroll* | to view both the envelope and the letter and then scroll to view just the envelope |
| Step 4 | *Save* | the document as *Johnson Letter With Envelope* and close it |

Kelly also wants you to create a mailing label for an oversized envelope and a sheet of return address labels for B. D. Vickers.

chapter
eight

8.b Preparing and Printing Labels

You can create many different types of labels in many different sizes, such as mailing labels, name tags, file folder labels, and computer diskette labels, with the Envelopes and Labels command on the Tools menu. There are labels for dot matrix printers and laser printers. Dot matrix printers use labels that pass through the printer by tractor feed. Laser and ink jet printers use labels on sheets that enter the printer through the sheet feeder. If you are using a laser printer, be sure to buy labels designed specifically for laser printers. Using labels made for a copier in a laser printer may damage your printer. Word has built-in label formats for most types of Avery labels. If you are not using Avery labels, you can specify a similar Avery label format, or you can create a custom label format.

Printing Individual Labels

When you need just one label, you create it and then specify exactly which label on a sheet of labels to use by setting options in the Labels tab of the Envelopes and Labels dialog box. Kelly is sending a large, oversized envelope to one of the contacts on the *Envelope and Label List* document. She asks you to create an individual label for the envelope. The label you use is in the first row and first column on a sheet of Avery 5160-Address labels. To create an individual label:

Step 1	*Open*	the *Envelope And Label List* document located on the Data Disk
Step 2	*Move*	the insertion point to the address for Debbie Gonzales
Step 3	*Open*	the Envelopes and Labels dialog box
Step 4	*Click*	the Labels tab
Step 5	*Observe*	the address is inserted in the Address: text box

The default option is to print a full page of the same label. If you want to print a single label from a sheet of labels, you must specify the exact row and column position of the label. You can print a label that includes the return address in the User Information tab of the Options dialog box by inserting a check mark in the Use return address check box. As with envelopes, clicking the <u>O</u>ptions button enables you to select a label format or printer. Now you specify the label size and position.

Step 6	*Click*	the Si<u>n</u>gle label option button
Step 7	*Verify*	the Ro<u>w</u>: and <u>C</u>olumn: text boxes contain 1 to specify the label prints in the first row and first column of the label sheet
Step 8	*Click*	<u>O</u>ptions

The Label Options dialog box on your screen should look similar to Figure 8-4.

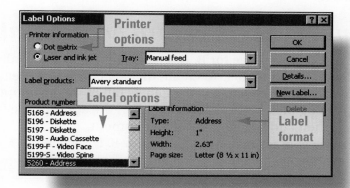

FIGURE 8-4
Label Options Dialog Box

The Printer information group contains options for selecting a Dot <u>m</u>atrix or <u>L</u>aser and ink jet printer as well as <u>T</u>ray options. You use the Label <u>p</u>roducts: list box to select an Avery or other label product list. The Product n<u>u</u>mber: list box contains the list of label products by product number. The Label information group contains a description of the label format for the label selected in the Product n<u>u</u>mber: list box. Use the <u>D</u>etails button to display margins, height, and width for the selected label. You can also change the **pitch** (space between the labels) and the number of labels in each row or column with the <u>D</u>etails button. Use the <u>N</u>ew Label button to create and save custom labels. When you save a new custom label, it is added to the Product n<u>u</u>mber: list.

Step 9	*Click*	5160 – Address in the Product n<u>u</u>mber: list box (scroll to view this option)

chapter
eight

| Step 10 | *Observe* | that the label type, height, and width appear in the Label information group |
| Step 11 | *Click* | OK |

You are ready to print the label, if instructed to do so. Otherwise, cancel the Gonzales label by canceling the dialog box.

| Step 12 | *Click* | Cancel |
| Step 13 | *Close* | the document without saving any changes |

Now you create a sheet of return address labels for B. D. Vickers that Kelly requested.

Printing a Sheet of Return Address Labels

The label product you use for B. D. Vickers return address labels is the Avery 5260-Address label. To create the labels you first create a new, blank document, then open the Labels tab in the Envelopes and Labels dialog box. Key the address, select the appropriate label options, and then add the labels to the document.

To create a sheet of return address labels for B. D. Vickers:

Step 1	*Create*	a new, blank document, if necessary
Step 2	*Open*	the Labels tab in the Envelopes and Labels dialog box
Step 3	*Verify*	the insertion point is in the Address: text box
Step 4	*Key*	B. D. Vickers Administrative Vice President Worldwide Exotic Foods, Inc. Gage Building, Suite 2100 Chicago, IL 60606-2000
Step 5	*Verify*	the Full page of the same label option is selected
Step 6	*Click*	Options
Step 7	*Click*	5260 - Address in the Product number: list box (scroll to view this option)
Step 8	*Click*	OK
Step 9	*Click*	New Document to create a document with labels

The new document containing a sheet of return address labels appears. Your screen should look similar to Figure 8-5.

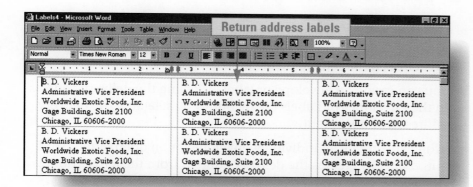

FIGURE 8-5
Sheet of Labels for
B. D. Vickers

Word organizes label text in a series of columns and rows called a **table**. Each intersection of a column and row is called a **cell**. Each cell of the table represents a label that contains B. D. Vickers return address.

| Step 10 | *Save* | the document as *Return Address Labels* and close it |

Because you saved the new label document you can use it later to create more labels, whenever Kelly needs more return address labels for B. D. Vickers.

**chapter
eight**

Summary

► You can send an envelope or a sheet of labels directly to a printer or you can add them to the current document. An individual label must be sent directly to the printer.

► You can create an envelope or label by keying the delivery address in the Envelopes or Labels dialog box or by selecting the delivery address in a document.

► When you create an individual envelope for an open letter, Word automatically creates the delivery address from the letter's address.

► Word automatically inserts a frame or box around the delivery address on an envelope document that enables you to reposition the delivery address.

► Word automatically adds the default return address from data found in the User Information tab of the Options dialog box, which you can change or omit.

► You can create an entire sheet of the same label or a sheet with individual labels at a specified position.

► You can select from a list of commonly used Avery labels or you can create your own custom label size.

Commands Review

Action	Menu Bar	Shortcut Menu	Toolbar	Keyboard
Create an individual envelope, label, or sheet of the same label	Tools, Envelopes and Labels			ALT + T, E

Concepts Review

Circle the correct answer.

1. To print a single label you must:
[a] open a document that contains the label address.
[b] specify the column and row on the label sheet.
[c] change the return address in the User Information dialog box.
[d] use a name tag label format.

2. A Size 10 business envelope is:
[a] 3⅝ × 6½ inches.
[b] 4⅛ × 9½ inches.
[c] 3⅝ × 9½ inches.
[d] 4⅛ × 6½ inches.

3. Labels are created and displayed in:
[a] table format.
[b] column format.
[c] Landscape orientation.
[d] only Print Preview.

4. You can modify the font, style, and size of addresses in the Envelopes and Labels dialog box with:
[a] the Font command on the menu bar.
[b] the CTRL + Z keys.
[c] the Font command on the shortcut menu.
[d] the Change Formatting button in the Envelopes and Labels dialog box.

5. To reposition the delivery address for an envelope:
[a] view the envelope in Print Preview.
[b] drag the default frame to a new location.
[c] delete the return address.
[d] change the return address in the User Information tab of the Tools, Options dialog box.

6. Which of the following is the default formatting style that Word uses when you key the envelope delivery address?
[a] Normal
[b] Envelope Address
[c] Heading 1
[d] Envelope Return

7. When you create a custom label, it is added to the:
[a] Label products list.
[b] Product number list.
[c] Label options list.
[d] Tray list.

chapter eight

Circle **T** if the statement is true or **F** is the statement is false.

T   F   1. You can create file labels in the Envelopes and Labels dialog box.

T   F   2. The return address can be omitted when creating envelopes.

T   F   3. You can send an envelope directly to a printer or save it with the letter for printing later.

T   F   4. If you save an envelope with the letter, Word places the envelope at the bottom of the letter.

T   F   5. The USPS approved envelope format is mixed case with punctuation.

T   F   6. You cannot create custom labels.

T   F   7. Envelopes and labels must be printed on a laser printer.

T   F   8. The Details button on the Labels tab allows you to change the margins, pitch, and number of labels on a sheet.

T   F   9. The default envelope font is Times New Roman 10 point.

T   F   10. You can specify envelope rotation, face up or face down, and manual or tray feed in the Labels Options dialog box.

Skills Review

Exercise 1

1. Create envelopes for each of the addresses below. Use the Times New Roman 12-point font and the open punctuation, uppercase delivery address format. Create each envelope as a separate document.

   Mr. Thomas Williams　　　　　　*Ms. Barbara Robins*
   Williams Products Company　　　*Sunrise Orange Growers*
   293 East Road　　　　　　　　　*698 Orange Grove Drive*
   Houston, TX 77024-2087　　　　　*Miami, FL 33153-7634*

2. the Size 10 (4⅛ × 9½ in) envelope size.

3. Omit the return address.

4. Save the Williams envelope as *Williams Envelope*. Save the Robins envelope as *Robins Envelope*.

5. Preview and print the envelopes and close the documents.

Exercise 2

1. Create envelopes for each of the addresses below. Use the Arial 12-point font and the open punctuation, uppercase delivery address format. Create each envelope as a separate document.

   Mr. Alex Pyle　　　　　　　*Ms. Alice Yee*
   Office Supplies, Inc.　　　　*Raceway Park*
   20343 Blue Sage Drive　　　*632 Raceway Drive*
   Shreveport, LA 71119-3412　*Sebring, FL 33870-2156*

2. Use the Size 6¾ (3⅝ × 6½ in) envelope size.

3. Omit the return address.

4. Save the Pyle envelope as *Pyle Envelope*. Save the Yee envelope as *Yee Envelope*.

5. Preview and print the envelopes and close the documents.

Exercise 3

1. Create a sheet of labels for the following address. Use the Avery 5160 label product for laser printers.

2. Format the address in the USPS style.
Ms. Ramona Mendez
Southwest Services, Inc
3426 Main Street
Dallas, TX 72345-1235

3. Add the labels to a new document.

4. Save the document as *Mendez Labels*.

5. Preview, print, and close the document.

Exercise 4

1. Open the *Envelope And Label List* document located on the Data Disk.

2. Create a sheet of Avery 5260 product laser labels for John Delany as a new document.

3. Save the document as *Delany Labels*.

4. Preview, print, and close the document.

Exercise 5

1. Open the *Wilson Advertising Letter* located on the Data Disk.

2. Create a Size 10 envelope.

3. Key your name and address as the return address.

4. Add the envelope to the document.

5. Do not save the new return address as the default return address.

6. Reposition the delivery address ½ inch to the right.

7. Save the document as *Wilson Advertising Letter With Envelope*.

8. Preview, print, and close the document.

Exercise 6

1. Open the *Wilson Advertising Letter* document located on the Data Disk.

2. Create a sheet of return labels using the Avery 5160 product for laser printers.

3. Format the labels with Times New Roman 10-point font and the uppercase and open punctuation style.
(*Hint:* Remove the punctuation, select the address, right-click the address, and click Font.)

4. Add the labels to a new document.

5. Save the label document as *Wilson Labels*.

6. Preview and print the label document and close both documents.

chapter eight

Exercise 7

1. Create a sheet of name tag labels using the Avery 5362 product for laser printers. Add the labels to a new document.

2. Key the following names into the labels (*Hint:* Press the TAB key to move to the next label):
Janice Greene
Frances Carmichael
Carlos Armondo
Sarah Winters
Felix Martinez

3. Select the entire document and change the font to Arial 20 point.

4. Apply the bold and center align formats.

5. Save the document as *Name Tags*.

6. Preview, print, and close the document.

Exercise 8

1. Create the following letter. Set the appropriate margins for a block format letter.

Current date

Mr. Raul Rodriguez
Rodriguez Food Suppliers
355 Allen Drive
Houston, TX 77042-3354

Dear Mr. Rodriguez:

Congratulations on starting your own business. Given the growth of the specialty food industry, I know you will be successful.

Please send me a catalog explaining and illustrating your product lines. I hope we can do business together.

Yours truly,

Davita Washington
Purchasing Agent

ka

2. Create a 6¾ (3⅝ × 6½ in) size envelope and format the delivery address in the approved USPS format.

3. Omit the return address.

4. Add the envelope to the document.

5. Save the document as *Solicitation Letter With Envelope.*

6. Create a sheet of return address labels using the Avery 2160 product for laser printers.

7. Add the labels to a new document.

8. Save the document as *Rodriguez Labels.*

9. Preview and print the sheet of labels and close the documents.

Case Projects

Project 1

One of the purchasing department employees frequently creates return address labels and wants to be able to do this more quickly. You suggest using the AutoText feature. Create an AutoText entry for B. D. Vickers' return address. Using this AutoText entry, create a sheet of return address labels. Save, preview, and print the labels.

Project 2

You have been asked to add the POSTNET code and FIM-A code to an envelope but are not sure what these are. Using the Office Assistant, search online Help for information about these two codes. Create an unbound report document describing these two codes and explaining how to insert them on an envelope. Save, preview, and print the document. Attach a sample envelope with the codes inserted.

Project 3

Kelly Armstead has asked you how to print just the envelope attached to a document. Using the Office Assistant, research how to print only the envelope when it is attached to a document. Create an interoffice memorandum to Kelly explaining how

to do this. Save, preview, and print the memorandum. Then open an existing document with an attached envelope and print only the envelope following the instructions in your memo to Kelly.

Project 4

At next week's "brown bag" lunch and training session for the purchasing department clerical staff, the discussion topic is "Printing Envelopes and Labels." You are presenting information on inserting an address from an electronic address book. Use the Office Assistant to locate information on your topic. Create an unbound report document describing techniques for doing this. With your instructor's permission, describe the process to a group of classmates.

Project 5

The purchasing department is having an "open house" holiday celebration and B. D. Vickers asks you to create a letter inviting three top Chicago-area distributors. Using fictitious data, create three letters in the block format with appropriate margins inviting each distributor. Attach an envelope in the approved USPS format to each letter. Save, preview, and print each document.

chapter eight

Project 6

Several important clients and their families are visiting the Chicago office next week and you have been asked to prepare a list of Chicago-area sites and facilities the families can enjoy during their visit. Connect to your ISP, launch your Web browser, and search for Chicago-area sites of interest to visitors. Print at least five Web pages. Create an interoffice memorandum to B. D. Vickers describing the sites of interest. Save, preview, and print the memorandum.

Project 7

You have been asked to find out how to automatically add the company graphic logo to the return address each time you create an envelope. Using the Office Assistant, research how to do this. Create an interoffice memorandum to Kelly Armstead describing how to add a graphic logo to the return address automatically. Save, preview, and print the memorandum.

Project 8

Worldwide Exotic Foods is going to sponsor an evening at a sports event for Chicago-area youth groups and you need to prepare a list of possible events. Connect to your ISP, launch your Web browser, and search for sports events in the Chicago area. Print at least three Web pages. Create an interoffice memorandum to Kelly Armstead describing the sports events. Save, preview, and print the memorandum.

Working with Documents

Chapter Overview

When you edit existing documents, it is sometimes necessary to quickly locate and replace certain text or formatting with different text or formatting. Also, large documents often require additional identifying text such as the date or page number added to the top or bottom of each page. In this chapter, you learn how to find and replace text, create page and section breaks, create and edit headers and footers, and use hyphenation.

Case profile

The human resources department regularly creates documents that are distributed to all Worldwide Exotic Foods employees. Jody Haversham, administrative assistant to B. J. Chang, the Vice President of Human Resources, has several completed documents, including training materials for an Internet class, that need some final editing and formatting before they can be printed and distributed.

chapter nine

9.a Finding and Replacing Text

As you work on existing documents, you may want to move quickly to a certain statement or to each heading in your document. Word can locate a word, phrase, special character, or format each time it occurs in a document. You can search for upper or lowercase text with or without formatting. You can search for whole words or for characters. For example, Word can find the three characters "our" in words such as "hour" or "your" or can find only the whole word "our." **Wildcards**, special search operators, such as "?" or "*", enable you to search for text patterns. The "?" represents any single character. For example, you can use "r?t" to search for three characters beginning with "r" and ending with "t." The "*" represents any series of characters. To search for words ending in "ed" you can use the search pattern "*ed." You can search for words that sound alike but are spelled differently. You can search for all word forms: noun, verb, adjective, or adverb. After Word finds the characters or words, you can edit them manually or replace them automatically with other text.

Finding Text

Jody asks you to open a document, *Internet Training*, find each instance of the uppercase characters "ISP" as a whole word (so you won't stop at that letter combination in other words), and then apply bold formatting to those characters.

To open the document and the Find and Replace dialog box:

Step 1	*Open*	*Internet Training* document located on the Data Disk
Step 2	*Save*	the document as *Internet Training Revised*
Step 3	*Click*	Edit
Step 4	*Click*	Find
Step 5	*Click*	More, if necessary, to expand the dialog box

The Find and Replace dialog box expands to show the options. The dialog box on your screen should look similar to Figure 9-1.

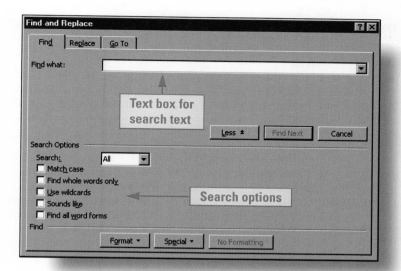

FIGURE 9-1
Find and Replace
Dialog Box

> **QUICK TIP**
>
> You can find and replace formatting, special characters, and nonprinting elements (such as tab formatting marks) with the Format and Special buttons in the Find and Replace dialog box.

Notice that "All" is the default option selected in the Search Options group. This means that Word will search the entire document, regardless of the position of the insertion point. You can specify that Word find only text with the exact case by turning on the Match case option. To find the uppercase characters "ISP" as a whole word and bold each instance:

Step 1	*Key*	ISP in the Find what: text box
Step 2	*Click*	the Match case check box to insert a check mark, if necessary
Step 3	*Click*	the Find whole words only check box to insert a check mark, if necessary
Step 4	*Remove*	the check marks from the remaining check boxes, if necessary
Step 5	*Click*	Less to collapse the dialog box
Step 6	*Click*	Find Next

The first instance of the text "ISP" is selected. When the Find and Replace dialog box opens it becomes the active window and the Word application window becomes inactive (the title bar is gray). To edit or delete the selected text you must activate the Word document window. If the Find and Replace dialog box hides the selected text or the toolbar buttons, you can drag it out of the way.

Step 7	*Click*	the Word document window to activate the window (the title bar is blue when the window is active)
Step 8	*Click*	the Bold button **B** on the Formatting toolbar

You continue to find and bold each instance of the text "ISP." When all the instances of the text "ISP" are found, Word opens a Confirmation dialog box telling you the search is finished.

Step 9	*Click*	Find Next in the Find and Replace dialog box
Step 10	*Click*	the Bold button **B** on the Formatting toolbar to activate the Word window and format the text in one step
Step 11	*Continue*	to find and bold the text "ISP"
Step 12	*Click*	OK to close the Confirmation dialog box when it opens
Step 13	*Click*	Cancel to close the Find and Replace dialog box

Jody instructs you to find each instance of the phrase "electronic mail" in the *Internet Training Revised* document and change it to "e-mail."

Replacing Text

Often you want to search for a word, phrase, special character, or format and replace it with a different word, phrase, special character, or format. You can have Word replace the text or formatting automatically without adding it manually each time. To replace the phrase "electronic mail" with the word "e-mail" in the *Internet Training Revised* document:

Step 1	*Click*	Edit
Step 2	*Click*	Replace
Step 3	*Key*	electronic mail in the Find what: text box
Step 4	*Press*	the TAB key to move the insertion point to the next text box
Step 5	*Key*	e-mail in the Replace with: text box
Step 6	*Verify*	that Options: Match Case appears below the Find what: text box (the Whole words only option automatically turns off when you search for multiple words)
Step 7	*Click*	Find Next and verify that the phrase "electronic mail" is selected
Step 8	*Click*	Replace
Step 9	*Drag*	the dialog box out of the way and scroll to view the selected text, if necessary

The first instance of the phrase "electronic mail" is replaced with the word "e-mail" and Word automatically highlights the next occurrence of the phrase. Your screen should look similar to Figure 9-2.

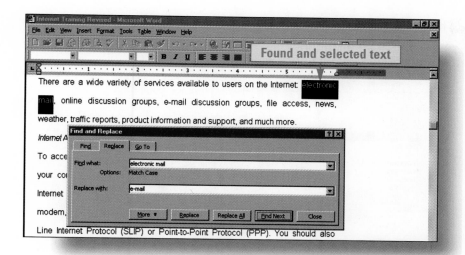

FIGURE 9-2
Replacing Text

CAUTION TIP

Be careful using the Replace All button in the Find and Replace dialog box to replace text in a document with which you are unfamiliar. Replacing all instances of certain characters or words may cause unexpected replacements and create errors in your document.

The Find and Replace dialog box remembers the last search options you set. Always review and turn on or off the search options before each new search. You can also search for and replace formatting as well as text. Always use the No Formatting button to turn off any formatting options set from the previous search before you begin a new search.

When another match is found, you can replace it by clicking the Replace button. If you want to leave the text unchanged, click the Find Next button to skip that occurrence of the text. If you want to replace every occurrence of the text without reviewing each one, click the Replace All button. When no more matches exist, a Confirmation dialog box opens informing you that Word finished searching the document.

Step 10	*Click*	Replace
Step 11	*Click*	OK to close the Confirmation dialog box
Step 12	*Close*	the Find and Replace dialog box
Step 13	*Save*	the document

While reviewing the *Internet Training Revised* document, Jody notices an error on page two and asks you to correct it.

Using Go To to Locate Specific Elements

When you need to edit text on a specific page, you can go to that page quickly. The Go To feature moves a specific item within your document, including a page, section, or line. You can go to that item by clicking the Go To command on the Edit menu to open the Go To tab in the Find and Replace dialog box.

To move the insertion point to the second page and correct the text:

| Step 1 | *Click* | Edit |
| Step 2 | *Click* | Go To |

The G<u>o</u> To tab in the Find and Replace dialog box opens. The dialog box on your screen should look similar to Figure 9-3.

FIGURE 9-3
G<u>o</u> To Tab in the Find and Replace Dialog Box

In this tab you select the document item you wish to go to in the G<u>o</u> to what: list. Notice that Page is the default choice. If you want to go to another page, simply enter the page number in the <u>E</u>nter page number: text box and click the Go <u>T</u>o button (which appears in place of the Next button when a page number is entered).

Step 3	*Key*	2 in the <u>E</u>nter page number: text box
Step 4	*Click*	Go <u>T</u>o

The insertion point moves to the top of page two and the Find and Replace dialog box remains open. The dialog box remains open so you can search through a document and make multiple changes without reopening it. When you are finished, you close the dialog box.

Step 5	*Close*	the dialog box
Step 6	*Move*	the insertion point before the word "computers" in the first line on page two
Step 7	*Key*	of and press the SPACEBAR
Step 8	*Save*	the document

In addition to Go To, Word has other ways to navigate through a document.

Navigating Through a Document

In addition to navigating through a document by using the G<u>o</u> To command, the horizontal and vertical scroll bars, or by moving the insertion point with the mouse and keyboard, you can browse a document by selecting a document item. You use the Select Browse

---

M OUSE **TIP**

You can open the G<u>o</u> To tab in the Find and Replace dialog box by double-clicking the status bar (not a mode indicator). You can also go to specific items within your document with the Select Browse Object button and the Next and Previous buttons located below the vertical scroll bar.

Object feature to select a field, endnote, footnote, comment, section, heading, picture, or table document item.

You can also open the <u>G</u>o To and Fin<u>d</u> tabs in the Find and Replace dialog box with the Select Browse Object. The default option for the Select Browse Object is to browse by page. To review the Select Browse Object:

Step 1	*Click*	the Select Browse Object button 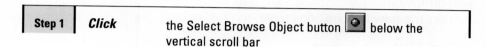 below the vertical scroll bar

The Select Browse Object grid opens immediately below the Select Browse Object button. The grid on your screen should look like Figure 9-4.

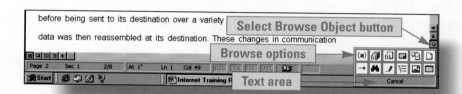

FIGURE 9-4
Select Browse Object Grid

Each icon represents an item by which to browse. You can point to each icon and observe the item name in the text area. When you see the item you want to browse by, click its icon.

Step 2	*Point to*	the first icon on the Select Browse Object grid
Step 3	*Observe*	the text "Browse by Field" in the text area
Step 4	*Continue*	to review each icon on the grid by pointing to it
Step 5	*Point to*	the text area of the grid
Step 6	*Observe*	the text "Cancel"
Step 7	*Click*	Cancel to close the grid without selecting a browse item

The paragraph headings in the *Internet Training Revised* document are italic. Jody asks you to find all the instances of italic formatting and replace it with the Words Only underline style. To use the Select Browse Object to do this:

Step 1	*Move*	the insertion point to the top of the document
Step 2	*Click*	the Select Browse Object button 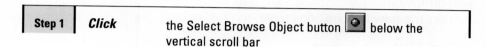 below the vertical scroll bar

chapter
nine

| Step 3 | *Click* | the Find icon on the Select Browse Object grid |
| Step 4 | *Click* | the Replace tab |

This is the same Find and Replace dialog box you used earlier. First you remove the text you last searched for ("electronic mail"), and then you set the new find options to search for italic formatting.

Step 5	*Delete*	the text in the Find what: text box
Step 6	*Click*	More, if necessary
Step 7	*Click*	Format
Step 8	*Click*	Font to open the Font dialog box
Step 9	*Click*	Italic in the Font style: list in the Font tab
Step 10	*Click*	OK

Next you remove the "e-mail" text from the Replace with: text box and set the underline formatting option. To set the Replace with: formatting:

Step 1	*Press*	the TAB key to select the contents of the next text box
Step 2	*Delete*	the text in the Replace with: text box
Step 3	*Click*	Format
Step 4	*Click*	Font
Step 5	*Click*	Regular in the Font style: list box
Step 6	*Click*	the Underline style: list arrow and click the Words only option
Step 7	*Click*	OK
Step 8	*Click*	the Match case check box to remove the check mark
Step 9	*Click*	the Less button to collapse the dialog box

The dialog box options on your screen should look like Figure 9-5.

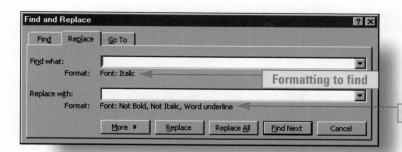

FIGURE 9-5
Find and Replace Options
for Formatting

Step 10	*Click*	Replace <u>A</u>ll
Step 11	*Click*	OK to confirm Word has replaced all 12 instances of the italic formatting with underlined words
Step 12	*Close*	the dialog box
Step 13	*Scroll*	the document to review the formatting changes to the paragraph headings
Step 14	*Save*	the document

Word inserts an automatic page break when the text you key extends beyond the limits of a single page. Jody reminds you to set the appropriate margins for the unbound report document *Internet Training Revised*, and then review and modify the page breaks.

9.b Inserting Page Breaks

Word automatically determines how much text will fit on a page based on the margins, font, font size, and paper size. A **page break** identifies where one page ends and another begins. There are two types of page breaks: a soft, or automatic, page break and a hard, or manual, page break. Word inserts an **automatic page break** when a page is full of text. In Normal view, an automatic page break appears as a dotted horizontal line from the left to the right margins. You can also create your own **manual page break** at any point on a page; a manual page break appears as a dotted horizontal line from the left to right margins containing the words "Page Break" in the center.

Before you review the pagination of the *Internet Training Revised* document, you need to reset the margins. To set margins for an unbound report:

Step 1	*Set*	2-inch top and 1-inch left and right margins
Step 2	*Zoom*	the document to Page Width, if necessary, to see all the text at the right margin

| Step 3 | *Scroll* | the document to view all the automatic page breaks (the dotted line extending from the left to right margins) then scroll the document to view the first page break |

Some of the automatic page breaks in *Internet Training Revised* occur in awkward places in the document. For example, there is a page break two lines after the paragraph heading "User Names." A better place for that page break to occur is immediately before the paragraph heading so that both the paragraph heading and the following paragraph text are on the same page. Changing the position of the page breaks in a document is called **repagination**. You cannot move or delete an automatic page break. Instead, you must insert a manual page break at some point above the automatic page break. Word then repaginates the entire document from the position of the manual page break.

To insert a manual page break immediately above the paragraph heading "User Names":

Step 1	*Go to*	page 4
Step 2	*Scroll*	to view the User Names paragraph heading at the bottom of the page
Step 3	*Move*	the insertion point to the left margin of the paragraph heading
Step 4	*Click*	Insert
Step 5	*Click*	Break

The Break dialog box that opens on your screen should look similar to Figure 9-6.

FIGURE 9-6
Break Dialog Box

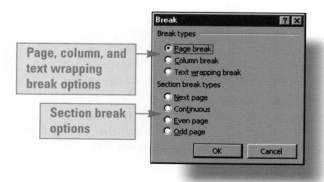

Page, column, and text wrapping break options

Section break options

The default option, <u>P</u>age Break, is already selected.

Step 6	*Click*	OK
Step 7	*Scroll*	the document to see that Word repaginated the document from the new manual page break

As you continue to edit the *Internet Training Revised* document, you can add or remove pages or text or replace the formatting. When you do this, the manual break you just inserted may then be incorrect. If you no longer want a manual page break to occur at a certain position, you can move or delete it.

To delete the manual page break:

Step 1	*Go to*	page 4
Step 2	*Click*	the manual page break dotted line above the paragraph heading "<u>U</u>ser <u>N</u>ames" in the selection bar to select it
Step 3	*Press*	the DELETE key
Step 4	*Observe*	the automatic page break in its original position two lines below the paragraph heading

When you delete the manual page break, Word repaginates the document and inserts automatic page breaks as necessary. Jody wants you to create a title page with 1-inch top and bottom margins using the three lines of text at the top of page one. She wants the text centered vertically and horizontally on the page. Now you create the title page.

9.c Creating Sections with Different Formatting

When you need to format part of a document with different margins, such as a title page, you can insert a section break. A **section break** stores the section formatting such as the margin settings and appears as a double dotted line with the words "Section Break" in the center of the line. Section breaks are inserted automatically when you format a portion of a document with different margins, headers, footers, columns, or page orientation. You also can insert a manual section break and then apply the formatting. To create a new page for title page of the *Internet Training Revised* document:

| Step 1 | *Move* | the insertion point to the left margin of the first paragraph heading "Introduction To The Internet" on the first page |
| Step 2 | *Open* | the Break dialog box |

Table 9-1 describes the four types of section breaks that appear in the Break dialog box.

TABLE 9-1
Types of Section Breaks

Type	Description
Next Page	creates a page break and begins the new section on the next page
Continuous	begins the new section on the same page
Even page	begins the new section on the next even-numbered page
Odd page	begins the new section on the next odd-numbered page

Step 3	*Click*	the Next page option button
Step 4	*Click*	OK
Step 5	*Observe*	the double dotted line with the text "Section Break (Next Page)" above the paragraph heading and the section number, Sec 2, on the status bar
Step 6	*Move*	the insertion point to the top of the document and observe the section number, Sec 1, on the status bar

To change the margins and vertically center the text in Section 1:

Step 1	*Open*	the Page Setup dialog box
Step 2	*Change*	the top margin to 1 inch and verify that the Apply to: list box contains "This section"
Step 3	*Change*	the vertical alignment to Center and verify that that the Apply to: list box contains "This section"
Step 4	*Click*	OK

Now that the appropriate margins are set for each section of the document, you need to verify the remaining page breaks. Whenever a page break occurs one or two lines below a paragraph heading, you insert a manual page break above the paragraph heading to keep the heading and its paragraph together. To review the page breaks:

Step 1	*Scroll*	the document to the next automatic page break at the paragraph heading "How the Internet Began"
Step 2	*Click*	at the left margin of the paragraph heading and insert a manual page break
Step 3	*Continue*	by inserting page breaks at the paragraph headings "Services Available On The Internet" and "Transmission Speeds"
Step 4	*Print Preview*	the document in two rows of five pages

Your screen should look similar to Figure 9-7.

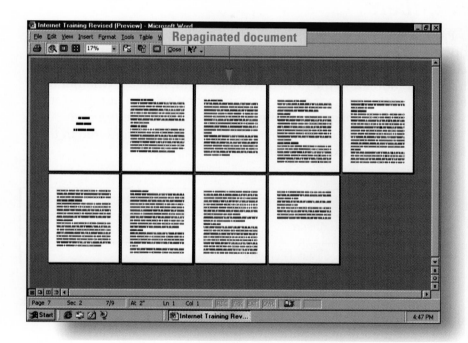

FIGURE 9-7
Document with Section and Page Breaks

| Step 5 | *Close* | Print Preview |
| Step 6 | *Save* | the document |

Because the *Internet Training Revised* document contains many pages, you need to use page numbers. You insert page numbers in the header or footer of a document.

chapter
nine

9.d Creating and Modifying Headers and Footers

Headers and footers allow text to appear on every page of a document above or below the top and bottom margins and body text area. **Header** text appears at the top of each page and **footer** text appears at the bottom of each page. You can specify that headers or footers print on every page or only on certain pages. For example, you can create headers and footers for every page except the first page, or for even- or odd-numbered pages.

 Creating, Inserting, and Modifying Page Numbers

Page numbers are always inserted at the top or bottom of a document as a header or footer. One way to insert page numbers is to click the Page Numbers command on the Insert menu, specify either header or footer and the horizontal alignment, indicate whether or not to show the number on the first page, and select a number format.

You won't put a page number on the title page of the *Internet Training Revised* document. To insert page numbers centered in the footer on all pages except the first page:

Step 1	*Move*	the insertion point to the top of the document, if necessary
Step 2	*Click*	Insert
Step 3	*Click*	Page Numbers

The Page Numbers dialog box that opens on your screen should look similar to Figure 9-8.

FIGURE 9-8
Page Numbers Dialog Box

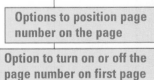

| Step 4 | *Verify* | Bottom of page (Footer) is selected in the Position: list box |

Step 5	*Click*	the Alignment: list arrow
Step 6	*Click*	Center
Step 7	*Click*	the Show number on the first page check box to remove the check mark
Step 8	*Click*	OK

Word switches to Whole Page zoom in Print Layout view.

| Step 9 | *Scroll* | to view the page number at the bottom of each page except the first page |
| Step 10 | *Zoom* | the document to 100% and scroll to view the bottom of the second page |

The page number 2 appears in light gray in the footer area at the bottom of the page. You can change the format of page numbers to be upper and lowercase alphabetic characters or upper and lowercase Roman numerals. To format the page numbers as lowercase Roman numerals:

| Step 1 | *Open* | the Page Numbers dialog box |
| Step 2 | *Click* | Format |

The Page Number Format dialog box that opens on your screen should look similar to Figure 9-9.

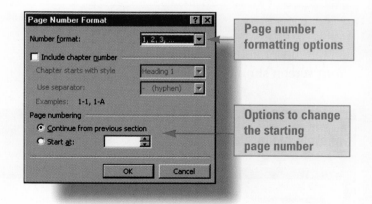

Page number formatting options

Options to change the starting page number

FIGURE 9-9
Page Number Format
Dialog Box

You can change the number format by selecting a format from the Number format: list. If you want to change the starting page number, you can click the Start at: option button and then key the new starting page number in the adjacent text box.

chapter
nine

Step 3	*Click*	the Number format: list arrow
Step 4	*Click*	the lowercase Roman numeral option (i, ii, iii …)
Step 5	*Click*	OK twice to close both dialog boxes
Step 6	*Scroll*	to view the bottom of page two and observe that the page number is changed from "2" to "ii"
Step 7	*Switch*	to Normal view and move the insertion point to the top of the document
Step 8	*Save*	the document

In addition to the page numbers, the document needs identifying text on each page beginning with page two. Jody wants the company name at the left margin of a header on all even-numbered pages and the text "Internet Training" at the right margin of a header for all odd-numbered pages.

Creating Alternate Headers and Footers

If you want to add more than page numbers to a header or footer, you use the Header and Footer command on the View menu. This command switches to Print Layout view, activates the header or footer pane (in which you can key text and add page numbers or the date), and displays the Header and Footer toolbar. To activate the header and footer panes in the *Internet Training Revised* document:

Step 1	*Click*	View
Step 2	*Click*	Header and Footer
Step 3	*Zoom*	the document to Page Width, if necessary, to see the text at the right margin

Your screen should look similar to Figure 9-10.

FIGURE 9-10
Header Pane and Header
and Footer Toolbar

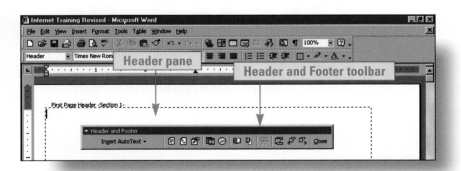

Notice that the First Page Header – Section 1 – pane, enclosed in dashed lines, contains the insertion point. When you removed the page number from the first page, Word created different header and footer panes for the first page and the rest of the text.

Step 4	*Observe*	the First Page Header – Section 1 – pane at the top of the first page
Step 5	*Review*	the Header and Footer toolbar buttons using the ScreenTips feature
Step 6	*Click*	the Show Next button ▣ on the Header and Footer toolbar

The Header – Section 2 – pane appears. Any text you key in this pane appears at the top of every page in Section 2 of the *Internet Training Revised* document.

| Step 7 | *Click* | the Switch Between Header and Footer button ▣ on the Header and Footer toolbar |

The Footer – Section 2 – pane appears. Any text you key in this pane appears at the bottom of every page in Section 2 of the *Internet Training Revised* document. Notice the footer pane contains the page number you already inserted and modified.

By default the header and footer panes have preset tabs: a Center tab at 3 inches and a Right tab at 6 inches. These tab settings allow you to center and right align text in the pane and are based on the 1¼-inch default left and right margin settings. Because the *Internet Training Revised* document has 1-inch left and right margins, the tab stops in the Footer – Section 2 – pane are not at the correct positions.

| Step 8 | *Remove* | the existing tab stops |
| Step 9 | *Set* | a center-aligned tab stop at the 3¼-inch position and a right-aligned tab stop at the 6½-inch position |

You can create headers and footers for alternate pages, as well as every page. Alternate headers and footers allow flexibility in positioning header and footer text. You want alternate header text on the even-numbered and odd-numbered page. You set the document for

---

QUICK TIP

You key and format text in the header or footer panes just as you do in the body of a document. When the header or footer pane is active, the body text in the document is light gray or "inactive" and cannot be edited.

When you are viewing a header or footer in Print Layout view, you can quickly activate the body text or the header or footer pane by double-clicking whichever is inactive (light gray). Depending on your document's layout, Word creates separate header and footer panes for each section, for the first page of each section, and for odd and even pages in each section.

chapter nine

alternate header and footer panes in the Layout tab of the Page Setup dialog box.

To create alternate header and footer panes for Section 2:

Step 1	*Click*	the Switch between Header and Footer button on the Header and Footer toolbar
Step 2	*Click*	the Page Setup button on the Header and Footer toolbar to open the Layout tab in the Page Setup dialog box
Step 3	*Click*	the Different odd and even check box to insert a check mark
Step 4	*Click*	OK
Step 5	*Observe*	the Even Page Header – Section 2 – pane

To key the company name at the left margin for each even-numbered page:

Step 1	*Key*	Worldwide Exotic Foods, Inc.
Step 2	*Click*	the Show Next button on the Header and Footer toolbar to view the Odd Page Header – Section 2 – pane
Step 3	*Remove*	the existing tab stops
Step 4	*Set*	a 6½-inch right tab stop
Step 5	*Press*	the TAB key
Step 6	*Key*	Internet Training
Step 7	*Print Preview* the document in two rows of six pages
Step 8	*Observe*	the differently formatted first page in Section 1, page numbers and the odd and even page headers in Section 2 (zoom each page, if necessary, to verify the header and footer)

Your screen should look similar to Figure 9-11.

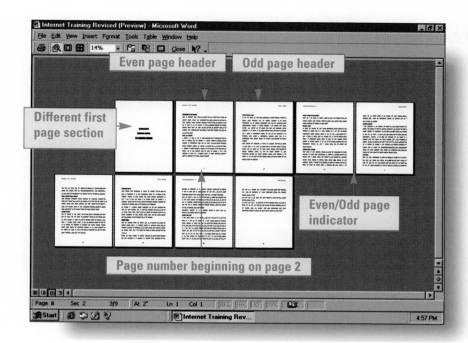

FIGURE 9-11
Different First Page and
Section Formatting

| Step 9 | *Close* | Print Preview |
| Step 10 | *Save* | the document and close it |

The human resources department is beginning computer software training classes next month that are available to all employees. Jody drafted a bulletin to insert in all paycheck envelopes at the next pay period. She is not satisfied with the way the text wraps and asks you hyphenate words in the document.

9.e Using Hyphenation

Hyphens are used to join words, such as "drag-and-drop," and to split long words at the right margin. Because word wrap moves a word to the next line if it is too long to fit within the set right margin, left-aligned text may have a very ragged right margin or justified text may have large spaces between words. The end result is less text on a page. **Hyphenation** splits words at the right margin, creating a smoother right margin or smaller spaces between words and more text on the page. The best time to hyphenate a document is after you have keyed, edited, and formatted the text. The Hyphenation subcommand under the Language command on the Tools menu provides options to hyphenate text automatically or manually.

chapter
nine

You hyphenate the *Training Commitment* document to improve its text wrapping. To open the document and turn on automatic hyphenation:

Step 1	*Open*	the *Training Commitment* document located on the Data Disk
Step 2	*Zoom*	the document to Page Width, if necessary, to view the text at the right margin
Step 3	*Observe*	the ragged right margin
Step 4	*Click*	Tools
Step 5	*Point to*	Language
Step 6	*Click*	Hyphenation

The Hyphenation dialog box that opens on your screen should look similar to Figure 9-12.

FIGURE 9-12
Hyphenation Dialog Box

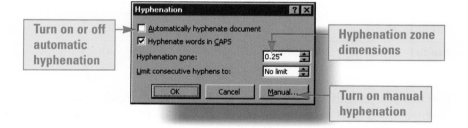

Turn on or off automatic hyphenation

Hyphenation zone dimensions

Turn on manual hyphenation

The **hyphenation zone** defines the distance from the right margin where you want to hyphenate your document. Words that fall into the hyphenation zone are hyphenated. A large zone increases the right margin raggedness because fewer words require hyphens. A small zone reduces the right margin raggedness, because more words require hyphens. Because too many consecutive hyphenated words make a document harder to read, you can limit the number of consecutively hyphenated words.

| Step 7 | *Click* | the Automatically hyphenate document check box to insert a check mark |
| Step 8 | *Click* | OK |

Word automatically hyphenates four words: communication, receive, assigned, and keystrokes. The right margin is less ragged. To control which words are hyphenated, you use manual hyphenation.

To undo the automatic hyphenation and manually hyphenate the *Training Commitment* document using a 0.3 inch hyphenation zone:

Step 1	*Click*	the Undo button on the Standard toolbar
Step 2	*Open*	the Hyphenation dialog box
Step 3	*Key*	.3 in the Hyphenation <u>z</u>one: text box
Step 4	*Click*	<u>M</u>anual

The Manual Hyphenation dialog box opens with a suggestion for hyphenating the word "com-mu-ni-ca-tion." The flashing insertion point indicates where the word is hyphenated if you click <u>Y</u>es to accept the suggestion. You can click another hyphenation position to modify the suggestion and then click <u>Y</u>es to accept it. If you don't want to hyphenate that word, click <u>N</u>o. To manually hyphenate the document:

Step 1	*Click*	the word at the first (com-) hyphenation position
Step 2	*Click*	<u>Y</u>es
Step 3	*Observe*	the next suggested hyphenation "as-signed"
Step 4	*Click*	<u>N</u>o
Step 5	*Accept*	the last suggested hyphenation "key-strokes"
Step 6	*Click*	OK to confirm the hyphenation is complete
Step 7	*Scroll*	the document to review the hyphenation
Step 8	*Save*	the document as *Training Commitment Revised* and close it

Certain hyphenated words (such as e-mail) should not be broken at the right margin.

Nonbreaking Hyphens

The *Fall Schedule* document contains several hyphenated words that you don't want to split between lines. **Nonbreaking hyphens** are used to prevent hyphenated words from breaking at the right margin. To insert nonbreaking hyphens in a document:

| Step 1 | *Open* | the *Fall Schedule* document located on the Data Disk |
| Step 2 | *Observe* | the hyphenated text "left-aligning" that breaks at the right margin |

chapter
nine

Step 3	*Select*	the hyphen following the word "left"
Step 4	*Press*	the CTRL + SHIFT + HYPHEN (-) keys to insert a nonbreaking hyphen
Step 5	*Observe*	the hyphenated text "left-aligned" wrapped to the left margin
Step 6	*Change*	the hyphen in the text "built-in" to a nonbreaking hyphen
Step 7	*Save*	the document as *Fall Schedule Revised*

Sometimes you want to control where a word is hyphenated if it cannot fit at the right margin. You use optional or soft hyphens to do this.

Optional Hyphens

Optional hyphens join words that can be split if they do not fit at the right margin. An optional hyphen breaks a word or phrase only when it does not fit at the right margin. If the word or phrase appears anywhere else in the line, the optional hyphen does not appear in the document. To insert text and an optional hyphen in the *Fall Schedule Revised* document:

Step 1	*Move*	the insertion point after the text "using" and the space at the end of the second line in the large paragraph following the heading *"Intermediate Word Processing"*
Step 2	*Key*	AutoCorrect, using and press the SPACEBAR
Step 3	*Move*	the insertion point between the o and the C in AutoCorrect
Step 4	*Press*	the CTRL + HYPHEN (-) keys to insert an optional hyphen
Step 5	*Observe*	the word AutoCorrect is hyphenated and broken between two lines

To see how the optional hyphen works, you change the margins so that the word "AutoCorrect" does not have to be hyphenated. To view the hyphenated word "AutoCorrect" when it appears at the beginning of the line:

Step 1	*Change*	the right margin to 1½ inch
Step 2	*Observe*	the word "AutoCorrect" at the beginning of the third line of the paragraph and the hyphen disappears
Step 3	*Change*	the right margin to 1¼ inch
Step 4	*Observe*	the word "AutoCorrect" is again hyphenated

| Step 5 | *Save* | the document |

When you need to print a document on paper that is wider than it is tall, you change the page orientation.

9.f Setting Page Orientation

The default page orientation is called **portrait** orientation, which means the paper is taller than it is wide. You can also print documents in **landscape** orientation, which means the paper is wider than it is tall. You want to change the page orientation for the *Fall Schedule Revised* document. To change the orientation:

Step 1	*Open*	the Page Setup dialog box
Step 2	*Click*	the Paper Size tab
Step 3	*Observe*	the default option is Portrait and the document in the preview is taller than it is wide
Step 4	*Click*	the Landscape option button
Step 5	*Observe*	in the preview that the document is now wider than it is tall
Step 6	*Set*	the top margin to 2 inches and the left and right margins to 1.5 inches
Step 7	*Print Preview*	the document to review the new page orientation
Step 8	*Close*	Print Preview
Step 9	*Save*	the document as *Fall Schedule In Landscape Orientation* and close it

Jody will print the training material documents you finished and distribute them at the Internet class.

chapter
nine

Summary

- ► Word can locate a character, word, phrase, special character, or format each time it occurs in a document.

- ► You can search for characters, words, phrases, special characters, or formats, and replace them with other text or formats individually or all at one time.

- ► The Go To command moves the insertion point to a specific item within your document, such as the top of the page.

- ► The Select Browse Object button provides options for browsing your document by item, such as pictures, comments, or tables.

- ► Word creates an automatic page break when text fills a page whose length is determined by the margins, font, font size, and paper size.

- ► You can insert a manual page break to remove an automatic page break.

- ► A section break allows you to change the margins and headers or footers for different parts of a document.

- ► You can insert page numbers at the top or bottom of every page—or all pages except the first page—and then format the page numbers.

- ► Header text appears at the top of the designated pages and footer text appears at the bottom of designated pages.

- ► You can use different header or footer text on the first page or on even- or odd-numbered pages.

- ► The best time to hyphenate words is after all text is keyed, edited, and formatted.

- ► The Hyphenation tool can hyphenate all possible words automatically or can suggest words for you to hyphenate manually.

- ► Nonbreaking hyphens are used to prevent hyphenated words from breaking at the right margin.

- ► Optional hyphens break a word or phrase only when it does not fit at the right margin.

- ► You can print pages in Portrait (8½ × 11) or Landscape (11 × 8½) orientation.

Commands Review

Action	Menu Bar	Shortcut Menu	Toolbar	Keyboard
Search for specific text or item	Edit, Find			ALT + E, F CTRL + F
Search and replace specific text or item	Edit, Replace			ALT + E, E CTRL + H
Go to a specific document element	Edit, Go To		Double-click the status bar (not a mode indicator)	ALT + E, G CTRL + G F5
Navigating through a document by item				
Insert Page or Section Breaks	Insert, Break			ALT + I, B
Creating and modifying Headers and Footers	View, Header and Footer			ALT + V, H
Insert page numbers	Insert, Page Numbers			ALT + I, U
Use Hyphenation tool	Tools, Language, Hyphenation			ALT + T, L, H
Nonbreaking hyphen				CTRL + SHIFT + HYPHEN
Optional hyphen				CTRL + HYPHEN
Nonbreaking space				CTRL + SHIFT + SPACEBAR
Change page orientation	File, Page Setup, Paper Size tab			ALT + F, U, S

Concepts Review

Circle the correct answer.

1. Hyphens are used to:
 [a] separate number ranges.
 [b] split long words at the right margin.
 [c] split long words at the left margin.
 [d] add interest to a document.

2. You create alternate header and footer panes in the:
 [a] Margins tab in the Page Setup dialog box.
 [b] Header and Footer tab in the Print Setup dialog box.
 [c] Layout tab in the Print dialog box.
 [d] Layout tab in the Page Setup dialog box.

3. Which Find option allows you to avoid search results that include the individual characters of a word inside other words?
 [a] Match case
 [b] Find whole words only
 [c] Sounds like
 [d] Find all word forms

4. The default option for the Select Browse Object button is to Browse by:
 [a] Picture.
 [b] Comment.
 [c] Find.
 [d] Page.

5. When a page fills with text, Word inserts a(n):
 [a] manual page break.
 [b] temporary page break.
 [c] permanent page break.
 [d] automatic page break.

6. When you want to format part of a document with different margins or page orientation, you insert a:
 [a] manual page break.
 [b] header.
 [c] section break.
 [d] hyphen.

chapter nine

7. Page numbers are always inserted in:
[a] Roman numerals.
[b] a header or footer.
[c] a hyphenated format.
[d] the body text.

8. Repagination means to:
[a] change the line spacing in a document.
[b] format text characters with the Italic format.
[c] insert headers and footers.
[d] change the position of page breaks.

9. The best time to hyphenate text is:
[a] at each page break.
[b] as you key it.
[c] before you format it.
[d] after keying, editing, and formatting it.

10. The actions of the Next and Previous buttons below the vertical scroll bar are controlled by the:
[a] Find and Replace dialog box.
[b] Hyphenation button.
[c] CTRL + SHIFT + HYPHEN (-) keys.
[d] Select Browse Object button.

Circle **T** if the statement is true or **F** if the statement is false.

T F 1. The <u>F</u>ind command locates a word, phrase, or format in a document and replaces it with a word, phrase, or format.

T F 2. A page break identifies where one page ends and another begins.

T F 3. The Select Browse Object button can be used to display only the Find and Replace dialog box.

T F 4. When you use the <u>R</u>eplace command, you can only replace text from the insertion point forward.

T F 5. You must be in Print Layout view to see the header and footer panes.

T F 6. Word automatically changes the position of the center and right tab stops in the header and footer panes when you change a document's margins.

T F 7. You use Portrait orientation to print on paper that is taller than it is wide.

T F 8. Word determines how much text fits on a page based on the margins, font, font size, and paper size settings.

T F 9. An optional hyphen is used to prevent hyphenated words from breaking at the right margin.

T F 10. You can use special search operators like "?" and "*" to search for text patterns.

Skills Review

Exercise 1 C

1. Open the *British Columbia Report* document located on the Data Disk.

2. Change the font for the entire document to Arial, 12 point.

3. Change the top margin to 2 inches, the left margin to 1½ inches, and the right margin to 1 inch.

4. Automatically hyphenate the document using the default hyphenation zone.

5. Go to the top of page 2. Change the top margin to 1 inch and apply it from the position of the insertion point forward in the document.

6. Insert a page number at the bottom center of each page.

7. Save the document as *British Columbia Report Revised*.

8. Preview, print, and close the document.

Exercise 2

1. Open the *British Columbia Report* document located on the Data Disk.

2. Find each occurrence of the text "British Columbia" and replace it with "New York." (*Hint:* Remember to clear any formatting that is set in the dialog box.)

3. Change the font for the entire document to Times New Roman 12 point.

4. Change the left margin to 1 inch.

5. Find the text "In contrast" and insert a page break before the paragraph beginning with the text.

6. Create a header with the text "New York Analysis Report" centered, boldfaced, and Times New Roman 12 point. (*Hint:* don't forget to change the center tab stop setting to agree with the left and right margin settings.)

7. Switch to the footer and insert a page number at the bottom center of the page. (*Hint:* Don't forget to change the center tab stop setting to agree with the left and right margin settings.)

8. Omit the header and footer on page 1 by creating blank first page header and footer panes.

9. Save the document as *New York Report.*

10. Preview, print, and close the document.

Exercise 3

1. Open the *Inventory Report* document located on the Data Disk.

2. Find each occurrence of the text "warehouse" and replace it with "plant."

3. Indent the bulleted list ½ inch on the left side.

4. Indent the numbered list ½ inch on the left and right sides.

5. Change the top margin to 2 inches and the left and right margins to 1 inch.

6. Automatically hyphenate the text.

7. Go to the top of page 2. Change the top margin to 1 inch and apply it from the position of the insertion point forward.

8. Create a Section 2 header containing centered and bold text "Inventory Report." (*Hint:* Make sure you turn off the Same as Previous button on the Header and Footer toolbar so the header will not appear in Section 1. Don't forget to adjust the center tab stop.)

9. Switch to the Section 2 footer and insert a page number at the bottom center of the page. (*Hint:* Make sure you turn off the Same as Previous button on the Header and Footer toolbar so the footer will not appear in Section 1. Don't forget to adjust the center tab stop.)

10. Format the page number in the lowercase Roman numeral style.

11. Save the document as *Inventory Report Revised.*

12. Preview, print, and close the document.

Exercise 4

1. Open the *New York Report* document you created in Exercise 2.

2. Zoom the document to Page Width and manually hyphenate it with a 0.4 hyphenation zone.

3. Save the document as *New York Report With Manual Hyphenation.*

4. Preview, print, and close the document.

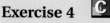

Exercise 5

1. Create the following document. Use the default font and set the margins for a block format letter.

Current date

Mr. T. J. Olsen
13567 Mason Park Drive
East Melbourne VIC 3002
Australia

Dear Mr. Olsen:

Thank you for your inquiry about teaching positions in our Melbourne office. Our Melbourne office is not currently planning on expanding their training staff. However, we will keep your resume on file for six months and will contact you if there is an opening in the Melbourne office teaching staff.

In the meantime, Mr. Olsen, we are forwarding your resume to the Vancouver branch at your request.

Sincerely,

B. J. Chang
Vice President of Human Resources

jh

2. Find each instance of the name Olsen and replace it with Nance using the Select Browse Object button.

3. Find each instance of the word "Melbourne" and replace it with "Vancouver" except in the letter address.

4. Find each instance of the word "six" without formatting and replace it with the word "*six*" with italic formatting.

5. Create a Size 10 envelope with the Delivery Point barcode and omit the return address.

6. Add the envelope to the document.

7. Save the document as *Nance Letter With Envelope.*

8. Preview, print, and close the envelope and letter.

Exercise 6

1. Open the *Vancouver Warehouse Report* document located on the Data Disk.

2. Create a title page using a Next Page section break immediately before the paragraph heading <u>Audit Methods</u>.

3. Use 1-inch top, bottom, left, and right margins for the title page in Section 1.

4. Center the title text vertically between the left and right margins.

5. Change the Section 2 margins to 2-inch top and 1-inch left and right margins.

6. Move the insertion point to the top of the document and view the Header and Footer toolbar.

7. Using the Header and Footer toolbar buttons create a different first page header and footer pane for Section 1 and leave both the first page header and footer blank.

8. Using the Header and Footer toolbar buttons view the Section 2 header and create a different odd and even header and footer panes for Section 2.

9. Insert a page number at the right margin for the even page header and at the left margin for the odd page header. (*Hint:* Remember to adjust the right-aligned tap stop to the right margin, if necessary.)

10. Save the document as *Vancouver Warehouse Report With Title Page*.

11. Preview, print, and close the document.

Exercise 7

1. Open the *Welcome To The World Wide Web* document located on the Data Disk.

2. Change the margins to the appropriate margins for an unbound report.

3. Using the Replace tab in the Find and Replace dialog box find all instances of the phrase "World Wide Web" and change it to "WWW."

4. Using the Replace tab in the Find and Replace dialog box find all text formatted with the Times New Roman, 14-point font and change it to Times New Roman, 12 point, bold.

5. Horizontally justify the document text below the title.

6. Change the line spacing for the entire document to 1.7.

7. Scroll the document and review the page breaks.

8. Insert a manual page break if an automatic page break occurs 1 to 3 lines below a paragraph heading.

9. Use the Page Numbers command on the Insert menu to insert centered page numbers in footers on all pages. Use the (A, B, C) page number format.

10. Check the spelling and grammar.

11. Save the document as *Welcome To The WWW*.

12. Preview, print, and close the document.

Exercise 8

1. Open the *Welcome To The WWW* document created in Exercise 6.

2. Create a separate title page for the title line.

3. Format the title page with a 1-inch top margin and vertically centered text.

4. Omit the page number on the title page.

chapter nine

5. Change the page number format for Section 2 to uppercase Roman numerals and show the page number on the first page of Section 2.

6. Find the hyphenated text "dial-up and "e-mail" and create nonbreaking hyphens.

7. Save the document at *Welcome To The WWW Revised*.

8. Preview, print, and close the document.

Exercise 9

1. Open the *Legislative Update* document located on the Data Disk.

2. Change the page orientation to landscape.

3. Change the top and bottom margins to .75 inch and the left and right margins to 1 inch.

4. Save the document as *Landscape Legislative Update*.

5. Print and close the document.

Case Projects

Project 1

Prepare a three-paragraph block format letter for B. J. Chang's signature to Ms. Helen Alexander, 1400 W. Highlands Avenue, Melbourne, VIC, 20006, Australia. Thank Ms. Alexander for her resume and interest in employment as an inventory control specialist with Worldwide Exotic Foods, Inc. Advise Ms. Alexander that there is an opening in the Melbourne warehouse and you are forwarding her resume to the Melbourne warehouse manager who will contact her to set up an appointment for an interview. Save the document but do not close it. Replace each instance of the word "Alexander" with the word "Stackhouse." Replace each instance of the word "Melbourne" in the body of the letter with the word "Sydney." Save the document with a new name. Add an envelope with no return address to each letter, save each letter again, and preview and print both letters and envelopes.

Project 2

Belinda Montez, an assistant secretary in the human resources department, needs help with inserting page breaks and section breaks in her documents. Using the Office Assistant, research troubleshooting page and section breaks. Write

Belinda an interoffice memorandum describing the most common page and section break problems and suggest a solution based on what you learned from your research. Save, preview, and print the document.

Project 3

B. J. Chang asks you to find several Web pages that provide information for human resources professionals, including any online magazines devoted to the human resources field. Connect to your ISP, load your Web browser, and search for Web pages with information for human resources professionals. Print at least four Web pages. Write B. J. Chang an interoffice memorandum describing what you found on the Web. Save, preview, and print the memorandum.

Project 4

You want to practice hyphenating documents automatically and manually. Using the Office Assistant, review how to hyphenate documents—including the use of optional and nonbreaking hyphens. Open three documents of your choice and automatically hyphenate each document. Review each document and create nonbreaking and optional hyphens as necessary. Save each document with a new name and print it. Open two documents of your choice and manually hyphenate the documents. Save the documents with new names and print them. Create a three-page document that includes a title page and two pages of text. The title page should include the title "Using Word Features," your name, and the current date centered vertically and horizontally on the page. The text pages should describe in your own words how to search for and replace text and formatting, how to use the Select Browse Object feature, how to create different types of headers and footers, and how to use different hyphenation options. Create different first page headers and footers and leave them blank. Insert page numbers centered at the bottom of the page on pages two and three beginning with number 2. Insert your name as a header at the left margin of each even-numbered page and your school's name at the right margin of each odd-numbered page (except the first page). Use hyphenation as necessary. Save, preview, and print the document.

Project 5

B. J. Chang wants to post several open positions on the Web and asks you which Web sites to use. Connect to your ISP, load your Web browser, and search for Web sites that allow companies to post job openings. Print at least three pages. Write an interoffice memorandum to B. J. Chang recommending at least two Web sites. Discuss the reasons for your recommendations. Save, preview, and print the memorandum.

Project 6

You are working with Jody and Belinda on the new employee handbook and they have questions about creating the headers and footers for the handbook. Jody asks how to adjust the horizontal and vertical position of headers and footers and Belinda asks how to insert the chapter number and title in footers. Using online Help, look up

answers to these questions. Create an interoffice memorandum to both Jody and Belinda listing their questions and your answers. Save, preview, and print the document. With your instructor's permission, use the memo as a guide to show a classmate how to adjust the horizontal and vertical position of headers and footers and how to insert a chapter number and title in footers.

Project 7

Jody wants to know how to use the Special button in the expanded Find and Replace dialog box. Open a large document of your choice and experiment finding items on the Special button list. Also experiment finding items and replacing them with other items on the Special button list. Write Jody an interoffice memorandum describing how to use the Special button and suggesting how she can use the list to expedite editing her documents.

Project 8

Belinda has a large document and she wants to find every instance of a three-letter word that begins with "s" and ends with "t." It does not matter what the middle character is. She also misspelled the name "Cathy" throughout the document by spelling it "Kathy" and wants to find and correct each instance. Finally, she needs to find all words that begin with "program" such as "programming" and "programmed" and apply bold formatting. Using Word Help features determine the Find and Replace options Belinda can use to accomplish her goals with the large document. Create a two-page, unbound report for Belinda describing in your own words how to use all the options in the Find and Replace dialog box, and giving specific examples of how to use each option. Insert page numbers in the top right corner on both pages in a header using the Roman numeral style. Add your name at the left margin and the current date at the right margin in a footer on both pages. Save, preview, and print the report.

Working with Columns and Drawing Objects

Chapter Overview

Columns are used in many documents—from annual reports to brochures to newsletters. Often lines and shapes are added to documents to make certain text stand out or to create an interesting and attractive format. In this chapter, you learn how to key and edit text in columns and create and modify lines and objects.

LEARNING OBJECTIVES

► Creating and using newspaper-style columns
► Using the drawing toolbar

Case profile

The human resources department distributes the company newsletter each month. Jody Haversham assigns you the task of creating and formatting the company newsletter for September. The newsletter is one page of text, formatted with a title and two-column body text. As space permits, Jody asks you to insert an AutoShape object to add interest and draw attention to some aspect of the newsletter.

chapter ten

10.a Creating and Using Newspaper-Style Columns

So far, you've worked with documents that have only a single column of text from margin to margin. You can also create multi-column documents, such as advertising brochures or newsletters, using **newspaper-style columns**, which divide a document into two or more vertical columns placed side-by-side on a page. When you format a document with columns, text fills the length of one column before moving to the next column. You can create two, three, four, or more newspaper-style columns of equal or unequal width for an entire document or for selected text in a document.

The Columns button on the Standard toolbar displays a grid from which you specify the number of equally spaced columns you want. By default, the Columns button applies column formatting to the whole document or to the active section. To apply column formatting to a portion of the document, first select the text to be formatted and then select the number of columns from the Columns button grid. Word automatically inserts a continuous section break before and, if necessary, after the selected text in columns.

Jody hands you a hard copy of the September newsletter text, shown in Figure 10-1. After you key and format the text, you change the body text to a two-column format.

To create the September newsletter:

Step 1	Key	the document in Figure 10-1
Step 2	Save	the document as *September Newsletter*
Step 3	Zoom	the document to Page Width, if necessary, to view all the text at the right margin

You create a continuous section break at the first paragraph heading and then apply the column formatting to the body text section.

Step 4	Move	the insertion point to the left margin of the first paragraph heading "Annual Conference"
Step 5	Open	the Break dialog box
Step 6	Click	the Continuous option button
Step 7	Click	OK

chapter
ten

FIGURE 10-1
September Newsletter
Text

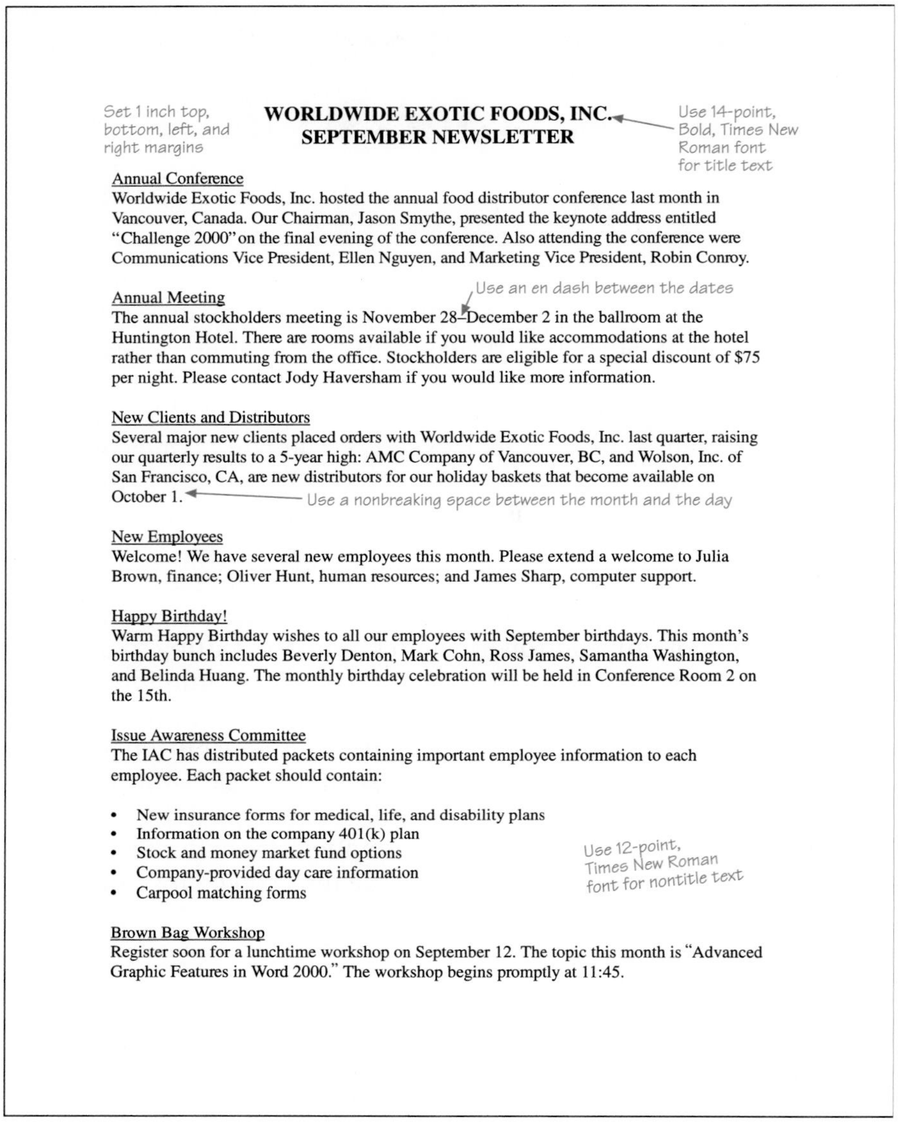

Set 1 inch top,
bottom, left, and
right margins

WORLDWIDE EXOTIC FOODS, INC.
SEPTEMBER NEWSLETTER

Use 14-point,
Bold, Times New
Roman font
for title text

<u>Annual Conference</u>
Worldwide Exotic Foods, Inc. hosted the annual food distributor conference last month in Vancouver, Canada. Our Chairman, Jason Smythe, presented the keynote address entitled "Challenge 2000" on the final evening of the conference. Also attending the conference were Communications Vice President, Ellen Nguyen, and Marketing Vice President, Robin Conroy.

Use an en dash between the dates

<u>Annual Meeting</u>
The annual stockholders meeting is November 28–December 2 in the ballroom at the Huntington Hotel. There are rooms available if you would like accommodations at the hotel rather than commuting from the office. Stockholders are eligible for a special discount of $75 per night. Please contact Jody Haversham if you would like more information.

<u>New Clients and Distributors</u>
Several major new clients placed orders with Worldwide Exotic Foods, Inc. last quarter, raising our quarterly results to a 5-year high: AMC Company of Vancouver, BC, and Wolson, Inc. of San Francisco, CA, are new distributors for our holiday baskets that become available on October 1. ← Use a nonbreaking space between the month and the day

<u>New Employees</u>
Welcome! We have several new employees this month. Please extend a welcome to Julia Brown, finance; Oliver Hunt, human resources; and James Sharp, computer support.

<u>Happy Birthday!</u>
Warm Happy Birthday wishes to all our employees with September birthdays. This month's birthday bunch includes Beverly Denton, Mark Cohn, Ross James, Samantha Washington, and Belinda Huang. The monthly birthday celebration will be held in Conference Room 2 on the 15th.

<u>Issue Awareness Committee</u>
The IAC has distributed packets containing important employee information to each employee. Each packet should contain:

- New insurance forms for medical, life, and disability plans
- Information on the company 401(k) plan
- Stock and money market fund options
- Company-provided day care information
- Carpool matching forms

Use 12-point,
Times New Roman
font for nontitle text

<u>Brown Bag Workshop</u>
Register soon for a lunchtime workshop on September 12. The topic this month is "Advanced Graphic Features in Word 2000." The workshop begins promptly at 11:45.

The title is in Section 1 of the document and the body text is in Section 2. You create two equally spaced newspaper-style columns in Section 2.

Step 8	*Verify*	the insertion point is in Section 2
Step 9	*Click*	the Columns button [icon] on the Standard toolbar
Step 10	*Move*	the mouse pointer to the second column indicator on the grid
Step 11	*Observe*	the text "2 Columns" at the bottom of the grid

| Step 12 | *Click* | the second column indicator on the grid |

Word creates the newspaper-style columns and automatically switches to Print Layout view. You can view multiple columns in Print Layout view or Print Preview, but not in Normal view. When the text in the first column reaches the bottom of the page, the remaining text shifts automatically to the next column. This can create uneven columns lengths. For example, the second column in the *September Newsletter* document is not as long as the first column. To view the columns:

| Step 1 | *Zoom* | the document to Whole Page to view the two newspaper-style columns |
| Step 2 | *Zoom* | the document to 75% so you can read the text |

To make the newsletter more attractive, you can balance the column length.

Balancing Column Length

To balance column length, you can insert manual column breaks that force text into the next column. Manual column breaks are inserted with an option in the Break dialog box. Manual column breaks can be deleted and recreated, if necessary, as you continue to edit the document. To insert a manual column break in the *September Newsletter* document:

Step 1	*Move*	the insertion point to the left margin of the line beginning with the text "Brown" below the paragraph heading "New Employees" in column one
Step 2	*Open*	the Break dialog box
Step 3	*Click*	the Column Break Option button
Step 4	*Click*	OK
Step 5	*Zoom*	the document to Whole Page and review the more even column lengths
Step 6	*Click*	the Undo button on the Standard toolbar to remove the manual column break

Another way to use manual column breaks is to keep related text together in columns. For example, look at the heading and two lines of the following paragraph at the bottom of column one in the *September Newsletter* document. The remaining paragraph text flows to the top of

C

chapter
ten

column two. It would be easier to read if both were in the same column. You can keep both the paragraph heading and following paragraph text together by inserting a manual column break. To insert a manual column break at the bottom of column one:

Step 1	*Zoom*	the document to 75% so you can read the text
Step 2	*Move*	the insertion point to the left margin of the last paragraph heading in column one
Step 3	*Insert*	a manual column break

The paragraph heading and two lines move to the top of column two with the remaining paragraph text. However, this column break does not create even column lengths. You decide to see how the document looks with other column formats.

Revising the Column Structure

The Columns dialog box provide a variety of formatting options that save you time creating newspaper-style columns. The five preset newspaper-style column formats are: One column, Two columns, Three columns, Left column, and Right column. The One, Two, and Three column formats create even column widths. The Left and Right column formats create uneven column widths. You can also add a horizontal line as a divider between the columns.

Word cannot remove a manual column break when it applies a different column format to text. So to reformat columns, you should first remove any manual column breaks. You do this moving the insertion point to the right of the column break and pressing the BACKSPACE key. To revise the column structure:

Step 1	*Verify*	the insertion point is at the top of column two
Step 2	*Press*	the BACKSPACE key
Step 3	*Click*	Format
Step 4	*Click*	Columns

The Columns dialog box that opens on your screen should look similar to Figure 10-2.

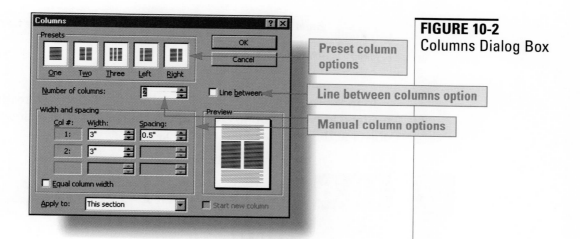

FIGURE 10-2
Columns Dialog Box

Preset column options

Line between columns option

Manual column options

First you try two newspaper-style columns with uneven widths.

Step 5	*Click*	<u>R</u>ight in the Presets group
Step 6	*Click*	OK
Step 7	*Zoom*	the document to Whole Page and review the columns

The text is in a wide left column and narrow right column. To try three evenly spaced columns with lines between them:

Step 1	*Open*	the Columns dialog box
Step 2	*Click*	<u>T</u>hree in the Presets group
Step 3	*Click*	the Line <u>b</u>etween check box to insert a check mark
Step 4	*Click*	OK

The text now appears in three evenly spaced columns with a vertical line between each column. You decide you liked two evenly spaced columns for the document. To modify the *September Newsletter* document:

Step 1	*Open*	the Columns dialog box
Step 2	*Click*	T<u>w</u>o in the Presets group
Step 3	*Click*	the Line <u>b</u>etween check box to remove the check mark
Step 4	*Click*	OK
Step 5	*Insert*	a manual column break before the last paragraph heading at the bottom of column one

M O U S E   T I P

You can change column widths by dragging the column indicator on the horizontal ruler with the mouse.

chapter
ten

| Step 6 | *Zoom* | the document to 75% so you can read the text |
| Step 7 | *Save* | the document |

To make the *September Newsletter* document more interesting to readers, Jody asks you to create and format an attractive drawing object at the bottom of column two.

C 10.b Using the Drawing Toolbar

Word provides a special toolbar, called the Drawing toolbar, which provides tools for creating and editing drawing objects in a document. **Drawing objects** are graphic items such as shapes, curves, and lines that can be created and edited with tools on the Drawing toolbar. For example, you can draw lines, arrows, rectangles, squares, ovals, special preset shapes called **AutoShapes**, and three-dimensional shapes by selecting the kind of object you want and then drawing the object with the mouse pointer. You can edit drawing objects to add text and color.

notes
It is a good idea to use the ScreenTips feature to review the buttons on each toolbar with which you are unfamiliar. For the remainder of this book it is assumed that each time a new toolbar is introduced you review the toolbar buttons before continuing with the step-by-step activities.

Jody suggests you draw a line below the text in column two and then add a "Congratulations!" banner below the text in column two. To view the Drawing toolbar and draw a line below the text in column two:

Step 1	*Move*	the insertion point to the bottom of column two
Step 2	*Click*	the Drawing button on the Standard toolbar to display the Drawing toolbar
Step 3	*Click*	the Line button on the Drawing toolbar
Step 4	*Move*	the mouse pointer to the left margin of column two approximately ¼ inch below the text (it becomes a drawing crosshair pointer)
Step 5	*Press & Hold*	the left mouse button

| Step 6 | *Drag* | approximately three inches to the right |
| Step 7 | *Release* | the mouse button to create the line |

Notice the small white squares at either end of the line. These are **sizing handles**, which you drag with the mouse pointer to change the size and shape of a drawing object. When you place the mouse pointer on a sizing handle, it becomes a black, two-headed sizing pointer that you use to drag the sizing handle in the desired direction. If you drag a corner sizing handle, the object maintains its vertical and horizontal proportion. The sizing handles also indicate an object is selected. To deselect the line object:

| Step 1 | *Click* | in the document outside the line object |

You use the AutoShapes tool to quickly draw special shapes such as stars and banners.

Using the AutoShapes Tool

The AutoShapes tool has many different preset shapes you can draw with the mouse pointer. To draw an AutoShape, you first select the shape to draw, move the mouse pointer to the appropriate location in the document, press and hold the left mouse button, and then drag downward and to the right to draw the shape. When the AutoShape object is the correct size, you release the mouse button.

To create the banner AutoShape in the newsletter:

| Step 1 | *Click* | the AutoShapes button AutoShapes ▾ on the Drawing toolbar |
| Step 2 | *Point to* | Stars and Banners |

The AutoShapes menu and Stars and Banners palette you see on your screen should look similar to Figure 10-3.

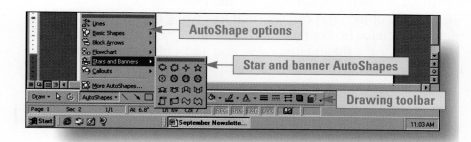

QUICK TIP

C To view a collection of pictures (also called **clips**) drawn with the AutoShapes tool, click the More AutoShapes command on the AutoShapes menu. Scroll to view the individual AutoShapes clips. To insert a clip in your document, right-click the clip and then click Insert.

FIGURE 10-3
AutoShapes Stars and Banners Palette

chapter
ten

Step 3	*Click*	the Down Ribbon option on the Stars and Banners grid (second column, the third row)
Step 4	*Move*	the mouse pointer to the left boundary of column two in the white space approximately ¼ inch below the line drawing object
Step 5	*Press & Hold*	the mouse button
Step 6	*Drag*	down approximately two inches and to the right approximately three inches
Step 7	*Release*	the mouse button to create the banner drawing object
Step 8	*Observe*	the sizing handles on the boundary of the banner object, indicating the object is selected
Step 9	*Deselect*	the banner object

The banner object on your screen should look similar to Figure 10-4.

FIGURE 10-4
Down Ribbon
Drawing Object

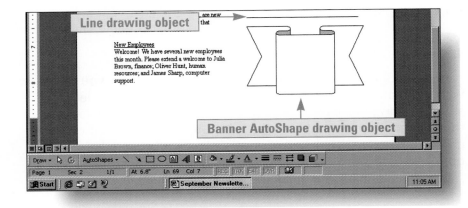

The banner drawing object is no longer selected. You can add text, shadow, and color to a drawing object.

Modifying Drawing Objects

To modify, or edit, a drawing object, you must first select it. Then you can use buttons on the Drawing toolbar to add fill (inside) color, line (border) color, a shadow effect, and even a three-dimensional effect to the object. You can also edit a drawing object with a shortcut menu and dialog box options.

You change the fill and line color, and add a blue shadow effect to the banner object. To modify the banner object:

Step 1	*Right-click*	the banner object

| Step 2 | *Click* | Format AutoShape |
| Step 3 | *Click* | the Colors and Lines tab, if necessary |

The Format AutoShape dialog box that opens on your screen should look similar to Figure 10-5.

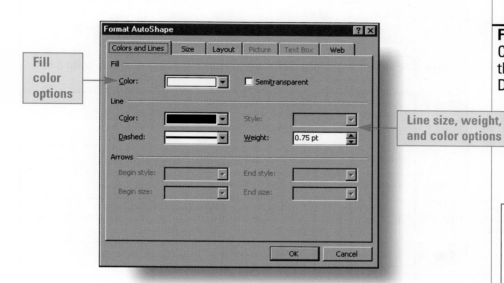

Fill color options

Line size, weight, and color options

FIGURE 10-5
Colors and Lines Tab in the Format AutoShape Dialog Box

Step 4	*Click*	the Fill Color: list arrow
Step 5	*Click*	Red (first column, third row)
Step 6	*Click*	the Line Color: list arrow
Step 7	*Click*	Blue (sixth column, second row)
Step 8	*Click*	OK
Step 9	*Click*	the Shadow button ▣ on the Drawing toolbar
Step 10	*Click*	Shadow Style 2 on the Shadow grid (second column, first row)
Step 11	*Click*	the Shadow button ▣ on the Drawing toolbar
Step 12	*Click*	Shadow Settings to display the Shadow Settings toolbar
Step 13	*Click*	the Shadow Color button list arrow 🖳▾ on the Shadow Settings toolbar
Step 14	*Click*	Blue on the Shadow Color grid (sixth column, second row)
Step 15	*Close*	the Shadow Settings toolbar

M O U S E   T I P

C You can insert pictures in your document by clicking the Insert Clip Art button on the Drawing toolbar to open the Clip Gallery. Then select and insert a picture.

You can insert specially formatted text by clicking the Insert WordArt button on the Drawing toolbar.

chapter
ten

Because the banner is meant to draw attention to the New Employees, you add the text "Congratulations!" to the banner. You can add text to a drawing object with a shortcut menu. To add and edit text to the banner object:

Step 1	*Right-click*	the banner object
Step 2	*Click*	Add Te**x**t
Step 3	*Observe*	the insertion point inside the banner object
Step 4	*Press*	the ENTER key twice to move the insertion point down two lines
Step 5	*Key*	Congratulations!
Step 6	*Select*	the text
Step 7	*Center*	the text
Step 8	*Change*	the font size to 14
Step 9	*Click*	the Font Color button list arrow [A ▾] on the Drawing toolbar
Step 10	*Click*	Blue (sixth column, second row)

If the text area in the banner object is too small to contain the formatted text on one line, the text wraps to the next line. You can increase the size of the object, if necessary, so the text fits on one line. To size the banner object, if necessary:

Step 1	*Move*	the insertion point to the lower-right corner sizing handle (the mouse pointer becomes a black, two-headed sizing pointer)
Step 2	*Drag*	the sizing handle down and right approximately ¼ inch or until the formatted text fits inside the banner object without wrapping to the next line
Step 3	*Deselect*	the banner object
Step 4	*Save*	the document

The banner drawing object on your screen is now red with a blue boundary, blue shadow effect, and blue text. Some drawing objects can have a three-dimensional shape. Instead of the banner object, you decide to use a three-dimensional rectangle object.

Creating and Modifying 3-D Shapes

When you no longer want a drawing object in your document, you can select and delete it. To select an object that contains text, move the mouse pointer to the object's boundary. The mouse pointer then becomes a move or selection pointer. (If you move the pointer to the text area of an object, it becomes an I-beam.) To select and delete the banner object:

Step 1	**Move**	the mouse pointer to the banner object's boundary
Step 2	**Click**	the banner object's boundary with the move or selection pointer to select the object
Step 3	**Press**	the DELETE key

In place of the banner object, you draw a rectangle and then add color, text, and a three-dimensional effect. To create and modify a rectangle drawing object:

Step 1	**Click**	the Rectangle button ▢ on the Drawing toolbar
Step 2	**Move**	the mouse pointer to the left margin of column two in the white space below the line
Step 3	**Drag**	down approximately one inch and to the right approximately three inches to create the rectangle object
Step 4	**Select**	the rectangle drawing object, if necessary
Step 5	**Click**	the Fill Color button list arrow 🎨 ▾ on the Drawing toolbar
Step 6	**Click**	Orange on the Fill Color grid (second color, second row)
Step 7	**Click**	the 3-D button 📦 ▾ on the Drawing toolbar
Step 8	**Click**	3-D Style 1 on the grid (first style, first row)
Step 9	**Click**	the 3-D button 📦 ▾ on the Drawing toolbar
Step 10	**Click**	3-D Settings to view the 3-D Settings toolbar

QUICK TIP

🅲 You can add interest to your documents by adding borders and shading to selected paragraphs. Select the paragraph text and then click the Borders and Shading command on the Format menu to view border and shading options.

chapter
ten

You can turn on or off the 3-D effect, tilt the 3-D object, change its shape and direction, change the lighting effect for any side, change the surface composition, and change the color with buttons on this toolbar. You lighten the color on the front surface of the object.

Step 11	*Click*	the Lighting button on the 3-D Settings toolbar
Step 12	*Click*	the button in the center of the grid
Step 13	*Close*	the 3-D Settings toolbar

Next you key text in the rectangle and format it. To add text:

Step 1	*Right-click*	the 3-D rectangle object
Step 2	*Click*	Add Te<u>x</u>t
Step 3	*Key*	Congratulations! two lines from the top of the object
Step 4	*Select*	the text
Step 5	*Format*	the text with 22 point, bold, white color font, and center alignment

Now that the rectangle is complete, you can resize and reposition it. To size and move the rectangle object:

Step 1	*Verify*	the rectangle object is selected
Step 2	*Drag*	the lower-right sizing handle down and to the right approximately ¼ inch with the black, double-headed sizing pointer
Step 3	*Drag*	the rectangle object from the bottom boundary of the object with the selection or move pointer until it is positioned attractively below the line
Step 4	*Deselect*	the object
Step 5	*Click*	the Drawing button on the Standard toolbar to close the Drawing toolbar
Step 6	*Save*	the document and close it

The completed newsletter looks much more attractive and interesting with the added drawing objects.

Summary

▶ Newspaper-style columns are appropriate for documents like brochures or newsletters.

▶ When you use newspaper-style columns, the text fills the length of one column before moving to the next column.

▶ You can create newspaper-style columns for an entire document or for a section of a document.

▶ You can select text and create columns from the selected text, or you can insert a section break and then create columns for the text in a specific section.

▶ You can view text columns in Print Layout view or Print Preview, but not in Normal view.

▶ When you use the Columns button on the Standard toolbar, Word creates columns that are equal in width by default.

▶ You can create columns of unequal width by using one of the two preset unequal-width column options or by specifying the exact column width in the Columns dialog box.

▶ You can add a vertical divider line between columns.

▶ Drawing objects—such as shapes, lines, and curves—are graphic items that you draw and edit with buttons on the Drawing toolbar.

▶ AutoShapes are special preset shapes—such as stars, banners, and flowchart symbols—that you draw with the mouse pointer.

▶ You can add fill and line color and three-dimensional shapes to drawing objects with buttons on the Drawing toolbar.

chapter ten

Commands Review

Action	Menu Bar	Shortcut Menu	Toolbar	Keyboard
Create columns of text	Format, Columns			ALT + O, C
Insert a column break	Insert, Break			ALT + I, B CTRL + SHIFT + ENTER
View the Drawing toolbar	View, Toolbars, Drawing	Right-click any toolbar, click Drawing		ALT + V, T, DOWN ARROW, ENTER
Format a drawing object		Right-click the object, click Format (object name)	Various buttons on the Drawing toolbar	

Concepts Review

SCANS

Circle the correct answer.

1. Which of the following is not a preset option for creating columns in the Columns dialog box?
   [a] Right
   [b] Center
   [c] Left
   [d] Two

2. Which of the following is not an AutoShapes category?
   [a] Basic Shapes
   [b] Block Arrows
   [c] Hearts and Flowers
   [d] Stars and Banners

3. When you use the Columns button, columns are automatically created with:
   [a] unequal column widths.
   [b] equal column widths.
   [c] divider lines.
   [d] justified alignment.

4. To add a special effect to a drawing object, you can click the:
   [a] Shadow button on the Drawing toolbar.
   [b] 3-D button on the Standard toolbar.
   [c] Fill Color button on the Formatting toolbar.
   [d] AutoShapes command on the menu bar.

5. To balance columns of uneven length, you should insert a(n):
   [a] page break.
   [b] even page section break.
   [c] column break.
   [d] line break.

6. To prevent a document title from becoming part of a column you can:
   [a] insert a section break below the title.
   [b] apply a 14-point font to the title.
   [c] center and bold the title.
   [d] indent the title.

7. When you add text to a drawing object, and move the mouse pointer to the text area, it becomes a(n):
   [a] move pointer.
   [b] sizing handle.
   [c] sizing pointer.
   [d] I-beam.

8. Before you apply different column formats, you should remove the manual:
   [a] page breaks.
   [b] section breaks.
   [c] column breaks.
   [d] line breaks.

9. You can use sizing handles to:
[a] format drawing objects.
[b] position text in newspaper-style columns.
[c] change the size and shape of drawing objects.
[d] draw preset stars, banners, and other graphic items.

10. To draw a straight line, square, or oval you use a button on the Drawing toolbar and the:
[a] CTRL key
[b] ALT key.
[c] SHIFT key.
[d] TAB key.

Circle **T** if the statement is true or **F** is the statement is false.

T F   1. With newspaper-style columns, text fills one column before moving to the next column on a page.

T F   2. Columns appear on the screen only in Print Layout view.

T F   3. You can redistribute text in columns by inserting a manual page break.

T F   4. The insertion point must be in the document section formatted in columns to revise the number of columns.

T F   5. You can change column width by dragging the column marker on the horizontal ruler.

T F   6. You can view vertical lines between columns in Normal view.

T F   7. You cannot create a manual column break with shortcut keys.

T F   8. Columns are created in unequal width when you use the Columns button.

T F   9. To draw an AutoShape you first select the shape, press the left mouse button, and drag down and to the right.

T F   10. You create three-dimensional shapes with a button on the Formatting toolbar.

Skills Review

Exercise 1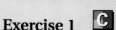

1. Open the *Legislative Update* document located on the Data Disk.

2. Insert a continuous section break below the second title line "LEGISLATIVE UPDATE."

3. Format the text in Section 2 with two columns of even width.

4. Insert column breaks so that the columns are approximately the same lengths.

5. Add a vertical line between the columns.

6. Switch to Normal view and select the two lines of title text in Section 1.

7. Expand the characters in the title text by 0.5 points. (*Hint:* Use the Character Spacing tab in the Font dialog box.)

8. Save the document as *Legislative Update With Columns*.

9. Preview, print, and close the document.

chapter ten

Exercise 2

1. Create a new, blank document.

2. Display the Drawing toolbar.

3. Draw a rectangle and fill it with blue. Change the line color to yellow. Change the line style to 2¼ point.

4. Draw an arrow to the right of the rectangle and format it with red using the Line Color button. Change the arrowhead style to Arrow Style 7 using the Arrow Style button.

5. Draw an oval below the rectangle and fill it with yellow. Change the line color to red. Change the line style to 6 point (three narrow and one wide line option). Add the text "Oval" in red, 14-point font in the center of the oval.

6. Using the SHIFT key and the Rectangle button, draw a square below the arrow and fill it with orange. Add the 3-D Style 17 to the square. Change the lighting effect to brighten the top of the 3-D object. Change the 3-D color to gold. (*Hint:* Use the 3-D Color button on the 3-D Settings toolbar.)

7. Using the SHIFT key and the Oval button draw a circle below the square and fill it with purple. Change the line color to orange. Add a light orange shadow effect to the circle.

8. Save the document as *Drawing Objects*.

9. Preview, print, and close the document.

Exercise 3

1. Open the *Announcements* document located on the Data Disk.

2. Find all instances of underlined text and replace it with no underline and Small Caps effect.

3. Format the entire document in two columns of uneven width using the <u>R</u>ight preset option.

4. Select the entire document and justify the text.

5. Save the document as *Announcements Revised*.

6. Preview, print, and close the document.

Exercise 4

1. Create a new, blank document.

2. Center the title "AutoShapes" in Arial, 14-point, bold font.

3. Display the Drawing toolbar.

4. Using the AutoShapes tool, draw five AutoShapes of your choice anywhere in the document.

5. Use fill and line color as desired.

6. Add text to two of the AutoShapes.

7. Format the text as desired.

8. Save the document as *AutoShape Examples*.

9. Preview, print, and close the document.

Exercise 5

1. Open the *Chicago Warehouses Audit* report located on the Data Disk.

2. Format the body text (not the title) in two columns of even width.

3. Insert a manual column break at the paragraph beginning "A consulting company…."

4. Save the document as *Chicago Warehouses Audit With Columns*.

5. Preview, print, and close the document.

Exercise 6

1. Create the following document. Use a 2-inch top and 1-inch left and right margins. Use the Times New Roman 10-point font for the body text and 12-point bold font for the title text.

2. Use newspaper-style columns for the body text beginning with "Pink Beach" paragraph heading.

3. Insert a manual column break to more evenly space the columns.

WORLDWIDE EXOTIC FOODS, INC.
TRAVEL SERVICES SPRING RECOMMENDATION
BONAIRE

On this sleepy island only 50 miles off the coast of Venezuela, where pink flamingos outnumber people, scuba diving is the sport of choice among visitors. Bonaire takes an enlightened approach to its marine environment, with the entire perimeter of the island from the high-water mark to 200 feet below deemed a protected park with restricted coral taking and spear fishing. Many attractions are described below.

Pink Beach
The prettiest stretch of sand on the island, Pink Beach lies on the southwestern shore and really does takes on a pinkish hue in the late afternoon sun. The powder-soft sand and bathwater-calm water makes it perfect for swimming, snorkeling, and scuba diving.

Salt Flats and Slave Huts
On the southern end of the island, huge white pyramids of industrial salt—looking like misplaced mounds of snow—are harvested by the Akzo Salt Antilles Company. The salt industry, which began in the early 19th century, formerly employed African slaves, who worked the fields by day, then slept in cramped huts (which can still be seen along the roadside) by night, returning to their homes in Rincon only on weekends.

Kralendijk
The quiet capital city of this serene island has only one main street—J. A. Abraham Boulevard, which turns into Kaya Grandi.

Boca Cai
At the mouth of La Bay on the eastern side of the island, this serene beach boasts mountainous heaps of conch shells, left there by fishermen. On weekends, particularly Sundays, Boca Cai is the place to be as two snack shacks open their doors, a meringue band strikes up the tunes, and locals and in-the-know visitors congregate for food, fun, music, and cold beverages.

---

4. Save the document as *Travel Services Recommendation*.

5. Preview, print, and close the document.

Exercise 7

1. Create the following document. Use a 2-inch top and 1-inch left and right margins. Use the Arial 10-point font for the body text and 12-point bold font for the title text.

2. Use three columns of equal width for the body text and insert the appropriate manual column breaks. Add a vertical line between the columns.

3. Save the document as *Office Technology Society*.

4. Preview, print, and close the document.

OFFICE TECHNOLOGY SOCIETY

OTS PURPOSE
Our primary purpose is to offer a symposium to exchange ideas among business and academic members. This knowledge facilitates research that helps the office workplace.

Secondarily, we advise the public on changes in office information technology in the areas of analysis, design, and administrative decision support.

OTS ACTIVITIES
- **Newsletter** – Published monthly. Update activities, conferences, research projects.

- **Journal** – Contains major excerpts from the research projects taken on by the members.

- **Research Conference** – A two-day annual conference where ideas and trends in office technology are discussed and papers are presented.

OTS MEMBERSHIP
1. Faculty members and students in the office technology field.

2. Administrators in business and government who manage office technology for their organizations.

3. Administrators, research directors, and vendors in the field of office technology.

Exercise 8

1. Open the *Training Commitment* document located on the Data Disk.

2. Create two newspaper-style columns of even width for the entire document.

3. Insert a column break at the "About Our Courses" paragraph.

4. Display the Drawing toolbar.

5. Draw a straight line across the bottom of the columns from the left margin of column one to the right margin of column two.

6. Draw a 24-point star AutoShape approximately two inches tall and two inches wide below the line and fill it with yellow. Change the border around the star to blue. (*Hint:* Use the Line Color button list arrow.)

7. Center the text "Our Training Commitment" on three lines near the center of the object and format the text with 14-point font.

8. Size the star, if necessary, to accommodate the new font size.

9. Zoom the document to Whole Page and reposition the star object close to the center of the page below the line with the mouse pointer then zoom back to 100%.

10. Select the line object and use the Line Style button to format the line with the 2¼ point style. (*Hint:* Click the line to select it.)

11. Save the document as *Training Commitment With Columns.*

12. Preview, print, and close the document.

Case Projects

Project 1

You are the secretary for the local chapter of the Office Technology Society and you prepare a quarterly newsletter for all chapter members. Create a newsletter titled "OFFICE TECHNOLOGY BULLETIN" with two newspaper-style columns of body text containing fictitious data for the following paragraph headings:

> Membership Drive
>
> New Members
>
> Annual Conference
>
> User Tips for Word 2000
>
> Hot Internet Sites

Add a line between the columns. Add an appropriate drawing object at the bottom of column two. Using online Help, review the "about graphics" topic, then use the Insert Clip Art and Insert WordArt buttons on the Drawing toolbar to insert metafiles, bitmaps, WordArt and other graphic objects in the newsletter. Insert at least five objects. Reposition two objects. Delete two objects. Use the Borders and Shading dialog box to apply borders and shading to selected paragraphs in the newsletter. Save, preview, and print the document.

Project 2

Jody Haversham is transferred to another department. Bill Martin, the new administrative assistant to B. J. Chang, is having trouble preparing the monthly employee newsletter. He does not know how to change column widths or balance the column text so that the newsletter has an attractive appearance; he asks you for help. Create an interoffice memorandum to Bill describing how to use the Office Assistant to troubleshoot problems with columns. Include two paragraphs explaining how to change column widths and balance column text. Save, preview, and print the memorandum.

chapter ten

Project 3

Your new assignment in the human resources department is to fill in for the corporate librarian while she is at a conference. Joe Beck in the finance department requests a list of investment-oriented online magazines and newsletters. Connect to your ISP, load your Web browser, and search for investment-oriented online newsletters and magazines. Print at least two Web pages. Write an interoffice memo to Joe describing the results of your search. Use two evenly-spaced columns separated by a line for the Web page descriptions. Add an appropriate AutoShape drawing object to the memo. Attach the Web pages you printed.

Project 4

Bill Martin drops by your desk to tell you about the AutoShape pictures he discovered. You want to experiment using these AutoShapes and then tell Kelly Armstead and Jody Haversham about them. Create a new, blank document. Display the Drawing toolbar, click the More AutoShapes command on the AutoShapes menu. Explore the contents of the More AutoShapes dialog box. Explore inserting AutoShape pictures in the blank document. Write an interoffice memorandum to both Kelly and Jody describing the AutoShapes pictures and suggesting ways they can use them in their documents. Save, preview, and print the memo.

Project 5

Chris Lofton, the manager of the word processing department, calls and asks for your help. The word processing department is experiencing delays in getting final documents to the authors. Chris thinks a flowchart illustrating an efficient workflow in the department will help identify any bottlenecks. You agree to help by creating the flowchart. Use the Flowchart and Lines options on the AutoShapes button to create a flowchart of an efficient workflow that includes keying, proofreading, editing, and printing documents. Add text and color to the drawing objects in the flowchart. Save, preview, and print the flowchart.

Project 6

The human resources department is helping a neighborhood civic association to hold its annual fund-raising bake sale by providing clerical support for the association. You are asked to create a flyer announcing the bake sale that can be copied and posted at neighborhood stores. Create an $8\frac{1}{2} \times 11$-inch flyer using fictitious data announcing the bake sale. Include a map showing the major roads and specific intersections and address of the building where the bake sale is to be held. (*Hint:* Use AutoShapes and other drawing objects to create the map.) Include formatting drawing objects to highlight the event. Assume the flyer is to be printed on white paper on a color printer. Use color in the fonts and drawing objects. Save, preview, and print the flyer.

Project 7

Bill Martin calls and asks for help. B. J. Chang wants a list of Web-based training classes covering office technology topics and Bill is not familiar with the WWW. You agree to search for the Web sites and write a memo to Chang. Connect to your ISP, load your Web browser, and search for Web sites providing online classes in office technology topics. Print at least three Web pages. Write an interoffice memorandum to B. J. Chang describing the results of your search. Use columns and drawing objects to make the memo more interesting. Save, preview, and print the memorandum. Attach the Web pages to the memorandum.

Project 8

While working on the September newsletter, you noticed three AutoShape lines with which you are unfamiliar: the Curve, the Freeform, and the Scribble lines. You want to know how to use these line drawing tools. Using the Office Assistant, research how to use these three tools. Create a new, blank document and experiment using each of the tools. Save, preview, and print the document.

Using Tables to Organize Information

Chapter Overview

Certain columnar data included in a document, such as budgets and price lists, needs to be organized in a logical manner so that it is easier to read and understand. You could use tabs to organize this data, but usually it is simpler to place it in a table. In this chapter you learn how to create and edit tables, format them attractively, use formulas to perform calculations, and switch text to tables and back again.

Learning Objectives

► Create and format tables
► Revise tables and modify table structure
► Use special table features
► Switch between text and tables

Case profile

The marketing and sales departments at Worldwide Exotic Foods, Inc. are getting ready for the busy holiday shopping season and need assistance preparing correspondence and reports. You are assigned to handle the work overflow for both departments. First you create a letter about advertising budgets, then you create a holiday price list cover sheet, and finally you format the latest phone extension list for the company's sales representatives. You use tables in each document.

chapter eleven

C **11.a** Creating and Formatting Tables

R. D. Jacobson, the media director for the marketing department, gives you a page of handwritten notes and asks you to use the notes to create a letter to the advertising agency that develops the media buying plans for Worldwide Exotic Foods. The letter contains the media budget for this year's holiday season. Jacobson's executive assistant, Maria Betancourt, suggests you organize the budget data in a table. You begin by creating a new, blank document and keying part of text. To create the letter:

Step 1	*Create*	a new, blank document
Step 2	*Set*	the appropriate margins for a block format letter
Step 3	*Key*	the current date, letter address, salutation, and first two body paragraphs shown in Figure 11-1
Step 4	*Press*	the ENTER key twice
Step 5	*Zoom*	the document to Page Width, if necessary, to view the text at the right margin

The next part of the letter contains the table of information. A **table** is a grid organized into columns and rows. A **column** is a set of information that runs down the page. A **row** runs across the page. A **cell** occurs at a column and row intersection. First, you create the table grid and key the data in the table cells. You can then add or remove the table border, format the text using the same formatting features you use for the body text, size the table, and position the table on the page.

The Insert Table button on the Standard toolbar displays a grid from which you select the number of rows and columns for the table by dragging the mouse pointer down and across the grid. To create a table with 5 rows and 4 columns:

Step 1	*Click*	the Insert Table button on the Standard toolbar
Step 2	*Move*	the mouse pointer to the upper-left cell in the grid
Step 3	*Observe*	the text "1 x 1 Table" at the bottom of the grid, indicating one row and one column are selected
Step 4	*Drag*	the mouse pointer down five rows and across four columns (until you see 5 x 4 Table at the bottom of the grid)

FIGURE 11-1
Completed Dynamic
Advertising Letter

Current date

Ms. Sue Wong
Account Executive
Dynamic Advertising Agency
3268 West International Blvd.
Dallas, TX 75211-1052

Dear Ms. Wong:

Please extend our thanks and congratulations to everyone at the Dynamic Advertising Agency
who works on the Worldwide Exotic Foods, Inc. account. Because of the outstanding media
program developed by your team last year, we experienced outstanding holiday sales.

We anticipate holiday sales for this year to exceed last year. Therefore, we are increasing this
year's media budget by 20%. The budget is detailed below:

Worldwide Exotic Foods, Inc. Media Budget				
Branch Office	**Holiday Baskets**	**Beverage Baskets**	**Gift Certificates**	**Total**
Chicago	$133,175.45	$55,321.89	$11,500.98	$199,998.32
London	74,768.90	46,987.37	10,589.32	132,345.59
Melbourne	97,509.52	30,890.00	1,561.25	129,960.77
Vancouver	458,321.89	138,079.43	15,345.95	611,747.27
Total	$763,775.76	$271,278.69	$38,997.50	$1,074,051.95

We can discuss these budget figures in detail at our media program meeting next week.

Sincerely,

R. D. Jacobson
Media Director

xx

Step 5	*Release*	the mouse button to create the table

Step 6	*Save*	the document as *Dynamic Advertising Letter*

The insertion point automatically appears in the first cell of the table.
Whenever the insertion point is in the table, column markers also
appear on the horizontal ruler. Word inserts table nonprinting
formatting marks, called end-of-cell and end-of-row marks, in the table.
You use these formatting marks to select cells, rows, and columns.

Step 7	*Click*	the Show/Hide button ¶ on the Standard toolbar to view the table formatting marks, if necessary

chapter
eleven

Your screen should look similar to Figure 11-2.

FIGURE 11-2
Table Grid,
Column Markers, and
Formatting Marks

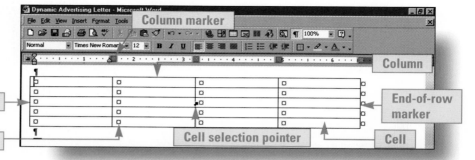

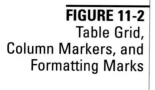

QUICK TIP

Remember that the selection bar runs from the ruler to the View buttons along the document's left margin.

To key text in a table you must move the insertion point from cell to cell.

Moving the Insertion Point in a Table

You can use the I-beam and the keyboard to move the insertion point from cell to cell. You do not press the ENTER key. Pressing the ENTER key creates a new line inside the cell. To move the insertion point with the I-beam, just click in the appropriate cell. To use the keyboard, press the appropriate ARROW key, press the TAB key to move one cell to the right, or press the SHIFT + TAB keys to move one cell to the left. Table 11-1 lists keyboard methods for moving the insertion point in a table.

TABLE 11-1
Table Movement Keys

Location	Keys	Location	Keys
One cell down	DOWN ARROW	First cell in a row	ALT + HOME
One cell right	TAB (RIGHT ARROW, if the cell is empty)	Last cell in a row	ALT + END
One cell left	SHIFT + TAB (LEFT ARROW, if the cell is empty)	First cell in a column	ALT + PAGE UP
One cell up	UP ARROW	Last cell in a column	ALT + PAGE DOWN

CAUTION TIP

By default, the table is created with thin, black borders that print. If you do not want to print a border you can remove it by moving the insertion point inside the table, opening the Borders and Shading dialog box, and clicking the None preset option on the Borders tab.

To move the insertion point in the table:

Step 1	*Click*	the middle of the first cell of the second row
Step 2	*Press*	the UP ARROW key
Step 3	*Continue*	to practice moving the insertion point in the table using Table 11-1 as your guide

| Step 4 | *Move* | the insertion point to the first cell (upper-left corner) in the table |

Now you are ready to key the text in the table.

Keying Text in Tables

You key the column headings in the first row of the table, called the **heading row**, and then key the branch office budget data in the following rows. Do not worry about keying the Totals row or column now; you add these later. As you key the numbers, do not align them in the cells. You align the numbers later. If you accidentally press the ENTER key while keying data in a cell, press the BACKSPACE key to remove the paragraph mark and blank line from the cell. To key the column headings:

Step 1	*Verify*	the insertion point is in the first cell in the first row
Step 2	*Key*	Branch Office and press the TAB key
Step 3	*Key*	Holiday Baskets and press the TAB key
Step 4	*Key*	Beverage Baskets and press the TAB key
Step 5	*Key*	Gift Certificates and press the TAB key

The insertion point moves to the first cell in the second row. Now you can key the rest of the data.

Step 6	*Key*	Chicago and press the TAB key
Step 7	*Continue*	to key the remaining data in the Branch Office, Holiday Baskets, Beverage Baskets, and Gift Certificates columns for the Chicago, London, Melbourne, and Vancouver branches, as shown in Figure 11-1 (*do not key the total text or numbers*)
Step 8	*Save*	the document

In addition to moving the insertion point from cell to cell, you also select cells, rows, and columns to format or delete the contents or to insert or delete the cells, rows, and columns.

Selecting Cells, Rows, and Columns

Before you can format the table contents, you must select the cells that contain the text. If you move the mouse pointer to the lower-left corner of a cell, to the selection bar to the left of a row, or to the top of

chapter
eleven

a column, the mouse pointer becomes a selection pointer. You can also select parts of a table with the keyboard. Table 11-2 lists mouse pointer and keyboard selection techniques.

TABLE 11-2
Table Selection Methods

Selection	Mouse	Keyboard
Cell	Move the mouse pointer inside the left boundary of a cell and click	Move the insertion point to the cell and press the SHIFT + END keys
Several cells	Drag across the cells with the selection pointer or the I-beam	Move the insertion point to the first cell, press and hold the SHIFT key, and then press the UP, DOWN, LEFT, or RIGHT ARROW key
Column	Move the mouse pointer to the top of the column until it becomes a vertical selection pointer then click, or press and hold the ALT key and click a cell in the column with the I-beam pointer	Move the insertion point to the first cell in the column, hold down the SHIFT key, and press the ALT + PAGE DOWN keys
Row	Click the selection bar at the left of the row, or double-click any cell in a row with the selection pointer	Move the insertion point to the first cell in the row, hold down the SHIFT key, and press the ALT + END keys
Table	Drag to select all rows or all columns (including the end-of-row marks) with the selection pointer	Move the insertion point to any cell, press the NUMLOCK key on the numeric keypad to turn off the Number Lock feature, and press the ALT + 5 keys (the 5 key on the numeric keypad).

M E N U   T I P

You can point to the Select command on the Table menu and then click Table, Column, Row, or Cell to select all or part of the table containing the insertion point.

To select a row, column, and cell in the table:

Step 1	*Move*	the mouse pointer to the left of the first row in the selection bar
Step 2	*Click*	the selection bar
Step 3	*Move*	the mouse pointer to the top of the second column (the mouse pointer becomes a small black selection pointer)
Step 4	*Click*	the column with the selection pointer
Step 5	*Move*	the mouse pointer just inside the left cell boundary in last cell in the last row (the mouse pointer becomes a small black selection pointer)
Step 6	*Click*	the cell with the selection pointer

| Step 7 | *Continue* | to select cells, rows, columns, and the entire table using Table 11-2 as your guide |
| Step 8 | *Move* | the insertion point to the first cell in the first row |

You can delete both the contents of a table and the table grid. To delete the contents of a cell, row, or column, simply select the cell, row, or column and press the DELETE key. To delete the entire table grid or a cell, row, or column, you must use a menu command. First move the insertion point to the table column, row, or cell, point to the Delete command on the Table menu, and click Table, Columns, Rows, or Cells. To delete the first row of the table:

Step 1	*Click*	Table
Step 2	*Point to*	Delete
Step 3	*Click*	Rows

The row is deleted. Because you want to use the entire table in the letter, you restore it.

| Step 4 | *Click* | the Undo button on the Standard toolbar |

Now you are ready to format the table text.

Changing Cell Formats

To help distinguish the column labels from the rest of the data, you format them. You format text in a table just like you do in the body of a document. To add bold and center the column headings:

Step 1	*Select*	the first row containing the column headings
Step 2	*Click*	the Bold button **B** on the Formatting toolbar
Step 3	*Click*	the Center button on the Formatting toolbar
Step 4	*Click*	any cell to deselect the row
Step 5	*Save*	the document

Later you shade the cells. Now, you add the table heading and the column and row totals.

CAUTION TIP

When you select all or part of a table and then press the DELETE key, only the contents in the selected part of the table are deleted. To use the DELETE key to delete an entire table, you must also select a portion of the text or a blank line above or below the table before pressing the DELETE key.

chapter
eleven

11.b Revising Tables and Modifying Table Structure

Once you create a table, you often need to modify it by inserting rows or columns for additional data, or by deleting unused rows and columns. For the table in the letter, you need to insert a row at the top of the table for the table heading, a row at the bottom of the table for the column totals, and a column at the right of the table for the row totals.

Inserting Rows and Columns

To insert rows or columns, first select the number of rows or columns you want to insert. For example, to insert two rows, select two rows in the table. Then you click the Insert command on the Table menu to insert the rows or columns above or below the selected row and left or right of the selected column. The inserted row retains the formatting from the original row. To add a new row at the top of the table using the Table menu:

Step 1	*Move*	the insertion point to any cell in the first row
Step 2	*Click*	Table
Step 3	*Point to*	Insert
Step 4	*Click*	Rows Above

A new row is inserted at the top of the table. To insert a column at the end of the table, you select the end-of-row marks just like you select a column. To insert a new column at the end of the table:

Step 1	*Select*	the end-of-row marks with the vertical selection pointer
Step 2	*Right-click*	the selection
Step 3	*Click*	Insert Columns
Step 4	*Observe*	the new column inserted to the left of the end-of-cell marks
Step 5	*Click*	the first cell in the new column
Step 6	*Observe*	that the cell is set for bold font and centered alignment, the same as other cells in the row

---

MOUSE TIP

When you select a table row, the Insert Table button on the Standard toolbar becomes the Insert Rows button. When you select a cell or column, the Insert Table button becomes the Insert Cell or Insert Column button.

The cells in the new column retain the same formatting as other cells in their respective rows. When you add a new column, the overall table size doesn't change but the column widths adjust to accommodate the new column. Notice the column heading "Beverage Baskets" now wraps to two lines and the row height increases to accommodate the new line. The remaining column labels fit on the first text line in each cell. The column labels are more attractive if they are aligned vertically at the bottom of each cell. There are nine cell alignment options, which combine the horizontal options (left, right, and center) with the vertical options (top, bottom, and center). To change the vertical alignment:

Step 1	*Select*	the column labels row
Step 2	*Right-click*	the selected row
Step 3	*Point to*	Cell Alignment
Step 4	*Click*	Align Bottom Center button on the palette
Step 5	*Move*	the insertion point to any cell in the first column

A table heading in the first row helps identify the data in the table. Currently the first row has five cells, one for each column. You only need one cell for a table heading.

Merging Cells

You can combine, or **merge**, cells vertically or horizontally by first selecting the cells to be merged and then clicking the Merge Cells command on the Table menu or a shortcut menu. You can also divide, or **split**, cells vertically or horizontally. Before you key and format the table heading, you must combine or merge the five cells in the first row into one cell. To merge the cells in the first row:

Step 1	*Select*	the first row
Step 2	*Right-click*	the selected row
Step 3	*Click*	Merge Cells

The first row of the table now contains one large cell. To key the two-line table heading:

| Step 1 | *Key* | Worldwide Exotic Foods, Inc. |
| Step 2 | *Press* | the ENTER key to create a new line in the cell |

C

chapter eleven

Step 3	*Key*	Media Budget

Step 4	*Observe*	that the two-line table heading is centered and bold and the row height increases to accommodate the second line of the heading

You now need to add a row at the bottom of the table for the category totals. You can do this with the TAB key. To add a row to the bottom of the table:

Step 1	*Move*	the insertion point to the last cell in the last row
Step 2	*Press*	the TAB key to add a new row to the bottom of the table

Your screen should look similar to Figure 11-3 with the insertion point in the first cell of the new row.

FIGURE 11-3
Table with New Row and Column

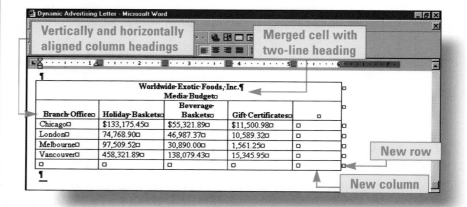

Step 3	*Save*	the document

Now that the total column and row are inserted, you calculate the total for each row and column.

Performing Calculations in a Table

You could manually calculate the total for each column and each row and then key it in the appropriate cell; however, if you later change the numbers or insert additional rows or columns, you must manually recalculate and rekey the totals. Instead, you can insert a formula that adds the contents of all the cells in the column or row. Then if you make any changes, you can update the formula to show the new total. You insert formulas with the F<u>o</u>rmula command on the

Table menu. You insert the column totals first. To insert the row heading and total formulas in the last row:

Step 1	*Key*	Total in the first cell in the last row
Step 2	*Press*	the TAB key
Step 3	*Click*	T̲able
Step 4	*Click*	F̲ormula

The Formula dialog box that opens on your screen should look similar to Figure 11-4.

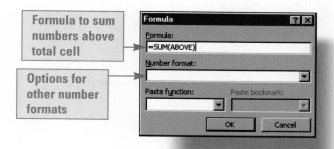

Formula to sum numbers above total cell

Options for other number formats

FIGURE 11-4
Formula Dialog Box

The most common calculation for a table is addition. You can also subtract, multiply, divide, and calculate averages, percentages, and minimum or maximum values in a table. Unless you indicate otherwise, Word assumes the calculation you want to perform is addition. Based on the position of the insertion point and the cells containing numbers, Word inserts an addition formula in the F̲ormula: text box. For example, if the insertion point is in a column, Word inserts a formula to sum the numbers in the cells *above* the insertion point. If the numbers are in a row, Word inserts a formula in the F̲ormula: text box to sum the numbers in the cells to the *left* or *right* of the insertion point.

Because the insertion point is in the last cell of a column, Word assumes you want to add the numbers in the cells above the insertion point. You accept the =SUM(ABOVE) formula.

Step 5	*Click*	OK

The sum of the numbers in the Holiday Baskets column appears in the cell. Once you create a formula, you can repeat it in other cells by using the R̲epeat Formula command on the E̲dit menu or by pressing

**chapter
eleven**

the CTRL + Y keys. To calculate the totals for the Beverage Baskets and Gift Certificates columns:

Step 1	Press	the TAB key to move the insertion point to the Beverage Baskets column
Step 2	Press	the CTRL + Y keys
Step 3	Press	the TAB key
Step 4	Press	the CTRL + Y keys

The totals for the Beverage Baskets and Gift Certificates columns appear in the cells. Now you can create a formula to calculate the total media budget for the Chicago branch office and then repeat that formula for the other branch offices and the grand total. To key the column heading and insert the row totals:

Step 1	Move	the insertion point to the last cell in the heading row
Step 2	Key	Total
Step 3	Press	the DOWN ARROW key
Step 4	Open	the Formula dialog box
Step 5	Verify	that the formula in the Formula: text box is =SUM(LEFT)
Step 6	Click	OK
Step 7	Repeat	the formula for the remaining cells in the column
Step 8	Save	the document

The table is almost complete; however, you need to align the numbers on the decimal points.

Using Tab Stops in Tables

You can set tab stops for table cells in the same way you set them for body text by selecting the tab alignment and clicking the tab-stop position on the horizontal ruler. You can set tab stops for individual cells or a group of selected cells.

To align all the numbers for each column at one time, you first select all the cells containing numbers. When you select cells containing numbers and then insert a tab stop, Word automatically aligns the numbers without inserting a tab character in the cell. To select the cells and insert a decimal tab stop:

Step 1	*Select*	all the cells containing numbers
Step 2	*Select*	the Decimal Tab alignment button
Step 3	*Move*	the mouse pointer to the 2¼-inch position on the horizontal ruler

Your screen should look similar to Figure 11-5.

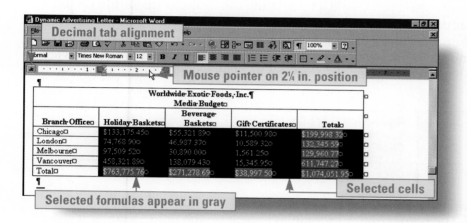

FIGURE 11-5
Table with Selected Cells

| Step 4 | *Click* | the horizontal ruler at the 2¼ position |
| Step 5 | *Deselect* | the cells |

Now that the numbers are aligned, you can resize the table.

Changing Row Height and Column Width

Now that the table contents are complete, you want to resize the cells' heights and widths to fit the data. A quick way to resize the table is to use the <u>A</u>utoFit options on the <u>T</u>able menu. You can have Word size or fit each column to match the column's contents. This method creates a column width that accommodates the widest cell contents in that column. Word can also resize the entire table to fit within the document margins or format rows for uniform height and columns for uniform width.

To have Word fit the entire table with evenly distributed columns (columns with the same width):

| Step 1 | *Verify* | the insertion point is in the table |

chapter
eleven

Step 2	*Click*	T<u>a</u>ble
Step 3	*Point to*	<u>A</u>utoFit
Step 4	*Click*	Distribute Columns Evenl<u>y</u>

You decide to see how the table looks without a border and with shaded column label cells.

Adding Borders and Shading to Tables

Borders and shading can make a table more attractive and easier to read. When you create a table using the Insert Table button on the Standard toolbar or <u>I</u>nsert Table command on the T<u>a</u>ble menu, Word automatically adds a border around each cell in the table. You can modify or remove this border and add shading from the Borders and Shading dialog box. To open the Borders and Shading dialog box:

Step 1	*Right-click*	the table
Step 2	*Click*	<u>B</u>orders and Shading
Step 3	*Click*	the <u>B</u>orders tab, if necessary

The border options for tables appear on the <u>B</u>orders tab. You can select one of the five preset border options or customize the table border. If you remove the table's printing border, the table appears with light gray gridlines. These nonprinting **gridlines** provide a visual guide as you work in a table. The nonprinting gridlines can be turned on or off with the Show <u>G</u>ridlines or Hide <u>G</u>ridlines commands on the T<u>a</u>ble menu. You remove the border and view the nonprinting gridlines.

| Step 4 | *Click* | the <u>N</u>one border option in the Setting: group |
| Step 5 | *Click* | OK |

The light gray nonprinting gridlines should appear. However, if the gridlines were previously turned off they do not appear. To turn on the gridlines, if necessary, and Print Preview the document:

Step 1	*Click*	T<u>a</u>ble
Step 2	*Click*	Show <u>G</u>ridlines, if necessary
Step 3	*Print Preview*	the document to see that the light gray gridlines do not print

---

Q UICK   TIP

You can resize individual rows and columns by setting row height or column width properties with the Table Properties command on the T<u>a</u>ble menu.

M OUSE   TIP

Word will automatically widen a column as you key text, if necessary. You also can drag the column boundaries inside a table or the column markers on the horizontal ruler to change the width of a column.

| Step 4 | *Close* | Print Preview |

You realize that the information in the table was easier to read with the default border. To reapply the default border and add shading to the column label row:

Step 1	*Open*	the <u>B</u>orders tab in the Borders and Shading dialog box
Step 2	*Click*	the Gri<u>d</u> option
Step 3	*Click*	OK
Step 4	*Select*	the second row, which contains the column heading text
Step 5	*Open*	the <u>S</u>hading tab in the Shadings and Borders dialog box
Step 6	*Click*	the Gray-10% color on the color grid (the third color in the first row)
Step 7	*Click*	OK
Step 8	*Deselect*	the row

The table is now complete and you need to finish the letter. To key the remaining body text and closing:

Step 1	*Move*	the insertion point to the blank line below the table
Step 2	*Press*	the ENTER key
Step 3	*Key*	the last body paragraph, closing, and your initials, using Figure 11-1 as your guide
Step 4	*Save*	the document and close it

The finished letter is ready for R. D. Jacobson's signature.

11.c Using Special Table Features

Bill Blake, an account executive in the marketing department, asks you to help create the new holiday sales price list. While he compiles the price list, he wants you to create a cover sheet for the document. You decide to do this by drawing tables in which you key the cover sheet text. Figure 11-6 shows the finished cover sheet.

chapter
eleven

FIGURE 11-6
Completed Holiday
Price List Cover Sheet

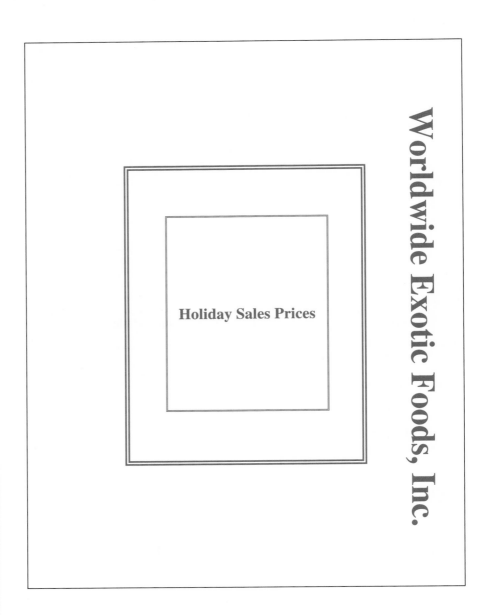

FIGURE 11-6
Completed Holiday
Price List Cover Sheet

Several features enable you to be very creative with tables. You can draw complex tables that have cells of different heights or a different number of columns per row, create side-by-side tables, change text direction inside a table cell, and even create a table inside a table cell. You can also reposition and size a table you draw with the mouse pointer.

Drawing Tables

You can also draw a table with the mouse pointer. When you use the Insert command on the Table menu or the Insert Table button on the Standard toolbar, you create a table grid of uniformly sized and positioned columns and rows. Drawing a table with the mouse pointer gives you the flexibility to determine the size and position of rows and columns. The Tables and Borders toolbar contains tools for drawing, erasing, and formatting a table. To begin the holiday sales price cover sheet, you create a new, blank document, change the margins, and view the Tables and Borders toolbar:

Step 1	*Create*	a new, blank document
Step 2	*Set*	the top, bottom, left, and right margins to ½ inch
Step 3	*Click*	the Tables and Borders button [icon] on the Standard toolbar

Word switches to Print Layout view, the mouse pointer changes to the pencil pointer when positioned in the document, and the Tables and Borders toolbar opens. Unless it has been previously repositioned, the Tables and Borders toolbar appears in its own window near the top of the document. You reposition the Tables and Borders toolbar below the Formatting toolbar to keep it out of the way.

Step 4	*Drag*	the Tables and Borders toolbar by its title bar up until it attaches directly below the Formatting toolbar
Step 5	*Click*	the Draw Table button [icon] on the Tables and Borders toolbar to display the pencil pointer, if necessary

Before you draw a table, you set the table border style, width, and color, or you can turn off the default border. To select a border style, line width and color:

Step 1	*Click*	the Line Style button list arrow [icon] on the Tables and Borders toolbar
Step 2	*Click*	the thin double line border option (the eighth option)
Step 3	*Click*	the Line Weight button list arrow [icon] on the Tables and Borders toolbar
Step 4	*Click*	the 2¼ pt option
Step 5	*Click*	the Border Color button [icon] on the Tables and Borders toolbar
Step 6	*Click*	Red (the first color in the third row)

To draw the table, you position the pencil pointer in the document where you want the upper-left corner of the table to begin. Thin

MENU TIP

You can view the Tables and Borders toolbar and pencil pointer by clicking the Dra<u>w</u> Table command on the <u>T</u>able menu.

MOUSE TIP

You can also use buttons on the Tables and Borders toolbar to add borders and shading to text paragraphs.

chapter
eleven

guidelines appear on the horizontal and vertical ruler, indicating the current position of the pencil pointer. You then drag diagonally toward the location of the lower-right corner of the table to create the external table boundaries. You continue to use the pencil pointer to draw the row and column boundaries inside the table. To draw the table:

| Step 1 | *Move* | the pencil pointer 1 inch below the top margin and 1 inch to the right of the left margin |

Your screen should look similar to Figure 11-7.

FIGURE 11-7
Pencil Pointer

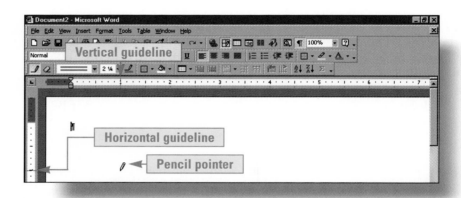

Step 2	*Drag*	diagonally to the right until the guideline on the horizontal ruler is at the 6-inch position and the guideline on the vertical ruler is at the 8½-inch position
Step 3	*Release*	the mouse button to create the external table boundaries
Step 4	*Zoom*	the document to Whole Page, if necessary

You use the pencil pointer to draw row and column boundaries inside the table. To create column and row boundaries with a red, 1-point, single border style:

Step 1	*Click*	the single line option (the second option) in the Line Style button list on the Tables and Borders toolbar
Step 2	*Click*	the 1 pt option in the Line Weight button list on the Tables and Borders toolbar
Step 3	*Click*	Red (the first color in the third row) in the Border Color button on the Tables and Borders toolbar
Step 4	*Move*	the pencil pointer inside the top boundary of the table approximately 1 inch from the left boundary of the table

Step 5	*Drag*	down to the bottom boundary until a dashed line column boundary appears
Step 6	*Release*	the mouse button to create the column boundary
Step 7	*Draw*	a second column boundary at any position inside the table
Step 8	*Draw*	a row boundary approximately 1 inch from the top of the table
Step 9	*Draw*	two additional row boundaries at any position

You now have a 4×3 table (four rows and three columns) with unevenly distributed columns and rows. You can turn off the Draw Table feature to switch back to an I-beam.

| Step 10 | *Click* | the Draw Table button ✎ to turn off the pencil pointer |

You can move the insertion point; select cells, rows, and columns; size the cells, rows, and columns; and key text in the cells just as you can when you create a table using the toolbar or menu commands. You sized the previous table using AutoFit sizing options; you can also size individual column widths or row heights. A quick way to do this is with the mouse pointer. To widen the first column and row:

Step 1	*Zoom*	the document to 75% so that it is easier to see
Step 2	*Move*	the mouse pointer to the right boundary of the first column (the mouse pointer becomes a sizing pointer)
Step 3	*Drag*	the column boundary to the right approximately ½ inch
Step 4	*Move*	the mouse pointer to the bottom boundary of the first row (the mouse pointer becomes a sizing pointer)
Step 5	*Drag*	the row boundary up approximately ½ inch

Actually, you don't need the table divided into rows and columns for the cover sheet. If you draw a column or row boundary that you don't need, or draw it in the wrong place, it is easy to erase it by turning the pencil pointer into an eraser. To erase the row and column boundaries:

Step 1	*Zoom*	the document to Whole Page
Step 2	*Click*	the Eraser button on the Tables and Borders toolbar
Step 3	*Drag*	the eraser pointer over a column boundary to erase it

C

chapter eleven

Step 4	*Drag*	the eraser pointer over a row boundary to erase it
Step 5	*Erase*	the remaining column and row boundaries leaving only the external table boundaries
Step 6	*Click*	the Eraser button 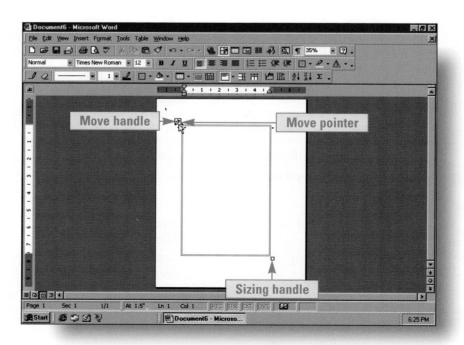 on the Tables and Borders toolbar to turn it off

When the pencil and eraser pointers are turned off, the mouse pointer becomes the I-beam when positioned over a table cell. When you place the I-beam in the table, two new objects are added to the table: a move handle that appears above the upper-left corner of the table and a sizing handle that appears below the lower-right corner of the table. You drag the **move handle** to reposition the table and the **sizing handle** to resize the entire table. You decide to move the table up on the page and make it a little smaller. To reposition and resize the table using the move handle and the sizing handle:

Step 1	*Move*	the mouse pointer to the move handle above the upper-left corner of the table (the mouse pointer becomes a move pointer with four black arrows)

Your screen should look similar to Figure 11-8.

FIGURE 11-8
Table Move Handle
and Move Pointer

Step 2	*Drag*	the move handle up approximately ¼ inch to reposition the table

Step 3	**Move**	the mouse pointer to the sizing handle below the lower-right corner of the table
Step 4	**Drag**	the sizing handle up approximately 1 inch

To make the cover page more interesting, you key title text in a second table inside the first table.

Nesting Tables

To help organize text on a page, you can create a table inside another table cell. Creating tables inside other tables is called **nesting**. You can nest tables when you need to organize a subset of data inside a larger table or to create a decorative effect. To create a nested table:

> **QUICK TIP**
>
> You can also create nested tables using the Insert Table button or command.

Step 1	**Set**	a thin double line, ¾ point, red boundary using buttons on the Tables and Borders toolbar
Step 2	**Click**	the Draw Table button 🖉 on the Tables and Borders toolbar to turn on the pencil pointer, if necessary
Step 3	**Draw**	a smaller table inside the larger table, approximately 2½ inches wide and 3 inches long and equidistant from the top, bottom, left, and right boundaries of the larger table
Step 4	**Position & Size**	the smaller table attractively near the center of the larger table
Step 5	**Zoom**	the document to 75% and scroll to view the smaller table
Step 6	**Verify**	the insertion point is inside the smaller table
Step 7	**Key**	Holiday Sales Prices
Step 8	**Format**	the text with bold and change the font to a larger point, red font

You decide to try different text alignment options. To change the vertical and horizontal alignment of the text in the nested table:

Step 1	**Verify**	the insertion point is in the smaller table
Step 2	**Click**	the Align button list arrow 🔲▾ on the Tables and Borders toolbar
Step 3	**Click**	the Align Center button 🔲
Step 4	**Deselect**	the text

chapter eleven

The text is aligned vertically and horizontally between the nested table boundaries.

Creating Side-by-Side Tables

Side-by-side tables provide greater flexibility in organizing information on a page. For example, in a sales brochure you might have lists of products in multiple side-by-side tables. You could also use side-by-side tables without borders to add a special text effect on a page. You do this for the holiday sales prices cover sheet. To create a new table without borders to the right of the nested tables:

Step 1	*Zoom*	the document to Whole Page
Step 2	*Select*	the No Border option from the Line Style list
Step 3	*Draw*	a long narrow table to the right of the nested tables beginning at the top margin and ending at the bottom margin leaving at least ½ inch between the tables

In addition to the horizontal and vertical alignment of text in a table cell, you can also change the text direction. You add the name of the company rotated so that it is read from top to bottom in the table.

C

Rotating Text in Tables

Changing the direction of text in a table cell allows you to add a special effect to the text. It also works well to rotate long column headings over narrow columns of data. Rotated text retains its horizontal and vertical formatting. You want the company name to appear vertically against the right boundary of the new table. To change the text direction:

Step 1	*Zoom*	the document to 75%
Step 2	*Click*	the Draw Table button on the Tables and Borders toolbar to turn off the pencil pointer, if necessary
Step 3	*Verify*	the insertion point is in the new table
Step 4	*Click*	the Change Text Direction button ▥ on the Tables and Borders toolbar until the directional arrows on the button face are pointing up
Step 5	*Change*	the alignment to Align Center Right using the Alignment button ▤▾ on the Tables and Borders toolbar
Step 6	*Key*	Worldwide Exotic Foods, Inc.
Step 7	*Format*	the text with bold, 48 point, red font

Step 8	*Zoom*	the document to Whole Page

Before you complete the cover sheet, you want to center the nested tables vertically and horizontally on the page.

Positioning Tables on the Page

You can horizontally align a table in relation to the edge of the page, the margins, or column boundaries. Tables can also be vertically aligned in relation to the top and bottom of the page, the top and bottom margins, or the top and bottom of a paragraph. The Table tab in the Table Properties dialog box provides options for positioning a table on the page. To position the table:

Step 1	*Right-click*	the large table in the nested tables
Step 2	*Click*	Table Properties
Step 3	*Click*	the Table tab, if necessary

The Table Properties dialog box that opens on your screen should look similar to Figure 11-9.

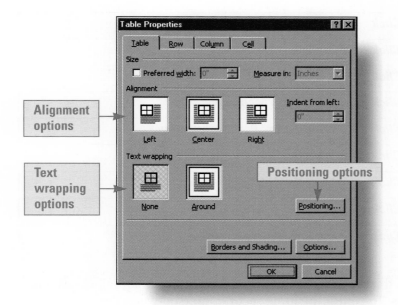

FIGURE 11-9
Table Properties
Dialog Box

INTERNET TIP

Tables, rather than columns, are used to organize information on a Web page. Many of the options in the Table Properties dialog box are used to create tables on Web pages. Use the dialog box Help button to review all the options in the dialog box.

Step 4	*Click*	Positioning

chapter
eleven

The Table Positioning dialog box that opens on your screen should look similar to Figure 11-10.

FIGURE 11-10
Table Positioning
Dialog Box

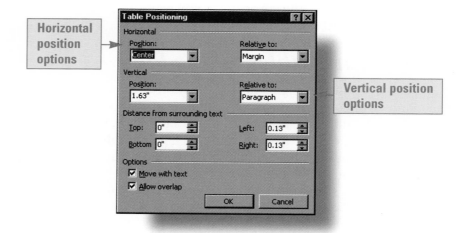

The options in the Horizontal and Vertical groups allow you to specify the position of the table in relation to the edges of the page, the margins, a newspaper-style column, or a text paragraph. You can also specify the distance the table boundaries should be from surrounding text. You center the table between the left and right margins.

Step 5	*Click*	the Horizontal Position: list arrow
Step 6	*Click*	Center, if necessary
Step 7	*Click*	the Horizontal Relative to: list arrow
Step 8	*Click*	Margin, if necessary
Step 9	*Click*	the Vertical Position: list arrow
Step 10	*Click*	Center
Step 11	*Click*	the Vertical Relative to: list arrow
Step 12	*Click*	Margin, if necessary
Step 13	*Click*	OK in each dialog box

The nested tables are centered vertically and horizontally between the margins. To center the long, second table between the top and bottom margins:

Step 1	*Right-click*	the long, second table
Step 2	*Click*	Table Properties

Step 3	*Click*	<u>P</u>ositioning
Step 4	*Select*	Center from the Vertical Posi<u>t</u>ion: list
Step 5	*Select*	Margin, if necessary, from the Vertical R<u>e</u>lative to: list
Step 6	*Click*	OK in each dialog box
Step 7	*Save*	the document as *Holiday Sales Prices* and close it
Step 8	*Close*	the Tables and Borders toolbar

Now Bill can add the holiday price list to the cover sheet.

11.d Switching Between Text and Tables

Selena Jackson, a secretary in the sales department, asks you to format a list of sales representatives and their telephone extensions. She already created the list using tab stops and tab characters to separate the information for each sales representative, but she thinks the list is easier to work with in a table. Instead of creating a table and keying the list again, you decide to convert the existing list to a table.

Data in tables is usually easier to manipulate, format, and calculate than the same data in text columns separated by tabs or other characters. You can convert text columns separated by tab characters, commas, or other characters to a table. You can also convert a table of rows and columns into text columns.

Converting Text to a Table

To convert text to a table you first select the text and then point to the Con<u>v</u>ert command on the <u>T</u>able menu and click the Text to Table command. To open Selena's existing document and select the text to convert to a table:

Step 1	*Open*	the *Sales Representatives* document located on the Data Disk
Step 2	*Select*	the columns of text separated by tab formatting marks, beginning with the Jones row and ending with the Aguilar row
Step 3	*Click*	<u>T</u>able
Step 4	*Point to*	Con<u>v</u>ert

chapter
eleven

Step 5	*Click*	Te_x_t to Table

The Convert Text to Table dialog box that opens on your screen should look similar to Figure 11-11.

FIGURE 11-11
Convert Text to Table
Dialog Box

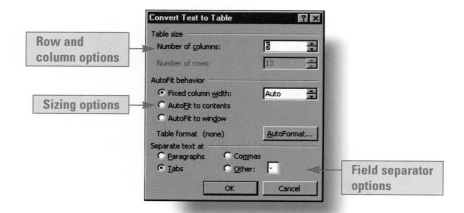

You specify the number of columns and rows as well as the size of the cells using AutoFit options in this dialog box. You also identify the character that separates columns so Word knows when to create a new column in the table. For example, the data in the *Sales Representatives* document is separated by tab formatting marks. Each time Word identifies a tab formatting mark, it places the data to the right of the tab formatting mark in the next column in the table. Word recognizes that the selected text contains five columns of text separated by tab formatting characters and sets those options for you. You can change the AutoFit option to control column width. Word also provides several automatic formats you can apply to a table. These automatic formats contain column width settings, shading, and font formatting.

To create a five-column table formatted with the Colorful 2 AutoFormat:

Step 1	*Verify*	the Number of _c_olumns: text box contains five and the _T_abs option button is selected
Step 2	*Click*	_A_utoFormat

The Table AutoFormat dialog box that opens on your screen should look similar to Figure 11-12.

You can preview how a table looks with each of the AutoFormats in the Forma_t_s: list in the Preview area of the dialog box. Some AutoFormats can be modified to remove or add borders and shading to specific columns and rows in the table. Because your table does not have a heading row, you select the Colorful 2 AutoFormat and then remove the heading row formatting.

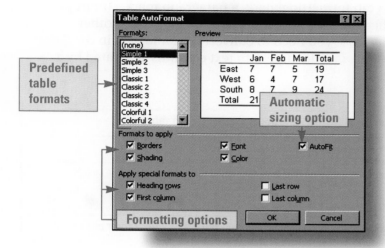

FIGURE 11-12
Table AutoFormat
Dialog Box

Step 3	*Click*	Colorful 2 in the Formats: list box
Step 4	*Observe*	the table preview and the darkly shaded heading row
Step 5	*Click*	the Heading rows check box to remove the check mark
Step 6	*Observe*	the table preview heading row is formatted like the remaining rows
Step 7	*Observe*	the AutoFit (to contents) check box contains a check mark
Step 8	*Click*	OK in each dialog box

MENU TIP

To save formatting time, you can apply one of the Word automatic table formats to any table by first selecting the table and then clicking the Table AutoFormat command on the Table menu or the Table AutoFormat button on the Tables and Borders toolbar.

The table is created with the Colorful 2 AutoFormat and the column widths automatically are sized to fit the contents. By default the table is left aligned. You can horizontally align a table by selecting the entire table and clicking a horizontal alignment button on the Formatting toolbar.

To center the table horizontally:

Step 1	*Verify*	the entire table is selected, including the end-of-row marks
Step 2	*Click*	the Center button ☰ on the Formatting toolbar
Step 3	*Deselect*	the table
Step 4	*Save*	the document as *Sales Representatives Revised*

CAUTION TIP

If you select the entire table by selecting columns, remember to also select the end-of-row marks.

Selena finds the new format much easier to read.

chapter
eleven

MOUSE **TIP**

You can quickly convert text uniformly separated by comma, tab characters, or other characters into a table by selecting the text and clicking the Insert Table button on the Standard toolbar.

MENU **TIP**

If you create a large table that flows to more than one page, you can repeat the heading row on each subsequent page by moving the insertion point to the heading row and clicking the Heading Rows Repeat command on the Table menu.

Converting a Table to Text

Sometimes you need to convert data organized in a table to text separated by a tab formatting mark, a paragraph mark, comma, or some other character in order to import the data into another application. Suppose you need to convert the table data in the *Sales Representatives Revised* document to text columns separated by a comma. To begin:

Step 1	*Move*	the insertion point inside the table
Step 2	*Click*	Table
Step 3	*Point to*	Convert
Step 4	*Click*	Table to Text
Step 5	*Click*	the Commas option button to select the column separator character
Step 6	*Click*	OK
Step 7	*Deselect*	the text
Step 8	*Observe*	that the data in each row of text is now separated by commas rather than a table columns
Step 9	*Save*	the document as *Converted Table* and close it

Converting table data to text columns enables you to format the same information in different ways without having to rekey it.

Summary

▶ You can place data in a table so that it is easier to read and understand.

▶ A table is a grid organized into rows and columns.

▶ A column is a set of information that runs down a page, and a row is a set of information that runs across a page.

▶ A cell is the intersection of a column and a row.

▶ You can move the insertion point between cells in a table using the mouse or the keyboard.

▶ Cells, rows, and columns in a table can be selected to insert, delete, or format the cells, rows, or columns.

▶ You can merge multiple cells vertically and horizontally into one cell.

▶ You can create formulas in tables to add, subtract, multiply, divide, and calculate averages, percentages, and identify minimum or maximum values in a column or row.

▶ You can change the column widths for one column in a table or multiple columns, using the mouse or the AutoFit commands on the Table menu.

▶ You position tables on the page with options in the Table Properties dialog box or with the mouse pointer.

▶ You can set tab stops for one or more table columns.

▶ Word provides several preset table formats, called AutoFormats, you can apply to a table.

▶ You can draw a complex table with the Draw Table feature, and then format the table and its contents with the Tables and Borders toolbar options.

▶ You can nest tables by drawing a table inside another table cell, and you can place tables side by side.

▶ Text separated by commas, paragraph marks, or other characters can be converted to a table.

▶ Tables can be converted to text that is separated by commas, paragraph marks, or other characters.

▶ You can format text in table cells just as you format paragraph text.

chapter eleven

Commands Review

Action	Menu Bar	Shortcut Menu	Toolbar	Keyboard
Create a table	Table, Insert, Table or Draw Table			ALT + A, I, T or ALT + A, B
Delete a table or table component	Table, Delete, Table, or Columns, or Rows, or Cells	Right-click selected table component, click Delete		ALT + A, D, T or C or R or E
Insert rows, columns, or cells in a table	Table, Insert, Columns to the Left Columns to the Right Rows Above Rows Below Cells	Right-click selected table component, click Insert		ALT + A, I, L or R or A or B or E
Change column width for selected column(s)	Table, Table Properties or AutoFit		Drag the column boundary or the column marker on the horizontal ruler	ALT + A, R or A
To align a table on the page	Table, Table Properties	Right-click table, click Table Properties	Drag move pointer	ALT + A, R
Align text horizontally and vertically		Right-click cell, click Cell Alignment		
Add formula to a table	Table, Formula			ALT + A, O
Repeat formulas	Edit, Repeat Formula			ALT + E, R CTRL + Y F4
Update a selected formula		Right-click a formula field, click Update Field		F9
Merge cells vertically or horizontally	Table, Merge Cells	Right-click selected cells, Merge Cells		ALT + A, M
Insert a tab formatting mark in a cell				CTRL + TAB
Add borders and shading to a table	Format, Borders and Shading	Right-click table, Borders and Shading		ALT + O, B
Change text direction		Right-click cell, click Text Direction		
Draw a table	Table, Draw Table			ALT + A, B
Apply a built-in automatic format	Table, Table AutoFormat			ALT + A, F
Convert text to a table	Table, Convert, Text to Table			ALT + A, V, X
Convert a table to text	Table, Convert, Table to Text			ALT + A, V, B
Split cells vertically or horizontally	Table, Split Cells			ALT + A, P
Split a table	Table, Split Table			ALT + A, T
Distribute rows and columns evenly	Table, Autofit, Distribute Rows Evenly or Distribute Columns Evenly	Right-click selected columns or rows, click Distribute Columns Evenly or Distribute Rows Evenly		ALT + A, N or Y
Repeat a heading row on all pages of the table	Table, Heading Rows Repeat			ALT + A, H
Change pencil pointer to eraser pointer				SHIFT

Concepts Review

SCANS

Circle the correct answer.

1. A table:
[a] is a grid organized in columns and rows.
[b] must be created with a button on the Standard toolbar.
[c] cannot be formatted with character formats like bold and paragraph formats like borders and shading.
[d] has columns labeled 1, 2, 3 and rows labeled A, B, C.

2. You can change the width of a column in a table by:
[a] pressing the TAB key.
[b] dragging a row boundary between two rows.
[c] clicking the Column Width command on the Table menu.
[d] dragging a column boundary on the horizontal ruler.

3. The gray table gridlines:
[a] automatically appear when you create a table.
[b] cannot be turned on and off.
[c] print with the table.
[d] provide visual help when working in a table without borders.

4. A cell is:
[a] a set of information that runs down a page.
[b] a set of information that runs across the page.
[c] the intersection of a column and row.
[d] a grid of columns and rows.

5. You cannot move the insertion point in a table with the:
[a] I-beam.
[b] TAB key.
[c] UP ARROW and DOWN ARROW keys.
[d] SPACEBAR.

6. You can create a table with the:
[a] Insert, Table commands on the Table menu.
[b] Draw Table button on the Standard toolbar.
[c] Table command on the Format menu.
[d] Insert Table button on the Formatting toolbar.

7. To update a formula in a table, press the:
[a] F8 key.
[b] SHIFT + F9 keys.
[c] ALT + F9 keys.
[d] F9 key.

8. Nested tables allow you to:
[a] move a table with the mouse pointer.
[b] size a table with the mouse pointer.
[c] place a table inside another table.
[d] add, subtract, multiply, and divide values.

9. The best way to align the numbers 973.32, 734.871, 34.972 in table columns is to:
[a] left-align the numbers.
[b] set a decimal tab stop.
[c] right-align the numbers.
[d] center the numbers.

10. Which of the following formatting options is not available on the Tables and Borders toolbar?
[a] vertical and horizontal text alignment
[b] text rotation
[c] line color, style, and width
[d] bold

chapter eleven

Circle **T** if the statement is true or **F** if the statement is false.

T   F   1. You cannot repeat the heading row when the table flows to a second page.

T   F   2. To delete a table's content and structure, first select the table and then press the DELETE key.

T   F   3. Rows can be inserted above or below the selected rows.

T   F   4. Cells can be merged horizontally but not vertically.

T   F   5. To move the insertion point to the next cell, press the ENTER key.

T   F   6. Tab stops are set for table cells in the same manner as body text.

T   F   7. The default table border cannot be removed or modified.

T   F   8. The pencil pointer is used to draw tables.

T   F   9. Creating tables inside other tables is called stacking.

T   F   10. Once text is converted to text in a table, it cannot be converted back to plain text.

Skills Review

Exercise 1

1. Open the *Annual Sales Data* document located on the Data Disk.

2. Change the top margin to 1½ inches and the left margin and right margins to one inch.

3. Select text separated by tab formatting marks and convert the text to a table using the Classic 2 table AutoFormat. Modify the AutoFormat to remove the borders.

4. Center the table on the page using the Center button on the Formatting toolbar.

5. Right-align the column headings and numbers in their cells.

6. Add a row to the bottom of the table and a column at the end of the table.

7. Key the word "Total" in the first cell of the new row and column.

8. Insert a formula in the last cell of the 1997 column to sum the values.

9. Repeat the formula for the 1998 and 1999 columns.

10. Insert a formula in the last cell of the Chicago row to sum the values.

11. Repeat the formula for the London, Melbourne, and Vancouver branches.

12. Save the document as *Annual Sales Data Revised*.

13. Preview, print, and close the document.

Exercise 2

1. Open the *Regional Deli Sales* document located on the Data Disk.

2. Select the five rows of text and convert the text to a table. (*Hint:* The separator character is a dash.)

3. Insert a row between North and East regions using the Insert Rows button on the Standard toolbar.

4. Key the following text in the row: Central, 28,975.33, 54,333.45, and 78,125.54.

5. Insert a column at the end of the table.

6. Key "Total Sales" in the first cell of the column.

7. Insert a row at the bottom of the table and title it "Total Sales."

8. Calculate the total for each column and row.

9. Right-align the numbers in the cells.

10. Adjust the column widths by dragging the column boundaries with the mouse pointer so that each column is just wide enough for the largest cell contents.

11. Center and bold the heading row.

12. Align the heading row text at the bottom center of each cell.

13. Center the table on the page.

14. Save the document as *Regional Deli Sales Revised*.

15. Preview, print, and close the document.

Exercise 3

1. Open the *Annual Sales Data Revised* document you created in Exercise 1.

2. Remove the automatic formatting. (*Hint:* Click in the table, click the Table AutoFormat command on the Table menu, click the (none) option in the Formats: list.)

3. Display the Tables and Borders toolbar.

4. Use the pencil pointer to draw a double-line, ¾-point, black border around the table.

5. Use the pencil pointer to draw single-line, ¾-point, black border column boundaries.

6. Add Gray-10% shading to the top and bottom row. (*Hint:* Use the Shading Color button on the Tables and Borders toolbar.)

7. AutoFit the table to the window (between the left and right margins).

8. Save the document as *Annual Sales Data With AutoFit*.

9. Preview, print, and close the document.

Exercise 4

1. Create a new, blank document.

2. Create a 7 × 4 table with the Insert Table button on the Standard toolbar

3. Key the data below:

District	Selling Expenses	Employee Expenses	Overhead
Central	$49,100.60	$12,421.00	$13,921.99
Eastern	41,756.72	5,523.42	8,992.33
Midwest	64,871.86	4,819.89	9,655.76
Mountain	59,256.36	7,085.07	6,332.99
Southern	45,817.32	12,253.57	16,322.86
Western	51,857.52	9,528.88	11,661.30

4. Select the first row and add bold formatting to the text.

5. Insert a row at the bottom of the document and a column at the left of the document.

6. Add the text "Total" to the first cell in the new row and column.

7. Display the Tables and Borders toolbar.

chapter eleven

8. Use the AutoSum button on the Tables and Borders toolbar to insert the total for each column. (Do not repeat the first formula.)

9. Use the Formula command on the Table menu to add the Central row. Repeat the formula for the remaining rows.

10. Change the value for Chicago Selling Expenses to $59,100.60. (*Hint:* The Selling Expenses total, Central total, and grand total do not change automatically.)

11. Select the Selling Expenses total cell and press the F9 key to update the formula. Select the Central total cell and press the F9 key to update the Central total. Select the grand total cell and press the F9 key to update the grand total.

12. Set a decimal tab for the cells that contain numbers.

13. AutoFit the table to the contents.

14. Select the first row and align the contents centered at the bottom of the cell using the Alignment button on the Tables and Borders toolbar.

15. Insert a row at the top of the document and merge the cells using buttons on the Tables and Borders toolbar.

16. Key the following title text in the new first row.
Worldwide Exotic Foods, Inc.
District Expense Report
Fourth Quarter

17. Change the font to 14 point.

18. Use the Borders and Shading dialog box to apply a 1½-point grid border to the table.

19. Center the table between the left and right margins.

20. Save the document as *District Expense Report.*

21. Preview, print, and close the document.

Exercise 5 C

1. Open the *Adjusted Costs Memo* document located on the Data Disk.

2. Display the Tables and Borders toolbar.

3. Draw a 7 × 4 table with no border below the memo body text.

4. Distribute the rows and columns evenly.

5. Merge the cells in the first row.

6. Key the following heading text centered and bolded in two lines in the first row.
EXECUTIVE SUPPORT DIVISION
Adjusted Costs for Second Fiscal Quarter

7. Key the following data in the remaining rows.

Item	Budgeted	Actual	Difference
Executive Secretaries	$2,455,000	$2,256,000	−$199,000
Administrative Assistants	390,600	475,900	85,300
Equipment	960,000	840,000	−120,000
Telecommunications	476,000	450,600	−25,400
Miscellaneous	76,000	60,000	−16,000

8. Align the numbers at the bottom right using the Align button on the Tables and Borders toolbar.

9. Underline and center the column heading text in the second row at the bottom of each cell.

10. Align the "Item" titles at the bottom left of the cell.

11. AutoFit the table to the contents.

12. Center the table between the left and right margins.

13. Save the document as *Adjusted Costs Memo Revised*.

14. Preview, print, and close the document.

Exercise 6

1. Create a new, blank document and insert the text TRIVIA INFORMATION ABOUT SELECTED STATES centered in 14-point font at the top of the document.

2. Display the Tables and Borders toolbar and draw two side-by-side tables beginning at the left margin using the border style of your choice. Make the first table approximately 1½ inches wide and 5 inches long and the second table approximately 4 inches wide and 5 inches long. Leave ½ inch white space between the tables.

3. Draw a narrow column approximately .3 inch at the left side of each table.

4. Format the first cell in each table to rotate the text vertical up (read from bottom to top) and align center left.

5. Key NAME in the first cell in the first table and format the text with the 18-point, bold font.

6. Key NICKNAME in the first cell in the second table and format the text with the 18-point, bold font.

7. Format the second cell in each table to align the text centered vertically and horizontally in the cell.

8. Key the following double-spaced text in the second cell of the first table: *Arkansas, Arizona, Colorado, Connecticut, Nebraska, New Mexico, Texas, Washington*.

9. Key the following double-spaced text in the second cell of the second table: *The Natural State, Grand Canyon State, Centennial State, Constitution State, Cornhusker State, America's Land of Enchantment, The Lone Star State, The Evergreen State*.

10. Center each table vertically between the top and bottom margins.

11. Save the document as *State Trivia*.

12. Preview, print, and close the document.

Exercise 7

1. Create the following document. Set the appropriate margins for a block format letter.

2. The company information and column titles in the table should be centered and boldfaced. Use the default black grid. The expense data should be right aligned. Finally, the Sales District numbers should be centered.

3. Calculate the total for each column.

4. Change the column width of each column as necessary.

5. Center the table horizontally.

6. Save the document as *Burns Letter With Table*.

chapter eleven

Current date

Mr. Daniel Burns
Vice President
Burns Consulting, Inc
250 Main, Suite 1230
Chicago, IL 60615-1203

Dear Daniel:

We finally completed the second quarter expense report for the Vancouver office and look
forward to your suggestions on reducing these expenses. See the details below:

VANCOUVER OFFICE EXPENSE REPORT			
Second Quarter			
Sales District	Telephone	Supplies	Misc.
1	$1,400.60	$806.86	$300.60
2	1,660.36	736.96	334.36
3	986.30	85.00	453.56
4	1,246.88	443.77	564.33
5	1,766.99	999.99	434.66
Total	$7,061.13	$3,072.58	$2,087.51

I will be meeting with the managers of each sales district to review these expenses next week.
After the reviews, I will e-mail our estimated expenses for the fourth quarter to you.

Sincerely,

Lisa Harrison
Accounting Manager

xx

Exercise 8

1. Create a new, blank document.
2. Use the Draw Table feature to create the following document.
3. Draw the first table beginning at the left margin with a single, 3-point, red border. Make the table approximately
   3½ inches wide and 3 inches long. Center the table horizontally.
4. Draw the second table inside the first table with a single 1½-point, red border. Make the second table
   approximately 2¾ inches wide and 2 inches long. Center the table horizontally.
5. Draw a column boundary (vertical line) down the middle of the second table.
6. Draw five row boundaries (horizontal lines) across the second table.

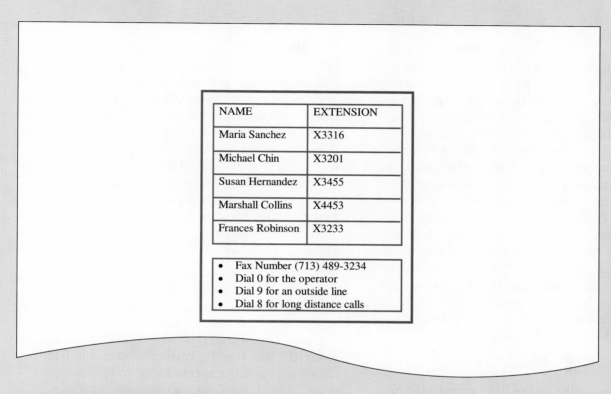

NAME	EXTENSION
Maria Sanchez	X3316
Michael Chin	X3201
Susan Hernandez	X3455
Marshall Collins	X4453
Frances Robinson	X3233

- Fax Number (713) 489-3234
- Dial 0 for the operator
- Dial 9 for an outside line
- Dial 8 for long distance calls

7. Distribute the rows and column evenly.

8. Draw a third table below the second table. Make this table approximately 2¾ inches wide and ½ inch long. Center the third table horizontally.

9. Key the text shown in the table.

10. Save the document as *Extension List*.

11. Preview, print, and close the document.

Case Projects

Project 1

A marketing department coworker, Ella Cohen, wants to know how to insert information from a database or other data source into a Word document as a table. Use online Help to locate the topic "Inserting information from a database into a Word document." Write an interoffice memorandum to Ella describing the process. Save, preview, and print the memo.

Project 2

R. D. Jacobson asks you to create an interoffice memo to five Vancouver sales representatives advising them of the profit (sales minus expenses) for the third quarter on the Extravaganza Basket product. Use a table to present the data for the five sales representatives by listing the sales, expenses, and profit for each. Then calculate the total sales, total expenses, and total profit for the branch. Use fictitious data. Format and position the table attractively on the page. Save, preview, and print the memo.

chapter eleven

Project 3

Maria Betancourt does not understand the concept of Word fields, such as the formula field or date and time field, and asks for your help. Use the Office Assistant to search online Help for information on Word fields. Print and review the information. Open the Options dialog box and use the Help button to review the Field options in the View tab. Create an interoffice memorandum to Maria describing Word fields and how to use the options on the View tab to view the fields. Use a table to organize the information about the View tab options. Save, preview, and print the memo. With your instructor's permission, use the memo as a guide to describe Word fields to a classmate. Then open a document that contains a date and time or formula field and demonstrate how to use the View tab field options.

Project 4

R. D. Jacobson asks you to help locate a list of firms that provide Web-based advertising. Connect to your ISP, load your Web browser, and search for companies who provide advertising services on the Web. Print at least five home pages. Create an interoffice memorandum to R. D. Jacobson listing your Web sources and a brief description of their services. Organize your Web source list in an attractively formatted and positioned table. Save, preview, and print the memo.

Project 5

Create a letter and an accompanying envelope to the president of WholeSale Food Distributors from M. D. Anderson, Sales Director, advising the president of the total sales data for the first quarter for five products. Use an attractively formatted and positioned table to itemize the product sales for January, February, and March. Calculate the total sales by product and month. Use fictitious data. Save, preview, and print the letter.

Project 6

Bill Blake has a big marketing presentation he will be putting together soon. In preparation for helping him, you practice drawing and formatting tables with the Tables and Borders toolbar. Create a new, blank document and display the Tables and Borders toolbar. Explore drawing various tables including nested tables. Use all the buttons on the toolbar, including changing the text orientation inside a cell to format the tables. Save, preview, and print the document.

Project 7

R. D. Jacobson assigns you to write a memorandum to all sales and marketing department employees advising them how to save a Word document to the company FTP site on the Internet. Use the Office Assistant to research how to save a Word document to an FTP site. Use the keywords "saving to FTP," click the Save a Document topic and follow appropriate links. Create a memorandum that describes an FTP site with step-by-step instructions on how to save a document to an FTP site. Use a table to organize the steps. Save, preview, and print the document.

Project 8

During lunch Maria Betancourt tells you that the features on the Tables and Borders toolbar can also be used to create and format borders around text. You want to explore doing this. Open an existing document that contains several text paragraphs. Display the Tables and Borders toolbar and use the toolbar buttons to draw borders around the paragraphs. Select a paragraph and convert it to a table with a border. Modify several borders. Save the document with a new name, preview it, and print it.

Using Styles and Templates

Chapter Overview

Styles and templates help reduce the time you need to format documents you create repeatedly, such as schedules, fax coversheets, or reports. Styles let you try out various looks for your document quickly, or you can create a template containing styles so you focus on the content rather than the formatting of future documents. This chapter shows you how to use built-in styles and templates, as well as how to create and modify custom styles and templates.

LEARNING OBJECTIVES

► Create and apply styles
► Edit styles
► Use templates and wizards to create documents

Case profile

Worldwide Exotic Foods, Inc. human resources department often distributes documents to employees throughout the company. Bill Martin asks you to format the winter training schedule for him. He asks you to use styles so he can add items to the schedule using the same formats. The public affairs officer, Viktor Winkler, handles investor and customer inquiries from around the world. Viktor's assistant is out of the office for two weeks and he asks you to prepare several fax coversheets and a calendar.

chapter twelve

12.a Creating and Applying Styles

Instead of copying formats from one paragraph or character to another, you can create styles. A **style** is a group of formats assigned a unique name. A style allows you to format text easily by applying all the specified formats at one time. You can use multiple styles within the same document. Styles are saved with the current document or a template, such as the Normal template, upon which the document is based. Table 12-1 below lists the two kinds of Word styles.

TABLE 12-1
Types of Word Styles

Style	Description
Paragraph	Determines the appearance of a paragraph, including text alignment, tab stops, indentation, line spacing, page breaks, borders and shading, numbered and bulleted lists, numbered headings, and the paragraph's position in the page layout
Character	Determines the appearance of selected text, including font, size, bold, italic, underline, and effects such as all caps

You can use the styles that come with Word or you can create your own.

Applying Built-in Styles

Word provides more than 90 built-in paragraph and character styles for formatting a document. You can apply the built-in styles to format selected text from the Style Preview list (also called simply the Style list), which you view by clicking the Style button list arrow on the Formatting toolbar. By default, only five built-in styles appear in the Style Preview. You can view the other built-in styles by holding down the SHIFT key as you view the Style Preview. Built-in styles can be used as is or they can be modified for the current document. If no built-in style contains the formats you want, you can create a custom style.

Bill creates a notice of future training schedules to be posted on the employee bulletin boards and asks you to format the document in a way that draws the attention of employees. You use styles to quickly format the document. To view the Style Preview:

Step 1	*Open*	the *Winter Schedule* document located on the Data Disk
Step 2	*Click*	the Style button list arrow Normal ▼ on the Formatting toolbar

The list of built-in styles that appears on your screen should look similar to Figure 12-1.

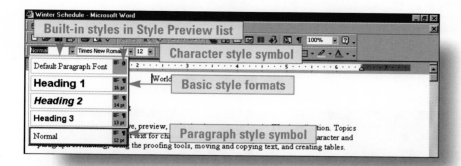

FIGURE 12-1
Style Preview

A bold, underlined letter "**a**" indicates a character style. A paragraph mark (¶) indicates a paragraph style. Notice the alignment and font size indicators. Each style name is displayed with its character formatting, providing an example of the style. The character style Default Paragraph Font formats selected text with the underlying paragraph style font, which is based on the paragraph style Normal. The paragraph style Normal is Times New Roman, 12 point, single-spaced, and left-aligned. By default, the Normal paragraph style is applied to all the text in a document that is based on the Normal template. The paragraph styles Heading 1, 2, and 3 format selected paragraphs to stand out from the Normal text as titles by making the font larger, boldfaced, or italicized—or by changing spacing above and below the paragraph.

Step 3	*Press*	the ESC key to close the style list

Because a paragraph style affects entire paragraphs, you can position the insertion point anywhere in a paragraph to select the paragraph before you apply a paragraph style. To apply character styles to an entire word, you position the insertion point in the word. If you are formatting a group of characters, you must select all the characters you want to format.

To format the document title, paragraph headings, and date line paragraphs, you decide to use Word built-in styles. To apply the Heading 1 style to the two title lines of the *Winter Schedule* document:

Step 1	*Select*	the two title lines
Step 2	*Click*	the Style button list arrow [Normal ▼] on the Formatting toolbar

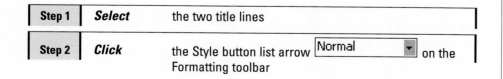

C A U T I O N   T I P

When you open a document created with an earlier version of Word, the five basic styles shown in the Style Preview reflect the styles in the original Normal template on which the document is based, not on the Word 2000 Normal template. For example, the default font size for the Normal style is 10 point for documents created in Word 97. If you open a document created in Word 97 the Style Preview shows the Normal style as 10 point.

M E N U   T I P

You can apply a style to selected characters or paragraphs by clicking the S̲tyle command on the F̲ormat menu.

chapter
twelve

Step 3	*Observe*	that the Heading 1 style contains bold, left-aligned, 16-point font formatting
Step 4	*Click*	Heading 1 in the Style Preview
Step 5	*Move*	the insertion point to the top of the document

Your screen should look similar to Figure 12-2.

FIGURE 12-2
Heading 1 Style Applied to Title Text

The Heading 1 style is applied to the selected text. Notice that the spacing between the two lines is also altered. In addition to the formatting you observed in the Style Preview, the Heading 1 style adds white space above and below each line. You can view the formatting components of each style from within the document.

Viewing Styles in a Document

When you position the insertion point in a paragraph, the Style button on the Formatting toolbar lists the name of the style used to format the paragraph. Figure 12-2 shows the insertion point in the first paragraph (the first title line) and the Heading 1 style name in the Style button. However, you cannot always tell the exact formatting from the style name or even by looking at the formatted text. If you want to see a list of all the formatting elements contained in the style, you click the paragraph with the What's This? help pointer.

To convert the mouse pointer to the What's This? help pointer and view the Heading 1 style formatting:

| Step 1 | *Press* | the SHIFT + F1 keys |
| Step 2 | *Click* | the first title line |

The Reveal Formats box, itemizing the paragraph and character styles of the Heading 1 style, appears. Your screen should look similar to Figure 12-3.

MENU TIP

You can convert the mouse pointer to the "What's This" help pointer by clicking the What's This? command on the Help menu.

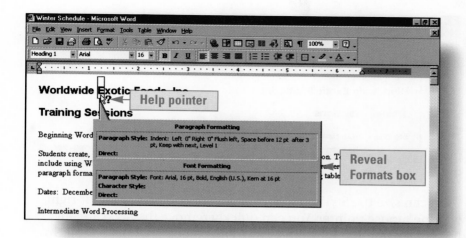

FIGURE 12-3
Heading 1 Style Paragraph
and Font Formatting

Any paragraph or character style applied to the selected text appears in the box. The list also includes any formatting you applied to the text using the Font or Paragraph command on the Format menu or the Formatting toolbar. After reviewing the formats in the Reveal Formats box, you can close it.

Step 3	*Press*	the ESC key

When working in Normal view, you can see the names of all the paragraph styles applied in the document without moving the insertion point from paragraph to paragraph. To do this, you set a space, called the **Style area**, to the left of the left margin and the selection bar on the screen. To create a ¾ inch Style area:

Step 1	*Click*	Tools
Step 2	*Click*	Options
Step 3	*Click*	the View tab, if necessary
Step 4	*Key*	.75 in the Style area width: text box
Step 5	*Click*	OK

The Style area appears at the left of the screen, which should look similar to Figure 12-4.

**chapter
twelve**

FIGURE 12-4
Document with Style Area

Style area

You can size the Style area by dragging the boundary left or right with the mouse pointer. You can quickly remove the Style area by dragging the boundary all the way to the left edge of the screen. To remove the Style area:

| Step 1 | *Move* | the mouse pointer to the Style area boundary line (it becomes a sizing pointer) |
| Step 2 | *Drag* | the Style area boundary line left until it disappears |

When there is no built-in style with the formatting combination you want, you can create a custom style.

Creating Custom Styles

Custom styles can be created in the Style dialog box or by example from formatted text. When you create styles in the Style dialog box, you can base the new style on another style or specify the style to be applied to the following paragraph.

To create styles by example, change the formatting of the selected text, click in the text box of the Style button, key a new style name, and press the ENTER key. Word creates the new style. You want to format all the paragraph headings for the *Winter Schedule* with the 12 point, bold, Arial, Small Caps, and a 2¼-inch text shadow border. First you reformat the "Beginning Word Processing" paragraph heading, and then you create a custom style by example based on the reformatted text. To change the font size and font style, and add a special text effect to the "Beginning Word Processing" paragraph heading:

MENU TIP

You can click the Style command on the Format menu to open the Style dialog box and create a custom style.

Step 1	*Select*	the "Beginning Word Processing" paragraph
Step 2	*Open*	the Font tab in the Font dialog box
Step 3	*Select*	the Arial, Bold, 12 point, Small Caps options
Step 4	*Click*	OK

The text shows the new font, font style, font size, and Small Caps effect. To add a 2¼-inch shadow border to the paragraph heading text:

Step 1	*Verify*	the "Beginning Word Processing" paragraph heading is selected
Step 2	*Open*	the Borders tab in the Borders and Shading dialog box
Step 3	*Click*	the Shadow Setting: option
Step 4	*Click*	2¼ pt in the Width: list
Step 5	*Click*	Text in the Apply to: list
Step 6	*Click*	OK
Step 7	*Deselect*	the text and leave the insertion point in the paragraph

A 2¼ pt shadow border is added to the paragraph. Your screen should look similar to Figure 12-5.

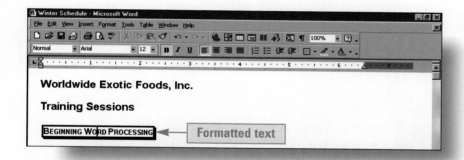

FIGURE 12-5
Formatted Heading Text

You can create a style based on the formatted text by moving the insertion point to the formatted text and then keying the style name in the Style button text box. By keying custom style names in all uppercase, you can distinguish your custom styles from the built-in styles. To create a custom style:

Step 1	*Verify*	the insertion point is in the "Beginning Word Processing" paragraph heading
Step 2	*Click*	the Style button text box [Normal ▼] on the Formatting toolbar
Step 3	*Key*	COURSE LEVEL
Step 4	*Press*	the ENTER key
Step 5	*Observe*	the COURSE LEVEL paragraph style name in the Style button text box

chapter twelve

The custom style makes it quick and easy to format other paragraphs the same way. You can apply the COURSE LEVEL style to the remaining paragraph headings by selecting the style from the Style Preview or by repeating the last action. To apply the custom style to the remaining paragraph headings:

Step 1	*Select*	the paragraph heading "Intermediate Word Processing"
Step 2	*Click*	the Style button list arrow `Normal ▼` on the Formatting toolbar
Step 3	*Observe*	that the custom style, COURSE LEVEL, is added to the Style Preview for this document
Step 4	*Click*	COURSE LEVEL
Step 5	*Select*	the paragraph heading "Advanced Word Processing"
Step 6	*Press*	the CTRL + Y keys to repeat the style formatting

The COURSE LEVEL paragraph style is applied to the title paragraphs.

Step 7	*Save*	the document as *Winter Schedule Revised*

notes Word can also automatically create styles as you key text. For example, when you key and format a document title or paragraph heading, Word interprets your formatting choices as modifications to a heading style. If you want to use the automatic style creation feature you can turn the option on (or off) in the AutoFormat As You Type tab in the AutoCorrect dialog box.

After reviewing the *Winter Schedule Revised* document you decide to change some of the style formatting. You can modify styles by overriding the style formatting with different formatting or by redefining the formatting contained in the style.

C 12.b Editing Styles

You override formatting applied by style when you select the text and apply different formatting from the Formatting toolbar or a dialog box. When you override style formatting, the new formats apply to only the selected text. The style itself is not affected. The Heading 1 style has left aligned the two title lines. You want to center the lines but retain the rest of the Heading 1 style formatting. To override the Heading 1 style by centering the lines manually:

Step 1	*Select*	the first title line
Step 2	*Click*	the Center button  on the Formatting toolbar
Step 3	*Observe*	that the second title line formatted with the Heading 1 style is not affected
Step 4	*Center*	the second title line

When you want to edit a style and have the changes automatically applied to all text in the current document formatted with that style, you redefine (or modify) the style itself. To redefine a style by example, you select text formatted with the style, change the formatting, and then rename the style with the same name.

You want to emphasize the date lines by applying a style. To apply the Heading 3 style to the date lines:

Step 1	*Select*	the first date line
Step 2	*Apply*	the Heading 3 style from the Style Preview
Step 3	*Select*	the second date line
Step 4	*Press*	the CTRL + Y keys

The 13-point font in the Heading 3 style is too large for the date line. Also, Bill inserted tab formatting marks between the dates and there are no custom tab stops set to arrange the dates attractively. You want to edit the Heading 3 style to have a 12-point font and left tab stops set at the 1-inch, 2.5-inch, and 4-inch positions. To reformat the text:

Step 1	*Select*	the first date line
Step 2	*Change*	the font size to 12
Step 3	*Set*	a left-aligned tab at the 1- , 2.5- , and 4-inch positions on the horizontal ruler
Step 4	*Click*	the Heading 3 style name in the Style button text box to select it
Step 5	*Press*	the ENTER key to rename the style with the same name

The Modify Style dialog box that opens on your screen should look similar to Figure 12-6.

M E N U   T I P

You can redefine a style with options in the Style dialog box. Open the Style dialog box by clicking the Style command on the Format menu.

chapter twelve

FIGURE 12-6
Modify Style Dialog Box

Option to update style with formatting changes

Option to revert to previous style formats

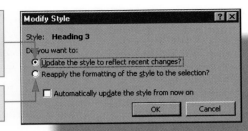

The default option is to redefine, or update, the style based on the changes made to the selected text. The other option is to return the selected text to its original, unmodified style. When you select the default option, all text formatted with the modified style is automatically reformatted.

Step 6	*Click*	OK
Step 7	*Observe*	that the second date line is automatically reformatted with the redefined Heading 3 style
Step 8	*Deselect*	the text
Step 9	*Save*	the document

When you no longer need a custom style in a document, you can delete it. This keeps the Style Preview shorter and easier to use. When you delete a custom style, any text in the document formatted with the custom style returns to the Normal style. To delete the COURSE LEVEL style:

Step 1	*Click*	Format
Step 2	*Click*	Style
Step 3	*Click*	COURSE LEVEL in the Styles: list box
Step 4	*Click*	Delete
Step 5	*Click*	Yes in the confirmation dialog box
Step 6	*Close*	the Style dialog box
Step 7	*Observe*	that the Course Level style is deleted and the Normal style is applied to the paragraph headings
Step 8	*Close*	the document without saving any changes

You can use the Style Gallery button in the Theme dialog box to preview sample documents based on Word templates, the current

CAUTION TIP

You can delete custom styles, but you cannot delete built-in styles.

QUICK TIP

The Organizer enables you to copy styles from document to document and from template to template. You open the Organizer dialog box by clicking the Templates and Add-Ins command on the Tools menu and then clicking the Organizer button or by clicking the Organizer button in the Style dialog box.

document with styles from templates, or a list of styles. To open the Theme dialog box, click Theme on the Format menu. When you copy a template in the Style Gallery to your document, styles with the same name override the style formatting currently in the document. Styles with names not in your document are added to the document. Unique styles in your document are not affected.

Viktor Winkler sends many faxes in response to customer and investor inquiries. He asks you to create a fax cover sheet. You can base the new cover sheet document on one of the Word fax templates.

12.c Using Templates and Wizards to Create Documents

Every document you create in Word is based on a template. A **template** is a master document or model that contains any text, formats, styles, macros, and AutoText that you want to include in a particular kind of document. Templates enable you to prepare documents more quickly because they supply many of the settings that you would otherwise need to create—such as margins, tabs, alignment, and formatted non-variable text. Each time you click the New button on the Standard toolbar you create a new document based on the Normal template. Another example is a letter template that contains the margin settings for a block format letter, the date field, and a standard closing including the writer's signature area.

There are two types of templates: global templates and document templates. The Normal template is an example of a **global template**, which means its settings are available for all documents. **Document templates** supply settings that affect only the current document and help you automatically format letters, faxes, memos, reports, manuals, brochures, newsletters, and special documents, such as Web pages. Word provides many built-in document templates and you can easily create your own.

You use a document template to create the cover sheet. To create a fax cover sheet based on a template:

Step 1	*Click*	File
Step 2	*Click*	New

chapter
twelve

Step 3	*Click*	the Letters & Faxes tab, if necessary
Step 4	*Double-click*	the Contemporary Fax icon
Step 5	*Observe*	that a new document is created based on the Contemporary Fax template and Word switches to Print Layout view
Step 6	*Zoom*	the document to 75%

The document is preformatted with graphics, text boxes, heading text, lines, and placeholders. **Placeholders** are areas in which you key the variable information. Your screen should look similar to Figure 12-7.

FIGURE 12-7
Document Based on the
Contemporary Fax
Template

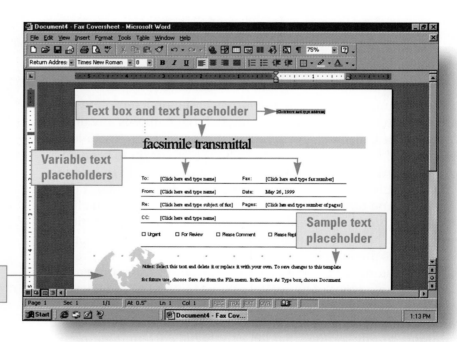

All you need to do to complete the fax is to key the appropriate variable information in the [Click here and type…] placeholders. After you click a variable text placeholder to select it, you key the appropriate text. Then press the F11 key to move to the next placeholder. To key the company name and address:

Step 1	*Zoom*	the document to 100% so you can read the text and placeholders
Step 2	*Observe*	that the current date already appears in the Date: placeholder because the date area contains a date field
Step 3	*Click*	the address placeholder text box in the upper-right corner of the document

| Step 4 | *Key* | Worldwide Exotic Foods, Inc.
Gage Building, Suite 1200
Riverside Plaza
Chicago, IL 60606-2000 |
| Step 5 | *Press* | the F11 key to select the next placeholder |

To key the remaining variable text:

Step 1	*Key*	John Washington, Software Inc.
Step 2	*Press*	the F11 key
Step 3	*Key*	312-555-0098 in the Fax: placeholder
Step 4	*Press*	the F11 key
Step 5	*Key*	Viktor Winkler in the From: placeholder
Step 6	*Press*	the F11 key twice
Step 7	*Key*	Speaking Engagement in the Re: placeholder
Step 8	*Press*	the F11 key
Step 9	*Key*	2 in the Pages: placeholder
Step 10	*Press*	the F11 key
Step 11	*Press*	the Delete key to delete the CC: placeholder
Step 12	*Press*	the F11 key
Step 13	*Key*	X in the Urgent placeholder check box
Step 14	*Select*	the Notes: text below the check box placeholders (do not select the word and colon "Notes:")
Step 15	*Key*	I am happy to accept your invitation to speak at the Software Inc. executive committee luncheon tomorrow. Attached is a draft of my speech.
Step 16	*Save*	the document as *Washington Fax* and close it

During the day, Viktor Winkler asks you to create several fax cover sheets for him. To save time, you decide to create a custom fax cover sheet template that already contains the company name, address, and Viktor Winkler's name.

Creating a Custom Template

You can create your own templates by making changes to the current document and saving it as a template. You can also use one of the Word templates as a basis for your custom template. You use the

chapter
twelve

Contemporary Fax template as the basis for the Winkler fax template. To create a custom template:

Step 1	*Open*	the Letters & Faxes tab in the New dialog box
Step 2	*Click*	the Template option button to create a new template based on another template
Step 3	*Double-click*	the Contemporary Fax icon

A template document named Template1 – Fax Coversheet opens. Now you can replace the placeholders with text that never changes. To add text to the template:

Step 1	*Select*	the address placeholder text box in the upper-right corner of the document
Step 2	*Key*	Worldwide Exotic Foods, Inc. Gage Building, Suite 1200 Riverside Plaza Chicago, IL 60606-2000
Step 3	*Press*	the F11 key three times
Step 4	*Key*	Viktor Winkler
Step 5	*Delete*	the Notes: text (do not delete the word and colon "Notes:")

Next you customize the heading text at the top of the document.

Step 6	*Select*	the text "facsimile transmittal" near the top of the document
Step 7	*Key*	Fax Cover Sheet

You need to save the changes you made to the template, just as you do with a document. To save the template:

Step 1	*Open*	the Save As dialog box
Step 2	*Observe*	that Save in location defaults to the Templates folder
Step 3	*Observe*	the file type is Document Template
Step 4	*Save*	the template as *Winkler Coversheet* and close it

The next time Viktor asks for a fax cover sheet, you can create one quickly based on the *Winkler Coversheet* template. To test the custom template:

Step 1	*Open*	the General tab in the New dialog box
Step 2	*Observe*	the new *Winkler Coversheet* template icon
Step 3	*Double-click*	the *Winkler Coversheet* template icon
Step 4	*Create*	a one-page fax to Beryl Davis, 312-555-7890, for review with a note confirming receipt of the new brochure listing government offices in the Chicago area
Step 5	*Save*	the fax as *Davis Fax* and close it

When you no longer use a template, you can delete it by opening the New dialog box, right-clicking the template icon, and clicking <u>D</u>elete. Your fax assignments for Viktor are complete so you want to delete the template. To delete the *Winkler Coversheet* template:

Step 1	*Open*	the General tab in the New dialog box
Step 2	*Right-click*	the *Winkler Coversheet* icon
Step 3	*Click*	<u>D</u>elete
Step 4	*Click*	<u>Y</u>es to confirm the deletion
Step 5	*Cancel*	the New dialog box

You can also modify the Normal template to change the default settings. Common defaults that users change are the font style, font size, and margin settings. Viktor Winkler uses the same margins and fonts for all public affairs correspondence. You can create a custom template for his correspondence or you can modify the margins and font settings in the Normal template so that every document you create contains the preferred margin and font settings.

Creating a New Document with a Wizard

A **wizard** is a series of dialog boxes that asks questions and uses your answers to lay out and format a document. You can use wizards to create legal pleadings, letters, fax cover sheets, envelopes, labels, memos, meeting agenda, calendars, resumes, and Web Pages. The wizard icons are located in the various tabs in the New dialog box along with the template icons. Viktor Winkler asks you to create a calendar he

chapter
twelve

can use to plan his travel schedule for next month. You use the Calendar Wizard to do this quickly. To create a one-month calendar:

Step 1	*Open*	the New dialog box
Step 2	*Click*	the Other Documents tab
Step 3	*Double-click*	the Calendar Wizard icon
Step 4	*Observe*	the Calendar Wizard dialog box options

When you work in a Wizard, you can cancel your actions with the Cancel button, return to the previous step with the <Back button, move to the next step with the Next> button, and complete the document with the Finish button. These buttons appear at the bottom of the dialog box.

Step 5	*Click*	Next> to choose a style for your calendar
Step 6	*Click*	the Boxes and borders option button
Step 7	*Click*	Next> to choose a the paper orientation
Step 8	*Click*	the Landscape option button
Step 9	*Click*	Next> to choose the calendar date
Step 10	*Select*	the next month and current year from the Month and Year list boxes
Step 11	*Click*	Next> to complete your calendar choices
Step 12	*Click*	Finish

The completed calendar document appears on your screen. You can click inside each day block and key text. When you click the calendar you can see the object's boundaries, which you can click to select the content and change its formatting. To review the calendar:

Step 1	*Scroll*	to view the calendar
Step 2	*Click*	the first blank day box at the top of the calendar to view the calendar border
Step 3	*Click*	the calendar object border to select the contents
Step 4	*Change*	the font size to 18 and remove the bold formatting
Step 5	*Save*	the document as *Viktor's Calendar* and close it

Wizards, templates, and styles make it easy to create consistently formatted documents quickly, letting you focus on the content of your documents.

Summary

▶ A style is a group of formats assigned a unique name.

▶ Styles help you save time by applying several different formats at once.

▶ There are two kinds of styles: paragraph styles and character styles.

▶ Styles are saved with the document and can be added to the template on which the document is based so that the styles are available to all new documents based on that template.

▶ Word has more than 90 built-in styles; however, only five built-in styles appear in a new document by default. You can choose to display all the built-in styles, if desired.

▶ Styles can be viewed in a Style area on the screen to the left of the document text.

▶ You can review the formatting components of a style by changing the mouse pointer to the What's This? help pointer and clicking the formatted text.

▶ You can create custom styles and can modify built-in styles in the Style dialog box. You can also create styles by example, using the Style button on the Formatting toolbar.

▶ A template is a model document. The default model is the Normal template.

▶ You can modify the Normal template by opening it and making changes to it. Also, you can change the font, font size, and margin settings in the Normal template in the Font and Page Setup dialog boxes.

▶ Word has many letter, fax, Web page, and other templates you can use to create your own documents.

▶ You can create a custom template by using another Word document as an example and saving it as a template. You can also use a Word template as the basis for the new custom template.

▶ You can create a variety of documents following a step-by-step process called a wizard.

chapter twelve

Commands Review

Action	Menu Bar	Shortcut Menu	Toolbar	Keyboard
Apply a style to selected text	Format, Style		Normal ▼	ALT + O, S CTRL + SHIFT + S CTRL + SHIFT + N (Normal style) ALT + CTRL + 1 (Heading 1 style) ALT + CTRL + 2 (Heading 2 style) ALT + CTRL + 3 (Heading 3 style) CTRL+ SHIFT + L (List style)
Repeat a style	Edit, Repeat Style			ALT + E, R CTRL + Y F4
Display all built-in styles			Press the SHIFT key and click the Normal ▼ list arrow	
Display the formatting applied to text in a box	Help, What's This?			ALT + H, T SHIFT + F1
Close the box containing formatting information				ESC
Display styles in the Style Area of the document	Tools, Options View tab			ALT + T, O
Create custom styles	Format, Style		Click the text area of Normal ▼ and type style name	ALT + O, S
Modify a style	Format, Style		Click the text area of Normal ▼ and press ENTER	ALT + O, S
View and/or copy styles from Word templates to the current document	Tools, Templates and Add-Ins			ALT + T, I
Base a document on a template or wizard	File, New			ALT + F, N
Go to the next field in a document based on a Word template				F11
Go to the previous field in a document based on a Word template				SHIFT + F11

Concepts Review   SCANS

Circle the correct answer.

1. A paragraph style does not:
  [a] include font, font size, and line spacing.
  [b] affect the entire selected paragraph.
  [c] determine the overall appearance of a paragraph.
  [d] affect only selected text characters.

2. Which of the following is not a basic style in the Style Preview?
  [a] Heading 1
  [b] Heading 3
  [c] Default Character Font
  [d] Normal

3. **You cannot see which style is applied to a paragraph by:**
   [a] selecting the paragraph and observing the Style button.
   [b] clicking the Style Gallery command on the Format menu.
   [c] setting a Style area down the left side of the screen.
   [d] moving the insertion point to a paragraph and then opening the Style dialog box.

4. **A template is a:**
   [a] place to store documents.
   [b] tool to apply a combination of formats at one time.
   [c] model document.
   [d] way to view the styles in your document.

5. **To view the entire list of styles in the Style Preview press the:**
   [a] ALT key and click the Style Preview list arrow.
   [b] CTRL key and click the Style Preview list arrow.
   [c] BACKSPACE key and click the Style Preview list arrow.
   [d] SHIFT key and click the Style Preview list arrow.

6. **A character style:**
   [a] determines the overall appearance of a paragraph.
   [b] must be applied to entire words.
   [c] must be created by example.
   [d] determines the appearance of selected text.

7. **The Normal template:**
   [a] must be opened before you can edit it.
   [b] is used to create documents when you click the Open button on the Standard toolbar.
   [c] cannot be edited in the Font and Page Setup dialog boxes.
   [d] contains the default font and margin settings.

8. **Entering a custom style name in uppercase characters:**
   [a] defines the style as a paragraph style.
   [b] makes the name easier to read.
   [c] distinguishes the custom style from a built-in style.
   [d] creates a style by example.

9. **Which template do you use each time you click the New button on the Standard toolbar?**
   [a] Paragraph template
   [b] Normal template
   [c] Font template
   [d] Formatting template

10. **The bold, underlined letter "a" indicates:**
    [a] a paragraph style.
    [b] the Normal template.
    [c] a character style.
    [d] the Style Gallery.

Circle **T** if the statement is true or **F** if the statement is false.

T   F   1. A style allows you to format text easily by applying many different formats at one time.

T   F   2. Word provides exactly 65 built-in styles.

T   F   3. You can create custom styles with the Formatting toolbar or the Style command on the Format menu.

T   F   4. You can delete built-in styles.

T   F   5. You can use the Style Gallery button on the Formatting toolbar to apply, create, or modify styles.

T   F   6. A character style determines the overall appearance of a paragraph.

T   F   7. The Reveal Formats box shows only character styles.

chapter twelve

T   F   8. After you edit a style, you must manually reapply the style to the formatted text.

T   F   9. Built-in styles cannot be modified.

T   F   10. You can use the Style Gallery to preview and copy styles to your document.

Skills Review

Exercise 1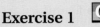

1. Open the *Word Outline* document located on the Data Disk.

2. Apply the built-in Heading 1 style to the title "WORD FOR WINDOWS."

3. Apply the built-in Heading 2 style to the topic headings. (The topic headings are in 12-point font.)

4. Save the document as *Word Outline With Built-in Styles*.

5. Preview, print, and close the document.

Exercise 2

1. Open the *Word Outline* document located on the Data Disk.

2. Create a style by example to center and add bold formatting to the title "WORD FOR WINDOWS." Name the style TITLES.

3. Create a style by example to bold and underline the topic headings. (The topic headings are in 12-point font.) Name the style HEADINGS.

4. Apply the HEADINGS style to the topic headings.

5. Apply the built-in List Bullet 2 style to the subtopics. (The subtopics are in 10-point font.) (*Hint:* Use the SHIFT key to view all the style in the Style Preview.)

6. Save the document as *Word Outline With Custom Styles*.

7. Preview, print, and close the document.

Exercise 3

1. Open the *Word Outline With Custom Styles* document created in Exercise 2.

2. Modify the TITLES style using the Style list box on the Formatting toolbar so that the title is Arial, 16 point, italic, no bold.

3. Modify the HEADINGS style using the Style list box on the Formatting toolbar so that the headings are Arial, 12 point, bold, Small Caps effect, no underline.

4. Save the document as *Word Outline With Custom Styles Revised*.

5. Preview, print, and close the document.

Exercise 4

1. Open the *Preparing For A Speech* document located on the Data Disk.

2. Create a style that indents the body of the document 0.25 inches from the left and right margins, double spaces the body of the document, and uses justified alignment. Name the style LAYOUT.

3. Create a style that makes the document title boldfaced and centered. Name the style TITLES.

4. Create a style to format the paragraph headings with a double underline and 1.5 line spacing. Name the style SIDEHEAD.

5. Apply the styles in the document.

6. Save the document as *Preparing For A Speech With Styles*.

7. Preview, print, and close the document.

Exercise 5

1. Open the *Preparing For A Speech With Styles* document created in Exercise 4.

2. Edit the SIDEHEAD style so that the side headings are bold and italic instead of underlined.

3. Change the LAYOUT style so that the line spacing is 1.5.

4. Save the document as *Preparing For A Speech Revised*.

5. Preview, print, and close the document.

Exercise 6

1. Use the Elegant Memo template to create a memorandum to Viktor Winkler from yourself with a copy to Bill Martin.

2. Describe the new Winkler Coversheet template and how to use it in the body of the memorandum.

3. Save the memorandum as *Winkler Memo*.

4. Preview, print, and close the document.

Exercise 7

1. Create a new custom fax coversheet for Bill Martin, with a copy to B. J. Chang, based on the Professional Fax template. (*Hint:* Enlarge the text box that contains the company name so that the text does not wrap to two lines.)

2. Save the custom template as *Martin Fax*.

3. Preview, print, and close the document.

Exercise 8

1. Create an interoffice memo using the Memo Wizard.

2. Use the Contemporary style, the default title text, and the Date, From, and Subject header lines. Send the memo to Jody Haversham with a copy to Viktor Winkler. Add your initials as the writer's initials. Do not include a header or footer. The subject is "Using Wizards."

3. Key a brief paragraph describing how to create a document using a wizard.

4. Save the document as *Memo Created With A Wizard*.

5. Preview, print, and close the document.

Exercise 9

1. Create the following document using built-in styles.

2. Save the document as *Public Affairs Officer*.

3. Preview, print, and close the document.

chapter twelve

Public Affairs Officer

Viktor Winkler

Investor and Customer Inquiries

Annual Reports

401(k) Reports

Customer Service

Government Liaison

13th District Election Committee

Food Distributors PAC

Registered Lobbyist

Civic and Business Liaison

Heltrep Foundation

Speakers Bureau

Youth First Committee

Mayor's Council

Case Projects

Project 1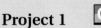

Viktor Winkler's assistant, Bob Thackery, returns from vacation and is impressed with the documents you formatted. He wants to know how to apply, create, and modify styles using the Style dialog box and asks you for help. Because you created your custom styles using the Style button, you need to research how to use the Style dialog box. Open the Style dialog box with the Style command on the Format menu. Use the dialog box Help tool to review the options and buttons in the dialog box, and then close it. Use the Office Assistant to research creating and modifying paragraph and character styles using the options in the Style dialog box. Write Bob an interoffice memorandum, based on a memo template, explaining how he can use the Style dialog box to save time formatting documents. Save, preview, and print the memo.

Project 2

The human resource department frequently receives unsolicited resumes from people around the world who want to work for Worldwide Exotic Foods. Company policy is to thank the sender for the resume and advise them that their resume will be kept on file for six months. If a position becomes available, the sender will be contacted to arrange for an interview. To save time in responding to unsolicited resumes, Bill asks you to create a block format custom letter template with B. J. Chang's signature line. The only variable data keyed in documents based on this new custom template is the letter address and the name portion of the salutation. The date, the "Dear" portion of the salutation, the body text, the closing, the signature line, and the typist's initials are fixed text, sometimes called boilerplate text, in the template. Create, save, preview, and print the template. Then create two letters, including attached envelopes, to fictitious persons using the new custom letter template. Save, preview, and print the letters and envelopes.

Project 3

Viktor Winkler needs a list of government Web sites containing information of interest to Worldwide Exotic Foods, Inc. management and employees. He asks you to compile such a list. Connect to your ISP, load your Web browser, and search the Web for government Web pages of interest. Print at least five Web pages. Create a list of the Web sites of interest. Use built-in and custom styles to format the list. Save, preview, and print the list.

Project 4

Lydia Montez, a receptionist in the human resources department, is having trouble using styles. Sometimes her styles change unexpectedly, some paragraphs formatted with the same style look different, and she cannot see all the styles she wants to use in the Style Preview. You agree to research these problems and then tell her how to solve them. Using the Office Assistant, review how to troubleshoot problems you might encounter when using styles. Create a new document, with at least four paragraphs, that describes each of Lydia's style problems and suggests a solution for each one. Use styles to format the document. Save and print the document. With your instructor's approval, use the document as a guide to show a classmate how to solve these and other style problems.

Project 5

Bill Martin wants to preview the styles used in several Word templates and then copy the styles into a new document he is creating. He asks you

how to do this. Using the Office Assistant, research how to view or copy styles from another template into your document using the Style Gallery. Write Bill and interoffice memorandum explaining how to do this. Use styles to format your memorandum. Save, preview, and print the memorandum.

Project 6

Viktor Winkler wants to include current U. S. government international travel warnings in a bulletin he wants faxed to each branch office and posted in the employee lounge area to warn traveling employees. He asks you to locate the government page where international warnings are listed. Print the page. Create a document that lists the travel warnings. Format the document using custom paragraph and character styles. Save, preview, and print the document.

Project 7

Several human resources employees ask you how they can access styles contained in other documents when working in their documents. Using the online Help features, research how to use settings from another document by attaching a different template to a document and by using the Organizer feature. Practice attaching a different template and updating styles and copying styles to a document using the Organizer. Create a document itemizing how to use both techniques to use settings from other documents. Save, preview, and print the document. With your instructor's permission, demonstrate these techniques to several classmates.

Project 8

To save time in creating interoffice memos, Lydia asks you to create a human resources interoffice memorandum template. She wants you to use the Professional Memo template as the basis for the custom template, but she does not want the page number at the bottom of the page. Create the custom memo template—making any other changes you think appropriate to styles, layout, and formatting. Save, preview, and print the document.

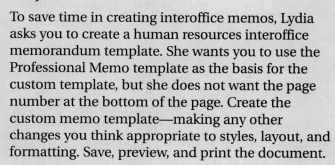

Generating an Outline

Chapter Overview

An outline is a way to structure information logically. You can use an outline to organize ideas and information into topics and subtopics for a large document, such as a report, proposal, or presentation. An outline is also a good way to construct multilevel lists. In this chapter you learn to create and modify outlines.

LEARNING OBJECTIVES

- ▶ Organize a document in Outline view
- ▶ Modify an outline
- ▶ Use Outline Numbered formats to create outlines

Case profile

Worldwide Exotic Foods, Inc. is planning a major presentation for investors, distributors, and other invited guests, during a company-sponsored picnic at the International Food Distributors annual conference in London. The executive assistant, Marisa DaFranco, asks you to help prepare the food list for the caterers and the chairperson's presentation outline.

chapter thirteen

13.a Organizing a Document in Outline View

An **outline** consists of headings and body text organized by level of importance into major headings and subheadings. Body text is paragraph text below an outline heading. Major headings are called level one headings. Each major heading can have subheadings, called level two headings. Each level two heading can have its own subheadings at level three, and so forth.

Marisa is preparing the food list for the company picnic and needs to organize the information for the caterer. She gives you the handwritten document in Figure 13-1 and asks you to create an outline with three heading levels.

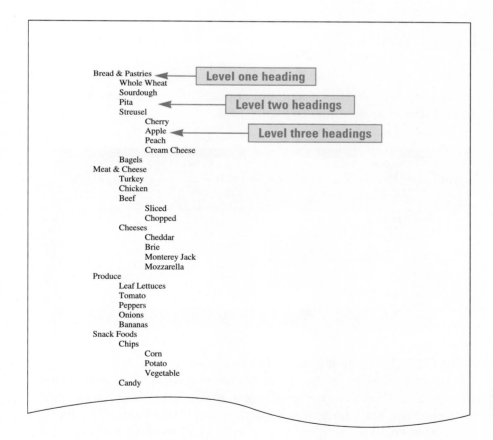

FIGURE 13-1
Catering List Outline

chapter
thirteen

MENU TIP

You can view a document in Outline view by clicking the Outline command on the View menu.

You begin by keying the text in Figure 13-1 in one single spaced column at the left margin. Do not manually indent any of the text. The text is indented when you create the outline.

To key the menu:

Step 1	*Key*	the text in Figure 13-1 in one single spaced column at the left margin
Step 2	*Save*	the document as *Catering Food List*

Word has two tools you can use to create outlines. You can create an outline in Outline view using heading or level styles and you can create outlines using formats in the Outline Numbered tab in the Bullets and Numbering dialog box.

To create the outline using styles:

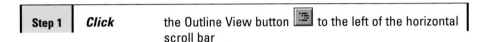

Step 1	*Click*	the Outline View button [icon] to the left of the horizontal scroll bar

The *Catering Food List* document appears in Outline view. Your screen should look similar to Figure 13-2.

FIGURE 13-2
Outline View

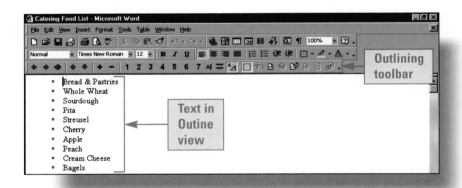

The Outlining toolbar appears below the Formatting toolbar whenever you are in Outline view. To create an outline in Outline view, you "promote" or "demote" headings to different levels of importance in the outline. You can do this as you key text into a blank document, or you can open an existing document, select the heading, and promote or demote it to the appropriate level. You use the Promote and Demote buttons on the Outlining toolbar to apply heading styles that indicate the outline levels.

Figure 13-1 indicates the text "Bread & Pastries," "Meat & Cheese," "Produce," and "Snack Foods" are major headings. To begin the outline by promoting the "Bread & Pastries" major heading to level one:

Step 1	*Verify*	the insertion point is in the first heading "Bread & Pastries"
Step 2	*Click*	the Promote button ⬅ on the Outlining toolbar
Step 3	*Observe*	the Bread & Pastries text is formatted with the Heading 1 style, making it a major or level one heading

The text beginning with "Whole Wheat" and ending with "Streusel" are level two subheadings. To demote the next four paragraphs to level two:

| Step 1 | *Select* | the text beginning with "Whole Wheat" and ending with "Streusel" |
| Step 2 | *Click* | the Demote button ➡ on the Outlining toolbar |

Word indents the level two headings and applies the Heading 2 style. The headings beginning with "Cherry" and ending with "Cream Cheese" are level three headings. To demote the next four paragraphs to level three:

| Step 1 | *Select* | the text beginning with "Cherry" and ending with "Cream Cheese" |
| Step 2 | *Click* | the Demote button ➡ on the Outlining toolbar |

The level three headings are indented and formatted with the Heading 3 style. To promote the heading "Bagels" to level two:

| Step 1 | *Select* | the text Bagels |
| Step 2 | *Click* | the Promote button ⬅ on the Outlining toolbar twice |

Bagels is promoted to level two. To promote the "Meat & Cheese" text to level one:

| Step 1 | *Select* | the "Meat & Cheese" text |
| Step 2 | *Click* | the Promote button ⬅ on the Outlining toolbar twice |

**chapter
thirteen**

Your screen should look similar to Figure 13-3.

FIGURE 13-3
Outline Levels Marked

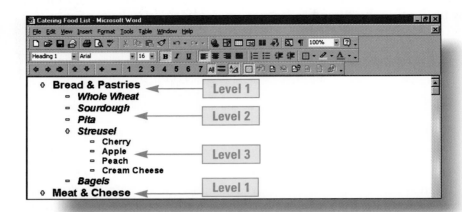

The plus sign (+) next to an outline level indicates that the outline level contains subheadings. The minus sign (–) next to an outline level indicates that the outline level does not contain subheadings. You can use the TAB key to demote text to a lower outline level and the SHIFT + TAB keys to promote text to a higher outline level. To demote the text beginning with "Turkey" and ending with "Beef" to level two:

Step 1	*Select*	the text beginning with "Turkey" and ending with "Beef"
Step 2	*Press*	the TAB key
Step 3	*Select*	the text beginning with "Sliced" and ending with "Chopped"
Step 4	*Press*	the TAB key to demote the selected text to level three

Next you use the SHIFT + TAB to promote text to a higher outline level. To promote "Cheeses" to level two:

Step 1	*Select*	the text "Cheeses"
Step 2	*Press & Hold*	the SHIFT key
Step 3	*Press*	TAB key twice to promote the text to level two
Step 4	*Release*	the SHIFT key
Step 5	*Complete*	the outline using Figure 13-1 as your guide
Step 6	*Save*	the document as *Catering List Outline*

MENU TIP

You can use the Increase Indent and Decrease Indent commands on the shortcut menu to demote or promote heading text.

Because you use outlines to organize ideas and information for large documents or presentations, you sometimes want to review outlines by heading level. This allows you to focus on the document structure. You can review an outline by heading level with the Show Heading buttons on the Outlining toolbar. Outline view indicates that a section contains more detail in two ways. The plus sign (+) to the left of a heading indicates it contains subheadings. When you hide the subheadings, a gray line appears below headings that contain additional detail, whether a subheading or body text. To see different level headings:

Step 1	*Click*	the Show Heading 1 button 1 on the Outlining toolbar
Step 2	*Observe*	only the level one headings are visible
Step 3	*Observe*	the gray line below the level one headings
Step 4	*Click*	the Show Heading 2 button 2 on the Outlining toolbar
Step 5	*Observe*	both the level one and two headings are visible
Step 6	*Click*	the Show All Headings button All on the Outlining toolbar
Step 7	*Observe*	all the headings are visible

> **MOUSE TIP**
>
> To show (expand) or hide (collapse) levels of detail in an outline, move your insertion point to the outline level you wish to expand or collapse and click the Expand or Collapse button on the Outlining toolbar. This affects only the selected levels.

Marisa likes the way the outline looks, but asks you to add two new subheadings under "Candy" and add a numbering scheme so that each outline level is numbered differently. She also asks you to move the entire Meat & Cheese group headings to the top of the outline.

13.b Modifying an Outline

After you create an outline, you can change it by adding and moving headings. To add a heading to the outline, move the insertion point to the location where you want the heading to begin, press the ENTER key to create a new line, and key the new heading. You can promote or demote the new headings as needed. To add two new headings:

Step 1	*Move*	the insertion point to the end of the document
Step 2	*Press*	the ENTER key
Step 3	*Click*	the Demote button ➡ on the Outlining toolbar

chapter thirteen

Step 4	*Key*	Chocolate
Step 5	*Press*	the ENTER key
Step 6	*Key*	All Other

You can move a heading by selecting it and clicking the Move Up or Move Down buttons on the Outlining toolbar. This moves the heading and all its subheadings up or down one position at a time in the outline. To select a heading and all its subheadings, click the plus sign (+) to the left of the heading.

A quick way to move a heading and its subheadings up or down several positions in the outline is to drag the heading's plus sign. As you drag the plus sign a horizontal positioning line appears on the screen indicating where the heading group is placed when you release the mouse pointer.

To select and move the Meat & Cheese major heading and subheadings to the top of the list:

Step 1	*Drag*	the plus sign (+) to the left of the Meat & Cheese level one text up until the horizontal line is positioned above the Bread & Pastries heading at the top of the document

Your screen should look similar to Figure 13-4.

FIGURE 13-4
Repositioning a Major
Heading

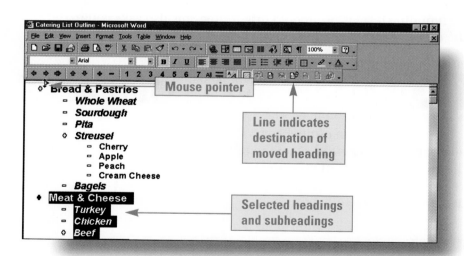

Step 2	*Release*	the mouse button to position the Meat & Cheese heading and subheadings at the top of the document
Step 3	*Deselect*	the text
Step 4	*Save*	the document

Creating an Outline Style Numbered List

Another way to modify an outline is to add numbers to each outline heading. This helps the reader follow the document structure from more important to less important headings. You can add numbers to the outline levels using the O*u*tline Numbered tab in the Bullets and Numbering dialog box. This is more effective than numbering the levels manually because if you rearrange the outline order Word updates the numbers automatically. To add numbers to the outline:

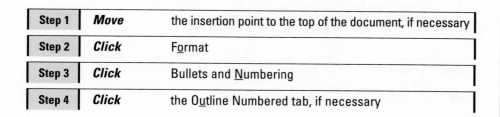

Step 1	*Move*	the insertion point to the top of the document, if necessary
Step 2	*Click*	F*o*rmat
Step 3	*Click*	Bullets and *N*umbering
Step 4	*Click*	the O*u*tline Numbered tab, if necessary

The dialog box you see on your screen should look like Figure 13-5. You select and customize the numbering scheme in this dialog box.

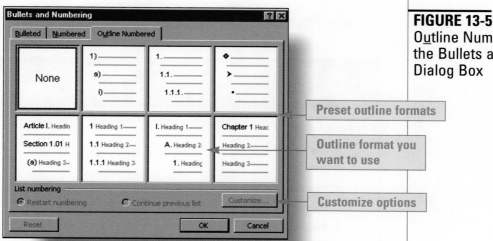

FIGURE 13-5
O*u*tline Numbered Tab in the Bullets and Numbering Dialog Box

notes

Unless otherwise noted, the activities in this chapter assume the O*u*tline Numbered formats contain their default settings. If the formats are customized, the Reset button is active when the format is selected. Click the Reset button, if it is active, to return the format to its default settings. It is recommended that you return all O*u*tline Numbered formats to their default settings before you proceed with the remaining activities in this chapter.

chapter
thirteen

To apply the I., A., 1. (Heading 1, 2, 3) format:

Step 1	***Double-click***	the third format option in the second row
Step 2	***Observe***	the numbering added to the outline headings and subheadings

In Outline view you cannot view the horizontal ruler with the indent marker and tab stops settings that control the position of the heading and subheadings in the outline. To view these settings, you must switch to Print Layout or Normal view.

Step 3	***Switch***	to Normal view
Step 4	***Scroll***	to view the entire list
Step 5	***Scroll***	to view the "Produce" and "Snack Foods" major headings on the screen
Step 6	***Observe***	the spacing between the heading number and the heading text for both headings

Your screen should look similar to Figure 13-6.

FIGURE 13-6
Heading Number and Text
Spacing

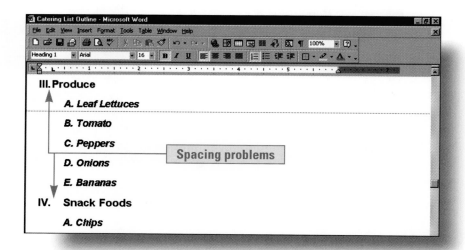

The "Produce" heading aligns immediately to the right of the heading number and the "Snack Foods" heading aligns at the next default tab stop. Word automatically indents each heading level in ½-inch increments beginning with level two. Also, Word inserts a custom left-aligned tab stop ¼ inch to the right of each heading's indent marker. When the heading number increases to three positions, the default ¼-inch tab stop position is not sufficient to properly align the heading text. Also notice that the level three headings appear indented too far to the right. To more attractively align the level one and level three headings, you must customize the outline number format for both levels. To customize the Outline Numbered format:

Step 1	*Open*	the Outline Numbered tab in the Bullets and Numbering dialog box
Step 2	*Verify*	the I., A., 1. (Heading 1, 2, 3) format is selected
Step 3	*Click*	Customize
Step 4	*Click*	the More button to expand the dialog box

The dialog box you see on your screen should look similar to Figure 13-7.

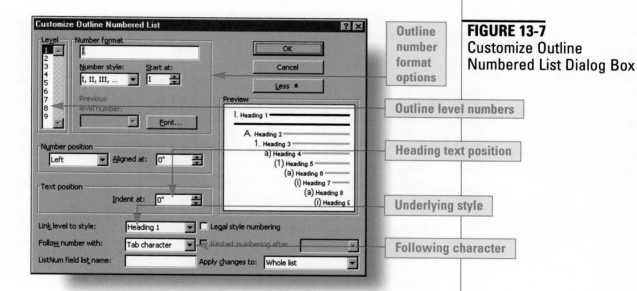

Outline number format options

Outline level numbers

Heading text position

Underlying style

Following character

FIGURE 13-7
Customize Outline Numbered List Dialog Box

When you customize the Outline numbered format, you do it one level at a time. First select the heading number you want to modify from the Level list and then change the numbering style, font, beginning number, or indentation positions. You can apply your changes to the whole list or at the position of the insertion point. To change the level one heading indentation so that it's ½ inch to the right of the heading number:

| Step 1 | *Verify* | that 1 is selected in the Level list |
| Step 2 | *Observe* | the position of the Heading 1 text in the Preview |

chapter
thirteen

| Step 3 | *Key* | .5 in the Indent at: text box |
| Step 4 | *Observe* | the new position of the Heading 1 text in the Preview |

Now you change the indentation for the level three number and heading text to ¾ inch.

Step 5	*Click*	3 in the Level list
Step 6	*Key*	.75 in the Aligned at: text box to change the number indentation
Step 7	*Key*	.75 in the Indent at: text box to change the heading text indentation
Step 8	*Click*	OK
Step 9	*Scroll*	to view the new level one and level three heading positions
Step 10	*Save*	the document

Marisa wants you to add a title to the outline. The best way to add a title to an outline created with heading styles in Outline view is to switch to Normal view, create a blank line at the top of the document, and then key and format the text. If you create a title in Outline view, you may not be able to see the title's formatting changes or its positioning.

To key and center the title "Catering Menu:

Step 1	*Verify*	the document is in Normal view
Step 2	*Move*	the insertion point to the top of the document
Step 3	*Press*	the ENTER key
Step 4	*Move*	the insertion point to the top of the document
Step 5	*Press*	the BACKSPACE key to remove the outline number
Step 6	*Key*	and center the title Catering Food List
Step 7	*Save*	the document and close it

Now Marisa wants you to add paragraph numbering to a report and create the chairperson's presentation as a formal topic outline.

MOUSE **T**IP

You also can insert body text below an outline topic while in Outline view. To do this, move the insertion point to the end of the heading under which you plan to add text, press the ENTER key to add a line, and click the Demote to Body Text button on the Outlining toolbar.

13.c Using Outline Numbered Formats to Create Outlines

Using Outline view is one way to create an outline. Another way is to work directly with the Outline Numbered formats in the Bullets and Numbering dialog box in Normal or Print Layout view. You can use the Outline Numbered formats to add numbering to text paragraphs or lists.

Outlining a Document by Assigning Outline Levels to Paragraphs

Numbered text paragraphs are often used in reports and proposals. While in London, the chairperson is also meeting with the London branch manager to discuss a research report on stores in the London branch. Marisa asks you to add paragraph numbering to the research report. To open the document and add paragraph numbering:

Step 1	*Open*	the *London Research* document located on the Data Disk
Step 2	*Select*	the entire document
Step 3	*Open*	the Outline Numbered tab in the Bullets and Numbering dialog box
Step 4	*Double-click*	the third option in the first row (1, 1.1, 1.1.1)
Step 5	*Deselect*	the text and review the new paragraph numbering

Paragraphs 3. and 4. are subparagraphs of paragraph 2 so you need to modify the paragraph numbering by demoting the paragraphs to the next lower level. You can use the TAB and SHIFT + TAB keys to promote and demote numbered paragraphs just like in an outline. To demote paragraphs 3. and 4.:

Step 1	*Select*	paragraphs 3. and 4.
Step 2	*Press*	the TAB key
Step 3	*Deselect*	the paragraphs and observe the new subparagraph numbering (2.1 and 2.2)
Step 4	*Save*	the document as *London Research Revised* and close it

chapter thirteen

Creating a Formal Topic Outline

When you need to create a formal topic outline, you can use a modified Outline Numbered format. A formal topic outline has a 2-inch top margin with an uppercase, centered title followed by three blank lines. Each major heading is numbered with Roman numerals followed by a period. The numerals are decimal aligned on the periods (for example, the I. and IV. heading numbers are aligned on the period). You double space before and after each major heading. The subheadings are single spaced and the number for each new subheading level (A., 1.) begins immediately below the text of the previous heading.

To create the chairperson's presentation as a formal topic outline, you apply a modified Outline Numbered format and then key the text in the outline. The chairperson will expand the outline later by providing the appropriate body text and formatting. To create the margins and title of a formal outline:

Step 1	*Create*	a new, blank document
Step 2	*Set*	a 2-inch top margin
Step 3	*Center*	the title "PRESENTATION OUTLINE" on the first line
Step 4	*Press*	the ENTER key four times
Step 5	*View*	the formatting marks
Step 6	*Move*	the insertion point to the left margin

Next you select and customize an Outline Numbered format. To create and customize the formal outline:

Step 1	*Open*	the Outline Numbered tab in the Bullets and Numbering dialog box
Step 2	*Click*	the second outline option (1, a, i) in the first row
Step 3	*Click*	Customize

To conform to the formatting standards for a formal topic outline, you must change the number style to Roman numerals for level one, uppercase alphabetic characters for level two, and Arabic numbers for level three. The character following the number must be changed to a period. The level one number alignment must be changed to Right aligned so that the numbers align on the period at the end of each number. The indentation for levels two and three must be modified to align the number with the text above it. You start by modifying the outline format for level one.

Step 4	*Verify*	1 is selected in the Level list
Step 5	*Click*	the Number style: list arrow
Step 6	*Click*	I, II, III
Step 7	*Click*	in the Number format text box
Step 8	*Replace*	the closing parenthesis with a period
Step 9	*Change*	the Number position to Right
Step 10	*Key*	.25 in the Aligned at: text box
Step 11	*Observe*	the changes to the level one heading in the Preview

You repeat the same series of actions for the level two headings. To modify the level two indentations, numbering style and following character:

Step 1	*Click*	2 in the Level list
Step 2	*Change*	the Number style to A, B, C
Step 3	*Replace*	the closing parenthesis with a period
Step 4	*Change*	the Aligned at: text box to .5 inch
Step 5	*Change*	the Indent at: text box to .85 inch

To modify the level three indentations, numbering style, and following character:

Step 1	*Click*	3 in the Level list
Step 2	*Change*	the Number style to 1, 2, 3
Step 3	*Change*	the closing parenthesis to a period
Step 4	*Change*	the Aligned at: text box to .85 inches
Step 5	*Change*	the Indent at: text box to 1.2 inches
Step 6	*Click*	OK

The indented first number automatically appears. You promote or demote headings by clicking the Increase or Decrease Indent buttons on the Formatting toolbar or by pressing the TAB key or the SHIFT + TAB keys before you key the text.

chapter
thirteen

To key the first heading:

Step 1	*Key*	MARKETING FORECAST
Step 2	*Press*	the SHIFT + ENTER keys to insert a New Line formatting mark (small return arrow) at the end of the MARKETING FORECAST heading and move the insertion point to a new line

Your screen should look similar to Figure 13-8.

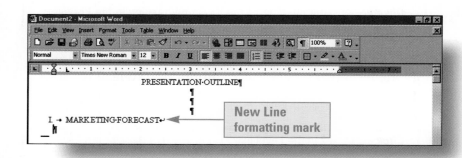

FIGURE 13-8
New Line Formatting Mark

Step 3	*Press*	the ENTER key to move the insertion point to the next line and continue the outline numbers

The next outline heading is automatically numbered at the same level as the previous heading which is level one. However, you now want to key level two headings. You demote the insertion point to the next level.

Step 4	*Click*	the Increase Indent button on the Formatting toolbar to move the insertion point to the next level and insert the A. outline number
Step 5	*Key*	Projected Sales
Step 6	*Press*	the ENTER key
Step 7	*Key*	Sales Stars!
Step 8	*Press*	the ENTER key

Next, key the level three headings below "Sales Stars!"

Step 9	*Press*	the TAB key
Step 10	*Key*	Wilson, Betancourt, and Fontaine, pressing the ENTER key after each heading

QUICK TIP

To add a double space between the major heading and any subheadings you can insert a New Line formatting mark that adds a blank line without outline numbers by pressing the SHIFT + ENTER keys. A **New Line formatting mark** creates a new line inside an existing paragraph formatting mark. You then press the ENTER key to create a new paragraph and begin the next numbered heading line.

Step 11	*Key*	Lu
Step 12	*Press*	the SHIFT + ENTER keys to insert a New Line formatting mark
Step 13	*Press*	the ENTER key

The next heading is level one. To promote the insertion point and key the second level one heading:

Step 1	*Click*	the Decrease Indent button ⊞ twice on the Formatting toolbar
Step 2	*Key*	ADVERTISING CAMPAIGN
Step 3	*Press*	the SHIFT + ENTER keys to insert a New Line formatting mark
Step 4	*Press*	the ENTER key to create the next heading line
Step 5	*Press*	TAB key to demote the insertion point to level two
Step 6	*Key*	Media Budget
Step 7	*Press*	the ENTER key
Step 8	*Press*	the TAB key to demote the insertion point
Step 9	*Key*	TV, Radio, and Web banners, pressing the ENTER key after each heading
Step 10	*Press*	the SHIFT + TAB keys to promote the insertion point
Step 11	*Key*	Print Ads
Step 12	*Press*	the ENTER key
Step 13	*Press*	the TAB key to demote the insertion point
Step 14	*Key*	Newspapers and Magazines pressing the ENTER key after Newspapers
Step 15	*Save*	the document as *Presentation Outline* and close it

The chairperson will base the conference presentation on this outline.

CAUTION TIP

When you customize an Outline Numbered format, it remains customized until you reset the format's options. Unless you want to permanently change the options, you should open the Outline Numbered tab in the Bullets and Numbering dialog box, select the customized format, and reset it when you are finished using the format.

chapter thirteen

Summary

► An outline is a way of organizing the ideas and information presented in a long document or presentation.

► Outline view automatically creates outlines from text formatted with built-in heading styles or Outline level: formats from the Paragraph dialog box.

► You can view different levels of an outline in Outline view.

► After you create an outline, you can change it by adding headings at any level or by moving headings to different levels and adding numbering or body text.

► You can modify headings by promoting them to a higher level or demoting them to a lower level.

► You can apply numbering to outline headings or document paragraphs using the Outline Numbered options in the Bullets and Numbering dialog box.

► The New Line formatting mark can be used to create a blank line inside an existing paragraph formatting mark.

Commands Review

Action	Menu Bar	Shortcut Menu	Toolbar	Keyboard
Display your document in Outline view	View, Outline			ALT + V, O ALT + CTRL + O
Display your document in Normal view	View, Normal			ALT + V, N ALT + CTRL + N
Promote a heading		Right-click a heading, click Decrease Indent		ALT + SHIFT + LEFT ARROW TAB
Demote a heading		Right-click a heading, click Increase Indent		ALT + SHIFT + RIGHT ARROW SHIFT + TAB
Expand the view of a heading				ALT + SHIFT + PLUS SIGN
Collapse the view of a heading				ALT + SHIFT + HYPHEN
Move a heading up or down			Drag the selected heading up or down	

Concepts Review

Circle the correct answer.

1. Outlines created in Outline view are not:
[a] a way of viewing a document to organize ideas and information.
[b] a way to arrange text in a document.
[c] easily created using built-in heading styles or Outline level: formats.
[d] automatically numbered.

2. You can add numbers to an outline created with the built-in heading styles by clicking the:
[a] Borders and Shading command on the Insert menu.
[b] Page Numbering command on the Insert menu.
[c] Heading Numbering command on the Format menu.
[d] Bullets and Numbering command on the Format menu.

3. Outline body text is:
[a] text added below an outline heading.
[b] the body of a letter.
[c] a subheading.
[d] an index.

4. Which of the following buttons is not on the Outlining toolbar?
[a] Expand
[b] Collapse
[c] All
[d] Show Level 12

5. The Outline level: formats are located in the:
[a] Font dialog box.
[b] Paragraph dialog box.
[c] Bullets and Numbering dialog box.
[d] Tabs dialog box.

6. To hide the subheadings for a selected major heading, click the:
[a] Expand button.
[b] Demote to Body Text button.
[c] All button.
[d] Show Heading 1 button.

7. You can reposition a major heading and its subheadings at one time by dragging:
[a] the minus sign (–) to the left of the major heading.
[b] the major heading text.
[c] the plus sign (+) to the left of the major heading.
[d] a subheading text.

8. Outlines created in Outline view are composed of:
[a] headings and body text.
[b] paragraph numbers.
[c] body text and numbers.
[d] formatting and fonts.

9. To create a formal topic outline, you can:
[a] modify and apply an Outline Numbered format.
[b] apply the Formal Topic Outline style.
[c] indent each subheading 1 inch.
[d] click the Formal Topic Outline command on the Insert menu.

10. Which numbering scheme is used for numbering paragraphs in reports and proposals?
[a] I, II, III
[b] Heading 1, Heading 2, Heading 3
[c] 1, 1.1, 1.1.1
[d] A, B, C

chapter thirteen

Circle **T** if the statement is true or **F** is the statement is false.

T   F   1. An index is a way of organizing the ideas and information that you want to present in a long document or report.

T   F   2. Outlines cannot have more than two levels.

T   F   3. You use the Promote button to move a major heading and its subheadings to the top of the document.

T   F   4. The Demote button moves a heading level to the next lower level.

T   F   5. When you press the ENTER key, Word automatically creates a new heading at the same level.

T   F   6. You can key an outline using Outline Numbered formats only in Outline view.

T   F   7. When you customize an Outline Numbered format, it automatically reverts to its original default settings the next time you open Word.

T   F   8. When you key and format an outline document title in Normal view, you can see the formatting and positioning changes you make.

T   F   9. You should use the Outline level: formats in the Paragraph dialog box when you do not want to change heading formats.

T   F   10. Press the SHIFT + ENTER keys to create a New Line formatting mark.

Skills Review

Exercise 1   C

1. Open the *Different Documents* document located on the Data Disk.

2. Select the text.

3. Open the Outline Numbered tab in the Bullets and Numbering dialog box and reset any customized formats.

4. Apply the fourth format in the first row to the document.

5. Center the title BUSINESS CORRESPONDENCE two lines above the outline.

6. Save the document as *Different Documents Outline*.

7. Preview, print, and close the document.

Exercise 2   C

1. Open the *Understanding The Internet* document located on the Data Disk.

2. Insert a centered page number at the bottom of each page including the first page.

3. Select all the text below the document title.

4. Apply paragraph numbering using the 1, 1.1, 1.1.1 Outline Numbered format to the selected paragraphs.

5. Use the TAB key or SHIFT + TAB keys to promote or demote the paragraph headings and following text paragraphs appropriately. The paragraph headings in all uppercase are level one headings; they should be numbered 1, 2, 3, and so forth. The paragraph text following the level one headings should be numbered as level two (1.1, 2.1). The paragraph headings in mixed case bold and Italic are level three headings and should be numbered 1.1.1, 1.1.2 and so forth. The paragraph text following the level three headings is level four (1.1.1.1, 1.1.2.1).

6. Save the document as *Numbered Paragraphs*.

7. Preview, print, and close the document.

Exercise 3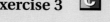

1. Open the *Suppliers And Distributors* document located on the Data Disk.

2. Move the "Suppliers" subheadings so that they appear in alphabetical order.

3. Move the "Distributors" subheadings so that they appear in alphabetical order.

4. Switch to Normal view and add the centered title Suppliers and Distributors at the top of the document.

5. Save the document as *Suppliers And Distributors Revised*.

6. View Level 2 headings in Outline view.

7. Print the document in Outline view showing only level one and two headings.

8. Show all levels of detail.

9. Switch to Normal view.

10. Preview, print, and close the document.

Exercise 4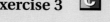

1. Open the *Top Sales* document located on the Data Disk in Outline view. Promote and demote the headings beginning with UNITED STATES. The headings in all uppercase are level one headings. The bold headings are level two headings. The remaining headings are level three.

2. Apply the 1, 1.1, and 1.1.1 Outline Numbered format.

3. Add the centered title TOP SALES at the top of the document in Normal view.

4. Save the document as *Top Sales Outline*.

5. Preview, print, and close the document.

Exercise 5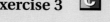

1. Open the *Top Sales Outline* document you created in Exercise 4 in Outline view.

2. Move the "AUSTRALIA" major heading and all subheadings above the "UNITED STATES" major heading.

3. Move the "UNITED STATES" major heading and all subheadings below the "GREAT BRITAIN" heading.

4. Save the document as *Top Sales Outline Revised*.

5. Preview, print and close the document.

Exercise 6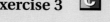

1. Use the data in the following document and a modified Outline Numbered format to create a formal topic outline following the rules outlined in this chapter. Title the outline "SALES OPPORTUNITIES."

2. Save the document as *Sales Opportunities*.

3. Preview, print, and close the document.

chapter thirteen

INTRODUCTION
TYPES OF STORES
  The Mall
    Suburban
    Inner city
  The Strip Center
  The Boutique
    Mom-and-Pop Stores
    The Eclectic Boutique
  The Gourmet Store
SHOPPER PERSONALITIES
  The Sale Hunter
  The Gourmet
  The Browser
  The Catalog Shopper
CONCLUSION

Exercise 7

1. Open the *Sales Opportunities* document created in Exercise 6.

2. Move the "SHOPPER PERSONALITIES" major heading and subheadings above the "TYPES OF STORES" heading.

3. Key the following information below the "SHOPPER PERSONALITIES" heading and subheadings. Do not apply the italic formatting:
SHOPPING SEASONS
  Valentine's Day
  Easter
  Mother's Day
  Father's Day
  Fall
  Christmas

4. Save the document as *Sales Opportunities Revised*.

5. Reset the Outline Numbered format you modified back to its defaults.

6. Preview, print, and close the document.

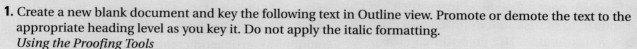

Exercise 8

1. Create a new blank document and key the following text in Outline view. Promote or demote the text to the appropriate heading level as you key it. Do not apply the italic formatting.

Using the Proofing Tools
  Using the Spelling and Grammar Command
  Using the Thesaurus Command
  Using AutoCorrect
    Customizing AutoCorrect
    Setting AutoCorrect Exceptions
  Creating and Applying Frequently Used Text
    Inserting Standard AutoText
    Inserting Custom AutoText
    Editing, Saving, Printing, and Deleting AutoText Entries
  Inserting Dates with AutoComplete

2. Apply the Chapter 1 Heading 1 Outline Numbered format.

3. Save the document as *Proofing Topics*.

4. Preview, print, and close the document.

Case Projects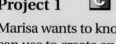

Project 1

Marisa wants to know which keyboard shortcuts she can use to create an outline. Using the online Help tools, identify the keyboard shortcuts used to create an outline in Outline view. Create an Outline Numbered list document itemizing these keyboard shortcut key combinations. Save, preview, and print the document.

Project 2

Because of your experience creating outlines, you are asked to prepare a short presentation to the executive staff of Worldwide Exotic Foods on the differences between creating an outline in Outline view and creating an outline using an Outline Numbered formats. Use the Office Assistant to review the differences between these methods. Create an outline for your presentation using either of the methods. Save, preview, and print the outline. With your instructor's permission, use your outline to discuss and demonstrate the differences between the two methods.

Project 3

Marisa wants you to create an outline from an existing document, but she does not want you to change the formatting. You know you can use the Outline level: formats in the Paragraph dialog box to do this, but you have never used this method. Use the Office Assistant and the dialog box Help tool to review how to use the Outline level: formats. Create an outline using an Outline numbered format itemizing the steps for using the Outline level: formats. Open two documents of your choice and use the Outline level: formats in the Paragraph dialog box to create an outline. Save, preview, and print the document.

Project 4

The chairperson wants to stay at an historic inn and visit several historic sites following the conference in London. Marisa asks you to locate several inns and suggest sites of interest around the London area. Connect to your ISP, load your Web browser, and search the Web for historic inns

chapter thirteen

and sites of interest in the London area. Print at least five Web pages. Create an interoffice memorandum to Marisa that itemizes and describes your research. Use an outline in the memorandum to list the inns and historic sites. Key the outline using an Outline Numbered format. Save, preview, and print the memo.

Project 5 C

Marisa tells you she would like to be able to see the actual formatting of a document when working in Outline view but finds it time-consuming to switch back and forth between Normal and Outline view as she works. You think she can view a document in both Normal and Outline view at the same time by splitting the screen. Use the Office Assistant to look up how to split the screen into two independent viewing panes. Also look up working in Outline view and viewing document formatting at the same time in Normal or Print Layout view. Create an outline itemizing how to see an outline in Normal or Print Layout view while you create it in Outline view. Save, preview, and print the outline. With your instructor's permission, use your outline as a guide and demonstrate the process to a classmate.

Project 6 C

The chairperson is extending the trip to London to include side trips to Wales and Scotland. Marisa asks you to find information on accommodations, ground transportation (auto rental, train), and guided tours to Wales and Scotland. Connect to your ISP, load your Web browser, and search for this information on the Web. Print at least five Web pages. Create an outline listing your research results. Save, preview, and print the outline.

Project 7 C

The current issue of the International Association of Executive Assistants monthly newsletter includes an article on creating outlines in Word. The article mentions using a shortcut menu in the Document Map to expand or collapse level headings in an outline. You want to see how this works and then show Marisa how to use the Document Map with outlines. Use the Office Assistant to review the Document Map feature, if necessary. Open several outlines of your choice and view the Document Map. Use a shortcut menu in the Document Map to show different outline levels and to expand and collapse outline levels. Write an interoffice memorandum to Marisa that includes an outline of the steps needed to view the Document Map and use the shortcut menu to view different levels of detail. Save, preview, and print the memo.

Project 8 C

The chairperson compliments you on the quality of your work and asks you to create an outline listing each department at Worldwide Exotic Foods, Inc. in which you worked and the Word features you used to create documents for the department. Create a formal topic outline using a modified Outline Numbered format. List each department in which you worked as major headings and the Word features you used to create documents for the department as subheadings. Include at least three levels of detail. Save, preview, and print the outline.

Creating Documents for the Internet or an Intranet

Chapter Overview

Organizations of every kind use Web sites to advertise and sell their products and services to the millions of potential customers who browse the Web each day. In addition, companies have intranets where they post Web pages that only their employees can access. In this chapter, you learn how to save documents as HTML, how to create your own Web pages from a template, and how to test and publish your Web pages to the Internet.

LEARNING OBJECTIVES

- ► **Save as a Web page**
- ► **Create a Web page**
- ► **Test and publish Web pages**

Case profile

The Worldwide Exotic Foods, Inc. Web site development committee wants to create a corporate Web site with a home page and individual branch office pages. You are assigned to assist Nat Wong, the committee chairperson, in creating the Web site using Word 2000. You create a home page for Worldwide Exotic Foods to promote the company's specialty food products and branch offices, and provide support to employees creating individual Web pages.

14

chapter fourteen

notes The activities in this chapter assume you have read Chapter 4 in the Office unit and are familiar with the Internet and the World Wide Web. It is also assumed that you are using the Internet Explorer 4.0 or later version Web browser.

C | 14.a Saving as a Web Page

CAUTION TIP

C When you save a Word document as a Web page, some of the Word formatting may not be visible when you view the Web page in your Web browser. When you reopen the Web page in Word, all the original formatting is available. This is called "roundtrip HTML" or "roundtrip documents." For more information, see online Help.

Many organizations are using the Web to communicate with customers and suppliers. Additionally, many organizations use their internal Web or intranet to communicate with employees by publishing Web pages that contain employee handbooks, policies and procedures, computer help-desk tips, and other useful information. Typically, this kind of information was previously made available to employees in printed form.

You can quickly publish documents to the Web or your company intranet by converting Word documents to Web pages. You do this by saving them as HTML documents. An HTML document is a document formatted as a Web page. All Web pages are based on HyperText Markup Language, or **HTML**, which uses codes, called **tags**, to identify the parts of a Web page—such as the title, headings, body—or graphic images, such as bullets. When a Web browser reads the Web page, it formats the Web page for the screen based on these HTML tags. You can save any existing Word document as an HTML document simply by clicking the Save as Web Page command on the File menu. Word automatically inserts the appropriate HTML tags for you.

Kelly Armstead needs help converting the *Vancouver Warehouse Report* to a Web page. She already created the document in Word, and wants to publish the document to the company intranet. You agree to create the Web page for her. To create a Web page from an existing document:

QUICK TIP

C The Web Page Wizard in the Web Pages tab in the New dialog box allows you to create multipage Web sites by entering a title and location, specifying the pages types to include, and applying a design theme.

Step 1	*Open*	the *Vancouver Warehouse Report* document located on the Data Disk
Step 2	*Click*	File
Step 3	*Click*	Save as Web Page

The Save As dialog box that opens on your screen should look similar to Figure 14-1.

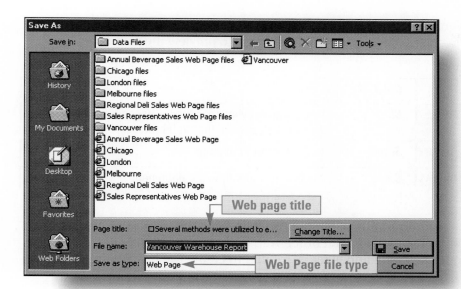

FIGURE 14-1
Save As Dialog Box

The Save As dialog box opens with Web Page in the Save as type: text box. In addition to the filename identification, you can create a title for the Web page. The **title** of a Web page is the text that appears in the title bar of a Web browser when the page loads. This information becomes part of the bookmark or URL when you save a bookmark or favorite URL in a Web browser and some search engines use this text as the keywords for indexing a Web page. If you don't supply a document title, Word uses the first few words of unformatted document text as the title. You want the filename to be the title of the document.

Step 4	*Observe*	the Page title: text
Step 5	*Click*	Change Title
Step 6	*Key*	Vancouver Warehouse Report in the Page title: text box
Step 7	*Click*	OK
Step 8	*Observe*	the new Page title: text
Step 9	*Save*	the Web page as *Vancouver Warehouse Report Web Page* in the location specified by your instructor
Step 10	*Click*	Continue to save the document and accept any automatic modifications made for the browser

After the save is complete, Word automatically switches to Web Layout view. You work in Web Layout view when you want to view the background color, text wrapping, or the position of graphics in Web pages or in Word documents that are to be read online. To see how your document looks in a Web browser, click the Web Page Preview command on the File menu. When you preview your document as a Web page,

chapter
fourteen

Word saves a copy of your document as a temporary file and then opens the copy in your default Web browser. To preview the Web page:

Step 1	*Click*	File
Step 2	*Click*	We<u>b</u> Page Preview to view the *Vancouver Warehouse Report* Web page in the Web browser
Step 3	*Scroll*	to review the Web page
Step 4	*Close*	the browser and then the document

Kelly can publish the document on the company intranet. Nat Wong has created the branch office Web pages for the Worldwide Exotic Foods Web site and is ready for you to create the home page.

14.b Creating a Web Page

To create a Web page in Word 2000, you can use one of the Web templates on the Web Pages tab in the New dialog box. The templates contain preset formatting and sample text you replace with your own text. You can also create a blank, unformatted Web page with the Web Page icon on the General tab in the New dialog box. Use this icon when you want to create a Web page with your own formatting and text options.

After selecting the appropriate template, you use many familiar word processing tools, such as tables, styles, alignment, and font formatting to help you create attractive and professional-looking Web pages.

The Worldwide Exotic Foods home page contains information about the company's business purpose, and a list of the branch office locations followed by the company's contact information. You begin the home page by creating a new, blank Web page. Then you add a title, apply a design theme, insert text, bullets, and a horizontal divider line. To create a new, blank Web page:

Step 1	*Open*	the General tab in the New dialog box
Step 2	*Double-click*	the Web Page icon

A blank Web page appears in Web Layout view. Nat wants you to use the company name as the title for the home page. You add a Web page title to a blank Web page in the document's properties. To add a title:

Step 1	*Click*	File

Step 2	*Click*	Properties
Step 3	*Click*	the Summary tab, if necessary
Step 4	*Key*	Worldwide Exotic Foods, Inc. in the Title: text box
Step 5	*Click*	OK

The Word title bar shows the blank document temporary name, not the new title. The new title appears in the title bar only when the page is loaded in a Web browser. It is a good idea to preview the Web page in a browser as you create or modify it so you can verify the quality and accuracy of your work before you complete the page. You want to verify that the new title "Worldwide Exotic Foods, Inc." appears in the browser title bar. To preview the Web page:

Step 1	*Click*	File
Step 2	*Click*	Web Page Preview
Step 3	*Observe*	the new title in the title bar of the Web browser
Step 4	*Close*	the Web browser

Now you want to add a design theme to the page. It is faster to apply a design theme to your Web page than to format each element individually. The Theme command on the Format menu allows you to preview and select a Web page **theme** that contains coordinated background, horizontal divider line, bullet, and text colors. You decide to look at the various themes that come with Word. To preview different themes:

| Step 1 | *Click* | Format |
| Step 2 | *Click* | Theme |

The Theme dialog box that opens on your screen should look similar to Figure 14-2.

notes It is assumed that all the themes are installed. See your instructor, if necessary, to install missing themes.

MOUSE TIP

In Web Layout view the New button on the Standard toolbar becomes the New Web Page button and is used to create a new, blank Web page.

MENU TIP

File properties are identifying details about a document such as the document's size, the dates the document was created or modified, a descriptive title, the author's name, the subject, and keywords that identify important topics in the document. You can view the open document's properties by clicking the Properties command on the File menu. For more information on viewing and setting properties, see online Help.

chapter
fourteen

FIGURE 14-2
Theme Dialog Box

You can select a theme from the Choose a Theme: list box and preview the background, headings, bullet, horizontal divider line, and text formats associated with the theme in the Sample of theme: area. Some of the themes' colors, graphics, and background images can be modified with options in this dialog box. You can set a default theme from the Theme dialog box. When you select a theme, Word sets the Bullets button on the Formatting toolbar with the theme bullet color and style, adds the theme horizontal divider line button to the Borders palette on the Formatting toolbar, and modifies the Normal and heading styles to match the theme.

Step 3	*Click*	Blends in the Choose a Theme: list
Step 4	*Observe*	the sample theme in the Sample of theme Blends: area
Step 5	*Continue*	to review the different themes
Step 6	*Click*	Geared Up Factory in the Choose a Theme: list
Step 7	*Click*	the Vivid Colors, Active Graphics, and Background Image check boxes to insert a check mark, if necessary
Step 8	*Click*	OK

The background image is applied to the page, the Bullets button option is modified, the horizontal divider line style is added to the Borders palette, and the Style Preview contains styles based on the chosen theme. To add the company name as a centered heading at the top of the page:

Step 1	*Click*	the Heading 1 style in the Style Preview
Step 2	*Key*	WORLDWIDE EXOTIC FOODS, INC.

Step 3	*Center*	the text
Step 4	*Press*	the ENTER key

Because tabs and newspaper-style columns are not supported by HTML, tables are used to organize information like the branch office names attractively on Web pages. You key the company's business purpose, called a mission statement, into a 1 × 1 table centered below the heading. Below the mission statement you key the branch office names as a bulleted list inside another 1 × 1 table. To insert the mission statement:

Step 1	*Create*	a 1 × 1 table on the line below the heading
Step 2	*Remove*	the table border
Step 3	*Show*	the gridlines, if necessary
Step 4	*Key*	Worldwide Exotic Foods, Inc. is the world's fastest growing distributor of specialty food items. Our mission is to provide our customers with an extensive and unusual selection of meats, cheeses, pastries, fruits, vegetables, and beverages.
Step 5	*Center*	the table horizontally
Step 6	*Center*	the text inside the table cell
Step 7	*Click*	at the left margin below the table
Step 8	*Click*	File
Step 9	*Click*	Save as Web Page
Step 10	*Save*	the Web page as *Worldwide Home Page* to the location specified by your instructor
Step 11	*Preview*	the Web page to make sure the text looks like what you expected
Step 12	*Close*	the Web browser

Nat wants viewers who load the home page to be able to locate each branch office. You create a bulleted list of the branch office locations below the mission statement. To add a table and the branch office bulleted list:

Step 1	*Press*	the ENTER key to move the insertion point down one line
Step 2	*Create*	a 1 × 1 table and remove the border

CAUTION TIP

Animated graphics turned on with the Active Graphics option in the Theme dialog box can be viewed only in a Web browser.

When you save a Web page, Word automatically creates a folder for the page at the same location. This folder contains the graphic images, such as bullets or horizontal divider lines, used in the Web page.

QUICK TIP

You can use AutoCorrect, the Spelling and Grammar checker, and other Word features when you create a Web page.

chapter
fourteen

Step 3	*Drag*	the right table boundary to the left until the table is approximately two inches wide
Step 4	*Center*	the table horizontally
Step 5	*Move*	the insertion point into the table
Step 6	*Apply*	the Heading 4 style
Step 7	*Key*	Visit Our Branch Offices
Step 8	*Center*	the text in the cell
Step 9	*Press*	the TAB key to create a new row
Step 10	*Apply*	the Normal style

Your screen should look similar to Figure 14-3.

FIGURE 14-3
Tables in a Web Page

Step 11	*Click*	the Bullets button on the Formatting toolbar
Step 12	*Key*	Chicago and press the ENTER key
Step 13	*Continue*	by adding London, Melbourne, and Vancouver to the bulleted list
Step 14	*Save*	the Web page
Step 15	*Preview*	the Web page and close the Web browser

C Horizontal lines are used frequently in Web pages to break the text into logical segments. You want to insert a horizontal line to separate the branch office names from the end-of-page contact information. In Web Layout view you can use the Click and Type feature to position the insertion point anywhere on the page. To add a centered horizontal divider line below the branch office names:

| Step 1 | ***Double-click*** | the center position below the bulleted list with the Click and Type pointer shown in Figure 14-4 |

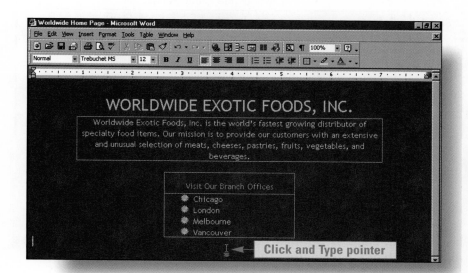

FIGURE 14-4
Click and Type Pointer

Step 2	***Click***	the Borders button list arrow ▦▾ on the Formatting toolbar
Step 3	***Click***	the Horizontal Line button ▤ on the Borders palette
Step 4	***Save***	the Web page
Step 5	***Preview***	the Web page and close the Web browser

It is important that viewers of your Web page have a way to contact you about the Web page. Because most viewers are looking for current information, it is also important to include the date the Web page was updated. Finally, to protect the contents of your Web page, you should add a copyright notice. To key the contact, update date, and copyright information below the horizontal divider line:

| Step 1 | ***Move*** | the insertion point to the left margin below the horizontal divider line |

QUICK TIP

The Click and Type feature is available in Print Layout or Web Layout view. **Click and Type** automatically applies the formatting needed to center, left align, or right align the text when you double-click the center, right side, or left side of a blank page. It also can left indent and apply left or right text wrapping. As you move the Click and Type pointer to a new position, it changes shape to show you which formatting will be applied. For more information on using Click and Type, see online Help.

**chapter
fourteen**

QUICK TIP

You can insert the © symbol with AutoCorrect by keying (c).

Step 2	*Key*	Worldwide Exotic Foods, Inc. Gage Building, Suite 2100, Riverside Plaza Chicago, IL 60606-2000 Contact us with questions or comments about this Web site. Updated 11/21/99 © 1999, Worldwide Exotic Foods, Inc.
Step 3	*Select*	all the text below the horizontal divider line
Step 4	*Apply*	the Heading 6 style
Step 5	*Center*	the text and then deselect it
Step 6	*Save*	the Web page
Step 7	*Preview*	the Web page and close the Web browser

Because the Web page is longer than one screen, Nat suggests you add a hyperlink at the bottom of the page that viewers can click to move quickly back to the top of the page. Nat asks you to create hyperlinks to each branch office Web page using the branch office bulleted list. These hyperlinks make it convenient for viewers to access each branch office page from the home page.

Creating Hyperlinks

A **hyperlink**, commonly called a **link**, is text or a picture that provides a shortcut to another document or to another location in the same document. When you position the mouse pointer on a hyperlink, it becomes a hand pointer. When you click a hyperlink, the associated document opens.

When viewers browse the Web looking for information, they often decide whether or not to explore a Web site based on the information they can see as a Web page loads. Because of this, you should position all important information and hyperlinks as close to the top of the page as possible. To help viewers navigate easily through a Web site, each page should include **navigational links**, hyperlinks to important areas of the same page and to all other significant pages at the site. A well-designed Web page contains an internal navigational link at the bottom of each page to move viewers quickly back to the top of the page without scrolling. You add an internal navigational link below the contact information at the bottom of the page. Internal links can be made to text formatted with the Word built-in heading styles or to a reference point at the destination position called a **bookmark**. Because the Web page formatting may change later, Nat asks you to use a bookmark. To insert a bookmark at the top of the page:

INTERNET TIP

You can create hyperlinks between two Word documents or between a Word document and a Web page. Additionally, you can create hyperlinks between different Office 2000 applications.

Step 1	*Move*	the insertion point to the top of the page

| Step 2 | *Click* | Insert |
| Step 3 | *Click* | Bookmark |

The Bookmark dialog box that opens on your screen should look similar to Figure 14-5.

FIGURE 14-5
Bookmark Dialog Box

You create a bookmark by assigning it a name and adding it to a list of available bookmarks. Bookmark names must begin with an alphabetic character. You can use numbers following the first character but you cannot use spaces. Use the underscore to separate words in a bookmark name instead of a space. You should use a descriptive name so that you can easily remember what the bookmark references later.

| Step 4 | *Key* | Top in the Bookmark name: text box |
| Step 5 | *Click* | Add |

Next you create a hyperlink between text at the bottom of the page and the bookmark. To insert the hyperlink text:

Step 1	*Move*	the insertion point to the bottom of the document
Step 2	*Press*	the ENTER key
Step 3	*Center*	the insertion point
Step 4	*Key*	Top of Page
Step 5	*Select*	the Top of Page text
Step 6	*Click*	the Insert Hyperlink button ![button] on the Standard toolbar

> **QUICK TIP**
>
> **C** You can insert graphic objects in a Web page. When you save your document as a Web page, all graphic objects, including pictures, AutoShapes, WordArt, text boxes, and so forth, are saved in GIF, JPEG, or PNG format. For more information on graphic file types for Web pages, see online Help.

chapter
fourteen

The Insert Hyperlink dialog box that opens on your screen should look similar to Figure 14-6.

FIGURE 14-6
Insert Hyperlink
Dialog Box

Link to: Places Bar

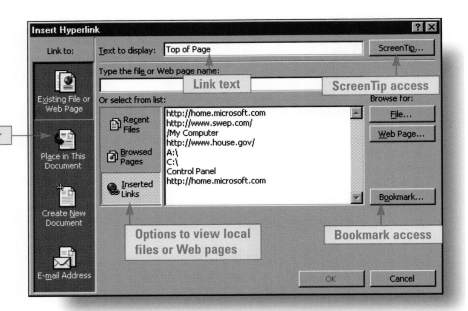

MENU TIP

Hyperlinks can be text, pictures, or drawing objects. You can insert pictures and drawing objects in a Web page with the Picture or Object commands on the Insert menu and you can use the AutoShapes feature to add drawing objects to a Web page.

You can create hyperlinks to existing external files or Web pages, locations in the current document, new external documents, and e-mail addresses in this dialog box. The selected text "Top of Page" appears in the Text to display: text box and appears on the Web page. You can create a custom ScreenTip for the hyperlink that appears whenever a viewer points to a link. You create a hyperlink to the Top bookmark and include a customized hyperlink ScreenTip.

Step 7	*Click*	the Place in This Document icon in the Link to: Places Bar
Step 8	*Observe*	the list of headings and bookmarks
Step 9	*Click*	Top in the Select a place in this document: list box
Step 10	*Click*	ScreenTip to open the Set Hyperlink ScreenTip dialog box
Step 11	*Key*	Return to the Top of the Page in the ScreenTip text: text box
Step 12	*Click*	OK to close the Set Hyperlink ScreenTip dialog box
Step 13	*Click*	OK to close the Insert Hyperlink dialog box

After you create hyperlinks, whether internal or external, you should test them to ensure they work correctly.

To test the Top internal navigational link:

Step 1	*Save*	the Web page
Step 2	*Preview*	the Web page
Step 3	*Position*	the mouse pointer on the <u>Top of Page</u> link at the bottom of the page to see the hand pointer and custom ScreenTip.

Your screen should look similar to Figure 14-7.

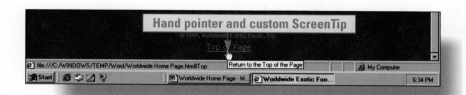

FIGURE 14-7
Hand Pointer and Custom
ScreenTip

Step 4	*Click*	the <u>Top of Page</u> link
Step 5	*Observe*	that you are viewing the top of the Web page
Step 6	*Close*	the Web browser

Often viewers who visit your Web page will want to contact you. To make it easy for them to provide feedback or request information you can add your e-mail address as a hyperlink on every Web page at your Web site. When clicked, the link opens the viewer's e-mail message composition window and automatically inserts your e-mail address in the To: address line. This type of hyperlink is called a **mailto: link**. To create a mailto: link in the contact information at the bottom of the home page:

Step 1	*Move*	the insertion point immediately before the word "with" in the sentence beginning "Contact us" at the bottom of the Web page
Step 2	*Key*	at staff@wwide.xeon.net
Step 3	*Press*	the SPACEBAR to have Word automatically create the mailto: link
Step 4	*Position*	the mouse pointer on the new link to view the mailto: ScreenTip

chapter
fourteen

| Step 5 | *Save* | the Web page |
| Step 6 | *Preview* | the Web page and close the Web browser |

Now you are ready to create external hyperlinks to the branch office Web pages.

Creating External Hyperlinks

You can create hyperlinks to other pages at your Web site and to pages at other Web sites. As with internal hyperlinks, external hyperlinks can be both pictures and text. You need to create external hyperlinks to each of the branch office pages that Nat created. To create an external hyperlink to the Chicago branch office home page:

Step 1	*Select*	the text Chicago in the bulleted list
Step 2	*Right-click*	the selected text
Step 3	*Click*	Hyperlink to open the Insert Hyperlink dialog box
Step 4	*Click*	the Existing File or Web Page icon in the Link to: Places Bar

You can key the path and filename of the external file to which you are linking, select the path and filename from lists of recently viewed local files or Web pages, or browse through the files stored on a diskette, hard drive, or network server to locate the appropriate file. You locate the Chicago branch office page by browsing.

Step 5	*Click*	File in the Browse for: area to open the Link to File dialog box
Step 6	*Switch*	to the disk drive and folder where the Data Files are stored
Step 7	*Double-click*	Chicago
Step 8	*Change*	the hyperlink ScreenTip to Chicago Branch Office
Step 9	*Click*	OK in each dialog box
Step 10	*Continue*	to create external hyperlinks with custom ScreenTips to the London, Melbourne, and Vancouver branch office home pages
Step 11	*Save*	the Web page
Step 12	*Preview*	the Web page and close the Web browser

If you decide you don't want to use a particular theme you can remove it or replace it with another theme. Before you test the links, Nat reviews the Web page and decides that the theme colors are too dark. He suggests you replace it with the theme he used for the branch office pages. To replace the theme:

Step 1	*Open*	the Theme dialog box
Step 2	*Double-click*	Cactus in the Choose a <u>T</u>heme: list box
Step 3	*Observe*	the changes to the background, text, bullets, horizontal line, and hyperlinks
Step 4	*Save*	the Web page
Step 5	*Preview*	the Web page and close the Web browser
Step 6	*Close*	the *Worldwide Home Page* document

After you complete all the Web pages at a Web site, you should review the pages and test all the links.

14.c Testing and Publishing Web Pages

Remember that potential viewers of a Web site can live anywhere in the world. Because of this, it is very important that you test the "look" of your Web pages by previewing them in different browsers, if possible. If you have access to a browser other than the one you already used to preview your pages, you should use it to open the *Worldwide Home Page* and observe any differences between how the page looks in your default browser and the other browser. To open the Web browser and load the *Worldwide Home Page*:

Step 1	*Open*	the Web browser
Step 2	*Click*	<u>F</u>ile
Step 3	*Click*	<u>O</u>pen
Step 4	*Click*	<u>B</u>rowse to locate and then open *Worldwide Home Page* Web page
Step 5	*Observe*	how the Web page looks

chapter
fourteen

Before you give the home page file to Nat, you should test all the hyperlinks. This way you can ensure they work and ensure viewers can focus on your message (rather than any problems). To test the hyperlinks and review the Web site:

Step 1	*Click*	the <u>Chicago</u> hyperlink
Step 2	*Test*	all the hyperlinks on the Chicago page and then return to the home page
Step 3	*Continue*	to load and review all the branch office pages from the home page
Step 4	*Close*	the browser when all the pages are reviewed and all the hyperlinks are verified

The final test of your Web pages is to have several people (both inside and outside of your organization) review the pages for their look, clarity, ease of use, interest, and so forth. Weigh their suggestions carefully, and revise your Web pages as necessary. It is a good idea to also carefully proofread the Web page text.

When you are satisfied with the look and content of your Web pages, you can make them available on the Web by publishing them to a Web server. **Publishing** is the process of transferring your Web pages to a Web server. You can save your Web pages directly to a Web server with options in the Save As dialog box or you can publish your Web pages using an FTP (File Transfer Protocol) program to transfer your Web page files over the Internet to a Web server. Once your Web pages are stored on the Web server, other users can access them.

Summary

▶ Word 2000 contains HTML editing tools that are shortcuts for entering HTML tags to create a Web page.

▶ You can use the Web Page Wizard and Web page templates to create new Web page documents. You can also save an existing Word document as a Web page.

▶ You can add a Web page title to the document's properties or in the Save As dialog box.

▶ Word provides Web page themes with coordinated background color and graphics, bullets, horizontal lines, and text.

▶ A table is an effective way to organize Web page content.

▶ Horizontal lines break a Web page into logical segments.

▶ You can use bulleted lists to itemize text on a Web page.

▶ Text, pictures, and drawing objects can be used to create external hyperlinks to other documents or internal hyperlinks to different locations in the same document.

▶ You should include navigational links to the home page, the top of the current page, and all other Web pages to each Web page at your site.

▶ You can add a custom ScreenTip to each hyperlink.

▶ After you complete all the pages at your Web site you should review them by testing all the links, running the spelling checker and proofreading the contents, and having others review the pages for their look, clarity, and ease of use.

▶ When you are satisfied with the look and content of your Web pages, you can make them available on the Web by publishing them to a Web server.

chapter fourteen

Commands Review

Action	Menu Bar	Shortcut Menu	Toolbar	Keyboard
Create a Web page	File, New		⬛ in Web Layout View	ALT + F, N
Switch to Web Layout view	View, Web Layout		⬛	ALT + V, W
Save a Web page	File, Save as Web Page			ALT + F, G
Preview a Web page	File, Web Page Preview			ALT + F, B
Add a title to a Web page	File, Properties			ALT + F, I
Create a bulleted list			⬛	ALT + O, N
Insert a horizontal line			⬛▾	
Apply a design theme	Format, Theme			ALT + O, H
Create a hyperlink	Insert, Hyperlink	Right-click selected link text, click Hyperlink	⬛	ALT + I, I
Create a bookmark	Insert, Bookmark			ALT + I, K

Concepts Review

Circle the correct answer.

1. To add a title to a Web page, you click the:
[a] Options command on the Edit menu.
[b] Properties command on the Edit menu.
[c] Internet Options command on the View menu.
[d] Properties command on the File menu.

2. To apply a preset design to a Web page click the:
[a] Color command on the Format menu.
[b] Scheme command on the Insert menu.
[c] Theme command on the Format menu.
[d] Background command on the View menu.

3. You organize information on a Web page with:
[a] columns.
[b] bookmarks.
[c] tables.
[d] links.

4. The Web page title appears in the:
[a] title bar in Web Layout view.
[b] Insert Hyperlink dialog box.
[c] top of a Web page of a Web browser.
[d] title bar of a Web browser.

5. When you save a Web page, Word automatically:
[a] opens the Insert Hyperlink dialog box.
[b] creates a subfolder at the same location as the Web page.
[c] applies a theme.
[d] browses for files.

6. Horizontal lines are used in Web pages to:
[a] link external pages.
[b] format text.
[c] break text into logical segments.
[d] move quickly to the top of a Web page.

7. Publishing is the process of:
[a] setting a document's properties.
[b] adding a Web page title.
[c] creating a bookmark.
[d] transferring a Web page to a Web server.

8. In order to encourage viewers to provide feedback on your Web site, you should:
[a] have fewer than 10 Web pages.
[b] link to other Web sites.
[c] use a consistent color scheme.
[d] insert a mailto: link on each page at the site.

9. The final test of your Web pages is to:
[a] check the spelling and grammar.
[b] proofread them.
[c] have others review them.
[d] publish them.

10. HTML is an abbreviation for:
[a] Hyperbolic Markup Language.
[b] HyperText Formatting Language.
[c] HyperText Markup Language.
[d] Hypersensitive Formatting Language.

Circle **T** if the statement is true or **F** is the statement is false.

T F 1. Animated graphics can be viewed only in Web Layout view.

T F 2. Hyperlinks can be text but not pictures.

T F 3. Web pages are created with HTML.

T F 4. You cannot use the Word proofing tools to check the spelling and grammar of your Web pages.

T F 5. A Web page title is the heading text often centered at the top of the page.

T F 6. It is not important to preview your Web page in a Web browser as you create it.

T F 7. After you create and test your Web pages, you can publish them to a Web server so others can access them.

T F 8. A hyperlink is commonly called a link.

T F 9. You can view the HTML tags that structure a Web page by viewing the source file.

T F 10. The Click and Type feature allows you to double-click anywhere on a document in Web Layout or Print Layout view to position the insertion point.

Skills Review

Exercise 1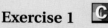

1. Create a new Web page using the Personal Web Page template.

2. Add your name as the title in the document properties.

3. Replace the main heading sample text with your name in all uppercase characters.

4. Complete the Work Information, Favorite Links, Contact Information, Current Projects, Personal Interests, and Revised Date using your own information.

5. Preview the Web page and make any necessary corrections.

6. Change the theme to a theme of your choice.

7. Save the Web page with your name as the filename.

8. Preview, print, and close the Web page.

Exercise 2   C

1. Create a new Web page using the Frequently Asked Questions template.

2. Complete the Web page by stating and answering the following questions:
How do I create a Web page from a template?
Where can I find the Web page templates?
What is a template?

3. Select and delete the table of contents text and buttons and related text for the questions:
Why doesn't...?
Who is...?
When is...?

4. Insert the current date as the last revised date.

5. Apply the theme of your choice.

6. Save the Web page with the title and filename *Frequently Asked Questions.*

7. Preview, print, and close the Web page.

Exercise 3   C

1. Open the *Office Information Automation Society* document located on the Data Disk.

2. Apply the Nature theme with vivid colors, animated graphics, and background image.

3. Format the main heading with the Heading 2 style and center it.

4. Add a centered horizontal line below the main heading.

5. Format the paragraph headings with the Heading 3 style.

6. Add bullets to the items below each paragraph heading.

7. Insert a top of page bookmark at the top of the page.

8. Use the AutoShapes feature to draw a blue filled up arrow object centered approximately 1½ lines below the last line of text. Insert a hyperlink from the arrow object to the top of page bookmark. Use the text "Top of the Page" as a customized ScreenTip. (*Hint:* Right-click the selected up arrow drawing object to open the Insert Hyperlink dialog box)

9. Save the Web page as *OIAS Web Page.*

10. Preview, print, and close the Web page.

Exercise 4   C

1. Open the *Commonly Misused Words* document located on the Data Disk.

2. Apply the Loose Gesture theme with vivid colors, animated graphics, and background image.

3. Center the major heading COMMONLY MISUSED WORDS formatted with the Heading 1 style one line above the first paragraph.

4. Format the first paragraph with the Heading 3 style.

5. Insert a centered horizontal line between the first paragraph and the list of descriptions.

6. Format the list of descriptions with the Heading 4 style.

7. Add bullets to the list of descriptions.

8. Insert a bookmark at the top of the page.

9. Insert a hyperlink to the top of the page bookmark centered below the text.

10. Save the Web page with the title "Commonly Misused Words" and filename *Misused Words Web Page*.

11. Preview, print, and close the Web page.

Exercise 5

1. Create a new Web page with the Web Page icon on the General tab in the New dialog box or the New Web Page button on the Standard toolbar in Web Layout view.

2. Add the title Worldwide Sales Department to the file properties.

3. Apply the Blueprint theme with vivid colors, active graphics, and background image.

4. Center the major heading "SALES INFORMATION" formatted with the Heading 1 style.

5. Insert a centered horizontal line below the major heading.

6. Create a 1 × 1 centered table approximately four inches wide and remove the border.

7. Apply the Heading 2 style.

8. Key and center the text "Sales Report Links" in the table.

9. Create a new row and apply the Heading 4 style.

10. Turn on the Bullets feature and key the following filenames in the second row.
    Sales Representatives Web Page
    Annual Beverage Sales Web Page
    Regional Deli Sales Web Page

11. Browse to create a hyperlink from each bulleted item to the file on the Data Disk. Modify the ScreenTip for each hyperlink to contain the filename.

12. Save the Web page as *Sales Information Web Page*.

13. Print and close the Web page.

14. Open the Web browser, load the *Sales Information Web Page* and test the links.

15. Close the Web browser when finished.

Exercise 6

1. Open the *Winter Schedule* document located on the Data Disk.

2. Select the two date paragraphs and convert the text to a table without a border.

3. Bold the date table contents.

chapter fourteen

4. AutoFit the table to the contents and then center the table horizontally. (*Hint:* Select all the columns and double-click any column boundary.)

5. Apply the Expedition theme with vivid colors and active graphics. Turn off the background image.

6. AutoFit the table to the contents again.

7. Apply the Heading 1 style to the major heading and center it.

8. Apply the Heading 2 style to the "Training Sessions" subheading and center it.

9. Apply the Heading 3 style to each of the paragraph headings.

10. Insert a centered horizontal divider line following the "Training Sessions" subheading, each date table, and the last paragraph on the page.

11. Create a bulleted list from the text following each paragraph heading. (*Hint:* Each sentence in the paragraph should be a new paragraph with a bullet.)

12. Add a top of page bookmark and an AutoShape hyperlink with the modified ScreenTip "Top of Page" below the last horizontal divider line.

13. Save the document as a Web page with the title "Training Schedule" and the filename *Winter Schedule Web Page.*

14. Preview, print, and close the Web page.

Exercise 7

1. Open the *Policy #113* document located on the Data Disk.

2. Apply the theme of your choice and format the document attractively using the theme options.

3. Save the document as a Web page with the title "Policy #113" and filename *Policy #113 Web Page* then preview, print and close it.

4. Open the *Policy #152* document located on the Data Disk.

5. Apply the theme of your choice and format the document attractively using the theme options.

6. Save the document as a Web page with the title "Policy #152" and filename *Policy #152 Web Page* and then preview, print and close it.

7. Create a new, blank Web page and apply the theme of your choice. Use the theme formatting options to format the page as desired.

8. Insert the major heading PERSONNEL POLICIES centered at the top of the page and text hyperlinks to the *Policy #113 Web Page* and *Policy #152 Web Page* files. Modify the ScreenTip for each hyperlink appropriately.

9. Save the new Web page with the title "Personnel Policies" and the filename *Personnel Policies Web Page.*

10. Open the Web browser, load the *Personnel Policies* Web page, and test the links.

11. Close the Web browser when finished.

Exercise 8

1. Open the *Preparing For A Speech* document located on the Data Disk.

2. Save the document as a Web page formatted with a theme of your choice. Use the title "How to Prepare for a Speech" and the filename *Preparing For A Speech Web Page.*

3. Add the appropriate navigational links.

4. Preview, print, and close the Web page.

Case Projects

Project 1

The sales manager, Dick Montez, asks you to create a Web page describing Worldwide Exotic Foods new holiday products. Create a blank Web page and apply the theme of your choice. Use fictitious information about five holiday products for the headings, text, and bulleted lists. Format the page attractively. Save, preview, and print the Web page.

Project 2

Nat Wong thinks it would be helpful for you to learn more about creating a Web page with the HyperText Markup Language (HTML) and suggests you locate online guides for working with HTML. Connect to your ISP, load your Web browser, and search for Web sites that provide information on how to create Web pages using HTML. Print at least four Web pages. Write Nat an interoffice memorandum describing the results of your research. Save, preview, and print the memo.

Project 3

Jody Haversham calls to ask for help formatting and saving an existing document as a Web page. Create an outline detailing the steps Jody should follow to open, apply a theme, format, preview, and save an existing document as a Web page. Save, preview, and print the outline. With your instructor's permission, use the outline to demonstrate the process to a classmate.

Project 4

Mary Boyer, the marketing department representative to the Web site development committee, asks you to research online options for getting the company Web site noticed. Connect to your ISP, load your Web browser, and search for Web sites that provide information on publicizing Web sites. Print at least five Web pages. Write an interoffice memorandum to Mary with a CC: to the Web site development committee describing your research. Include your recommendation on how to use these options to publicize the Worldwide Exotic Foods Web site. Save, preview, and print the memo.

Project 5

Nat wants to know how to use the Web Page Wizard icon in the Web Pages tab of the New dialog box to create multiple Web pages at one time and he asks you review the process. Use the Web Page Wizard icon to launch the wizard. Review each of the wizard steps using the dialog box Help tool. Follow the Wizard instructions to create a sample multiple-page Web site. Write Nat an interoffice memorandum describing how to use the wizard. Save, preview, and print the memo.

Project 6

Viktor Winkler, the public affairs officer, wants to add a Web page to the company intranet that provides hyperlinks to important government Web sites. He asks you to create the Web page. Using the template and theme of your choice, create a Web page that contains hyperlinks to ten local, state, and federal Web sites. Save, preview, and print the Web page.

Project 7

The human resources department decides to place the employee newsletter on the company intranet. Jody asks you to create the employee newsletter Web page for December. Use one of the columnar Web page templates and create an employee newsletter Web page using fictitious data. Replace the template theme with a theme of your choice. Using online Help, review the different file formats for graphic objects inserted in a Web page, then insert clip art, WordArt, photographs, and other graphics to enhance the Web page. After saving the Web page, review the associated graphics folder and identify the file type for each graphic—GIF, JPEG, or PNG. Create a document that contains a list of the graphics by file type. Save, preview, and print the Web page and document.

Project 8

Kelly Armstead is having trouble creating Web pages and asks for your help. When she saves existing Word documents as Web pages, some of the formatting is different when she views the Web page in a browser. Use the Office Assistant to search for information on Web pages. Look for an explanation of the formatting differences when Word documents are saved as Web pages and then viewed in the Microsoft Internet Explorer Web browser. Create an outline itemizing the differences. Save, preview, and print the outline.

Creating Multiple Letters with Mail Merge

Chapter Overview

Businesses commonly send the same letter to multiple addressees or create multiple envelopes or labels from a list of delivery addresses. This is done quickly with a process called mail merge. In this chapter you learn to create multiple letters using the mail merge process.

Learning Objectives

► Create a main document
► Create a data source
► Merge a main document and a data source

Case profile

The marketing department sends a letter to potential new customers to arrange a meeting with a sales representative. The letter consists of a standard text combined with names and addresses and other variable information to create a series of personalized form letters. You key the letter in one document, key the names and addresses in a second document, and then combine both documents to create the form letters.

chapter fifteen

15.a Creating a Main Document

The mail merge process is useful when the same text is repeated in many documents. For example, suppose the same letter must be sent to 1,000 customers. You can use the mail merge process to easily prepare 1,000 letters with just two documents! One document contains the letter content and **merge fields**, special codes that are placeholders for a specific data item or variable text such as the customer's name, address, and salutation. The second document contains the variable data that corresponds to the merge fields in the first document; that is, the actual names, addresses, and salutations for each customer. You then use the Mail Merge command on the Tools menu to combine these two documents to create 1,000 individual letters (often called form letters).

The document that contains the merge field codes and non-variable text is called the **main document**. You create a main document by keying the non-variable text and then inserting merge field codes for the variable text. A **data source** is a document that contains the variable text for each merge field in the main document. A data source can be another Word document, an Excel worksheet, an Access table or query, or Outlook contacts.

The marketing department wants to send the appointments letter to three new businesses in Texas. You begin by creating a new main document and keying the non-variable text. To set up the letter for the main document:

QUICK TIP

When a main document contains the current date you should insert the date as a date field. This allows you to use the main document multiple times without having to rekey the date.

Step 1	*Create*	a new, blank document, if necessary
Step 2	*Set*	the appropriate margins for a block format letter
Step 3	*Key*	the document text shown in Figure 15-1, inserting the current date as a date field
Step 4	*Save*	the document as *Marketing Letter*

The Word Mail Merge Helper provides a step-by-step guide to creating multiple letters using the mail merge process. To create the main document:

| Step 1 | *Click* | Tools |
| Step 2 | *Click* | Mail Merge |

Current date

Dear :

Congratulations on your new business venture. We, at Worldwide Exotic Foods, Inc., wish you many years of success.

Worldwide Exotic Foods, Inc. is one of the fastest-growing distributors of specialty food items in the world, distributing our products from our branch offices in Chicago, Illinois, Melbourne, Australia, Vancouver, Canada, and London, England. We specialize in supplying high-quality and unusual food products to enterprises like yours.

My associate and I are traveling to next week and will call to arrange an appointment as soon as we arrive. We appreciate the opportunity to meet with you to discuss how your company can benefit from our unique product lines.

Sincerely,

Joan Bradford
Marketing Representative

si

The Mail Merge Helper dialog box that opens on your screen should look similar to Figure 15-2.

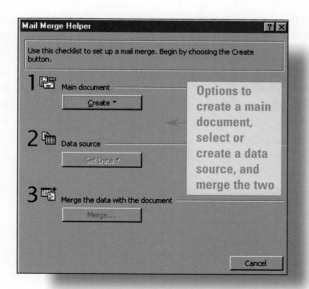

chapter
fifteen

The Mail Merge Helper dialog box contains options for creating and editing the main document and the data source and then merging them to create multiple documents. To begin, you must specify the merge type for main document and then define the active document *Marketing Letter* as the main document. The merge type can be envelopes, labels, a form letter that contains the same content but is sent to different addressees, or a catalog. A catalog is a list containing some common text and some variable text, such as a telephone list. You want to create form letters using the active document.

Step 3	*Click*	Create to view a list of main document merge types
Step 4	*Click*	Form Letters
Step 5	*Click*	Active Window to indicate the active document is the main document

The merge type, Form Letters, and the main document name and location appear below the Create button. You use the Edit button to switch to the main document so you can make any necessary text edits and insert the appropriate merge field codes. Before you can insert the merge field codes, you must define a data source.

 # 15.b Creating a Data Source

A data source is a document that contains the variable text to be inserted at each merge field code in the main document. When you merge documents, you can specify an existing data source or you can create a new data source. You can use a variety of existing sources as a data source for a Word mail merge such as a list of variable text in a Word document, an Excel worksheet, an Access table or query, or the Outlook Contact list. When you create a data source using the Mail Merge Helper, it consists of rows and columns of data in a table. Each column is called a **data field** and contains similar information. All the data fields for one item appear in a single row called a **data record**. For example, the data record for a customer consists of a row of data fields and each field contains a single piece of the customer's data such as the name, address, or telephone number.

You need to create a new data source for the three form letters. To create a new data source:

| Step 1 | *Click* | Get Data in the Mail Merge Helper dialog box to view a list of data source options |
| Step 2 | *Click* | Create Data Source |

The Create Data Source dialog box that opens on your screen should look similar to Figure 15-3.

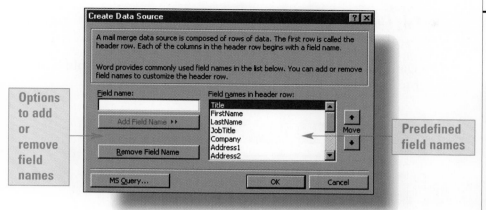

FIGURE 15-3
Create Data Source
Dialog Box

QUICK TIP

Separating data into many logical data fields makes your data source more flexible. For example, by creating separate data fields for the title, first name, and last name, you can use each data field in more than one location in the main document. By creating separate data fields for the city, state, and postal code, you can sort the data source by these data fields. Alternatively, you can select records for a specific city, state, or postal code to be merged with the main document. Data fields can contain text, or they can be left blank. By default, Word does not print blank lines if a data field is empty.

You can add custom field names to the data source by keying a descriptive one-word name in the Field name: text box and then clicking the Add Field Name button in the Create Data Source dialog box.

When creating a new data source, you first define a row of column headers called **field names** that identify the data fields. The Create Data Source dialog box opens with a list of commonly used field names that you can remove or add to as needed. The data fields you need for the *Marketing Letter* main document are the title (Mr., Mrs., Ms.), first name, last name, company name, street address, city, state, and postal code. The dialog box includes these field names as well as field names you do not need. To customize the header row, you must remove unwanted field names—Job Title, Address2, Country, HomePhone, and WorkPhone. You do not need to add any custom field names to the list.

Step 3	*Click*	JobTitle in the Field names in header row: list box
Step 4	*Click*	Remove Field Name
Step 5	*Click*	Address2 in the Field names in header row: list box
Step 6	*Click*	Remove Field Name
Step 7	*Continue*	to remove the Country, HomePhone, and WorkPhone fields
Step 8	*Verify*	that the header row contains the Title, FirstName, LastName, Company, Address1, City, State, and PostalCode field names
Step 9	*Click*	OK
Step 10	*Save*	the data source document as *Marketing Data Source*

After you save the data source, you have a choice of whether to enter the variable data records in the data source document or to edit the main document by inserting the appropriate merge field codes. You

**chapter
fifteen**

continue by adding the variable data records to the data source. To add records to the data source:

| Step 1 | *Click* | Edit <u>D</u>ata Source |

The Data Form dialog box that opens on your screen should look similar to Figure 15-4.

FIGURE 15-4
Data Form Dialog Box

Field names defined in the data source

The Data Form dialog box is an efficient way to add, edit, or delete records. The <u>V</u>iew Source button displays the data source in a table format, which allows you to see more than one record at a time. Each field name is listed in the Data Form dialog box followed by a text box for keying or editing data. Press the TAB key to move the insertion point to the next text box. Press the SHIFT + TAB keys to move the insertion point to the previous text box. To enter data for the first record:

Step 2	*Verify*	the insertion point is in the Title: text box
Step 3	*Key*	Mr.
Step 4	*Press*	the TAB key
Step 5	*Key*	Joseph in the FirstName: text box
Step 6	*Press*	the TAB key
Step 7	*Key*	Smythe in the LastName: text box
Step 8	*Press*	the TAB key twice (there is no data for the company field for this record)
Step 9	*Key*	1900 Post Oak Road in the Address1: text box
Step 10	*Press*	the TAB key
Step 11	*Key*	Houston in the City: text box

Step 12	*Press*	the TAB key
Step 13	*Key*	TX in the State: text box
Step 14	*Press*	the TAB key
Step 15	*Key*	77088-2399 in the PostalCode: text box
Step 16	*Click*	Add New

The Add New button opens a blank data form. Notice the number 2 in the Record text box, indicating that this is the second record in the data source. You can use the scroll buttons to scroll forward and back to view specific records. To enter data for the other two records:

Step 1	*Key*	record 2 for Mr. Robert Davila, Alamo Tea Shoppe, 3305 Elmridge Street, San Antonio, TX 78201-1407
Step 2	*Create*	a new record
Step 3	*Key*	record 3 for Ms. Elizabeth Ramirez, Diet Delite, 1301 Fairview Avenue, Dallas, TX 75243-1003

Because you modified the *Marketing Data Source* document, you should save it again. However, you cannot save the data source from the Data Form dialog box. To save the data source, you must display it in the table format which shows each data record in a separate row and the Database toolbar below the Formatting toolbar. To view the data records in the table format and then save the document:

Step 1	*Click*	View Source
Step 2	*Observe*	the data source in a table format and the Database toolbar below the Formatting toolbar
Step 3	*Save*	the *Marketing Data Source*

In the table format, when the text is too long to fit in a data field it wraps to the next line in the cell. However, the text prints appropriately when you merge it with the main document. If you key the data directly in the data source table you can use the ENTER key to create multiple lines within a field. For example, you might have two lines in the address field of one record and three lines in the address field of another record. If you key data in the Data Form dialog box, you cannot key multiple lines of data in each text box.

Now that you have completed the new data source document, you can edit the *Marketing Letter* main document to insert the merge field codes. Then you merge the two documents to create three form letters.

**chapter
fifteen**

C 15.c Merging a Main Document and a Data Source

You can use a button on the Database toolbar to switch to the *Marketing Letter* main document so you can edit it. When you view the main document, a new toolbar, the Mail Merge toolbar, appears below the Formatting toolbar. You use buttons on this toolbar to insert the merge field codes, preview the mail merge results, and then merge to create the form letters.

Inserting Merge Fields

To complete the main document, you need to insert the merge field codes that correspond to the data fields in the data source. You do this directly in the main document. To view the main document:

Step 1	*Click*	the Mail Merge Main Document button on the Database toolbar
Step 2	*Observe*	the *Marketing Letter* main document and the Mail Merge toolbar below the Formatting toolbar
Step 3	*Move*	the insertion point to the third blank line following the date
Step 4	*Press*	the ENTER key
Step 5	*Click*	the Insert Merge Field button Insert Merge Field ▾ on the Mail Merge toolbar

A list of all the field names available in the data source appears. You insert the appropriate merge field code from this list.

| Step 6 | *Click* | Title |
| Step 7 | *Observe* | that the merge field "«Title»" is inserted into the document at the insertion point (the merge field may be shaded) |

When you insert merge fields for the inside address and the salutation, you must also key the appropriate spaces and punctuation in your document, just as you would if you were keying an individual inside address or salutation. To insert the remaining merge fields and appropriate punctuation:

Step 1	*Press*	the SPACEBAR
Step 2	*Click*	the Insert Merge Field button `Insert Merge Field ▾` on the Mail Merge toolbar
Step 3	*Click*	FirstName
Step 4	*Press*	the SPACEBAR
Step 5	*Click*	the Insert Merge Field button `Insert Merge Field ▾` on the Mail Merge toolbar
Step 6	*Click*	LastName
Step 7	*Press*	the ENTER key
Step 8	*Continue*	to insert the company, street address, city, state, and postal code merge field codes with the appropriate spacing and punctuation

After inserting all the merge fields, the inside address should look similar to Figure 15-5.

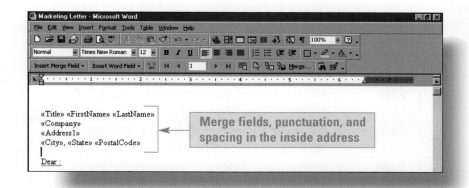

FIGURE 15-5
Merge Fields for an
Inside Address

Because you created the data source with small, logical data fields you can use these fields in more than one place in the main document. For example, you can use the title and last name fields in the salutation as well as the letter address. To insert merge field codes in the salutation:

Step 1	*Move*	the insertion point before the ":" in "Dear :"
Step 2	*Insert*	the Title merge field code

chapter
fifteen

| Step 3 | *Press* | the SPACEBAR |
| Step 4 | *Insert* | the LastName merge field code |

You use the city field to supply the missing word in the first sentence of the last body paragraph. To insert the city field:

Step 1	*Move*	the insertion point after the first word "to" in the first sentence of the last body paragraph
Step 2	*Press*	the SPACEBAR
Step 3	*Insert*	the City merge field code
Step 4	*Save*	the *Marketing Letter* document

Now you are ready to combine the *Marketing Letter* main document and the *Marketing Letter Data Source* document to create individual letters for each record in the data source.

Previewing Merged Data

In order to verify the accuracy of the merged data and the format of the merged letter documents, it is a good idea to preview the letters before you actually complete the merge process. The View Merged Data button on the Mail Merge toolbar creates a preview of the merged letters. To preview the merged letters:

Step 1	*Click*	the View Merged Data button on the Mail Merge toolbar
Step 2	*Observe*	that the data from the first record in the data source replaces the merge fields in the letter
Step 3	*Verify*	that the merge fields are replaced by the correct text and that the spacing and punctuation are correct
Step 4	*Click*	the Next Record button on the Mail Merge toolbar
Step 5	*Observe*	the merged second letter
Step 6	*Preview*	the third record
Step 7	*Click*	the View Merged Data button to turn off the preview

After you confirm that the documents merge correctly, you complete the process by merging the main document and data source to a new document or directly to a printer.

Merging to a New Document

When you need to keep a copy of your merged letters on disk as part of your permanent records or create the letters now but print them later, you can merge to a new document. Because you are going to print the letters later, you decide to merge the main document and the data source to a new document. To merge to a new document:

Step 1	*Click*	the Merge to New Document button ▣ on the Mail Merge toolbar
Step 2	*Observe*	the new document named Form Letters1 contains the three merged letters
Step 3	*Scroll*	to view the Next Page section breaks between the letters
Step 4	*Save*	the Form Letters1 document as *Marketing Letter Merged*
Step 5	*Save*	the *Marketing Letter* and *Marketing Letter Data Source* documents
Step 6	*Close*	any open documents

Saving a merged document created from a large data source may not be desirable or necessary because most organizations retain a printed copy of all correspondence for their files and the saved file requires disk storage space. Rather than use disk space to save a large merged document, you can quickly merge the documents again.

Merging Directly to a Printer

If you have access to a printer and you have verified the accuracy of the merged document, it is often more efficient to merge the main document and data source directly to a printer. When you merge directly to a printer, no new document is created. This can save time and computer resources by eliminating the need to create and store a merged document. To merge directly to the printer, click the Merge to Printer button on the Mail Merge toolbar. Be careful when merging directly to a printer. Merging documents that contain errors is costly because of the extra time and paper supplies needed to correct and remerge the data. It is a good idea to always preview and verify the merge results before you merge directly to a printer.

chapter
fifteen

Summary

- ▶ A mail merge combines two documents—one containing text and merge field codes and the other containing variable data—to create multiple documents.

- ▶ The document that contains the merge field codes and any non-variable text is called the main document.

- ▶ The document that contains the variable text is called the data source.

- ▶ A data source is made up of a header row, data records, and data fields.

- ▶ You can enter data in a data source in a data form or directly into a table.

- ▶ You should always preview a mail merge to verify the accuracy of the merge field codes, punctuation, and formatting of the main document, as well as the accuracy of the data in the data source.

- ▶ A main document and a data source can be merged to a new document or directly to a printer.

Commands Review

Action	Menu Bar	Shortcut Menu	Toolbar	Keyboard
Display the Mail Merge Helper	Tools, Mail Merge			ALT + T, R
Insert a merge field into a main document			Insert Merge Field ▾	ALT + SHIFT + F
Display the main document when viewing the data source				
Display the Data Form dialog box				ALT + SHIFT + E
Preview a merge from the main document				ALT + SHIFT + K
Merge to a new document				ALT + SHIFT + N
Merge to a printer				ALT + SHIFT + M

Concepts Review

Circle the correct answer.

1. Separating data into logical data fields:
[a] makes creating the main document more difficult.
[b] takes less disk space when you save the document.
[c] makes the data source less flexible.
[d] makes the data source more flexible.

2. The merge process does not include:
[a] inserting a date field.
[b] defining the main document.
[c] getting the data source.
[d] previewing the results.

3. A data source does not contain:
[a] merge field codes.
[b] data records.
[c] data fields.
[d] header row.

4. To complete the merge process, you need:
[a] a main document only.
[b] a data source document only.
[c] a single blank document.
[d] both a main document and a data source document.

5. A data source cannot be a(n)
[a] Excel worksheet.
[b] Access table or query.
[c] Outlook Contacts list.
[d] Word main document.

6. The four types of mail merge main documents are:
[a] Form Letters, Envelopes, Mailing Labels, and Catalog.
[b] Basic Letters, Envelopes, Labels, and Lists.

[c] Form Letters, Envelopes and Mailing Labels, Directories, and Lists.
[d] Form Letters, Directories, Catalogs, and Envelopes.

7. Data fields:
[a] cannot contain multiple lines of text.
[b] cannot be left empty.
[c] are indicated by rows in a table.
[d] are indicated by columns in a table.

8. To insert merge field codes, you use the:
[a] Insert Merge Code button on the Formatting toolbar.
[b] Merge Field command on the Insert menu.
[c] Insert Merge Field button on the Database toolbar.
[d] Insert Merge Field button on the Mail Merge toolbar.

9. To switch between viewing the main document and viewing the data source document you can use buttons on the:
[a] Standard and Formatting toolbars.
[b] Drawing and Forms toolbars.
[c] Mail Merge and Database toolbars.
[d] Formatting and Database toolbars.

10. A data record is a(n):
[a] single row of related information in a data source table.
[b] column in a data source table.
[c] efficient way to add, edit, and delete entries in a data source.
[d] field in a main document.

chapter fifteen

Circle **T** if the statement is true or **F** if the statement is false.

T   F   1. The mail merge process takes data and text from two different documents and creates a combined document.

T   F   2. The Mail Merge Helper dialog box provides options for creating or getting a data source.

T   F   3. You insert merge field codes into a data source document.

T   F   4. Every record in a data source must contain corresponding text for each merge field code in a main document.

T   F   5. When you preview a merge, you can view only the first record.

T   F   6. It is not important to create small logical data fields in a data source you use for multiple merge tasks.

T   F   7. You can insert a merge field several times in a main document.

T   F   8. The first row in the data source is called the header row and contains field names.

T   F   9. The Data Form dialog box is an efficient way to add records to a data source.

T   F   10. The first step in the Mail Merge Helper dialog box is to create a data source.

Skills Review

Exercise 1   C

1. Create the following document. Set appropriate margins for a block format letter.

Current date

Dear :

As a valued distributor, you are invited to a special preview of our new product lines. The preview will be held on May 5 at the Starcrest Convention Center.

Our marketing representatives will be on hand to answer all your questions and an extensive buffet of product samples will be available throughout the day.

We look forward to seeing you!

Sincerely,

M. V. Jackson
New Product Development Manager

xx

2. Save the main document as *Product Preview Letter*.

3. Use the Mail Merge Helper to begin the mail merge process. Create a form letters main document using the active document, *Product Preview Letter*, as the main document.

4. Create a data source containing the following data:

Ms. Ellen Rickman	*Mr. William Roberts*
President	*Sales Manager*
Rickman Specialities, Inc.	*Ackman Foods*
1983 Second Avenue	*P.O. Box 2390*
St. Louis, MO 64072-2108	*St. Louis, MO 64033-2099*

5. Save the data source as *Product Preview Data*.

6. Edit the main document to insert the appropriate merge field codes. Preview the merge and make any necessary corrections.

7. Merge to a new document. Save the merged document as *Product Preview Merged*, and then print it.

8. Close all documents.

Exercise 2

1. Open the *Spring Conference Letter* document located on the Data Disk. Create a form letters main document using the active document as the main document.

2. Use Mail Merge Helper to merge the main document with an existing data source, *Spring Conference Data*, located on the Data Disk. (*Hint:* You open an existing data source in the Mail Merge Helper dialog box.)

3. Insert the appropriate merge fields into the main document. (*Hint:* Use the FirstName field in the salutation.)

4. Save the main document as *Spring Conference Main Letter*.

5. Merge to the printer.

6. Close all documents.

Exercise 3

1. Open the *After Holiday Sale Letter* located on the Data Disk. Create a form letters main document using the active document as the main document.

2. Use the Mail Merge Helper to merge the main document with the *After Holiday Sale Data* data source document located on the Data Disk.

3. After inserting the merge field codes, save the main document as *After Holiday Sale Main Letter*.

4. Preview the merge and make any necessary corrections.

5. Merge to a new document. Save the merged document as *After Holiday Sale Merged*, and then print it.

6. Close all documents.

chapter fifteen

Exercise 4

1. Create a block format letter based on the following text. Use the 12-point Arial font.

Dear:

Thank you for your recent order. It has been entered into our system and is being processed. Please verify the product information on the attached sheet.

If any of the information is incorrect, or you wish to contact Customer Service regarding this order, please call 201-555-4543 and refer to your order number.

We are pleased to welcome you as a customer, and look forward to serving you.

Sincerely,

Jon Hanson
Customer Service

XX

Attachment

2. Save the document as *Confirmation Letter*.

3. Use the Mail Merge Helper to begin the mail merge process. Create a form letters main document using the active document, *Confirmation Letter*, as the main document.

4. Create a data source containing the following data:

Mr. Phillip Gonzales	*Ms. Letica Garcia*
Rio Grande Electric Authority	*Odessa Mining & Manufacturing*
134 Santa Anna Blvd.	*3125 North Brazos*
Brownsville, TX 75021-3651	*Odessa, TX 79034-4321*

5. Save the data source as *Confirmation Data*.

6. Edit the main document to insert the merge field codes. Preview the merge and make any necessary corrections.

7. Merge to a new document. Save the merged document as *Confirmation Merged*, and then print it.

8. Close all documents.

Exercise 5

1. Open the *After Holiday Sale Main Letter* you created in Exercise 3 and display the Mail Merge Helper dialog box.

2. Create a data source containing the following data:

Mr. Joseph Wagner	*Ms. Jennifer Gardner*	*Mr. Glen Hubert*
Director of Sales	*Purchasing Agent*	*250 York Drive*
Nevada Lumber	*AAA Kitchen & Bath*	*Columbus, IN 47201-2845*
3255 Hillshire	*3421 Smyth Road*	
Reno, NV 89501-4899	*Amherst, MA 03031-1546*	

Ms. Donna Miller	*Dr. Stephen Holland*
302 Shadow Place	*457 East Sam Houston Drive*
Aztec, NM 87101-4811	*Asheboro, NC 27203,2141*

3. Save the data source as *District A Data*.

4. Edit the *After Holiday Sale Main Letter* document to insert the JobTitle merge field code on a new line below the Title, FirstName, and LastName fields.

5. Save the main document as *District A Main Letter*. Preview the merge and make any necessary corrections.

6. Merge to a new document. Save the merged document as *District A Merged*, and then print it.

7. Close all documents.

Exercise 6   C

1. Create the following document. Set appropriate margins for a block format letter.

Current date

Dear :

The Fall Conference for the National Food Producers Association will be held this year in Orlando, Florida, on October 12, 13, and 14. The attached brochure provides all the information you need to make your reservations and plan your conference schedule.

Stop by our hospitality suite at the Midtown Hotel during your stay.

Sincerely,

Randall Holmes
President

xx

Attachment

2. Save the document as *Fall Conference Letter*.

3. Use the Mail Merge Helper to begin the mail merge process. Create a form letters main document using the active document, *Fall Conference Letter*, as the main document.

4. Create a data source containing the following data:

Mr. Ronnie Cardinali	*Mrs. Janice Godel*	*Mr. Matthew Hall*	*Ms. Tammie Ferguson*
Lincoln Bakeries	*Agricom, Inc.*	*Billingsley Markets*	*Sampson Produce*
34215 Weston Street	*322 Randolph Street*	*839 Washington Avenue*	*2100 East Coast Drive*
Madison, WI 53701-3661	*Wheeling, WV 26003-1541*	*Tacoma, WA 98402-4856*	*McLean, VA 22101-1656*

5. Save the data source as *Fall Conference Data*.

6. Edit the main document to insert the merge field codes. Preview the merge and make any necessary corrections.

7. Merge to a new document. Save the merged document as *Fall Conference Merged*, and then print it.

8. Close all documents.

chapter fifteen

Exercise 7

1. Open the *Sales Promotion Letter* located on the Data Disk.

2. Use the Mail Merge Helper to begin the mail merge process. Create a form letters main document using the active document, *Sales Promotion Letter*, as the main document.

3. Create a data source containing the following data:

Mr. Jonathan Pyle	*Ms. Ellen Morgan*	*Ms. Rosalyn McGregor*
1900 W. 33rd Avenue	*1301 Main Street*	*5465 Braesmont*
Vancouver, BCV6N 3J5	*Edmonton, ABT6B 2X3*	*Calgary, ABT2M 4M2*
Canada	*Canada*	*Canada*

4. Save the data source as *Sales Promotion Data*.

5. Edit the main document to insert the merge field codes.

6. Save the main document as *Sales Promotion Main Letter*.

7. Preview the merge and make any necessary corrections.

8. Merge to a new document. Save the merged document as *Sales Promotion Merged*, and then print it.

9. Close all documents.

Exercise 8

1. Create the following document. Set appropriate margins for a block format letter.

Current date

Dear :

We would like your help on contributing to the Annual save the Mongoose fund. You have helped many causes in the past. We Know that once you read the enclosed information, you will give generously.

This is a new cause, and we will not bother you again if you do not want to help. Just return the enclosed envelope and mark "No".

Sincerely,

George Olson
Chairperson

xx

Enclosure

2. Save the main document as *Mongoose Fund Letter*.

3. Use the Mail Merge Helper to begin the mail merge process. Create a form letters main document using the active document, *Mongoose Fund Letter*, as the main document.

4. Create a data source containing the following data:

Ms. Kelli Kendall	*Ms. Amanda Price*	*Mr. Ryan Janezick*	*Mr. Yong Yu*
3452 Sunset Drive	*3420 California Avenue*	*212 Mountview Road*	*3092 Cherry Court*
Huntsville, AL 35804-2456	*Flagstaff, AZ 86001-4366*	*Durango, CO 81301-4254*	*Little Rock, AR 72201-4167*

5. Save the data source as *Mongoose Fund Data*.

6. Edit the main document to insert the merge field codes. Preview the merge and make any necessary corrections.

7. Merge to a new document. Save the merged document as *Mongoose Fund Merged*, and then print it.

8. Close all documents.

Case Projects

Project 1

The Worldwide Exotic Foods, Inc. operating departments send overflow work to the word processing department. Dorothy Davis, the marketing assistant, asks you to prepare form letters announcing the opening of the new New Mexico sales territory. The form letters will be sent to a list of prospective distributors in the northern New Mexico and Southern Colorado area. Create a main document with the appropriate text and a data source with at least three records. Use fictitious names and addresses for the records in the data source. Save, preview, and print the main document and data source document. Preview the merged data. Merge to a new document. Save, preview, and print the new merged document.

Project 2

Chris Lofton asks you to prepare a list of potential mail merge problems and possible solutions, which can be distributed to all the word processing staff. Using the Office Assistant to troubleshoot the mail merge process, create an unbound report document that lists at least five potential problems and provides a suggested solution for each problem. Save, preview, and print the document.

Project 3

Viktor Winkler, the public affairs officer, drops by the word processing department looking for volunteers to assist with a neighborhood youth group sponsored by Worldwide Exotic Foods, Inc.

You volunteer to send a letter announcing the new summer programs to each family whose children participate in after-school activities with the youth group. Create a main document with the appropriate text and a data source with at least five records. Use fictitious names and addresses for the records in the data source. Save, preview, and print the main document and the data source. Preview the merged data. Merge to a new document. Save, preview, and print the merged document.

Project 4

The executive assistant to the marketing vice president asks you to create a document that explains the procedures for distributing the weekly marketing report to all the branch managers and marketing representatives via e-mail. Using the Office Assistant, research how you can distribute the weekly reports to all the managers via e-mail. Create a new document containing at least three paragraphs describing the process of merging and distributing the results via e-mail. Save, preview, and print the document.

chapter fifteen

Project 5

Chris Lofton asks you to make a 15-minute presentation to a group of junior clerical assistants on how to merge form letters using Word. Create an outline detailing the topics you plan to cover in your presentation. Save, preview, and print the outline. With your instructor's permission, use the outline as your guide to describe the mail merge process to several classmates.

Project 6

The marketing department wants to add candy to the product line. Beth Able, a marketing representative, asks you to locate companies who sell handmade or unusual candies. Connect to your ISP and search for companies selling handmade or unusual candy products. Print at least three Web pages. Write Beth an interoffice memorandum listing the companies you find. Save, preview, and print the memorandum. Attach the Web pages. Create a data source containing the names and addresses of the three companies selling the candy products to be used by the marketing department in a later mail merge. Save, preview, and print the data source document.

Project 7

The accounting department needs to send a form letter to all outside sales representatives announcing the new expense reporting form that will be attached to the memo. Create a main document using fictitious information. Create a data source by keying the data directly into a table. Don't forget to create a header row for the table. Key at least three records using fictitious names and addresses. Merge the main document and the data source to a new document after previewing the merge. Save, preview, and print the main document, the data source document, and the merged document.

Project 8

The marketing department asks you to create a form letter to new distributors inviting them to tour the Worldwide Exotic Foods, Inc. offices next week. Create the main document with appropriate text and create a data source with at least five records. Use fictitious information and data in the main document and data source. View the main document with the data and then merge to a new document. Save, preview, and print the main document, the data source, and the merged document.

Using Other Mail Merge Features

Chapter Overview

In addition to form letters, organizations often need to create envelopes or labels for large mailings and prepare lists of information, such as addresses or telephone numbers. In this chapter you learn to use the Mail Merge Helper to create multiple envelopes and labels and special list documents called catalogs. Finally, you learn to edit a data source, merge specific data records, and add personalized text to form letters.

LEARNING OBJECTIVES

► Create multiple envelopes
► Generate labels
► Create catalogs
► Modify an existing data source
► Query data records
► Insert Fields

Case profile

The word processing department does a variety of mail merge projects. Chris Lofton asks you to create multiple envelopes and labels using an existing data source, create personalized form letters by keying additional text during the merge process, update an existing data source, and create a client list.

chapter sixteen

16.a Creating Multiple Envelopes

Organizations often send mail, such as form letters, to multiple addressees at one time. Instead of creating each envelope individually, you can create all the envelopes quickly with mail merge. You create multiple envelopes easily using the Mail Merge Helper to merge a new or existing data source with an envelope main document. Chris Lofton asks you to create Size 11 envelopes for all the data records in the *Mailing List* data source located on the Data Disk.

You create multiple envelopes in the same way that you created multiple letters: by defining a main document, getting a data source, and merging the two documents. To define the main document:

Step 1	*Create*	a new, blank document, if necessary
Step 2	*Open*	the Mail Merge Helper dialog box
Step 3	*Create*	an Envelopes main document using the active document
Step 4	*Get*	the *Mailing List* data source
Step 5	*Set up*	the main document
Step 6	*Click*	the Envelope Options tab in the Envelope Options dialog box, if necessary
Step 7	*Select*	a Size 11 (4 ½ x 10 ⅜ in) envelope
Step 8	*Click*	OK

The Envelope address dialog box that opens on your screen should look similar to Figure 16-1.

FIGURE 16-1
Envelope Address
Dialog Box

To create the envelope main document, you insert the appropriate merge field codes in the Sample envelope address: list box. Remember to key any necessary punctuation and spaces between the merge field codes. To insert the merge fields:

Step 1	*Click*	Insert Merge Field
Step 2	*Click*	Title
Step 3	*Press*	the SPACEBAR
Step 4	*Click*	Insert Merge Field
Step 5	*Click*	FirstName
Step 6	*Press*	the SPACEBAR
Step 7	*Click*	Insert Merge Field
Step 8	*Click*	LastName
Step 9	*Press*	the ENTER key
Step 10	*Continue*	to insert the Address1, City, State, and PostalCode merge fields with the appropriate punctuation and spacing

After inserting the merge fields the sample envelope address should look similar to Figure 16-2.

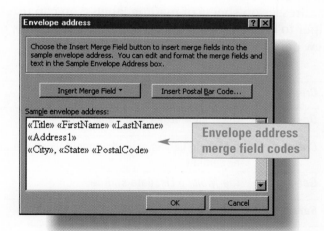

FIGURE 16-2
Merge Fields for an Envelope

Step 11	*Click*	OK
Step 12	*Close*	the Mail Merge Helper dialog box
Step 13	*Save*	the document as *Mailing List Envelopes*

chapter sixteen

You are now ready to merge the *Mailing List Envelopes* main document with the *Mailing List* data source. As with form letters, you should preview the merge to ensure accuracy. To preview the merge:

Step 1	*Preview*	the merge
Step 2	*Observe*	that the new document contains an envelope for each data record in the data source
Step 3	*View*	each record
Step 4	*Turn off*	the preview
Step 5	*Merge*	to a new document
Step 6	*Save*	the merged document as *Merged Envelopes*
Step 7	*Close*	all open documents

In addition to the envelopes, Chris also wants a sheet of mailing labels with the *Mailing List* data records.

16.b Generating Labels

If you need to print many addresses for envelopes and your printer does not have an automatic envelope feed tray, it is often quicker to print the addresses on sheets of mailing labels. You can use the Mail Merge Helper to create labels from an existing data source, or you can create a new data source. To create mailing labels:

Step 1	*Create*	a new, blank document, if necessary
Step 2	*Open*	the Mail Merge Helper dialog box
Step 3	*Create*	a Mailing Labels main document using the active document
Step 4	*Get*	the *Mailing List* data source
Step 5	*Set up*	the main document
Step 6	*Double-click*	5660 - Address in the Product number: list box (scroll to view this option)

The Create Labels dialog box opens. It looks similar to the Envelope address dialog box. To insert the merge field codes for the labels:

Step 1	*Insert*	the merge field codes with the appropriate spacing and punctuation

Step 2	*Click*	OK
Step 3	*Close*	the Mail Merge Helper dialog box
Step 4	*Observe*	that a table with field codes in each cell is created
Step 5	*Save*	the document as *Mailing List Labels*
Step 6	*Preview*	the merged labels
Step 7	*Turn off*	the preview
Step 8	*Merge*	to a new document
Step 9	*Save*	the document as *Merged Labels*
Step 10	*Close*	all open documents

Your next assignment is to create a list of distributor names and cities from the Mailing List data source.

16.c Creating Catalogs

In addition to form letters, envelopes, and labels, you can use the Mail Merge Helper to create catalogs. Catalogs are list merge documents that contain some non-variable text and variable data, such as telephone lists, client lists, product catalogs, and so forth.

The marketing department wants to discuss the status of certain distributors at their next staff meeting. Chris asks you to create a list of distributors containing the name and city from the data in the *Mailing List* data source. To begin:

Step 1	*Create*	a new, blank document, if necessary
Step 2	*Open*	the Mail Merge Helper dialog box
Step 3	*Create*	a Catalog main document using the active document
Step 4	*Get*	the *Mailing List* data source
Step 5	*Edit*	the main document

You are now ready to create the main document. When you create a catalog or list main document, any text you key in the main document is repeated with each data record that is merged. You key the text you want repeated and insert the merge fields only once for the entire document.

chapter sixteen

To edit the main document:

Step 1	*Set*	a left-aligned tab stop at 1 inch
Step 2	*Key*	Name:
Step 3	*Press*	the TAB key
Step 4	*Insert*	the FirstName merge field code
Step 5	*Press*	the SPACEBAR
Step 6	*Insert*	the LastName merge field code
Step 7	*Press*	the ENTER key
Step 8	*Key*	City:
Step 9	*Press*	the TAB key
Step 10	*Insert*	the City merge field code
Step 11	*Press*	the ENTER key twice to double space after each record

The main document on your screen should look similar to Figure 16-3.

FIGURE 16-3
Catalog Main Document

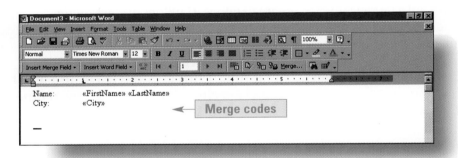

Step 12	*Save*	the document as *Distributor List*

You now merge the *Distributor List* main document and the *Mailing List* data source to a new document. To merge the catalog main document and the data source:

Step 1	*Preview*	the merge

Step 2	*Turn off*	the preview
Step 3	*Merge*	to a new document
Step 4	*Review*	the merged catalog document
Step 5	*Save*	the document as *Merged Distributor List*
Step 6	*Close*	all open documents

As you work with a data source in a variety of documents and for a variety or purposes, you find that it often must be updated and revised.

16.d Modifying an Existing Data Source

Even a well-constructed data source is usually modified over time to add new records, delete records that no longer belong in the data source, and add or remove data fields when the information retained in the data source changes. Chris asks you to update the *Mailing List* data source document by adding and deleting records.

Adding And Deleting Data Records

You can add or delete data records using the Data Form dialog box. You can also add and delete data records with the Database toolbar. To begin, you open the data source, view the Database toolbar, insert a new record, and key the data:

Step 1	*Open*	the *Mailing List* document located on the Data Disk
Step 2	*View*	the Database toolbar using the shortcut menu, if necessary
Step 3	*Click*	the Add New Record button ▦ on the Database toolbar
Step 4	*Observe*	the new, blank row at the bottom of the table and the insertion point in the first cell
Step 5	*Key*	the next record for: Ms. Roberta Davis 5465 Braesmont Houston, TX 77096-1347
Step 6	*Click*	the Add New Record button ▦ on the Database toolbar

chapter sixteen

| Step 7 | *Key* | the next record for:
Mr. David Yanklovic
6925 Spencer Road
Kent, WA 98032-6925 |

Chris tells you that Worldwide Exotic Foods no longer uses one of the distributors on the list. You need to delete that data record from the data source. When you delete a data record in the table format, the insertion point must be in the record. To delete a data record:

| Step 1 | *Move* | the insertion point to any field in the Steve Yang data record |
| Step 2 | *Click* | the Delete Record button  on the Database toolbar |

Over time, you might need to add or remove fields from a data source.

Adding Data Fields

You can add more information to an existing data source by adding new data fields. Chris asks you to add the name of the distributor's sales representative to each record in the *Mailing List* document. To add a new field for the sales representatives' names:

| Step 1 | *Click* | the Manage Fields button 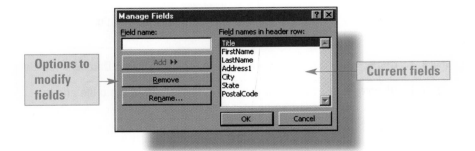 on the Database toolbar |

The Manage Fields dialog box that opens on your screen should look similar to Figure 16-4.

FIGURE 16-4
Manage Fields Dialog Box

Manage Fields   ? X

Field name:

	Field names in header row:
Add ►►	Title
Remove	FirstName LastName Address1
Rename...	City State PostalCode

Options to modify fields

Current fields

OK   Cancel

You add a custom field name for the sales representative and then key the data.

Step 2	*Key*	SalesRep in the <u>F</u>ield Name: text box
Step 3	*Click*	<u>A</u>dd
Step 4	*Click*	OK
Step 5	*Observe*	the SalesRep column added to the right side of the table
Step 6	*Key*	Malkovich in the SalesRep field in the first record
Step 7	*Press*	the DOWN ARROW key to move the insertion point to the SalesRep field in the second record
Step 8	*Key*	Wong
Step 9	*Continue*	by keying the following sales representatives names in the remaining records: Jackson; Overstreet; Ramirez; Raja; Nguyen
Step 10	*Save*	the data source as *Mailing List Revised* and close it

You can specify data records for a mail merge is by querying the data source for records that meet certain criteria. You need to merge only the records for distributors who are not in Texas.

16.e Querying Data Records

You can select certain records to merge with a main document by setting criteria for fields and field content in the records. This is called a data source **query**. Two ways to query a data source are to sort it or to filter it. You can sort data source records in ascending or descending order by specified field contents. For example, many large mailings should be sorted by postal code before being taken to the post office. To do this efficiently, you can sort the data records in ascending order by postal code before performing the merge.

To filter, or select, data records, you first must establish the data record selection criteria. You set these criteria by specifying a data field, a comparison operator, and a comparison value in this dialog box. There are several **comparison operators** such as "equal to," "not equal to," "less than," or "greater than." The **comparison value** is what the field should or should not contain to meet the criteria for selection. For example, to select all the records for distributors not located in Texas the data field criterion is the State field, the comparison operator criterion is "not equal to," and the comparison

QUICK TIP

It is easy to find specific records in a data source using the Data Form dialog box. You can scroll backward and forward using the scroll buttons to find the data record you want. If you know the data record number, you can key the record number in the GoTo text box.

You can also search the data source by the contents of a field by clicking the Find Record button on the Database toolbar to open the Find in Field dialog box. Key the search text in the Fi<u>n</u>d what: text box, select the field to search in the In fie<u>l</u>d: list, and then click the Find First button.

**chapter
sixteen**

value criterion is "TX." To query and merge selected records from the *Mailing List Revised* data source with the *Distributors Letter* main document:

Step 1	**Open**	the *Distributors Letter* document located on the Data Disk
Step 2	**Open**	the Mail Merge Helper dialog box
Step 3	**Create**	a Form Letters main document using the active document
Step 4	**Get**	the *Mailing List Revised* data source
Step 5	**Click**	Query Options
Step 6	**Click**	the Filter Records tab, if necessary

The Query Options dialog box that opens on your screen should look similar to Figure 16-5.

FIGURE 16-5
Filter Records Tab in the
Query Options Dialog Box

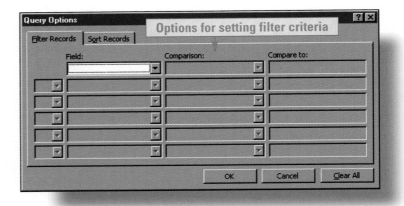

QUICK TIP

The And/Or text box on the left side of the Filter Records tab in the Query Options dialog box enables you to establish more than one set of criteria for record selection. Use "And" if records must meet all criteria; use "Or" if records must meet one criterion or the other.

To select records for those distributors *not* located in Texas:

Step 1	**Click**	the Field: list arrow
Step 2	**Click**	State (the data field criterion)
Step 3	**Click**	the Comparison: list arrow
Step 4	**Click**	Not equal to (the comparison operator)
Step 5	**Click**	in the Compare to: text box to position the insertion point
Step 6	**Key**	TX (the comparison value)

Step 7	*Click*	OK

Step 8	*Click*	<u>M</u>erge in the Mail Merge Helper dialog box

The Merge dialog box that opens on your screen should look similar to Figure 16-6.

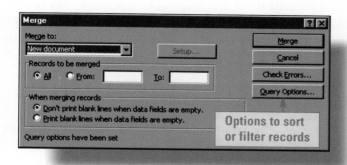

FIGURE 16-6
Merge Dialog Box

The Me<u>r</u>ge to: list box provides options for merging the main document and data source. You can merge to a new document or directly to the printer. If you have an e-mail system that works with Word, you also can merge to an e-mail address or fax number. The <u>S</u>etup button lets you identify the e-mail address or fax number for the merge. You can select whether to merge all the records (the default) or a group of records. You can select a group of records by keying the beginning record number in the <u>F</u>rom: text box and the ending record number in the <u>T</u>o: text box. The Check <u>E</u>rrors button allows you to establish how you want Word to report merge errors, such as missing merge fields in the main document, during the Mail Merge process. To specify selection criteria for a specific group of data records or to sort a group of data records, click the <u>Q</u>uery Options button.

Because you already selected the data records for distributors not in Texas, you can just complete the merge to a new document.

Step 9	*Verify*	the Me<u>r</u>ge to: list box contains New document

Step 10	*Click*	<u>M</u>erge in the Merge dialog box

Step 11	*Scroll*	to review the form letter document

Step 12	*Save*	the merged document as *Merged Query*

Step 13	*Close*	the document

In addition to the date field code that inserts the current date and the merge field codes that insert variable data from a data source, Word provides many other field codes you can use to control where and how text is inserted in a document.

**chapter
sixteen**

16.f Inserting Fields

C

QUICK TIP

You can have Word enter default text whenever you do not key specific text at the prompt by entering text in the Default fill-in text: text box. You can enter the same text for each merged data record by clicking Ask once. When you turn on this option, Word will prompt you for keyboard entry for the first data record and then use that input for all remaining data records.

Chris wants you to merge the *Mailing List Revised* data source filtered for distributors not located in Texas with a main document and then customize each merged letter during the merge process. You need to add text indicating each distributor's holiday discount as you merge queried records from the *Mailing List Revised* data source. One way to do this is to use the Fill-in field. The Fill-in Word field pauses the merge process so you can key variable text at the field location in each merged letter. To begin:

Step 1	*Verify*	the *Distributors Letter* document is open
Step 2	*Move*	the insertion point to the end of the last sentence in the body paragraph
Step 3	*Press*	the SPACEBAR
Step 4	*Click*	the Insert Word Field button [Insert Word Field ▾] on the Mail Merge toolbar
Step 5	*Click*	Fill-in

The Insert Word Field: Fill-in dialog box that opens on your screen should look similar to Figure 16-7.

FIGURE 16-7
Insert Word Field: Fill-in
Dialog Box

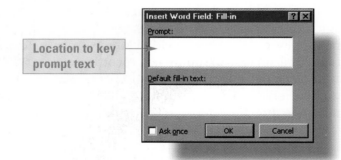

Location to key prompt text

The Fill-in field opens a prompt dialog box and pauses for keyboard input at the position of the field each time a data record is merged. You create the text for the prompt in this dialog box.

To create the prompt text:

MENU TIP

You can also insert field codes with the Field command on the Insert menu.

Step 1	*Key*	Key Discount Text in the Prompt: text box
Step 2	*Click*	OK
Step 3	*Observe*	the sample prompt dialog box

Step 4	*Verify*	the prompt text is keyed correctly
Step 5	*Click*	OK
Step 6	*Save*	the main document as *Fill-in Fields*

Once the field is set up, you can merge the main document and the data source. To begin the merge:

Step 1	*Click*	the Merge to New Document button ▦ on the Mail Merge toolbar
Step 2	*Observe*	that the prompt dialog box appears for the first data record
Step 3	*Key*	Your holiday discount is 15%.
Step 4	*Click*	OK
Step 5	*Observe*	that the prompt dialog box for the second data record contains the previously keyed text
Step 6	*Observe*	the message on the status bar indicating Word is merging record 2
Step 7	*Click*	OK to insert the same discount text in the second merged letter
Step 8	*Observe*	the prompt dialog box for the third letter
Step 9	*Key*	Your holiday discount is 20%.
Step 10	*Click*	OK

You have entered the fill-in information for the three records that meet the query criteria. Within a few seconds, a new Form Letters document appears with the merged letters. To review the customized form letters:

Step 1	*Scroll*	to view the customized letters
Step 2	*Verify*	the fill-in information for each letter
Step 3	*Save*	the merged document as *Merged Fill-in Fields*
Step 4	*Close*	all open documents

With the Fill-in field and other mail merge features, you can create any type of mailing Worldwide Exotic Food needs.

**chapter
sixteen**

Summary

▶ You can create multiple envelopes and labels using the mail merge process.

▶ You can create a list of information like a client list with a mail merge using a Catalog main document.

▶ Data records can be added and deleted from a data source using the Database toolbar or table features.

▶ Fields can be added or removed from a data source with the Database toolbar or table editing features.

▶ You can find specific records using the Data Form dialog box.

▶ Data records can be queried to filter or sort records for a mail merge.

▶ You can use special fields like the Fill-in field, which pauses for keyboard entry during a mail merge.

Commands Review

Action	Menu Bar	Shortcut Menu	Toolbar	Keyboard
Add a new record to a data source			▦	
Delete a record from a data source			▦	
Add or remove data fields from a data source			▦	
To query a data source for filtering or sorting			▦	
To insert a Word field			Insert Word Field ▾	

Concepts Review

Circle the correct answer.

1. You can add data records to a data source with a button on the:
  [a] Formatting toolbar.
  [b] Database toolbar.
  [c] Mail Merge toolbar.
  [d] Forms toolbar.

2. You can remove a record from a data source by clicking the:
  [a] Delete Record button on the Standard toolbar.

  [b] Delete button in the Data Form dialog box.
  [c] Remove button on the Database toolbar.
  [d] Delete button on the Mail Merge toolbar.

3. To select specific records for merging:
  [a] insert the Fill-in field in a main document.
  [b] click the Get Data button in the Mail Merge Helper dialog box.
  [c] click the Query Options button in the Mail Merge Helper dialog box.
  [d] insert a merge field code.

4. **To create a telephone list, you would use a mail merge main document for a(n):**
   - [a] label.
   - [b] catalog.
   - [c] envelope.
   - [d] form letter.

5. **You can view the Database toolbar:**
   - [a] automatically by opening a main document.
   - [b] with a shortcut menu.
   - [c] by clicking the Database button on the Formatting toolbar.
   - [d] by clicking the Toolbar button in the Mail Merge dialog box.

6. **To add a new field to a data source you can click the:**
   - [a] Insert Merge Field button on the Mail Merge toolbar.
   - [b] Insert Word Fields button on the Mail Merge toolbar.
   - [c] Manage Fields button on the Database toolbar.
   - [d] Update Field button on the Database toolbar.

7. **When you filter records, you:**
   - [a] delete them from a data source.
   - [b] sort them for a mail merge.
   - [c] add them to a data source.
   - [d] select them for a mail merge.

8. **By default, Word merges:**
   - [a] only records selected in the Query Options dialog box.
   - [b] all records in the data source.
   - [c] only records from 1 to 50.
   - [d] only records sorted in alphabetical order.

9. **Which of the following is a comparison operator?**
   - [a] below
   - [b] next
   - [c] equal to
   - [d] following

10. **The comparison value is:**
   - [a] the number of merge fields in the main document.
   - [b] the number of records in a data source.
   - [c] what a data field should or should not contain when records are filtered.
   - [d] the number of fields in a data source.

Circle **T** if the statement is true or **F** if the statement is false.

T   F   1. You cannot add new data records when the data source is in the table format.

T   F   2. All data records must be included in a mail merge.

T   F   3. The Fill-in field prompts you for keyboard input during the merge.

T   F   4. Query options can be set to filter or sort a data source.

T   F   5. To delete a data record with a button on the Database toolbar, the insertion point must be at the top of the table.

T   F   6. You can add and delete fields in a data source.

T   F   7. When you create a catalog main document, you should add the document title at the top of the main document before the merge.

T   F   8. The Find in Field dialog box presents options for searching for specific records.

T   F   9. Only text that is repeated should be keyed in a catalog main document.

T   F   10. It is not possible to modify a data source after it is created.

chapter sixteen

Skills Review

Exercise 1

1. Use the Mail Merge Helper to create a Size 10 envelope for the data records in the *Sales Department List* data source document located on the Data Disk. There is no return address.

2. Save the envelope main document as *Sales Department Envelopes Main Document.*

3. Merge to a new document.

4. Save the merged envelope document as *Sales Department Envelopes.*

5. Print the envelopes and close all documents.

Exercise 2

1. Use the Mail Merge Helper to create mailing labels for the data records in the *Sales Department List* data source document located on the Data Disk.

2. Use the Avery label product number 5260 for laser printers.

3. Save the label main document as *Sales Department Labels Main Document.*

4. Merge to a new document.

5. Save the merged label document as *Sales Department Labels.*

6. Print the labels and close all documents.

Exercise 3

1. Open the *Mailing List* document located on the Data Disk.

2. Display the Database toolbar.

3. Open the Data Form dialog box.

4. Find all records where the contents of the State field are equal to TX.

5. Close the document without saving changes.

6. Close the Database toolbar.

Exercise 4

1. Open the *Sales Department List* data source document located on the Data Disk.

2. Add the following records to the data source using the Database toolbar:

Mr. Thomas Carson	*Mr. Huang Chin*	*Ms. Lauren Harvell*
48 South Street	*P.O. Box 1356*	*347 Smythe Street*
Dayton, OH 45424-1179	*Dayton, OH 45424-1895*	*Cleveland, OH 55432-2344*

3. Save the data source as *Sales Department List Revised.*

4. Close the *Sales Department List Revised* data source document.

5. Use the Mail Merge Helper to merge the *Sales Department List Revised* data source with the *Merge Application Letter* main document located on the Data Disk.

6. Edit the main document to insert the appropriate merge field codes in the main document including the city name in the first sentence of the second body paragraph following the word "our" and preceding the word "sales."

7. Save the main document as *Ohio Letters*.

8. Query the data source to include only those records for Ohio. (*Hint:* Open the Merge dialog box from the Mail Merge button on the Mail Merge toolbar and click the Query Options button.)

9. Close the Merge dialog box and preview the merged records.

10. Merge to a new document using the Mail Merge toolbar.

11. Save the merged document as *Ohio Merged Letters*.

12. Print and close the *Ohio Merged Letters* and close the *Ohio Letters* document.

13. Use a blank document and the Mail Merge Helper to create Size 10 envelopes for the merged letters. (*Hint:* Reset the query options to everyone in Ohio.)

14. Save the merged envelopes as *Ohio Envelopes*.

15. Print the merged envelopes and close all documents without saving any changes.

Exercise 5

1. Open the *Spring Conference Data* document located on the Data Disk.

2. Add the following record to the data source using table editing tools:
Mr. Edward Miles
Bountiful Harvest
8379 Madison Road
Edmonton, ABT6G 2R6
Canada

3. Delete the record for Mr. Mark Jefferson using table editing tools.

4. Save the data source as *Conference Data* and close it.

5. Open the *Spring Conference Letter* document located on the Data Disk.

6. Use the Mail Merge Helper to merge the *Spring Conference Letter* main document with the *Conference Data* document.

7. Edit the main document to insert the merge field codes.

8. Save the main document as *Conference Main Document*.

9. Preview the merged records.

10. Merge to a new document.

11. Save the merged document as *Conference Merged Letters*.

12. Print the merged document and close all documents.

13. Use a blank document and the Mail Merge Helper to create Avery 5662 – Address mailing labels for the merged letters. Because you want to use the USPS preferred style, *do not* include any punctuation when you insert the merge field codes.

14. Merge to a new document.

15. Select the entire document and change the case to Uppercase to agree with the USPS preferred style.

16. Delete the punctuation following the title.

17. Save the mailing labels as *Conference Mailing Labels*.

18. Print the mailing labels and close all documents without saving any changes.

chapter sixteen

Exercise 6

1. Create a new, blank document as the basis for a list of chefs invited to the spring conference. Set a left-aligned tab at 1½ inches and key the following text:
   Name:
   Restaurant:
   City:

2. Double-space after the last line of text.

3. Open the Mail Merge Helper and define the active document as a <u>C</u>atalog main document.

4. Get the *Conference Data* data source document created in Exercise 5.

5. Edit the main document to insert the merge field codes.

6. Save the main document as *Chef Main Document.*

7. Preview the merged records.

8. Merge to a new document.

9. Center the title text "Conference Chef List" in bold, 14-point font three lines above the first record.

10. Change the top margin to 2 inches.

11. Save the merged document as *Conference Chef List.*

12. Print the merged document and close all documents.

Exercise 7

1. Create a new, blank document as the basis for a telephone list for the human resources department in the Melbourne branch office.

2. Set a left-aligned tab at 1 inch and key the following text:
   Name:
   Company:
   Phone:

3. Double space after the last line of text.

4. Use the Mail Merge Helper to define the active document as a <u>C</u>atalog main document and to create a new data source.

5. Use the Title, FirstName, LastName, Company, and WorkPhone fields for the data source.

6. Save the data source as *Telephone List Data.*

7. Edit the data source to add the following records:
Mr. Steven Brice	*Dr. Michelle Samuel*	*Ms. Erica Moon*
Brice Services	*Mercy Hospital*	*Psychology Associates*
2-3315773	*2-3412990*	*2-6933597*

8. View the data source as a table, and save it again with the new records.

9. Edit the main document to insert the merge field codes including Title.

10. Save the main document as *Telephone List Main Document.*

11. Preview the merge.

12. Merge to a new document.

13. Add the title "Melbourne Human Resources Telephone List" three lines above the first record.

14. Save the merged document as *Melbourne Telephone List*.

15. Print the merged document and close all documents.

Exercise 8

1. Open the *Reservation Data* data source document located on the Data Disk.

2. Display the Database toolbar.

3. Add the data field "City" to the data source document.

4. Move the "City" column to the left of the "State" column using the Cut and Paste features.

5. Key the following text in the "City" column:
Record 1   *San Marcos*
Record 2   *Bandera*
Record 3   *New Braunfels*
Record 4   *San Antonio*

6. Save the data source as *Reservation Data Revised* and close it.

7. Hide the Database toolbar.

8. Open the *Rattlesnake Lodge Letter* main document located on the Data Disk.

9. Use the Mail Merge Helper to merge the *Rattlesnake Lodge Letter* main document with the *Reservation Data Revised* data source document.

10. Edit the main document to insert the merge field codes.

11. Insert the Fill-in Word field for the room number in the appropriate location in the second sentence of the second body paragraph.

12. Key "Key Room Number" in the Prompt: text box.

13. Save the main document as *Rattlesnake Lodge Letter Revised*.

14. Merge to a new document.

15. Key the following room numbers at each Fill-in prompt:
1B-109
2A-115
3A-120
4B-117

16. Save the merged document as *Rattlesnake Lodge Letter Merged*.

17. Print the merged document and close all documents.

18. Use a blank document and the Mail Merge Helper to create Size 10 envelopes for the merged letters.

19. Save the merged envelope document as *Rattlesnake Lodge Envelopes*.

20. Print the envelopes and close all documents without saving.

Case Projects

Project 1

During lunch with several executive assistants, you hear the term "switches" used in reference to formatting merged information and you want to know what switches are and how to use them. Using the Office Assistant, search for merging help topics. Find and review the topic on formatting merged information. Print the help topic and any referenced topics on switches. Write an interoffice memorandum to Chris Lofton describing how the word processing staff could use switches to format merged information. Save, preview, and print the document.

Project 2

The executive assistant to the vice president of marketing, frequently sends letters to customers announcing new products. He asks you to create several letters and a merged list. Create a data source with at least 10 records containing each customer's title, first name, last name, address, home phone, and work phone numbers. Be sure to have different city data for at least 5 of the records. Then create a main document form letter announcing a new product. Use fictitious information in your documents. Preview and then merge the form letter main document and the data source to a new document. Save, preview, and print the main document, data source, and the new merged document. Query the data source to include only records for customers who live in a specific city; merge the queried data source and main document directly to the printer. Create a telephone list main document with each customer's title, last name, home phone number, and work phone number. Preview and then merge the telephone list main document with the complete data source to a new document. Save, preview, and print the telephone list main document and the new merged document.

Project 3

Jody Haversham calls to ask you for tips on creating data source documents. Using the Office Assistant, review the requirements for mail merge data sources including which applications you can use to create a data source, tips for planning a new data source, and using documents with data separated by tabs or commas as a data source. Write Jody a memorandum describing how she can find the information in online Help. Save, preview, and print the memo.

Project 4

Chris Lofton wants you to train the word processing staff to use different Word fields to customize merge documents. Use the Office Assistant to research how to customize documents using the ASK, FILLIN, IF, and SET fields. Print the appropriate online Help pages. Create an outline of the field help topics to be used as a training tool. Save, preview, and print the outline.

Project 5

Several of the word processing staff have indicated an interest in learning more about the different grammatical styles used by authors submitting work to the department. You suggest the department acquire several writers' style manuals. Connect to your ISP and search online bookstores for writers' style manuals. Print at least three Web pages containing a description of a popular style manual. Write an interoffice memorandum to Chris Lofton recommending the department purchase one of the manuals. Save, preview, and print the memorandum. Create a data source with a record for each style manual. Create a catalog main document listing the style manual name, publisher, and cost. Include the repeating text "Style Manual," "Publisher," and "Cost." Preview and then merge the main document with the data source. Add a text title to the merged document. Save, preview, and print the main document, the data source, and the merged document.

Project 6

Roberta Becker, the assistant manager of the accounting department, needs to send out collection letters and you are given the assignment. Create a standard collection letter, to be signed by Roberta, that contains at least three short paragraphs; this will be used as a main document. Include the phrase *"your past due balance of"* in the first body paragraph. Create a data source document with at least five records containing the title, first name, last name, address, city, state, and postal code fields. Use fictitious data for the data records. Merge the two documents using a Fill-in field to insert the past due balance. Create Size 10 envelopes for the letters. Save, preview, and print all documents.

Project 7

Chris Lofton asks you to create a Web page for the company intranet that lists the instructions for submitting mail-merge work assignments to the word processing department. Consider what information is important for submitting mail merge word processing tasks to a centralized word processing department and then create a set of appropriate instructions others can follow to send their work to the department. Format the document with a theme and save it as a Web page. Print the Web page.

Project 8

James Washington, a new employee in the word processing department, is having trouble with the monthly distributor sales mailing. The last time the main document and data source documents were used, it was to prepare letters to the Ohio distributors. Now he wants to merge all the records in the distributors data source; however, each time he tries to do it, Word creates only the letters for the Ohio distributors. He asks for your help in solving the problem. Using the Office Assistant, look up the topic "Select data records from a data source." Review the topic and write James a memo describing how he can solve his problem. Save, preview, and print the memo.

chapter sixteen

Sorting Text and Data Records

Chapter Overview

Information in reports, tables, lists, or data sources might be entered in one order, but later would be more useful if organized in a different order. Rather than having to manually rearrange the data, you can have Word sort it. In this chapter you learn how to sort dates, lists, tables, and data source records.

LEARNING OBJECTIVES

- ▶ Sort by dates
- ▶ Sort lists, paragraphs, and tables
- ▶ Sort records to be merged

Case profile

The sales department maintains information about sales department employees, departmental policies and procedures, products, sales data, and distributors in Word reports, tables, and data source documents. Sales department activities often require that this information be rearranged from its original order. You are to rearrange a list of employee hire dates, a numbered list of products, report paragraphs, sales data in a table, and distributor records in data source.

chapter seventeen

17.a Sorting By Dates

The Sort feature enables you to rearrange lists of text, table rows, data source records, and document paragraphs quickly. You can sort text alphabetically or numerically, or chronologically. You can arrange as many as three criteria or sort fields at one time in **ascending** order (A-Z, 0-9, earliest to latest) or **descending** order (Z-A, 9-0, latest to earliest). A date separator is the character used to separate the month, day, and year. When sorting by date, Word recognizes the forward slash (/), hyphens (-), commas (,), and periods (.) as valid date separators. You can sort a list of dates that have different date separators.

The human resources department wants a list of new sales representatives organized by date of hire. A sales department clerical assistant created the list in alphabetical order and you need to reorder the list by date. You sort text in Word documents with the Sort commands on the T<u>a</u>ble menu or with buttons on the Tables and Borders or Database toolbars. To open the document and sort the list by date of hire:

Step 1	*Open*	the *List Of Dates* document located on the Data Disk
Step 2	*Observe*	that the dates in the list are formatted with different separator characters
Step 3	*Select*	the names and dates text
Step 4	*Click*	T<u>a</u>ble
Step 5	*Click*	<u>S</u>ort

The Sort Text dialog box that opens on your screen should look similar to Figure 17-1.

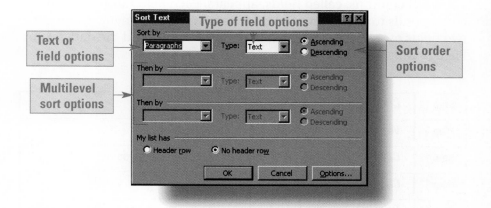

FIGURE 17-1
Sort Text Dialog Box

chapter
seventeen

You specify the text to sort and the sort order in this dialog box. Before you do that, you must specify the character that separates the columns of text so that Word can identify the individual columns.

Step 6	*Click*	Options

The Sort Options dialog box that opens on your screen should look similar to Figure 17-2.

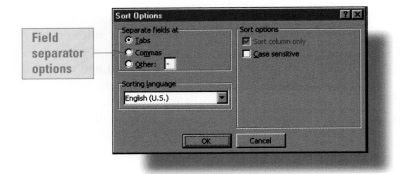

FIGURE 17-2
Sort Options Dialog Box

Field separator options

Tab characters separate the columns in the Sales Representatives document. Word correctly identifies the tab character as the column separator.

Step 7	*Verify*	the Tabs option button is selected
Step 8	*Click*	OK
Step 9	*Click*	the Sort by list arrow in the Sort Text dialog box

A list of columns, called **fields**, appears. Each field number in the list corresponds to a column of selected text in the document. There are two fields of selected text: the name text in Field 1 and the data text in Field 2. You select Field 2 and specify the sort order.

Step 10	*Click*	Field 2
Step 11	*Verify*	Date appears in the Type: list box
Step 12	*Click*	the Ascending option button, if necessary
Step 13	*Click*	OK
Step 14	*Observe*	the selected text is rearranged in ascending date order

Step 15	*Deselect*	the text
Step 16	*Save*	the document as *Sorted Dates* and close it

In addition to sorting dates, Word can also sort text in lists, body paragraphs, and tables.

17.b Sorting Lists, Paragraphs, and Tables

When you sort Word documents, text that begins with punctuation marks or symbols is listed first, text that begins with numbers is listed next, and text that begins with letters is listed last. Word ignores case unless specified, and then uppercase letters precede lowercase letters; for example, "C" precedes "c." When two items of text begin with the same character, Word looks at subsequent characters to determine which item is listed first.

Sorting Lists

Manny DaVito, a sales representative, has created a list of products. He wants you to number the list and rearrange it alphabetically in ascending order. The easiest way to number a list is with the Numbering button on the Formatting toolbar. When you sort the numbered list, Word renumbers the list automatically. To create a numbered list and sort it in ascending order:

Step 1	*Open*	the *List Of Products* document located on the Data Disk
Step 2	*Select*	the list of products
Step 3	*Click*	the Numbering button on the Formatting toolbar
Step 4	*Click*	Ta̲ble
Step 5	*Click*	S̲ort
Step 6	*Verify*	Paragraphs is selected in the S̲ort by list
Step 7	*Verify*	Text is selected in the Ty̲pe: list
Step 8	*Click*	the A̲scending option button, if necessary
Step 9	*Click*	OK
Step 10	*Deselect*	the text

| Step 11 | **Observe** | that the list of products is rearranged alphabetically in ascending order and renumbered |
| Step 12 | **Save** | the document as *Sorted Products* and close it |

You can also sort columns of text separated by tabs, commas, or other characters. The sales department receptionist must be able to quickly direct inquiries from distributors and customers to the appropriate sales representative. To help her do this, the sales manager requests a list of sales representatives sorted alphabetically by last name. She also wants a list sorted alphabetically by city within state. Finally, she wants a list sorted by postal code for Texas representatives. To sort the sales representatives list in ascending order by last name:

Step 1	**Open**	the *Sales Representatives* document located on the Data Disk
Step 2	**Select**	the five-column list
Step 3	**Open**	the Sort Text dialog box
Step 4	**Click**	the Sort by list arrow

Word identifies each column in the selected text as a field. Field 1 is the first column containing the last name. Field 5 is the last column containing the postal code.

Step 5	**Click**	Field 1
Step 6	**Click**	the Ascending option button, if necessary
Step 7	**Click**	OK
Step 8	**Deselect**	the text
Step 9	**Observe**	that the *Sales Representatives* document list is arranged in ascending alphabetical order by last name
Step 10	**Save**	the document as *Sales Representatives By Last Name*

Sometimes you need to sort a document by more than one field. For example, you want to arrange the *Sales Representatives By Last Name* list in ascending alphabetical order by state and then in ascending alphabetical order by city within each state. In this multilevel sort, the state is the most important or **primary field**, and the city is the next important, or **secondary field**. You could also sort the list by a third field, called the **tertiary field**. The primary field is defined with the Sort by list, the secondary field is defined with the first Then by list, and the tertiary field is defined with the second Then by list in the Sort Text dialog box. To sort the *Sales Representatives By Last Name* document list by city within state in ascending alphabetical order:

Step 1	*Select*	the five-column list
Step 2	*Open*	the Sort Text dialog box
Step 3	*Select*	Field 4 (the state field) in the Sort by list
Step 4	*Verify*	Text is selected in the Type: list for Field 4
Step 5	*Click*	the Ascending option button for Field 4, if necessary
Step 6	*Select*	Field 3 (the city field) in the first Then by list
Step 7	*Verify*	Text is selected in the Type: list for Field 3
Step 8	*Click*	the Ascending option button for Field 3, if necessary
Step 9	*Click*	OK
Step 10	*Deselect*	the text
Step 11	*Observe*	that the list is arranged in ascending order by city within state
Step 12	*Save*	the document as *Sales Representatives By City Within State*

You also can sort a portion of a list. You now want to sort the cities in Texas in ascending order by postal code. To select the text to be sorted and then specify the sort criteria:

Step 1	*Select*	the lines of text beginning with Aaron and ending with Nguyen
Step 2	*Open*	the Sort Text dialog box
Step 3	*Select*	Field 5 in the Sort by list
Step 4	*Click*	the Ascending option button for Field 5, if necessary
Step 5	*Click*	(none) in the Then by list to turn off the previous sort criteria
Step 6	*Click*	OK
Step 7	*Deselect*	the text
Step 8	*Observe*	that the lines of text for cities in Texas are arranged in ascending order by postal code
Step 9	*Save*	the document as *Texas Sort* and close it

**chapter
seventeen**

You can use the Cut and Paste commands to rearrange paragraphs in a document. However, if the paragraphs are adjacent to each other, it may be faster to sort them in a specific order.

Sorting Paragraphs

Word sorts body paragraphs following the same rules used to sort a numbered list mentioned earlier in this chapter. Based on these rules, numbers are arranged ahead of letters. The easiest way to sort body paragraphs in a specific order is to add a number to the beginning of each paragraph. The number represents the paragraph's order after the sort. For example, if you want a paragraph to be the third paragraph after the sort, key a 3 at the beginning of the paragraph. After the paragraphs are reordered, you can delete the numbers.

The sales manager asks you to reorganize the *Sales Department Expense Guidelines* document created by the previous administrative assistant. To open the document and number the paragraphs:

Step 1	*Open*	the *Sales Department Expense Guidelines* document located on the Data Disk
Step 2	*Key*	the following numbers as the first character of each body paragraph: 6 (paragraph 1) 1 (paragraph 2) 5 (paragraph 3) 2 (paragraph 4) 3 (paragraph 5) 4 (paragraph 6) 7 (paragraph 7)

Now you can rearrange the paragraphs.

Step 3	*Select*	the numbered paragraphs
Step 4	*Open*	the Sort Text dialog box
Step 5	*Select*	Paragraphs in the Sort by list, if necessary
Step 6	*Click*	the Ascending option button, if necessary
Step 7	*Click*	OK
Step 8	*Deselect*	the text
Step 9	*Scroll*	to view the paragraphs in ascending numeric order
Step 10	*Delete*	the numbers from the paragraphs
Step 11	*Save*	the document as *Sorted Paragraphs* and close it

Data organized in tables can be sorted using buttons on the Tables and Borders toolbar or the Database toolbar or with the Sort command on the Table menu.

Sorting Tables

Whenever you sort data in a table using the Tables and Borders or Database toolbar, you first must move the insertion point into the column to be sorted. Then you can sort the column using the Sort Ascending or Sort Descending buttons on the toolbars.

Marjorie Mason, a sales representative, is analyzing deli sales in five major marketing cities. She gives you a document containing deli sales organized in a table by item number assigned to each row and asks you to reorganize the data in ascending alphabetical order by city and then in descending order by product. To open the document and sort the data in ascending order by city:

Step 1	*Open*	the *Deli Sales Report* document located on the Data Disk
Step 2	*Move*	the insertion point to any cell in the City column
Step 3	*Display*	the Tables and Borders toolbar
Step 4	*Click*	the Sort Ascending button 🔼 on the Tables and Borders toolbar
Step 5	*Observe*	that the rows are now in alphabetic order by city
Step 6	*Save*	the document as *Deli Sales Sorted By City*

You can reorder the table in descending order by one column just as quickly. To sort the Bread column in descending order:

Step 1	*Move*	the insertion point to any cell in the Bread column
Step 2	*Click*	the Sort Descending button 🔽 on the Tables and Borders toolbar
Step 3	*Observe*	that the rows are now rearranged in descending order by the values in the Bread column
Step 4	*Save*	the document as *Deli Sales Sorted By Bread Value*

If you want to sort by more than one table column, you need to use the Sort dialog box, just as you did for lists. To return the table to its original order by item number using the Sort dialog box:

| Step 1 | *Click* | Table |

QUICK TIP

Word does not include the header row when sorting a table.

chapter
seventeen

Step 2	*Click*	<u>S</u>ort
Step 3	*Click*	the <u>S</u>ort by list arrow to display a list of column (field) names
Step 4	*Click*	#, if necessary
Step 5	*Click*	the <u>A</u>scending option button, if necessary
Step 6	*Click*	OK
Step 7	*Observe*	the table is returned to its original order
Step 8	*Close*	the document without saving any changes
Step 9	*Hide*	the Tables and Borders toolbar

Because records in a data source document are organized in a table, you can sort them just as you would any table.

17.c Sorting Records to be Merged

Data source records in a table can be arranged chronologically, alphabetically, or numerically in ascending or descending order based on the information in the data fields selected for sorting.

The sales manager asks you to create several letters to distributors announcing the sales promotion program for next year. To expedite mailing, the mail room manager requests you keep the letters in order by postal code. To do this, you use the mail merge tools to define the main document, get the data source, and query the data source to set the sort options. To begin the merge process:

Step 1	*Open*	the *Sales Promotion Letter* located on the Data Disk
Step 2	*Open*	the Mail Merge Helper dialog box
Step 3	*Create*	a Form <u>L</u>etters main document using the active document
Step 4	*Get*	the *Mailing List* data source located on the Data Disk
Step 5	*Edit*	the main document, inserting the appropriate merge field codes
Step 6	*Open*	the Merge dialog box
Step 7	*Open*	the S<u>o</u>rt Records tab in the Query Options dialog box

The Query Options dialog box you see on your screen should look similar to Figure 17-3.

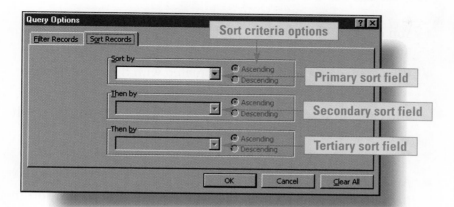

FIGURE 17-3
Sort Records Tab in the
Query Options Dialog Box

You specify the sort field in the data source.

Step 8	*Select*	PostalCode in the Sort by list
Step 9	*Click*	the Ascending option button, if necessary
Step 10	*Click*	OK
Step 11	*Merge*	to a new document
Step 12	*Verify*	that the letters are in ascending order by postal code
Step 13	*Save*	the merged document as *Letters By Postal Code*
Step 14	*Save*	the main document as *Merged Postal Code*
Step 15	*Close*	all open documents

No matter what order information is entered in reports, tables, lists, or data sources, you can sort the data to fit your needs.

**chapter
seventeen**

Summary

▶ You can sort dates that are separated by a forward slash, a comma, a period, and a hyphen.

▶ When you sort a numbered list created with the numbering feature, the list is automatically renumbered.

▶ You can sort text alphabetically, numerically, or chronologically, applying up to three criteria at one time.

▶ You can sort a selected portion of a list.

▶ An alternative to using cut-and-paste techniques to rearrange paragraphs in a document is to number the paragraphs, sort them, and then delete the numbers.

▶ You can use menu commands to sort records in a data source, or you can use buttons on the Database or Tables and Borders toolbar.

Commands Review

Action	Menu Bar	Shortcut Menu	Toolbar	Keyboard
Sort a numbered list, text in columns, paragraphs, or data records	Table, Sort		![A-Z] ![Z-A]	ALT + A, S

Concepts Review

Circle the correct answer.

1. Word can automatically:
   [a] select sort criteria.
   [b] format a sorted list.
   [c] renumber a sorted list.
   [d] arrange table text.

2. Columns to be sorted are called:
   [a] rows.
   [b] a data source.
   [c] fields.
   [d] date separators.

3. Which of the following is not a correct sorting rule?
   [a] Word first sorts text that begins with punctuation marks or symbols.
   [b] Word ignores case in a sort.
   [c] Word looks at subsequent characters when two items of text begin with the same character.
   [d] Word sorts letters before numbers.

4. To sort body paragraphs in a specific order, you can:
[a] cut and paste them.
[b] add a number indicating the sort order before the paragraphs and then sort them.
[c] select the paragraphs and then sort them alphabetically.
[d] insert Tab characters in the paragraphs and sort them.

5. Which of the following characters is not a valid date separator?
[a] period
[b] semicolon
[c] forward slash
[d] hyphen

6. You can sort data in tables by using buttons on the:
[a] Merge toolbar.
[b] Formatting toolbar.
[c] Standard toolbar.
[d] Tables and Borders toolbar.

7. When sorting text in columns, you must specify the:
[a] font.
[b] line spacing.
[c] text field and separator character.
[d] margins.

8. When sorting data records, you set:
[a] query options.
[b] record options.
[c] line options.
[d] paragraph options.

9. In a multilevel sort, you select the:
[a] primary, secondary, and tertiary fields.
[b] first, intermediate, and last fields.
[c] beginning, secondary, and final fields.
[d] starting, middle, and ending fields.

10. Information entered in one order might be more useful later when it is:
[a] requested by your manager.
[b] formatted.
[c] organized in a different order.
[d] stored on floppy disks.

Circle **T** if the statement is true or **F** is the statement is false.

T   F   1. You can only sort numbered lists and text in columns separated by tab characters.

T   F   2. When two items of text begin with the same character, Word looks at subsequent characters to determine which item is listed first.

T   F   3. Numbers can be added to the beginning of a paragraph to sort paragraphs in a specific order.

T   F   4. Ascending order is A-Z and 0-9.

T   F   5. Numbers are sorted after letters.

T   F   6. A sort can have a maximum of three criteria (fields) at one time.

T   F   7. When you sort data records, you select the header row as part of the sort.

T   F   8. You can sort a portion of a list.

T   F   9. The primary field is the least important sort criterion.

T   F   10. A date separator is the character used to separate month, day, and year.

chapter seventeen

Skills Review

Exercise 1

1. Open the *Review List* document located on the Data Disk.

2. Sort the list in ascending order by review date.

3. Save the document as *Review List Revised*.

4. Print and close the document.

Exercise 2

1. Open the *Chicago Warehouses Audit* document located on the Data Disk.

2. Number the three possible causes paragraphs 3, 1, and 2. (*Hint:* Place the number in front of the text for each bulleted item.)

3. Sort the numbered paragraphs in ascending order.

4. Delete the numbers at the beginning of each paragraph.

5. Save the document as *Chicago Warehouses Audit Revised*.

6. Print page one of the document and then close the document.

Exercise 3

1. Open the *Fall Conference Data* data source document located on the Data Disk.

2. Display the Database toolbar.

3. Sort the data records by company name in ascending order.

4. Save the document as *Fall Conference Data Sorted*.

5. Print and close the document.

6. Close the Database toolbar.

Exercise 4

1. Open the *Spring Conference Data* data source document located on the Data Disk.

2. Sort the data records by last name in ascending order using the Sort dialog box.

3. Save the document as *Spring Conference Data Sorted*.

4. Print and close the document.

Exercise 5

1. Open the *Monthly Sales Report* document located on the Data Disk.

2. Sort the list in ascending order by city within state.

3. Save the document as *Monthly Sales Report Sorted*.

4. Print and close the document.

Exercise 6

1. Open the *Dividing Words* document located on the Data Disk.

2. Center the title "Dividing Words" and format it with the bold, 14-point font.

3. Insert a blank line following the title.

4. Number the body paragraphs 3, 7, 2, 1, 6, 5, and 4. (*Hint:* Turn on the view of formatting marks to see the paragraph marks.)

5. Sort the numbered paragraphs in ascending order.

6. Delete the numbers at the beginning of each body paragraph.

7. Space the body paragraphs at 1.3 lines and add bullets.

8. Save the document as *Dividing Words Sorted*.

9. Print and close the document.

Exercise 7

1. Open the *Regional Deli Sales* document located on the Data Disk.

2. Convert the text to a table and apply the Columns 3 AutoFormat.

3. Right-align the cells containing numbers.

4. Center the table between the left and right margins.

5. Display the Tables and Borders toolbar.

6. Sort the list in ascending order by region.

7. Save the document as *Regional Deli Sales Sorted*.

8. Close the Tables and Borders toolbar.

9. Print and close the document.

Exercise 8

1. Create the following document.

2. Apply the Heading 2 style to the title and center it.

3. Turn on the automatic numbering feature in the AutoFormat as You Type tab of the AutoCorrect dialog box, if necessary, to automatically number the list as you key the text.

4. Sort the numbered list in descending alphabetical order.

5. Save the document as *Sales Districts Sorted*.

6. Print and close the document.

chapter seventeen

Revised Sales Districts

1. Texas
2. New Mexico
3. Minnesota
4. New York
5. California
6. Alaska
7. Washington
8. Alabama

Case Projects

Project 1

Bob Horseman, a clerical assistant in the sales department, created a document with a table that contains several columns of *unrelated* data. He wants to sort just one of the columns leaving the other column data in its original order and he asks for your help. Using the Office Assistant, review how to sort a single column in a table. Write Bob an interoffice memorandum explaining the process. Save, preview, and print the memorandum.

Project 2

The sales manager wants a list of the outside sales representatives and the number of customer calls each representative made during the previous month. Create a list containing three columns of information separated by tab characters. Include at least 15 sales representatives and key the first name in column 1, the last name in column 2, and the number of calls for the previous month in column 3. Use fictitious names and call data. Include at least two duplicate last names. Sort the list in an appropriate way. Save, preview, and print the list.

Project 3

The sales manager wants the sales staff to become more familiar with the Web and how to use it to locate information. You are asked to prepare a 30-minute presentation on how to find information on the Web using search engines and directories. Create an outline of your presentation listing several search engines and directories and how to use them. Include a section describing the differences between directories and search engines. List at least ten search engines and directories in the outline and then sort the list in ascending alphabetical order. Save, preview, and print the outline. With your instructor's permission, use the outline as a guide to conduct a 30-minute discussion on locating information on the Web.

Project 4

Beverly McDonald, a manager in the sales department, wants to send a welcome letter to ten new distributors. Create a main document welcome letter. Create a data source with ten records. Use fictitious data for the welcome letter and the data source. In order to process the outgoing mail more efficiently, the mail room supervisor requests all multiple mailings be sorted in postal code order. Merge the main document and the data source, with the data records sorted in ascending order by postal code. Save, preview, and print all documents.

Project 5

The human resources manager requests a list of birth dates for everyone in the sales department.

Create a list of at least ten employee names and birthdays using the mm/dd/yy format. Use different date separators in the list. Sort the list in ascending order by birth date. Save, preview, and print the list.

Project 6

David Wilson and Benica Washington, two clerical assistants in the sales department, are unfamiliar with sorting text in a Word document. Using the Office Assistant, research the rules for sorting text in a word document. Create an interoffice memorandum to David and Benica that describes the sorting rules. Save, preview, and print the memorandum.

Project 7

The sales department is sponsoring a softball game between Worldwide Exotic Foods, Inc. employees and several distributors' employees to raise money for a local children's hospital. The sales manager wants to give all participants a custom tee shirt and asks you to locate several companies that can create custom tee shirts. Connect to your ISP, load your Web browser, and search for companies who print and sell custom tee shirts. Save at least two Web pages. Write the sales manager an interoffice memorandum recommending one of the companies. Include a list of the companies and their addresses sorted by city within state. Save, preview, and print the memorandum.

Project 8

Sarah Bradley, the sales department receptionist, created a list of ten bulleted product items and now needs to rearrange the items. She thinks cutting and pasting each item takes too much time and asks you if there is a quicker way to rearrange them. Write Sarah an interoffice memorandum explaining how to use numbered paragraphs to quickly rearrange items in a bulleted list. Save, preview, and print the memorandum.

chapter seventeen

Using Macros

Chapter Overview

Organizations often create macros to save their employees time. Rather than performing a series of common tasks, they can automate them into one macro. Then employees need to select only one command to perform the entire group. In this chapter, you learn to record, run, edit, copy, rename, and delete macros.

LEARNING OBJECTIVES

► Create and apply macros
► Edit macros
► Copy, rename, and delete macros

Case profile

Several departments at Worldwide Exotic Foods want to automate routine word processing tasks by using macros. Chris Lofton, the word processing manager, asks you to tackle the project. You agree to learn how to record, edit, and run macros and then create the macros requested by each department. You create and modify a macro that prints two copies of any active document and you create a macro that performs a multilevel sort on five columns of text and then formats the text as a table.

**chapter
eighteen**

18.a Creating and Applying Macros

A **macro** is a set of commands saved together in one step to automate a multiple step task. Macros are especially useful for detailed, repetitive tasks that existing Word features—toolbar buttons, AutoCorrect, AutoText, styles, document templates, and so forth—do not perform efficiently. You can use a macro to speed up editing and formatting, to combine multiple commands, and to automate a series of tasks. For example, you could use a macro to create and format a header or footer or to convert text to a table and apply an AutoFormat to the table.

You can create a macro by writing the Word commands in the Visual Basic for Applications programming language. An alternative method of creating a macro is to turn on the macro recorder and record the macro by actually performing all the steps of a task, such as clicking menu commands, keying text, or moving the insertion point. As you complete each step, Word translates the actions into Visual Basic for Applications programming statements. For most macros that automate routine tasks, you simply record the steps to create the macro.

Applying a macro is called "running" it. You can run a macro by assigning it to a menu, toolbar, or keyboard shortcut and then clicking the menu command or toolbar button, or pressing the shortcut keys. By default, macros are stored in the Normal template so that they are available for all documents you open each time you start Word, but they may be stored in any template or document. For example, you may want to restrict a macro's use to a single document or template rather than use it with all documents. Individual macros are stored in **macro projects**, which are a group of macros stored in a document or template that you can copy, delete, or rename using the Organizer feature. The default name for macro projects is NewMacros.

Before you begin to record a macro, it is helpful to first write down all the steps in the task that you want to automate. Then you practice the steps to be certain you haven't accidentally omitted any steps. After you are certain that the written steps are correct, you record the macro. This technique helps you record the macro correctly the first time, so that you do not have to rerecord or edit it.

Worldwide Exotic Foods employees often print two copies of documents—one for their files and one to distribute. Chris asks you to automate this task by creating a macro that prints two copies of any active document, which users can run by clicking a command on the menu bar. To begin:

Step 1	**Write down**	the commands you click, in the exact order, to print two copies of any active document

---

QUICK TIP

You can create flexible, powerful macros that include instructions that you cannot record, by using the Visual Basic for Applications programming language. For more information on using the Visual Basic for Applications programming language, see online Help.

MENU TIP

You can create, record, run, edit, and delete macros with the <u>M</u>acro command on the <u>T</u>ools menu.

chapter
eighteen

| Step 2 | *Practice* | the steps until you are certain no steps have been omitted |

Once you know the steps are correct and complete, you can record the macro. To record the macro:

| Step 1 | *Create* | a new, blank document, if necessary |
| Step 2 | *Double-click* | the REC mode indicator on the status bar |

The Record Macro dialog box that opens on your screen should look similar to Figure 18-1.

FIGURE 18-1
Record Macro Dialog Box

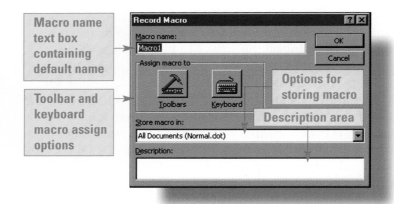

QUICK TIP

Keyboard shortcuts are a very efficient way to run frequently used macros. Click the Keyboard button in the Record Macro dialog box to assign one or more keys as a keyboard shortcut for a macro. Be careful not to assign key combinations already assigned to other shortcuts, such as the CTRL + C keys for copy. It is a good idea to use the ALT key instead of the CTRL or SHIFT key to avoid any conflict with the built-in keyboard shortcuts. If you try to assign a key combination that is already assigned, Word lists the existing keyboard assignment below the Press new shortcut key: text box.

You can use the Record Macro dialog box to assign a macro to a menu, toolbar button, or keyboard shortcut. The Store macro in: list allows you to store the macro in the attached template or in the document. If a macro is going to be used widely, it is a good idea to store it in the Normal template. If a macro is used only with a specific template or document, you can store it in that template or document. To help you remember what a macro does, you enter a short description of your macro in the Description: text box.

Because this macro is used on many documents, you store it in the Normal template. You name the macro and add a short description.

Step 3	*Key*	PRINTMACRO in the Macro name: text box
Step 4	*Key*	Prints two copies of the active document. in the Description: text box
Step 5	*Click*	Toolbars
Step 6	*Click*	the Commands tab, if necessary

The Commands tab in the Customize dialog box that opens on your screen should look similar to Figure 18-2.

FIGURE 18-2
Commands Tab in the Customize Dialog Box

> **QUICK TIP**
>
> The menu bar is a toolbar just like the Standard and Formatting toolbars. To add a macro to a specific menu, click the Toolbars button in the Record Macro dialog box and drag the macro to the appropriate menu.

To assign the PRINTMACRO command to the menu bar, you simply drag the macro command to the desired position.

Step 7	*Drag*	the Normal.NewMacros.PRINTMACRO command from the Commands: list to the menu bar

To make the command easier to read, you can edit the macro command text.

Step 8	*Right-click*	the Normal.NewMacros.PRINTMACRO command on the menu bar
Step 9	*Edit*	the Name: text box to contain only the text PRINTMACRO
Step 10	*Press*	the ENTER key to close the menu
Step 11	*Close*	the Customize dialog box

The Stop Recording toolbar appears and the mouse pointer now has a cassette icon indicating the macro recorder is turned on. Every keyboard and mouse action you perform is recorded when the macro recorder is turned on. The two buttons on the Stop Recording toolbar allow you to stop recording your actions or to pause recording your actions while you do something that is not part of the macro. Your screen should look similar to Figure 18-3.

**chapter
eighteen**

FIGURE 18-3
Document with Macro
Recorder Turned On

To record the steps in the print macro:

Step 1	*Click*	File
Step 2	*Click*	Print
Step 3	*Key*	2 in the Number of copies: text box
Step 4	*Click*	OK
Step 5	*Click*	the Stop Recording button ▣ on the Stop Recording toolbar

> ### CAUTION TIP
>
> When recording a macro, you can use the mouse to click commands and dialog box options, but you cannot use the mouse to move the insertion point or select, copy, or move text in the document window. Use the keyboard for these tasks.

The Stop Recording toolbar no longer appears and the REC mode indicator on the status bar is not bold, indicating that Word is no longer recording your keystrokes.

After you record a macro, you should test it to ensure it works properly. You run a macro to test it. To test the PRINTMACRO:

Step 1	*Open*	the *Chicago Warehouses Audit* document located on the Data Disk
Step 2	*Click*	the PRINTMACRO command on the menu bar
Step 3	*Observe*	that two copies of the active document print
Step 4	*Close*	the document

The sales department wants to print two copies of a sales representatives list formatted as a table. Because the list is used in a variety of ways, they do not want to permanently change the formatting. Chris asks you to create the macro that sorts five columns of text alphabetically by the first column and then the second column, converts the sorted text to a table, sizes and centers the table, and prints two copies. This macro applies only to this specific document, so you store it in the document and run it from the Macros dialog box.

This is a complex macro; therefore, it is important that you write down and practice the steps before you begin recording. To begin:

| Step 1 | *Write down* | the steps for the macro |
| Step 2 | *Practice* | the steps for the macro |

After writing down and practicing the steps you can begin recording the macro. To turn on the macro recorder:

Step 1	*Open*	the *Sales Representatives* document located on the Data Disk
Step 2	*Double-click*	the REC mode indicator on the status bar
Step 3	*Key*	TABLE in the Macro name: text box
Step 4	*Select*	Sales Representatives (document) in the Store macro in: list box
Step 5	*Key*	Sorts five columns of text in ascending order by last name and then first name; converts to a table; sizes and centers the table; prints two copies. in the Description: text box
Step 6	*Click*	OK

The Stop Recording toolbar appears and the mouse pointer now has a cassette icon attached, indicating the macro recorder is on and you can begin recording your actions. To select the five columns of text using the keyboard:

| Step 1 | *Move* | the insertion point to the beginning of the Jones line using the keyboard |
| Step 2 | *Press* | the CTRL + SHIFT + END keys to select from the insertion point to the end of the document |

Now you sort the selected text in ascending order. To sort the text:

Step 1	*Click*	Table
Step 2	*Click*	Sort
Step 3	*Select*	Field 1 in the Sort by list box, if necessary
Step 4	*Click*	the Ascending option button, if necessary

**chapter
eighteen**

Step 5	*Select*	Field 2 in the Then by list box
Step 6	*Click*	the Ascending option button, if necessary
Step 7	*Click*	OK

Now that the text is sorted correctly, you convert it to a centered table. To convert the text to a table and size and center it:

Step 1	*Click*	Table
Step 2	*Point to*	Convert
Step 3	*Click*	Text to Table
Step 4	*Click*	OK
Step 5	*AutoFit*	the table to the table's contents using the AutoFit command on Table menu
Step 6	*Center*	the table using the Table Properties dialog box
Step 7	*Print*	two copies of the document
Step 8	*Press*	the CTRL + Home keys to deselect the table and move the insertion point to the top of the document
Step 9	*Click*	the Stop Recording button ▣ on the Stop Recording toolbar
Step 10	*Observe*	the formatted table and two printed copies

Now that you've recorded the macro you want to remove all the formatting changes you made while recording it, and then run it to verify that it works. Because you didn't assign the macro to a keyboard, toolbar, or menu, you use the Macros dialog box to run it. To test the macro:

Step 1	*Undo*	all the previous formatting actions with the Undo button list arrow ↰▾ on the Standard toolbar
Step 2	*Move*	the insertion point to the top of the document
Step 3	*Click*	Tools
Step 4	*Point to*	Macro
Step 5	*Click*	Macros

The Macros dialog box that opens on your screen should look similar to Figure 18-4.

QUICK TIP

To correct a macro that is not running correctly, simply rerecord the steps and save it with the same name.

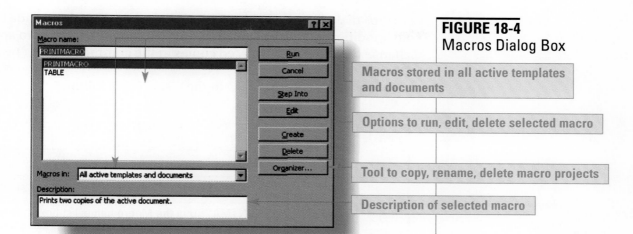

FIGURE 18-4
Macros Dialog Box

Macros stored in all active templates
and documents

Options to run, edit, delete selected macro

Tool to copy, rename, delete macro projects

Description of selected macro

You can run, edit, create, and delete macros in this dialog box. You run the TABLE macro.

| Step 6 | *Double-click* | TABLE in the Macro name: list box |
| Step 7 | *Observe* | that Word sorts the five columns of text, converts them to an automatically sized table, and prints two copies |

You need to save the document with the macro, but you do not want to save the new formatting. To remove the formatting and save the document with the macro:

| Step 1 | *Undo* | all the previous formatting actions |
| Step 2 | *Save* | the document as *Sales Representatives Automated* and close it |

Sometimes you need to modify macros. You do this by editing them with the Visual Basic Editor.

18.b Editing Macros

You use the Visual Basic Editor to create new macros or to edit existing macros. The **Visual Basic Editor** is a feature that contains its own windows, menus, and tools you use to write or revise the Visual Basic programming statements for a macro. Chris tells you that the PRINTMACRO must be modified to print three copies of the active document instead of two. Rather than record the entire macro again, you decide to edit it in the Visual Basic Editor by selecting it in the

**chapter
eighteen**

Macros dialog box and clicking the Edit button. You also decide to add the modification date as an additional comment to the macro and change the number of printed copies in the comments from "two" to "three."

To open the PRINTMACRO in the Visual Basic Editor:

Step 1	*Click*	Tools
Step 2	*Point to*	Macro
Step 3	*Click*	Macros
Step 4	*Click*	PRINTMACRO in the Macro name: list box, if necessary
Step 5	*Click*	Edit

The Visual Basic Editor window that opens should look similar to Figure 18-5.

FIGURE 18-5
Microsoft Visual Basic Editor

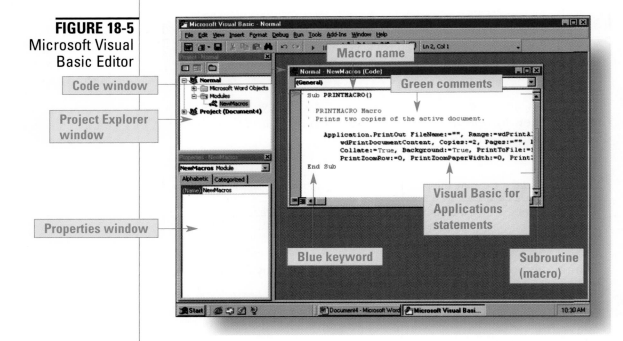

The Visual Basic Editor contains three windows: the Code window, the Project Explorer window, and the Properties window. The large Code window on the right displays the contents of a macro written in the Visual Basic for Applications programming language. When you recorded the PRINTMACRO macro, Word translated your recorded steps into this code. The Project Explorer window at the upper left displays a list of macro projects currently open; programmers use this window to add or delete macro project components and reorganize macro projects. If the Project Explorer window is not visible, you can open it by clicking the Project Explorer button on the Standard toolbar. The Properties window at the lower left allows programmers to change the settings or characteristics of a macro. If the Properties window is not visible, you can open it by clicking the Properties Window button on the toolbar. Because you are going to modify the code, you close the Project Explorer and Properties windows. To close the windows:

Step 1	*Click*	the Close button ❎ in the Project Explorer window
Step 2	*Click*	the Close button ❎ in the Properties window
Step 3	*Maximize*	the Code window, if necessary

The Visual Basic for Applications code is created in a special format called a **subroutine**. Macros are sometimes called subroutines. Each subroutine (macro) is part of a larger component, called a **module**. The subroutine (macro) begins with the reserved word, or **keyword**, "Sub" that's displayed in blue font; it ends with the keyword "End Sub"—also in blue font. Between these two keywords are the name of the subroutine (macro), any comments in green font, and the Visual Basic for Applications program statements that perform the macro tasks in black font. You want to add the modification date as a comment and change the comment text "two" to "three." To add and modify the comment text:

Step 1	*Move*	the insertion point to the end of the green comment line beginning with "Prints"
Step 2	*Key*	Modified on (*today's date*).
Step 3	*Select*	the text "two" and replace it with "three" in the first comment line

Now you want to edit the Visual Basic for Applications statement to print three copies instead of one. To edit the Visual Basic for Applications statement:

Step 1	*Select*	the number 2 in the code Copies:=2 in the Visual Basic for Applications statement
Step 2	*Key*	3
Step 3	*Restore*	the Code window to a smaller window

chapter eighteen

Step 4	*Click*	the Project Explorer button [icon] on the Standard toolbar to open the Project Explorer window
Step 5	*Click*	the Properties Window button [icon] on the Standard toolbar to open the Properties window
Step 6	*Drag*	the top of the Properties window down approximately 1 inch to size the window
Step 7	*Click*	<u>F</u>ile
Step 8	*Click*	<u>C</u>lose and Return to Microsoft Word

As before, you run the macro to verify that it works. To test the PRINTMACRO modifications:

Step 1	*Open*	the *Chicago Warehouses Audit* document located on the Data Disk
Step 2	*Run*	the PRINTMACRO macro
Step 3	*Close*	the document without saving changes

Because macro viruses can be a serious problem, Word provides a macro security feature to protect your computer files.

Changing the Security Level

A **virus** is a computer program that "infects" your computer by inserting copies of itself into other files. When this happens, the virus can infect still other files when the infected file is loaded into your computer's memory. Some viruses are harmful and may damage your hard disk, use computer memory that could otherwise be used by other programs, or destroy files. A **macro virus** is a virus included in a macro that is activated when the macro runs.

By default, Word sets a high security level that automatically disables any macros in a document when you open the document. Unless you switch to a lower security level, macros are disabled automatically without a warning message for any document that contains a macro you open, such as the *Sales Representatives Automated* document you created earlier. You can modify this security level so you can choose whether to open a document with macros enabled or disabled.

To modify the security level:

Step 1	*Click*	<u>T</u>ools
Step 2	*Point to*	<u>M</u>acro

Step 3	*Click*	Security

Step 4	*Click*	the Security Level tab, if necessary

The Security dialog box that opens on your screen should look similar to Figure 18-6.

FIGURE 18-6
Security Level Tab in the Security Dialog Box

> **CAUTION TIP**
>
> It is a good practice to install the most current version of anti-virus software on your computer system so that you can check routinely for computer viruses. Opening files you receive as e-mail attachments and downloading files from the Web may place your computer system at a higher risk for a virus infection. You should consider saving e-mail attachments and downloaded files to a disk and then checking them with your anti-virus software before opening them to avoid infection. To learn more about computer viruses and anti-virus software see your instructor, visit a local computer store, or search the Web for computer virus topics.

Because macro viruses can only damage your files when the macro runs, you might want to modify the security level so that you can choose to open a document with the macros enabled or disabled. The medium security level allows you to do this. If you are comfortable with the source of the document and trust that you are not exposing your system to a macro virus, you can then elect to open the document with the macros enabled. If you are not comfortable with the source of the document, you can choose to cancel the open process or open the document as read-only with the macros disabled.

You want to open the *Sales Representatives Automated* document you created earlier with the macro enabled. To do this, you can change the security level to medium.

Step 5	*Click*	the Medium option button, if necessary

Step 6	*Click*	OK

**chapter
eighteen**

You can see how the security level works by opening the *Sales Representatives Automated* document you created earlier. To open the document with macros enabled:

| Step 1 | **Open** | the *Sales Representatives Automated* document |
| Step 2 | **Click** | the Enable Macros button in the confirmation dialog box |

Despite the care you take to write down, practice, and then record a macro, you might find errors when you test it. If a macro is not working properly, you can work through it step-by-step to find the errors.

Debugging Macros

If you record a macro that doesn't run properly, you can look for errors in each Visual Basic for Applications statement by working through the macro one step at a time. A macro "bug" is an error in a Visual Basic for Applications statement. The process of stepping through the statements to find errors is called **debugging** the macro. Although the macro in the *Sales Representatives Automated* document should be working properly, you can use it to view the debugging process. To open the TABLE macro:

Step 1	**Open**	the Macros dialog box
Step 2	**Select**	the TABLE macro
Step 3	**Click**	Edit to open the Visual Basic Editor window

As you process the macro step by step, you can switch to the Word document to view the results of that step. To begin the debugging process:

Step 1	**Click**	Debug on the menu bar
Step 2	**Click**	Step Into
Step 3	**Observe**	the first line of the subroutine is highlighted and the left side of the Code window contains a yellow arrow pointing to the highlighted text
Step 4	**Press**	the F8 key to proceed to the first statement in the subroutine
Step 5	**Observe**	the statement that moves the insertion point down three lines is highlighted
Step 6	**Press**	the F8 key to run the highlighted statement and move to the next statement

---

CAUTION TIP

Extensive editing of complex macros requires some knowledge of the Visual Basic for Applications programming language and experience using the Visual Basic Editor. In many cases it is easier and faster to simply rerecord the macro. If a macro is not working properly, first review your written steps, then practice the steps again, and rerecord the macro with the same name.

Step 7	*Press*	the F8 key three times to finish running the statements that move the insertion point and select the five columns of text
Step 8	*Switch*	to the Word document using the taskbar button and observe the selected text
Step 9	*Switch*	to the Visual Basic Editor using the taskbar button
Step 10	*Continue*	to process each step of the macro by pressing the F8 key
Step 11	*Close*	the Visual Basic Editor and return to Word when finished
Step 12	*Close*	the document without saving any changes

When you have several macros, it is important to be able to organize them.

18.c Copying, Renaming, and Deleting Macros

Over time you may need to edit your macros to meet new processing requirements or delete those macros that are no longer useful. As you develop your macros, others in your workgroup may also want to use them. You can manage your macros using the Organizer, the Visual Basic Editor, or the options in the Macros dialog box.

Using the Organizer

You can access the Organizer from the Macros dialog box or from the Templates and Add-ins dialog box, both of which are opened from the Tools menu. From the Organizer dialog box, you can copy macros to other documents or templates, rename macros when necessary, and delete macros when they are no longer needed.

Chris asks you to copy the NewMacros macro project (which contains the PRINTMACRO macro) from the Normal template to another document, rename the PRINTMACRO in the new document, and then delete the PRINTMACRO from the Normal template. To open the new document and the Organizer dialog box:

Step 1	*Open*	the *Chicago Warehouses Audit* document located on the Data Disk
Step 2	*Open*	the Macros dialog box
Step 3	*Click*	Organizer

chapter
eighteen

The Macro Project Items tab in the Organizer dialog box that opens on your screen should look similar to Figure 18-7.

FIGURE 18-7
Macro Project Items Tab in
the Organizer Dialog Box

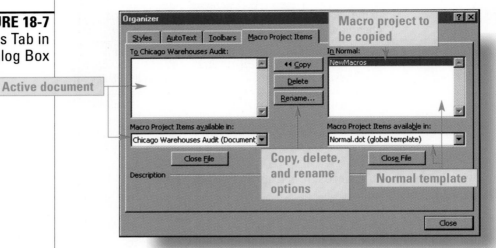

You copy, rename, and delete entire macro projects in this dialog box. Because you opened the *Chicago Warehouses Audit* document before you opened the Organizer dialog box, both the Normal template and the destination document are open and ready for the copy process. You copy the selected NewMacros project to the destination document.

Step 4	***Click***	the Copy button in the dialog box
Step 5	***Close***	the dialog box
Step 6	***Save***	the document as *Chicago Warehouses With Print Macro*

Using the Visual Basic Editor

You also can manage individual macros using the Visual Basic Editor. To rename the PRINTMACRO in the *Chicago Warehouses With Print Macro* document, you edit the name in the Visual Basic Editor. To edit the macro name:

Step 1	***Open***	the Macro dialog box
Step 2	***Select***	the Project.NewMacros.PRINTMACRO item in the Macro name: list box
Step 3	***Click***	Edit

Step 4	*Select*	the macro name PRINTMACRO following the blue keyword Sub in the Chicago Warehouses With Print Macro Code window
Step 5	*Key*	PrintsThree
Step 6	*Click*	File
Step 7	*Click*	Close and Return to Microsoft Word
Step 8	*Open*	the Macros dialog box and observe the new macro name "PrintsThree"

Using the Macros Dialog Box

Now you want to delete the PRINTMACRO macro from the NewMacros project in the Normal template. You can do this in the Macros dialog box.

To delete the PRINTMACRO in the Normal template:

Step 1	*Select*	PRINTMACRO, if necessary
Step 2	*Click*	Delete
Step 3	*Click*	Yes to confirm the deletion
Step 4	*Close*	the dialog box

Because the PRINTMACRO in the Normal template is no longer available, you must also remove the PRINTMACRO command from the menu bar. To remove the macro command:

Step 1	*Press & Hold*	the ALT key
Step 2	*Drag*	the PRINTMACRO command down into the document area
Step 3	*Release*	the mouse button and the ALT key
Step 4	*Save*	the *Chicago Warehouses With Print Macro* document and close it

You can use macros to automate many of your routine word processing tasks.

> ### QUICK TIP
>
> If the only open macro projects are in the Normal template, you might see a list of macro names without a macro project reference in the Macros dialog box.
>
> You can remove a macro command or button by opening the Customize dialog box and dragging the command or button off the menu or toolbar.

chapter eighteen

Summary

▶ A macro is a set of Word commands and instructions you can use to perform complex tasks in a single, automated step.

▶ Macros are especially useful when you perform detailed, repetitive tasks that you cannot accomplish efficiently with other Word features, such as toolbar buttons, AutoCorrect, AutoText, Styles, and document templates.

▶ You can assign a macro to a toolbar button, menu, or keyboard shortcut.

▶ When you record a macro, Word writes the instructions you record in a macro programming language called Visual Basic for Applications.

▶ By default, macros are stored in the Normal template, but they can be stored in any template or document.

▶ When recording a macro, you cannot use the mouse to move the insertion point or to select, copy, or move text in the document window. You can use the mouse to select menu commands.

▶ The process of stepping through a macro to find errors is called debugging the macro.

▶ You can copy, rename, or delete macro projects in the Organizer dialog box.

▶ You can copy, rename, or delete individual macros in the Macros dialog box or using the Visual Basic Editor.

▶ When you delete a macro, you should also remove the custom toolbar button or custom menu command that executes the macro.

▶ A macro virus is a potentially harmful program that might be included in a macro; the virus could damage your files or hard disk.

▶ By default Word sets a high security level that automatically disables any macros in a document when you open the document.

▶ You can modify the security level to allow you the choice of opening a document with macros enabled or disabled.

Commands Review

Action	Menu Bar	Shortcut Menu	Toolbar	Keyboard
Record a macro	<u>T</u>ools, <u>M</u>acro, <u>R</u>ecord New Macro		Double-click the REC mode indicator	ALT + T, M, R
Run or edit a macro	<u>T</u>ools, <u>M</u>acro, <u>M</u>acros Click a custom menu command assigned to the macro		Click a custom toolbar button assigned to the macro	ALT + T, M, M Press custom keyboard shortcut keys assigned to the macro ALT + F8

Concepts Review

Circle the correct answer.

1. A macro:
[a] cannot be recorded as you perform actions.
[b] can be created using the Word 2000 Basic programming language.
[c] is useful to perform tasks not covered by the toolbar buttons, AutoText, Styles, AutoCorrect, and templates.
[d] must be edited in the Word 2000 Basic Editor window.

2. You cannot run a macro by:
[a] double-clicking the REC mode indicator on the status bar.
[b] clicking a custom button on a toolbar.
[c] clicking a custom command on a menu.
[d] pressing keyboard shortcut keys.

3. By default, macros are stored in the:
[a] active document.
[b] Normal template.
[c] Macro template.
[d] Macros dialog box.

4. When you need to automate a task, you should first:
[a] open the Macros dialog box.
[b] turn on the recorder and record the steps to automate it.
[c] write down all the commands and instructions required in exact order.
[d] practice performing the task you want to automate.

5. Which of the following routine tasks is the best candidate for automation with a macro?
[a] inserting standard wording in a document
[b] adding a standard header and footer to multiple-page letters
[c] applying boldface or italic formatting to text
[d] creating a basic 4x3 table

6. A group of macros in a document or template are stored in:
[a] the Visual Basic Editor.
[b] macro projects.
[c] the Organizer.
[d] the Macros dialog box.

7. To select text or position the insertion point when recording a macro, you must use the:
[a] mouse.
[b] keyboard.
[c] ALT + M keys.
[d] Visual Basic Editor.

8. The process of looking for errors in a macro line by line is called:
[a] step-by-step processing.
[b] debugging.
[c] managing.
[d] editing.

chapter eighteen

9. The cassette icon on the mouse pointer means:
   [a] a macro is running.
   [b] every mouse and keyboard actions is being recorded.
   [c] you are deleting a macro.
   [d] you are renaming a macro.

10. Macros are also called:
   [a] keywords.
   [b] viruses.
   [c] debuggers.
   [d] subroutines.

Circle **T** if the statement is true or **F** is the statement is false.

T   F   1. Macros can be created or edited in the Macro Editor window.

T   F   2. You double-click the TRK mode indicator on the status bar to begin editing a macro.

T   F   3. You can copy, rename, or delete individual macros in the Organizer dialog box.

T   F   4. If a macro contains errors, you can edit it or simply rerecord it.

T   F   5. The Stop Recording toolbar has buttons for Stop Recording and Pause Recording actions.

T   F   6. A macro is an appropriate alternative when existing Word toolbar buttons, AutoCorrect, AutoText, styles, and document templates do not automate a task.

T   F   7. Macros can be created only by keying the Visual Basic for Applications code in the Visual Basic Editor code window.

T   F   8. Macros can be assigned to a command on the menu bar and to keyboard shortcuts, but not to any other toolbar.

T   F   9. A keyword is a reserved word in the Visual Basic for Applications language.

T   F 10. A macro virus can infect your computer system even if it is not executed.

Skills Review

SCANS

Exercise 1   C

1. Write down the steps to open a document, save it with a new name, print two copies, and close it.

2. Practice the steps to assure their accuracy.

3. Record a macro named OPENDOCUMENT to open the *Internet Training* document located on the Data Disk, save it as *Internet Macro*, print two copies, and close it.

4. Store the macro in the Normal template.

5. Assign the macro to the ALT + M keys.

6. Close all open documents and run the macro.

7. Select the OPENDOCUMENT macro in the Macros dialog box, open the Visual Basic Editor, and select and print the OPENDOCUMENT subroutine.

Exercise 2   C

1. Create a new, blank document.

2. Copy the NewMacros project created in Exercise 1 from the Normal template to the new document.

3. Save the document as *NewMacros Document*.

4. Edit the OPENDOCUMENT macro in the *NewMacros Document* to print one copy using the Visual Basic Editor.

5. Enter the text "Testing the modified macro." in the document.

6. Save the document to update the copy on the disk.

7. Run the macro from the Macros dialog box.

8. Close the document.

Exercise 3   C

1. Write down the steps to create a custom header and footer. Right-align the date in the header and center the page number in the footer.

2. Practice the steps to assure their accuracy.

3. Record a macro named HEADER to insert the custom header and footer.

4. Store the macro in the Normal template.

5. Assign the macro to a command on the menu bar.

6. Customize the macro command to read "Custom Header."

7. Open the *Understanding The Internet* document located on the Data Disk.

8. Run the macro.

9. Print and close the document without saving any changes.

10. Select the HEADER macro in the Macros dialog box, open the Visual Basic Editor window, select the HEADER subroutine (macro) in the code window, and print the selection.

Exercise 4   C

1. Write down the steps to open, print, and close three single-page documents of your choice from the Data Disk. (*Hint:* Use the SHIFT + Click or CTRL + Click methods of opening multiple documents.)

2. Practice the steps to assure their accuracy.

3. Record a macro named THREE to open, print, and close the documents.

4. Store the macro in the Normal template.

5. Run the macro from the Macros dialog box.

6. Select the THREE macro in the Macros dialog box, open the Visual Basic Editor, and select and print the THREE subroutine.

Exercise 5

1. Edit the THREE macro created in Exercise 4 in the Visual Basic Editor to rename it to THREEPAGES.

2. Select and print the THREEPAGES subroutine.

Exercise 6

1. Write down the steps to create a new interoffice memorandum template that sets appropriate margins and tab stops, text, formatting, and line spacing. Center the text MEMORANDUM at the top of the document. Insert the current date as a field and insert the name B. Michaels as the From: name. Position the insertion point at the left margin of the first body paragraph line.

2. Practice the steps to assure their accuracy.

3. Record a macro named MEMO to create the template.

4. Store the macro in the Normal template.

5. Assign the macro to a command on the menu bar.

6. Run the macro.

7. Save the document as *Michaels Memo Template*.

8. Print and close the document.

9. Open the MEMO macro in the Visual Basic Editor and select and print the MEMO subroutine.

Exercise 7

1. Write down the steps to sort in descending order the product list in the *List Of Products* document located on the Data Disk and then print the document.

2. Practice the steps to assure their accuracy.

3. Open the *List Of Products* document and record a macro named SORTPRINT to sort the list and print the document.

4. Store the macro in the document.

5. Undo all the previous actions with the Undo button on the Standard toolbar.

6. Save the document as *List Of Products Automated*.

7. Run the macro from the Macros dialog box.

8. Open the document in the Visual Basic Editor and select and print the SORTPRINT subroutine.

9. Close the document without saving any changes.

Exercise 8

1. Use the Macros dialog box to delete the OPENDOCUMENT, HEADER, THREEPAGES, and MEMO macros from the Normal template. (If you did not create all the macros, delete the ones you did create.)

2. Remove any macro commands from the menu bar using the ALT + Drag method.

Case Projects

Project 1

While you're showing Chris Lofton how to record a macro, a question arises about the purpose of the Microsoft Script Editor command on the Macro submenu. You decide to research the command. Using the Office Assistant, search for the "macro" topic. Open the "Using macros to automate tasks" subtopic and click the "Automating tasks in Web pages" link. Review the topic and the "using Web scripts" subtopics. Write Chris an interoffice memorandum describing, in general, how the command is used. Suggest to Chris how a Web script could be used on the company home page. Save, preview, and print the memorandum.

Project 2

Jody Haversham is eager to create a macro that applies a standard footer on her purchasing reports. The footer includes the text "Purchasing Department" at the left margin, a centered page number, and the current date at the right margin. She also wants to be able to run the macro using a keyboard shortcut. She asks for your help in recording the macro. Create an outline containing the steps required to record the macro. Save, preview, and print the outline. With your instructor's permission, use the outline to guide a classmate through the process of recording the macro.

Project 3

This week's edition of the *Secretarial Guide* e-mail newsletter contains a brief reference to the macros supplied by Word. You want to know more about them. Using the Office Assistant, review the topic called Using the macros supplied with Word. Write an interoffice memorandum to Chris Lofton describing three of the macros and how they can be used in the word processing department. Save, preview, and print the memorandum.

Project 4

Because of your experience using Word 2000, Chris asks you to update the macros chapter of the word processing department procedure manuals. Some of the junior operators are experiencing problems recording and running macros. Using the Office Assistant, research how to troubleshoot certain problems encountered when recording or running macros. Create an unbound report document describing five common problems and a suggested solution. Save, preview, and print the document.

Project 5

During lunch with Marisa DaFranco, the executive assistant to the chairperson, she tells you that her boss must be able to connect to the Internet when traveling both in the U. S. and internationally. She asks for your help in locating an Internet service provider that has local phone numbers in major U. S. cities, plus a 1-800 service for international calls. Connect to your ISP, launch your Web browser, and search the Web for pages that list Internet service providers. Review several Web pages to compare service and price. Print at least three Web pages. Write Marisa an interoffice memorandum describing the results of your research, recommending a service provider that meets the chairperson's needs. Save, preview, and print the memorandum.

chapter eighteen

Project 6

Kelly Armstead asks you to create a macro that centers the title text PURCHASING DEPARTMENT and formats it with Arial, 12-point font, with the words only underlined. After thinking about how to create the macro, you decide there are already ways to create, store, and insert preformatted text using existing Word features without creating a macro. Write Kelly an interoffice memorandum explaining why a macro is not necessary to accomplish the task and describing two Word features that she can use instead of a macro. Save, preview, and print the memorandum.

Project 7

Chris Lofton wants to publish a Web page to the company intranet that offers weekly tips on using Word 2000 and asks you to create the Web page. The first set of tips covers recording a macro. Using online Help and what you learned in this chapter, create a Web page with a bulleted list of five to ten tips for recording a macro. Apply the theme of your choice. Save, preview, and print the Web page.

Project 8

Nat Wong has recently upgraded to Word 2000 from the previous version of Word (Word 97) and he calls with concerns about whether or not his Word 97 macros will run properly in Word 2000. You agree to research the problem and get back to him. Using online Help, find the answer to Nat's question and then draft an e-mail message (using a new Word document) that provides the answer. Save, preview, and print the document.

Project 9

Marisa DaFranco, the executive assistant to the chairperson, tells you that the chairperson is also concerned about computer viruses that might be transmitted over the Internet. Connect to your ISP, launch your Web browser, and search the Web for pages that discuss Internet security and viruses. Print at least three Web pages. Write Marisa an interoffice memorandum describing the results of your research, including at least two paragraphs that describe how computer viruses are transmitted over the Internet and how to protect against possible infection. Save, preview, and print the memorandum.

Creating and Using Document Notations

Chapter Overview

Document notations are a helpful way to insert additional information, such as references and notes, into your documents. You can also browse through documents by notation or headings. In this chapter you learn how to create, revise, and delete footnotes and endnotes and how to insert comments and bookmarks. In addition, you use the Document Map to move quickly through a document.

LEARNING OBJECTIVES

- ► Create or revise footnotes and endnotes
- ► Insert comments
- ► Use bookmarks
- ► Use the Document Map

Case profile

Kelly Armstead calls to congratulate you on being elected secretary of the International Association of Executive Assistants. You spend several hours each week preparing correspondence, news releases, the newsletter, and library updates. You use document notations, including bookmarks that allow you to quickly reference specific topics, comments that add extra information, and footnotes or endnotes that identify the sources of quotations or facts you use in your documents.

chapter nineteen

C 19.a Creating or Revising Footnotes and Endnotes

A **footnote** or **endnote** is supplemental text added to the bottom of a page or end of the document that allows you to identify sources of quotations, facts, and ideas used in the document. You can also use footnotes or endnotes to insert incidental information that is not part of the document content. Footnotes appear at the bottom of the page that contains the text being noted; endnotes appear at the end of the document text or on a separate page at the end of the document. Each footnote or endnote is numbered consecutively. As you create, edit, add, or delete footnotes or endnotes, Word automatically updates the numbering to keep it sequential. You create footnotes and endnotes by clicking the Footnote command on the Insert menu.

 notes This chapter illustrates how to use the Word footnote and endnote features. The formatting rules for footnotes and endnotes vary by the type of source being quoted. You can review the formatting rules for footnotes and endnotes in different style guides. See Appendix C "Formatting Tips for Business Documents" for additional information about style guides.

As chapter secretary, your first task is to prepare chapter update information for the international newsletter, as shown in Figure 19-1. To create the newsletter:

Step 1	**Create**	a new, blank document, if necessary
Step 2	**Switch**	to Normal view, if necessary
Step 3	**Create**	the document shown in Figure 19-1
Step 4	**Save**	the document as *Chapter Update*

Potential association members who read the information in the *Chapter Update* document might want to contact a chapter. Contact information is not directly relevant to the document content so you decide to insert the information as footnotes.

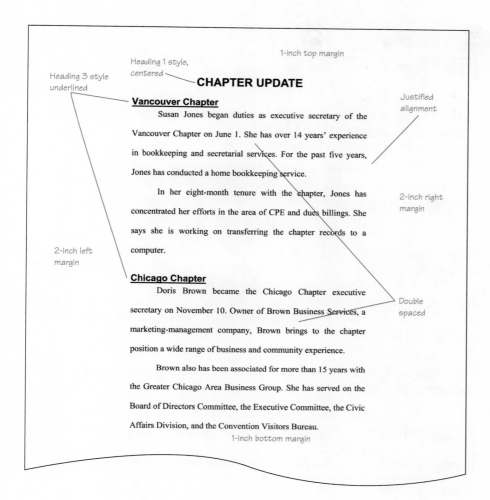

FIGURE 19-1
Chapter Update
Newsletter Information

Inserting Footnotes

Word footnotes consist of a **note reference mark**, a number or symbol placed next to the referenced text and the corresponding note, and the note text. When you create a footnote, Word inserts the appropriately numbered note reference mark at the location of the insertion point and in the **note pane**, a separate text area where you key the note text.

You insert the telephone number and e-mail address for each association chapter as the contact information. To insert the Vancouver chapter telephone number and e-mail address:

Step 1	*Move*	the insertion point after the text "Vancouver Chapter" on the second line of the first body paragraph

chapter
nineteen

Step 2	*Click*	Insert

Step 3	*Click*	Footnote

The Footnote and Endnote dialog box that opens on your screen should look similar to Figure 19-2.

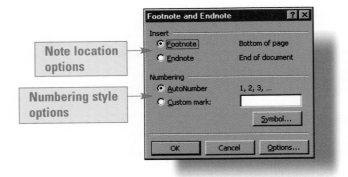

FIGURE 19-2
Footnote and Endnote
Dialog Box

By default, 1, 2, 3, ... is the automatic numbering pattern for footnotes. You accept the default AutoNumber option.

Step 4	*Click*	the Footnote option button, if necessary

Step 5	*Click*	the AutoNumber option button, if necessary

Step 6	*Click*	OK

Step 7	*Observe*	the note reference mark to the right of the "Vancouver Chapter" text

The note pane containing the insertion point opens at the bottom of your screen, which should look similar to Figure 19-3.

The Footnotes list box in the note pane displays the text "All Footnotes," which means that all the footnotes currently in the document appear in the pane. The other options in the list—Footnote Separator, Footnote Continuation Separator, and Footnote Continuation Notice—customize the appearance of the line or text associated with the selected item. For more information about these choices, see online Help. You key the Vancouver contact information in the note pane.

Step 8	*Key*	Vancouver Chapter telephone number (604-555-8495) and e-mail address (vanc@iaea.net)

Step 9	*Click*	Close in the note pane to close it

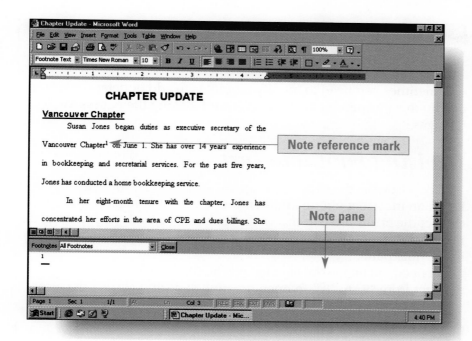

FIGURE 19-3
Note Pane with Footnote
Reference Mark

You repeat the same process to insert the footnote for the Chicago chapter. Word automatically uses the next consecutive number. To insert the Chicago contact information:

Step 1	**Move**	the insertion point after the text "Chicago Chapter" on the first line of the third body paragraph
Step 2	**Click**	Insert
Step 3	**Click**	Footnote
Step 4	**Verify**	the Footnote and AutoNumber options are selected
Step 5	**Click**	OK
Step 6	**Key**	Chicago Chapter telephone number (312-555-5639) and e-mail address (chic@iaea.net)
Step 7	**Close**	the note pane
Step 8	**Save**	the document as *Chapter Update With Footnotes*

You can view footnote text directly in the document in Print Layout view or Print Preview. You can also view the footnote text by positioning the mouse pointer over the note reference mark, which changes to a "sticky-note" style of icon that contains a ScreenTip with the footnote text. To view the Chicago Chapter footnote text:

Step 1	**Move**	the mouse pointer to the note reference mark after the text "Chicago Chapter"

QUICK TIP

To use a special symbol instead of numbers for the footnotes or endnotes reference marks, click the Custom mark: option button in the Footnote and Endnote dialog box and then key the symbol you want or click the Symbol button and insert the desired symbol from the Symbol dialog box.

**chapter
nineteen**

| Step 2 | **Observe** | the shape of the mouse pointer and the footnote text in the ScreenTip |

Sometimes you need to modify footnotes to add or delete text. You can do this by opening the note pane and making the necessary changes.

Revising Footnote Text

After reviewing the Chicago Chapter footnote text, you realize you keyed an incorrect phone number. You open the note pane and correct the error. You edit text in the note pane exactly as you do in the main document. All the formatting and editing features are available in the note pane.

You need to change the last digit in the Chicago Chapter phone number from "9" to "8." To open the note pane and correct the error:

Step 1	**Double-click**	the note reference mark following the text "Chicago Chapter"
Step 2	**Select**	the number "9" in the Chicago Chapter footnote
Step 3	**Key**	8
Step 4	**Close**	the note pane
Step 5	**Observe**	the note text in a ScreenTip
Step 6	**Print Preview**	the document
Step 7	**Observe**	the separator line and the note placement on the page
Step 8	**Close**	Print Preview

To change the numbering pattern for footnotes or the location of footnotes on the page, you can click the Footnote command on the Insert menu and then click the Options button to select different numbering or positioning options. Changes in the footnote options affect all the footnotes in the document. When you want the notes to appear together at the end of the document, you use endnotes instead of footnotes.

Inserting Endnotes

To insert endnotes you follow the same process as inserting footnotes except you click the Endnote option button in the Footnote and Endnote dialog box. As you create, edit, add, or delete endnotes, Word revises the numbering automatically to keep it sequential. By default, Word uses i, ii, iii, ... for endnote numbering.

MENU TIP

You can open the note pane by clicking the Footnotes command on the View menu.

QUICK TIP

You can edit footnotes and endnotes in Print Layout view. When you double-click the note reference mark in Print Layout view, the insertion point moves to the beginning of the selected footnote or endnote.

MOUSE TIP

Depending on the style guide you use, you might need to indent the first line from the left margin, or create a hanging indent so that all lines except the first line are indented from the left margin. To do this, switch to Print Layout view, select the footnotes, and use the First Line and Hanging Indent markers on the horizontal ruler to indent the lines as needed.

Because you expect to add more chapter update information to the document, it is more convenient to use endnotes placed on a separate page at the end of the document. You can quickly convert the current footnotes to endnotes. To convert the footnotes to endnotes:

Step 1	*Click*	View
Step 2	*Click*	Footnotes
Step 3	*Select*	both footnotes
Step 4	*Right-click*	the selected footnotes
Step 5	*Click*	Convert to Endnote
Step 6	*Close*	the note pane
Step 7	*Observe*	the new note reference marks in the document

Now that the footnotes are endnotes, you need to place them on their own page. To place the endnotes on a separate page at the end of the document:

Step 1	*Insert*	a manual page break immediately following the last sentence in the document
Step 2	*Print Preview*	the document in 1 x 2 pages to see the endnotes on a separate page
Step 3	*Close*	Print Preview
Step 4	*Save*	the document as *Chapter Update With Endnotes*

You can edit endnote text in the same way you edit footnote text. You can edit a footnote or endnote in Print Layout view by scrolling to view it and then moving the insertion point into the note text. Move the insertion point back into the document body when you've edited the note.

19.b Inserting Comments

When you need to add information that is not part of the document text, you use comments. **Comments** are hidden text placed in a document for informational purposes. You can use the Comments feature in several ways. For example, comments can serve as reminders about tasks that need to be completed or they can prompt you to get a question answered. When others review or edit a document, they can use comments to insert their notes rather than

MENU TIP

To convert footnotes to endnotes or vice versa, you can open the Footnote and Endnote dialog box, click the Options button, and then click the Convert button.

QUICK TIP

If you need to quickly find a particular footnote or endnote, you use the Go To tab in the Find and Replace dialog box.

MOUSE TIP

You can remove the separator line, if desired, by displaying the note pane, clicking Footnote Separator in the Footnote list box, selecting the line, and pressing the DELETE key.

chapter
nineteen

keying their notes directly into the text. This makes it easy to read and remove the notes by reviewing and deleting the comments. Word provides a special toolbar, the Reviewing toolbar, with buttons to insert, edit, and delete comments.

The hire date for Susan Jones in the *Chapter Update With Endnotes* document must be verified before the document is finalized. You add a comment to remind yourself to do this. To insert a comment:

Step 1	*View*	the Reviewing toolbar with the toolbar shortcut menu
Step 2	*Position*	the toolbar immediately below the Formatting toolbar, if necessary
Step 3	*Select*	the text "June 1" in the first body paragraph
Step 4	*Click*	the Insert Comment button on the Reviewing toolbar

The comment pane that opens at the bottom of the screen should look similar to Figure 19-4.

FIGURE 19-4
Comment Pane

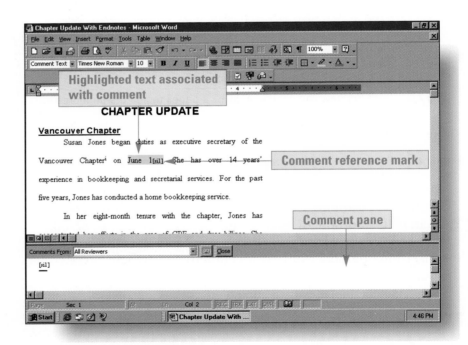

The comment pane, similar to the note pane, contains a comment reference mark—bracketed initials, and the number 1—and the insertion point so you can key the comment text. The initials are those listed in the <u>U</u>ser Information tab in the Options dialog box. The selected text is highlighted in yellow. You add the comment text.

| Step 5 | *Key* | Confirm this date with Dave. |
| Step 6 | *Close* | the comment pane |

You view comments by moving the mouse pointer to the yellow, highlighted text to open a ScreenTip containing the comment text. To view the comment text:

Step 1	*Move*	the mouse pointer to the yellow highlighted text "June 1"
Step 2	*Observe*	the mouse pointer shape and the comment text in the ScreenTip
Step 3	*Save*	the document as *Chapter Update With Comments*
Step 4	*Close*	the Reviewing toolbar

Word continues to consecutively number the comments, even when you add, delete, or revise them. If multiple reviewers comment on same document, their initials appear in the appropriate comment reference marks.

You expect more chapter secretaries to provide updated information for the newsletter. As the document gets larger, you need a way to quickly find each chapter's information. You can use bookmarks to do this.

19.c   Using Bookmarks

A **bookmark** is a reference point in a document. Bookmarks are helpful when you need an efficient way to locate text in a large document. The Bookmark feature places hidden brackets around referenced text, which allows Word to quickly locate and select the text. You insert and remove bookmarks with the Boo<u>k</u>mark command on the <u>I</u>nsert menu.

You want to quickly reference individual chapter paragraphs in the *Chapter Update With Comments* document. To insert a bookmark around the Vancouver paragraphs:

| Step 1 | *Select* | the two body paragraphs below the Vancouver paragraph heading |

chapter
nineteen

QUICK TIP

Bookmark names must begin with a letter and cannot contain spaces.

Step 2	*Click*	Insert
Step 3	*Click*	Bookmark
Step 4	*Key*	Vancouver in the Bookmark name: text box
Step 5	*Click*	Add
Step 6	*Deselect*	the text

You insert other bookmarks the same way. To add a bookmark for the Chicago paragraphs:

| Step 1 | *Select* | the two Chicago paragraphs |
| Step 2 | *Create* | a bookmark named "Chicago" |

Now that the bookmarks are in place, you test them. To locate the Vancouver text:

Step 1	*Double-click*	the status bar (not on a mode indicator) to open the Go To tab in the Find and Replace dialog box
Step 2	*Click*	Bookmark in the Go to what: list box
Step 3	*Select*	Vancouver in the Enter bookmark name: list box, if necessary
Step 4	*Click*	Go To
Step 5	*Close*	the Find and Replace dialog box
Step 6	*Observe*	that the bookmarked text is selected
Step 7	*Deselect*	the text
Step 8	*Go To*	the Chicago bookmark
Step 9	*Close*	the Find and Replace dialog box
Step 10	*Observe*	the bookmarked text
Step 11	*Deselect*	the text
Step 12	*Save*	the document as *Chapter Update With Bookmarks*

Another tool you can use to quickly locate text in a document is the Document Map.

19.d Using the Document Map

The **Document Map** feature helps you move the insertion point quickly to different paragraphs in a large document. When you turn on the Document Map your screen splits into two panes: the left pane contains the Document Map with a list of paragraph headings and the right pane contains the document text. When you click a heading in the Document Map, the insertion point moves to that paragraph heading in the document text in the right pane. To be recognized by the Document Map feature, the paragraph headings must be formatted with a built-in heading style (Heading 1 through 9) or an <u>O</u>utline-level: paragraph format (Level 1 through 9 in the Paragraph dialog box).

To open the Document Map for the *Chapter Update With Bookmarks* document:

Step 1	*Move*	the insertion point to the top of the document
Step 2	*Click*	the Document Map button 🔲 on the Standard toolbar
Step 3	*Observe*	the Document Map with headings in the left pane and the document text in the right pane

Your screen should look similar to Figure 19-5.

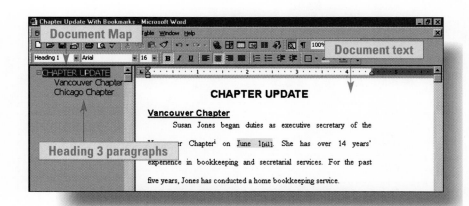

MENU TIP

You can view the Document Map by clicking the <u>D</u>ocument Map command on the <u>V</u>iew menu.

You can choose to view different levels of detail in the Document Map by right-clicking the Document Map to view the shortcut menu and then clicking the Heading level you want to see.

FIGURE 19-5
Document Map of Chapter Update

You can select how many levels of headings to view, just like when you work with an outline. If the Heading 3 paragraphs do not appear in the Document Map, you can display them. To show Heading 1 through Heading 3 paragraphs:

Step 1	*Right-click*	the Document Map pane

chapter
nineteen

MOUSE TIP

You can resize the Document Map by dragging the map pane's right boundary with the mouse pointer. You can close the Document Map by double-clicking its boundary.

MENU TIP

To quickly find a footnote, endnote, comment, or bookmark, click the Go To command on the Edit menu.

| Step 2 | *Click* | Show Heading 3 |

You can click any heading to move quickly to that location in the document. To move the insertion point to the Chicago Chapter paragraph:

| Step 1 | *Click* | the Chicago Chapter heading in the Document Map |
| Step 2 | *Observe* | that the insertion point moves to the Chicago Chapter paragraph heading in the right pane |

The helpfulness of the Document Map becomes even clearer when you work with a very long document. To close the Document Map and the document:

| Step 1 | *Click* | the Document Map button on the Standard toolbar |
| Step 2 | *Close* | the document without saving any changes |

You find the document notation features extremely helpful as you create documents.

Summary

► Creating footnotes and endnotes allows you to document sources of quotations, facts, and ideas used in a report.

► Word automatically numbers footnotes and endnotes as you create them and renumbers them sequentially as you add or remove them.

► You view and edit footnotes and endnotes in the note pane in Normal view.

► You can edit footnotes and endnotes directly in the document in Print Layout view.

► Footnotes can be deleted or converted to endnotes; endnotes can be deleted or converted to footnotes.

► Comments are hidden text that adds information to the document.

► Bookmarks are an efficient way to mark and then locate specific text in a large document.

► The Document Map quickly locates specific paragraph headings in a document.

Commands Review

Action	Menu Bar	Shortcut Menu	Toolbar	Keyboard
Insert a footnote	Insert, Footnote			ALT + I, N ALT + CTRL + F
Insert an endnote	Insert, Footnote			ALT + I, N ALT + CTRL + D
Insert a comment	Insert, Comment		🖉	ALT + I, M ALT + CTRL + M
Delete a comment		Right-click comment, click Delete Comment	🖉	
Insert a bookmark	Insert, Bookmark			ALT + I, K
Open the Document Map	View, Document Map		🖻	ALT + V, D
Move the insertion point to a specific footnote, endnote, bookmark, or comment	Edit, Go To			ALT + E, G CTRL + G F5

Concepts Review

Circle the correct answer.

1. You create a bookmark with the:
- **[a]** Insert command on the File menu.
- **[b]** Bookmark command on the Insert menu.
- **[c]** Insert command on the Format menu.
- **[d]** Bookmark command on the Edit menu.

2. Comments are:
- **[a]** hidden text that does not affect document text.
- **[b]** a quick way to find and select specific text.
- **[c]** a method of documenting sources of quotations, facts, and ideas.
- **[d]** viewed in the Document Map.

3. In Normal view, footnotes and endnotes are edited in the:
- **[a]** note pane.
- **[b]** Document Map.
- **[c]** Bookmark dialog box.
- **[d]** comment pane.

4. Endnotes:
- **[a]** are inserted at the bottom of each page.
- **[b]** show the user's initials in the reference mark.
- **[c]** can be placed on a separate page at the end of the document.
- **[d]** add hidden text to a document.

5. To view paragraph headings in the Document Map, they must be formatted with:
- **[a]** bold or underline formatting.
- **[b]** heading styles or outline-level paragraph formats.
- **[c]** uppercase formatting.
- **[d]** bookmarks.

6. The initials that appear in the comment reference can be modified in the:
- **[a]** Font dialog box.
- **[b]** note pane.
- **[c]** Options dialog box.
- **[d]** comment pane.

7. To quickly open the note or comments pane, you can:
[a] double-click the note or comment reference.
[b] drag the note or comment reference mark to the bottom of the screen.
[c] click the Note and Comments View button on the Reviewing toolbar.
[d] double-click the REC mode indicator on the status bar.

8. The Document Map allows you to:
[a] display reviewer notes.
[b] highlight text.
[c] quickly find specific text.
[d] browse a document by paragraph headings.

9. Footnotes and endnotes consist of the note text and a:
[a] bookmark.
[b] comment.
[c] review button.
[d] reference mark.

10. The default footnote numbering pattern is:
[a] A, B, C.
[b] I, II, III.
[c] i, ii, iii.
[d] 1, 2, 3.

Circle **T** if the statement is true or **F** is the statement is false.

T   F   1. Bookmarks are used to document sources of quotations, facts, and ideas in a report.

T   F   2. Footnotes are listed at the end of the document.

T   F   3. Word automatically numbers footnotes and endnotes inserted in a document.

T   F   4. If you decide to use endnotes instead of footnotes after the footnotes are created, you must delete the footnotes and then create the endnotes.

T   F   5. You can see the actual footnote at the bottom of each page when viewing the document in Print Layout view.

T   F   6. You insert, edit, and delete comments by using buttons on the Reviewing toolbar.

T   F   7. When you need to add information that is not part of the document, you insert a bookmark.

T   F   8. By default, endnotes appear on a separate page at the end of the document text.

T   F   9. A comment is a reference point in a document.

T   F   10. To quickly find a bookmark, comment, endnote, or footnote, you can use the Go To command on the Edit menu.

chapter nineteen

Skills Review

Exercise 1

1. Open *The Internet* document located on the Data Disk.

2. View the Document Map.

3. Show the Heading 2 levels.

4. Move to the "Internet Challenges" text.

5. Show all levels.

6. Move to the "Defining the Internet" text.

7. Close the Document Map.

8. Close the document without saving any changes.

Exercise 2

1. Open the *Answering The Telephone* document located on the Data Disk.

2. Add the following footnote at the end of the document. Indent the first line of the note.
John Spencer and Adrian Pruss, <u>The Professional Secretary's Handbook: Communication Skills</u> (New York: Barron's Educational Series, Inc., 1997), 63.

3. Add a bookmark at the last sentence. The bookmark name should be "promise."

4. Select the last sentence using the bookmark.

5. Print the selection.

6. Save the document as *Answering The Telephone With Footnote*.

7. Preview, print, and close the document.

Exercise 3

1. Open the *Answering The Telephone With Footnote* document you created in Exercise 2.

2. Convert the footnote to an endnote.

3. Place the endnotes on a separate page at the end of the document.

4. Remove the bookmark from the last sentence.

5. Save the document as *Answering The Telephone With Endnote*.

6. Preview, print, and close the document.

Exercise 4

1. Open the *Extending Your Vocabulary* document located on the Data Disk.

2. Add the following endnote at the end of the paragraph. Place the endnote on a separate page at the end of the document. Center the title "ENDNOTES" two lines above the endnote.
John Spencer and Adrian Pruss, <u>The Professional Secretary's Handbook: Communication Skills</u> (New York: Barron's Educational Series, Inc., 1997), 120.

3. Select the four vocabulary ranges at the end of the second sentence and insert a comment. The text for the comment should be "Give an example of each vocabulary range."

4. Save the document as *Extending Your Vocabulary With Endnote*.

5. Preview, print, and close the document.

Exercise 5

1. Open the *Extending Your Vocabulary With Endnote* document you created in Exercise 4.

2. Convert the endnote to a footnote.

3. The footnote should appear at the bottom of the page. Delete the page break and title "ENDNOTES."

4. Remove the comment from the second sentence. (*Hint:* Use a button on the Reviewing toolbar to remove the selected comment.)

5. Save the document as *Extending Your Vocabulary With Footnote*.

6. Preview, print, and close the document.

Exercise 6

1. Open the *Preparing Manuscripts* document located on the Data Disk.

2. Create the following endnotes. The first endnote appears at the end of the first sentence in the first paragraph. The second endnote appears at the end of the second paragraph. Indent the first line of each note.
Joseph Gibaldi, <u>MLA Style Manual and Guide to Scholarly Publishing</u>, 2nd ed. (New York: The Modern Language Association of America, 1998), 291.
John Grossman, ed. <u>The Chicago Manual of Style</u>, 14th ed. (Chicago: The University of Chicago Press, 1993), 495.

3. Place the endnotes on a separate page at the end of the document. Center the title "ENDNOTES" above the endnotes.

4. Switch to Print Layout view. Add a blank line between the two endnotes.

5. Insert a comment at the end of the first paragraph. The text should be "See what The Chicago Manual of Style recommends."

6. Save the document as *Preparing Manuscripts With Endnotes*.

7. Preview, print, and close the document.

chapter nineteen

Exercise 7

1. Open the *Preparing Manuscripts With Endnotes* document you created in Exercise 6.

2. Convert the endnotes to footnotes.

3. The footnotes should appear at the bottom of the page. Delete the page break and title "ENDNOTES."

4. Save the document as *Preparing Manuscripts With Footnotes*.

5. Preview, print, and close the document.

Exercise 8

1. Create the document shown below. Use the default margins and font.

> Worldwide Exotic Foods, Inc. is one of the fastest-growing distributors of specialty food items. Worldwide Exotic Foods has branch offices in Chicago, Illinois, Melbourne, Australia, Vancouver, Canada, and London, England, and specializes in supplying high-quality and unusual food products to customers around the world.

2. Add the following footnote at the end of the paragraph. Use an em dash between the company name and the Web page URL.
Worldwide Exotic Foods, Inc.—http://www.wwide.com

3. Save the document as *Company Profile With Footnote*.

4. Preview, print, and close the document.

Case Projects

Project 1

The next monthly meeting of the International Association of Executive Assistants includes a 10-minute presentation on troubleshooting working with footnotes and endnotes. You prepare the outline for the presentation. Using the Office Assistant, research footnote and endnote troubleshooting topics. Create an outline itemizing five troubleshooting topics, including possible solutions to the problem. Add a footnote reference to each topic, identifying the online Help page. Save, preview, and print the outline.

Project 2

You are writing an article about document notations for the next International Association of Executive Assistants newsletter; you want to include information about using style guides and documenting an online source. Using the keyword phrases "style guides" and "documenting online sources," search the Web for sites that describe style guides and how to document an online source. Print at least five Web pages. Using your Web sources, create an unbound report document describing several style guides and how to document an online source. Use footnotes or endnotes appropriately formatted for online sources to identify the sources of your information. Save, preview, and print the report.

Project 3

B. J. Chang asks you to prepare a three-paragraph report concerning a major Internet industry news topic for his next department meeting. You should include quotes from news sources. Using newspapers, magazines, and the Web, select a current news topic about the Internet and create an unbound report document discussing the topic. Add footnotes or endnotes referencing the source of any quotes, facts, or ideas used in the report including appropriately formatted online sources (refer to Project 2). Add an explanatory comment on any proper name used in the report. Save, preview, and print the report.

Project 4

Jody Haversham calls to ask how to change the number format of the footnotes in a document she just created. Research the topic and write Jody a brief explanatory interoffice memorandum explaining how to do this. Save, preview, and print the memorandum.

Project 5

Although she often creates very large documents, Marisa DaFranco has never used the Document Map. You want to explain to her how easy it is to use. Open the large document of your choice and create and/or format paragraph headings with the Outline level: paragraph formats found in the Paragraph dialog box. Preview and then save the document with a new name. Use the Document Map to review the document. Write Marisa an interoffice memorandum explaining how to use the Document Map and include the document formatting requirements. Save, preview, and print the memorandum.

Project 6

Marinda Jefferson, who works in the accounting department, often inserts follow-up comments in her documents. She wants the comment initials to be "acc" for the accounting department but doesn't know how to change them from her personal initials. If necessary, use online Help to research how to do this. Create an e-mail message on a blank document explaining to Marinda how to change the initials for her comments. Save, preview, and print the document.

chapter nineteen

Project 7

You created a large document that includes several comments and now you want to print the document and the comments. You ask Libby, who is in an office next door to the association office, if comments can be printed. She says she knows they can be printed, but she isn't certain how to do it. Review the print options in the Options dialog box, the Print dialog box, and any other Word source to find the answer to your question. Then, open a document of your choice and insert at least five comments at different locations in the document. Save the document with a new name, preview it, and print it together with the document comments.

Project 8

You know that Word inserts brackets ([ ]) around bookmarked text but have never seen these brackets when working with a document that contains bookmarks. You think viewing the brackets could help identify bookmarked text and want to know how to view them. Use online Help to research how to show the brackets associated with bookmarks. Open a document of your choice, insert a bookmark, and then view the brackets. Turn off the view of the brackets and close the document without saving any changes. Create a Web page, using the theme of your choice, to describe how to create and use bookmarks. Include step-by-step instructions that explain how to create, use, and delete bookmarks, and how to view the bookmark brackets. Save, preview, and print the Web page.

Using Desktop Publishing Features

Chapter Overview

Y ou can add a professional appearance to your documents by the attractive spacing of text, use of decorative borders and shading, and placement of graphics and specially formatted text called WordArt. In this chapter you learn how to apply these finishing touches to your documents.

LEARNING OBJECTIVES

- ▶ Use text flow options
- ▶ Appying borders and shading to paragraphs
- ▶ Create and edit WordArt special text effects
- ▶ Insert, position, and delete graphics
- ▶ Use the drop-cap effect
- ▶ Insert and edit text boxes
- ▶ Create watermarks

Case profile

Bill Martin, in the human resources department, is on vacation and you are assigned to assist B. J. Chang while Bill is out of the office. Bill has keyed several documents and has started formatting them. He leaves you instructions to use character spacing, borders and shading, graphics, and WordArt to give the documents an attractive, professional appearance.

chapter twenty

20.a Using Text Flow Options

Readers often give more credibility to the content of a document if the document is attractively arranged on the page; therefore, the appearance of the text is very important. Word provides text flow options that allow you to keep single lines from flowing to the top of an additional page, to control page breaks within paragraphs, to control the amount of space between paragraphs and characters, and to create "hard" spaces that keep text on the same line.

Controlling Widows and Orphans and Keeping Lines Together

Single lines stranded alone on a page can detract from a paragraph's appearance and message. A **widow** line is the last line of a paragraph that appears by itself at the top of a following page. An **orphan** line is the first line of a paragraph that appears by itself at the bottom of a page. By default the Word option that controls widow and orphan lines is turned on in the Line and Page Breaks tab of the Paragraph dialog box. Keeping lines together on a page prevents Word from placing a page break inside a paragraph. You can also prevent page breaks from occurring between selected paragraphs or force a manual page break to occur before a specific paragraph. You set these options in the Line and Page Breaks tab in the Paragraph dialog box.

The first document Bill wants you to complete is the November newsletter. You verify that the document is set for Widow/Orphan control. To view the Widow/Orphan control option and line break options:

Step 1	*Open*	the *November Newsletter* document located on the Data Disk
Step 2	*Open*	the Paragraph dialog box
Step 3	*Click*	the Line and Page Breaks tab

The dialog box that opens on your screen should look similar to Figure 20-1.

Step 4	*Verify*	the Widow/Orphan Control check box contains a check mark

FIGURE 20-1
Line and Page Breaks Tab
in the Paragraph Dialog Box

To change the default setting, you can remove the check mark from the Widow/Orphan control check box. You can also set other line break options in this tab.

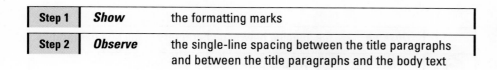

| Step 5 | *Use* | the dialog box Help button to review all the options |
| Step 6 | *Close* | the dialog box |

During pagination, Word won't split a paragraph between pages unless at least two lines appear on each page.

Adjusting Paragraph Spacing

Bill leaves instructions for you to modify the character spacing in the November newsletter title and to add extra white space after each line in the title. To review the title lines character and paragraph spacing:

| Step 1 | *Show* | the formatting marks |
| Step 2 | *Observe* | the single-line spacing between the title paragraphs and between the title paragraphs and the body text |

chapter
twenty

The single hard return between the first and second lines of the title and between the title and the following body text paragraphs do not add enough space. But two hard returns would add too much space. A half line of space after each title paragraph would provide an attractive amount of white space. In much typeset material, including the text you are reading, 12 points is the equivalent of a full line; 6 points is the equivalent of a half line. You can specify the number of points of white space before or after a paragraph in the Paragraph dialog box. To adjust the spacing of the title paragraphs:

| Step 1 | *Select* | the two title paragraphs in Section 1 |
| Step 2 | *Open* | the Indents and Spacing tab in the Paragraph dialog box |

The Spacing group provides options for changing the amount of white space between paragraphs. You add 6 points of white space after each line of the title.

Step 3	*Key*	6 in the After: text box
Step 4	*Click*	OK
Step 5	*Deselect*	the text

The spacing between the title paragraphs has changed to 6 points, or a half line. Now you want to make the title paragraphs easier to read by adding additional space between the characters.

Spacing Between Characters

The Character Spacing tab in the Font dialog box provides options for expanding or condensing the amount of space between the characters in your document. You expand the space between the characters of the two title paragraphs. The extra spacing makes the uppercase title easier to read. To add space between the characters in the title paragraphs:

Step 1	*Observe*	the spacing between characters in the title paragraphs
Step 2	*Select*	the two title paragraphs in Section 1
Step 3	*Open*	the Character Spacing tab in the Font dialog box

The Font dialog box on your screen should look similar to Figure 20-2.

Character spacing options

FIGURE 20-2
Character Spacing Tab in
the Font Dialog Box

The default character spacing in the Spacing: list box is Normal, based on the default spacing for the current font. You can expand or condense the spacing between characters by the amount you key or select in points in the Spacing By: text box. The Position: list box provides options for placing characters in relation to the **baseline**, the invisible horizontal line at the bottom of a line of text. You can place characters Raised above the baseline or Lowered below the baseline. The default position is Normal or on the baseline. Use the Position By: text box to specify the exact point measurement in relation to the baseline. To expand the space between the letters in the heading paragraphs:

Step 1	*Click*	the Spacing: list arrow
Step 2	*Click*	Expanded
Step 3	*Observe*	text is automatically expanded by 1 point in the By: text box
Step 4	*Key*	2 in the By: text box to change the setting to 2 points
Step 5	*Click*	OK
Step 6	*Deselect*	the text
Step 7	*Observe*	the new character spacing in the title lines

When you want words or characters separated by a space to always remain together on the same line, you can use a nonbreaking space.

QUICK TIP

Kerning changes the amount of space between any two adjacent characters in order to improve the overall appearance of the text. The amount of increase or decrease in the white space depends on the font you use and which characters you are modifying. For more information about kerning, see online Help.

chapter twenty

Inserting Nonbreaking Spaces

Nonbreaking spaces are "hard" spaces you insert in a document to keep text separated by the space on the same line. The birthday acknowledgment paragraph at the top of the second column in the *November Newsletter* document contains a reference to Conference Room 4. Because the text wraps to fit in the column, the number "4" wraps to the next line. It is easier to read the text if the number "4" remains with at least part of the preceding text. You insert a nonbreaking space to keep the text "Room 4" together on the same line.

To insert a nonbreaking space:

Step 1	***Select***	the space between the word "Room" and the number "4" in the paragraph at the top of the second column
Step 2	***Press & Hold***	the CTRL + SHIFT keys
Step 3	***Press***	the SPACEBAR
Step 4	***Observe***	that the word "Room" moves to the next line with the number "4" and a nonbreaking space symbol is inserted

Your screen should look similar to Figure 20-3.

FIGURE 20-3
November Newsletter

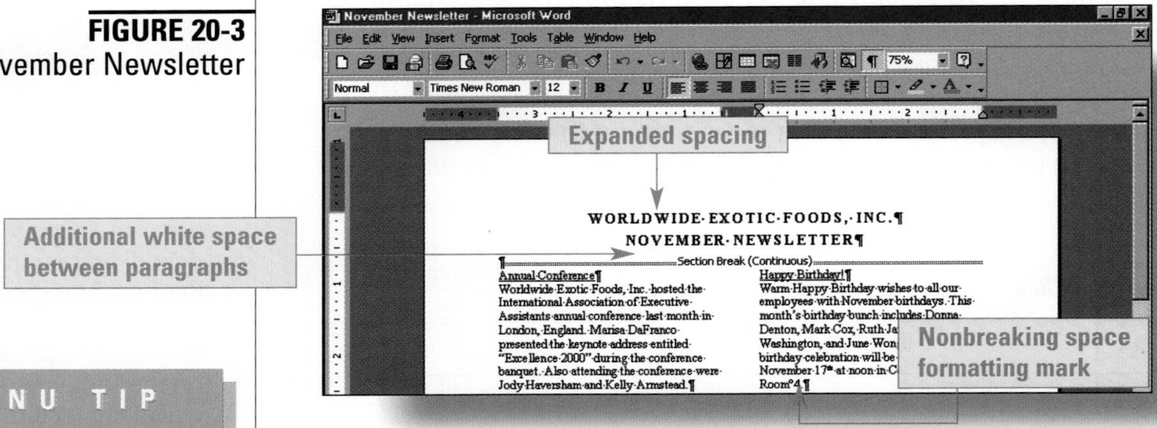

Step 5	***Save***	the document as *November Newsletter Revised*

You can use borders and shading to dress up documents, such as newsletters.

QUICK TIP

You can prevent a hyphenated word from breaking at the right margin by inserting a nonbreaking hyphen by pressing the CTRL + SHIFT + HYPHEN (-) keys.

MENU TIP

You can insert nonbreaking spaces by clicking the Symbol command on the Insert menu, clicking the Special Characters tab in the Symbol dialog box, and then double-clicking Nonbreaking Space.

20.b Applying Borders and Shading to Paragraphs

Borders and shading can make your document more pleasing to the eye and emphasize specific portions or items. You can apply borders to selected text and individual paragraphs. You can apply page borders to the entire document, a section, the first page of a section, or all pages except the first page. Borders and shading options are available in the Borders and Shading dialog box or with buttons on the Tables and Borders toolbar or the Formatting toolbar.

Applying and Modifying Paragraph Borders

You want to draw attention to the annual meeting reminder paragraph in the *November Newsletter Revised* document. You decide to place a border around it using the Tables and Borders toolbar. To select the paragraph and add a border:

Step 1	*Display*	the Tables and Borders toolbar
Step 2	*Select*	the "Reminder! Annual Meeting" paragraph heading and following paragraph in the first column
Step 3	*Apply*	a ½ point, single dashed line style, outside border using buttons on the Tables and Borders toolbar

The border appears around the selected paragraphs, but it doesn't stand out quite enough. You can modify a paragraph border by reselecting the paragraph, selecting different formatting options, and reapplying the border. To modify the border to a ¾ point, double-line style border:

Step 1	*Select*	the "Reminder! Annual Meeting" paragraph heading and the following paragraph, if necessary
Step 2	*Change*	the border to a ¾ point, double-line style, outside border using buttons on the Tables and Borders toolbar
Step 3	*Center*	the paragraphs inside the border
Step 4	*Deselect*	the text

To make the entire page more interesting you can add an art border around the edge of the page.

chapter
twenty

Creating and Modifying Page Borders

You can add, modify, or remove page borders with options in the Borders and Shading dialog box. You can choose from a preset border or create a custom border by selecting the line style, color, and width. Word also provides border art you can use as a page border. To add a page border to the *November Newsletter Revised* document:

Step 1	*Open*	the Page Border tab in the Borders and Shading dialog box

The dialog box tab that opens on your screen should look similar to Figure 20-4.

FIGURE 20-4
Page Border Tab in the
Borders and Shading
Dialog Box

Preset border options →

Border art list →

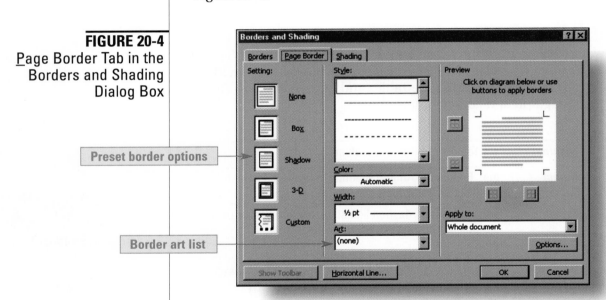

You want to add a border of flowers around the edge of the page. To do this, you select the border style and art.

Step 2	*Click*	the Box preset option
Step 3	*Click*	the Art: list arrow
Step 4	*Click*	the suns (the twentieth option)
Step 5	*Observe*	the border preview
Step 6	*Verify*	that the border is applied to Whole document
Step 7	*Click*	OK

| Step 8 | *Zoom* | the document to Whole Page to view the paragraph and page borders |

An alternative method to emphasize text is to add shading.

Applying Paragraph and Section Shading

Now that the document has a colorful border, you decide to add complementary shading to the title paragraphs in Section 1. You can add shading from the Shading tab in the Borders and Shading dialog box or with a button on the Tables and Borders toolbar. To add shading to the title paragraphs:

Step 1	*Select*	the two title paragraphs
Step 2	*Click*	the Shading Color button list arrow on the Tables and Borders toolbar
Step 3	*Click*	Gold (the second color in the seventh row)
Step 4	*Deselect*	the text

Your screen should look similar to Figure 20-5.

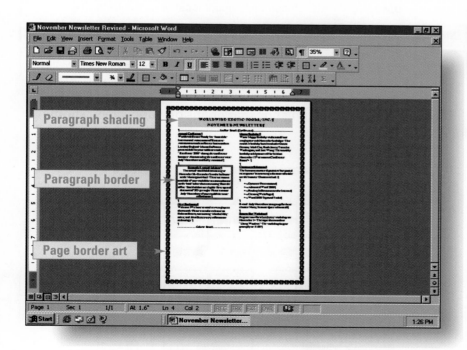

FIGURE 20-5
Newsletter with Page Border and Shaded Titles

> **QUICK TIP**
>
> By default, paragraph shading is applied from margin to margin. If you want the shading to appear with only the paragraph text, you can indent the paragraph from the left and right margins or select just the text and apply text shading.

| Step 5 | *Save* | the document and close it |

chapter
twenty

| Step 6 | **Close** | the Tables and Borders toolbar |

Bill wants you to add special text effects to a document announcing the latest travel bargain from Worldwide Exotic Foods, Inc. travel services. You create the special text effects with WordArt.

C 20.c Creating and Editing WordArt Special Text Effects

MENU TIP

You can create special text effects by clicking the <u>I</u>nsert menu, pointing to <u>P</u>icture, and then clicking the <u>W</u>ordArt command.

CAUTION TIP

Because a WordArt object is a drawing object and not regular text, you cannot use the Spelling & Grammar feature to check the WordArt object text spelling.

The **WordArt** feature allows you to draw and format objects that contain text. You can add special effects to WordArt object text by adding shadows and changing the text shape. You edit WordArt objects just like drawing objects to add fill color, change the line style or color, or add 3-D effects. You want to add a WordArt title to the partially completed *Bonaire* document. To open the document and the Drawing toolbar:

Step 1	**Open**	the *Bonaire* document located on the Data Disk
Step 2	**Display**	the Drawing toolbar
Step 3	**Click**	the Insert WordArt button on the Drawing toolbar

The WordArt Gallery dialog box that opens on your screen should look similar to Figure 20-6.

FIGURE 20-6
WordArt Gallery
Dialog Box

First, you select a WordArt style in this dialog box and then you key the WordArt text in the Edit WordArt Text dialog box. To create the WordArt:

Step 1	*Double-click*	the fourth WordArt style in the second row
Step 2	*Key*	BONAIRE in the Edit WordArt Text dialog box
Step 3	*Click*	48 in the <u>S</u>ize: list box
Step 4	*Click*	OK

The selected WordArt object and the WordArt toolbar both appear on your screen, which should look similar to Figure 20-7.

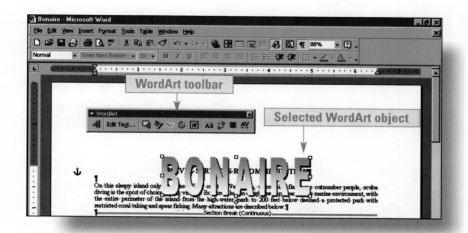

FIGURE 20-7
WordArt Object and Toolbar

You can now move, size, and edit this WordArt object just like any other drawing object. The Word Art drawing object is "anchored" or attached to the first paragraph. This means if you move the paragraph text, the Word Art object also moves with the text. You can edit the Word Art object to turn off the anchor with a shortcut menu. To move the WordArt object above the text and change its shape:

Step 1	*Drag*	the WordArt drawing object to center it above the "TRAVEL SERVICES RECOMMENDATION" text
Step 2	*Click*	the WordArt Shape button ![Abc] on the WordArt toolbar
Step 3	*Click*	the Wave 1 shape on the grid (the fifth shape in the third row)
Step 4	*Deselect*	the WordArt object
Step 5	*Save*	the document as *Bonaire Revised*

**chapter
twenty**

Now you want to insert a graphic image or picture to the Boca Cai text in the second column.

 ## 20.d Inserting, Positioning, and Deleting Graphics

Word comes with a set of pictures you can access from the Clip Gallery. You can import pictures into the Clip Gallery from other sources or you can insert pictures in your document from disk files without first importing them into the Clip Gallery.

 notes
Your Clip Gallery might contain different pictures than the ones used in this chapter. You can substitute pictures from those available in your Clip Gallery in the activities in this chapter, if necessary.

You want to insert a picture at the bottom of the *Bonaire Revised* document. To position the insertion point and open the Clip Gallery:

Step 1	*Press*	the CTRL + END keys to move the insertion point to the bottom of the document (bottom of the second column)
Step 2	*Press*	the ENTER key
Step 3	*Click*	the Insert Clip Art button 🖼 on the Drawing toolbar
Step 4	*Click*	the Pictures tab, if necessary

The Insert ClipArt window that opens on your screen should look similar to Figure 20-8.

In addition to importing clips from other sources, you can go directly to a special Web page containing additional clips and import them directly into the Clip Gallery with the Clips Online button. The Clip Gallery has its own Help files you can view by clicking the Help button at the top of the dialog box. You can first select a category of clip art (picture), and then insert the desired picture into your document. You can also quickly find clip art by searching the Clip Gallery using keywords.

To search for an appropriate picture using the keyword "sun":

Step 1	*Key*	sun in the Search for clips: text box
Step 2	*Press*	the ENTER key
Step 3	*Observe*	the search icon as Word searches the Clip Gallery for the appropriate pictures
Step 4	*Scroll*	to view the related clips that appear in the Pictures tab when the search is finished

You want to use the "summer" clip. To insert the clip:

| Step 1 | *Click* | the Summer icon (the large sunshine face with sunglasses) to view the pop-up menu |

Your screen should look similar to Figure 20-9.

You can insert the picture in your document, preview the picture in a larger view, add the picture to other Clip Gallery categories, and look for other pictures with similar style, color and shape, or by identifying keyword with buttons on this pop-up menu.

QUICK TIP

You can leave the Insert ClipArt dialog box open in a smaller window while you work on your document by clicking the Change to Small Window button in the upper-right corner of the dialog box.

MENU TIP

You can also use a shortcut menu in the Clip Gallery to insert or copy a picture or view a picture's properties by right-clicking a picture, and then clicking the appropriate command.

**chapter
twenty**

FIGURE 20-9
Selected Clip in the
Clip Gallery

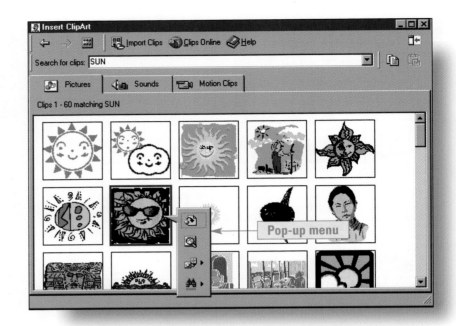

MOUSE TIP

You can use the drag-and-drop feature or copy and paste a picture from the Clip Gallery to your document. To use drag-and-drop, open the Insert ClipArt dialog box, locate the desired clip, and drag it out of the dialog box into your document. To copy and paste, open the Insert ClipArt dialog box, select the desired clip, click the Copy button at the top of the dialog box and then paste the clip into your document.

| Step 2 | *Click* | the Insert clip button 🔲 on the pop-up menu |
| Step 3 | *Close* | the Insert ClipArt window |

Now that the Summer clip is in the document, you need to move and resize it. First you click the picture to select it for editing, sizing, or repositioning. When you select a picture object, the Picture toolbar should appear. If is does not automatically appear, you can use the shortcut menu to show it. The Picture toolbar has buttons you use to edit the picture. You can size a picture object with the mouse by dragging a sizing handle—just as you size drawing objects. To select and size the Summer picture object:

| Step 1 | *Click* | the picture to select it |
| Step 2 | *Drag* | the lower-right corner sizing handle diagonally up approximately ½ inch |

Using Advanced Text Alignment Features with Graphics

The default layout for picture objects and text is for the picture to be in line with the text. **In line** means that the picture is in the same line as text that appears before or after it. When a picture is in line with text, you can position it with the alignment buttons on the Formatting toolbar, just as you would text. If you want text to wrap around or through the picture, you select the Square, Tight, Behind Text, or In Front of Wrapping styles from the Format Picture dialog box or the Text Wrapping button on the Picture toolbar. When you select one of these options, you can reposition the picture by dragging it to a new location with the mouse pointer.

You can delete a picture the same way you delete a drawing object, by selecting the object and pressing the DELETE key.

To edit the text wrapping and reposition the picture object:

Step 1	*Verify*	the picture object is still selected
Step 2	*Click*	the Text Wrapping button ▥ on the Picture toolbar
Step 3	*Click*	Square
Step 4	*Observe*	that the picture object now has clear sizing handles and the mouse pointer becomes a move pointer when placed on the object
Step 5	*Drag*	the picture object to the beginning of the Boca Cai paragraph heading

The text shifts to accommodate the picture object. Because Bill will be printing and copying the *Bonaire* document in black and white, you want to use a black-and-white picture instead of a color picture. You can edit the Summer picture colors. To change the picture colors to black and white:

Step 1	*Verify*	the picture object is still selected
Step 2	*Click*	the Image Control button ▥ on the Picture toolbar
Step 3	*Click*	Black & White
Step 4	*Deselect*	the picture object

Your screen should look similar to Figure 20-10.

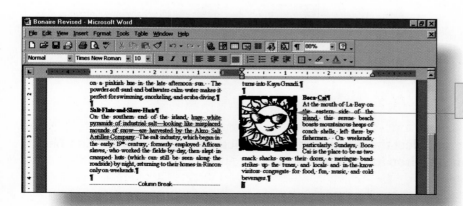

FIGURE 20-10
Summer Picture in Newsletter

Sized, positioned, and formatted picture

chapter twenty

Step 5	*Save*	the document

You also want to draw readers' attention to the first body paragraph in the document. You can do this with the drop-cap effect.

20.e Using the Drop-Cap Effect

A **drop cap** is an oversized capital first letter used to draw attention to the beginning of a paragraph or line of text. A drop cap can be positioned within the paragraph or to the left of the paragraph in the margin. You want to drop the character "O" in the word "On" at the beginning of the first paragraph.

To create a drop cap:

Step 1	*Click*	in the first body paragraph beginning "On this sleepy island" to select it
Step 2	*Click*	Format
Step 3	*Click*	Drop Cap

The Drop Cap dialog box that opens on your screen should look similar to Figure 20-11.

FIGURE 20-11
Drop Cap Dialog Box

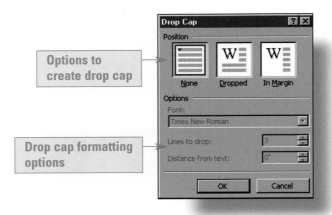

You select the position of the character, the font, and the number of lines to drop in this dialog box.

To drop the character three lines using the default font:

Step 1	**Double-click**	the <u>D</u>ropped icon
Step 2	**Deselect**	the text
Step 3	**Observe**	that the oversized character "O" dropped three lines at the beginning of the first paragraph

Your screen should look similar to Figure 20-12.

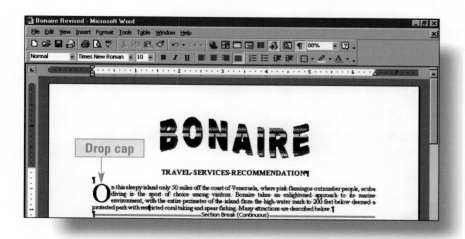

FIGURE 20-12
Dropped Cap Character

Step 4	**Save**	the document and close it

Text boxes allow you to easily reposition text in a document.

20.f Inserting and Editing Text Boxes

A **text box** is an invisible container for the text, tables, or charts you want to position in a document. By placing text in a text box, you can treat the text more like a graphic object than regular text. You format a text box in the same way you format an AutoShape. You format the text inside the text box just as you do with regular text.

Before he left, Bill created an announcement for the Office Technology Society. To draw the reader's eye to the OTS membership information,

MENU TIP

You can click the Text Box command on the <u>I</u>nsert menu to insert a text box.

QUICK TIP

A **callout** is a text box used to label a picture. Often the callout also includes a **leader**, or line, to draw the reader's eye from the picture to the label. You can use AutoShapes to create callouts with leaders.

chapter
twenty

he instructs you to place that portion of the text in a formatted text box and then position the text box at the right margin. To open the document, select the membership information, and create a text box:

Step 1	*Open*	the *Office Technology Announcement* document located on the Data Disk
Step 2	*Select*	the OTS MEMBERSHIP paragraph heading, numbered list, and following blank line
Step 3	*Click*	the Text Box button ▣ on the Drawing toolbar

A text box is placed around the text. Your screen should look similar to Figure 20-13.

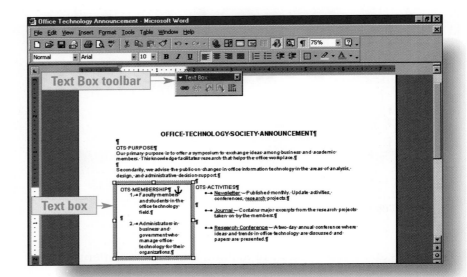

FIGURE 20-13
Membership Information in Selected Text Box

Not all the text inside the box is visible; therefore you need to size the text box and then reposition it. You can use the mouse pointer to size or reposition a text box. To size and reposition the text box:

Step 1	*Drag*	the middle sizing handle on the bottom boundary down until the remaining text appears
Step 2	*Drag*	the text box boundary up and to the right until the right edge of the text box is positioned at the right margin and the top of the text box is even with the OTS PURPOSE paragraph heading

QUICK TIP

You can create an empty text box and then key and format text inside the text box.

Step 3	*Deselect*	the text box
Step 4	*Save*	the document as *OTS Revised*
Step 5	*Zoom*	the document to Whole page to observe the text box placement

By default, a thin single-line border appears around a text box. You can add a customized border to a text box or remove the default border. You can also add fill color to a text box. To add a customized border and fill color:

Step 1	*Right-click*	the boundary of the text box
Step 2	*Click*	Format Text Box
Step 3	*Click*	the Colors and Lines tab, if necessary

You can add a solid-color fill that is semitransparent or completely opaque. To add a semitransparent fill color and a colored border:

Step 1	*Click*	the Color: list arrow in the Fill group
Step 2	*Click*	Light Turquoise (fifth color, fifth row)
Step 3	*Click*	the Semitransparent check box to select it
Step 4	*Click*	the Color: list arrow in the Line group
Step 5	*Click*	Red (first color, third row)
Step 6	*Click*	OK
Step 7	*Deselect*	the text box
Step 8	*Observe*	the formatted text box
Step 9	*Save*	the document and close it

Watermarks allow you to place a picture or graphic behind the text.

MENU TIP

You format a selected text box by clicking the Text Box command on the Format menu.

QUICK TIP

You can flow text from one text box to another by linking them. Insert an extra text box that is empty. Key text in another text box and then reduce its size so that not all of the text is visible. Right-click the text box and click the Create Text Box Link command. Click the empty text box. Any text not visible in the original text box "flows" into the empty text box. For more information on linking text boxes, see online Help.

chapter
twenty

20.g Creating Watermarks

A **watermark** is a picture or graphic image that appears faintly behind text in a document. You might use a watermark to add the text "DRAFT" or "CONFIDENTIAL" behind text or you can insert a company logo or picture as a watermark. To create a watermark, you first open the header and footer panes and then insert the Drawing object, AutoShape, or Graphic Watermark object. Even though the Watermark object is inserted into the header or footer pane, you can move it anywhere on the page after you position the picture behind the text.

The human resources department is hosting a retirement party for a long-time department employee, Richard Klaus. Bill leaves instructions for you to complete a memo inviting the department staff to the party. You open a partially completed memo and insert a WordArt watermark in the document. To insert a watermark:

Step 1	*Open*	the *Retirement Party Memo* document located on the Data Disk
Step 2	*View*	the header and footer panes
Step 3	*Insert*	the seniors picture from the Food & Dining category in the Clip Gallery
Step 4	*Close*	the Clip Gallery
Step 5	*Click*	the picture to select it

Before you can move a graphic watermark object, you must select the Behind Text wrapping option and then drag the Picture object to the desired position. To select the wrapping option and reposition the object:

Step 1	*Select*	the Behind Text wrapping option using the Picture toolbar
Step 2	*Enlarge*	the picture to approximately four times its original size using the mouse pointer
Step 3	*Reposition*	the picture attractively in the memo text using the mouse pointer

Contrast emphasizes the difference between the lighter and darker images in a picture. Adjusting the contrast can make the picture sharper and individual images stand out more. **Brightness** controls the relative darkness or lightness of the entire picture. If a picture is too dark, it is difficult to distinguish between individual images inside the picture. If a picture is too light, it has a washed-out appearance. Now you edit the picture for watermark shading and adjust its contrast and brightness. To edit the picture:

Step 1	*Verify*	the Picture object is selected
Step 2	*Click*	the Image Control button on the Picture toolbar
Step 3	*Click*	Watermark
Step 4	*Adjust*	the brightness and contrast using buttons on the Picture toolbar (the picture should be visible but very faint when the document is printed)
Step 5	*Close*	the header and footer panes
Step 6	*Observe*	the Watermark object behind the text
Step 7	*Save*	the document as *Retirement Party With Watermark* and close it

You can use watermarks along with the other desktop publishing features to create documents with attractive and professional appearances.

Summary

▶ Text flow options—such as controlling widow and orphan lines, line breaks, character spacing, nonbreaking spaces, and paragraph spacing—allow you to give your document a professional appearance.

▶ To add interest to your document, you can add borders and shading to individual paragraphs and pages.

▶ You can use WordArt drawing objects to add special text effects to your documents.

▶ You can insert, edit, and position pictures anywhere in a document.

▶ The drop-cap effect draws the reader's attention to a line or paragraph by enlarging the first character.

▶ You can treat text in a text box more like a graphic object than text.

▶ A watermark is a picture, graphic, or text box whose image appears faintly behind text in a document.

Commands Review

Action	Menu Bar	Shortcut Menu	Toolbar	Keyboard
Control Widow/Orphan lines and line breaks	Format, Paragraph	Right-click the text, click Paragraph		ALT + O, P
Change paragraph spacing	Format, Paragraph	Right-click the text, click Paragraph		ALT + O, P
Change character spacing	Format, Font	Right-click the text, click Font		ALT + O, F
Insert a nonbreaking space	Insert, Symbol			ALT + I, S CTRL + SHIFT + SPACEBAR
Add borders and shading	Format, Borders and Shading		various buttons on the Tables and Borders toolbar and the Formatting toolbar	ALT + O, B
Create WordArt drawing objects	Insert, Picture, WordArt			ALT + I, P, W
Insert a picture	Insert, Picture, Clip Art			ALT + I, P, C
Format a picture	Format, Picture	Right-click the picture, click Format Picture		ALT + O, I
Create a drop cap	Format, Drop Cap			ALT + O, D
Insert a text box	Insert, Text Box			ALT + I, X

Concepts Review

SCANS

Circle the correct answer.

1. Readers often give more credibility to a document's contents if the document is:
[a] double-spaced.
[b] printed in Landscape orientation.
[c] presented attractively on the page.
[d] unformatted.

2. A widow line is:
[a] an unformatted line of text.
[b] the first line of a paragraph that appears by itself at the bottom of the page.
[c] a poorly spaced line.
[d] the last line of a paragraph that appears by itself at the top of a following page.

3. Nonbreaking spaces are:
[a] used to wrap words or characters separated by a space.
[b] used only in text boxes.
[c] "hard" spaces that keep text together on the same line.
[d] used to hyphenate words.

4. An orphan line is:
[a] the first line of a paragraph appearing by itself at the top of a page.
[b] a line with extra spaces between the characters.
[c] the first line of a paragraph appearing by itself at the bottom of a page.
[d] the last line of a paragraph that appears by itself at the top of a following page.

chapter twenty

5. WordArt is a:
[a] text box with formatted text.
[b] container or box you insert around drawing objects.
[c] drawing object that contains special text effects.
[d] large capital letter in the first line of a paragraph.

6. By placing text in a text box, you can:
[a] change the orientation of text.
[b] edit the text shape.
[c] treat text more like a graphic object than text.
[d] enlarge the first character.

7. A drop cap is a(n):
[a] oversized capital letter.
[b] missing character.
[c] word positioned below the baseline.
[d] superscript character.

8. A watermark:
[a] must be inserted on the last page of a document.
[b] is a picture, text, or drawing object that appears faintly behind text in a document.
[c] is visible only in Normal view.
[d] cannot be moved or edited once it is created.

9. You add extra white space before and after a paragraph in the:
[a] Borders and Shading dialog box.
[b] Font dialog box.
[c] Paragraph dialog box.
[d] WordArt Gallery.

10. You can change the amount of white space between characters in the:
[a] Paragraph dialog box.
[b] WordArt Gallery.
[c] Font dialog box.
[d] Borders and Shading dialog box.

Circle **T** if the statement is true or **F** is the statement is false.

T   F   1. Once you insert a picture, you cannot move it to another location in your document.

T   F   2. The baseline is an invisible horizontal line at the bottom of a line of text.

T   F   3. Widow/Orphan control keeps the first and last lines of a paragraph with at least one other line of the paragraph on a page.

T   F   4. The WordArt feature allows you to draw and format objects that contain text effects.

T   F   5. Kerning changes the amount of space between two adjacent characters.

T   F   6. You cannot use AutoShapes or WordArt as watermark objects.

T   F   7. Paragraph borders extend from margin to margin.

T   F   8. Captions and callouts are used to format WordArt objects.

T   F   9. In-line pictures are those positioned behind the text.

T   F   10. A full line of spacing is 18 points and a half line of spacing is 9 points.

Skills Review

Exercise 1

1. Open the *Legislative Update* document located on the Data Disk.
2. Select the two-line title and expand the character spacing by 2 points.
3. Add 12-pt spacing after the "SENATE BILL 1004," "AWARD," and "WORKSHOPS" paragraphs.
4. Insert a nonbreaking space before the number "18" in the "SENATE BILL 1004" section.
5. Add a 2¼-pt, single-line style, preset shadow border around the two-line title. Add a Gray-15% shading fill.
6. Indent the two-line title 1 inch from the left and right margins.
7. Save the document as *Legislative Update Revised*.
8. Preview, print, and close the document.

Exercise 2

1. Open the *Legislative Update Revised* document you created in Exercise 1.
2. Remove the border and shading from the two-line title.
3. Change the page orientation to Landscape.
4. Change the top and bottom margins to ¾ inch and the left and right margins to 1 inch.
5. Apply a page border around the document. Select an art option of your choice.
6. Save the document as *Legislative Update With Page Border*.
7. Preview, print, and close the document.

Exercise 3

1. Open the *Announcements* document located on the Data Disk.
2. Format the entire document in two columns of even width.
3. Insert a manual column break at the paragraph beginning "Conference Travel."
4. Place the "For Sale" items in a text box.
5. Enlarge the text box until all the text is visible.
6. Drag the text box so it appears between the two columns and the text wraps appropriately around it.
7. Save the document as *Announcements With Text Box*.
8. Preview, print, and close the document.

Exercise 4

1. Open the *Legislative Update* document located on the Data Disk.
2. Insert a continuous section break below the second title line "LEGISLATIVE UPDATE."
3. Format the text in Section 2 with two columns of even width.
4. Insert a column break before the "Human resource" paragraph.
5. Insert a graphic image of your choice at the beginning of the first body paragraph. Change the wrapping style to square. Size the graphic so the paragraph text appears to the right of the graphic.

chapter twenty

6. Insert a graphic image of your choice at the beginning of the "The State University" paragraph. Change the wrapping style to square. Size the graphic so the paragraph text appears to the right of the graphic.

7. Save the document as *Legislative Update With Graphics*.

8. Preview, print, and close the document.

Exercise 5 [C]

1. Open the *Training Commitment* document located on the Data Disk.

2. Select the title "Our Training Commitment" and apply a 1-point, single-line border and Gray-10% shading to the selected text.

3. Repeat the text border and shading with the title "About Our Courses."

4. Format the "W" in Worldwide as a drop cap in the dropped position.

5. Format the first paragraph of the About Our Courses text with a drop cap in the dropped position.

6. Save the document as *Training Commitment With Drop Caps*.

7. Preview, print, and close the document.

Exercise 6 [C]

1. Open the *Southwest Civic Association Art Show* document located on the Data Disk.

2. Insert an appropriate graphic from the Clip Gallery as a watermark.

3. Size and move the watermark so it is centered vertically and horizontally behind the text. Adjust the brightness as necessary.

4. Save the document as *Southwest Civic Association Art Show With Watermark*.

5. Preview, print, and close the document.

Exercise 7 [C]

1. Open *The Internet* document located on the Data Disk.

2. Select the entire document. Change the line spacing to single and turn off the Widow/Orphan control option.

3. Scroll to the bottom of page 1. Notice that the last line of the "Services Available On The Internet" paragraph is at the top of page 2.

4. Print pages 1 and 2.

5. Select the entire document and turn on the Widow/Orphan control option. Notice that page 1 is repaginated correctly.

6. Print pages 1 and 2.

7. Close *The Internet* document without saving any changes.

Exercise 8 [C]

1. Open the *Summer Vacation* document located on the Data Disk.

2. Add the title "Summer Vacation" using WordArt. Format the WordArt object as desired.

3. Center the WordArt object at the top of the document. (*Hint:* You may need to insert some hard returns to move the paragraph text down to make room for the WordArt object.)

4. Save the document as *Summer Vacation With WordArt*.

5. Preview, print, and close the document.

Case Projects

Project 1

As the temporary administrative assistant to
B. J. Chang, part of your responsibilities is the
preparation of the monthly employee newsletter.
While creating this month's newsletter, you
experienced the following problems working with
pictures and other objects:

1. You cannot see the border around a drawing object.

2. When you edit the fill color of a drawing object with
   shadow or 3-D effect, the color of the shadow or 3-D
   effect doesn't change.

Use the Office Assistant to research these
problems. Create an outline that describes each
problem and suggests a solution for each. Save,
preview, and print the outline.

Project 2

Bill is creating a large report that contains several
tables, drawing objects, and pictures. He wants
to use captions for the objects and asks you to
research how to do this. Use online Help to
research ways to use captions in a large document.
Write Bill an interoffice memorandum describing
how to create and edit captions. Save and print the
document. Create an example sheet to attach to
Bill's memo that contains a table, picture, and
drawing object with captions. Save, preview, and
print the example document.

Project 3

You want to locate some new graphics (pictures) to
use in the employee newsletter and coworkers tell
you there are many Web sites that offer free
graphics you can download. Connect to your ISP,
load your Web browser, and search for Web sites

offering free graphics. With your instructor's
permission, download at least three new pictures.
Create a new, blank document and insert and label
each new picture. Save, preview, and print the
document. (*Caution:* Most graphics used on Web
pages or offered for sale at Web sites are
copyrighted. Be certain you do not download and
use any of these copyrighted graphics. If unsure,
contact the Webmaster at the site and ask
permission before you download the graphics.)

Project 4

The accounting department at Worldwide Exotic
Foods, Inc. sponsors a youth organization, which is
holding its annual fund-raising bake sale next
Saturday from 10:00 a.m. to 6:00 p.m. at the Civic
Association building. The accounting manager
asks you to create a flyer, which can be copied and
posted at local stores, to announce the bake sale.
Create an 8½ × 11-inch flyer using fictitious data.
The flyer should announce the bake sale and
contain the following additional information:

1. A map showing the major roads and specific
   intersection and address of the Civic Association
   building. (*Hint:* Explore the use of AutoShapes,
   rectangles, squares, circles, curves, lines, and text
   boxes to draw the map.)

2. Bitmap and metafile graphics and WordArt drawing
   objects to highlight the event. (*Hint:* Insert bitmap
   and metafile graphics or combine drawing objects to
   create your own graphics.)

Assume the flyer will be printed on white paper
and in color. Use color in the fonts, WordArt, and
drawing objects or graphics. Save, preview, and
print the flyer.

chapter twenty

Project 5

B. J. Chang is drafting a five-page report to management on projected training needs. He wants to dress up the report with page borders and wants you to create a sample report for his review. Create a five-page document including a title page. Apply a page border to only the title page. Number all the pages except the first page at the center bottom. Add a WordArt watermark "CONFIDENTIAL" to print on each page, including the title page. Create fictitious text for the title page, but leave the remaining pages blank. Save, preview, and print the document.

Project 6

It's time to create the December employee newsletter. Create the newsletter with the following topics: "Gifts for Tots," "New Employees," "Annual Holiday Party," and "Hot Web Sites." Add at least two brief paragraphs of text for each topic. Search the Web for interesting Web sites to include. Insert a paragraph that warns readers about downloading a copyrighted picture or copying Web page text that is copyrighted. Add two Web page references where the readers can find out more about copyright issues on the Web. Use columns, WordArt, drop caps, graphics, drawing objects, line, paragraph, and character spacing, and borders and shading to make the document interesting and attractive. Size, position, and delete the graphics as necessary. Save, preview, and print the document.

Project 7

Viktor Winkler, the public affairs officer, is experienced with earlier versions of Word and tells you that inserting a frame is the best way to reposition text in a document. You are not familiar with frames and always use text boxes to reposition text. Using the Office Assistant, research the difference between frames and text boxes. Write Viktor an interoffice memorandum explaining the difference and describing when to use frames and when to use text boxes. Save, preview, and print the memo.

Project 8

Beth Garza, a training specialist in the human resources department, needs help to prepare training materials that include pictures and callouts. You decide to create some examples for her review. Use the Office Assistant, if necessary, to research how to create callouts. Create a new, blank document and insert at least three pictures. Add callouts using different callout styles to the pictures. Save, preview, and print the example document. Write Beth an interoffice memorandum explaining how to create and edit callouts. Save, preview, and print the memo.

Creating Tables of Contents and Indexes

Chapter Overview

A table of contents and an index help make it easier for readers to locate specific sections, topics, or words in a long document, such as a report or employee training manual. In this chapter you learn to create and modify a table of contents and an index.

LEARNING OBJECTIVES

► **Create and modify a table of contents**
► **Create and modify an index**

Case profile

The human resources department is preparing several large documents. They want to include table of contents and indexes in the documents to help readers locate information quickly. Bill Martin asks you to create the tables of contents and indexes for these documents.

chapter
twenty
one
21

21.a Creating and Modifying a Table of Contents

A **table of contents** is a sequential list of the names and page numbers of each chapter's heading and section subheadings. It appears at the front of large reports or books, such as this one. You can list several levels of subsections and their corresponding page numbers in the table of contents, depending on the level of detail you want to maintain.

Identifying Table of Contents Entries with Heading Styles

The Word Table of Contents feature creates a table of contents automatically based on paragraphs you format with styles. When using Word built-in heading styles, the "Heading 1" style creates a first-level table of contents entry, the "Heading 2" style creates a second-level table of contents entry, and so on through nine heading levels. If you create and format your document headings with custom styles, then you can specify which heading style to use for each level in the table of contents.

Bill wants you to create a table of contents for the *Understanding The Internet* training document. You create a table of contents for this document by first identifying the paragraph headings to be included in the table of contents. Because you do not want to change the formats of the heading text, you first create custom styles by example for the two heading levels. To open the document and create custom styles by example:

Step 1	*Open*	the *Understanding The Internet* document located on the Data Disk
Step 2	*Select*	the heading text INTRODUCTION TO THE INTERNET on the first page
Step 3	*Create*	a custom style named LEVEL 1 based on the formats in the selected text
Step 4	*Apply*	the LEVEL 1 style to the INTERNET ACCESS (on page 2) and INTERNET CHALLENGES (on page 4) paragraph headings
Step 5	*Select*	the Defining the Internet paragraph heading on the first page
Step 6	*Create*	a custom style named LEVEL 2 based on the formats in the selected text

| Step 7 | *Apply* | the LEVEL 2 style to the How the Internet Began, Services Available on the Internet, Internet Service Providers, Internet Addresses, User Names, and Other Internet Access Methods paragraph headings |

Now you are ready to create the table of contents.

Creating a Table of Contents

After you apply the heading styles to the text, you move the insertion point to the location where you want to place the table of contents in the document. Generally, you place the table of contents on a separate page at the beginning of the document. To create a new first page for the table of contents:

Step 1	*Move*	the insertion point to the top of the document
Step 2	*Insert*	a page break
Step 3	*Move*	the insertion point to the new blank page

After you position the insertion point, you insert a table of contents by clicking the Index and Tables command on the Insert menu. To insert a table of contents:

Step 1	*Click*	Insert
Step 2	*Click*	Index and Tables
Step 3	*Click*	the Table of Contents tab (See Figure 21-1)

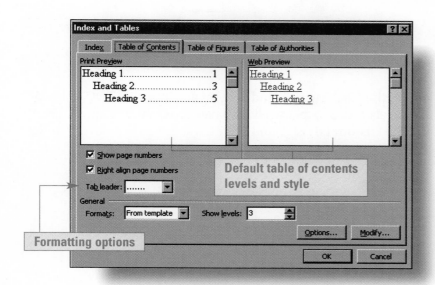

FIGURE 21-1
Table of Contents Tab in the Index and Tables Dialog Box

chapter
twenty-one

You specify the table of contents format in this dialog box. The Formats: list offers several built-in formats. To see how the various formats look, click a format in the Formats: list box and view a sample Table of Contents in the Print Preview or Web Preview box. The Tab leader: list box provides various tab leader options. You decide to use the Classic format with a dotted line leader.

Step 4	*Click*	Classic in the Formats: list
Step 5	*Click*	the Tab leader: list arrow
Step 6	*Click*	the first dotted line option

Because you are using custom styles to identify table of contents levels, you now must tell Word which custom style to use for level 1, level 2, and so forth. You do this in the Table of Contents Options dialog box. To specify custom table of contents levels:

| Step 1 | *Click* | Options |

The Table of Contents Options dialog box on your screen should look similar to Figure 21-2.

FIGURE 21-2
Table of Contents Options
Dialog Box

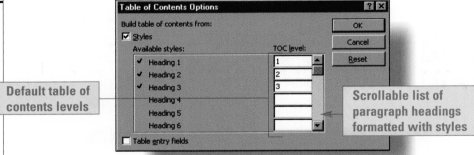

By default, the Heading 1, 2, and 3 styles are specified TOC (table of contents) levels 1, 2, 3 respectively. You can scroll the TOC level: list and mark the custom LEVEL 1 and LEVEL 2 styles as TOC level 1 and 2, respectively.

Step 2	*Scroll*	the TOC level: list to view the LEVEL 1 and LEVEL 2 custom styles
Step 3	*Key*	1 in the LEVEL 1 TOC level: text box
Step 4	*Key*	2 in the LEVEL 2 TOC level: text box
Step 5	*Click*	OK to close the Table of Contents Options dialog box
Step 6	*Click*	OK to close the Index and Tables dialog box and create the table of contents
Step 7	*Move*	the insertion point to the top of the document to select the table of contents and observe the entries

Your screen should look similar to Figure 21-3.

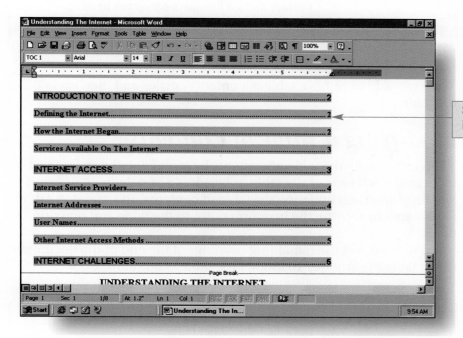

FIGURE 21-3
Understanding The Internet Table of Contents

Selected table of contents inserted on first page

Step 8	*Save*	the document as *Understanding The Internet With Classic TOC*

You can view specific text in the document by clicking a table of contents entry.

chapter
twenty-one

Using a Table of Contents to View Specific Text

The table of contents entries are linked to the referenced paragraph headings in the document. You can click any entry to move the insertion point in the document. To "jump" to a specific paragraph:

Step 1	*Move*	the mouse pointer to the Internet Service Providers table of contents entry
Step 2	*Observe*	that the mouse pointer becomes the pointing hand
Step 3	*Click*	the Internet Service Providers table of contents entry
Step 4	*Observe*	that the insertion point moves immediately to the Internet Service Providers paragraph heading
Step 5	*Close*	the Web toolbar that automatically appears whenever you click a link in a Word document

You can add or remove table of contents entries and then update the table.

Modifying a Table of Contents

You can modify the table of contents by modifying the styles used to identify each level of the table or by adding or deleting paragraph headings and then updating the table of contents. You update a table of contents by moving the insertion point to the table and pressing the F9 key.

You need to add the remaining headings at the end of the document to the table of contents. To modify the table of contents:

Step 1	*Apply*	the LEVEL 1 custom style to the LOADING A WEB PAGE heading text on page 7
Step 2	*Apply*	the LEVEL 2 custom style to the "Transmission Speeds" and "Security Issues" paragraph headings on page 6
Step 3	*Move*	the insertion point to the table of contents
Step 4	*Press*	the F9 key to update the table of contents with the new items
Step 5	*Double-click*	the Update entire table option button in the Update Table of Contents dialog box
Step 6	*Scroll*	the table of contents and observe the changes
Step 7	*Save*	the document

Another way to view a table of contents for documents that are going to be read online is with a frame.

Creating a Table of Contents in a Frame

A **frame** is a scrollable pane on your screen that contains information separate from the document text. Frames are used primarily to organize information on Web pages; however, for Word documents that are read online, you can place the table of contents in a frame when the heading text is formatted with built-in heading styles.

In addition to the printed version of a document, Bill plans to circulate a copy to be read online. He wants a table of contents placed in a frame. You open a document already formatted with heading styles and then create the table of contents. To create a table of contents in a frame:

Step 1	*Open*	the *Working With Frames* document located on the Data Disk
Step 2	*Click*	F̲ormat
Step 3	*Point to*	F̲rames
Step 4	*Click*	T̲able of Contents in Frame

A frame containing the table of contents links opens on left side of your screen and the Frames toolbar appears. Your screen should look similar to Figure 21-4.

QUICK TIP

You can also create a **table of authorities** for legal documents by marking the citations in a legal document and then creating a table of the citations using the Table of Authorities tab in the Index and Tables dialog box.

A **table of figures** is a list of the tables, graphs, or pictures in a document. You can use either captions or custom styles to create a table of figures. For more information on creating a table of figures or table of authorities, see online Help.

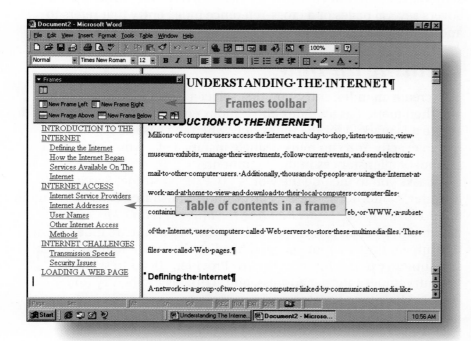

FIGURE 21-4
Table of Contents in a Frame

chapter
twenty-one

The table of contents in the frame is similar to paragraph heading text in the Document Map. Scroll bars appear in the frame if the text extends beyond the frame pane. To use the table of contents to view part of the document:

Step 1	*Scroll*	the frame to view the LOADING A WEB PAGE link at the bottom of the frame, if necessary
Step 2	*Click*	the LOADING A WEB PAGE link
Step 3	*Observe*	that the insertion point moves to that portion of the document
Step 4	*Save*	the document as *Working With Frames* and close it

To quickly find keywords in the text, Bill asks you to create an index for the document.

21.b Creating and Modifying an Index

An **index** is an alphabetical list of keywords and phrases matched to page numbers. It appears at the back of a long report or book, such as this one. You can create an index entry for a specific word, phrase, or symbol. You can also create a page range index entry for a topic that covers several pages or a cross-reference index entry that refers to another index entry.

Creating an Index

To create an index entry, you first select a word, phrase, or symbol and then mark it as an index entry. Index entries are case-sensitive and text is marked for the index only when the case and spelling match exactly. You can mark a single instance of a word, phrase, or symbol or all instances in the document.

Bill asks you to include the words "TCP/IP," "Internet Service Provider," "Internet address," and "Uniform Resource Locator" as main index entries in the *Understanding the Internet With Classic TOC* document. You can also create index subentries that are index entries that appear under a more general heading. You want to include "ISP" as a subentry under Internet Service Provider, "IP address" as a subentry under Internet address, and "URL" as a subentry under Uniform Resource Locator.

notes For the index activities, use the Find and Replace dialog box to search from the top of the document text (not the table of contents) for the words or phrases to index. Leave the dialog box open until instructed to close it.

To mark the text "TCP/IP" for the index:

Step 1	*Find*	the first instance of the text "TCP/IP"
Step 2	*Click*	Insert
Step 3	*Click*	Index and Tables
Step 4	*Click*	the Index tab, if necessary
Step 5	*Click*	Mark Entry

The Mark Index Entry dialog box that opens on your screen should look similar to Figure 21-5.

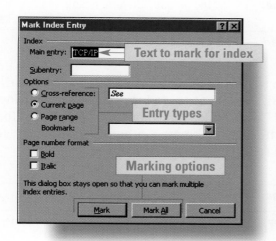

FIGURE 21-5
Mark Index Entry
Dialog Box

The selected text appears in the Main entry: text box. You can specify the format for the page number of the index entry by inserting a check mark in the Bold or Italic check box. Use the Mark button to mark the selected index entry for the current page only. Use the Mark All button to mark the first occurrence of the index entry in each paragraph. You mark all instances of the word "TCP/IP" for the index.

| Step 6 | *Click* | Mark All |
| Step 7 | *Leave* | the Mark Index Entry dialog box open until instructed to close it |

chapter twenty-one

All instances of the text "TCP/IP" are identified as index entries with the field code {XE "TCP/IP"}. You want to add the phrases Internet Service Provider, Internet address, and Uniform Resource Locator to the index. To add the remaining main index entries:

Step 1	*Find*	the phrase "Internet Service Provider" in the text (not in the table of contents or paragraph heading)
Step 2	*Mark*	all instances for the index
Step 3	*Find*	the phrase "Internet address" in the text (not in the table of contents or paragraph heading)
Step 4	*Mark*	all instances for the index
Step 5	*Find*	the phrase "Uniform Resource Locator" in the text (not in the table of contents or paragraph heading)
Step 6	*Mark*	all instances for the index

In addition to the previous phrases, you want to mark the text "ISP," "IP," and "URL" as subentries to Internet Service Provider, Internet address, and Uniform Resource Locator respectively. To do this, you must select the text and create a subentry index entry. To create the ISP subentry to Internet Service Providers:

Step 1	*Find*	the first instance of the text "ISP"
Step 2	*Key*	Internet Service Provider in the Main entry: text box
Step 3	*Key*	ISP in the Subentry: text box
Step 4	*Mark*	all instances for the index

To create the remaining subentries:

Step 1	*Find*	the phrase "IP address"
Step 2	*Create*	an index subentry for the text "IP address" for the main entry "Internet address"
Step 3	*Mark*	all instances for the index
Step 4	*Find*	the phrase "URL"

Step 5	*Create*	an index subentry for the text "URL" for the main entry "Uniform Resource Locator"
Step 6	*Mark*	all instances for the index
Step 7	*Close*	the Mark Index Entry and Find and Replace dialog boxes

After all the index entries are marked, you compile the index page.

Compiling an Index

After you have identified the index text, you specify where to place the index in the document, usually starting on a separate page at the end of a document. To insert an index at the end of the document:

Step 1	*Move*	the insertion point to the end of the document
Step 2	*Insert*	a page break
Step 3	*Open*	the Index tab in the Index and Tables dialog box

You specify the index format in this dialog box. The Formats: list box offers different appearance options. You can see how a format looks by clicking a format in the Formats: list and observing the sample Index in the Print Preview box. By default, all format appearances display the index text in two columns. You can change the number of columns by selecting a different number in the Columns: text box. You create the index in Classic format.

Step 4	*Click*	Classic in the Formats: list box, if necessary
Step 5	*Click*	OK
Step 6	*Switch*	to Whole Page zoom in Print Layout view
Step 7	*Observe*	the index page
Step 8	*Switch*	to Normal view
Step 9	*Save*	the document as *Understanding The Internet With Classic Index*

You can edit or delete an index entry after the index page is created.

Modifying an Index

Although compiling an index should be one of the last actions you perform in your document, you can revise it later if necessary. You can mark additional words or phrases as index entries and then update the index by moving the insertion point to the index and pressing the F9 key.

CAUTION TIP

You should compile the index with the formatting marks turned off. Although the hidden text won't print, it can affect pagination onscreen and cause incorrect page entries.

QUICK TIP

The AutoMark button on the Index tab of the Index and Tables dialog box allows you to open a concordance file that identifies specific words to use in an index. For more information about using a concordance file, see online Help.

chapter twenty-one

Because Word inserts index entries in a document as an index field, you edit, format, or delete index entries by modifying the field contents or deleting the field. When all changes are complete, you update the index page with the F9 key.

To view the index fields:

Step 1	*Show*	the formatting marks, if necessary
Step 2	*Scroll*	the document to see the XE (Index Entry) fields adjacent to the indexed text in the document
Step 3	*Move*	the insertion point to the top of page 3

Your screen should look similar to Figure 21-6.

FIGURE 21-6
TCP/IP XE
(Index Entry) Field

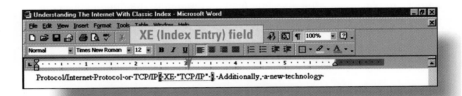

You decide that the TCP/IP entry doesn't need to be in your index. To delete the TCP/IP entry:

Step 1	*Select*	the first index field {XE "TCP/IP"} (including the brackets) located on page 3
Step 2	*Press*	the DELETE key
Step 3	*Select*	the second index field {XE "TCP/IP"} (including the brackets) located on page 3
Step 4	*Press*	the DELETE key

Now that you've deleted all the TCP/IP entries you need to update the index to remove the listing in the index. To update the index:

Step 1	*Move*	the insertion point to the index page
Step 2	*Press*	the F9 key to update the index
Step 3	*Observe*	the TCP/IP entries are removed when the index updates
Step 4	*Add*	the centered title INDEX to the page above the first continuous section break
Step 5	*Save*	the document and close it

Summary

► A table of contents appears at the beginning of a document and lists the headings that divide the document, such as chapters titles in a book.

► You can use built-in heading styles and custom styles to specify table of contents entries. After you format the heading text, you create the table of contents usually on the first page of the document.

► An index appears at the back of a document and matches keywords and phrases to page numbers.

► To create an index entry, you first select the index text and then mark it as an index entry. When all entries are marked, you create the index page.

► You can create cross-reference, current page, and page-range index entries.

► In addition to a table of contents, you can also create tables of figures or tables of authorities for legal documents.

Commands Review

Action	Menu Bar	Shortcut Menu	Toolbar	Keyboard
Insert a table of contents	Insert, Index and Tables			ALT + I, D
Mark a table of contents entry				ALT + SHIFT + O
Insert an index	Insert, Index and Tables			ALT + I, D
Mark an index entry				ALT + SHIFT + X
Update a table of contents or an index				F9

chapter twenty-one

Concepts Review

Circle the correct answer.

1. A table of contents is:
[a] created with bookmarks.
[b] a sequential list of headings and page numbers.
[c] generally located at the end of a document.
[d] a list of legal citations.

2. Creating a table of contents does not involve:
[a] defining where you want to place it in the document.
[b] identifying the text that will appear in the table.
[c] inserting the table.
[d] creating a list of figures.

3. An index:
[a] generally appears at the beginning of a document on a separate page.
[b] must be created from Word built-in heading styles.
[c] cannot be edited or changed.
[d] is an alphabetical list of keywords and phrases.

4. You can update a table of contents by:
[a] moving the insertion point to the table of contents and pressing the F9 key.
[b] selecting the table of contents and pressing the F11 key.
[c] saving the document.
[d] deleting the XE field code.

5. Which of the following steps is not part of creating an index?
[a] compiling the index
[b] identifying the words or phrases to be included in the index
[c] applying a heading style to the index text
[d] specifying where the index will appear in the document

6. To create a table of contents without changing the formatting of the paragraph heading:
[a] remove the formats after the table of contents is created.
[b] format the text with bold and italic.
[c] create and apply a built-in style.
[d] create and apply a custom style.

7. You can click a table of contents entry to:
[a] update the table.
[b] create an index entry.
[c] view the referenced document text.
[d] determine the number of levels in a table of contents.

8. To modify an index, you must edit or delete the:
[a] XE field code.
[b] table of contents entry.
[c] index page.
[d] AutoMark code.

9. A frame is:
[a] a list of pictures, tables, and graphics in a document.
[b] a panel that contains information separate from the document text.
[c] a Document Map.
[d] where an index is compiled.

10. To quickly find keywords and phrases in a document you should add a(n):
[a] table of contents.
[b] table of authorities.
[c] index.
[d] bookmark.

Circle **T** if the statement is true or **F** is the statement is false.

T   F   1. When you create a table of contents, you specify where the table is placed in the document after you identify the table headings.

T   F   2. You can click an index entry to view the referenced text in the document.

T   F   3. An index matches keywords and phrases to page numbers.

T   F   4. A table of contents usually appears at the front of a long report or book.

T   F   5. You can update a table of contents or index with the F12 key.

T   F   6. An index must always contain subentries.

T   F   7. You create a table of contents using built-in or custom heading styles.

T   F   8. A table of figures lists all the citations in a legal document.

T   F   9. A page range index provides a cross-reference to another index entry.

T   F   10. The Heading 2 style creates a first-level table of contents entry.

Skills Review

Exercise 1

1. Open the *Quality Task Force Report* document located on the Data Disk.

2. Place a page break between each topic.

3. Format each heading using the Heading 1 style.

4. Create a table of contents using the Formal format on a separate page at the beginning of the document.

5. Create an index for the words "quality" and "task force." Mark only the occurrences in the text, not in the table of contents.

6. Place the index in the Formal format on a separate page at the end of the document.

7. Save the document as *Quality Task Force Report With TOC*.

8. Print and close the document.

Exercise 2

1. Open the *Impressions* document located on the Data Disk.

2. Double-space the document.

3. Leave the IMPRESSIONS title text formatted with the Normal style.

4. Create a custom style by example for a LEVEL 1 and LEVEL 2 style. Format "Visual Impressions" using the LEVEL 1 style. All other headings should be formatted using the LEVEL 2 style.

5. Create a table of contents on a separate page before the text. Use the Classic format with a dotted-line style of tab leaders.

6. Save the document as *Impressions With TOC*.

7. Print and close the document.

chapter twenty-one

Exercise 3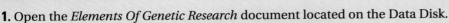

1. Open the *Compensation Procedures* document located on the Data Disk.

2. Double-space the document.

3. Create an index in the Classic format on a separate page at the end of the document using the following words:

paycheck   commissions
overtime   Personnel Board
holiday   vacation
terminated   retirement

4. Match case when searching for and marking words.

5. Save the document as *Compensation Procedures With Index.*

6. Print the index page.

7. Delete the retirement index item and update the index page.

8. Print the index page and close the document without saving any changes.

Exercise 4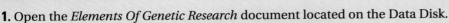

1. Open the *Elements Of Genetic Research* document located on the Data Disk.

2. Create an index in the Formal format on a separate page at the end of the document using the following words:

Cell   Diagnosis
Chromosome   Detection
DNA   Function
Gene   Replacement

3. Match case when searching for and marking words.

4. Save the document as *Elements Of Genetic Research With Index.*

5. Print the index page and close the document.

Exercise 5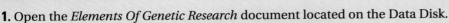

1. Open the *Vocabulary* document located on the Data Disk.

2. Double-space the entire document.

3. Create a custom style by example for the table of contents entries, using the paragraph headings.

4. Create a table of contents on a separate page before the text. Use the Classic format with a dotted-line style of tab leaders.

5. Print the table of contents page.

6. Create an index in the Classic format on a separate page at the end of the document using the following words:

literature   audience
extensive   listener
vocabulary   intelligence
dictionary

7. Match case when searching for and marking words.

8. Save the document as *Vocabulary With TOC.*

9. Print the index page and close the document.

Exercise 6

1. Open the *Word Processing Outline* document located on the Data Disk.

2. Format the heading text with built-in styles.

3. Create a table of contents containing only first-level headings. Use the Formal format with a dotted-line style of tab leaders. Insert the table of contents on the first page.

4. Save the document as *Word Processing Outline With TOC*.

5. Print the table of contents and close the document.

Exercise 7

1. Open the *Australia* document located on the Data Disk.

2. Create custom styles by example for the heading text. Left-aligned titles in uppercase text are first-level headings. All other titles are second-level headings.

3. Create a table of contents using the Fancy format. Place the table of contents on a separate page before the text.

4. Save the document as *Australia With TOC*.

5. Print the table of contents and close the document.

Exercise 8

1. Open the *End-User Model Curriculum Process* document located on the Data Disk.

2. Format the paragraph headings with a custom style.

3. Create a table of contents containing only first-level headings. Use the Classic format with dotted line style tab leaders. Place the table of contents on a separate page before the text.

4. Create an index of the following words. Do not mark the text "End User" that is underlined.

EURA	curriculum
End-User	group
EUCG	development
design	course
refinement	implementation

5. Match case when searching for and marking words.

6. Place the index in the Formal format on a separate page at the end of the document.

7. Save the document as *End-User Model Curriculum Process With Index*.

8. Print the table of contents and index page and close the document.

Case Projects

Project 1

Mary Whitt is drafting a legal document and wants to include a table of authorities. She asks for your help. Using the Office Assistant, research how to create and edit a table of authorities. Write Mary an interoffice memorandum describing the process. Save, preview, and print the memorandum.

chapter twenty-one

Project 2

Bill Martin asks you to create a company intranet Web page describing the steps needed to create and update a table of contents and an index. Create a Web page using the theme of your choice and list the procedures for creating a table of contents and an index. Save, preview, and print the Web page.

Project 3

Chris Lofton asks you to present a 15-minute "brown-bag" seminar for the word processing department. The topic of the seminar is "Creating and Inserting Tables of Contents and Indexes." Using the Office Assistant, research how to create a table of contents and an index. Create an outline that lists the major topics and subtopics for creating tables of contents and indexes. Save, preview, and print the outline. With your instructor's permission, use the outline as your guide and explain the processes to several classmates.

Project 4

After your presentation to the word processing department, participants ask the following questions:

1. Susan Tierney: "How can I create multiple tables of contents in one document?"

2. Mark Acton: "How can I format index entries?"

3. Libbie Daniels: "Can I create a cross-reference for an index entry?"

Use online Help to research the answers to these questions. Create an unbound report document that lists each question and gives an appropriate answer. Save, preview, and print the document.

Project 5

B. J. Chang asks you to prepare a list of animal protection and welfare groups that might be interested in receiving support from Worldwide Exotic Foods, Inc. Connect to your ISP, load your Web browser and search for Web pages sponsored by animal welfare and animal protection organizations. Print at least three Web pages. Write B. J. Chang a report describing the results of your research and recommending one of the organizations. Include a table of contents and an index. Save, preview, and print the report.

Project 6

You are asked to write a short article for the next monthly newsletter of the International Association of Executive Assistants. It should describe how to use a concordance file to create an index. Use the Office Assistant to learn how to create a concordance file and how to use it to create an index. Create an unbound report document that describes the process of creating and using a concordance file. Save, preview, and print the document.

Project 7

Olivia Rameriz, a training specialist in the human resources department, is creating some training materials. She asks your advice on how to create the table of contents. She does not want to use the existing paragraph headings for the table of contents entries. You suggest she might want to use embedded headings instead. Using online Help, research how to create embedded headings and then use the embedded heading to create a table of contents. Use a document of your choice to practice creating embedded headings. Write Olivia a memo that describes the process; attach a sample document. Save, preview, and print the memo.

Project 8

After Olivia creates the embedded headings for her document, she continues to get the error message "Error! Bookmark not defined" instead of page numbers when she creates the table of contents. Troubleshoot this error and create an e-mail to Olivia in Word that describes how to solve her problem. Save, preview, and print the e-mail message.

Working with Large Documents

Chapter Overview

Master documents enable you to work efficiently with large documents, such as books and reports. Subdocuments allow many people to work on a large document at the same time. You can track revisions to document each reviewer's edits or use cross-references to direct readers to a related section. Another timesaving feature is the ability to format and summarize the entire document automatically. In this chapter you learn to create and manage master documents, track revisions, add cross-references, use AutoFormat to quickly format an entire document, and use AutoSummarize to create a synopsis of a document.

LEARNING OBJECTIVES

► **Create master documents and subdocuments**
► **Create a cross-reference**
► **Track changes to a document**
► **Route documents**
► **Create multiple versions of a document**
► **Automatically format an entire document**
► **Automatically summarize a document**

Case profile

Jody Haversham, who transferred to the chairperson's office to be a special projects coordinator, is working on several large documents that require input from others. You work with Jody to create master and subdocuments, track changes to large documents, and use other techniques for sharing documents effectively and efficiently with others.

chapter twenty two

22.a Creating Master Documents and Subdocuments

The Master Document feature allows you to separate a large document into smaller, more manageable subdocuments. The **master document** is a file that organizes and displays a series of smaller, related individual files, called **subdocuments**. Subdocuments are stored in separate files with their own filenames. You can work on all the subdocuments in the master document or you can open and work in an individual subdocument. Subdocuments provide workgroup members access to different parts of a larger document at the same time while the master document keeps track of the subdocuments' overall structure.

You can format the master document as a whole or format each subdocument separately. For example, you can use one template in the master document and a different one in the subdocuments. You can also create a table of contents for the document as a whole in the master document or create a table of contents for each subdocument. And you can print either the master document or individual subdocuments.

Creating Subdocuments

You create a master document and subdocuments from an outline in Outline view using built-in heading styles or Outline level: paragraph formats. First identify the outline level where you want the sub-documents created with a built-in heading style or an Outline level: paragraph format. If you use custom styles and do not want to change the heading text formats, use the Outline level: paragraph formats. Word creates a subdocument each time that heading style or Outline level: paragraph format occurs in the document.

Jody is going to place a copy of a document on the network so that various members of her workgroup can update and modify individual portions of it. She wants you to open the document and create a master document with subdocuments for each major heading that appears in all uppercase characters. You do not want to change the current formatting, so you apply the Outline level: paragraph format Level 1 to the heading text and then create the subdocuments. To open the *Internet Master Document* and format the heading text:

| Step 1 | *Open* | the *Internet Master Document* document located on the Data Disk |

Step 2	*Select*	the INTRODUCTION TO THE INTERNET heading
Step 3	*Open*	the Indents and Spacing tab in the Paragraph dialog box
Step 4	*Click*	Level 1 in the Outline level: list
Step 5	*Click*	OK
Step 6	*Continue*	to apply the Level 1 Outline level: format to the INTERNET ACCESS, INTERNET CHALLENGES, and LOADING A WEB PAGE headings
Step 7	*Move*	the insertion point to the top of the document
Step 8	*Save*	the document as *Internet Master Document With Subdocuments*
Step 9	*Switch*	to Outline view

Your screen should look similar to Figure 22-1.

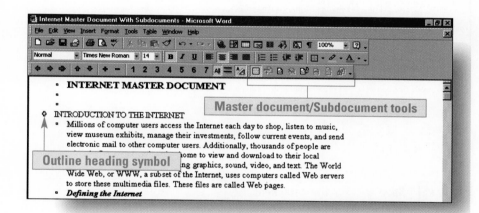

FIGURE 22-1
Document in Outline View

The buttons on the Outlining toolbar create, expand, collapse, combine, split, unlock, and remove subdocuments in the master document. You create subdocuments in your master document. To create the subdocuments:

| Step 1 | *Select* | the text from "INTRODUCTION TO THE INTERNET" to the end of the document |
| Step 2 | *Click* | the Create Subdocument button ▣ on the Outlining toolbar |

Subdocuments are created at each Level 1 heading. Each subdocument is enclosed in a box that contains the text for that subdocument, outline-heading symbols, and a small subdocument icon in the upper-left corner of the subdocument box.

chapter
twenty-two

Step 3 | ***Scroll*** | to view each subdocument and then return to the top of the document

After scrolling to the top of the document, your screen should look similar to Figure 22-2.

FIGURE 22-2
First Subdocument in Master Document

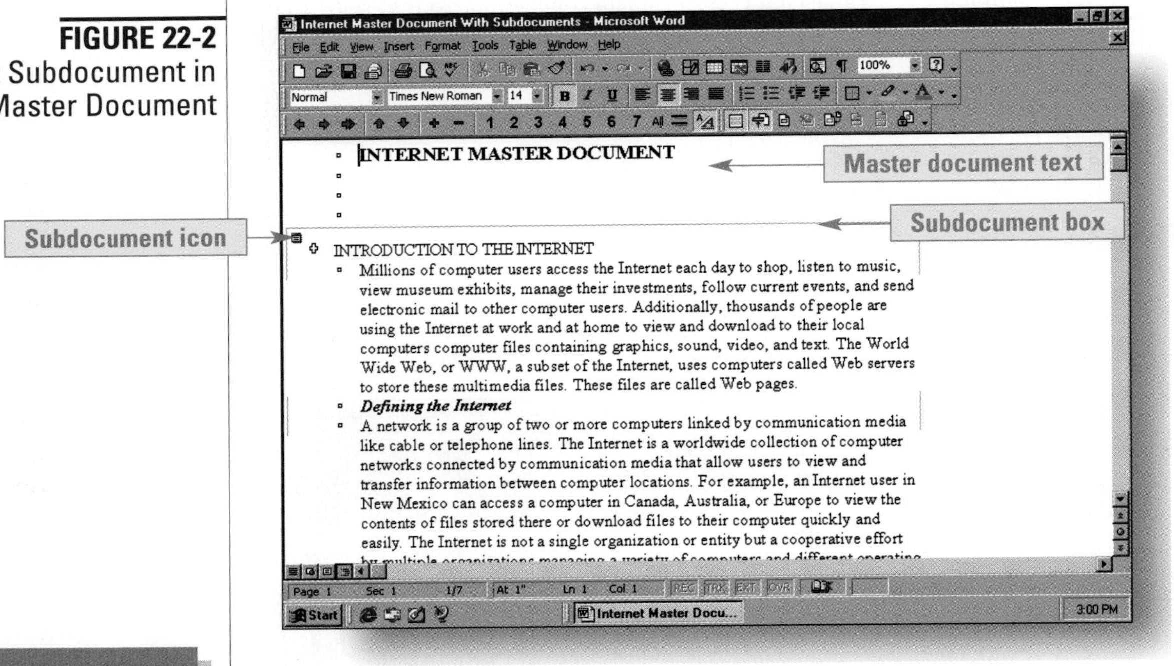

CAUTION TIP

Warning! Do not rename or move a subdocument using Windows Explorer, Windows NT File Manager, or MS-DOS. If you do, the master document will not be able to locate the sub-document. To rename a subdocument, display the master document in Outline view, open the subdocument in its own window, and save it with a new name. Then save the master document again.

Step 4 | ***Save*** | the document

Word saves each subdocument individually, so that you can work with each of them independently.

Saving Master Documents and Subdocuments

When you save a master document, Word saves each subdocument as a separate file with a filename based on the heading text for that subdocument. The subdocuments are saved automatically in the same location as the master document. When you saved the *Internet Master Document With Subdocuments*, the master document and subdocuments were saved to the same location.

To view the saved subdocuments files:

Step 1	*Open*	the Save As dialog box
Step 2	*Switch*	to the disk drive and folder where the *Internet Master Document With Subdocuments* document is stored
Step 3	*Observe*	that the four subdocuments *INTERNET ACCESS, INTERNET CHALLENGES, INTRODUCTION TO THE INTERNET,* and *LOADING A WEB PAGE* are also saved in the same location
Step 4	*Cancel*	the Save As dialog box
Step 5	*Close*	the document

You can edit subdocuments, split one subdocument into two or more subdocuments, or combine subdocuments into a single document.

Managing Subdocuments

Master documents give you the flexibility to maneuver and organize subdocuments. You can edit a subdocument in Outline view, or you can open a subdocument for viewing or editing in its own window. You can move subdocuments from one position to another within a master document. Finally, you can split a subdocument into two subdocuments and or combine two or more subdocuments into one subdocument.

When you open a master document, each subdocument is represented by a hyperlink. Simply click the hyperlink to display the subdocument in its own window for editing or printing. Or, expand the master document to show all the subdocuments in Outline view and work on the document as a whole.

To open the *Internet Master Document With Subdocuments* and manage the subdocuments:

| Step 1 | *Open* | the *Internet Master Document With Subdocuments* document |
| Step 2 | *Observe* | that the subdocuments are collapsed and each subdocument is represented by a hyperlink |

chapter
twenty-two

You can open an individual subdocument by clicking the hyperlink or you can expand all the subdocuments and work on them from the master document in Outline view. To open the *INTRODUCTION TO THE INTERNET* subdocument in its own window:

| Step 1 | *Click* | the INTRODUCTION TO THE INTERNET hyperlink |

The subdocument opens as a separate document in its own window. You can edit the subdocument as you would any Word document. After the subdocument is edited, you can save it with the <u>S</u>ave command on the <u>F</u>ile menu or the Save button on the Formatting toolbar. Because the subdocument and the master document are linked, Word automatically saves the changes to both the subdocument and the master document. You close the subdocument just like any other document.

| Step 2 | *Close* | the subdocument |
| Step 3 | *Observe* | that the INTRODUCTION TO THE INTERNET hyperlink in the master document is a different color, indicating that it is a "followed" link that has been used to "jump" to another document |

notes Whenever you use hyperlinks, Word automatically opens the Web toolbar. You can leave the toolbar open or close it with the shortcut menu. The figures in this chapter do not show the Web toolbar.

If you want to work on the subdocuments from within the master document, you can display the contents of all the subdocuments at one time. To expand the subdocuments:

| Step 1 | *Click* | the Expand Subdocuments button 🔲 on the Outlining toolbar |
| Step 2 | *Observe* | that the subdocuments replace their hyperlinks |

You can move individual topics within a subdocument or reposition an entire subdocument within the master document. You reposition a subdocument by selecting the subdocument and then dragging it to a new position. To reposition the INTERNET ACCESS subdocument after LOADING A WEB PAGE subdocument:

| Step 1 | *Click* | the INTERNET ACCESS subdocument icon |

Step 2	*Observe*	that the entire text of the subdocument is selected
Step 3	*Position*	the mouse pointer on the INTERNET ACCESS subdocument icon
Step 4	*Press & Hold*	the mouse button
Step 5	*Drag*	the INTERNET ACCESS subdocument icon downward with the move mouse pointer until a horizontal gray line appears immediately below the LOADING A WEB PAGE subdocument (do not drag to the bottom of the document)
Step 6	*Release*	the mouse button to reposition the subdocument
Step 7	*Deselect*	the subdocument text

You can combine two or more adjacent subdocuments into a single subdocument. When you save the file, Word saves only one file with name of the first subdocument. The other subdocument files are no longer linked to the master document and you can delete them. To combine the LOADING A WEB PAGE and INTERNET ACCESS subdocuments into a single subdocument:

Step 1	*Click*	the LOADING A WEB PAGE subdocument icon to select the subdocument
Step 2	*SHIFT + Click*	the INTERNET ACCESS subdocument icon to select the subdocument
Step 3	*Click*	the Merge Subdocument button 🖹 on the Outlining toolbar
Step 4	*Deselect*	the subdocument text
Step 5	*Scroll*	the document to view the combined subdocuments

You might need to split a large subdocument into more than one subdocument, or you might want to create a subdocument within another subdocument. You must place the insertion point at the position where you want the split to occur. To split a subdocument:

Step 1	*Move*	the insertion point before the "I" in the INTERNET ACCESS heading in the LOADING A WEB PAGE subdocument

QUICK TIP

You can delete a subdocument and its contents from a master document by selecting the subdocument and pressing the DELETE or BACKSPACE keys.

QUICK TIP

When you save the changes to the master document, Word saves the combined sub-documents with the filename of the first subdocument.

**chapter
twenty-two**

| Step 2 | *Click* | the Split Subdocument button ⊟ on the Outlining toolbar |
| Step 3 | *Observe* | that the combined subdocument is split into two subdocuments: LOADING A WEB PAGE and INTERNET ACCESS |

You can also create subdocuments within other subdocuments. You want to create a subdocument for the Internet Service Providers text in the INTERNET ACCESS subdocument. To open the subdocument and format the heading:

Step 1	*Double-click*	the INTERNET ACCESS subdocument icon to open the subdocument for editing
Step 2	*Apply*	the Outline level: LEVEL 1 paragraph format to the Internet Service Providers paragraph heading
Step 3	*Save*	the document as *INTERNET ACCESS* to update the copy on the disk (*Caution:* Word attempts to assign a new name to the document; save it with the original name *INTERNET ACCESS*)
Step 4	*Close*	the subdocument

To create the new subdocument:

Step 1	*Select*	the paragraph heading "Internet Service Providers" and the following paragraph in the INTERNET ACCESS subdocument
Step 2	*Click*	the Create Subdocument button ⊟ on the Outlining toolbar
Step 3	*Scroll*	to view a separate subdocument, Internet Service Providers, within the INTERNET ACCESS subdocument
Step 4	*Close*	the master document without saving any changes

Printing Master Documents and Subdocuments

You can print all or part of a master document, or you can print individual subdocuments. To print an entire master document, expand the subdocuments and then print the entire document from Normal view. To print an individual subdocument, open the subdocument and click the Print command on the File menu or the Print button on the Formatting toolbar. For more information on working with master documents and subdocuments, see online Help.

22.b Creating a Cross-Reference

When working with large documents that people read online, cross-reference hyperlinks help readers move quickly to related topics. You can create hyperlink cross-references for headings, bookmarks, footnotes, endnotes, tables, equations, figures, or numbered items. You can create a cross-reference to headings formatted with the built-in heading styles. If you are not using the built-in heading styles, you can create a hidden bookmark at the appropriate paragraph heading and then create a cross-reference to that bookmark. A **hidden bookmark** creates a reference point that is not visible in the document.

Jody asks you to include a hyperlink cross-reference for the first instance of the text "Web pages" to the subdocument heading LOADING A WEB PAGE in the *Internet Master Document With Subdocuments* document. To create a bookmark at the LOADING A WEB PAGE paragraph heading:

Step 1	*Open*	the *Internet Master Document With Subdocuments* document
Step 2	*Expand*	all the subdocuments
Step 3	*Select*	the LOADING A WEB PAGE paragraph heading
Step 4	*Open*	the Bookmark dialog box
Step 5	*Key*	WebPages in the Bookmark name: text box
Step 6	*Click*	the Hidden bookmarks check box to insert a check mark, if necessary
Step 7	*Click*	Add

You create the cross-reference to this bookmark. To enter the cross-reference text:

Step 1	*Move*	the insertion point to the end of the last sentence in the first paragraph under the INTRODUCTION TO THE INTERNET paragraph heading
Step 2	*Press*	the SPACEBAR
Step 3	*Key*	For more information, see
Step 4	*Press*	the SPACEBAR

chapter
twenty-two

Now you create a cross-reference from this location to the WebPages bookmark. To create the hyperlink cross-reference:

Step 1	*Click*	Insert
Step 2	*Click*	Cross-reference

The Cross-reference dialog box that opens on your screen should look similar to Figure 22-3.

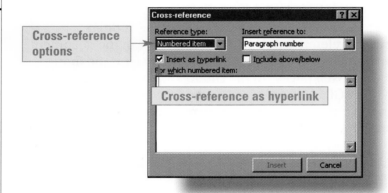

Cross-reference options

Cross-reference as hyperlink

You select the reference type and to what the cross-reference refers in this dialog box. For example, if you create a cross-reference to a heading formatted with the built-in heading styles, you select Heading in the Reference type: list and Heading text appears in the Insert reference to: list box. A list of all the formatted headings appears in the For which heading: list box. You then select the heading to which the cross-reference refers. Because you are using bookmarks, you select Bookmark from the Reference type: list, Bookmark text appears in the Insert reference to: list, and the available bookmarks appear in the For which bookmark: list.

Step 3	*Click*	Bookmark in the Reference type: list arrow, if necessary
Step 4	*Verify*	WebPages is selected in the For which bookmark: list box
Step 5	*Click*	the Insert as hyperlink check box to insert a check mark, if necessary
Step 6	*Click*	Insert
Step 7	*Close*	the dialog box
Step 8	*Observe*	that the text "LOADING A WEB PAGE" is added to the sentence as a hyperlink that is not underlined or colored
Step 9	*Key*	a period (.) following the LOADING A WEB PAGE link text

QUICK TIP

The cross-reference hyperlink refers to the text you selected for the bookmark, including any spaces or punctuation.

CAUTION TIP

Word inserts cross-references as fields. When you edit, delete, or move an item referred to in a cross-reference you must update the cross-reference field by selecting the cross-reference, right-clicking it, and clicking Update Field or pressing the F9 key. To update all the cross-references in the document, first select the entire document.

You decide to try the link to ensure it works properly. To test the hyperlink cross-reference:

Step 1	*Click*	the LOADING A WEB PAGE hyperlink
Step 2	*Observe*	that the insertion point moves to the bookmark text
Step 3	*Save*	the document

As you revise documents you can track changes so others can see your changes as well as the original text.

22.c Tracking Changes to a Document

Tracking changes enables members of a workgroup to suggest changes by keying them in the document. Later, one person can review all the changes and decide which ones to accept or reject. When reviewing or editing a document on your screen, you can choose to view highlighted changes with the original text, view the document in its original form, or view the document in its changed form. You can also specify how Word marks the changed text.

Jody asks you to make some revisions in the *Internet Master Document With Subdocuments* document and track the changes. Before you revise the document, you review the formatting options set for tracking changes. You also display the Reviewing toolbar, which provides buttons working with tracked changes. To display and position the Reviewing toolbar:

| Step 1 | *Display* | the Reviewing toolbar using the shortcut menu |
| Step 2 | *Drag* | the Reviewing toolbar immediately below the Outlining toolbar, if necessary |

Word can format any changes you make to a document in a variety of ways. To set the Track Changes formatting options:

| Step 1 | *Right-click* | the TRK mode indicator on the status bar |
| Step 2 | *Click* | Options |

**chapter
twenty-two**

The Track Changes dialog box that opens on your screen should look similar to Figure 22-4.

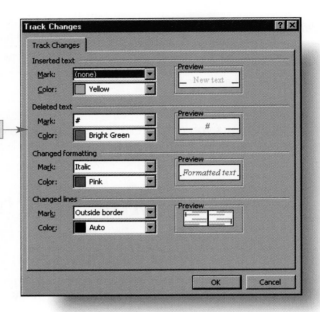

Color and format options for marking changes

You set the formats for the type of mark and the color for inserted text, deleted text, reformatted text, and changed lines in this dialog box. You want any text you insert to be changed to the red color, deleted text changed to blue, and any reformatted text changed to green. You also want the mark for inserted text to be an underline, for deleted text to be a strikethrough, and for changed formatting to be a double underline.

Step 3	*Click*	the Mark: list arrow in the Inserted text group
Step 4	*Click*	Underline
Step 5	*Click*	the Color: list arrow in the Inserted text group
Step 6	*Click*	Red
Step 7	*Change*	the Deleted text mark to a strikethrough and color to blue
Step 8	*Change*	the Changed formatting text mark to a double underline and color to green
Step 9	*Click*	OK

To turn on the Track Changes feature and begin modifying the document:

| Step 1 | *Click* | the Track Changes button 🖱 on the Reviewing toolbar |

Step 2	*Observe*	the TRK mode indicator on the status bar is bold indicating the Track Changes feature is turned on
Step 3	*Delete*	the word "computer" in the phrase "computers computer files" in the first paragraph of the INTRODUCTION TO THE INTERNET subdocument
Step 4	*Observe*	the deleted word appears in blue text with a blue strikethrough line
Step 5	*Observe*	the short vertical line to the left of the paragraph indicating a revision
Step 6	*Position*	the I-beam over the deleted text to display a ScreenTip with the editor's name, revision date and time, and revision type

When you change text to bold, italics, or other formats, Word indicates the change with green text. To change text formatting:

Step 1	*Bold*	the characters WWW in the phrase "or WWW" in the first paragraph of the INTRODUCTION TO THE INTERNET subdocument
Step 2	*Deselect*	the text
Step 3	*Observe*	the reformatted text appears in green

Any text you key in the document while tracking changes becomes red and underlined. To insert text:

Step 1	*Move*	the insertion point in front of the word "files" in the "These files are called Web pages." sentence in the first paragraph of the INTRODUCTION TO THE INTERNET subdocument
Step 2	*Key*	hypermedia
Step 3	*Press*	the SPACEBAR
Step 4	*Observe*	the inserted red underlined text and space

Your screen should look similar to Figure 22-5.

**chapter
twenty-two**

FIGURE 22-5
Tracked Changes Marked
in a Document

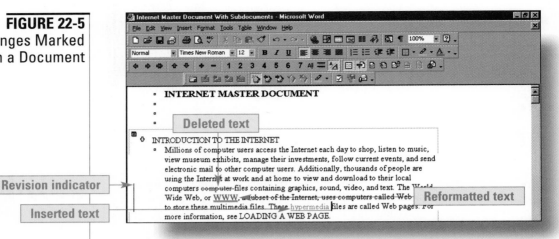

Deleted text

Revision indicator

Inserted text

Reformatted text

You can accept or reject changes with the Track Changes feature turned on or off. You can use buttons on the Reviewing toolbar or a shortcut menu to accept or reject each change to the document. You can also open a dialog box and accept or reject all changes at once, as well as review and accept or reject changes one by one. Because all changes to the document are made, you turn off the Track Changes feature and then accept the changes. To turn off the tracking of changes and accept all the changes:

MOUSE **TIP**

You can turn off the Tracked Changes feature by double-clicking the TRK mode indicator on the status bar or by clicking the Track Changes button on the Reviewing toolbar.

Step 1	*Click*	the Track Changes button on the Reviewing toolbar
Step 2	*Right-click*	the TRK mode indicator on the status bar
Step 3	*Click*	Accept or Reject Changes

The Accept or Reject Changes dialog box that opens on your screen should look similar to Figure 22-6.

FIGURE 22-6
Accept or Reject Changes
Dialog Box

Buttons to locate changes

Options to view changes

Options to accept or reject changes

You can accept all the changes without reviewing them, or cycle through the document accepting or rejecting individual changes. You want to accept all the changes.

Step 4	*Click*	A̲ccept All
Step 5	*Click*	Y̲es to confirm that you want to accept all the changes without reviewing them
Step 6	*Close*	the dialog box
Step 7	*Observe*	that the changes are incorporated into the original text
Step 8	*Save*	the document

When you want to make a document available to others for editing or reviewing you can route it via e-mail and then have it returned to you with their revisions.

22.d Routing Documents

When you work on a computer network, you may be able to route a document as an e-mail attachment so that others can review and edit it. You can route a document from one recipient to another so that each person can see the changes the previous person made or you can route a document to all recipients at one time. As the document is routed, you can track its status by having an e-mail message sent to you each time the document is routed to the next recipient. When all the recipients have reviewed the document, you can have it automatically returned to you with their revisions. You route a document by creating a routing slip with the recipients' addresses and the routing options.

notes To route documents through e-mail you need to have Microsoft Exchange (or other MAPI-compatible mail systems) or Lotus cc:Mail (or other VIM-compatible mail systems). Also, routing mail may not work across certain electronic mail gateways. The routing activities in this chapter assume you are using Microsoft Outlook 2000 and Microsoft Exchange on a network. See your instructor, if necessary, to confirm your mail routing capabilities and to get the additional instructions you need to route documents.

Jody wants you to route the INTRODUCTION TO THE INTERNET subdocument to several other people for their input. To open the subdocument and view the Routing Slip dialog box:

Step 1	*Double-click*	the INTRODUCTION TO THE INTERNET subdocument icon to open the subdocument

chapter twenty-two

Step 2	*Click*	<u>F</u>ile

Step 3	*Point to*	Sen<u>d</u> to

Step 4	*Click*	<u>R</u>outing Recipient

The Routing Slip dialog box that opens on your screen should look similar to Figure 22-7.

FIGURE 22-7
Routing Slip Dialog Box

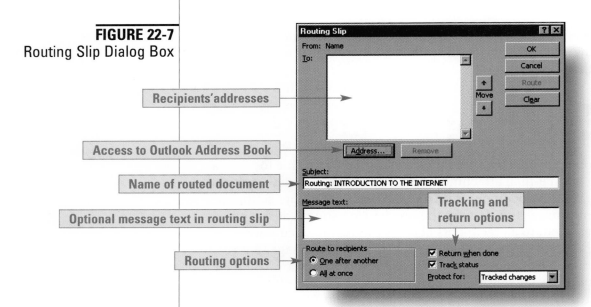

The <u>A</u>ddress button opens your Outlook address book where you select the e-mail address for the recipients. You key the subject in the <u>S</u>ubject: text box, add an optional note in the <u>M</u>essage text: text box, and choose the routing options in this dialog box. Unless you receive additional routing instructions from your instructor, cancel the Routing Slip dialog box without routing a document. To cancel the dialog box without routing:

Step 1	*Cancel*	the Routing Slip dialog box

Step 2	*Close*	the subdocument and master document

When you create a routing slip, an e-mail message is sent to each recipient in the <u>T</u>o: list box based on the routing options you selected. Each recipient receives the routed document as an e-mail message attachment. The recipient double-clicks the attachment icon in the e-mail message to open the Word 2000 application and the document. After reviewing and modifying the document, the recipient routes the document either to the next recipient in the list or to the originator of the document. To do that, they click the Word File menu, point to Send To, and click the Next Routing Recipient command.

22.e Creating Multiple Versions of a Document

Sometimes you modify a document and you want to keep copies of both the original version and the modified version. Rather than saving each version of the document as a separate files, you can save multiple versions of the same document in one file. Jody asks you to open the *Internet Master Document* document and let Word automatically format it. Before you format the document, you decide to save the original unformatted document as the original version of the document in a new file. Later, you save the formatted version in the same file. To open the document and save it with a new name:

| Step 1 | *Open* | the *Internet Master Document* located on the Data Disk |
| Step 2 | *Save* | the document as *Internet Master Document Versions* |

Before you make any changes to the document, you save it as the original version.

| Step 3 | *Click* | the Save Version button 🔲 on the Reviewing toolbar |

The Save Version dialog box that opens on your screen should look similar to Figure 22-8. You describe the version by adding comments in this dialog box.

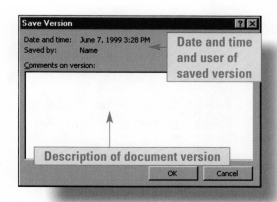

FIGURE 22-8
Save Version Dialog Box

chapter
twenty-two

MENU TIP

You can save a version by clicking the Versions command on the File menu.

Step 4	*Key*	Original version in the Comments on version: text box
Step 5	*Click*	OK
Step 6	*Observe*	that the original version of the document saves and the Versions mode indicator is added to the end of the status bar

Now you can modify the document and save it as a different version in the same file. When you want to quickly format a document you can have Word make all the formatting decisions for you.

22.f Automatically Format an Entire Document

When you need to format a document quickly, you can use the AutoFormat command on the Format menu to format the entire document based on the built-in styles. Word applies styles based on the position of text in the document. To expedite formatting the *Internet Master Document Versions* you decide to use the AutoFormat feature. Then you save the formatted document as the final version in the same file as the original version of the document. To automatically format the document:

Step 1	*Move*	the insertion point to the top of the document, if necessary
Step 2	*Click*	Format
Step 3	*Click*	AutoFormat

The AutoFormat dialog box that opens on your screen should look similar to Figure 22-9.

FIGURE 22-9
AutoFormat Dialog Box

Automatic formatting options

Document type options

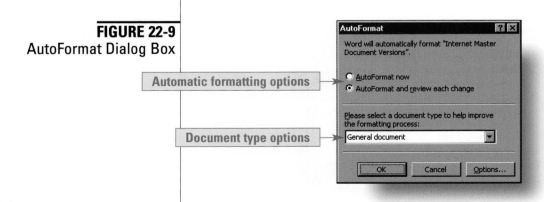

You can let Word format the entire document and then decide whether to review and accept or reject the formatting changes. You also choose on which type of document to base the automatic formatting: General document, Letter, or E-mail.

Step 4	*Click*	the AutoFormat and review each change option button, if necessary
Step 5	*Click*	the Please select a document type to help improve the formatting process: list arrow
Step 6	*Click*	General document, if necessary
Step 7	*Click*	OK
Step 8	*Click*	Review Changes in the AutoFormat dialog box

Word formats the document using built-in styles. Next, you find and accept or reject each of the changes Word made to the document. To review the changes:

Step 1	*Click*	Find in the Review AutoFormat Changes dialog box to move forward to the first change
Step 2	*Observe*	the referenced highlighted text and the comment Applied style Title in the dialog box
Step 3	*Click*	Find to select the next paragraph heading
Step 4	*Observe*	the referenced highlighted text and the comment Applied style Heading 1 in the dialog box
Step 5	*Continue*	to review several changes and then cancel the dialog box
Step 6	*Click*	Accept All to accept all the formatting changes without further review

You save the formatted document as a different version in the same file. To save the document as the final version:

Step 1	*Click*	the Save Version button 🖫 on the Reviewing toolbar
Step 2	*Key*	Final version in the Comments on version: text box
Step 3	*Click*	OK to save the final version in the same file as the original version

chapter twenty-two

You can look at all the saved versions in a file. To view both versions of the *Internet Master Document Versions* document:

Step 1	***Double-click***	the Versions mode indicator on the status bar
Step 2	***Observe***	the two versions of the document listed in the Versions in Internet Master Document Versions dialog box
Step 3	***Close***	the dialog box
Step 4	***Close***	the Reviewing toolbar

To quickly review a large document on your screen, you can summarize the key points.

22.g Automatically Summarize a Document

The AutoSummarize feature provides options to automatically summarize a document by highlighting key text within the document, creating a new document with the summary, inserting an executive-style summary at the top of the document, or hiding the document and displaying only the summary.

To automatically summarize the *Internet Master Document Versions* document by highlighting key text:

Step 1	***Click***	<u>T</u>ools
Step 2	***Click***	A<u>u</u>toSummarize

The AutoSummarize dialog box that opens on your screen should look similar to Figure 22-10.

Step 3	***Click***	the <u>H</u>ighlight key points option, if necessary
Step 4	***Click***	25% in the <u>P</u>ercent of Original: list, if necessary
Step 5	***Click***	OK

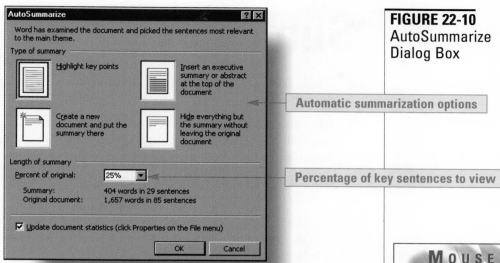

FIGURE 22-10
AutoSummarize
Dialog Box

Automatic summarization options

Percentage of key sentences to view

The key points are highlighted in yellow and the AutoSummarize toolbar appears. You can hide or show only the highlighted summary portion of the document, change the percentage of the document that is summarized, and remove the highlighting using the AutoSummarize toolbar. The Highlight/Show Only Summary button allows you to turn the highlighting off and view just the summarized text. If formatting marks are turned on, the Highlight/Show Only Summary button turns off the highlighting and displays all the text; the text that is not part of the summary has a dotted underline. To view only the summary:

Step 1	**Click**	the Highlight/Show Only Summary button [icon] on the AutoSummarize toolbar
Step 2	**Observe**	that only the 25% of the document that is the summary displays and the rest of the document is hidden
Step 3	**Click**	the Close button [Close] on the AutoSummarize toolbar to turn off the summarization
Step 4	**Save**	the document and close it

The AutoSummarize is a timesaving feature when you work with long documents.

MOUSE TIP

You can summarize more or less of the highest scoring sentences in a document by clicking the right or left arrows on the Percent of Original button on the Auto-Summarize toolbar.

CAUTION TIP

If the hidden text option is turned on in the View tab of the options box, the text that is not part of the summary has a dotted underline.

chapter
twenty-two

Summary

► The Master Document feature helps you separate a large document into smaller, more manageable subdocuments.

► You can create a master document by converting an existing document, combining existing documents into a master document, or by keying original text as an outline in Outline view.

► Word uses the built-in heading styles or paragraph Outline level: formats to identify subdocuments.

► When you save a master document, Word also saves each subdocument as a separate file and automatically assigns each subdocument filename.

► You can edit a subdocument in Outline view in the master document or open each subdocument individually in its own window for editing.

► You can split subdocuments into more than one subdocument or combine multiple subdocuments into one subdocument.

► You can print master and subdocuments together or individually.

► Cross-references for headings, bookmarks, footnotes, endnotes, tables, and figures can be added to a document as a hyperlink.

► The Track changes feature marks revisions to text that identify any insertions, deletions, or reformatting with distinctive colors and marks.

► You can review tracked changes and decide whether to accept or reject each change individually or all changes at once.

► Word can automatically format documents using the built-in styles, and you can accept or reject each formatting change.

► The AutoSummarize feature summarizes large documents based on a percentage of key sentences.

Commands Review

Action	Menu Bar	Shortcut Menu	Toolbar	Keyboard
Display a document in Outline view	View, Outline		⊞	ALT + V, O
Select a subdocument			Click the subdocument icon	
Move a subdocument			Drag the selected subdocument to the new location	
Select multiple subdocuments				SHIFT + Click the subdocument icons
Merge subdocuments			⊟	
Split subdocuments			⊟	
Create a subdocument			⊟	
Expand subdocuments			⊡	CTRL + \
Collapse subdocuments			⊡	CTRL + \
Insert a cross-reference	Insert, Cross-reference			ALT + I, R
Track changes	Tools, Track Changes	Right-click the TRK mode indictor on the status bar, click Track Changes	Double-click the TRK mode indicator on the status bar	ALT + T, T CTRL + SHIFT + E
Automatically format a document using built-in styles	Format, AutoFormat			ALT + O, A
Automatically summarize a document	Tools, AutoSummarize			ALT + T, U

Concepts Review

SCANS

Circle the correct answer.

1. **You create and manage master and subdocuments with buttons on the:**
   [a] Formatting toolbar.
   [b] Standard toolbar.
   [c] Outlining toolbar.
   [d] Master Document toolbar.

2. **Which of the following steps is not part of the process for creating a subdocument:**
   [a] format the outline-level text with Word built-in heading styles or paragraph outline-level formats.
   [b] identify the outline level where the subdocuments occur.
   [c] select the outline-level text to be included in the subdocuments.
   [d] switch to Normal view and select the text to be included in the subdocuments.

3. **Saving a master document:**
   [a] saves each subdocument with a filename consisting of the master document name and a number.
   [b] saves all subdocuments in a new folder created for subdocuments.
   [c] saves all subdocuments in the same location as the master document.
   [d] does not automatically save each subdocument.

chapter twenty-two

4. **You can let Word automatically format a document with:**
   [a] built-in styles.
   [b] a summary.
   [c] paragraph <u>O</u>utline level: formats.
   [d] versions.

5. **Word automatically summarizes a document based on the number of:**
   [a] keywords in each sentence.
   [b] styles applied to paragraph headings.
   [c] subdocuments in the document.
   [d] workgroup members to whom the document is routed.

6. **A master document is:**
   [a] a brief summary of a document.
   [b] one of a series of small, related files.
   [c] created when you track changes to a document.
   [d] a file that organizes and displays a series of smaller, related files.

7. **Word inserts cross-references as:**
   [a] paragraph headings.
   [b] fields.

[c] bookmarks.
[d] subdocuments.

8. **Tracking changes to a document:**
   [a] allows readers to quickly reference topics when reading a document on the screen.
   [b] enables members of a workgroup to key changes in a document that may be accepted or rejected.
   [c] allows you to store multiple versions of the same document in one file.
   [d] creates smaller, more manageable subdocuments.

9. **When you need to quickly format an entire document, you can use the:**
   [a] <u>A</u>utoText command.
   [b] <u>A</u>utoComplete command.
   [c] <u>A</u>utoFormat command.
   [d] <u>A</u>utoCorrect command.

10. **A locked subdocument:**
   [a] cannot be opened.
   [b] can be opened and modified.
   [c] has a Read-only sharing property.
   [d] cannot be expanded.

Circle **T** if the statement is true or **F** is the statement is false.

T   F   1. You can save multiple versions of a document in a single file.

T   F   2. You cannot create new subdocuments within an existing subdocument.

T   F   3. Word assigns a score to sentences containing keywords and then highlights a percentage of the most highly scored sentences when you automatically summarize a document.

T   F   4. When you combine subdocuments, remove subdocuments, or delete subdocuments, the original subdocument files are automatically removed from the folder in which they were saved.

T   F   5. Master documents can be edited only in Normal view.

T   F   6. You can turn on the Track Changes feature by double-clicking the REC mode indictor on the status bar.

T   F   7. Cross-references can be created as hyperlinks.

T   F   8. When you automatically format an entire document, you must accept all of the formatting changes.

T   F   9. Combined subdocuments are saved with the filename of the first subdocument.

T   F   10. You can print master documents but not subdocuments.

Skills Review

Exercise 1

1. Open the *Internet Report* document located on the Data Disk.

2. Automatically format the document and accept all formatting.

3. Display the document in Outline view and view only the first-level headings.

4. Select the first-level headings INTRODUCTION, ACCESS, CHALLENGES, and WEB PAGES and create subdocuments.

5. View all levels in the outline.

6. Save the master document as *Internet Report Master Document* and close it.

7. Verify that the four subdocuments are also saved in the same folder.

8. Open the *Internet Report Master Document* document and open each subdocument using the hyperlink. Print each subdocument before you close it.

9. Close the master document without saving any changes.

Exercise 2

1. Open the *Top Sales* document located on the Data Disk.

2. Apply the paragraph outline-level format Level 1 to the uppercase headings.

3. View the document in Outline view and verify the outline-level icon at the left of each uppercase heading.

4. Select the entire document and create the subdocuments.

5. Save the master document as *Top Sales Master Document* and close it.

6. Verify that the four subdocuments are saved in the same folder as the master document.

7. Open the *Top Sales Master Document* document and expand the subdocuments.

8. Add a blank line at the end of the master document.

9. Move the UNITED STATES subdocument to the end of the master document just before the last blank line.

10. Save the master document and subdocuments to update the copies on the disk.

11. Print and close the master document.

Exercise 3

1. Open the *Internet Report Master Document* document created in Exercise 1.

2. Expand the subdocuments.

3. Create a hidden bookmark named ACCESS for the Other Internet Access Methods subheading in the ACCESS subdocument.

4. Move the insertion point to the end of the first sentence in the INTRODUCTION subdocument.

5. Key "For more information, see" and insert the ACCESS hyperlink cross-reference. Add the appropriate spacing and punctuation.

chapter twenty-two

6. Save the document as *Internet Report Master Document With Cross-reference*.

7. Use the hyperlink cross-reference to view the referenced text.

8. Select the referenced paragraph heading and following paragraph and print the selection.

9. Close the document without saving.

10. Close the Web toolbar.

Exercise 4

1. Open the *Top Sales Master Document* document you created in Exercise 2.

2. Expand the subdocuments.

3. Select each subdocument by clicking the subdocument icon and then remove the subdocument formatting by clicking the Remove Subdocument button on the Outlining toolbar.

4. Switch to Normal view and remove any section breaks and blank lines.

5. Open the Reviewing toolbar.

6. Save the document as *Top Products*.

7. Change the Track Changes marks and color so that: (a) Inserted text is bold and green, (b) Deleted text is strikethrough and red, (c) Reformatted text is double underline and dark blue.

8. Turn on the Track Changes features.

9. Change the bold text to italic.

10. Add "Lettuce" to each Produce category.

11. Replace "Leaf Lettuces" in the GREAT BRITAIN, Produce category with "Tomato."

12. Save the document as a version with the comment Tracked Changes.

13. Accept all the changes.

14. Save the document as a version with the comment Updated Version.

15. Print the document and close it.

16. Close the Reviewing toolbar.

Exercise 5

1. Open the *Chicago Warehouses Audit* document located on the Data Disk.

2. Summarize the document 25% by highlighting key points.

3. Turn off the summarization.

4. Summarize the document 50% by inserting an executive summary at the top of the document.

5. Insert a page break between the executive summary and the full document.

6. Left align the paragraph headings in the executive summary and create a bulleted list for the three topics: Poor communication, Insufficient quality control, and Low morale and reduced worker productivity.

7. Save the document as *Executive Summary*.

8. Print the executive summary page and close the document.

Exercise 6

1. Open the *Different Documents* document located on the Data Disk.

2. Apply the Heading 3 style to the uppercase headings.

3. Switch to Outline view.

4. Select the entire document and create subdocuments.

5. Merge the TYPING LETTERS and TYPING BUSINESS CORRESPONDENCE subdocuments.

6. Open and print the merged TYPING LETTERS subdocument.

7. Delete the STATISTICAL COMMUNICATIONS subdocument. (*Hint:* Removing a subdocument with the Remove Subdocument button on the Outlining toolbar places the subdocument text in the master document. To completely delete subdocument text, select the subdocument and press the DELETE key.)

8. Save the master document as *Different Documents Master Document* and close it.

Exercise 7

(Complete this exercise only if you are on a network using Microsoft Exchange and Outlook 2000 for e-mail and have your instructor's permission to route a document to three classmates.)

1. Open the *Chicago Warehouses Audit* document located on the Data Disk and save it as *Important Chicago Information*.

2. Turn on the tracking of changes.

3. Create a routing slip addressed to three classmates to route the document from one classmate to another and then to return the document to you after all classmates have reviewed the document.

4. Add message text asking each classmate to make at least one change to the document before routing it to the next recipient or back to you.

5. When the document is returned to you, review the changes and accept them.

6. Save the document as *Updated Chicago Information*.

7. Print and close the document.

Case Projects

Project 1

Chris Lofton calls to ask for your help. The word processing department has just received the draft (on disk) of a new 15-chapter research report, which must be edited, formatted, and printed within 2 days. You suggest to Chris that a master document with subdocuments for Chapters 1–5, 6–10, and 11–15 be created so that three word processing specialists can work on the document at one time. Chris asks you to create a procedure memo for the operators describing in detail how they create, edit, save, and print the master document and subdocuments. Create, save, preview, and print the procedure memo.

chapter twenty-two

Project 2

You want to add a Web page to the company intranet that provides links to new Web sites of interest for your coworkers. Connect to your ISP, launch the Internet Explorer Web browser, and review the built-in "Best of the Web" Web site from the button on the Links bar. (If you are using a different browser, open a comparable Web page.) Review the links. Print at least three Web pages. Create a Web page using the theme of your choice containing text describing the Web sites and links to the Web sites. Save, preview, and print the Web page.

Project 3

While working on the research report, a word processing specialist called you for help solving several problems. Review online Help for solutions to the following problems:

1. Getting a File in use message when trying to open a master document or subdocument.

2. Not all the subdocument buttons are available on the Outlining toolbar.

3. When I open a subdocument, some cross-references are replaced by error messages.

Create an outline itemizing these problems and suggesting solutions. Save, preview, and print the outline. With your instructor's permission, use the outline as a guide to discuss how to solve these three problems with three classmates.

Project 4

Jody wants you to create a master document and subdocuments for an Internet training document and then consecutively number the pages and add page borders to the entire master document. Using online Help, research how to add page numbers and page borders to a master document and subdocuments. Create a master document with at least three subdocuments on Internet topics. Add consecutively numbered pages and a page border to all subdocuments in the master document. Save, preview, and print the master document.

Project 5

Jody wants you to add a cross-reference to the subdocuments you created in Project 4. Use a heading cross-reference instead of a bookmark cross-reference. Save the master document with a new name and print the cross-referenced text.

Project 6

Viktor Winkler stops by your desk to ask for help changing the Track Changes marks and colors. You agree to write Viktor the instructions on how to do this. Write Viktor an interoffice memorandum explaining how to change the marks and colors for tracking changes. Save, preview, and print the memo.

Project 7

Viktor Winkler suggests you save the memo you created in Project 5 as a Web page for the company intranet. Open the memo, apply the theme of your choice, make appropriate formatting changes, and save it as a Web page, preview it, and print it.

Project 8

Marisa DaFranco calls to ask for your suggestions on ways to distribute documents in the company. Using online Help, review all the topics for distributing documents to other people. Write Marisa an interoffice memorandum suggesting different ways to distribute documents; discuss the good and bad points of each method. Save, preview, and print the memorandum.

Using Online Forms

Chapter Overview

Filling in forms online (also called onscreen) speeds up the order-taking process and helps ensure accuracy because data is keyed only once, as the form is completed. Word can create form templates for documents such as invoices, routing slips, order forms, and schedules. Users complete onscreen documents based on these templates by filling in data (such as dates and amounts), marking check boxes, or selecting items from list boxes. In this chapter, you learn to create a form template and then complete a document based on the template.

Case profile

The Worldwide Exotic Foods sales department takes telephone orders and then manually prepares an order form. Later the accounting department imports this information into the company's databases. The sales manager believes the process could be more efficient if the sales representatives completed the order form online during the telephone conversation. You assist the sales manager in developing an online order form template.

Learning Objectives

► Create and modify a form
► Create a document based on a form template
► Set the default file location for workgroup templates

chapter twenty three

23.a Creating and Modifying a Form

A **form** is a document that contains non-variable informational text (called **boilerplate**) and spaces to enter variable information. Forms, such as Worldwide Exotic Foods' online order form, include boilerplate text as well as fill-in text boxes to key text and numerical data, check boxes to specify yes or no information, drop-down lists to select from a standard group, calculations of numerical data, and dates. You create forms as templates, using tables for the layout and Word form fields for the variable information.

notes This chapter assumes you are familiar with drawing and formatting tables using the Tables and Borders toolbar.

The Worldwide Exotic Foods sales manager wants you to create an order form that the sales representatives can complete online at the computer as they receive orders from customers. This form will contain the following variables:

1. Buyer's name and address (Sold to)
2. Shipping address (Ship to)
3. Sales Representative name
4. Order Date
5. Ship by Date
6. Shipping Method
7. Item Number
8. Item Description (Description)
9. Quantity Ordered (Qty Ordered)

The first step in creating an online form is to plan the framework and content. Draw the form on a sheet of paper so that you can visualize the way it looks. Include any text and form fields to ensure you have room for all the information. It is also helpful to ask an end user (such as a Worldwide Exotic Foods sales representative, in this case) to review your draft of the form and check for errors or omissions. After you are satisfied with the draft of the form, the next steps are to create a new form template, draw the table structure, enter boilerplate and form fields, and then save the template.

The reviewed and approved form, with variable data organized into four tables, is shown in Figure 23-1.

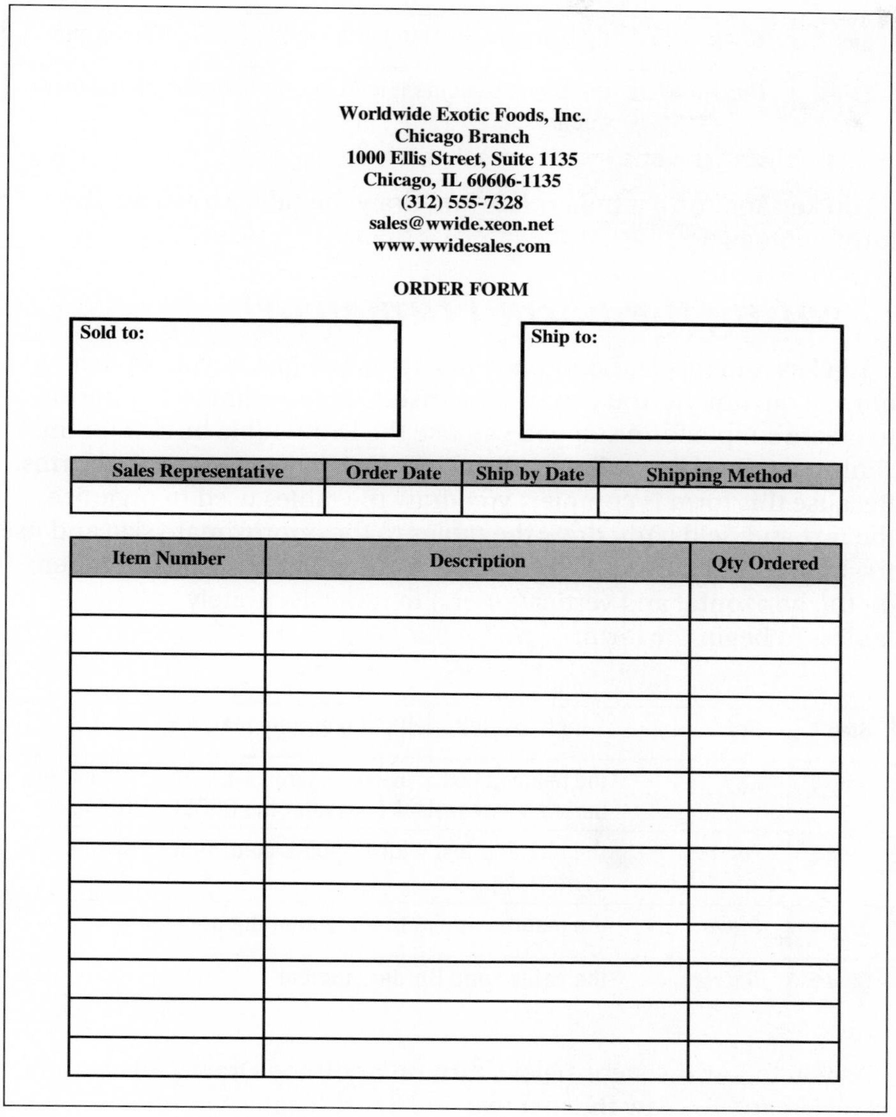

FIGURE 23-1
Completed Order Form

Worldwide Exotic Foods, Inc.
Chicago Branch
1000 Ellis Street, Suite 1135
Chicago, IL 60606-1135
(312) 555-7328
sales@wwide.xeon.net
www.wwidesales.com

ORDER FORM

Sold to:

Ship to:

Sales Representative	Order Date	Ship by Date	Shipping Method

Item Number	Description	Qty Ordered

Business forms often use tables to organize the placement of the text and form fields.

Creating a Form Template

After you are satisfied with the draft of the form, you begin by creating a new template. You create a form from a template so that each sales representative can open a new document that contains all the boilerplate and blank form fields ready for information. After the sales representative has filled in the form fields, the order can be saved separately. To create a new template:

Step 1	*Open*	the General tab in the New dialog box

chapter
twenty-three

| Step 2 | *Click* | the Template option button in the Create New group |
| Step 3 | *Double-click* | the Blank Document icon to create the blank template document |

You key and format boilerplate and draw the tables to create the form's framework.

Creating the Form Framework

You key and format boilerplate in a template just as you do in a normal document. You can use the Insert Table command or button to create simple forms, or you can use the Draw Table button on the Tables and Borders toolbar or Forms toolbar to create complex forms. Because this form is complex, you draw the tables used to organize the text and fields. You draw the tables to the approximate size and use the mouse pointer (and the ALT key so you can view actual numbers on the horizontal and vertical rulers) to more accurately size the tables. To begin the form:

Step 1	*Set*	1-inch top, left, right, and bottom margins
Step 2	*Key*	the heading text shown in Figure 23-1, with one blank line before and two blank lines after the ORDER FORM text
Step 3	*Format*	the heading text with 12-point, bold, Times New Roman, center-aligned
Step 4	*Move*	the insertion point to the end of the document
Step 5	*Display*	the Tables and Borders toolbar

As you follow the steps below, turn on or off the Draw Table feature as necessary. To draw the first two side-by-side tables for the Sold to: and Ship to: boxes on the form:

Step 1	*Select*	a 2¼ point single-line format
Step 2	*Draw*	a rectangle approximately 1-inch high and 2.65-inches wide, beginning at the left margin
Step 3	*Draw*	a rectangle of the same size, starting approximately 0.9 inch to the right of the first rectangle and ending at the right margin
Step 4	*Size*	the tables as needed, using the mouse pointer and the ALT key
Step 5	*Key*	the 12-point, bold, Times New Roman text in each table, as shown in Figure 23-1

You are drawing the tables to an approximate size; however, your screen should look similar to Figure 23-2.

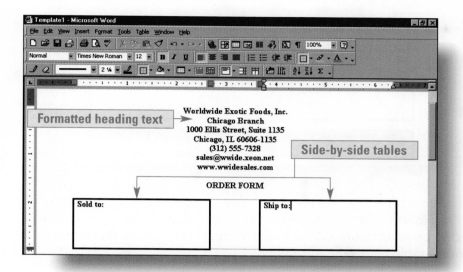

FIGURE 23-2
Side-by-Side Tables

C A U T I O N   T I P

When you draw similarly sized side-by-side tables, Word joins the tables by adding a cell without printable borders between the two tables.

The next table is a four-column table. To draw the four-column table below the first two tables:

Step 1	*Change*	the line weight to 1½ pt
Step 2	*Draw*	a rectangle, approximately ½-inch high, from the left margin to the right margin, starting approximately ¼ inch below the first two tables
Step 3	*Size*	the left and right borders with the mouse pointer and the ALT key, if necessary
Step 4	*Draw*	a row from the left to the right boundary of the table approximately ⅓ the height of the table
Step 5	*Draw*	four columns in the new table, as shown in Figure 23-1 (the first and fourth columns are approximately 2-inches wide and the second and third columns are approximately 1.01-inches wide)
Step 6	*Apply*	Gray-20% shading to the first row in the table
Step 7	*Key*	the 12-point, bold, Times New Roman text in the first row of the table, as shown in Figure 23-1
Step 8	*Center*	the text vertically and horizontally

Your screen should look similar to Figure 23-3.

**chapter
twenty-three**

FIGURE 23-3
Four-Column Table

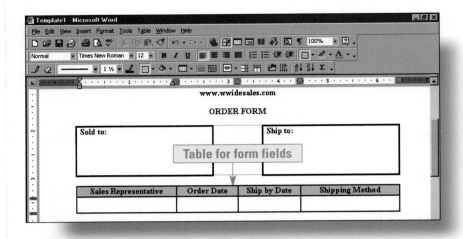

The fourth table contains three columns where sales representatives enter variable information about the items ordered. To draw the fourth table below the third table:

Step 1	*Draw*	a rectangle from the left margin to the right margin, starting approximately ¼ inch below the third table and ending approximately ½ inch from the bottom margin
Step 2	*Size*	the left and right and bottom borders with the mouse pointer and the ALT key, if necessary
Step 3	*Draw*	13 rows across the table
Step 4	*Distribute*	the rows evenly
Step 5	*Draw*	a column approximately 1.5 inches from the left border
Step 6	*Draw*	a column approximately 1.2 inches from the right border
Step 7	*Apply*	Gray-20% shading to the first row
Step 8	*Key*	the 12-point, bold, Times New Roman text in the first row, as shown in Figure 23-1
Step 9	*Center*	the text vertically and horizontally

To make the order form template easy to use, the sales manager wants a template icon for the order form to appear in the General tab of the New dialog box. Any template you save in the C:\Windows\Application Data\Microsoft\Templates folder appears in that location.

notes This chapter assumes you are saving your template so that the template icon appears on the General tab in the New dialog box. Your instructor may provide alternate instructions for saving and using your custom templates.

To save the order form template:

Step 1	**Save**	the template as *Order Form Template* in the C:\Windows\Application Data\Microsoft\Templates folder (or other folder as designated by your instructor)

After you construct the framework for your form, you insert form fields for the variable data.

Creating and Modifying a Form Control

A **form field** (sometimes called a **form control**) is a placeholder for a specific type of variable information in a specific place in a document, such as names and addresses. Text form fields provide space for user to key regular text, numbers, or dates, and perform calculations. Table 23-1 describes the various text form fields. Check Box form fields enable a user to select an option. Drop-Down form fields provide a list of variables from which a user can select.

Option	Description
Regular text	text, numbers, symbols, or spaces
Number	numbers only
Date	date only
Current date/ Current time	system date/time (you cannot change this field)
Calculation	=(formula) field to calculate numbers

TABLE 23-1
Text Form Field Descriptions

You insert form fields with buttons on the Forms toolbar. To display the Forms toolbar:

Step 1	**Close**	the Tables and Borders toolbar
Step 2	**Display**	the Forms toolbar using a shortcut menu
Step 3	**Review**	the buttons on the Forms toolbar using the SHIFT + F1 Help pointer

This order form requires the following fields:

1. Text form fields for the names, addresses, item numbers, and item description data
2. Number form field for the quantity ordered data

chapter twenty-three

3. Current date form field for the order date

4. Date form field for the ship by date

5. Check Box form fields to indicate the shipping method

6. Drop-Down form field to select the sales representative

You start by entering the text fields at the top of the form. To insert a Regular text form field for the Sold to: name:

Step 1	*Move*	the insertion point to the right of the "Sold to:" text in the first table
Step 2	*Set*	a left-aligned tab stop at approximately ¾ inch
Step 3	*Press*	the CTRL + TAB keys to insert a tab character formatting mark
Step 4	*Click*	the Text Form Field button ![abl] on the Forms toolbar
Step 5	*Verify*	the Form Field Shading button ![a] is pressed

Word inserts the form field into the table; your screen should look similar to Figure 23-4.

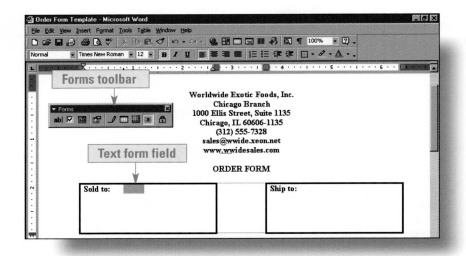

notes If the Bookmarks check box on the View tab in the Options dialog box is turned on, you see the nonprinting bookmark brackets around or adjacent to the form fields. The figures in this chapter show fields with the view of bookmark brackets turned off.

You need to specify the type of Text form field, the length of text the field accepts, and its format. To edit the form field:

| Step 1 | *Click* | the Form Field Options button  on the Forms toolbar |

The Text Form Field Options dialog box that opens on your screen should look similar to Figure 23-5.

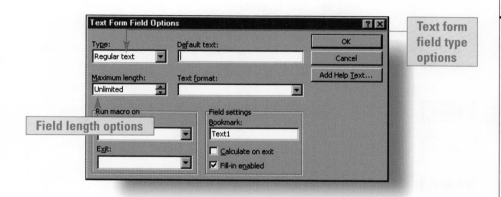

FIGURE 23-5
Text Form Field Options
Dialog Box

QUICK TIP

You can run macros automatically when the insertion point enters or exits an individual form field. For more information on running macros in a form, see online Help.

You select the type of Text form field in the Type: list box. Enter text you want shown by default in the Default text: text box. Specify the maximum number of characters the text form field can contain in the Maximum length: text box. Select a formatting option for the text form field in the Text format: list box.

You need four 25-character Regular text form field for the Sold to: name. You insert these form fields.

Step 2	*Verify*	Regular text is in the Type: list box
Step 3	*Double-click*	the Maximum length: text box to select its contents
Step 4	*Key*	25
Step 5	*Click*	OK

The form field is edited for 25-character regular text. Notice the form field is now a dark gray color, indicating it is selected. You need four 25-character Regular text form field for the Sold to: name and address. To insert the next three form fields:

| Step 1 | *Copy* | the dark gray shaded form field to the Clipboard |

Step 2	*Press*	the END key to move the insertion point to the right of the shaded form field, if necessary
Step 3	*Press*	the ENTER key
Step 4	*Press*	the CTRL + TAB keys to insert a tab character formatting mark
Step 5	*Paste*	the form field from the Clipboard at the insertion point
Step 6	*Continue*	by inserting tab character formatting marks and pasting the text form field until you have four fields in the Sold to: table

You also need four 25-character regular text form fields for the name and address in the Ship to: table. To insert these fields:

Step 1	*Move*	the insertion point to the right of the "Ship to:" text in the last column of the first table
Step 2	*Set*	a left-aligned tab stop at the 4.6-inch position on the horizontal ruler
Step 3	*Press*	the CTRL + TAB keys
Step 4	*Paste*	the form field from the Clipboard at the insertion point
Step 5	*Press*	the ENTER key
Step 6	*Continue*	to insert tab character formatting marks and paste the text form field until you have four fields in the Ship to: table

You use a Drop-Down form field to create a list of Sales Representative names. To create and format a Drop-Down form field:

Step 1	*Move*	the insertion point to the blank cell below the "Sales Representative" text in the third table
Step 2	*Click*	the Drop-Down Form Field button ▦ on the Forms toolbar
Step 3	*Double-click*	the drop-down form field

The Drop-Down Form Field Options dialog box that opens on your screen should look similar to Figure 23-6.

FIGURE 23-6
Drop-Down Form Field
Options Dialog Box

You key each item to appear in the drop-down list in the <u>D</u>rop-down item: text box. When you click the <u>A</u>dd button or press the ENTER key, the item appears in the <u>I</u>tems in drop-down list: list box. Use the Move buttons to reorder items in the list. Click the <u>R</u>emove button to remove selected items from the list. To create the drop-down list of sales representatives names:

Step 1	*Verify*	the insertion point is in the <u>D</u>rop-down item: text box
Step 2	*Key*	B. Collins
Step 3	*Click*	<u>A</u>dd
Step 4	*Key*	D. Rendell
Step 5	*Click*	<u>A</u>dd
Step 6	*Click*	OK

B. Collins, the first item in the list, appears in the cell. Later, when you open a new document based on this form template, the field will display a list box complete with a down arrow. You use the current system date for the Order Date. The buyer provides the Ship by Date when the order is taken. Word has two Text form fields for dates. The Order Date cell uses the Current date text form field, which is updated automatically with the system date. The Date text form field is used when the date data is entered in the form. You format both fields to contain a maximum of eight characters (which includes the date separator /) and to display the month as a two-digit number (suppressing the leading 0 for single digit months), the day of the month as a two-digit number, and the last two digits of the year.

**chapter
twenty-three**

To enter the Order Date text form field:

Step 1	*Move*	the insertion point to the blank cell below the "Order Date" text
Step 2	*Click*	the Text Form Field button [abl] on the Forms toolbar
Step 3	*Double-click*	the Text form field
Step 4	*Click*	the Type: list arrow
Step 5	*Click*	Current date
Step 6	*Key*	8 in the Maximum length: text box
Step 7	*Click*	the Date format: list arrow
Step 8	*Click*	M/d/yy
Step 9	*Click*	OK

The Current date form field, now displayed in the cell, contains the system date. You are now ready to insert a Text form field for the Ship by Date. To enter the Date text form field:

Step 1	*Move*	the insertion point to the blank cell below the "Ship by Date" text
Step 2	*Click*	the Text Form Field button [abl] on the Forms toolbar
Step 3	*Double-click*	the Text form field
Step 4	*Click*	Date in the Type: list
Step 5	*Key*	8 in the Maximum length: text box
Step 6	*Click*	M/d/yy in the Date format: list
Step 7	*Click*	OK

The Date form field is inserted. The sales representative completing the order form will enter data for this field.

Worldwide Exotic Foods, Inc. ships items on a "Rush" basis or on a "Regular" basis. You use a Check Box form field to indicate the shipping method. The Check Box form field is entered empty and the user simply moves to the check box and presses the SPACEBAR to insert an X indicating the correct shipping method. To insert the Check Box form fields:

Step 1	*Move*	the insertion point to the blank cell below the text "Shipping Method"
Step 2	*Key*	Rush
Step 3	*Press*	the SPACEBAR
Step 4	*Click*	the Check Box Form Field button ☑ on the Forms toolbar
Step 5	*Press*	the SPACEBAR twice
Step 6	*Key*	Regular
Step 7	*Press*	the SPACEBAR
Step 8	*Click*	the Check Box Form Field button ☑ on the Forms toolbar
Step 9	*Center*	all the fields vertically and horizontally in their cells using a shortcut menu

You use a 10-character Regular text form field for the Item Number. To insert the Item Number field:

Step 1	*Scroll*	the document to view the top rows in the last table
Step 2	*Move*	the insertion point to the first blank cell below the text "Item Number"
Step 3	*Insert*	a 10-character Regular text form field
Step 4	*Align*	the cell contents to the bottom left using a shortcut menu

You use a 30-character Regular text form field for the Item Description.

To insert the Description field:

Step 1	*Press*	the TAB key
Step 2	*Insert*	a 30-character Regular text form field
Step 3	*Align*	the cell contents to the bottom left using a shortcut menu

You use a 10-character Number text form field for the Quantity Ordered. When you specify a Number text form field, an error message is displayed if you attempt to enter nonnumeric data. To insert the Qty Ordered field:

Step 1	*Press*	the TAB key
Step 2	*Insert*	a 10-character Number text field
Step 3	*Align*	the cell contents to the bottom right using a shortcut menu

You must insert text form fields for each remaining line of the last table. This allows the sales representative to enter order data in all the rows of the table. Use the copy and paste feature to insert the remaining form fields in the last table. To copy the form fields:

Step 1	*Copy*	the fields in row 2 to all the remaining rows in the table

You can add a help message to a form field that appears on the status bar whenever the insertion point is in the form field. Help for a form field can also be assigned to the F1 key. Use status bar help messages for short reminders. For more complex instructions, assign the help message to the F1 key. You want to add a help message to the Ship by Date. To add a help message:

Step 1	*Double-click*	the Ship by Date field
Step 2	*Click*	Add Help Text
Step 3	*Click*	the Status Bar tab, if necessary

The Form Field Help Text dialog box that opens on your screen should look similar to Figure 23-7.

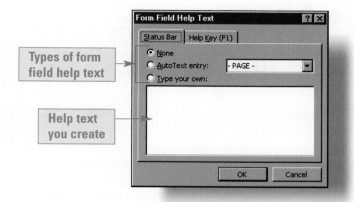

Types of form
field help text

Help text
you create

FIGURE 23-7
Status Bar Tab in the Form
Field Help Text Dialog Box

You set the type of help message and key the help text in this dialog box. You create your own help message text for the status bar.

Step 4	*Click*	the Type your own: option button
Step 5	*Key*	Remember to ask for the Ship by Date
Step 6	*Click*	OK in the Form Field Help Text dialog box
Step 7	*Click*	OK in the Text Form Field Options dialog box
Step 8	*Deselect*	the form field

After inserting all the form fields, you must protect the template.

Protecting the Form Template

When you **protect** the template, you provide access to only the form fields. Users cannot edit the boilerplate or the form structure of a protected form. They can only enter information in the fields.

You turn off the shading so that the form is easier to read and then you protect the form template by clicking the Protect Form button on the Forms toolbar. To protect the template:

Step 1	*Click*	the Form Field Shading button on the Forms toolbar
Step 2	*Click*	the Protect Form button 🔒 on the Forms toolbar
Step 3	*Close*	the Forms toolbar
Step 4	*Save*	the template and close it

QUICK TIP

To modify a form template, open the template and turn off the protection. Make the desired changes, protect the form, and save it again as a template.

C

MENU TIP

You can protect the template document by clicking the Protect Document command on the Tools menu.

**chapter
twenty-three**

23.b Creating a Document Based on a Form Template

To complete an online form, you first create a new document based on the form template and then you fill in the variable information. The sales manager asks you to test the order form by recording an order from a major customer for one item. To create a new order form document based on the *Order Form Template*:

Step 1	*Open*	the General tab in the New dialog box
Step 2	*Double-click*	the Order Form Template icon

A new document based on the *Order Form Template* opens. Because the document is protected for forms, you can only enter data in each text field, select data from the drop-down list box, or use a check box. The remaining portions of the document cannot be edited unless you turn off the protection with the Unprotect Document command on the Tools menu.

The insertion point is in the location of the first field where you must enter data. To move to the next field, press the TAB key. Press the SHIFT + TAB keys to move back to the previous field. You can also click the field where you want to enter data. To enter the variable data:

Step 1	*Key*	Mary Bowlin
Step 2	*Press*	the TAB key to move to the next line in the Sold to: box
Step 3	*Key*	75 West Highlands Street
Step 4	*Press*	the TAB key to move to the next line in the Sold to: box
Step 5	*Key*	Sydney NSW 20003
Step 6	*Press*	the TAB key to move to the next line in the Sold to: box
Step 7	*Key*	Australia
Step 8	*Press*	the TAB key to move to the first line in the Ship to: box
Step 9	*Key*	Same in the Ship to: box

QUICK TIP

When you unprotect the document, you can update selected form fields by pressing the F9 key. You can toggle between a form field and the field results by pressing the SHIFT + F9 keys. You can toggle between all form fields and all field results by pressing the ALT + F9 keys.

Step 10	*Click*	the current Sales Representative name to view the drop-down list
Step 11	*Click*	D. Rendell
Step 12	*Press*	the TAB key to move the Ship by: date field
Step 13	*Observe*	the help message on the status bar
Step 14	*Key*	the current date using two digits for month, day, and year
Step 15	*Press*	the TAB key to move to the Rush check box
Step 16	*Press*	the SPACEBAR to insert an X in the Rush check box
Step 17	*Press*	the TAB key twice to move to the first Item Number field
Step 18	*Key*	4568YZ
Step 19	*Press*	the TAB key to move to the first Description field
Step 20	*Key*	Holiday Meat and Cheese Basket
Step 21	*Press*	the TAB key to move to the first Quantity field
Step 22	*Key*	15

The form template works correctly and should save the sales representatives a lot of time as they take customer orders.

Forms can be printed on plain paper or on preprinted forms. To print the form on plain paper, simply print the document as you would any Word document. To print only the variable data in the current document on a preprinted form click the Print data only for forms check box in the Print tab of the Options dialog box.

To save, print, and close the document:

| Step 1 | *Save* | the document as *Completed Order Form* |
| Step 2 | *Print* | the document on plain paper and close it |

Now that you have tested the form template, you want to save it to another location and delete it from the default templates folder. To save the *Order Form Template*:

| Step 1 | *Open* | the Open dialog box |

chapter twenty-three

Step 2	*Switch*	to the C:\Windows\Application Data\Microsoft\Templates folder
Step 3	*Copy*	the *Order Form Template* document using a shortcut menu
Step 4	*Switch*	to the folder where your completed files are stored
Step 5	*Paste*	the *Order Form Template* document in the folder using a shortcut menu
Step 6	*Close*	the Open dialog box

Now you can remove the original copy of the *Order Form Template* document. To delete the custom form template from the New dialog box:

Step 1	*Open*	the General tab in the New dialog box
Step 2	*Right-click*	the *Order Form Template* icon
Step 3	*Click*	Delete
Step 4	*Click*	Yes to confirm the deletion
Step 5	*Close*	the New dialog box

23.c   Setting the Default File Location for Workgroup Templates

When templates are used by many members of the same workgroup, it is a good idea to have the network system administrator store the templates as read-only or on a server with limited access permissions. This helps to prevent users from inadvertently altering the templates. So that Word can locate your workgroup templates, you can set the default file location for them in the File Locations tab in the Options dialog box. To review the File Locations tab:

Step 1	*Open*	the Options dialog box
Step 2	*Click*	the File Locations tab
Step 3	*Observe*	the Workgroup templates option in the File types: list

You change the location by selecting the Workgroup templates option, clicking the <u>M</u>odify button to open the <u>M</u>odify Location dialog box, and then browsing to select the disk drive and folder that contains the templates. For now, you close the Options dialog box without changing the Workgroup templates location.

Step 4	*Close*	the dialog box

The Worldwide Exotic Foods sales representives will be able to process customer orders much more efficiently with the online form you created.

**chapter
twenty-three**

Summary

▶ Online forms can be used to create invoices, routing slips, order forms, and schedule documents. Users quickly fill in the variable information on a document based on a form template.

▶ Form templates can include boilerplate text, fill-in text fields, check boxes, drop-down lists, calculations, and dates.

▶ Before creating a form, you should design it on paper and then have your design reviewed by an end user.

▶ Tables provide a good framework for organizing forms.

▶ Help messages can be added to fields in a form template. You can specify that these help message appear on the status bar or display when the user presses the F1 key.

▶ Form templates must be protected, to prevent accidental changes to the text or fields in documents based on the form template.

▶ By changing a print option, you can specify that documents based on a form template be printed on plain paper or on preprinted forms.

▶ You can save the variable data entered into an onscreen form without saving the form's boilerplate or framework. This enables you to import the data into other applications such as Excel or Access.

Commands Review

Action	Menu Bar	Shortcut Menu	Toolbar	Keyboard
Create a new template	File, New, Template option			ALT + F, N ALT + T
Insert a tab character in a table				CTRL + TAB
Insert a Text form field			ab|	
Insert a Check Box form field			☑	
Insert a Drop-Down list form field				
Set form field options		Right-click form field, click Properties	or Double-click form field	
Display the Forms toolbar	View, Toolbars, Forms	Right-click toolbar, click Forms		ALT + V, T, DOWN ARROW to Forms, SPACEBAR
Move to the next field			Click field	TAB, or F11 (Word template)
Move to the previous field			Click field	SHIFT + TAB SHIFT + F11 (Word template)
Show contents of a drop-down list			Click list arrow	F4 ALT + DOWN ARROW
Move up or down a drop-down list				UP ARROW DOWN ARROW
Make a selection from a drop-down list			Click item	ENTER
Mark or unmark a check box field			Click check box	SPACEBAR key an X
Show Help for a form field			Click form field and read the status bar	F1 (unless set as status bar message)
Update a selected field				F9
Switch between viewing a field code and its results				SHIFT + F9
Switch between viewing all field codes and their results				ALT + F9
Activate form fields and protect a form template	Tools, Protect Document Forms option		🔒	ALT + T, P, F ALT + F
Set print options to print only variable data from a form	File, Print Tools, Options, Print tab			ALT + F, P ALT + T, O ALT + O ALT + P

Concepts Review

SCANS

Circle the correct answer.

1. You protect a form template before you save it so that:
[a] an icon for the template appears in the New dialog box.
[b] users can easily modify the form template's boilerplate and framework.
[c] users cannot accidentally change the non-variable text or framework of documents based on the template.
[d] the template design can be reviewed by end users.

2. Which of the following is not a Text form field type:
[a] Date.
[b] Number.
[c] Current date.
[d] Previous date.

3. Non-variable form text is called:
[a] switches.
[b] fields.
[c] controls.
[d] boilerplate.

4. The first step in creating an online form is to:
[a] plan and sketch the form.
[b] enter the variable data in each field.
[c] protect the form.
[d] create a new, blank template.

5. The framework for online forms is based on:
[a] templates.
[b] dialog boxes.
[c] drawing objects.
[d] tables.

6. A Regular text field can contain:
[a] only dates.
[b] only the system date.
[c] text, numbers, symbols, or spaces.
[d] numbers used in calculations.

7. A form field is sometimes called:
[a] a switch.
[b] boilerplate.
[c] an option.
[d] a control.

8. Check Box form fields allow the user to:
[a] answer yes or no by inserting an X.
[b] insert the current date in a field.
[c] key variable text in the field.
[d] select a variable from a list.

9. The date field format that includes "MMM" displays the month as:
[a] a number without a leading 0 for single-digit months.
[b] a number with a leading 0 for single-digit months.
[c] the month in two alphabetical characters.
[d] the month in three alphabetical characters.

10. You can assign a form field help message to the:
[a] F10 key.
[b] F1 key.
[c] F11 key.
[d] F4 key.

Circle **T** if the statement is true or **F** if the statement is false.

T   F   1. Word provides three kinds of form fields for online forms: text, check box, and drop-down list.

T   F   2. You cannot edit a document created from a protected form template.

T   F   3. When you protect a form, template users can enter data only in the form fields.

T   F   4. Documents based on a form template must always be printed on plain paper.

T   F   5. You can save variable data entered into a form without saving a form's boilerplate or framework.

T   F   6. Drop-down list form fields allow the user to select from a list of variables.

T   F   7. Drawing multiple tables is the best way to structure a complex form.

T   F   8. The first step in creating a form is to immediately create a new template and start designing the form on the screen.

T   F   9. Filling in forms onscreen slows down the process and increases errors.

T   F   10. You use the CTRL or CTRL + TAB keys to move from field to field when completing an online form.

Skills Review

Exercise 1   C

1. Open the *Time Sheet* document located on the Data Disk.

2. Format the first row of the table with Gray-20% shading.

3. Format the entire table with a 2¼-pt outside border and a ¾-pt inside border.

4. Set left-aligned tabs in the tables as appropriate for inserting the form fields.

5. Insert the form fields listed in the following table.

Variable	Field Options
Name:	Regular text, 25 characters
Date:	Current date; 8 characters, M/d/yy format
Dept.:	Drop-Down, with the following departments: Accounting, Legal, Sales
Status:	Check Box Exempt Check Box Non-exempt
For week ended:	Date; 8 characters, M/d/yy format
Hours worked:	Number; 2 characters
Supervisor:	Drop-Down; with following names: Roberto Rivas, Elizabeth Washington, Joseph Yang

chapter twenty-three

6. Protect the template.

7. Save the template as *Time Sheet Template* so that an icon appears in the General tab of the New dialog box.

8. Print and close the template document.

9. Create a new document based on the *Time Sheet Template* template. Use the following data:
Your name
Today's date
Accounting Department
Non-exempt status
For week ended today
40 hours worked
Supervisor, Elizabeth Washington

10. Save the document as *Completed Time Sheet*.

11. Preview, print, and close the document.

Exercise 2

1. Create the following form template.

2. The three-line heading and the text INSURANCE APPLICATION are 12-point bold.

3. Use tables to create a framework for the form and format the tables with a 10% shading and 2¼-pt outside border.

4. Set left-aligned tabs within the tables as appropriate for inserting the form fields.

5. Insert the appropriate form fields listed in the following table.

Variable	Field Options
Date:	Current date; 8 characters, M/d/yy format
SS #:	three number fields: 3, 2, and 4 characters
Name:	Regular text; 25 characters
Date of Birth:	Date; 8 characters, M/d/yy format
Address:	Regular text, 25 character for each of two lines of text
Home Phone:	Regular text, 15 characters
Gender:	Check Boxes (Female and Male)
Employer:	Regular text, 25 characters
Employer Phone:	Regular text, 15 characters
Type of Coverage:	Drop-Down, with the following list: Automobile, Homeowners, Renters
Replacement Value:	Number, 15 characters, #,##0 format
Yes or No question:	Check Boxes
Automobile use:	Check Boxes
Number of drivers:	Number, 2 characters for each category
Length of time at current address:	Number, 2 characters for each category

MCBRIDE INSURANCE AGENCY
3414 W. SECOND STREET
CHICAGO, IL 60616-3414

INSURANCE APPLICATION

| Date: | SS #:   -   - |

| Name: | Date of Birth: |

| Address: | Home Phone: |
| | Gender: Female   Male |

| Employer: |

| Employer Phone: |

| Type of Coverage: | Replacement Value: |

1. Has your driver's license been revoked, suspended or have you been convicted for driving under the influence of alcohol or drugs within the last five years?

| Yes | No |

2. Do you use your automobile for:

| Business | Pleasure |

3. Number of drivers in the household:

| Under 25 | Over 25 |

4. How long have you lived at your current address?

| Years | Months |

_____   _____
Applicant's Signature   Date

chapter twenty-three

6. Protect the form.

7. Save the form template as *Insurance Form Template* so that an icon appears in the General tab of the New dialog box.

8. Close the form template.

9. Create a new document based on the *Insurance Form Template* template using the data in the following table.

Field	Text
SS #	123-45-6789
Name	Elvira Jefferson
Date of Birth	03/25/57
Address	7890 Sycamore Avenue Chicago, IL 60603-1124
Home Phone	(312) 555-7823
Gender	Female
Employer	Worldwide Exotic Foods, Inc.
Employer Phone	(312) 555-8752
Key of Coverage	Automobile
Replacement Value	Skip
Driver's license	No
Automobile use	Pleasure
Number of drivers	2 over 25
Length of time at current address	Skip

10. Save the document as *Jefferson Form*.

11. Preview, print, and close the document.

12. Create a new document based on the *Insurance Form Template* using the data in the following table.

Field	Text
SS #	789-23-3390
Name	Henry Lincoln
Date of Birth	07/10/42
Address	14 East 11th Street Chicago, IL 60613-5467
Home Phone	(312) 555-9195
Gender	Male
Employer	Worldwide Exotic Foods, Inc.
Employer Phone	(312) 555-2548
Key of Coverage	Renters
Replacement Value	60,000
Driver's license	Skip
Automobile use	Skip
Number of drivers	Skip
Length of time at current address	5 years and 3 months

13. Save the document as *Lincoln Form*.

14. Preview, print, and close the document.

Exercise 3

1. Open the *Registration Form* document located on the Data Disk.

2. Format the form with tables, borders, and shading of your choice.

3. Set left-aligned tabs in the tables as appropriate for inserting the form fields.

4. Insert the form fields listed in the following table.

Variable	Field Options
Date	Current Date; 8 characters, M/d/yy format
Name	Regular text; 25 characters
Address	Regular text, 25 characters for each of two lines
Telephone Number	Regular text, 15 characters
Number of Dependent Children	Number, 2 characters
Registration Fee	Check Boxes for each category
Youth Group	Drop-Down, with the following list: West Side Youth, Central City Youth, East Side Youth

chapter twenty-three

5. Add appropriate help message to display on the status bar for each registration fee form field.

6. Protect the template form.

7. Save the template form as *Registration Form Template* so that an icon appears on the General tab in the New dialog box.

8. Print and close the template form.

9. Create a new document based on the *Registration Form Template* using the data in the following table.

Field	Text
Name	Millicent Ho
Address	1174 Rosebud Lane Chicago, IL 60623-2589
Telephone Number	(312) 555-4963
Number of Dependent Children	3
Registration Fee	Family
Youth Group	West Side Youth

10. Save the document as *Ho Form*.

11. Preview, print, and close the document.

Exercise 4

1. Create the following form template.

WORLDWIDE EXOTIC FOODS, INC.
SALES DEPARTMENT
EXPENSE REPORT

NAME:
DATE:

DATE	DESCRIPTION	EXPENSE

2. Set a 1½-inch top margin, and use the default left, right, and bottom margins. Key all text in 12-point Times New Roman, except the title. Format the title text as 12-point, bold Arial and centered.

3. The Date column should be ¾" wide. The Description column should be 3¾" wide. The Expense column should be 1" wide.

4. Center the Date column and set a decimal tab for the Expense column.

5. Format the table with 10% shading, a ¾-pt inside border, a 2¼-pt outside border, and a 2¼-pt bottom border for row 1.

6. Center the table between the left and right margins.

7. Insert the form fields listed in the following table.

Variable	Field Options
Name	Regular text, unlimited characters
Date	Date text, 8 characters, M/d/yy format
Date (in table)	Date text, 8 characters, M/d/yy format
Description	Regular text, unlimited characters
Expense	Number unlimited characters, first cell $#,##0.00;($#,##0.00) format, other cells #,##0.00 format

8. Remove the form field shading and protect the form.

9. Save the form template as *Expense Report Form* so that an icon appears on the General tab in the New dialog box.

10. Print and close the template document.

Exercise 5   C

1. Create a new document based on the *Expense Report Form* template you created in Exercise 4.

2. Enter the data listed in the following table.

Field	Text
Name	Clifford McDaniels
Date	current date in M/d/yy format
Date	6/27/99
Description	Airline tickets
Expense	350.75
Date	6/30/99
Description	Hotel accommodations
Expense	750.25
Date	6/30/99
Description	Rental car
Expense	220.12

chapter twenty-three

3. Unprotect the form.

4. Enter the text "Total" in the Description column in the cell below "Rental car."

5. Delete the form field in the cell below the last expense. (*Hint:* Display nonprinting characters.)

6. Enter a formula to calculate the total expenses. Format the formula with the $#,##0.00;($#,##0.00) format.

7. Save the document as *McDaniels Expense Form*.

8. Preview, print, and close the document.

Exercise 6

1. Create the following form template.

REGISTRATION FORM

Date
Name
Department
Address
Phone Number
Course Name
Course Date

---

2. Set a 1½-inch top margin, and use the default left, right, and bottom margins.

3. Add a 3-point box border around the form text.

4. Key text in 12-point Arial. Bold and center the text REGISTRATION FORM.

5. Set a left-aligned tab at 1½ inches.

6. Insert the appropriate form fields listed in the following table.

Variable	Field Options
Date	Current date, 8 characters, M/d/yy format
Name	Regular text, unlimited characters
Department	Regular text, unlimited characters
Address	Regular text, unlimited characters for each of two lines of text
Phone Number	Regular text, 15 characters
Course Name	Drop-Down, with the following courses: Beginning Microsoft Word Intermediate Microsoft Word Advanced Microsoft Word Beginning Microsoft Excel Intermediate Microsoft Excel Advanced Microsoft Excel Beginning Microsoft PowerPoint Intermediate Microsoft PowerPoint
Course Date	Date text, 8 characters, M/d/yy format

7. Remove the form field shading and protect the form.

8. Save the form template as *Training Form Template* so that an icon appears on the General tab in the New dialog box.

9. Print and close the template document.

Exercise 7   C

1. Create a new document based on the *Training Form Template* you created in Exercise 6.

2. Enter the data listed in the following table.

Field	Text
Name	Janet Holiday
Department	Accounting
Address	3850 West Union Drive Chicago, IL 60605-1135
Phone Number	(312) 555-8900
Course Name	Advanced Microsoft Word
Course Date	8/5/99

3. Save the document as *Holiday Registration*.

4. Preview, print, and close the document.

chapter twenty-three

Exercise 8

1. Create the following form template.

WORLDWIDE EXOTIC FOODS, INC.
TRAINING SEMINAR EVALUATION

Date	Course Name	Instructor Name

	Excellent	Very Good	Good	Fair	Poor
Instructor's Knowledge of Subject					
Instructor's Presentation Skills					
Course Content					
Effectiveness of Printed Material					
Pace of Class					
Overall Evaluation					
Facilities					

2. The title text is 12-point, bold Arial and centered. The remainder of the text is 10-point Times New Roman.

3. Use tables to create the framework for the form.

4. Insert the appropriate form fields listed in the following table.

Variable	Field Options
Date	Current date, 8 character size, M/d/yy format
Course Name	Drop-Down, with the following courses: Beginning Microsoft Word Intermediate Microsoft Word Advanced Microsoft Word Beginning Microsoft Excel Intermediate Microsoft Excel Advanced Microsoft Excel Beginning Microsoft PowerPoint Intermediate Microsoft PowerPoint Instructor Name
Instructor Name	Drop-Down with the following names: Janice Benevides Tamicka Johnson Brenda Wang David Oliver Frances D'Aversa
Excellent, Very Good, Good, Fair, Poor	Check boxes for each of the following: Instructor's Knowledge of Subject Instructor's Presentation Skills Course Content Effectiveness of Printed Materials Pace of Class Overall Evaluation Facilities

5. Remove the form field shading and protect the form.

6. Save the form template as *Training Evaluation Template* so that an icon appears on the General tab in the New dialog box.

7. Print and close the template document.

Exercise 9

1. Copy the following templates to a different location using the Open dialog box and then delete them from the General tab in the New dialog box.
Time Sheet Template
Insurance Form Template
Registration Form Template
Expense Report Form
Training Form Template
Training Evaluation Template

chapter twenty-three

Case Projects

Project 1

Beverly Williams, the manager of the office services department, needs help creating the online forms used in the department. She asks you to solve the following problems:

1. No arrow on drop-down lists in documents created from a form template.

2. Sometimes {FORMTEXT}, {FORMCHECKBOX}, or {FORMDROPDOWN} appear instead of form fields.

3. The form fields don't work properly.

Use the Office Assistant to research solutions to these problems. Write Beverly an interoffice memorandum describing each problem and suggesting a solution. Save, preview, and print the memo.

Project 2

The sales manager asks you to create an online form that the shipping department can use to record items shipped. The information needed on the form is: customer billing name, address, and telephone number; shipping address; order date and ship date; and description and quantity of items shipped. Sketch the layout of the form. With your instructor's permission, have a classmate review the form. Then draw and size the tables to create the layout. Insert the appropriate field codes. Protect, save, and print the template form. The orders will be printed on preprinted forms. Create three orders using the order form template. Use fictitious data for each form. Save, preview, and print the data for each order form.

Project 3

The accounting department wants to create invoice forms that contain calculations. The accounting manager asks you how to do this. Using the Help tools, review how to use the Calculation text form field. Write the manager, Bill Wilson, an interoffice memorandum explaining how to use the Calculation text form field in an Invoice online form template. Save, preview, and print the memo.

Project 4

Chris Lofton, the manager of the word processing department, is concerned about the workflow in the department. To avoid delays and enhance scheduling, you are asked to design an online form employees can complete when they send their work to the department. Sketch a draft of an appropriate online form. With your instructor's approval, have the form reviewed by a classmate. Create a form template based on the reviewed draft. Save, preview, and print the template document. Create an interoffice memorandum to all word processing department users with instructions on how to complete the form. Attach a sample of the form to the memorandum. Save, preview, and print the memorandum.

Project 5

The sales manager wants to see several examples of Web pages that use online forms to gather data. Connect to your ISP, launch your Web browser, and search for Web sites that use online forms. Save at least five Web pages. Write the sales manager an interoffice memorandum describing the Web sites that use online forms and the kind of information gathered by the forms. Save, preview, and print the memo.

Project 6

The sales manager has reviewed your memorandum on online forms for Web pages (from Project 5) and now wants to know how to create a form on a Web page using Word. Connect to your ISP and search the Web for information on how to create online forms. Also review online Help for information on how to do this. Create an unbound report document containing instructions for creating a Word Web page that contains an online form. Create a sample Web page with an online form, including fields for the name, address, telephone number, and e-mail address. Save, preview, and print the report and the form.

Project 7

The accounting department creates several invoices each day using an online form template. Because the invoice data is used in other applications, the accounting manager wants to save only the variable data for each invoice and asks you if this can be done. Using the Office Assistant, locate the online forms topics and review the "Save the data from a form in Word for use in a database" topic. Write the accounting manager an interoffice memorandum describing the process. Save, preview, and print the memorandum.

Project 8

Kelly Armstead in the purchasing department needs an online Purchase Order form. Draft the form and then create the form as a template. Create at least three purchase orders using the template and fictitious data. Save, preview, and print the template and the purchase order documents.

chapter twenty-three

Creating and Modifying Charts

Chapter Overview

Readers can usually more quickly understand and analyze numerical data when it is presented visually as well as in a list of figures. For example, sales growth and budgets can be represented as pie or bar charts, and the employee structure of a company or department is immediately evident from an organization chart. Some documents require formulas or other mathematical equations. In this chapter you learn how to create and modify data charts, organization charts, and equations.

LEARNING OBJECTIVES

► Create and modify charts
► Import data into charts
► Create an organization chart
► Create equations

Case profile

The Worldwide Exotic Foods accounting department is preparing quarterly financial reports for the sales at each of the four branches. In addition to including the actual numerical figures, they include charts to provide a picture of these numbers. The accounting manager, Bill Wilson, asks you to prepare the charts for these financial reports.

chapter
twenty
four

24.a   Creating and Modifying Charts

C

Microsoft Graph 2000 Chart is a supplementary application that comes with Office. With this application you can present numerical information as a **chart**, a picture or graphic of data or the relationship between sets of data. Common styles of charts are bar charts, pie charts, and line charts.

Creating a Chart

Bill Wilson, the accounting manager, plans to send an interoffice memorandum to all branch office and department managers reporting the third quarter sales data. In addition to the message and a table with the sales data, he wants you to include a chart illustrating the sales data. First, you create the interoffice memo and table shown in Figure 24-1.

FIGURE 24-1
Morris Memo

TO: All Branch Office and Department Managers

FROM: E. Morris
          Financial Vice President

DATE: October 25, 1999

SUBJECT: Third Quarter Sales Results

I would like to congratulate all branch managers on the outstanding results for the third quarter. This year' hird quarter results exceed all previous years by more than 20%!
     s t

Please be certain to discuss the results illustrated in the table and chart below at your next staff meeting.

Branch	Catalog Sales	Online Sales	Special Promotions	Total
WORLDWIDE EXOTIC FOODS, INC. THIRD QUARTER SALES REPORT ($000)				
Chicago	$33,175	$55,322	$11,500	$99,997
London	74,769	46,987	10,589	132,345
Melbourne	97,510	30,890	27,561	155,961
Vancouver	58,322	38,079	15,346	111,747
Total	$263,776	$171,278	$64,996	$500,050

**chapter
twenty-four**

To create the memo:

Step 1	*Create*	a new, blank document
Step 2	*Set*	the appropriate margins for an interoffice memorandum
Step 3	*Key*	the memo headings and text shown in Figure 24-1
Step 4	*Create*	the table shown in Figure 24-1 (key "Special Promotion" on two lines by pressing the ENTER key after "Special")
Step 5	*AutoFit*	the table to the contents and center the table
Step 6	*Save*	the document as *Third Quarter Memo*

You want to create a column chart based on the data in the table and center the chart horizontally below the table. To create a chart from the data in the table:

Step 1	*Select*	rows 2 through 7 of the table (the title is in row 1)
Step 2	*Click*	Insert
Step 3	*Point to*	Picture
Step 4	*Click*	Chart

In a few seconds, the Microsoft Graph 2000 Chart window opens. A **datasheet**, a grid of rows and columns in which you can enter, edit, or format data, appears. The datasheet contains the selected table data. You can also key the numerical data and text labels directly in the datasheet or you can import data from another program, such as Excel, into the datasheet. A default 3-dimensional column chart based on the data in the datasheet also appears on the screen. Your screen should look similar to Figure 24-2.

After you enter or import data in the datasheet, you choose the chart type, style, and formatting. The Standard and Formatting toolbars provide buttons to quickly change the chart type, the data orientation, the color or pattern of a data series, and the text formatting.

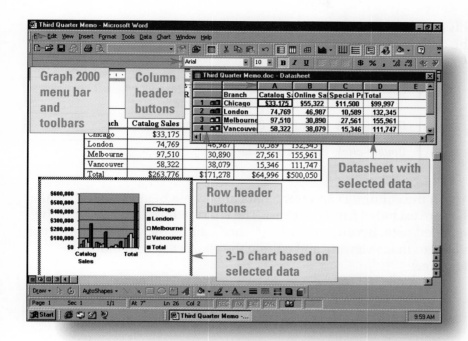

FIGURE 24-2
Graph 2000 Datasheet
and Chart

QUICK TIP

You can copy and paste link data from a spreadsheet application into a datasheet. When data is linked, any changes made to the original data are reflected in the data in the datasheet. Therefore, changes made to the data in the spreadsheet automatically update the Word document chart. For more information on importing and linking spreadsheet files, see Microsoft Graph online Help.

The datasheet contains the data you selected in the Word table. You can enlarge the datasheet to view all the columns and rows with data by dragging the datasheet boundaries with the mouse pointer. When you are finished with the datasheet, you can hide it to better view and edit the chart. To enlarge the datasheet:

| Step 1 | *Move* | the mouse pointer to the lower-right corner of the datasheet where it becomes a sizing pointer |
| Step 2 | *Drag* | the corner of the datasheet down and to the right until you can view columns A through D and rows 1 through 5 |

You realize you selected extra data. If you include data that should not be part of the chart, it is easy to remove it.

Removing Chart Data

You can include or exclude data from the chart by including or excluding rows and columns in the datasheet. You exclude columns or rows by double-clicking the column or row heading. Excluded columns and rows appear light gray in the datasheet. You can restore previously excluded data by double-clicking the column or row heading.

The data you selected in the Word table includes the total data by sales category and by branch. It is not appropriate to include totals in

**chapter
twenty-four**

this chart because you want to compare the sales details. To exclude the total data column and row:

Step 1	*Position*	the mouse pointer in the datasheet where it becomes a large white plus sign pointer
Step 2	*Double-click*	the column D header button
Step 3	*Double-click*	the row 5 header button

Both the column D and row 5 data are now light gray, indicating that they are excluded from the chart. The chart redraws to show only the included data. Because you are finished editing the datasheet, you can hide it to make viewing and editing the chart easier. To hide the datasheet:

| Step 1 | *Click* | the View Datasheet button 🔲 on the Standard toolbar |

The chart is composed of specific areas. The **chart area** comprises the entire chart. The **category or X-axis** is the data that appears along the bottom of the chart. Similarly, the **value or Y-axis** is the data that appears down the left side of the chart. The **plot area** contains the **data markers,** which illustrate each data value or point. **Walls** are the area that forms the background for the grid; walls provide a 3-D effect. Printable **gridlines** help the reader's eye follow the data markers. The **legend** identifies which data marker color represents each category of the original data. When you place the mouse pointer on a chart area, a ScreenTip appears to identify it. Figure 24-3 illustrates the specific chart areas.

FIGURE 24-3
Chart Areas

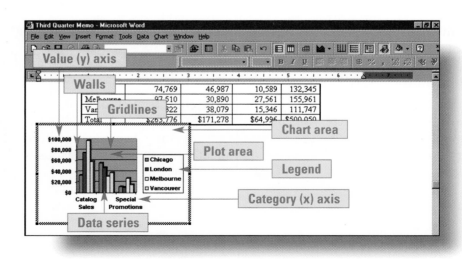

Now you are ready to size and format the chart.

Sizing a Chart

The chart has a hatch-mark boundary, indicating that it is selected and in an editing window. You use the sizing handles to resize the selected chart with the mouse, as you do with other objects. The "Online Sales" data text does not appear between "Catalog Sales" and "Special Promotions" at the bottom of the chart because the chart is too narrow. To widen the chart object and view the ScreenTips:

Step 1	**Drag**	the middle-right sizing handle to the right approximately 2 inches
Step 2	**Observe**	that the text "Online Sales" appears along the x-axis
Step 3	**Move**	the mouse pointer to upper-right corner of the chart
Step 4	**Observe**	the ScreenTip "Chart Area"
Step 5	**Move**	the mouse pointer to the gray area that forms the grid background
Step 6	**Observe**	the ScreenTip "Walls"
Step 7	**Continue**	to move the mouse pointer to different parts of the chart to identify the value (y) axis, category (x) axis, data markers, corners, gridlines, plot area, and legend

When you are finished creating a chart, you can close the Graph 2000 application and return to the document.

Closing Graph 2000 and Returning to the Document

After you create a chart, you should close the Graph 2000 application and return to your Word document. This inserts the chart as an object into your document. To return to the document:

| Step 1 | **Click** | in the document area outside the chart object |

The Graph 2000 application closes and the chart object is inserted into your document. You select a chart object by clicking it. You can size a selected chart object with the mouse, just as you do with other objects. By default a chart object is inserted in line with the text; therefore, you can use the alignment buttons on the Formatting toolbar to position it on the page.

You want to center the chart below the table. To select and center the chart object:

| Step 1 | **Click** | the chart to select it |

QUICK TIP

To position the chart object with the mouse pointer, you must first format the object with a wrapping option in the Layout tab of the object's Format dialog box.

chapter
twenty-four

Step 2	*Click*	the Center button 📑 on the Formatting toolbar
Step 3	*Deselect*	the chart object by clicking in the document outside the object
Step 4	*Scroll*	to view the chart

Your screen should look similar to Figure 24-4.

FIGURE 24-4
Centered Chart Object

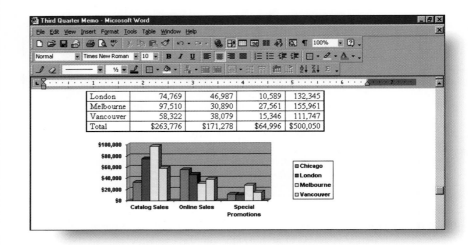

You can edit a chart object to change the chart type, add titles, change data marker colors, and format the text.

Modifying a Chart

To make a chart more attractive you can change the chart type, add and format titles, change the position of the legend, format the axes and legend text, and change the scale of the value axis. Also, if you do not have a color printer, you can change the default pastel data markers colors to black or gray, or add patterns. You can also change the plot area color.

To edit the chart object:

Step 1	*Double-click*	the chart object to open Graph 2000
Step 2	*Hide*	the datasheet
Step 3	*Scroll*	to view the entire chart, if necessary

You can use menu commands, a shortcut menu, and toolbar buttons to edit chart components. First, you want to change the chart type to a 2-dimensional column chart.

M ENU   TIP

You can open Graph 2000 to edit its components by selecting the chart, clicking the Edit menu, pointing to Chart Object, and then clicking the Edit command, or by right-clicking the chart object, pointing to Chart Object, and clicking Edit.

To change the chart type:

Step 1	*Click*	the Chart Type button list arrow ▨ on the Standard toolbar
Step 2	*Click*	the Column Chart button ▥ on the palette
Step 3	*Observe*	that the chart is a two-dimensional column chart

To more clearly identify the chart, you can add chart titles.

Adding and Formatting Titles

You can add titles for the chart, the category (*x*) axis, and the value (*y*) axis to better identify these chart components. To add a chart title:

Step 1	*Right-click*	the chart area
Step 2	*Click*	Chart Options
Step 3	*Click*	the Titles tab, if necessary

The Chart Options dialog box that opens on your screen should look similar to Figure 24-5.

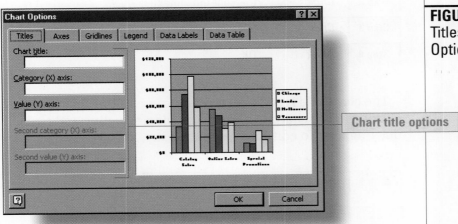

FIGURE 24-5
Titles Tab in the Chart Options Dialog Box

The Chart Options dialog box contains options for adding titles and data labels, positioning the legend, formatting the axes, adding or removing gridlines, and creating data tables.

| Step 4 | *Key* | Third Quarter Sales in the Chart title: text box |
| Step 5 | *Observe* | that the chart preview changes to include the new chart title |

| Step 6 | *Click* | OK |
| Step 7 | *Press* | the ESC key to deselect the chart title object |

You change the font, font size, font color, and add boldface or italic formatting to the title text by first selecting the chart title object and then opening the object's Format dialog box. One way to select any individual chart object is to use the Chart Objects list on the Standard toolbar. To select the chart title object:

Step 1	*Click*	the Chart Objects button list arrow
		Chart Area ▾ on the Standard toolbar
Step 2	*Click*	Chart Title
Step 3	*Observe*	that the chart title is selected

When you select an individual chart component, the Format *chart component* button on the Standard toolbar opens the selected component's Format dialog box. To format the chart title:

Step 1	*Click*	the Format Chart Title button 🖻 on the Standard toolbar
Step 2	*Click*	the Font tab, if necessary
Step 3	*Change*	the font to Times New Roman, 12 point
Step 4	*Click*	OK

The chart title is still selected. You can edit the chart title text by clicking in the chart title box and keying, selecting and replacing, or deleting text. To edit the chart title text:

Step 1	*Move*	the insertion point to the end of the word "Sales" in the chart title text
Step 2	*Press*	the SPACEBAR
Step 3	*Key*	by Branch
Step 4	*Press*	the ESC key twice to remove the insertion point from the chart title box and deselect the chart title

You can also reposition chart components.

MENU TIP

You can edit a selected chart component by clicking the S̲elected Object command on the F̲ormat menu, or by right-clicking a chart component and then clicking the F̲ormat Object command.

CAUTION TIP

You can open the Format dialog box for an individual chart component, such as the title or legend, by double-clicking it. Be careful when you use this method. It is very easy to double-click an adjacent chart component in error and open the wrong Format dialog box. When using the double-click method, you should always verify the dialog box title before you begin choosing formatting options. If you accidentally open the wrong Format dialog box, simply cancel it and try again.

Repositioning the Legend

You can select a chart component, such as the chart title or legend, and drag it to a new position with the mouse pointer. You want to move the legend from the right side of the chart to below the category (*x*) axis. If you drag the legend to the new position, the chart does not redraw to accommodate it and the legend might overlap the category (*x*) axis title and names. The best way to position the legend object is with the Format Legend dialog box. To select the legend and open the Format Legend dialog box:

Step 1	***Right-click***	the legend boundary
Step 2	***Click***	F<u>o</u>rmat Legend
Step 3	***Click***	the Placement tab, if necessary

The Format Legend dialog box that opens on your screen should look similar to Figure 24-6.

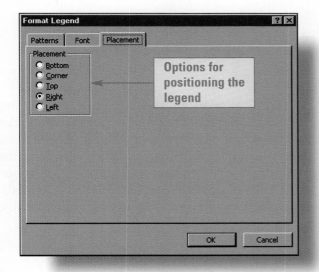

FIGURE 24-6
Placement Tab in the Format Legend Dialog Box

| Step 4 | ***Double-click*** | the <u>B</u>ottom option button to reposition the legend |
| Step 5 | ***Press*** | the ESC key to deselect the legend object |

The legend is positioned below the chart and category (*x*) axis and the chart redraws to accommodate the legend's new position. To make the chart easier to read, you can also format the plot area.

chapter
twenty-four

Editing the Plot Area

The plot area is the gray area between the value (*y*) axis and category (*x*) axis. It is often easier to read a chart printed in black and white, if the plot area is white and the plot area boundaries are black. To change the plot area color and boundary color:

Step 1	*Double-click*	the gray plot area
Step 2	*Verify*	the Format Plot Area dialog box opens
Step 3	*Click*	the Color: list arrow in the Border group
Step 4	*Click*	Black
Step 5	*Click*	White on the Color grid in the Area group
Step 6	*Observe*	the Sample plot area in the lower-left corner of the dialog box
Step 7	*Click*	OK
Step 8	*Deselect*	the plot area

The plot area is set to print attractively in black-and-white. Next you want to change the values that appear along the *y*-axis.

Editing the Value (Y) Scale

The Graph 2000 application establishes a default scale for the value (*y*) axis based on the selected data and the size of the chart. The scale begins with the smallest or minimum data value and goes to the largest or maximum data value charted. Instead of listing every number between the minimum and maximum values, only the numbers for a specific increment are shown. You can edit this value (y) scale to control the data markers height by changing the minimum, maximum, and scale increments. You want the increment to be $25,000.

notes For the remaining activities in this chapter, you can use the menu, toolbar, shortcut, or mouse method to open the Format dialog box for a chart object.

To change the value (y) scale:

Step 1	*Open*	the Scale tab in the Format Axis dialog box for the value (*y*) axis
Step 2	*Key*	25000 in the Major unit: text box
Step 3	*Click*	OK

| Step 4 | *Deselect* | the value (*y*) axis chart object |
| Step 5 | *Observe* | that the value (*y*) increment is changed to $25,000 |

Sometimes a chart does not display the data in the appropriate grouping or orientation.

Changing the Data Orientation

Because of the arrangement of the data in the original table, Graph 2000 assumes the chart orientation is based on the rows of data. Because of this, each row in the table is plotted as a data series. With the data series plotted by rows, the chart compares the three sales categories by branch. Bill wants the chart to compare branch office sales rather than sales by category. You can change the data orientation to columns to compare branch offices. To change the data orientation to columns:

| Step 1 | *Click* | the By Column button ▦ on the Standard toolbar |
| Step 2 | *Observe* | that the data are now presented by branch |

Because the memo will be printed in black and white, you decide to change the data marker colors and patterns to make the printed chart more attractive.

Editing a Data Series

You can change the data series colors to make the chart more legible or attractive. If you do not have a color printer, you can change the data series area and boundary colors to black or gray shades. You can also add a pattern to a data series. To edit a data series you must first select the series markers. You can select the entire series at once or one marker in the series at a time. To change the Catalog Sales data series:

Step 1	*Click*	any marker in the Catalog Sales data series (any light blue marker) to select the data series
Step 2	*Open*	the Patterns tab in the Format Data Series dialog box
Step 3	*Click*	Black in the Area color grid
Step 4	*Click*	OK
Step 5	*Observe*	that the Catalog Sales data series is now black

CAUTION TIP

If you accidentally click outside a chart when editing it, Graph 2000 closes and you are working in your document. To reopen Graph 2000 and continue editing the chart, double-click the chart object.

QUICK TIP

To select one marker in a data series, first click any marker in the series to select the entire series. Then click a specific marker in the series to select that marker.

**chapter
twenty-four**

You want to change a second data series to a pattern. To edit the Online Sales data series:

Step 1	*Select*	the Online Sales data series
Step 2	*Open*	the Patterns tab in the Format Data Series dialog box
Step 3	*Click*	Fill Effects in the Area group
Step 4	*Click*	the Pattern tab, if necessary

The Fill Effects dialog box that opens on your screen should look similar to Figure 24-7.

FIGURE 24-7
Pattern Tab in the Fill
Effects Dialog Box

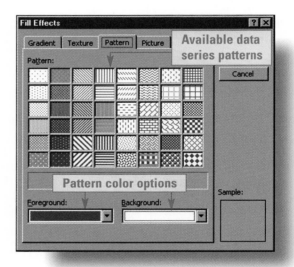

Step 5	*Click*	the Light vertical tile (fourth pattern in the first row)
Step 6	*Click*	Gray-40% in the Foreground: list
Step 7	*Click*	Gray-25% in the Background: list
Step 8	*Click*	OK in each dialog box
Step 9	*Deselect*	the chart object and return to the document

You can use drawing objects to enhance a chart's appearance.

Enhancing a Chart with Drawing Objects

You can add non-title text and drawing objects, such as arrows, to enhance a chart's appearance and draw attention to specific elements.

You want to add the text "Great Performance!" and an arrow pointing to the Melbourne catalog sales data marker. To add the non-title text:

Step 1	***Double-click***	the chart to edit it
Step 2	***Hide***	the datasheet, if necessary
Step 3	***Key***	Great Performance! to place the text in a text box
Step 4	***Drag***	the "Great Performance!" text box above the top gridline at the right edge of the chart
Step 5	***Deselect***	the text box
Step 6	***Display***	the Drawing toolbar
Step 7	***Draw***	an arrow pointing from the "Great Performance!" text to the Melbourne Catalog Sales data marker
Step 8	***Deselect***	the chart object and return to the document

The chart object on your screen should look similar to Figure 24-8.

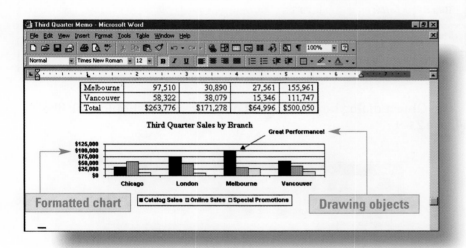

FIGURE 24-8
Completed Chart with Drawing Objects

Step 9	***Save***	the document and close it

If you have data in another application, you can import it into the Graph 2000 datasheet and chart it.

24.b Importing Data into Charts

Bill wants you to create a document that shows a chart of the third quarter pastries sales. You import the data from an Excel worksheet into the Graph 2000 datasheet and create a chart based on the imported data. You can open Microsoft Graph 2000 with a datasheet that contains sample data and then replace that data with the imported data. To create a new document and create a chart:

Step 1	*Create*	a new, blank document
Step 2	*Key*	Pastries Sales
Step 3	*Format*	the text with 14-point, bold, Times New Roman, center-aligned
Step 4	*Press*	the ENTER key twice
Step 5	*Click*	Insert
Step 6	*Click*	Object
Step 7	*Click*	the Create New tab, if necessary

The Object dialog box that opens on your screen should look like Figure 24-9.

FIGURE 24-9
Create New Tab in the
Object Dialog Box

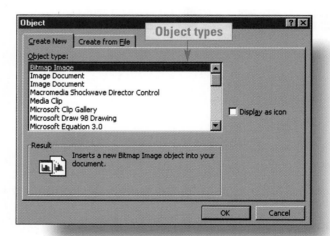

Step 8	*Double-click*	Microsoft Graph 2000 Chart in the Object type: list

The datasheet opens containing sample data. You replace the sample data with the imported data. To import the data from the Excel worksheet:

| Step 1 | **Click** | the Import File button 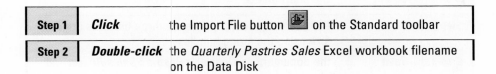 on the Standard toolbar |
| Step 2 | **Double-click** | the *Quarterly Pastries Sales* Excel workbook filename on the Data Disk |

The Import Data Options dialog box that opens on your screen should look similar to Figure 24-10.

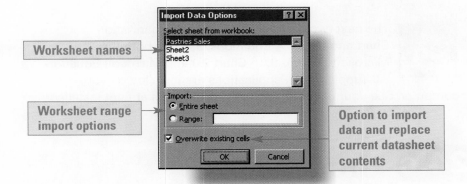

Worksheet names

Worksheet range import options

Option to import data and replace current datasheet contents

FIGURE 24-10
Import Data Options
Dialog Box

The data you want to import begins in cell A5 (column A, row 5) and ends in cell D9 (column D, row 9) in the Pastries Sales worksheet in the workbook. The group of cells beginning in A5 and ending in D9 is called a range and is written A5:D9. You specify the worksheet and data range to import in this dialog box.

Step 3	**Select**	Pastries Sales in the <u>S</u>elect sheet from workbook: list, if necessary
Step 4	**Click**	the R<u>a</u>nge option button
Step 5	**Key**	A5:D9 in the R<u>a</u>nge: text box
Step 6	**Click**	the <u>O</u>verwrite existing cells check box to insert a check mark, if necessary
Step 7	**Click**	OK
Step 8	**Observe**	that the pastries sales data replaces the sample data in the datasheet
Step 9	**Hide**	the datasheet
Step 10	**Deselect**	the chart object and return to the document

To finish up this document, you just need to format the chart object by sizing it. To resize the chart object:

Step 1	*Select*	the chart object
Step 2	*Size*	the chart object approximately three times its original size using the sizing handles
Step 3	*Save*	the document as *Quarterly Pastries Sales Report* and close it

Another type of chart you can create shows the relationship between people in an organization.

notes   The next two sections, Creating an Organization Chart and Creating Equations, assume both the Microsoft Organization Chart 2.0 and Microsoft Equation 3.0 supplemental applications are installed on your computer. See your instructor if these applications are not installed.

24.c Creating an Organization Chart

An **organization chart** shows the hierarchical reporting relationships between people in an organization. An organization chart identifies these reporting relationships by placing employees in different levels on the chart, the top level being the primary reporting relationship. For example, the president of an organization would be shown at the first level on an organization chart, vice presidents at the second level, managers at the third level, and so forth.

The accounting manager needs an organization chart for the accounting department and asks you to create one. You can create an organization chart with the Microsoft Organization Chart 2.0 supplementary application. To create a new document:

Step 1	*Create*	a new, blank document
Step 2	*Key*	Worldwide Exotic Foods, Inc. Accounting Department Organization Chart
Step 3	*Format*	the three heading lines with 18-point, bold, Times New Roman and center them
Step 4	*Press*	the ENTER key twice

With the heading text in place, you can open the supplemental program and create the organization chart. To create a blank organization chart:

Step 1	**Open**	the Create New tab in the Object dialog box
Step 2	**Double-click**	the MS Organization Chart 2.0 in the Object type: list
Step 3	**Maximize**	the Microsoft Organization Chart window

An organization chart consists of linked boxes, each of which contains the name and title of one person in the organization. Whenever you add boxes, change their size, or move them, Organization Chart redraws the complete chart. When working with a large chart, it is faster to create new boxes while viewing the chart in actual size or 200% of actual size, because only the part of the chart that is visible is redrawn. For now, you view the chart at 50% of actual size so that all the boxes are visible while the chart is being created and edited. To change the view:

| Step 1 | **Click** | View |
| Step 2 | **Click** | 50% of Actual |

The entire chart is now visible. Your screen should look similar to Figure 24-11.

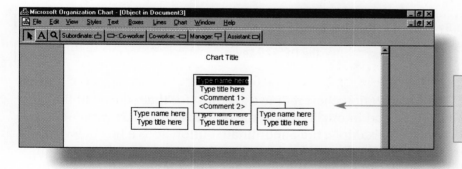

FIGURE 24-11
Microsoft
Organization Chart

Default
organization chart
text boxes viewed
at 50% zoom

Bill wants to include the following personnel on the organization chart: B. J. Wilson, Accounting Manager; M. S. Morales, Assistant Manager Payables; A. L. Smith, Assistant Manager Receivables; F. W. Gordon, Payables Clerk; and T. J. Chu, Receivables Clerk. The accounting manager is placed at the first level of the chart, the assistant accounting managers are placed at the second level of the chart, and the clerks are placed at the third level of the chart. To enter the accounting manager in the chart:

| Step 1 | **Key** | B. J. Wilson in the Type name here selected area of the first-level box |

MENU TIP

When you open Organization Chart, a new chart is created based on one of two chart templates. You can change the template and other default options with the Options command on the Edit menu.

chapter
twenty-four

Step 2	*Press*	the ENTER key
Step 3	*Key*	Accounting Manager in the Type title here selected area of the first-level box
Step 4	*Click*	outside the box to deselect it

To enter the information for the two assistant managers at the second level in the chart:

Step 1	*Click*	the first box on the second level to select the box
Step 2	*Key*	M. S. Morales
Step 3	*Press*	the ENTER key
Step 4	*Key*	Assistant Manager
Step 5	*Press*	the ENTER key
Step 6	*Key*	Payables
Step 7	*Continue*	by adding A. L. Smith, Assistant Manager, Receivables to the second box on the second level

Because there are only two employees at this second level, you don't need the third box in the second level. To delete the extra box:

| Step 1 | *Click* | the third box to select it |
| Step 2 | *Press* | the DELETE key |

The organization chart redraws to adjust for the removal of the box. You can add additional boxes to the organization chart with toolbar buttons. For example, the Subordinate button adds a box below an existing box. The Co-worker buttons add a box to the left or right of boxes at the same level. The clerks are subordinates of the assistant managers. To add subordinates to Morales and Smith:

Step 1	*Click*	the Subordinate button Subordinate: on the Organization Chart toolbar
Step 2	*Click*	anywhere in the Morales box
Step 3	*Key*	F. W. Gordon
Step 4	*Press*	the ENTER key

Step 5	*Key*	Payables Clerk
Step 6	*Continue*	by adding T. J. Chu, Receivables Clerk, as a subordinate of Smith

When you close the Organization Chart application and return to the document, an organization chart object is inserted into the document. To close Organization Chart 2.0 and return to your document:

Step 1	*Click*	File
Step 2	*Click*	Exit and Return to Document
Step 3	*Click*	Yes to confirm you want to update the chart
Step 4	*Observe*	the selected organization chart object in the document

You can edit the organization chart to change the box fill and border colors, the text colors, and the arrangement of the boxes by double-clicking the organization chart object, selecting some or all the boxes with a shortcut menu, and making formatting choices from the menu bar. To edit the organization chart object and select all the boxes:

Step 1	*Double-click*	the organization chart object
Step 2	*Right-click*	the chart background
Step 3	*Point to*	Select
Step 4	*Click*	All

Bill asks you to format the chart text to match other departmental documents. To change the font and font size:

Step 1	*Click*	Text
Step 2	*Click*	Font
Step 3	*Change*	the font to 12-point Times New Roman
Step 4	*Click*	OK
Step 5	*Return*	to the document and update the chart
Step 6	*Observe*	the reformatted organization chart object
Step 7	*Save*	the document as *Accounting Organization Chart* and close it

**chapter
twenty-four**

When you need to insert special mathematical symbols or formulas in a document, you can use the Equation 3.0 supplemental application.

24.d   Creating Equations

The Microsoft Equation 3.0 supplementary application allows you to create and edit mathematical and scientific equations. The equations you create with Microsoft Equation 3.0 are inserted as objects in your document. These equations do not calculate; however, they do print with the appropriate structure and format for an equation.

You need to insert the formula used to calculate the average age of the accounting department employees in an insurance report. To insert the equation:

Step 1	**Open**	the *Insurance Report* document located on the Data Disk
Step 2	**Move**	the insertion point to the blank line below the line beginning "The formula for"
Step 3	**Open**	the Create New tab in the Object dialog box
Step 4	**Double-click**	Microsoft Equation 3.0 in the Object type: list box

The Equation 3.0 application opens. Your screen should look similar to Figure 24-12.

FIGURE 24-12
Microsoft Equation 3.0
Window

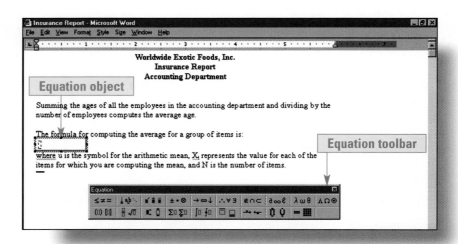

You use buttons on the Equation toolbar to insert symbols into the equation object. The first character in the equation is the Greek character μ.

To insert the μ character into the equation:

| Step 1 | *Click* | the Greek characters (lowercase) button λ ω θ on the Equation toolbar |
| Step 2 | *Click* | the μ symbol (first symbol, fourth row) |

Next, you enter the rest of the formula to calculate the average age of the accounting department employees.

Step 3	*Key*	=
Step 4	*Click*	the Fraction and radical templates button ▦ √▯ on the Equation toolbar
Step 5	*Click*	the first template (first column, first row)
Step 6	*Click*	the Summation templates button Σ▯ Σ▯ on the Equation toolbar
Step 7	*Click*	the first template (first template, first row)
Step 8	*Key*	X
Step 9	*Click*	the Subscript and superscript templates ▮ ▯ on the Equation toolbar
Step 10	*Click*	the second template on the first row (second template, first row)
Step 11	*Key*	i
Step 12	*Click*	the slot at the bottom of the fraction to move the insertion point
Step 13	*Key*	N

The equation is complete. To close Equation 3.0, return to the document, and position the equation object:

Step 1	*Click*	anywhere in the document outside the equation object
Step 2	*Select*	the equation object and center it
Step 3	*Deselect*	the equation object

chapter
twenty-four

Your screen should look similar to Figure 24-13.

FIGURE 24-13
Completed Equation in
Document

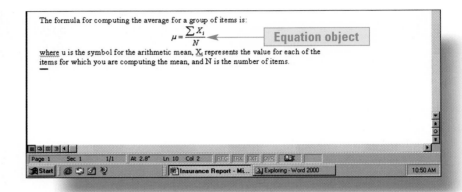

The formula for computing the average for a group of items is:

$$\mu = \frac{\sum X_i}{N}$$ ← Equation object

where u is the symbol for the arithmetic mean, X_i represents the value for each of the items for which you are computing the mean, and N is the number of items.

| Step 4 | *Save* | the document as *Insurance Report with Equation* and close it |

The Equation Editor enables you to insert formulas or other mathematical equations into any document.

Summary

► Numerical data can be presented as a picture called a chart.

► You can use the Microsoft Graph 2000 Chart application to create charts by entering the data, importing the data, or selecting the data in a Word table.

► You can hide or display the datasheet that contains the data for your chart.

► You remove data from a chart by deselecting the data in the datasheet or by deleting a data series in a chart.

► You can size a chart object by dragging a sizing handle with the mouse.

► You can edit an existing chart by opening the Graph 2000 application and working with the chart object in an editing window.

► Individual chart components can be selected and formatted in the appropriate Format dialog box or with toolbar buttons.

► You can enhance the appearance of a chart by adding descriptive text and drawing objects.

► Organization charts show the relationship between people in an organization and are created with the Microsoft Organization Chart 2.0 application.

► You can create correctly formatted mathematical equations—complete with symbols—with Microsoft Equation 3.0.

chapter twenty-four

Commands Review

Action	Menu Bar	Shortcut Menu	Toolbar	Keyboard
Create a chart	Insert, <u>O</u>bject, Microsoft Graph 2000 Chart			ALT + I, O
Edit an existing chart in your document	<u>E</u>dit, Chart <u>O</u>bject, <u>E</u>dit	Right-click the chart object, point to Chart <u>O</u>bject, click <u>E</u>dit	Double-click the chart object	ALT + E, O, E
Format a selected chart object	F<u>o</u>rmat, selected chart object	Right-click the chart object, click the F<u>o</u>rmat command	Double-click the chart object Chart Area ▾ 	ALT + O, then the underlined character in the selected chart object command
Create an organization chart	Insert, <u>O</u>bject Microsoft Organization Chart 2.0			ALT + I, O
Create an equation	Insert, <u>O</u>bject Microsoft Equation 3.0			ALT + I, O

Concepts Review

Circle the correct answer.

1. A chart is a(n):
  [a] table containing data.
  [b] clip from the ClipArt Gallery.
  [c] equation.
  [d] picture of numerical data or the relationship between people in an organization.

2. One way to remove data from a chart is to select the data series markers and press the:
  [a] ALT key.
  [b] SHIFT + ALT keys.
  [c] CTRL key.
  [d] DELETE key.

3. You can deselect a chart component by:
  [a] pressing the TAB key.
  [b] pressing the SHIFT key.
  [c] pressing the ESC key.
  [d] clicking the Format Object button.

4. An organization chart shows:
  [a] a picture of numerical data.
  [b] the relationship between people in an organization.
  [c] a properly formatted mathematical or scientific equation.
  [d] a grid of rows and columns.

5. The best way to reposition the legend in a chart is to:
  [a] select a new position in the Format Legend dialog box.
  [b] drag it to the new position with the mouse.
  [c] select a new position in the Format Data Series dialog box.
  [d] double-click it.

6. You can include or exclude data in a chart by:
[a] clicking the Data Erase button.
[b] selecting the data and pressing the ALT key.
[c] double-clicking a column or row header button.
[d] dragging the data out of the chart.

7. Which of the following is not a chart component?
[a] value (y) axis.
[b] chart title.
[c] data marker.
[d] Fraction and Radical template.

8. To change the orientation of the data in a chart, you can click the:
[a] Flip Data button.
[b] Data Orientation button.
[c] By Rows button.
[d] Rotate Data button.

9. Plot area gridlines:
[a] identify which data marker color represents each category.
[b] underline the data along the bottom of the chart.
[c] help a reader's eyes follow the data markers.
[d] illustrate each data value.

10. Equations inserted with Equation 3.0:
[a] do not print.
[b] cannot be edited once inserted.
[c] do not calculate.
[d] cannot be repositioned once inserted.

Circle **T** if the statement is true or **F** if the statement is false.

T   F   1. You can change the default scale for the value (y) axis for a chart.

T   F   2. You cannot change the chart type once a chart is created.

T   F   3. Chart components can be edited but they cannot be moved.

T   F   4. You can edit a chart component by right-clicking it to display a shortcut menu, and then clicking the Format (object) command.

T   F   5. The only way to create a chart in Word is to select data from a Word table.

T   F   6. The Microsoft Equation 3.0 application is used to create organization charts.

T   F   7. Non-title text and drawing objects can be added to enhance the appearance of a chart.

T   F   8. The default chart type is a two-dimensional bar chart.

T   F   9. It is harder to understand and analyze numerical data when presented visually in a chart.

T   F   10. You use a datasheet to construct an equation.

chapter twenty-four

Skills Review

Exercise 1

1. Open the *City Sales Report* document located on the Data Disk.

2. Select rows 2 through 6 of the table and create a two-dimensional column chart. (*Caution:* When years appear as numbers in the first row of the table, Chart 2000 assumes they are values and creates a data series for them.)

3. Add the chart titles. Use "Sales Report" for the chart title and "Units" for the value (y) title.

4. Size and position the chart attractively on the page.

5. Key the years 1997, 1998, and 1999 in individual text boxes. Position each text box below the appropriate series of values.

6. Save the document as *City Sales Report With Chart.*

7. Print the document.

8. Edit the chart. Format the chart title with 16-point Times New Roman. Position the legend at the bottom of the chart. Change the plot area to white with no border. Change the data series colors to colors and patterns of your choice. Turn off the gridlines.

9. Add the text "Great Job!" and an arrow that points to the Chicago, 1998 data marker.

10. Save the document as *Revised City Sales.*

11. Preview, print, and close the document.

Exercise 2

1. Open the *Division Expense Report* document located on the Data Disk.

2. Select rows 2 through 7 of the table and create a pie chart illustrating Supplies Expense by division.

3. Change the data series orientation to columns to see all the pie slices.

4. Do not display a legend. (*Hint:* Hide the legend in the Chart Options dialog box.)

5. Use "Supplies" as the chart title.

6. Format the plot area to display no borders and no area color.

7. Show label and percent data labels. (*Hint:* Use the Data Labels tab in the Chart Options dialog box.) Remove the leader lines.

8. Change the font size of the data labels to 10 point.

9. Size and position the chart attractively below the table.

10. Select each individual data label and position it more attractively with the mouse.

11. Save the document as *Division Expense Report With Chart*.

12. Print the document.

13. Edit the pie chart to change the chart type to a 3-D pie chart. (*Hint:* Use the Chart Type button on the Graph 2000 Standard toolbar to select the 3-D pie chart type.)

14. Edit the position of the data labels, if necessary.

15. Edit the chart title to read "Supplies Expense."

16. Save the document as *Division Expense Report Revised*.

17. Preview, print, and close the document.

Exercise 3   C

1. Create a new, blank document.

2. Create a chart based on the sample data in Graph 2000.

3. Import the *Third Quarter Bread Sales* workbook, Sales Units worksheet data, range A1:D4 into the datasheet to replace the sample data.

4. Change the chart to a two-dimensional bar chart.

5. Add the chart title "Third Quarter Sales" and the value (*y*) title "Units."

6. Enhance the chart text, titles, and data series using the appropriate formatting dialog boxes.

7. Save the document as *Third Quarter Bread Sales*.

8. Preview, print, and close the document.

Exercise 4   C

1. Open the *Marketing Organization Chart* located on the Data Disk.

2. Double-click the organization chart to edit it.

3. Select all the boxes and change the boxes color to red and the boxes border style to a style of your choice. (*Hint:* Use the Boxes command on the Organization Chart menu bar.)

4. Select all the boxes and change the text color to white.

5. Select all the boxes and change the organization chart style to the vertical style. (*Hint:* Use the Styles command on the Organization Chart menu bar.)

6. Add an assistant to T. J. Edwards named B. Rivera with the job title "Executive Assistant."

7. Update the organization chart in the document.

8. Make the organization chart smaller so that chart appears on the same page as the three heading lines, if necessary.

chapter twenty-four

9. Change the font color of the heading text to red.

10. Save the document as *Organization Chart Revised*.

11. Preview, print, and close the document.

Exercise 5

1. Open the *Third Quarter Bread Sales* document you created in Exercise 3.

2. Use the Formatting toolbar to format the chart title with 12-point Times New Roman.

3. Change the color of the data series to colors and patterns of your choice.

4. Save the document as *Enhanced Third Quarter Bread Sales*.

5. Preview, print, and close the document.

Exercise 6

1. Open the *Support Expenses* document located on the Data Disk.

2. Select the rows 2 through 7 in the table and create a two-dimensional column chart comparing the budgeted and actual expenses for all item categories.

3. Edit the datasheet to widen columns A and B by double-clicking the boundary between the column header buttons. Edit the datasheet to omit column C and row 5.

4. Change the value (*y*) Major increment scale to 1,000,000.

5. Edit the data series to print attractively in black and white.

6. Format, size, and position the chart attractively below the table.

7. Save the document as *Support Expenses With Chart*.

8. Preview, print, and close the document.

Exercise 7

1. Open the *Support Expenses With Chart* document you created in Exercise 6.

2. Change all data series colors back to automatic.

3. Omit the Budget data and include the Miscellaneous category.

4. Change the chart type to a 3-D pie.

5. Change the data orientation to columns.

6. Add the chart title "Actual Expenses."

7. Remove the plot area border.

8. Add percent data labels.

9. Size and position the chart attractively below the table.

10. Save the document as *Actual Expenses*.

11. Preview, print, and close the document.

Exercise 8

1. Open the *Interest Rate* document located on the Data Disk.

2. Between the two paragraphs, insert the following formula, which computes the interest owed on a loan for a specific time period. (*Hint:* Format the X in italic using the <u>O</u>ther command on the <u>S</u>tyle menu.)

$$I = P \; x \; \frac{R}{12}$$

3. Center the equation between the left and right margins.

4. Enlarge the equation object approximately ½ inch, using the lower-right-corner sizing handle.

5. Save the document as *Interest Rate Equation*.

6. Preview, print, and close the document.

Case Projects

Project 1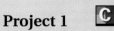

Jody Haversham calls to ask for your help creating charts in Word. Open a document that contains a chart you created in this chapter and edit the chart. Use the SHIFT + F1 Help feature to review the buttons on the Standard and Formatting toolbars in the Graph 2000 window. Write Jody an interoffice memorandum describing at least five graph buttons and how to use them. Save, preview, and print the memo.

Project 2

The accounting manager asks you to create a chart from a Word table that is part of a customer letter. Include data labels on the chart for one data marker in a series. Create a letter to a fictitious customer that includes a Word table with three columns of fictitious sales data. Create a chart from the table and format the chart attractively. Add a data label to the largest (value) data marker. Position the chart attractively below the table. Save, preview, and print the letter and accompanying envelope.

Project 3

Because of your experience creating charts in the accounting department, Chris Lofton asks you to present a 30-minute review on how to create charts using Graph 2000 to the word processing specialists. Create an outline with three levels of detail for the presentation, itemizing the topics you should cover. Save, preview, and print the outline. Create a new document that contains a table with two columns. In the first column, list the main topics of the presentation. In the second column, list the amount of time you expect to use covering the topic. Create a pie chart that uses the table data to illustrate the percentage of time devoted to each main topic. Save, preview, and print the table and chart.

Project 4

The shipping manager wants to put the shipping department organization chart on the company intranet. Create an organization chart for the shipping department using fictitious data. Include three levels in your chart. Apply the theme of your choice and save the document as a Web page. Preview and print the Web page.

chapter twenty-four

Project 5

Kelly Armstead has created a chart in a Word document based on data in a table. Now she must update the table by adding two additional columns and three additional rows of data. She wants to know how to update the chart after she adds the new data to the table. Use the Office Assistant to research how to add data to a chart. Write Kelly an interoffice memorandum explaining the process. Save, preview, and print the memo. Open a document containing a Word table and create a chart from the table. Add two additional columns and three additional rows of data to the chart using fictitious data. Save the document with a new name, preview it, and print it.

Project 6

Chris Lofton wants to add a Web page to the company intranet that contains an example of an equation created with Microsoft Equation 3.0 and a brief explanation of the steps to create the equation. Open a document containing an equation or create a new equation, add a brief description of how the equation was created, and save the document as a Web page. Preview and print the Web page.

Project 7

Marisa DaFranco, the executive assistant to the chairperson, called to request your help. She needs an organization chart that shows the managers of the word processing, accounting, sales, marketing, human resources, and purchasing departments and their executive or administrative assistants. Also include any other staff positions known to you. Using fictitious data, create the chart. Leave the name blank but include the box for each position even if you do not know the name. Format the organization chart attractively. Save, preview, and print the document.

Project 8

Jon Swenson, a chartered accountant in the Vancouver branch office, would like to know more about the Microsoft Equation 3.0 application. Open Microsoft Equation 3.0 and, using its online Help, locate and review the Equation Editor basics topic. Write Jon an interoffice memorandum describing the application and how to use it. Save, preview, and print the memo.

Managing Files

Chapter Overview

Managing your Word document files is a very important task. During the course of a business day, you may need to move files to a different folder, copy or rename them, or quickly print them. You also may need to protect important documents from unauthorized changes or add additional identifying text to documents to help locate them later. In this chapter you learn how to search for specific files by various file properties, how to protect files from unauthorized changes, and how to add comments to file properties. You also learn to use a shortcut menu to move, copy, rename, and print files from the Open dialog box.

LEARNING OBJECTIVES

- ► Search for specific files
- ► Use a shortcut menu to manage files
- ► Protect documents
- ► Add comments to the file properties

Case profile

You are promoted to the position of administrative assistant to Randall Holmes, the president of Worldwide Exotic Foods, Inc. The president thinks that publishing standardized company-wide procedures for locating, identifying, and protecting important Word document files saves time and reduces errors. He asks you to set up the procedures for managing Word document files.

chapter
twenty
five
25

notes This chapter assumes you are using the entire set of Data Files that accompany this book. Your instructor may modify some of the hands-on activities if you do not have access to the entire set of Data Files.

25.a Searching For Specific Files

Before you begin to work on an existing document, you need to open it. If you do not know the name of the file or where it's stored, you can use the Find dialog box to search for the file based on its file properties. File **properties** are details about a file that help identify it, including a descriptive filename, the author's name, or the file type.

Using the File Name Property

If you know that the filename of the document you want to find starts with a certain letter, you can search any folder and its subfolders or an entire drive for files that begin with that letter. You want to find Word document files beginning with "c" located on the Data Disk. To open the Find dialog box:

Step 1	*Open*	the Open dialog box
Step 2	*Switch*	to the disk drive and folder where the Data Files are stored, if necessary
Step 3	*Click*	the Tools button [Tools ▾] on the dialog box toolbar
Step 4	*Click*	Find

The Find dialog box that opens on your screen should look similar to Figure 25-1.

You specify your search criteria (or rules) in this dialog box. You can select one or more file properties, set conditions for each property, look for files in specific locations, and save your search to use again later. The find process is not case-sensitive, so you can use either "c" or "C" in your search criteria to find a list of files beginning with "c."

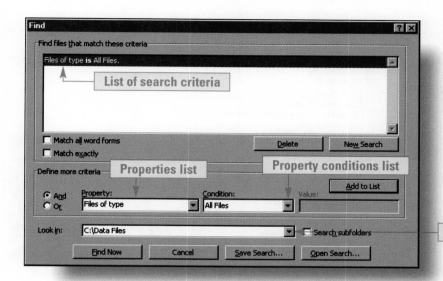

FIGURE 25-1
Find Dialog Box

The criteria from the previous search are still listed; you need to delete them before you add the new criteria. To delete any previous criteria except the default file type criteria and add new search criteria:

Step 1	*Click*	New Search to delete any previous search criteria
Step 2	*Click*	File name in the Property: list, if necessary
Step 3	*Click*	begins with in the Condition: list
Step 4	*Key*	c in the Value: text box
Step 5	*Click*	Add to List
Step 6	*Observe*	the new search criteria in the find files that match these criteria list box
Step 7	*Click*	Find Now to create the list of Word documents on the Data Disk beginning with "c"

The Open dialog box reappears, showing only those files that begin with "c." The filename c* appears in the File name: text box. The * is called a **wildcard character,** a symbol that represents an unlimited number of unknown characters following the character "c." Your dialog box should look similar to Figure 25-2.

**chapter
twenty-five**

FIGURE 25-2
List of Word Documents
That Begin With "c"

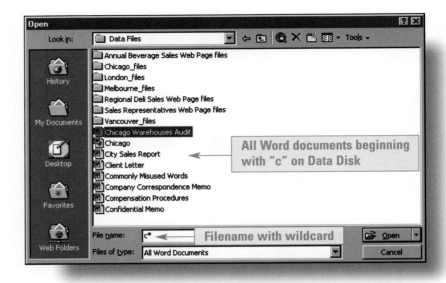

If you don't recall any information about the filename, you can search for a file based on its content.

Using the Contents Property

You can search for files that contain specific words in the document. In addition, you can select what types of files to search for. To find all the files (not just the Word documents) on the Data Disk that include the phrase "Vancouver branch:"

Step 1	*Open*	the Find dialog box from inside the Open dialog box
Step 2	*Click*	the New Search button to clear all criteria items except the file-type criteria
Step 3	*Click*	Delete to remove the All Word Documents file-type criteria
Step 4	*Click*	Files of type in the Property: list, if necessary
Step 5	*Click*	All Files in the Condition: list
Step 6	*Click*	Add to List
Step 7	*Click*	Contents in the Property: list
Step 8	*Click*	includes phrase in the Condition: list
Step 9	*Key*	Vancouver branch in the Value: list
Step 10	*Click*	Add to List
Step 11	*Observe*	the new search criteria
Step 12	*Click*	Find Now

The Open dialog box displays Word and Excel files that contain the phrase "Vancouver branch." Your dialog box should look similar to Figure 25-3.

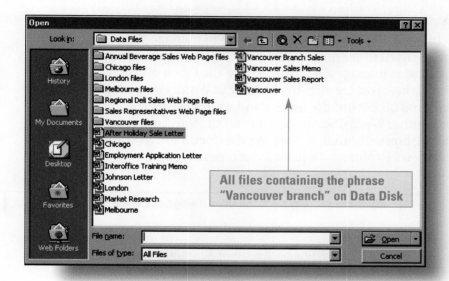

FIGURE 25-3
All Files Containing Phrase
"Vancouver branch"

You can also locate files by date.

Using Date Properties

You can search for files by the dates on which you created or modified files. This is helpful if you do not know the filename, but can remember the time frame during which you worked on the file. To view a list of all recently modified files:

Step 1	**Switch**	to the disk drive and folder where your completed Data Files are stored
Step 2	**Open**	the Find dialog box
Step 3	**Delete**	the "includes phrase" criteria (do not delete the All Files criteria)
Step 4	**Click**	Last modified in the Property: list
Step 5	**Click**	this month in the Condition: list
Step 6	**Click**	Add to List
Step 7	**Click**	Find Now
Step 8	**Observe**	that the Open dialog box lists the files you modified this month

Locating files by date is helpful when you want to back up a group of newer files or delete a group of outdated files.

chapter
twenty-five

QUICK TIP

You can also use a shortcut menu to manage your files in the Save As dialog box.

25.b Using a Shortcut Menu to Manage Files

Instead of using Windows Explorer to manage your files, you can use a shortcut menu to open, print, move, copy, delete, rename, or otherwise manage a file from inside the Open dialog box. This saves time when you are already working in Word. For example, if you are working on a Word document and a co-worker asks for a hard copy of another Word document, you can quickly print it from the Open dialog box without first opening the document in Word (or opening Windows Explorer). To print a document from the Open dialog box:

| **Step 1** | ***Right-click*** | any file in the Open dialog box to view the shortcut menu |

Your dialog box should look similar to Figure 25-4.

FIGURE 25-4
Shortcut Menu in Open
Dialog Box

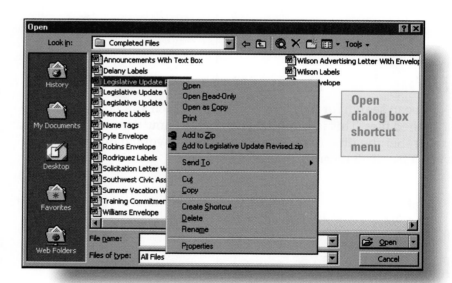

MOUSE TIP

You can use the SHIFT + Click method to select multiple adjacent files and the CTRL + Click method to select multiple nonadjacent files in the dialog box. Then right-click the selection to perform a common task, such as printing all selected files.

| **Step 2** | ***Click*** | Print |

In addition to locating files, you might also want to make sure others don't access or change certain documents.

25.c Protecting Documents

There are several ways to protect a document from unauthorized changes. In Chapter 23 you learned how to protect an online form so that users can only key the variable data in the document. You can also protect other types of documents. You can assign a password to prevent others from opening a document or you can assign a password that allows others to open the document but prevents them from modifying it. You can have Word recommend that others open specific documents as "read-only." If they open the file as "read-only" and modify it, they must save file with a different name. Finally, you can specify that individuals who review documents online can add comments—but not tracked changes—to the document. To review the different ways to protect a document, use the Office Assistant to search online Help using the keywords "protect document."

You want to protect the *Chicago Warehouses Audit* document by assigning a password that must be used to open the document. You give the document a new name and password-protect it.

To rename and password-protect the *Chicago Warehouses Audit* document:

Step 1	*Open*	the *Chicago Warehouses Audit* document located on the Data Disk
Step 2	*Open*	the Save As dialog box
Step 3	*Click*	the Tools button `Tools ▾` on the dialog box toolbar
Step 4	*Click*	General Options

The Save tab from the Options dialog box opens in its own dialog box. The dialog box you see on your screen should look similar to Figure 25-5.

When you key password characters in the password text boxes, you see only asterisks (*). This prevents others from learning the password. After you key the password, you to confirm it by keying it again in a confirmation dialog box.

CAUTION TIP

When you create a password be sure to write it down and store it in a safe place for future reference. If you lose or forget the password you will not be able to open the password-protected document!

QUICK TIP

A password can have any combination of letters, numbers, spaces, and symbols up to a maximum of 15 characters. Passwords are case-sensitive so if you use upper- and lowercase letters when you assign a password, users who try to open the document must also use the same upper- and lowercase letters.

**chapter
twenty-five**

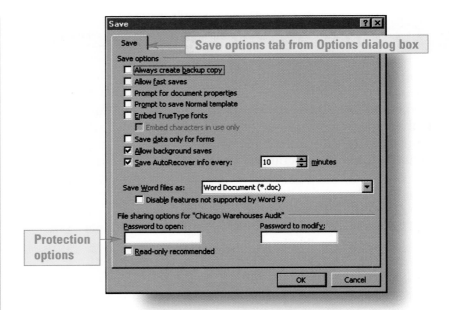

FIGURE 25-5
Save Options

To set the password to open the document:

Step 1	*Key*	Password in the <u>P</u>assword to open: text box
Step 2	*Click*	OK
Step 3	*Key*	Password in the Confirm Password dialog box
Step 4	*Click*	OK
Step 5	*Save*	the document as *Password Protected Document* and close it

To test the password protection you open the document and enter the password:

Step 1	*Open*	the *Password Protected Document* you just saved
Step 2	*Key*	Password in the Password dialog box
Step 3	*Click*	OK
Step 4	*Close*	the document without saving any changes

QUICK TIP

To remove the password protection from a document, open the document using the password, and then open the Save tab in the Options dialog box. Select and delete the password and click the OK button. Then save the document to update the copy on the disk.

You also set the read-only recommendation and modification password for a document in the Save tab in the Options dialog box.

25.d Adding Comments to the File Properties

In addition to the filename, file type, location, size, and dates, document properties include document statistics—such as the number of words in the document. You can also add user information, such as special comments, to the document properties.

To add comments to the *Chicago Warehouses Audit* document:

Step 1	*Open*	the *Chicago Warehouses Audit* document located on the Data Disk
Step 2	*Click*	File
Step 3	*Click*	Properties
Step 4	*Click*	the Summary tab

The Properties dialog box you see on your screen should look similar to Figure 25-6.

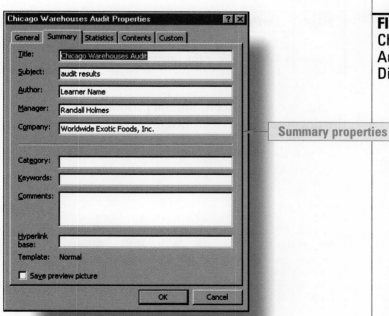

MENU TIP

You can right-click a filename in the Open dialog box and click Properties to display the Properties dialog box for the selected file. You can click the Properties command on the Tools button list in the Open dialog box to view the document properties dialog box for a selected file.

FIGURE 25-6
Chicago Warehouses Audit Properties Dialog Box

chapter twenty-five

You can use the user comments and data you add in the Summary tab to search for files. You want to be able to locate all warehouse audit documents. One way to do this is to add searchable comment text to each document that deals with warehouse audits. To add the comment text:

Step 1	*Click*	in the Comments: text box
Step 2	*Key*	warehouse audit
Step 3	*Click*	OK
Step 4	*Save*	the document as *Chicago Warehouses Audit With Summary Comment* and close it

You verify that you can locate the file from the comment you just added. To search for the document using the Comments text:

Step 1	*Open*	the Find dialog box
Step 2	*Change*	the search criteria to look for Word documents with the phrase "warehouse audit" in the Comments property
Step 3	*Click*	Find Now
Step 4	*Verify*	the *Chicago Warehouses Audit With Summary Comment* file is listed
Step 5	*Cancel*	the Open dialog box

Adding comments to the file properties ensures you can always find the document you need when you want it.

QUICK TIP

You can print document properties by opening the document, and then selecting the Document properties option in the Print what: list in the Print dialog box.

Summary

▶ You can search for specific files by file properties using the options in the Find dialog box, which you open from the Tools button list in the Open dialog box.

▶ File properties include the filename, file type, location, file size, date created, date modified, last date accessed, user summary information, and document statistics.

▶ You can use a shortcut menu in the Open dialog box to perform many file management tasks, such as opening, printing, moving, copying, deleting, and renaming files.

▶ You can view file properties by opening the document's Properties dialog box from the File menu, the Open dialog box shortcut menu, or by clicking the Properties command on the Tools button list in the Open dialog box.

▶ You can add information to a document property like comments and then search for files based on the comments text.

Commands Review

Action	Menu Bar	Shortcut Menu	Toolbar	Keyboard
Open the Find dialog box			Tools ▾	
View file properties	File, Properties	Right-click a filename, click Properties	Tools ▾	ALT + F, I

Concepts Review

Circle the correct answer.

1. You use features in the Find dialog box to:
[a] save a file.
[b] search for a file.
[c] print a file.
[d] display file properties.

2. Which of the following items is not a file property?
[a] Last modified
[b] Files of type
[c] Contents
[d] Application size

3. When entering search value criteria, use the wildcard "*" to represent:
[a] only the first character.
[b] an unlimited number of unknown characters.
[c] the letter "c."
[d] one unknown character.

4. Which search criteria will find all files whose filename begins with "b"?
[a] File name ends with b* and Files of type is All Word Documents.
[b] File name begins with b* and Files of type is All Files.
[c] File name begins with b* and Files of type is All Word Documents.
[d] File name includes b* and Files of type is All Files.

5. Which of the following is not a search condition for the Last modified property?
[a] yesterday
[b] today
[c] tomorrow
[d] this week

6. To prevent unauthorized access to a document you should:
[a] mark it "read-only" recommended.
[b] password-protect it to open.

[c] password-protect it for comments.
[d] password-protect it for tracked changes.

7. Which information category is not part of the Summary tab in the Properties dialog box?
[a] title
[b] subject
[c] keywords
[d] file size

8. Which search criteria finds all Word documents that contain the phrase "audit report" in the document Comments property?
[a] Files of type is All Word Documents and Contents includes "audit report."
[b] Files of type is All Files and Comments includes phrase "audit report."
[c] Files of type is All Files and Contents includes "audit report."
[d] Files of type is All Word Documents and Comments includes phrase "audit report."

9. If you password-protect a document, you should be careful to:
[a] mark the document "read-only."
[b] write down the password and save it in a safe place.
[c] turn on the track changes feature.
[d] insert a comment.

10. If you open a file marked "read-only" and then modify it, you must:
[a] password-protect it.
[b] save it with a new name.
[c] store it on a different disk.
[d] save it with the same name.

Circle **T** if the statement is true or **F** if the statement is false.

T F   1. You can search for different types of files based on the condition of file properties.

T F   2. You cannot delete search criteria once you select it.

T F   3. If you are already working in Word and need to move, copy, rename, or print a different document, you should first open Windows Explorer.

T F   4. The Properties dialog box can be opened using a shortcut menu in the Open dialog box.

T F   5. You can copy but not move a file using a shortcut menu in the Open dialog box.

T F   6. Word keeps track of document statistics, such as the number of words, in the Properties dialog box.

T F   7. If you can't remember the name of a file, you can search for it by one of several dates.

T F   8. If you see a file listed in the Open dialog box that you want to print, you must first open the file and then print it.

T F   9. A password can have any combination of letters, numbers, spaces, and symbols up to a maximum of 25 characters.

T F   10. To change the way files and folders are listed in the Open dialog box, you click the Tools button and then click a list option.

Skills Review

Exercise 1

1. Open the Open dialog box and then view the contents of the Data Disk.

2. Open the Find dialog box and search for all files beginning with "m."

3. Print one of the files using a shortcut menu.

4. Add the comment "comment example" to the document's properties.

5. Save the document as *Document With Comment Example*.

6. Print the document properties by selecting the Document properties option in the Print what: list in the Print dialog box and close the document.

Exercise 2

1. Open the Open dialog box and search the Data Disk for all Word files that begin with "w."

2. Open the Properties dialog box for the *Winter Schedule* document and add the following to the Summary tab:

Title	Winter Schedule
Subject	Class schedule
Author	Your name
Manager	Instructor name
Company	School name
Category	schedule
Keywords	course
Comments	Data provided by registrar

chapter twenty-five

3. Save the document as *Winter Schedule With Summary.*

4. Print the document properties by selecting the Document properties option in the Print what: list in the Print dialog box and close the document.

5. Open the Open dialog box search for all Word documents containing the school name in the Company property.

6. Open the *Winter Schedule With Summary* document and password-protect it to open.

7. Save the document as *Protected Winter Schedule With Summary* and close it.

Exercise 3   C

1. Open the Open dialog box and search the Data Disk for all Word documents whose filename contains the character "x."

2. Open the *Enhanced Text* document from the search list using a shortcut menu.

3. Add the "special search text" to the Comments property

4. Protect the document using the password "Modification" so that others cannot modify it.

5. Save the document as *Protected Enhanced Text.*

6. Print the document properties and close the document.

7. Open the *Protected Enhanced Text* using the appropriate password and create a bulleted list from the body text.

8. Save the document as *Protected Enhanced Text With Bullets.*

9. Print and close the document.

Exercise 4   C

1. Open the Open dialog box and search your completed Word documents for all files modified this week.

2. Add your name as the author to the properties for each document.

3. Save each document to update the copy on the disk and print the document properties for each document.

4. Close all open documents when finished.

Exercise 5   C

1. Open the Open dialog box and search for all files containing your name in the Author property.

2. Protect one document as "read-only" and save the document with a new name.

3. Print the document.

4. Open the read-only protected document; attempt to modify it and then close it.

Exercise 6

1. Open the Open dialog box and search the Data Disk for all Word documents that have at least three pages.

2. Select both files using the SHIFT + Click method and print them at one time using a shortcut menu.

Exercise 7

1. Open the Open dialog box and search the Data Files for all Word documents whose filename includes the word "world."

2. Open the *Worldwide Outline* document properties dialog box using a shortcut menu and add the text "PowerPoint presentation" as the subject property.

3. Save the document as *Worldwide Outline With Summary*.

4. Print the document properties and close the document.

Exercise 8

1. Open the Open dialog box and search the Data Disk for all Word documents whose contents include the word "travel."

2. Protect the *Bonaire* document by using the password "vacation" so that others cannot open it.

3. Save the document as *Protected Bonaire* and close it.

Case Projects

Project 1

As the recently promoted administrative assistant to the president you are replacing an employee who resigned after several years of employment. You must frequently find documents created before you were hired. The president cannot provide filenames for the documents. While you have successfully searched for files by various criteria, you often experience the following problems: (a) The wrong files sometimes appear after a search. (b) When you use a saved search, sometimes the files you previously found are no longer found. (c) You know that a file is in the folder whose contents are displayed in the Open dialog box but you don't see the filename. Use the Office Assistant to troubleshoot searching for files. Create an unbound report document describing each problem and its suggested solution. Save, preview, and print the document.

Project 2

After receiving several questions from other employees about file properties, you decide to create a Web page for the company intranet that contains an explanation and examples of file properties. Use the Office Assistant to review the "About file properties" topic in online Help and then create a Web page that describes file properties and gives examples of different types of file properties. Use a theme of your choice. Save, preview, and print the Web page.

Project 3

The president asks you how to change the setup on his personal computer so that the new company intranet Web search page (instead of the default search page) appears when he clicks the Search the Web button in the Open dialog box or on the Web toolbar. Use the Office Assistant to research how to set the default search page. Then create an interoffice memorandum to the president describing the process. Save, preview, and print the document.

Project 4

Jody Haversham meets you for lunch and asks how she can use passwords to protect her confidential documents from being opened by others and how

chapter twenty-five

to protect her nonconfidential documents from being modified by others. Use online Help to research how to use passwords, if necessary. Write Jody an interoffice memorandum suggesting how to protect confidential documents and how to protect documents from unauthorized changes. Save, preview, and print the memo.

Project 5

Bill Martin, in human resources, calls to ask for your help in locating a Word document. He cannot remember the name but knows he created the document last week. Write Bill an e-mail message suggesting how he can search for the document. Save and print the e-mail message.

Project 6

Jody Haversham calls you and she is very upset and asks for your help. She used a password to protect a confidential document and now she cannot open the document when she keys the password. Search online Help for suggestions on troubleshooting passwords. Create an e-mail message to Jody suggesting ways to prevent this problem. Save and print the e-mail message.

Project 7

Kelly Armstead is preparing a document she plans to route to several reviewers and she wants to protect the document so that the reviewers can add only comments and not make changes. She also wants to be sure that only authorized reviewers can open the document. She asks for your help in preparing the document. Use the Office Assistant to search for topics on tracking changes and how to prepare copies of a document to be reviewed. Write Kelly a memo describing what she should do to protect her document. Save, preview, and print the memo.

Project 8

Bill Martin uses the same search criteria several times a week to create a list of Word documents and he asks you if there is an easy way to repeat the same search without recreating the search criteria each time. Use the Office Assistant, if necessary, to review the "search for files" topic. Write Bill an e-mail message describing how he can use the same search criteria multiple times without recreating them. Save and print the e-mail message.

Integrating Word with Other Office 2000 Applications

Chapter Overview

A nother very important feature of the Word application is the ability to integrate data with other Office 2000 applications. This means you can create documents with the application most suited to that information and use the same information in other application documents. In this chapter you learn to integrate Word with Excel, PowerPoint, and Access and to send e-mail messages directly from Word using Outlook 2000.

Case profile

Randall Holmes asks you to work with Marisa DaFranco, the executive assistant to the chairperson, to prepare the documents for the third quarter sales meeting. Working with Marisa, you combine information from Excel worksheets, PowerPoint slide show presentations, and Access database information with Word documents.

LEARNING OBJECTIVES

- ► Integrate Excel worksheet data with Word
- ► Create Excel worksheets in Word
- ► Use hyperlinks to connect Office 2000 documents
- ► Integrate PowerPoint presentations with Word
- ► Integrate Access database information with Word
- ► Send e-mail messages from Word

integration

WX.a Integrating Excel Worksheet Data with Word

The Excel 2000 application is designed to analyze and perform calculations on numerical data rather than prepare text documents. You enter data in Excel **workbooks** that contain **worksheets** consisting of columns and rows similar to Word tables. Then you use Excel special features, which are more flexible and comprehensive than Word table features, to analyze and format the numerical data. When you have a large set of numerical data including calculations, you should use an Excel worksheet instead of a Word table to take advantage of these special features. It is possible to enter, format, and calculate numerical data in an Excel worksheet and then integrate that data into a Word document in several ways. You can:

1. insert an Excel file into a Word document
2. copy and paste Excel worksheet data or a chart into a Word document
3. embed Excel data or a chart in a Word document
4. link Excel data or a chart to a Word document
5. import Excel data into a Microsoft Graph 2000 Chart datasheet and place the chart object in a Word document.

When you **insert** an Excel file into a Word document, the data is placed in a Word table that must be edited with Word table features. When you use the Copy and Paste commands, the data are pasted into a Word table. Neither option maintains a link to the original Excel data—that is, the Word document includes a copy of the data but it does not maintain any connection to the Excel workbook. Any changes you make to the data in the Word document do *not* appear in the original Excel workbook. Use the insert or copy and paste option when you want to include Excel data in a Word document in a table format, and when you want to edit the data with Word editing features. Do not use these options if you want to edit the data with Excel editing features or if you want to edit the data in the original Excel workbook.

When you **embed** Excel data, you place a copy of the data in a Word document as an object that you can edit only with Excel menu commands and toolbar buttons. However, the embedded data maintains no link or connection with the original Excel workbook. Any changes you make to the data in the Word document do *not* appear in the original Excel workbook. Use the embed method when you want to include Excel data in a Word document and want to edit the data with the Excel features instead of Word features.

QUICK TIP

When sharing data between Excel and Word, Excel is usually the **source,** or originating, application and Word is usually the **destination,** or target, application. However, you can embed and link Word text into an Excel worksheet. For example, you can paste Word text such as a date into the Excel formula bar; or, you can "paste link" a lengthy piece of text from a Word document into a worksheet cell or paste Word text into a text box on a worksheet.

When you **link** Excel worksheet data to a Word document, the data are displayed in the Word document but stored and edited in the Excel workbook. You must make any changes to the data in the original Excel workbook. When you open the Word document, the data is automatically updated to reflect the changes in the original Excel workbook. Use the link method when the Excel workbook data changes frequently.

notes The activities in this chapter assume you are familiar with the Excel, PowerPoint, and Access applications. If necessary, your instructor will provide additional information about these applications before you begin these activities.

Inserting an Excel File into a Word Document

You insert an Excel file into a Word document in a few steps. Open a Word document and then click the Fi_l_e command on the _I_nsert menu. Select the workbook file, the desired worksheet, and any range of cells if appropriate, then insert the data. The data are inserted into a Word table that often requires substantial formatting to provide a professional presentation of the data. For more information on inserting an Excel worksheet into a Word document, see online Help.

Copying and Pasting Excel Data into a Word Document

To include Excel data in a Word document and then edit the data with Word editing features, you can copy the data from an Excel worksheet and then paste it into a Word document. You use this method to paste data from an Excel worksheet located in the *Worldwide Exotic Foods Sales Report* workbook into the *Worldwide Memo* document. To open the Excel and Word files:

Step 1	*Open*	the *Worldwide Memo* document located on the Data Disk
Step 2	*Move*	the insertion point to the end of the document
Step 3	*Open*	the Excel application and the *Worldwide Exotic Foods Sales Report* Excel workbook located on the Data Disk and maximize the Excel window, if necessary
Step 4	*Click*	the Sales Data worksheet tab, if necessary

You want to use the data in the group of cells (called a **range**) that start in cell A1 and end in cell F10. To copy the worksheet data to the Office Clipboard:

Step 1	*Move*	the mouse pointer to cell A1 (the pointer becomes a large white plus pointer)
Step 2	*Drag*	down and to the right to cell F10 to select the range of cells A1:F10
Step 3	*Right-click*	the selected range of cells
Step 4	*Click*	Copy

The Excel data is stored on the Office Clipboard. To switch to the Word application and paste the data into the *Worldwide Memo* document:

Step 1	*Click*	the *Worldwide Memo* document button on the taskbar
Step 2	*Right-click*	at the insertion point
Step 3	*Click*	Paste
Step 4	*Zoom*	the document to Page Width, if necessary
Step 5	*Observe*	that the worksheet data are pasted into a Word table
Step 6	*Hide*	the table gridlines, if necessary

Your screen should look similar to Figure WX-1.

FIGURE WX-1
Excel Data Pasted into a
Word Table

Excel data pasted into a Word table

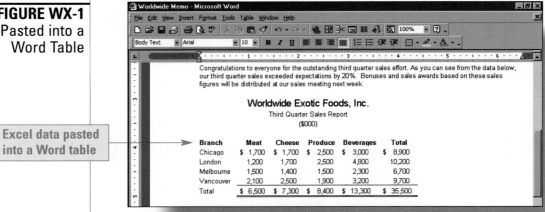

You can edit the data and format the table just as you would any Word table. To reposition the table:

Step 1	**Center**	the table between the left and right margins
Step 2	**Zoom**	the document back to 100%, if necessary
Step 3	**Save**	the document as *Worldwide Memo With Pasted Data* and close it (leave the Excel application and workbook open)

Embedding Excel Worksheet Data in a Word Document

Sometimes you need to share data between Excel and Word but still want to edit the data with the Excel menus and toolbars. In this case, you insert the Excel worksheet data into the Word document as an embedded object. Embedding leaves the data in its original Excel format and you must edit it with Excel features.

The Excel data copied from *Worldwide Exotic Foods Sales Report* is still on the Office Clipboard. You need to reopen the *Worldwide Memo* document and then paste the Excel data into it as an embedded object using the Paste Special command. To create an embedded object:

Step 1	**Open**	the *Worldwide Memo* document located on the Data Disk
Step 2	**Move**	the insertion point to the end of the document
Step 3	**Click**	Edit
Step 4	**Click**	Paste Special

The Paste Special dialog box that opens on your screen should look similar to Figure WX-2.

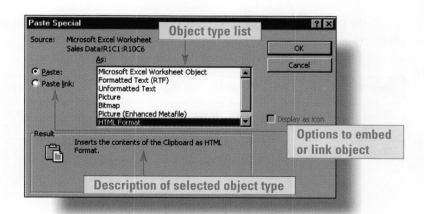

FIGURE WX-2
Paste Special Dialog Box

integration

The eight data types allow you to insert an Excel object, data in a table, pictures, or HTML format. You can click a data type in the <u>A</u>s: list box and view its description in the Result box. The <u>D</u>isplay as icon option inserts an icon representing the worksheet data in the Word document. Double-clicking the icon in the destination document displays the worksheet data. To embed the worksheet data:

Step 1	***Click***	the <u>P</u>aste: option button, if necessary
Step 2	***Double-click***	Microsoft Excel Worksheet Object in the <u>A</u>s: list box
Step 3	***Observe***	the embedded Excel object sizing handles and smaller size
Step 4	***Deselect***	the object by clicking in the document outside the object
Step 5	***Save***	the document as *Worldwide Memo With Embedded Data*

You can edit the embedded worksheet object by double-clicking the object to view the Excel menu bar, toolbars, and worksheet grid. When you edit an embedded object, you are editing the data *only* in the Word document (although you use the Excel features). You are *not* editing the data in the original Excel source file. You reposition the selected Excel embedded object by selecting a layout option in the Format Object dialog box. To reposition the embedded object:

Step 1	***Right-click***	the object
Step 2	***Click***	Format <u>O</u>bject
Step 3	***Click***	the Layout tab
Step 4	***Double-click***	the <u>I</u>n line with text option
Step 5	***Center***	the object using the Formatting toolbar

To edit the embedded worksheet object and then verify that no changes are made to the data in the Excel source file:

Step 1	***Double-click***	the worksheet object to view the Excel features
Step 2	***Observe***	the Excel menu bar and toolbars and the data in an Excel worksheet grid
Step 3	***Observe***	that the title bar indicates you are still working in the Word application

To turn off the gridlines and edit the data in cell B7:

Step 1	*Click*	Tools
Step 2	*Click*	Options and click the View tab, if necessary
Step 3	*Click*	the Gridlines check box to remove the check mark
Step 4	*Click*	OK
Step 5	*Click*	cell B7 (column B and row 7) to make it the active cell
Step 6	*Key*	2,500
Step 7	*Press*	the ENTER key
Step 8	*Observe*	the recalculated totals in cells F7, B10, and F10
Step 9	*Click*	anywhere in the document outside the embedded worksheet object to deselect it

The data in the worksheet object have changed. To verify that no changes have been made to the original Excel workbook:

Step 1	*Click*	the Excel button on the taskbar
Step 2	*Observe*	that the gridlines still appear and that the data in B7 and the totals in F7, B10, and F10 did not change
Step 3	*Switch*	back to the *Worldwide Memo With Embedded Data* document using the taskbar
Step 4	*Save*	the document and close it

Linking Excel Worksheet Data to a Word Document

When you link data between an Excel worksheet and a Word document, the Word destination file contains only a reference, or pointer, to the data—although the data are visible in the document. The data exist only in the Excel source file. When you edit linked data, you actually open the source application and file and do all your editing in the source file. When you change data in the source file, the data displayed in the destination file are updated.

It is a good idea to link data between files when you do not need a copy of the data in the destination file. Linking data between files saves disk space because the same information is not duplicated in both the source file and the destination file. However, the source file must be available at all times to provide the data for the destination file. If you move or rename the source file without updating the link in

integration

the destination file, an error may occur when the destination file looks for the linked data. For more information on breaking, modifying, and reestablishing links, see online Help.

You want to insert a linked Excel object in the *Worldwide Memo* document and then edit the original source worksheet to update the linked document. To begin:

MENU TIP

C You can insert Excel data into a Word document in a Word table with the Paste Special command on the Edit menu, and the Formatted Text (rtf) option in the Paste Special dialog box.

Step 1	Open	the *Worldwide Memo* document located on the Data Disk
Step 2	Move	the insertion point to the end of the document
Step 3	Switch	to the Sales Data worksheet in the *Worldwide Exotic Foods Sales Report* workbook
Step 4	Turn off	the gridlines using the View tab in the Options dialog box
Step 5	Select	the range A1:F10, if necessary
Step 6	Copy	the selected range to the Clipboard
Step 7	Switch	to the *Worldwide Memo* document

To paste the Excel data as a linked object:

Step 1	Open	the Paste Special dialog box
Step 2	Click	the Paste link: option button
Step 3	Double-click	Microsoft Excel Worksheet Object in the As: list
Step 4	Change	the object layout to In line with text and center it

A linked Excel worksheet object appears in the *Worldwide Memo* document. This object is a reference to the *Worldwide Exotic Foods Sales Report* source file. The data does not exist in the *Worldwide Memo* document and cannot be edited in the *Worldwide Memo* document. You need to change the Vancouver branch produce sales to $2,500. To edit the object:

CAUTION TIP

Because you did not save the changes to the *Worldwide Exotic Foods Sales Report* workbook, the next time you open *Worldwide Memo With Linked Worksheet Data*, the linked Excel object contains the original values and gridlines because it is linked to the original workbook.

Step 1	Close	the Excel application and the *Worldwide Exotic Foods Sales Report* from the taskbar without saving changes to the workbook or saving the large Clipboard item
Step 2	Double-click	the linked Excel object to open the Excel application and *Worldwide Exotic Foods Sales Report* workbook
Step 3	Observe	that the Sales Data worksheet is active
Step 4	Maximize	the Excel application window, if necessary

Step 5	*Turn off*	the gridlines in the View tab of the Options dialog box
Step 6	*Click*	cell D9 to make it the active cell
Step 7	*Key*	2,500
Step 8	*Press*	the ENTER key to enter the data in the cell
Step 9	*Switch*	to the *Worldwide Memo* document using the taskbar
Step 10	*Observe*	that the Vancouver produce data and all relevant subtotals and totals in the linked Excel object are changed
Step 11	*Deselect*	the linked Excel object
Step 12	*Save*	the document as *Worldwide Memo With Linked Worksheet Data* and close it

<aside>
M OUSE TIP

You also can use the drag-and-drop method to link Excel worksheet data in a Word document by right-dragging the selected worksheet range to the Word document.
</aside>

Leave the Excel application and workbook open for the next section.

WX.b Creating Excel Worksheets in Word

Sometimes you may have a few lines of numerical data to enter directly into a Word document and you would like to use the more comprehensive Excel features to format the data or perform calculations on it. Instead of first entering and formatting the data in an Excel workbook and then creating an embedded Excel object in the Word document, you can simply insert a blank Excel worksheet object directly into the Word document and key and format the data in the blank worksheet object. You use the Object command on the Insert menu or the Insert Microsoft Excel Worksheet button on the Standard toolbar to do this.

Inserting a Blank Embedded Excel Object

You want to insert a blank embedded Excel object into the *Worldwide Memo* document and then add and format the data and calculate several totals. To insert a blank embedded Excel object:

| Step 1 | *Open* | the *Worldwide Memo* document located on the Data Disk |
| Step 2 | *Move* | the insertion point to the end of the document |

Step 3	*Click*	the Insert Microsoft Excel Worksheet button ▣ on the Standard toolbar
Step 4	*Drag*	to select four rows and three columns (4 × 3 Spreadsheet) on the grid and then release the mouse button
Step 5	*Observe*	the blank embedded Excel worksheet object inserted in the document

You can size the object with the mouse to view more columns or rows. To view two more columns:

Step 1	*Drag*	the middle right sizing handle three positions to the right to view columns A through F
Step 2	*Drag*	the middle bottom sizing handle down to view rows 1 through 13
Step 3	*Center*	the object and deselect it
Step 4	*Save*	the document as *Worldwide Memo With New Worksheet Object*

The object is currently blank except for the gridlines, which are visible on the screen but do not print. To edit the blank embedded Excel object, simply double-click it. Then you manually enter the text and data in the worksheet object and use the Excel formatting features to format them. To enter the data:

Step 1	*Double-click*	the object to edit it
Step 2	*Enter*	the title data in Figure WX-3 in cells A1, A2, and A3 (key an apostrophe before you key ($000) to create a text entry)
Step 3	*Enter*	the remaining data shown in Figure WX-3 in cells A5:F10

To center the titles across the range in combined cells:

Step 1	*Select*	the range A1: to F1
Step 2	*Click*	the Merge and Center button ▦ on the Formatting toolbar
Step 3	*Select*	the range A2:F2
Step 4	*Click*	the Merge and Center button ▦ on the Formatting toolbar
Step 5	*Center*	the contents of cell A3 over the range A3:F3

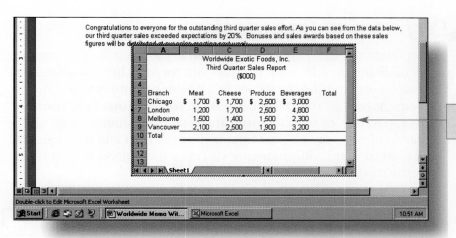

FIGURE WX-3
Worksheet Data

Embedded Excel object with data and formatting

Next you center the content of cells without merging them and you apply special formats to the numbers. To format the rest of the worksheet:

Step 1	*Center*	the contents in the range B5:F5 using the Center button
Step 2	*Select*	the range B7:F9
Step 3	*Right-click*	the selected range and click Format Cells
Step 4	*Click*	the Number tab in the Format Cells dialog box
Step 5	*Click*	Accounting in the Category: list
Step 6	*Key*	0 in the Decimal places: text box
Step 7	*Click*	None in the Symbol: list, if necessary
Step 8	*Click*	OK to change the selected range to the Accounting format, no decimal, and no $ symbol
Step 9	*Format*	the cells in the range B6:F6 and B10:F10 with the Accounting format, no decimal, and the $ symbol
Step 10	*Select*	the range B10:F10
Step 11	*Add*	a Top and Double Bottom border to the cells using the Borders button on the Formatting toolbar
Step 12	*Turn off*	the gridlines in the View tab of the Options dialog box
Step 13	*Save*	the document

Next you add the total calculations.

integration

Performing Calculations

Calculations in Excel are called **formulas**. You want to add formulas to calculate the total for each product and for each branch office. The easiest way to total the values in a row or column is to use the AutoSum button on the Standard toolbar. You can total each column or row separately, or you can insert the total calculations for all the rows and columns at one time by selecting the data and the adjacent blank total row and column before you click the AutoSum button. To insert the total calculations at one time:

Step 1	*Select*	the range B6:F10
Step 2	*Click*	the AutoSum button Σ on the Standard toolbar
Step 3	*Observe*	the total calculations are inserted in the total row and column cells
Step 4	*Deselect*	the embedded worksheet object
Step 5	*Save*	the document and close it

Instead of using Copy and Paste or Paste Special commands to include data from another application, you can create a hyperlink to the data.

QUICK TIP

You can create a hyperlink to a Web page or Office 2000 document in a Word document by keying the URL or network path and pressing the SPACEBAR. The option to automatically create hyperlinks as you key is in the AutoFormat as You Type tab in the AutoCorrect dialog box.

WX.c Using Hyperlinks to Connect Office 2000 Documents

You can create hyperlinks to link Word documents to each other or to link documents created in other Office applications, such as Excel or PowerPoint. You can also create hyperlinks between two Word documents. This is an excellent alternative to embedding or linking data maintained in other Office applications. Earlier you used embedding and linking to integrate the sales data maintained in an Excel workbook with a Word memo. This workbook also contains a chart that was not embedded or linked in the memo. Now you want to use a hyperlink in the memo, instead of embedding or linking the data, so that a reader can "jump" to the Excel workbook and view all the workbook's contents, including the chart.

CAUTION TIP

You must edit the hyperlink if the path changes.

To open the *Worldwide Memo* document and insert additional text:

Step 1	**Open**	the *Worldwide Memo* document located on the Data Disk
Step 2	**Move**	the insertion point to the end of the document
Step 3	**Key**	Click the link to view the sales data and chart

When you select a specific cell, the text inside the cell becomes the hyperlink text. To insert a hyperlink to the *Worldwide Exotic Foods Sales Report* workbook using the right-drag method:

Step 1	**Switch to**	the *Worldwide Exotic Foods Sales Report* workbook using the taskbar
Step 2	**Click**	cell A2 to select it
Step 3	**Move**	the mouse pointer to the bottom boundary of the cell (the mouse pointer becomes a left-facing arrow pointer shape when placed on the boundary)
Step 4	**Right-drag**	the cell A2 boundary to the *Worldwide Memo* document button on the taskbar
Step 5	**Pause**	for the document Word window to open (do not release the mouse button)
Step 6	**Continue**	to right-drag until the dashed line insertion point appears immediately before the word "link" in the last sentence in the document and then release the mouse button
Step 7	**Click**	Create Hyperlink Here
Step 8	**Position**	The insertion point between the hyperlink text and the word "link" using the keyboard and then press the SPACEBAR
Step 9	**Save**	the document as *Worldwide Memo With Hyperlink*
Step 10	**Close**	the Excel workbook from the taskbar without saving any changes

To test the link:

Step 1	**Click**	the Third Quarter Sales Report hyperlink
Step 2	**Observe**	that the Excel application and *Worldwide Exotic Foods Sales Report* workbook open
Step 3	**Close**	the Excel application and workbook
Step 4	**Close**	the *Worldwide Memo With Hyperlink* document

MENU TIP

You can insert a hyperlink with the Copy/Paste as Hyperlink commands on the Edit menu, or by right-dragging a selection from the source application into the destination application and clicking Create Hyperlink Here.

You also can create hyperlinks by keying the link text, selecting the link text, and then clicking the Hyperlink command on the Insert menu and entering the filename and path or browse to locate the linked file in the Insert Hyperlink dialog box.

MOUSE TIP

Select the link text and then open the Insert Hyperlink dialog box by clicking the Insert Hyperlink button on the Standard toolbar. Enter the filename and path or browse to locate the linked file in the dialog box.

integration

WX.d Integrating PowerPoint Presentations with Word

The PowerPoint 2000 application provides tools for creating slides and audience handout materials for presentations. You can integrate a PowerPoint presentation with Word in several ways. You can copy and paste PowerPoint information into Word documents, or you can embed or link PowerPoint slides into a Word document just as you do with Excel worksheet data or charts. Additionally, you can send PowerPoint items, such as slides, notes pages, or an outline to Word to be edited or printed. You can also create a PowerPoint presentation from a Word outline.

Creating a PowerPoint Presentation from a Word Outline

You can create a Word outline using built-in heading styles and then send that outline to PowerPoint to create slides. PowerPoint uses the built-in heading styles to identify individual slides or bulleted items on a slide. Marisa has already created a topic outline in Word using the built-in heading styles and asks you to create the presentation based on her topic outline. To open the topic outline and create a PowerPoint presentation:

Step 1	*Open*	the *Worldwide Outline* document located on the Data Disk
Step 2	*Click*	File
Step 3	*Point to*	Send To
Step 4	*Click*	Microsoft PowerPoint
Step 5	*Observe*	that the PowerPoint application opens in Normal view and contains bulleted list slides based on the Word outline

Your screen should look similar to Figure WX-4.

MENU TIP

You can also bring a Word outline into PowerPoint by clicking the Open command on the PowerPoint File menu (or the Open button on the Standard toolbar), and then changing the Files of type: to All Outlines. Switch to the appropriate disk drive and folder and open the Word outline. For more information, see online Help.

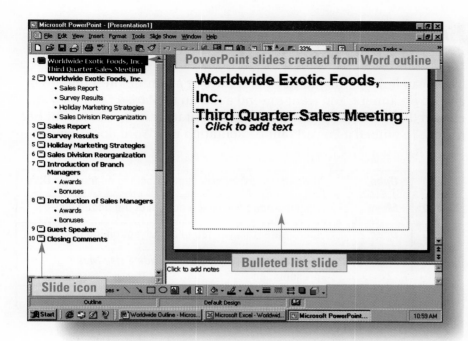

FIGURE WX-4
New PowerPoint
Presentation from
Word Outline

PowerPoint creates a new bulleted list slide for each topic formatted with the Heading 1 style and a bulleted list detail item for each topic formatted with the Heading 2 style. You edit text on a PowerPoint slide just as you edit text in Word. The first slide should be a title slide. To convert the bullet slide to a title slide, you can change the slide layout. To change the slide layout:

Step 1	*Click*	the Common Tasks button Common Tasks ▾ on the Formatting toolbar
Step 2	*Click*	Slide Layout
Step 3	*Double-click*	the Title slide layout (first layout, first row) in the Slide Layout dialog box
Step 4	*Format*	the text as desired
Step 5	*Click*	the Common Tasks button Common Tasks ▾ on the Formatting toolbar
Step 6	*Click*	Apply Design Template and apply a presentation design of your choice to the slides
Step 7	*Save*	the presentation as *Worldwide Sales Meeting*
Step 8	*Close*	the PowerPoint application and presentation
Step 9	*Close*	the *Worldwide Outline* document without saving any changes

integration

Embedding a PowerPoint Presentation in a Word Document

You can link or embed individual slides or an entire presentation in a Word document. You want to send a memo to Marisa DaFranco and embed the *Worldwide Sales Meeting* presentation in the memo for her review. To embed a PowerPoint presentation in a Word document:

Step 1	**Open**	the *DaFranco Memo* document located on the Data Disk
Step 2	**Move**	the insertion point to the bottom of the document
Step 3	**Open**	the Create from File tab in the Object dialog box
Step 4	**Browse**	to locate and open the *Worldwide Sales Meeting* presentation
Step 5	**Click**	OK to close the Object dialog box

In a few seconds, the presentation is inserted into the Word document as an embedded object. To format the object and view the slide show:

Step 1	**Zoom**	the document to Whole Page
Step 2	**Center**	the selected object
Step 3	**Size**	the object to approximately half its current size, using the mouse pointer, and then deselect it
Step 4	**Save**	the document as *DaFranco Memo With Presentation*
Step 5	**Double-click**	the presentation object to run the slide show
Step 6	**Click**	the left mouse button to advance each slide
Step 7	**Close**	the document without saving any changes when the slide show is complete

Sending a PowerPoint Presentation to Word

Another way to integrate a PowerPoint presentation with Word is to send part or all of a presentation to Word. Marisa wants a copy of the *Worldwide Sales Meeting* presentation in a format suitable for adding speaker notes. She wants to key the speaker notes in a Word

QUICK TIP

To embed or link a single slide from a PowerPoint presentation into a Word document, select the slide icon in PowerPoint Normal or Outline view, and use the Copy/Paste Special commands and Paste or Paste Link the slide object.

document. To do this, you can send the presentation slides to Word. To send the *Worldwide Sales Meeting* presentation to Word:

Step 1	**Open**	the PowerPoint application and the *Worldwide Sales Meeting* presentation created earlier, if necessary
Step 2	**Click**	F<u>i</u>le
Step 3	**Point to**	Sen<u>d</u> To
Step 4	**Click**	Microsoft <u>W</u>ord

The Write-Up dialog box that opens on your screen should look similar to Figure WX-5.

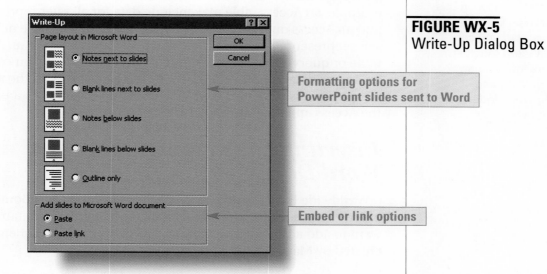

FIGURE WX-5
Write-Up Dialog Box

Formatting options for PowerPoint slides sent to Word

Embed or link options

This dialog box has options for the Word document format as well as for whether to embed or link the slides to the Word document. You select the Bl<u>a</u>nk lines next to slides format and embed the slides.

Step 5	**Click**	the Bl<u>a</u>nk lines next to slides option button
Step 6	**Click**	the <u>P</u>aste option button, if necessary
Step 7	**Click**	OK
Step 8	**Zoom**	the document to Whole Page, if necessary
Step 9	**Observe**	the embedded slide objects inserted into a table

integration

| Step 10 | *Save* | the document as *Worldwide Sales Meeting Notes* and close it |
| Step 11 | *Close* | the PowerPoint application and presentation |

WX.e Integrating Access Database Information with Word

Data in an Access database is maintained in **Access tables**. An **Access query** is a subset of an Access table that meets specific criteria. For example, an Access table may include data for all sales representatives and an Access query created from that table may include only the sales representatives from a specific division. Data from an Access table or query can be inserted into a Word document. You can also use an Access database table or query as the data source in the mail-merge process or import a Word document converted to a text file into the Access application.

Inserting an Access Query into a Word Document

Worldwide Exotic Foods, Inc. maintains information about its branch office vice presidents and sales managers in an Access database. You want to add a list of the vice presidents to an interoffice memorandum created by Marisa. To open the memorandum:

| Step 1 | *Open* | the *Confidential Memo* document located on the Data Disk |
| Step 2 | *Move* | the insertion point to the bottom of the document |

To insert an Access query as a linked object:

| Step 1 | *Display* | the Database toolbar |
| Step 2 | *Click* | the Insert Database button 🔲 on the Database toolbar |

The Database dialog box that opens on your screen should look similar to Figure WX-6.

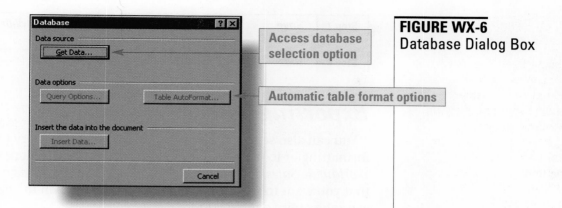

FIGURE WX-6
Database Dialog Box

You insert the Vice President query data into the *Worldwide Sales* database located on the Data Disk.

Step 3	*Click*	the Get Data button in the Database dialog box
Step 4	*Switch*	to the Data Disk
Step 5	*Change*	the Files of type: field to MS Access Databases
Step 6	*Double-click*	*Worldwide Sales* in the Look in: list box
Step 7	*Click*	the Queries tab in the Microsoft Access dialog box
Step 8	*Click*	Vice President Query
Step 9	*Click*	the Link to Query check box to insert a check mark, if necessary
Step 10	*Click*	OK to select the query

The Access data appears in a Word table when you insert it. You can automatically format the table with the Table AutoFormat button. To automatically format the table and insert the query data:

Step 1	*Click*	the Table AutoFormat button
Step 2	*Double-click*	Colorful 1 in the Formats: list box
Step 3	*Click*	Insert Data
Step 4	*Click*	OK in the Insert Data dialog box to insert all the records
Step 5	*Observe*	that the Access query data appear in your document as a formatted Word table
Step 6	*AutoFit*	the table to the window

integration

| Step 7 | *Save* | the document as *Confidential Memo With Vice President Data* and close it |
| Step 8 | *Hide* | the Database toolbar |

Exporting Access Data to Word

You can also send (or **export**) an Access table or query to Word for formatting or to use as a data source in a Word mail merge. The *Worldwide Sales* database includes information on sales managers that you want to send to a Word document. To open the database and send the query data to Word:

Step 1	*Open*	the Access application and the *Worldwide Sales* database located on the Data Disk
Step 2	*Click*	the Queries icon in the Objects bar
Step 3	*Select*	the Sales Managers Query
Step 4	*Click*	the OfficeLinks button list arrow on the Access Standard toolbar
Step 5	*Click*	Publish It with MS Word

In a few seconds, the Sales Managers Query data is sent to Word as a Rich Text Format file (.rtf) named Sales Manager Query. (A Rich Text Format file is a text file containing formatting.) The file is stored in the folder that is open when you send the data.

Step 6	*Save*	the document as *Worldwide Sales Managers* as a Word document type and close it
Step 7	*Close*	the Access application and database
Step 8	*Delete*	the *Sales Managers Query* (.rtf) document from the active folder in the Open dialog box

C Merging a Document Using Alternate Data Sources

You can personalize interoffice memorandums or form letters by merging names and addresses maintained in an Access table or query with a Word document. You can do this a couple of ways. You can open the document in Word and use the Mail Merge Helper to open the database table or query as your data source. You can also merge a table or query with a Word document from Access by using the OfficeLinks button on the Standard toolbar. You want to send an interoffice memorandum to all vice presidents and sales managers and their names are maintained in the Employees table in the *Worldwide Sales* database. To merge the Employees table data with a Word memo:

Step 1	*View*	the tables objects, if necessary
Step 2	*Select*	the Employees table, if necessary
Step 3	*Click*	the OfficeLinks button list arrow ▨ ▾ on the Standard toolbar
Step 4	*Click*	Merge It with MS Word

The Microsoft Word Mail Merge Wizard dialog box opens. The dialog box on your screen should look similar to Figure WX-7.

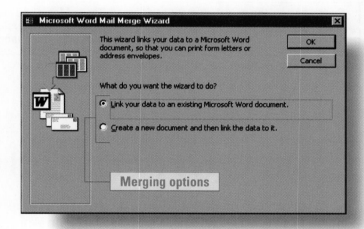

FIGURE WX-7
Microsoft Word Mail Merge Wizard

Step 5	*Verify*	the Link your data to an existing Microsoft Word document. option is selected
Step 6	*Click*	OK
Step 7	*Open*	the *Bonus Memo* document located on the Data Disk

In a few seconds the memo opens as a merge main document. You insert merge fields from the Employees table. Then you preview the merge and merge to a new document. To modify the memo:

Step 1	*Move*	the insertion point to the TO: variable text position
Step 2	*Click*	the Insert Merge Field button [Insert Merge Field ▾] on the Merge toolbar

integration

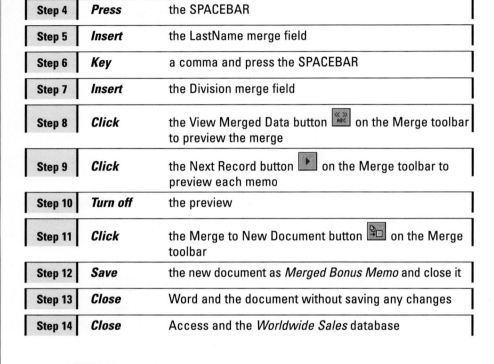

Step 3	*Click*	FirstName
Step 4	*Press*	the SPACEBAR
Step 5	*Insert*	the LastName merge field
Step 6	*Key*	a comma and press the SPACEBAR
Step 7	*Insert*	the Division merge field
Step 8	*Click*	the View Merged Data button ⟨⟨» on the Merge toolbar to preview the merge
Step 9	*Click*	the Next Record button ▶ on the Merge toolbar to preview each memo
Step 10	*Turn off*	the preview
Step 11	*Click*	the Merge to New Document button on the Merge toolbar
Step 12	*Save*	the new document as *Merged Bonus Memo* and close it
Step 13	*Close*	Word and the document without saving any changes
Step 14	*Close*	Access and the *Worldwide Sales* database

WX.f Sending E-mail Messages from Word

If you have Outlook 2000 or Outlook Express 5.0 designated as your e-mail client, you can send e-mail messages directly from Word. If you are using a different e-mail client, the Word e-mail features and options may vary. When you send an e-mail message directly from Word, it is automatically sent in HTML format, which means the message can contain animated graphics, multimedia objects, and other Web page features. Recipients can read the e-mail message in HTML format with a Web browser or with an e-mail client like Outlook 2000 that supports the HTML format.

notes

The following activities assume you are using Outlook 2000 or Outlook Express 5.0 as your e-mail client. Your instructor may provide additional instructions if you are using a different e-mail client. If you have e-mail capability, your instructor may supplement the following activity to include sending and replying to e-mail messages.

To create and send a new message:

Step 1	*Switch*	to the Word application, if necessary
Step 2	*Open*	the General tab in the New dialog box
Step 3	*Double-click*	the E-mail Message icon
Step 4	*Observe*	the e-mail header that appears below the Formatting toolbar

Your screen should look similar to Figure WX-8.

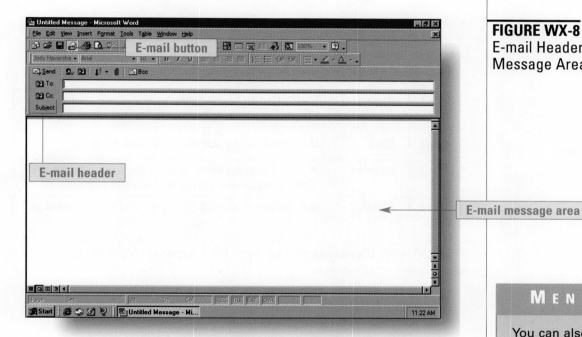

FIGURE WX-8
E-mail Header and
Message Area

To complete the message you key or insert from the Address Book the To: and Cc: e-mail addresses, key the subject, and then key and format the message. You can use the buttons at the top of the e-mail header to send the message, check keyed e-mail addresses against the Address Book or open the Address Book, assign a high or low priority to messages, attach files to messages, and view or hide a blind carbon copy address line. Click the Send button above the e-mail header to send the message. You can print the message content with the Print command or Print button, but the message header does not print. If you save the message document, the e-mail header information is saved and appears with the message contents when you open the document.

M E N U T I P

You can also send the current document to someone via e-mail or attach the current document to an e-mail message directly from Word by clicking the File menu, pointing to Send To, and clicking the appropriate e-mail command.

To complete the message:

Step 1	*Key*	marisa@wwide.xeon.net in the To: text box
Step 2	*Key*	Sales Meeting in the Subject: text box
Step 3	*Key*	Marisa, can you meet with me at 3 p.m. to discuss the sales meeting materials? in the message area
Step 4	*Key*	your name two lines below the message
Step 5	*Save*	the message document as *Marisa Message* and close it without sending it

You can also create or open a document and send it to someone via e-mail directly from Word. The document becomes the e-mail message content. To send a current document via e-mail:

Step 1	*Open*	the *DaFranco Memo With Presentation* document created earlier in this chapter
Step 2	*Click*	the E-mail button 🖃 on the Standard toolbar
Step 3	*Observe*	the e-mail header opens and the *Worldwide Memo With Slide Show* document is in the message content area
Step 4	*Close*	the document without saving or sending the message

With Word, it's easy to send e-mail messages with or without document attachments.

MOUSE **TIP**

You can attach a document to an e-mail message created directly in Word by clicking the Attach File button in the e-mail header.

Summary

▶ You can insert an Excel worksheet into a Word document as a Word table or you can copy and paste Excel data into a Word document as a Word table.

▶ You can copy and paste data maintained in Office documents, such as Excel workbooks, into a Word document as an embedded or linked object.

▶ Embedding data in a Word document inserts a copy of the data into its original source format; the data must be edited with the source application features.

▶ Linking data in a Word document places a reference or pointer in the Word document, but the data continue to reside in the source application and must be edited in the source application.

▶ A PowerPoint slide show can be based on an imported Word outline created with built-in heading styles.

▶ You can link a PowerPoint presentation to a Word document and then view it from the Word document.

▶ Data from a database application, such as Access, can be inserted into a Word document as a table.

▶ Excel worksheet data and Access database data can be used as a data source for a Word mail merge.

▶ An alternative to embedding or linking data is to insert a hyperlink that allows the reader of a Word document to "jump" to the linked Office document.

▶ If you have Outlook 2000 or Outlook Express 5.0 as your e-mail client, you can create and send e-mail messages directly from Word.

integration

Commands Review

Action	Menu Bar	Shortcut Menu	Toolbar	Keyboard
Insert Excel worksheet data as a Word table	Edit, Copy Edit, Paste	Right-click selected worksheet range, click Copy Right-click at insertion point, click Paste	 	ALT + E, C ALT + E, P
Embed Excel worksheet data into a Word document	Insert, Object Edit, Copy and then Edit, Paste Special, Paste	Use drag-and-drop or right-drag and click Copy Here Note: the Paste Special command does not appear on the Word shortcut menu		ALT + I, O ALT + E, C and then ALT + E, S, P
Link Excel worksheet data to a Word document	Edit, Paste Special, Paste Link	Right-drag and click Insert Excel object here		ALT + E, S, L
Create a blank embedded Excel object	Insert, Object			ALT + I, O
Create a PowerPoint presentation from a Word outline	File, Send To, Microsoft PowerPoint			ALT + F, D, P
Import a Word outline to create a PowerPoint slide show	From PowerPoint: File, Open, All Outlines			ALT + F, O
Link a PowerPoint presentation to a Word document	Insert, Object, Link to File option			ALT + I, O, L
Send a PowerPoint presentation to Word	From PowerPoint: File, Send To, Microsoft Word			ALT + F, D, W
Import an Access table or query into a Word document				
Send an Access table or query to Word	From Access: File, Save As/Export			ALT + F, A
Create hyperlinks between Word and Office documents	Insert, Hyperlink			ALT + I, I CTRL + K

Concepts Review

Circle the correct answer.

1. **You can link Excel worksheet data to a Word document with the:**
   [a] Copy and Paste buttons on the Standard toolbar.
   [b] Copy and Paste Special commands.
   [c] Link button on the Standard toolbar.
   [d] Link command on the Edit menu.

2. **When you insert an Excel file into a Word document, the data are:**
   [a] linked.
   [b] embedded.
   [c] hyperlinked.
   [d] placed in a Word table.

3. **To edit data in an embedded Excel worksheet object in a Word document you use the:**
   [a] Excel menu bar and toolbars in Word.
   [b] Excel menu bar and toolbars in Excel.
   [c] Word menu bar and toolbars in Word.
   [d] Word menu bar and toolbars in Excel.

4. **When you link data maintained in another Office application to Word, the Word document:**
   [a] cannot be edited.
   [b] contains a copy of the actual data.
   [c] contains a hyperlink.
   [d] contains a reference to the original source document and application.

5. **You can use the drag-and-drop method to embed Excel worksheet data in a Word document by:**
   [a] dragging a range of Excel data to the Word button on the taskbar while pressing the CTRL key.
   [b] displaying both applications side by side and dragging a selected range of Excel data into the Word application window while pressing the ALT key.
   [c] dragging a range of Excel data to the Word button on the taskbar while pressing the SHIFT key.
   [d] dragging a range of Excel data to the Word button on the taskbar while pressing the SPACEBAR.

6. **When you want to insert a blank embedded Excel object into a Word document, you can click the:**
   [a] Object command on the Insert menu.
   [b] Create Worksheet button on the Formatting toolbar.
   [c] Import Excel command on the File menu.
   [d] Office Links button on the Word Standard toolbar.

7. **When you create a PowerPoint presentation from a Word outline, the Word outline must be:**
   [a] linked to a PowerPoint presentation.
   [b] formatted with built-in heading styles.
   [c] copied to PowerPoint first.
   [d] sent to PowerPoint with the Send Word command on the File menu.

integration

8. **You can create and send an e-mail directly from Word by clicking the:**
   [a] E-mail button on the Formatting toolbar.
   [b] E-mail command on the Tools menu.
   [c] E-mail icon in the New dialog box.
   [d] E-mail command on the File menu.

9. **If you use the Paste command to place Excel data in a Word document you create a(n):**
   [a] Word table.
   [b] embedded Excel object.
   [c] linked Excel object.
   [d] hyperlink.

10. **Calculations in Excel are called:**
    [a] hyperlinks.
    [b] equations.
    [c] formulas.
    [d] sums.

Circle **T** if the statement is true or **F** is the statement is false.

T   F   1. When you link an Excel worksheet object to a Word document, the data must be edited in the Word application with Excel features.

T   F   2. If you want to modify the data only in the Word document using the source application's tools, you should link the data.

T   F   3. When you Paste link Excel data into a Word document, the data is placed in a Word table.

T   F   4. To have data in the destination application automatically reflect changes made in the source application, you should embed the data.

T   F   5. You can send a PowerPoint slide show to Word to create speaker notes and handout materials.

T   F   6. When you embed data, any changes you make to the original data are reflected in the embedded object.

T   F   7. Hyperlinks can be used only between Word documents and Web pages on the Internet.

T   F   8. You cannot attach a file to an e-mail message created and sent directly from Word.

T   F   9. An Access query is a subset of an Access table.

T   F   10. When you send an e-mail message from Word it is automatically formatted in HTML format.

Skills Review

SCANS

Exercise 1

1. Open the *Vancouver Sales Memo* document located on the Data Disk.

2. Open the Excel application and the *Vancouver Branch Sales* workbook located on the Data Disk.

3. Copy the Sales Report data in the range A1:F10 and paste the data as an embedded worksheet object below the first body paragraph.

4. Change the object layout to Inline with text and center it.

5. Save the document as *Vancouver Sales Memo With Embedded Object*.

6. Print and close the document.

7. Close the Excel application and workbook.

Exercise 2   C

1. Open the *Vancouver Sales Memo* document located on the Data Disk.

2. Open the Excel application and the *Vancouver Branch Sales* workbook located on the Data Disk.

3. Copy the Sales Report data in the range A1:F10 and paste the data as a linked object below the first body paragraph.

4. Change the object layout to Inline with text and center it.

5. Close the Excel application and workbook without saving changes. Do not save the large Clipboard item.

6. Edit the linked Excel worksheet object to right-align the column headings in cells B5:F5, and change the sales figures for Meat to 1,000 for North, 800 for South, 1,300 for East, and 900 for West. Turn off the display of gridlines.

7. Save the workbook as *Modified Vancouver Branch Sales* and close the Excel application.

8. Save the word document as *Vancouver Sales Memo Revised*.

9. Print and close the document.

Exercise 3   C

1. Open the *Australia Outline* document located on the Data Disk.

2. Create a PowerPoint presentation from the outline.

3. Change the Slide 1 layout to Title.

4. Apply a presentation design of your choice and format the text as desired.

5. Save the presentation as *Australia Highlights*.

6. Print the presentation with three slides per page.

7. Close the PowerPoint application and presentation.

8. Close the Word document without saving any changes.

Exercise 4   C

1. Open the *Vancouver Sales Memo With Embedded Object* document created in Exercise 1.

2. Modify the second sentence in the first paragraph to refer to a hyperlink.

3. Select and delete the embedded object.

4. Create a hyperlink to the *Vancouver Branch Sales* Excel workbook and place it in the second sentence in the first paragraph that refers to the linked workbook.

5. Close the Excel application and workbook.

6. Test the hyperlink in the Word document by clicking it.

7. Save the Word document as *Vancouver Sales Memo With Hyperlink*.

8. Print and close the document.

integration

Exercise 5 ⒸC

1. Open the PowerPoint application and the *Australia Highlights* presentation.

2. Send the presentation to Word and use the Write-Up layout of your choice.

3. Close the PowerPoint application and presentation.

4. Save the Word document as *Australia Handout.*

5. Print and close the Word document.

Exercise 6 ⒸC

1. Open the *District A Sales Decline* document located on the Data Disk.

2. Double space the document. Center and single-space the stores and their locations.

3. Save the document as *Modified Sales Decline.*

4. Open the Excel application and open the *District A Sales Report* workbook located on the Data Disk.

5. Copy the District A Sales Report data in the range A1:H11 and paste the data as an embedded worksheet object at the bottom of the document.

6. Close the Excel application and workbook without saving any changes. Do not save the large Clipboard item.

7. Save and print the document.

8. Edit the embedded object to change the sales figures for Store A5 to 68,000 for November, 59,100 for December, 57,850 for January, 59,150 for February, 58,000 for March, 67,100 for April, and 66,900 for May.

9. Save the document as *Edited Sales Decline.*

10. Print and close the document.

Exercise 7 ⒸC

1. Open the *London Personnel* database located on the Data Disk.

2. Export the Employees table to a Word document.

3. Edit the exported Access data using Word editing features.

4. Save the document as *London Personnel* as a Word document type.

5. Print and close the document.

Exercise 8 ⒸC

(Complete this Project if you are using Outlook 2000 or Outlook Express as your e-mail client.)

1. Create a new blank e-mail message to a classmate from inside Word using the E-mail icon in the New dialog box.

2. Use a classmate's e-mail address provided by your instructor.

3. The subject of the message is "Sales Meeting."

4. The message text is: "Please confirm your attendance at the sales meeting on Thursday."

5. Sign the message with your name.

6. Send the message, if possible.

7. Save the message document as *Sales Meeting Confirmation*, print and close it.

Case Projects

Project 1

Marisa DaFranco calls to tell you that whenever she double-clicks a linked Excel object in one of her Word documents, see gets a "cannot edit" error message. She asks you how to solve the problem. Using the Office Assistant, research troubleshooting linking and sharing data with other programs. Create an e-mail message to Marisa telling her how to solve the problem. Save and print the e-mail message.

Project 2

Margaret Nguyen, the administrative assistant to the vice president of marketing, is responsible for some of the sales meeting presentations. She asks you to create a PowerPoint presentation announcing the new holiday sales campaign and then send it to her in a memo for her review. She will format the slides in the presentation after reviewing it. Create a new Word outline using built-in heading styles and containing fictitious sales campaign topics. Then create a PowerPoint slide presentation from the outline. Save and print the presentation slides. Create an e-mail message to Margaret from inside Word and attach the presentation file. Save and print the e-mail message.

Project 3

Chris Lofton, the word processing manager, asks you to give a short presentation to the word processing specialists on the difference between embedding and linking objects. Use online Help to review the explanation of linked objects and embedded objects. Then create a Word outline using built-in styles of the topics you plan to cover

in the presentation. Send the Word outline to PowerPoint to create a presentation. Format the presentation as desired and print it. Send the PowerPoint presentation to Word using a Write Up style of your choice. Save and print the Word document. With your instructor's permission, open the PowerPoint presentation and, using the presentation and the Word handout document, explain the difference between linked and embedded objects to a group of classmates.

Project 4

Jody Haversham calls and asks for your help in reconnecting a linked Excel object in one of her documents. She renamed the Excel source workbook and now Word cannot find the source file. Using the Office Assistant, search for the "Reconnecting a linked object when the source moves or is renamed" topic. After reviewing the topic, write Jody an e-mail message listing step-by-step instructions on reconnecting a linked object to a renamed source file. Save and print the e-mail message.

Project 5

Kelly Armstead has a Word document that contains a list of contact names and addresses. She wants to import the Word information into her Outlook 2000 contacts folder and asks for your help. Use online Help to research how to do this, then write Kelly an e-mail message describing what she needs to do. Save and print the e-mail message.

integration

Project 6

Marisa DaFranco wants to know if there is any shortcut method to create linked objects, shortcuts, or hyperlinks when sharing information between Word and other Office 2000 documents. You think she can use the right-drag technique to do this. Using the Word document and Excel workbook of your choice practice creating linked objects, shortcuts, and hyperlinks using right drag. Write Marisa an e-mail message explaining how to create each of these items using the right-drag method. Save and print the e-mail message.

Project 7

The Vancouver branch manager wants to review the data in the *Vancouver Branch Sales* workbook before he leaves his office for a two-week sales trip. He asks you to e-mail the data. Open the *Vancouver Branch Sales* workbook and copy the range A1:F10 to the Clipboard. Create a new e-mail message in Word. Address it to the Vancouver branch manager using a fictitious e-mail address. Add appropriate subject and message text and paste the copied data into a Word table. Save and print the e-mail message.

Project 8

You want to know what online Help is available from the Web. Connect to your ISP and click the Office on the Web command on the Help menu. Review the available help topics. Send an e-mail message to several classmates describing what they can expect to find when they click the Office on the Web command on the Help menu. Save and print the e-mail message.

Working with Windows 98

T Appendix Overview

The Windows 98 operating system creates a workspace on your computer screen, called the desktop. The desktop is a graphical environment that contains icons you click with the mouse pointer to access your computer system resources or to perform a task such as opening a software application. This appendix introduces you to the Windows 98 desktop by describing the default desktop icons and showing how to access your computer resources, use menu commands and toolbar buttons to perform a task, and select dialog box options.

LEARNING OBJECTIVES

► Review the Windows 98 desktop
► Access your computer system resources
► Use menu commands and toolbar buttons
► Use the Start menu
► Review dialog box options
► Use Windows 98 shortcuts
► Understand the Recycle Bin
► Shut down Windows 98

A appendix

A.a Reviewing the Windows 98 Desktop

Whenever you start your computer, the Windows 98 operating system automatically starts and the Windows 98 desktop appears on your screen. To view the Windows 98 desktop:

| Step 1 | *Turn on* | your computer and monitor |
| Step 2 | *Observe* | the Windows 98 desktop, as shown in Figure A-1 |

FIGURE A-1
Windows 98 Desktop

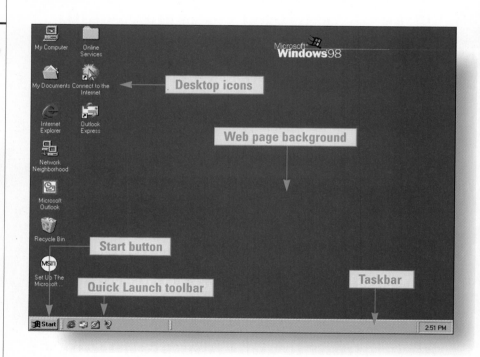

The Windows 98 desktop contains three elements: icons, background, and taskbar. The icons represent Windows objects and shortcuts to opening software applications or performing tasks. Table A-1 describes some of the default icons. By default, the background is Web-page style. The taskbar, at the bottom of the window, contains the Start button and the Quick Launch toolbar. The icon types and arrangement, desktop background, or Quick Launch toolbar on your screen might be different.

The Start button displays the Start menu, which you can use to perform tasks. By default, the taskbar also contains the **Quick Launch toolbar**, which has shortcuts to open Internet Explorer Web browser, Outlook Express e-mail software, and Internet channels, as well as to switch between the desktop and open application windows. You can customize the Quick Launch toolbar to include other toolbars.

Icon	Name	Description
🖥	My Computer	Provides access to computer system resources
📁	My Documents	Stores Office 2000 documents (by default)
🅔	Internet Explorer	Opens Internet Explorer Web browser
📇	Microsoft Outlook	Opens Outlook 2000 information manager software
🗑	Recycle Bin	Temporarily stores folders and files deleted from the hard drive
🖧	Network Neighborhood	Provides access to computers and printers networked in your workgroup

TABLE A-1
Common Desktop Icons

A.b Accessing Your Computer System Resources

The My Computer window provides access to your computer system resources. To open the My Computer window:

Step 1	*Point to*	the My Computer icon 🖥 on the desktop
Step 2	*Observe*	a brief description of the icon in the ScreenTip
Step 3	*Double-click*	the My Computer icon 🖥 to open the My Computer window shown in Figure A-2

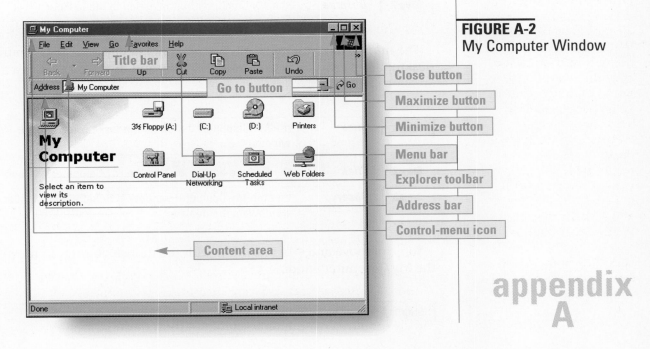

FIGURE A-2
My Computer Window

appendix
A

Point means to place the mouse pointer on the command or item. **Click** means to press the left mouse button and release it. **Right-click** means to press the right mouse button and release it. **Double-click** means to press the left mouse button twice very rapidly. **Drag** means to hold down the left mouse button as you move the mouse pointer. **Right-drag** means to hold down the right mouse button as you move the mouse pointer. **Scroll** means to use the application scroll bar features or the IntelliMouse scrolling wheel.

A window is a rectangular area on your screen in which you view operating system options or a software application, such as Internet Explorer. Windows 98 has some common window elements. The **title bar**, at the top of the window, includes the window's Control-menu icon, the window name, and the Minimize, Restore (or Maximize), and Close buttons. The **Control-menu icon**, in the upper-left corner of the window, accesses the Control menu that contains commands for moving, restoring, sizing, minimizing, maximizing, and closing the window. The **Minimize** button, near the upper-right corner of the window, reduces the window to a taskbar button. The **Maximize** button, to the right of the Minimize button, enlarges the window to fill the entire screen viewing area above the taskbar. If the window is already maximized, the Restore button appears in its place. The **Restore** button reduces the window size. The **Close** button, in the upper-right corner, closes the window. To maximize the My Computer window:

| Step 1 | *Click* | the Maximize button ⬜ on the My Computer window title bar |
| Step 2 | *Observe* | that the My Computer window completely covers the desktop |

When you want to leave a window open, but do not want to see it on the desktop, you can minimize it. To minimize the My Computer window:

| Step 1 | *Click* | the Minimize button ▬ on the My Computer window title bar |
| Step 2 | *Observe* | the My Computer button added to the taskbar |

The minimized window is still open but not occupying space on the desktop. To view the My Computer window and then restore it to a smaller size:

Step 1	*Click*	the My Computer button on the taskbar to view the window
Step 2	*Click*	the Restore button 🗗 on the My Computer title bar
Step 3	*Observe*	that the My Computer window is reduced to a smaller window on the desktop

You can move and size a window with the mouse pointer. To move the My Computer window:

| Step 1 | *Position* | the mouse pointer on the My Computer title bar |

| Step 2 | *Drag* | the window down and to the right approximately ½ inch |
| Step 3 | *Drag* | the window back to the center of the screen |

Several Windows 98 windows—My Computer, My Documents, and Windows Explorer—have the same menu bar and toolbar features. These windows are sometimes called **Explorer-style windows**. When you size an Explorer-style window too small to view all its icons, a vertical or horizontal scroll bar may appear. A scroll bar includes scroll arrows and a scroll box for viewing different parts of the window contents.

To size the My Computer window:

Step 1	*Position*	the mouse pointer on the lower-right corner of the window
Step 2	*Observe*	that the mouse pointer becomes a black, double-headed sizing pointer
Step 3	*Drag*	the lower-right corner boundary diagonally up approximately ½ inch and release the mouse button
Step 4	*Click*	the right scroll arrow on the horizontal scroll bar to view hidden icons
Step 5	*Size*	the window twice as large to remove the horizontal scroll bar

You can open the window associated with any icon in the My Computer window by double-clicking it. Explorer-style windows open in the same window, not separate windows. To open the Control Panel Explorer-style window:

| Step 1 | *Double-click* | the Control Panel icon |
| Step 2 | *Observe* | that the Address bar displays the Control Panel icon and name, and the content area displays the Control Panel icons for accessing computer system resources |

A.c Using Menu Commands and Toolbar Buttons

You can click a menu command or toolbar button to perform specific tasks in a window. The **menu bar** is a special toolbar located below the window title bar that contains the File, Edit, View, Go, Favorites, and Help menus. The **toolbar**, located below the menu bar, contains shortcut "buttons" you click with the mouse pointer to execute a variety of commands. You can use the Back and Forward

---

QUICK TIP

The Explorer-style windows and the Internet Explorer Web browser are really one Explorer feature integrated into Windows 98 that you can use to find information on your hard drive, network, company intranet, or the Web. Explorer-style windows have a Web-browser look and features. You can use Internet Explorer to access local information by keying the path in the Address bar or clicking an item on the Favorites list.

MOUSE TIP

You can display four taskbar toolbars: Quick Launch, Address, Links, and Desktop. The Quick Launch toolbar appears on the taskbar by default. You can also create additional toolbars from other folders or subfolders and you can add folder or file shortcuts to an existing taskbar toolbar. To view other taskbar toolbars, right-click the taskbar, point to Toolbars, and then click the desired toolbar name.

appendix
A

buttons on the Explorer toolbar or the Back or Forward commands on the Go menu to switch between My Computer and the Control Panel. To view My Computer:

Step 1	Click	the Back button ⇐ on the Explorer toolbar to view My Computer
Step 2	Click	the Forward button ⇒ on the Explorer toolbar to view the Control Panel
Step 3	Click	Go on the menu bar
Step 4	Click	the My Computer command to view My Computer
Step 5	Click	the Close button ☒ on the My Computer window title bar

A.d Using the Start Menu

The **Start button** on the taskbar opens the Start menu. You use this menu to access several Windows 98 features and to open software applications, such as Word or Excel. To open the Start menu:

| Step 1 | Click | the Start button 🔲 Start on the taskbar to open the Start menu (see Figure A-3) |

FIGURE A-3
Start Menu

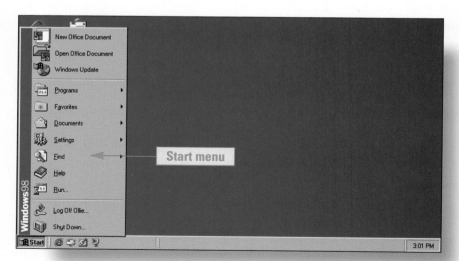

| Step 2 | Point to | Programs to view the software applications installed on your computer |
| Step 3 | Click | the desktop outside the Start menu and Programs menu to close them |

A.e Reviewing Dialog Box Options

A **dialog box** is a window that contains options you can select, turn on, or turn off to perform a task. To view a dialog box:

Step 1	*Click*	the Start button **🄰Start** on the taskbar
Step 2	*Point to*	Settings
Step 3	*Point to*	Active Desktop
Step 4	*Click*	Customize my Desktop to open the Display Properties dialog box
Step 5	*Click*	the Effects tab (see Figure A-4)

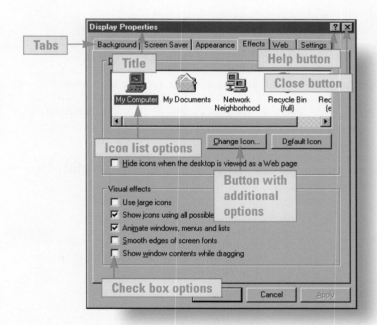

Step 6	*Click*	each tab and observe the different options available *(do not change any options unless directed by your instructor)*
Step 7	*Right-click*	each option on each tab and then click <u>W</u>hat's This? to view its ScreenTip
Step 8	*Click*	Cancel to close the dialog box without changing any options

QUICK TIP

Many dialog boxes contain sets of options on different pages organized on **tabs** you click. Options include drop-down lists you view by clicking an arrow, text boxes in which you key information, check boxes and option buttons you click to turn on or off an option, and buttons that access additional options.

FIGURE A-4
Effects Tab in the Display Properties Dialog Box

**appendix
A**

A.f Using Windows 98 Shortcuts

You can use the drag-and-drop method to reposition or remove Start menu commands. You can also right-drag a Start menu command to the desktop to create a desktop shortcut. To reposition the Windows Update item on the Start menu:

Step 1	*Click*	the Start button on the taskbar
Step 2	*Point to*	the Windows Update item
Step 3	*Drag*	the Windows Update item to the top of the Start menu

To remove the Windows Update shortcut from the Start menu and create a desktop shortcut:

Step 1	*Drag*	the Windows Update item to the desktop
Step 2	*Observe*	that the desktop shortcut appears after a few seconds
Step 3	*Verify*	that the Windows Update item no longer appears on the Start menu

To add a Windows Update shortcut back to the Start menu and delete the desktop shortcut:

Step 1	*Drag*	the Windows Update shortcut to the Start button on the taskbar and then back to its original position when the Start menu appears
Step 2	*Close*	the Start menu
Step 3	*Drag*	the Windows Update shortcut on the desktop to the Recycle Bin
Step 4	*Click*	Yes

You can close multiple application windows at one time from the taskbar using the CTRL key and a shortcut menu. To open two applications and then use the taskbar to close them:

| Step 1 | *Open* | the Word and Excel applications (in this order) from the Programs menu on the Start menu |

Step 2	*Observe*	the Word and Excel buttons on the taskbar (Excel is the selected, active button)
Step 3	*Press & Hold*	the CTRL key
Step 4	*Click*	the Word application taskbar button (the Excel application taskbar button is already selected)
Step 5	*Release*	the CTRL key
Step 6	*Right-click*	the Word or Excel taskbar button
Step 7	*Click*	Close to close both applications

You can use the drag-and-drop method to add a shortcut to the Quick Launch toolbar for folders and documents you have created. To create a new subfolder in the My Documents folder.

Step 1	*Click*	the My Documents icon on the desktop to open the window
Step 2	*Right-click*	the contents area (but not a file or folder)
Step 3	*Point to*	New
Step 4	*Click*	Folder
Step 5	*Key*	Example
Step 6	*Press*	the ENTER key to name the folder
Step 7	*Drag*	the Example folder to the end of the Quick Launch toolbar (a black vertical line indicates the drop position)
Step 8	*Observe*	the new icon on the toolbar
Step 9	*Close*	the My Documents window
Step 10	*Position*	the mouse pointer on the Example folder shortcut on the Quick Launch toolbar and observe the ScreenTip

You remove a shortcut from the Quick Launch toolbar by dragging it to the desktop and deleting it, or dragging it directly to the Recycle Bin. To remove the Example folder shortcut and delete the folder:

Step 1	*Drag*	the Example folder icon to the Recycle Bin
Step 2	*Click*	Yes
Step 3	*Open*	the My Documents window
Step 4	*Delete*	the Example folder icon using the shortcut menu
Step 5	*Close*	the My Documents window

**appendix
A**

A.g Understanding the Recycle Bin

The **Recycle Bin** is an object that temporarily stores folders, files, and shortcuts you delete from your hard drive. If you accidentally delete an item, you can restore it to its original location on your hard drive if it is still in the Recycle Bin. Because the Recycle Bin takes up disk space you should review and empty it regularly. When you empty the Recycle Bin, its contents are removed from your hard drive and can no longer be restored.

A.h Shutting Down Windows 98

It is very important that you follow the proper procedures for shutting down the Windows 98 operating system when you are finished, to allow the operating system to complete its internal "housekeeping" properly. To shut down Windows 98 correctly:

| Step 1 | *Click* | the Start button ![Start] on the taskbar |
| Step 2 | *Click* | Sh<u>u</u>t Down to open the Shut Down Windows dialog box shown in Figure A-5 |

FIGURE A-5
Shut Down Windows
Dialog Box

You can shut down completely, restart, and restart in MS-DOS mode from this dialog box. You want to shut down completely.

| Step 3 | *Click* | the <u>S</u>hut down option button to select it, if necessary |
| Step 4 | *Click* | OK |

Managing Your Folders and Files Using Windows Explorer

Appendix Overview

Windows Explorer provides tools for managing your folders and files. This appendix introduces the Windows Explorer options of expanding and collapsing the folder view, creating new folders, renaming folders and files, deleting folders and files, and creating desktop shortcuts.

LEARNING OBJECTIVES

► Open Windows Explorer
► Review Windows Explorer options
► Create a new folder
► Move and copy folders and files
► Rename folders and files
► Create desktop shortcuts
► Delete folders and files

appendix

notes   The default Windows 98 Custom folder options are used in the hands-on activities and figures. If you are using the Windows 95 operating system, your instructor will modify the hands-on activities and your screen will look different.

B.a Opening Windows Explorer

You can open Windows Explorer from the <u>P</u>rograms command on the Start menu or from a shortcut menu. To open Windows Explorer using a shortcut menu:

Step 1	*Right-Click*	the Start button **Start** on the taskbar
Step 2	*Click*	Explore
Step 3	*Maximize*	the Windows Explorer window, if necessary (see Figure B-1)

FIGURE B-1
Windows Explorer
Window

QUICK TIP

You can also use the My Computer Explorer-style window to manage your files and folders. If you are using Windows 95, the list of disk drives and folders is called the **Tree pane**.

The window below the menu bar, toolbar, and Address bar is divided into two panes: The **Explorer Bar** on the left shows the computer's organizational structure, including all desktop objects, My Computer objects, and the disk drive folders. The **Contents pane** on the right shows all subfolders and files for the folder selected in the Explorer Bar. The panes are divided by a **separator bar** that you drag left or right to resize the panes.

B.b Reviewing Windows Explorer Options

You can view disk drive icons, folders, and files (called **objects**) for your computer by selecting an item from the Address bar list or by clicking an object in the Explorer Bar. To view all your computer's disk drives and system folders:

Step 1	*Click*	the Address bar list arrow
Step 2	*Click*	My Computer to view a list of disk drives and system folders in the Contents pane
Step 3	*Click*	the (C:) disk drive object in the Explorer Bar to view a list of folders (stored on the C:\ drive) in the Contents pane

You can expand or collapse the view of folders and other objects in the Explorer Bar. To collapse the view of the C:\ drive in the Explorer Bar:

Step 1	*Click*	the minus sign (–) to the left of the (C:) disk drive object in the Explorer Bar
Step 2	*Observe*	that the C:\ drive folders list is hidden and the minus sign becomes a plus sign (+)
Step 3	*Click*	the plus sign (+) to the left of the (C:) disk drive object in the Explorer Bar
Step 4	*Observe*	that the list of folders stored on the C:\ drive is again visible

You can view a folder's contents by clicking the folder in the Explorer Bar or double-clicking the folder in the Contents pane. To view the contents of the folder that contains the Data Files:

| Step 1 | *Click* | the disk drive in the Explorer Bar where the Data Files are stored |

appendix
B

| Step 2 | *Double-click* | the Data Files folder in the Contents pane (scroll, if necessary) to view a list of Data Files and folders |

You can resize and reposition folders and files in the Contents pane and add more details about the file size, type, and date modified. To change the size and position of the Data Files and folders:

Step 1	*Click*	the Views button list arrow 🔲▾ on the Explorer toolbar
Step 2	*Click*	Large Icons to view horizontal rows of larger folder and file icons in the Contents pane
Step 3	*Click*	Small Icons on the Views button list to view horizontal rows of smaller folder and file icons in the Contents pane
Step 4	*Click*	Details on the Views button list to view a vertical list of folders and files names, sizes, types, and dates modified
Step 5	*Click*	List on the Views button list to view a simple list of the files and folders

B.c Creating a New Folder

You can create a new folder for an object in the Explorer Bar or the Contents pane. To add a folder to the My Documents folder in the C:\ drive folder list:

Step 1	*Click*	the My Documents folder in the Explorer Bar to select it (scroll, if necessary)
Step 2	*Click*	File
Step 3	*Point to*	New
Step 4	*Click*	Folder
Step 5	*Observe*	the newly created folder object in the Contents pane with the selected temporary name New Folder

To name the folder and refresh the Explorer Bar view:

Step 1	*Key*	Practice Folder
Step 2	*Press*	the ENTER key
Step 3	*Observe*	the new folder name in the Contents pane
Step 4	*Click*	View

| Step 5 | *Click* | Refresh |
| Step 6 | *Observe* | that the My Documents folder has a plus sign, indicating that the folder list can be expanded |

B.d Moving and Copying Folders and Files

You select folders and files by clicking them. You can then copy or move them with the Cut, Copy and Paste commands on the Edit menu or shortcut menu, the Copy and Paste buttons on the Explorer toolbar, or with the drag-and-drop or right-drag mouse methods. To copy a file from the Data Files folder to the Practice Folder using the right-drag method:

Step 1	*View*	the list of Data Files in the Contents pane
Step 2	*Right-drag*	any file to the My Documents folder in the Explorer Bar and pause until the My Documents folder expands to show the subfolders
Step 3	*Continue*	to right-drag the file to the Practice Folder subfolder under the My Documents folder in the Explorer Bar
Step 4	*Click*	Copy Here on the shortcut menu
Step 5	*Click*	the Practice Folder in the Explorer Bar to view the copied file's icon and filename in the Contents pane

B.e Renaming Folders and Files

Sometimes you want to change an existing file or folder name to a more descriptive name. To rename the copied file in the Practice Folder:

Step 1	*Verify*	the icon and filename for the copied file appears in the Contents pane
Step 2	*Right-click*	the copied file in the Contents pane
Step 3	*Click*	Rename
Step 4	*Key*	Renamed File
Step 5	*Click*	the Contents area (not the filename) to accept the new filename

---

MOUSE TIP

You can use the SHIFT + Click method to select adjacent multiple folders and files in the Contents pane by clicking the first item to select it, holding down the SHIFT key, and then clicking the last item. You can use the CTRL + Click method to select nonadjacent files and folders in the Contents pane by clicking the first item, holding down the CTRL key, and then clicking each additional item.

MENU TIP

You can quickly copy a file to a disk from a hard disk or network drive, create a desktop shortcut, or send the file as an attachment to an e-mail message by right-clicking the file, pointing to Send To, and clicking the appropriate command.

appendix
B

B.f Creating Desktop Shortcuts

You can add a shortcut for folders and files to the Windows desktop by restoring the Windows Explorer window to a smaller window and right-dragging a folder or file icon to the desktop. You can also right-drag a folder or file icon to the Desktop icon in the Explorer Bar inside the Windows Explorer window. To create a desktop shortcut to the Practice Folder using the Desktop icon:

Step 1	*Expand*	the My Documents folder in the Explorer Bar, if necessary, to view the Practice Folder subfolder
Step 2	*Right-drag*	the Practice Folder to the Desktop icon at the top of the Explorer Bar
Step 3	*Click*	Create Shortcut(s) Here
Step 4	*Minimize*	the Windows Explorer window to view the new shortcut on the desktop
Step 5	*Drag*	the Shortcut to Practice Folder desktop shortcut to the Recycle Bin to delete it
Step 6	*Click*	Yes
Step 7	*Click*	the Exploring-Practice Folder taskbar button to maximize the Windows Explorer window

B.g Deleting Folders and Files

When necessary, you can delete a folder and its contents or a file by selecting it and then clicking the Delete command on the File menu or shortcut menu, or pressing the DELETE key. You can also delete multiple selected folders and files at one time. To delete the Practice Folder and its contents:

Step 1	*Click*	the Practice Folder in the Explorer Bar to select it, if necessary
Step 2	*Press*	the DELETE key
Step 3	*Click*	Yes to send the folder and its contents to the Recycle Bin

---

Formatting Tips for Business Documents

Appendix Overview

Most organizations follow specific formatting guidelines when preparing letters, envelopes, memorandums, and other documents to ensure the documents present a professional appearance. In this appendix you learn how to format different size letters, interoffice memos, envelopes, and formal outlines. You also review a list of style guides and learn how to use proofreader's marks.

LEARNING OBJECTIVES

- ▶ Format letters
- ▶ Insert mailing notations
- ▶ Format envelopes
- ▶ Format interoffice memorandums
- ▶ Format formal outlines
- ▶ Use proofreader's marks
- ▶ Use style guides

appendix

C

C.a Formatting Letters

The quality and professionalism of a company's business correspondence can affect how customers, clients, and others view a company. That correspondence represents the company to those outside it. To ensure a positive and appropriate image, many companies set special standards for margins, typeface, and font size for their business correspondence. These special standards are based on the common letter styles illustrated in this section.

Most companies use special letter paper with the company name and address (and sometimes a company logo or picture) preprinted on the paper. The preprinted portion is called a **letterhead** and the paper is called **letterhead paper**. When you create a letter, the margins vary depending on the style of your letterhead and the length of your letter. Most letterheads use between 1 inch and 2 inches of the page from the top of the sheet. There are two basic business correspondence formats: block format and modified block format. When you create a letter in **block format**, all the text is placed flush against the left margin. This includes the date, the letter address information, the salutation, the body, the complimentary closing, and the signature information. The body of the letter is single spaced with a blank line between paragraphs.[1] Figure C-1 shows a short letter in the block format with standard punctuation.

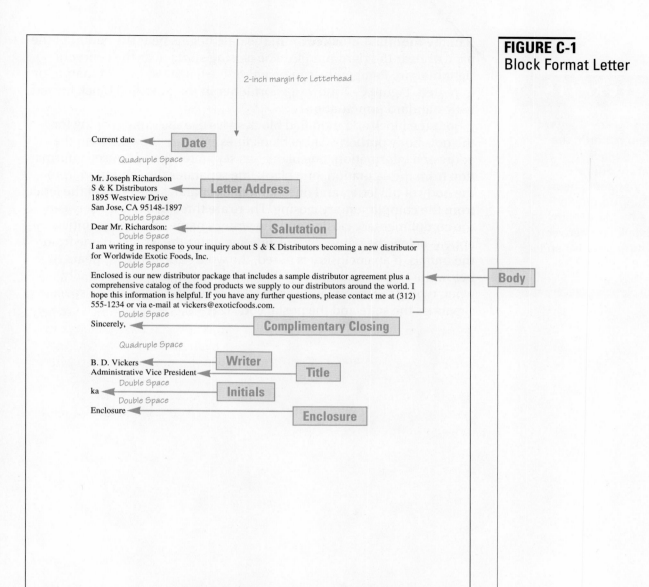

FIGURE C-1
Block Format Letter

2-inch margin for Letterhead

Current date — **Date**

Quadruple Space

Mr. Joseph Richardson
S & K Distributors — **Letter Address**
1895 Westview Drive
San Jose, CA 95148-1897
Double Space
Dear Mr. Richardson: — **Salutation**
Double Space
I am writing in response to your inquiry about S & K Distributors becoming a new distributor
for Worldwide Exotic Foods, Inc.
Double Space
Enclosed is our new distributor package that includes a sample distributor agreement plus a — **Body**
comprehensive catalog of the food products we supply to our distributors around the world. I
hope this information is helpful. If you have any further questions, please contact me at (312)
555-1234 or via e-mail at vickers@exoticfoods.com.
Double Space
Sincerely, — **Complimentary Closing**

Quadruple Space

B. D. Vickers — **Writer**
Administrative Vice President — **Title**
Double Space
ka — **Initials**
Double Space
Enclosure — **Enclosure**

**appendix
C**

QUICK TIP

When you key a letter on plain paper in the modified block format, the return address usually appears near the right margin and above the date, with one blank line between the return address and the date.

In the **modified block format**, the date begins near the center of the page or near the right margin. The closing starts near the center or right margin. Paragraphs can be either flush against the left margin or indented. Figure C-2 shows a short letter in the modified block format with standard punctuation.

Both the block and modified block styles use the same spacing for the non-body portions. Three blank lines separate the date from the addressee information, one blank line separates the addressee information from the salutation, one blank line separates the salutation from the body of the letter, and one blank line separates the body of the letter from the complimentary closing. There are three blank lines between the complimentary closing and the writer's name. If a typist's initials appear below the name, a blank line separates the writer's name from the initials. If an enclosure is noted, the word "Enclosure" appears below the typist's initials with a blank line separating them. Finally, when typing the return address or addressee information, one space separates the state and the postal code (ZIP+4).

FIGURE C-2
Modified Block
Format Letter

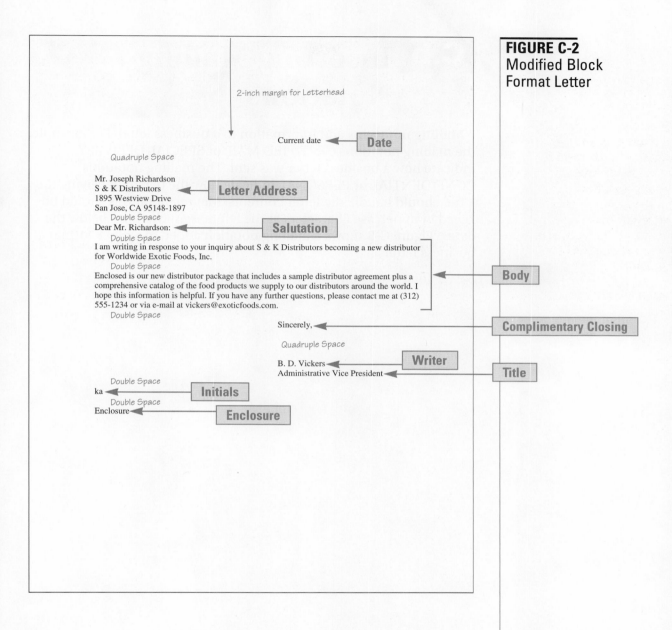

2-inch margin for Letterhead

Current date   **Date**

Quadruple Space

Mr. Joseph Richardson
S & K Distributors   **Letter Address**
1895 Westview Drive
San Jose, CA 95148-1897
Double Space
Dear Mr. Richardson: **Salutation**
Double Space
I am writing in response to your inquiry about S & K Distributors becoming a new distributor
for Worldwide Exotic Foods, Inc.
Double Space
Enclosed is our new distributor package that includes a sample distributor agreement plus a   **Body**
comprehensive catalog of the food products we supply to our distributors around the world. I
hope this information is helpful. If you have any further questions, please contact me at (312)
555-1234 or via e-mail at vickers@exoticfoods.com.
Double Space

Sincerely,   **Complimentary Closing**

Quadruple Space

B. D. Vickers   **Writer**
Administrative Vice President   **Title**
Double Space
ka   **Initials**
Double Space
Enclosure   **Enclosure**

**appendix
C**

C.b Inserting Mailing Notations

Mailing notations add information to a business letter. For example, the mailing notations CERTIFIED MAIL or SPECIAL DELIVERY indicate how a business letter was sent. The mailing notations CONFIDENTIAL or PERSONAL indicate how the person receiving the letter should handle the letter contents. Mailing notations should be keyed in uppercase characters at the left margin two lines below the date.[2] Figure C-3 shows a mailing notation added to a block format business letter.

FIGURE C-3
Mailing Notation on Letter

Current date
Double Space
CERTIFIED MAIL   ← | **Mailing Notation** |
Double Space
Mr. Joseph Richardson
S & K Distributors
1895 Westview Drive
San Jose, CA 95148-1897

Dear Mr. Richardson:

I am writing in response to your inquiry about S & K Distributors becoming a new distributor for Worldwide Exotic Foods, Inc.

Enclosed is our new distributor package that includes a sample distributor agreement plus a comprehensive catalog of the food products we supply to our distributors around the world. I hope this information is helpful. If you have any further questions, please contact me at (312) 555-1234 or via e-mail at vickers@exoticfoods.com.

Sincerely,

B. D. Vickers
Administrative Vice President

ka

Enclosure

**appendix
C**

C.c Formatting Envelopes

Two U. S. Postal Service publications, *The Right Way* (Publication 221), and *Postal Addressing Standards* (Publication 28) available from the U. S. Post Office, provide standards for addressing letter envelopes. The U. S. Postal Service uses optical character readers (OCRs) and barcode sorters (BCSs) to increase the speed, efficiency, and accuracy in processing mail. To get a letter delivered more quickly, envelopes should be addressed to take advantage of this automation process.

Table C-1 lists the minimum and maximum size for letters. The post office cannot process letters smaller than the minimum size. Letters larger than the maximum size cannot take advantage of automated processing and must be processed manually.

TABLE C-1
Minimum and Maximum
Letter Dimensions

Dimension	Minimum	Maximum
Height	3½ inches	6⅛ inches
Length	5 inches	11½ inches
Thickness	.007 inch	¼ inch

The delivery address should be placed inside a rectangular area on the envelope that is approximately ⅝ inch from the top and bottom edge of the envelope and ½ inch from the left and right edge of the envelope. This is called the **OCR read area**. All the lines of the delivery address must fit within this area and no lines of the return address should extend into this area. To assure the delivery address is placed in the OCR read area, begin the address approximately ½ inch left of center and on approximately line 14.[3]

The lines of the delivery address should be in this order:

1. any optional nonaddress data, such as advertising or company logos, must be placed above the delivery address
2. any information or attention line
3. the name of the recipient
4. the street address
5. the city, state, and postal code (ZIP+4)

The delivery address should be complete, including apartment or suite numbers and delivery designations, such as RD (road), ST (street), or NW (northwest). Leave the area below and on both sides of the delivery address blank. Use uppercase characters and a sans serif font (such as Arial) for the delivery address. Omit all punctuation except the hyphen in the ZIP+4 code.

Figure C-4 shows a properly formatted business letter envelope.

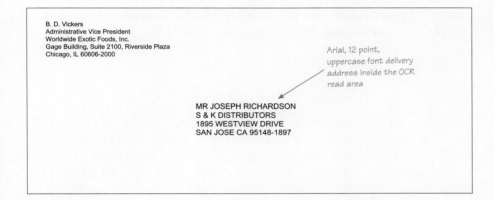

QUICK TIP

Foreign addresses should include the country name in uppercase characters as the last line of the delivery address. The postal code, if any, should appear on the same line as the city.

FIGURE C-4
Business Letter Envelope

appendix
C

C.d Formatting Interoffice Memorandums

Business correspondence that is sent within a company is usually prepared as an **interoffice memorandum**, also called a **memo**, rather than a letter. There are many different interoffice memo styles used in offices today, and word processing applications usually provide several memo templates based on different memo styles. Also, just as with business letters that are sent outside the company, many companies set special standards for margins, typeface, and font size for their interoffice memos.

A basic interoffice memo should include lines for "TO:", "FROM:", "DATE:", and "SUBJECT:" followed by the body text. Memos can be prepared on blank paper or on paper that includes a company name and even a logo. The word MEMORANDUM is often included. Figure C-5 shows a basic interoffice memorandum.

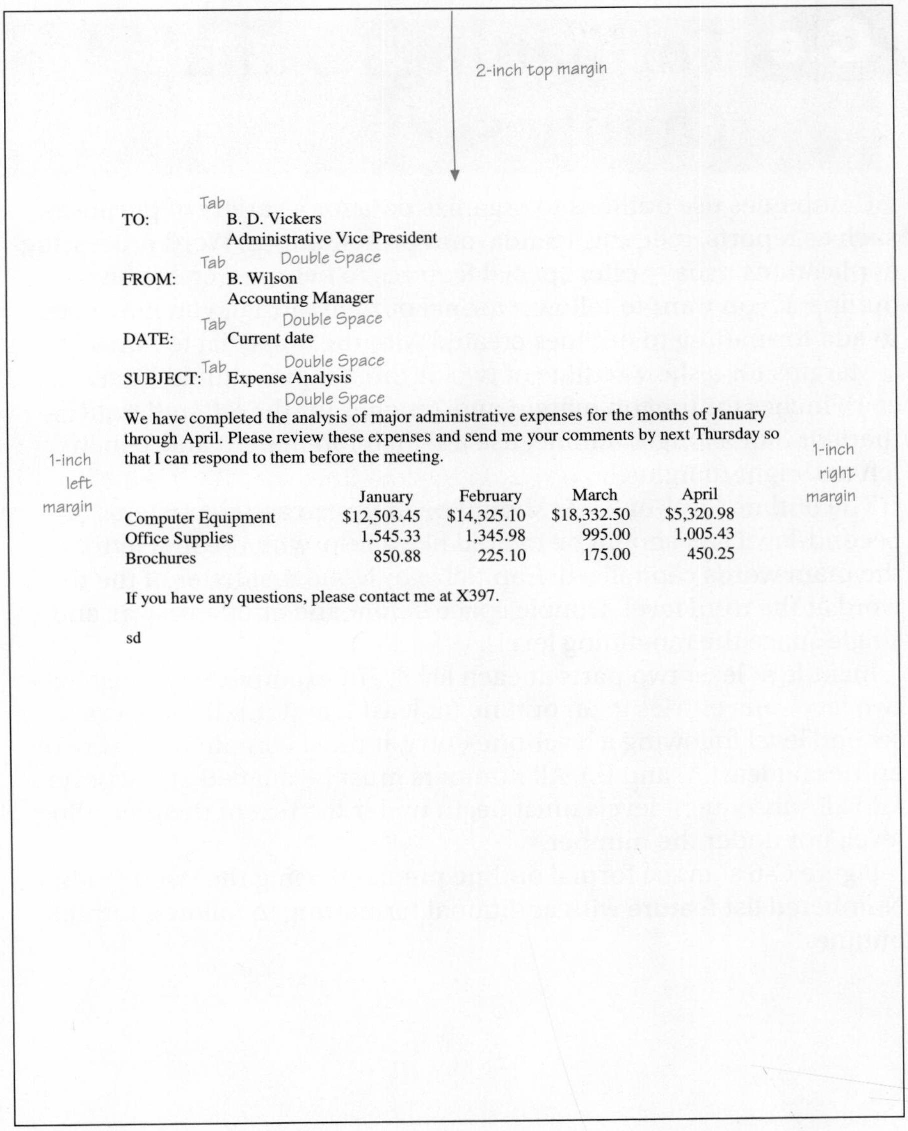

FIGURE C-5
Interoffice Memorandum

2-inch top margin

TO: _{Tab} B. D. Vickers
              Administrative Vice President
       _{Tab}   Double Space
FROM: B. Wilson
              Accounting Manager
       _{Tab}   Double Space
DATE: Current date
       _{Tab}   Double Space
SUBJECT: Expense Analysis
              Double Space

We have completed the analysis of major administrative expenses for the months of January through April. Please review these expenses and send me your comments by next Thursday so that I can respond to them before the meeting.

	January	February	March	April
Computer Equipment	$12,503.45	$14,325.10	$18,332.50	$5,320.98
Office Supplies	1,545.33	1,345.98	995.00	1,005.43
Brochures	850.88	225.10	175.00	450.25

If you have any questions, please contact me at X397.

sd

1-inch left margin

1-inch right margin

appendix
C

C.e Formatting Formal Outlines

Companies use outlines to organize data for a variety of purposes, such as reports, meeting agenda, and presentations. Word processing applications usually offer special features to help you create an outline. If you want to follow a formal outline format, you may need to add formatting to outlines created with these special features.

Margins for a short outline of two or three topics should be set at 1½ inches for the top margin and 2 inches for the left and right margins. For a longer outline, use a 2-inch top margin and 1-inch left and right margins.

The outline level-one text should be in uppercase characters. Second-level text should be treated like a title, with the first letter of the main words capitalized. Capitalize only the first letter of the first word at the third level. Double space before and after level one and single space the remaining levels.

Include at least two parts at each level. For example, you must have two level-one entries in an outline (at least I. and II.). If there is a second level following a level-one entry, it must contain at least two entries (at least A. and B.). All numbers must be aligned at the period and all subsequent levels must begin under the text of the preceding level, not under the number.[4]

Figure C-6 shows a formal outline prepared using the Word Outline Numbered list feature with additional formatting to follow a formal outline.

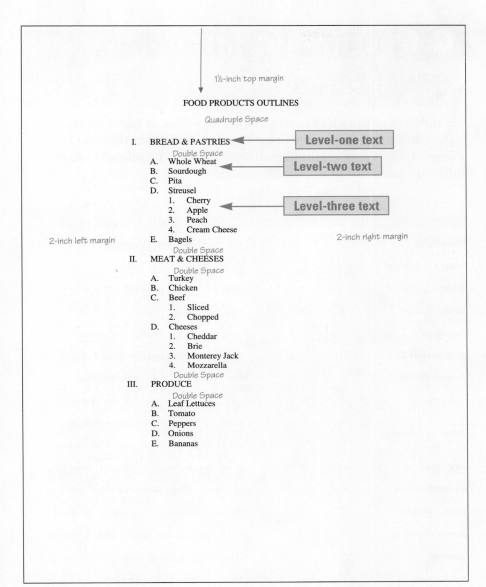

1½-inch top margin

FOOD PRODUCTS OUTLINES

Quadruple Space

I.   BREAD & PASTRIES ← Level-one text

   Double Space
   A.   Whole Wheat ← Level-two text
   B.   Sourdough
   C.   Pita
   D.   Streusel
       1.   Cherry ← Level-three text
       2.   Apple
       3.   Peach
       4.   Cream Cheese
   E.   Bagels

   Double Space

II. MEAT & CHEESES

   Double Space
   A.   Turkey
   B.   Chicken
   C.   Beef
       1.   Sliced
       2.   Chopped
   D.   Cheeses
       1.   Cheddar
       2.   Brie
       3.   Monterey Jack
       4.   Mozzarella

   Double Space

III. PRODUCE

   Double Space
   A.   Leaf Lettuces
   B.   Tomato
   C.   Peppers
   D.   Onions
   E.   Bananas

2-inch left margin

2-inch right margin

FIGURE C-6
Formal Outline

appendix
C

C.f Using Proofreader's Marks

Standard proofreader's marks enable an editor or proofreader to make corrections or change notations in a document that can be recognized by anyone familiar with the marks. The following list illustrates standard proofreader's marks.

Defined		Examples
Paragraph	⁋	⁋ Begin a new paragraph at this
Insert a character	∧	point. Insrt a letter here.
Delete	ℓ	Delete these words. Disregard
Do not change	stet or ...	the previous correction. To
Transpose	tr	transpose is to around turn.
Move to the left	⌐	⌐Move this copy to the left.
Move to the right	⌐	Move this copy to the right.
No paragraph	No ⁋	No ⁋Do not begin a new paragraph
Delete and close up		here. Delete the hyphen from
		pre-empt and close up the space.
Set in caps	Caps or ≡	a sentence begins with a capital
Set in lower case	lc or /	letter. This Word should not
Insert a period	⊙	be capitalized. Insert a period⊙
Quotation marks	⌄ ⌄	Quotation marks and a comma
Comma	⋀	should be placed here he said.
Insert space	#	Space between thesewords. An
Apostrophe	⌄	apostrophe is whats needed here.
Hyphen	=	Add a hyphen to Kilowatthour. Close
Close up	◠	up the extra spa ce.
Use superior figure	⌄	Footnote this sentence. Set
Set in italic	Ital. or —	the words, sine qua non, in italics.
Move up	⌐	This word is too low. That word is
Move down	⌐	too high.

C.g Using Style Guides

A **style guide** provides a set of rules for punctuating and formatting text. There are a number of style guides used by writers, editors, business document proofreaders, and publishers. You can purchase style guides at a commercial bookstore, an online bookstore, or a college bookstore. Your local library likely has copies of different style guides and your instructor may have copies of several style guides for reference. Some popular style guides are *The Chicago Manual of Style* (The University of Chicago Press), *The Professional Secretary's Handbook* (Barron's), *The Holt Handbook* (Harcourt Brace College Publishers), and the *MLA Style Manual and Guide to Scholarly Publishing* (The Modern Language Association of America).

appendix
C

Endnotes

[1] Jerry W. Robinson et al., *Keyboarding and Information Processing* (Cincinnati: South-Western Educational Publishing, 1997).

[2] Ibid.

[3] Ibid.

[4] Ibid.

Index

Special Characters

A

B

C

E

I

N

S

T